HANDBOOK OF
Individual Therapy

HANDBOOK OF
Individual Therapy

edited by
Windy Dryden

SAGE Publications
London • Thousand Oaks • New Delhi

Previous editions have been published as *Individual Therapy in Britain* (1984) and *Individual Therapy: A Handbook* (1990).

This edition published 1996.

 SAGE Publications Ltd
6 Bonhill Street
London EC2A 4PU

SAGE Publications Inc
2455 Teller Road
Thousand Oaks, California 91320

SAGE Publications India Pvt Ltd
32, M-Block Market
Greater Kailash – I
New Delhi 110 048

British Library Cataloguing in Publication data

A catalogue record for this book is available from the British Library.

ISBN 0 8039 7842 1
ISBN 0 8039 7843 X (pbk)

Library of Congress catalog record available

Typeset by Mayhew Typesetting, Rhayader, Powys.
Printed in Great Britain by The Cromwell Press Ltd, Broughton Gifford, Melksham, Wiltshire.

To Louise

Contents

Preface

The two preceding editions of this handbook attempted to fill a gap in the market by having British authors write on well-established approaches to individual therapy for a British readership. In this third edition, the most successful elements of the previous editions have been retained. Contributors were once again asked to keep firmly to a common structure (Appendix 1) in writing their chapters on the different therapeutic approaches (Chapters 2–13), there is a chapter placing therapy in a social context (Chapter 1), and chapters are included on research and training as they pertain to individual therapy (Chapters 14 and 15).

As before, I have sought feedback on the previous edition and have incorporated the following suggestions into this edition. First, many people who use this book for training purposes asked me to omit the comparison chapter. They said that the inclusion of this chapter in the second edition inhibited the creative thought of trainees when they came to compare and contrast different therapeutic approaches. After much thought I have acceded to this suggestion. Second, I received quite a few requests to reinstate the chapter on Rational-Emotive Therapy (now known as Rational Emotive Behaviour Therapy), which appeared in the first edition of this volume but was omitted from the second. I was happy to respond to these requests. All other chapters have been updated or completely rewritten. The book ends as the two previous editions did with information on clinical services and training opportunities offered by every approach (see Appendix 2).

I welcome feedback on this handbook and hope that once again readers will join me in thanking all the contributors for a job very well done.

Windy Dryden, London

The Editor and Contributors

The Editor

Windy Dryden is Professor of Counselling at Goldsmiths College, University of London. He has authored or edited over 95 books including *Facilitating Client Change in Rational Emotive Behaviour Therapy* (Whurr Publishers, 1995) and *Daring to be Myself: A Case of Rational-Emotive Therapy*, written with Joseph Yankura (Open University Press, 1992). In addition, he edits 12 book series in the area of counselling and psychotherapy including the *Brief Therapy and Counselling* series (Wiley) and *Developing Counselling* (Sage). His major interests are in Rational Emotive Behaviour Therapy, eclecticism and integration in psychotherapy and, increasingly, writing short, accessible self-help books for the general public.

The Contributors

Mark Aveline has been a consultant medical psychotherapist in Nottingham since 1974. His chief interests are in the development of a range of effective psychotherapies, suitable for NHS practice, and teaching the necessary skills at undergraduate, post-qualification and specialist levels. He enjoys group and focal therapy and programming in 4th Dimension, a relational database. He is a member of the Governing Board of the United Kingdom Council for Psychotherapy (1992–), chair of the Training Committee of the South Trent Training in Dynamic Psychotherapy (1984–), President of British Association for Counselling (1994–), chair of the Psychotherapy Training Specialist Advisory Committee of the Royal College of Psychiatrists (1995–) and UK Vice-President elect of the Society for Psychotherapy Research (1995–). He is co-editor of *Group Therapy in Britain* (Open University Press, 1988) and *Research Foundations for Psychotherapy Practice* (Wiley, 1995) and author of *From Medicine to Psychotherapy* (Whurr Publishers, 1992).

Michael Barkham trained as a clinical psychologist and then spent 10 years working at the MRC/ESRC Social and Applied Psychology Unit, University of Sheffield. He was involved in comparative studies of contrasting brief therapies focusing on both outcomes and processes and has published widely in scientific journals. In 1995 he took up post as Senior Lecturer in Clinical Psychology and Deputy Director of the Psychological Therapies Research Centre at the University of Leeds. He is currently UK Vice-President of the international body of the Society for Psychotherapy Research.

Ann Casement is a Training Analyst and Director of Training at the Association of Jungian Analysts in London. She is a member of the International Association of Analytical Psychologists and is in private practice as an analyst. In addition, she is a Fellow of the Royal Anthropological Institute. She lectures, writes and teaches on analytical psychology and anthropology. She is an assistant editor of the *Journal of Analytical Psychology*, as well as a regular contributor to *The Economist* and has written articles for the Science Section and reviewed books for that publication for many years. She also contributes to other journals. She is a member of the Governing Board of the United Kingdom Council for Psychotherapy (1995–), and chair of the Analytical Psychology Section of that umbrella organization. She has convened two national conferences for the four UK Jungian groups, the first in May 1993, and the second, 'The Jungians Today', in November 1995.

Petrūska Clarkson is a Consultant Chartered Counselling and Clinical Psychologist, UKCP registered psychotherapist, accredited supervisor and accredited organizational consultant. She is Chair of the Board of Examiners for the British Psychological Society Diploma in Counselling Psychology, Honorary Reader in the Psychology of Supervision at Surrey University and on the Ethics Committee of the British Association for Psychoanalytic and Psychodynamic Supervision. She is the principal founder of several organizations (including BIIP and Metanoia), the author of eight books (including *Transactional Analysis – An integrated approach*), several University validated Diploma courses and 90 professional papers/chapters – many in the *Transactional Analysis Journal*. She has been internationally active for some 25 years as supervisor and teacher of advanced training/educational programmes for supervisors, psychologists and individual and group psychotherapists and counsellors and is a prizewinner for contribution to theory in Transactional Analysis. Petrūska is also now at PHYSIS, London.

Jenny Clifford is a full-time speech and language therapist in the National Health Service. She has a psychology degree and is an Adlerian counsellor and supervisor and an International Adlerian trainer. She is co-director of the Institute for Adlerian Psychology and co-chairperson of ICASSI (International Committee for Adlerian Summer Schools and Institutes). She co-authored a chapter on 'Family counselling with children who stutter; an Adlerian approach' in Celia Levy (ed.) *Stuttering Therapies: Practical Approaches* (London: Croom Helm, 1987), and was co-author, with Charlotte Padfield and Elizabeth Smith, of an article on using the Adlerian approach with adults who stammer, in *Speech Therapy in Practice*, 4(6) 1989.

Cassie Cooper is a Kleinian psychotherapist/psychologist, formerly Head of Services for students at the Harrow Campus of the University of Westminster and Course Leader for its Diploma in Counselling Skills and ancillary counselling courses.

She is the author of many papers on psychotherapy and counselling published in learned journals and has contributed chapters in textbooks on these subjects. Current publications include chapters in M. Jacobs (ed.) *Charlie, an Unwanted Child* (Open University Press, 1995), Ved P. Varma (ed.) *Stresses in Psychotherapists* (Routledge, 1996), and R. Woolfe and W. Dryden (eds) *Handbook of Counselling Psychology* (Sage Publications, 1996). She is currently Editor of the newsletter of the British Psychological Society (Psychotherapy Section) and

Counselling Consultant to Age Concern UK. In addition, she has a large clinical practice.

Peggy Dalton is a member of the PCP Centre Group and is involved in teaching personal construct psychology. She works independently as a psychotherapist and counsellor with children and young people as well as adults. She is joint author with Fay Fransella of *Personal Construct Counselling in Action* (Sage Publications, 1990) and with Gavin Dunnett of *A Psychology for Living* (Wiley, 1992). Her most recent book, *Counselling People with Communication Problems* (Sage Publications, 1994), focuses on her particular interest in speech, language and voice problems.

Emmy van Deurzen-Smith is an existential psychotherapist, a chartered counselling psychologist and a philosopher. She is Professor and Dean at the School of Psychotherapy and Counselling at Regent's College. She is the founder and an honorary life member of the Society for Existential Analysis and has published and lectured widely on the subject of existential psychotherapy, including *Existential Counselling in Practice* (Sage Publications, 1988) and *Everyday Mysteries* (Routledge, in press). Emmy is a past chair of the United Kingdom Council for Psychotherapy and at present serves as External Relations Officer to the European Association for Psychotherapy.

Fay Fransella is Director of the Centre for Personal Construct Psychology and an active member of its operating arm, the PCP Centre Group. She is also Emeritus Reader in Clinical Psychology, University of London. The eight books she has authored include *Inquiring Man* written with Don Bannister (Routledge, 3rd edition, 1986), *Personal Construct Counselling in Action*, written with Peggy Dalton (Sage Publications, 1990) and *George Kelly* (Sage Publications, 1995). She is on several committees connected with the United Kingdom Council for Psychotherapy, of which the PCP Centre has long been a member. Through this membership all those completing the Centre's Diploma in PCP Psychotherapy are registered as UKCP psychotherapists. In addition, she is involved in the teaching and practice of psychotherapy as well as running psychotherapy supervision groups.

Maria Gilbert has extensive experience in adult education, organizational consultancy and psychotherapy, as well as in the supervision and training of psychotherapists and psychotherapists' supervisors in Transactional Analysis, Gestalt Psychotherapy and Integrative Psychotherapy. She is a teaching and supervising transactional analyst (with clinical speciality) of the International Transactional Analysis Association, a teaching member of the Gestalt Psychotherapy Training Institute and recognized supervisor with the British Association for Counselling.

Judith Hemming, formerly a teacher and teacher trainer, has been in private practice as a Gestalt psychotherapist for the past 10 years, having trained in a variety of Gestalt and other approaches in Britain and America since 1980. She is an associate teaching and supervising member of the Gestalt Psychotherapy Training Institute and offers training and supervision for several institutes in Britain and abroad. She specializes and has written about Gestalt Couples

Therapy and her current research interest lies in integrating Bert Hellinger's family systemic work with Gestalt practice. She is Associate Editor of the *British Gestalt Journal*.

Stirling Moorey is a Consultant Psychiatrist and Honorary Senior Lecturer at St Bartholomew's Hospital, London. He is responsible for providing a cognitive-behaviour therapy service to the City & Hackney. He has written on the clinical applications of cognitive therapy, and has published outcome studies evaluating the effectiveness of cognitive therapy in improving the quality of life of people with cancer. He is co-author, with Dr Steven Greer, of *Psychological Therapy for Patients with Cancer* (Oxford: Heinemann Medical Books, 1989) and co-editor, with Dr Matthew Hodes, of *Psychological Treatment in Disease and Illness* (London: Gaskell Publications, 1993).

Geraldine O'Sullivan is a Consultant Psychiatrist at West Herts Community NHS Trust. She works in general adult psychiatry and maintains a special interest in behaviour therapy and eating disorders. She has researched and published papers on behaviour therapy in the management of phobic and obsessive-compulsive disorders. She has also examined the interaction between behaviour therapy and pharmacological treatments.

Malcolm Parlett is a Gestalt Psychotherapist, clinical supervisor, trainer and organizational consultant in private practice, resident in Bristol. He is Editor of the *British Gestalt Journal*. He has a background in qualitative research in education and has held visiting professorships at three universities. He has been centrally involved in the development of Gestalt therapy training and professionalization in Britain since the early 1980s and one of his major interests is in new applications of the Gestalt philosophy and methods. His chief research interests are in field theory, about which he has written several articles, and in mind–body relationships and Gestalt bodywork.

David Pilgrim works as an NHS Consultant Clinical Psychologist in Blackburn, Lancashire and is a Senior Research Fellow at the Universities of Liverpool and Salford. His interests span psychology, sociology and social policy and he has published widely in all three disciplines about the topic of mental health. His books include *Clinical Psychology Observed* (Routledge, 1992), with Andy Treacher; *A Sociology of Mental Health and Illness* (Open University Press, 1993) and *Mental Health Policy in Britain* (Macmillan, 1996), both with Anne Rogers. Currently he is trying to write a book about psychotherapy and society.

David Livingstone Smith is Principal Lecturer in Psychotherapy and Counselling at Regent's College in London, where he directs the MA in Psychotherapy and Counselling. He has published widely on psychoanalysis and related subjects in the professional journals and is the author of *Hidden Conversations: An Introduction to Communicative Psychoanalysis* (Routledge, 1991). His major interests concern the interface of psychotherapy, philosophy and science, and he is at present engaged in research into Freud's philosophy of mind in relation to contemporary ideas in analytic philosophy and cognitive science.

Brian Thorne is Director of Student Counselling and of the Centre for Counselling

Studies, University of East Anglia, Norwich. He is also a founder member of the Norwich Centre and a Director of Person-Centred Therapy (Britain). His books include *Person-Centred Counselling in Action,* co-authored with Dave Mearns (Sage Publications, 1988), *Person-centred Therapy: Therapeutic and Spiritual Dimensions* (Whurr Publishers, 1991) and *Carl Rogers* (Sage Publications, 1992). His current major interests are the European developments in person-centred therapy (he holds appointments in Paris and Vienna) and the relationship between therapy and the Western spiritual tradition. In addition to his contributions to the counselling and psychotherapy literature he also edits the *Wounded Pilgrim* series for the religious publishers, Darton, Longman and Todd and is the author of *Behold the Man* (Darton, Longman & Todd, 1991).

Keith Tudor is a certified transactional analyst (EATA) and a registered psychotherapist (UKCP). He is also a qualified social worker and an accredited counsellor (BAC). He is in private practice in Sheffield offering counselling and psychotherapy, working with individuals – both adults and children – and with groups. He is a Director of Temenos, a 'place set aside' which offers services in the field of human relations: training, consultancy and research under which auspices he is a director of a Diploma Course in Person-Centred Counselling. He is an Honorary Research Fellow at King's College, London, where he has conducted research into mental health promotion and into masculinity and violence. He is the author of over 20 articles in the field of mental health and social policy, counselling and psychotherapy and of *Mental Health Promotion* (Routledge, 1996) and *Counselling in Groups* (Sage Publications, forthcoming).

1

British Psychotherapy in Context

David Pilgrim

This chapter will be about a form of psychological practice (psychotherapy) but will not be written from a psychological perspective. That is, some attempt will be made to go outside the boundaries of academic and therapeutic psychology and draw upon other bodies of knowledge, notably sociology, social history and economics, in order to offer some account of the way in which British psychotherapy has been shaped by its social context. Attempts at developing a sociology of psychological knowledge have produced some fruitful and provocative ideas but, by and large, they have not captured the sustained attention of psychotherapists (see e.g. Holland, 1977; Ingleby, 1985). I hope to build upon these, and other undervalued works, in order to re-focus the attention of therapists on the social origins of their own practice. This social perspective is necessary in order to correct some patterns of faulty reasoning evident within writings in the field. In particular, there is a tendency to view the history of ideas and practices associated with psychotherapy as a history of great people or, less speciously, a history of great ideas. Within these inadequate accounts, it is assumed that a single variable, e.g. genius, or brilliance of theory, or scientific credibility, can account for why this, rather than that, version of theory and practice took root and flourished, while others were marginalized or superseded.

In the first edition of this book (Dryden, 1984) authors, to varying degrees, cited biographical details of innovators or the persuasiveness of new arguments, e.g. the irresistible thoughts of Meichenbaum in relation to 'cognitive-behaviourism', when placing their topic in its British context. To be clear about this, I am not arguing that clever people have no role in history nor that the cogency of particular theoretical innovations have no relevance. What I am emphasizing is that these are weak rationales, *in themselves*, to account for sociohistorical developments in the field of psychotherapy, unless they are placed into a wider socioeconomic context.

The tendency on the part of these authors to offer incomplete accounts of their therapy in context may be a function of the subdivision of intellectual labour (Braverman, 1974). Because of the compartmentalization of academic skills and knowledge, psychologists and psychotherapists not surprisingly, in the main, reason psychologically. Psychological models, no matter how reflexive they are at the individual level (e.g. Kelly, 1955), cannot account for their own existence as *social* phenomena (Holland, 1981). Having introduced these cautions, I want to begin to focus on those factors which need to be invoked in order to build up a picture of psychotherapy in its British social context. The factors include the following:

1 *Politics* e.g. the politics of mental health professionalism; the relationship between professional structures in the field of mental health and the development

of individual psychotherapy; the sociology of the mental health professions, with particular emphasis on professional dominance.

2 *Economics* e.g. variations over time in socioeconomic conditions and their influence on policies concerning the social control of psychological distress; the role of the mental hospital in the past and its absence in the future; the link between war and peace economies and psychotherapy.

3 *British culture* e.g. the role of cultural traditions in Britain in influencing the legitimacy of particular psychotherapeutic forms of knowledge; philosophical continuities in British intellectual life; and the role of foreign intellectual labour in Britain.

It can be seen that even in this summarized form, the complex of social variables noted is extensive. Before moving on to explore some of this complexity, within the constraints of space in this chapter, a particular assumption needs to be declared. Human systems, which are the context for the emergence of knowledge forms including psychotherapy, are open systems. As such, they defy complete description as they are in dynamic flux over time. Consequently, descriptions and, sometimes, explanations can be offered about the past but predictions are precarious. As with Freud's emphasis on learning after the event within, and about, individuals, I assume that the past is easier to make sense of than the future in relation to the social world. Now that these assumptions have been outlined, psychotherapy in Britain will be explored in relation to political, economic and cultural factors in its history.

Victorian roots

Britain is a favoured focus for social historians of psychiatric practice (e.g. Scull, 1979; Donnelly, 1983). The reasons for this are not exactly clear but one explanation could be that as the oldest capitalist country, its forms of social organization represented prototypes for elsewhere. As far as the early signs of psychotherapy are concerned, moral therapy emerged within the expanding state asylum system in the 19th century, and descriptions of the events in England and France are described by Scull (1979) and Castel (1985) respectively. Moral therapy can be viewed as an early attempt to operate psychological rather than physical methods to correct mental disorder. Its roots in the charity sector at the Quaker Retreat in York, at the beginning of the 19th century, led to it being commonplace in the rhetoric of social reformers, but it transferred poorly to the state asylum system (Digby, 1985). Whether it represented a more humane form of intervention than chains and sedation is a moot point.

While it emphasized the inhuman tendency in early biological psychiatry (Bynum, 1974), Castel (1985) describes it as 'authoritarian pedagogy', with the tyranny of social conformity replacing the tyranny of physical interference. However it is evaluated, it is certainly true that its utility for the state was linked closely to its value in re-socializing deviants. As its name suggests, this was done within an overall moral regime, which depended on a mixture of benign and authoritarian paternalism, in order to reverse deviant conduct.

As far as future trends were concerned, what was important about moral treatment was that it offered *both* individual and collective rationales for changing conduct. Falret, reviewing the scene in the mid-19th century (cited by Castel, 1985), considered that the blanket application of the rules of moral therapy within an institution were necessary because of the inexact state of the science or art of this brand of medicine at the time. He hoped that refinements of moral therapy as it developed would allow *each patient to be treated individually*.

Ultimately moral therapy failed to become the dominant rational in Victorian psychiatry not because of its inadequacy as a version of social control for the state, but because of the offence it caused to the profession of medicine (Scull, 1979). The primary need of the state was for mental disorder to be segregated in order to leave the economic system free to operate uncontaminated by the unemployed or unemployable (Barham, 1984). The success or otherwise of particular treatment methods were a secondary political consideration. To this day all rationales for changing mental disorder (as opposed to containing or controlling it) have proved to fall well short of ideal; this is as true for biological as for psychological models.

Mainstream medicine in the 19th century, and for a long time to come, was characterized by a biological rather than psychological or social model of aetiology and treatment. Consequently, moral therapy constituted, *inter alia*, an ideological opposition to biodeterminism and physical treatment methods. According to Scull and Bynum, a strategic error of Tuke, the patriarch of moral therapy at York, was his terminology ('treatment', 'illness', and so on, which were medical terms although Tuke was not a physician) along with a deliberate emphasis on the ordinary non-expert features of his approach (such as paternalism and kindness, which were not peculiar to experts). This error made Tuke's approach vulnerable to attack from biological psychiatrists, who could thereby protect their status and salaries. The use of medical terminology poses problems to this day when non-physicians use it in relation to a client group over which they hope to have some jurisdiction (Pilgrim, 1987). Today the term 'psychotherapy' remains problematic for non-medical practitioners, in terms of their claiming autonomous status in health care contexts.

What is implicit in this description and needs to be considered in itself now is the dominant role of medicine (Freidson, 1970). The position argued by most social historians of British psychiatry is that in the mid-19th century, the medical profession as a whole (Parry and Parry, 1976) and in its psychiatric specialization (Scull, 1979; Baruch and Treacher, 1978) succeeded in gaining a legal mandate on behalf of the state to have sole jurisdiction over deviance-as-illness. As far as Victorian psychiatry was concerned, the profession established a position of dominance in three ways. First, it established a legal monopoly of jurisdiction over forms of deviance which could be framed as illness (in the Lunacy Act, 1842 and the General Medical Act, 1858). Second, it secured a territorial base to control and to work from: the mental hospital. Third, it offered a conceptual framework of mental disorder which would guarantee that medicine would be in permanent control of knowledge about mental disorder (biodeterminism). Moral therapy or any *subsequent* psychological model would need to be warded off, as would any move towards de-carceration. Although medicine exploited moral therapy for rhetorical purposes at times, emphasizing its humanitarianism, in practice this prototype of psychotherapy was marginalized in the Victorian asylum system.

Warfare and British psychotherapy

Following the demise of moral therapy, asylum-based, biological psychiatry began to consolidate its position at the turn of this century. Despite the seminal developments surrounding psychoanalysis and its derivatives at this time, depth psychology merely provoked vociferous antipathy from the medical profession. It is true that it commanded some version of allegiance from a very small number of physicians, some of whom were quite prestigious (Glover, Murray, Ernest Jones, Forsyth, Eder, Trotter, Hart and Stanford Read). However, the bulk of the profession were ignorant of, or indifferent or hostile to, the 'new psychology'. Developments in the latter were barely reported or cited in medical journals. Leaders of the medical profession such as Mercier conducted a campaign to boycott psychoanalysis as a morally corrupting influence. Stone (1985) reports a meeting held at the BMA (Neurological Section) in which the audience stood up and left the room before the beginning of a discussion on a paper presented by Jones and Eder. As Stone notes, the status of psychoanalysis and its psychotherapeutic derivatives was dramatically changed by the outbreak of the First World War.

Until this event, the great bulk of interest on the part of asylum doctors had been in madness. After all, during a peace economy it is the disruptive influence of the mad (and other pauper deviants such as criminals and handicapped people) that stands out as being of political importance to the state. Warfare brings a different set of problems as far as managing the population is concerned. Before 1914, neurologists, not 'mad-doctors', were more likely to take a psychological interest in the less disturbed (neurotic) part of the population. This interest was intensified during the war years. Not only were biological psychiatrists displaced by neurologists and psychologists for practical reasons when shell-shock was being described and treated, but the whole edifice of Kraepelinian psychiatry, which gave self-congratulatory accounts of its own performance in peacetime (Doerner, 1970), was being shaken. Biodeterminism in Victorian psychiatry largely depended on the unproved, elitist assumption that mental disorder was a result of genetically inherited degeneracy. What the war spawned was a large number of stalwart British soldiers (volunteers in the lower ranks and commissioned officers and gentlemen) who were mentally breaking down. It was out of the question to tolerate the unpatriotic notion that these men were in any sense degenerate. Environmentalist and psychological ideas could thus find a new type of legitimacy on the mental health scene.

The war had vital consequences. It helped legitimize the role of verbal psychotherapy within medicine. For a while it undermined the power of asylum doctors and their biodeterministic ideas. As Stone notes about this time: 'If psychotherapists had been the hero of the piece, the asylum doctors had been its villains' (1985: 236). The war also contributed to the emergence of a psychological discourse in Britain. Psychoanalytical and other psychological ideas about shell-shock flourished in the immediate post-war period. In 1919 the first section in the British

Psychological Society to be established within this current was the Medical Section. Along with the Medico-Psychological Association (later the Royal College of Psychiatrists) the BPS was becoming a forum for psychological ideas.

Asylum doctors were so out of favour with the government after the First World War that none were appointed to the Royal Commission on Lunacy and Mental Disorder in 1924 (Armstrong, 1980). This led to a gap between policy and practice during the inter-war period. In 1930 the Mental Treatment Act was passed, which was a relatively liberal piece of legislation encouraging both voluntary patients, and outpatient, rather than inpatient, treatment. Following on the 1924 Commission, such legislation took the form it did because of the temporary marginalization of asylum doctors at the level of mental health policy formation. However, their practical authority was gradually being re-established in the asylum system. The outpatient clinics established to mop up after the war, responding to neuroses psychotherapeutically, were competing with business as usual in the hospitals, which were returning to their traditional peacetime role of segregating the disruptive mad. Whatever the 1930 Act said, old-fashioned inpatient psychiatry was returning to an ascendant position.

During this period, Klein and the Freuds came and settled in Britain. This imported a crucial developing tension within psychoanalysis about the role of very early infantile experience, which dated back to a dispute between Anna Freud and Klein at the Innsbruck Conference in 1927 (Roazen, 1974). A vital point to make here is that the existence in England of such esteemed psychoanalytical mentors did not, in the inter-war period, produce an impact on mainstream psychiatry. None the less, the scene was set for some crucial developments after the defeat of Nazism. Although the practical impact of psychoanalysis was warded off by asylum doctors, theoretical creativity in the inter-war period was not stymied. Moreover, within this creativity were elaborate psychoanalytical debates about warfare itself, which were available to military authorities (Richards, 1986b). Following on from this first point, the anticipation of a recurrence of the problems of the First World War led military authorities to seek to pre-empt, where possible, psychological difficulties. Not surprisingly, psychoanalysts found themselves to be favoured advisers on military selection, morale and psychotherapy during the course of the war and its aftermath. These included Rees, Bion, Rickman, Main and Foulkes. This grouping, as with the psychotherapists of the First World War, temporarily displaced asylum doctors as far as state-recognized psychiatric leadership was concerned.

Another result of the Second World War was that the previous emphasis on individual psychotherapy was altered. The pressure to see more 'soldier-patients' led to the military psychoanalysts experimenting with both group therapy and ward democracy as an enabling process (the beginnings of the therapeutic community movement in Britain). Bion's seminal work on group dynamics, *Experiences in Groups* (Bion, 1959) is characterized at times by the genuine humility of an individual therapist trying to make sense of fresh psychological data (group processes).

This shift, from an individual to a group model, was to have important implications for post-war developments in NHS mental health services, as group rather than individual work could be offered as being more cost-effective, and therapeutic community regimes could paradoxically be cited in defence of institutional psychiatry. Maxwell Jones, who, as well as Main, developed the work of the military psychoanalysts in the NHS during the 1950s, comments wryly that his medical colleagues would 'wheel me out' whenever a benign picture of psychiatry was required (Jones, 1984). (This has echoes of the Victorian times when moral treatment was used for purposes of humanitarian rhetoric.)

Welfarism and psychotherapy

As with the First World War, the Second World War led to a period of optimism about psychotherapeutic developments in Britain. Returning from the war, Tavistock Clinic practitioners hoped that through their 'Operation Phoenix' they could spread the psychoanalytical word to mental health services throughout the newly formed NHS (Dicks, 1970). However, this was not be. Most psychoanalytical practice remained ghettoized around Hampstead, with the important exceptions of Main's development at the Cassel in south London and Sutherland exporting a version of the Tavistock to Edinburgh. Although, in principle, the NHS held out the possibility of psychotherapy (both group and individual) being offered, like other interventions, free at the time of need, history was to repeat itself as far as a post-war decline in psychotherapy was concerned.

In the 1950s psychodynamic psychotherapy was opposed on two fronts. The first, and most predictable, was once more from biological psychiatry. The invention of major tranquillizers strengthened the claims being made about chemotherapy facilitating the 'open door' policy in mental hospitals and enabling patients to stay in the community. This myth, since still colluded with by all but the most honest academic psychiatrists, does not tally with what is known about the changing psychiatric population. Inpatient numbers began to drop *before* the introduction of major tranquillizers (Scull, 1977; Busfield, 1986). None the less, the authoritative claims of biological psychiatry with its chemical solutions to personal problems moved, once more, into the ascendancy during the post-war period.

Psychotherapy was facing opposition on another front though, this time from a non-medical, nascent profession. A precondition of clinical psychology being established, as a profession separate from medicine, was that it could appeal to a set of cultural values deeply embedded in British life (positivism and empiricism). By contrast, the high status of psychoanalysis in Britain, during two historical wartime epochs, was a cultural aberration. This was possible because psychoanalysis was imported into *medicine*. With the exception of the odd 'lay' (non-medical) analyst, British psychoanalysis, as elsewhere, was one of several *medical* clubs. Once it was incorporated, albeit under conditions of initial vilification, into the dominant profession of medicine, psychoanalysis gained substantial protection from the hostile intellectual currents traditional to Britain.

Psychoanalysis is a case *par excellence* of a European style of thought. It goes beyond the given, commonsense view of reality favoured by the British. It is not rationalistic but a psychology of the *irrational*. Though sternly intellectual as a form of therapeutic practice in one sense, it is a profound psychology of the emotions (primitive anxiety, sexual desire, murderous hatred, and so on). It is not surprising that when the first substantial history was written of British psychology it revealed that outside its medical enclave, psychoanalysis did not find favour with mainstream academic psychology between the wars, any more than did behaviourism (Hearnshaw, 1964). At the risk of generalizing about my own culture, the British tend to treat emotionality *and* elaborate intellectual theorizing with equal suspicion.

In the context of these anomalies surrounding psychoanalysis in Britain, a new profession, clinical psychology, emerged in the 1950s. There is an irony in the beginnings of the profession in Britain. While, as argued above, psychoanalysis was, metaphorically, an enemy alien in British intellectual life, gaining sanctuary within the prestigious boundaries of the mature profession of medicine, this was also true in a more direct personal sense of the man inheriting a leadership role within British differential psychology. The irony is compounded when we can now reflect that this man was to gain notoriety for, among other things, championing the vilification of psychoanalysis. Eysenck, a German in England during the war years, gained the protection of Aubrey Lewis at Mill Hill from 1942 and later the Institute of Psychiatry (Gibson, 1981). This psychiatric paternalism was to provide another irony, in the light of Eysenck's later moves to subvert the therapeutic monopoly of medicine, and thus initiate clinical psychology's boundary disputes with psychiatry (Eysenck, 1958).

In the early 1950s, Eysenck began to rehearse the strategic considerations needed for the emergence of clinical psychology. One aspect of his strategy was to make a bid for legitimacy for the new profession based upon challenging the other major psychological model operating in a health context (psychoanalysis) (Eysenck, 1952). It cannot be a coincidence that a preoccupation with the denigration of psychoanalysis, and its psychotherapeutic derivatives, has gone hand in glove with clinical psychology differentiating itself from medicine and marking out an area of separate epistemological validity. This post-war challenge to the dominance of psychoanalysis was one reason, amongst others, why therapeutic psychology was to develop into an eclectic mixture of theoretical positions. However, *en route* to this eclecticism were other vital stages of maturation.

Initially, British clinical psychology was not characterized by therapy of any description. Until the late 1950s the scientific (or 'scientistic', depending on one's ideology) approach to psychology was mainly represented by the British psychometric tradition. Eysenck was the most recent trustee of the latter, which dates back to Galton via Burt, Spearman and Pearson (Hearnshaw, 1964). As Anderson (1969) points out, Eysenck was part of a wider movement of cultural renewal in Britain, entailing a number of white émigrés (exemplified by Karl Popper) who were faithful to British empiricism. Émigrés not in a position to champion the latter were passed over, in terms of academic status, or failed to settle in Britain. Immigrant intellectual workers willing to work hard at systematizing British traditions were welcomed and well rewarded.

Eysenck's importance cannot be underestimated but it should be emphasized that his leadership role was established as a result of the British intellectual values he championed. His host culture incorporated him, amongst others, to re-energize the flagging empiricist discourse in Britain. Eysenck and Popper joined with native defenders of the faith, like Russell and Ayer, to define what types of knowledge claim could legitimately be made about mental life. As Holland (1977) has noted, this British climate of naive positivism and empiricism in the main could resist the penetration of grander 'continental' idealist and materialist theoretical systems, derived from, say, Husserl, Marx, Freud, Lévi-Strauss or Lacan. (The term 'continental' in English usage, to mean mainland Europe, itself reveals the Anglocentrism epitomized by the classic headline 'Channel fogbound – Europe isolated'.)

Clinical psychology, although a new profession, was thus being built upon old conservative foundations. When it came to the second phase of its development, during the 1960s, the scientific model of psychological change advocated was based on long-established assumptions. Behaviour therapy was a sort of atavistic return to the innovations of Scottish physiology, where Whytt discovered the conditioned reflex 150 years before Pavlov (Millenson, 1969), and philosophical notions associated with Hobbes, Locke, Hume, the Mills and Spencer. Hobbes provided a blueprint for both associationism and behaviourism in *Leviathan* (1651) and 50 years later Locke even gave a cognitive-behavioural account of the aetiology of phobias (see Woodworth and Sheehan, 1964: 62).

Indeed, the shaping of their views abroad, in revolutionary Russia by Pavlov and Kornilov and frontier-expanding America by Thorndike and Watson, marks another irony about the logical consequences of British empiricism. The latter leads to a preoccupation with methodological rigour at the expense of theorizing, which is devalued and so falls into disuse. It is no exaggeration to claim that every major theoretical debate in the human sciences has taken place between positions shaped into coherent forms in countries outside of Britain. However, Britain has been the *host* to these debates in and between both behavioural and psychodynamic psychology, since the Second World War.

As Hearnshaw (1964) notes in relation to British psychology, theoretical systems-building has not been popular during its academic maturation this century. Moreover, because philosophers retarded the academic differentiation of psychology (from philosophy on one side and medicine on the other) British psychology severed its attachments eventually from the philosophical roots of its own traditions, by developing more applied than theoretical interests. Consequently, empiricism manifested in both psychometrics and behaviour therapy was expressed in ways which were naive. In particular, this took the form of *methodological* behaviourism associated with the Maudsley training course in clinical psychology and the efforts made by psychiatrists (Marks and Gelder) there to claw back therapeutic authority from the newer profession. The courses on nurse therapy at the Maudsley have their roots in the confluence of methodological behaviourism and medical power. As well as being technique oriented (directed in the main at symptom reduction rather than elaborate functional analysis) they emphasize the traditional division of labour between doctors and nurses, with the former diagnosing and therapeutic tasks being delegated to the latter. This situation prompted Blackman, a British academic advocate of American radical behaviourism, to comment:

> British psychology appears to have an unduly crude and ill-formulated view of contemporary behaviourism, and this must be a source of concern when one sees the *techniques* of behaviour modification being enthusiastically advocated by clinical psychologists who

have little respect for, or facility in, the functional analysis of behaviour. It is probably inevitable that members of other professions may turn to behaviour modification merely as a set of effective techniques. (Blackman, 1979: 39)

The problem with Blackman's lament is that it is essentially moralistic and does not go any way to account for *why* the situation he describes exists. British psychologists failed to 'respect' functional analysis because they are acculturated generally not to theorize too much. Likewise, nurses carry out prescribed techniques because their profession has been in this type of structural relationship with medicine for a hundred years. Having no knowledge base of its own, nursing traditionally follows the epistemological contours and professional directives of medicine. (Of course this is now changing, with nursing studies being integrated more into *higher* rather than further education in Britain, but the changes are very recent and still quite slow.)

The heyday of behaviour therapy in British clinical psychology during the late 1960s and early 1970s gave way to a period of eclecticism (Richards, 1983). In academic psychology the popularity of behaviourism was replaced by cognitivism, which culminated in a peculiar and arguably paradoxical trend towards 'cognitive-behaviour therapy'. Mackay (1984) notes a certain inertia within Britain concerning this trend compared to other countries. However, it should also be noted that, as would be expected, given our poor track record on theorizing, philosophical concerns about the contradictions of integrating cognitivism with behaviourism, rather than practitioner inertia, emerged abroad rather than here.

By 1980 British clinical psychology had become eclectic to a point where even verbal psychotherapy was now being integrated. Although Eysenck retained his intense hostility towards psychoanalysis and verbal psychotherapy during the 1980s, the bulk of the profession no longer had need for this old debate. After all, with the publication of the Trethowan Report on the role of psychologists in the health service (DHSS, 1977), structural autonomy from medicine was becoming a possibility, which no longer depended on the posturing of 1952. During this phase, clinical psychologists were keen to boast the advantages of eclecticism and in a thoroughgoing debate in the *British Journal of Clinical Psychology* (1983: 22, 2), which gave over rare space to theoretical rather than empirical issues, only a British expatriate in Australia, Yates (1983), tried to defend the faults of integration. A series of contributors from both sides of the Atlantic (Murray, Wachtel, Messer and Davis) queued up to point out the errors of his ways.

As far as psychotherapy was concerned, then, eclecticism eventually predominated within clinical psychology, with neophytes in the profession demonstrating theoretical agnosticism and ambivalence. Smail (1982) noted ironically that in this period clinical psychology had become 'homogenised and sterilised'. Consistent with this trend, no fewer than three full chapters of this book's first edition (Dryden, 1984) contained lengthy pleas for eclecticism. My concern here is not to evaluate whether eclecticism is a good or bad thing; rather it is to highlight its over-determined emergence in a certain historical context in Britain.

Whatever its merits and demerits, eclecticism was, in Britain, an inevitability brought about by five main factors. First, as already mentioned, the lack of thoroughgoing theorizing in British academic psychology meant that no coherent model existed. Second, linked to this, both psychoanalysis, as a powerful cultural aberration, and methodological behaviourism, as an expression of British empiricist orthodoxy, were here to stay. Both, in some form or other, had to find a place within professional structures. Thus in all of the main mental health professions, both traditions began to coexist. Third, this coexistence was facilitated by a breakdown during the 1960s in the hegemony of what Anderson (1969) describes as 'aggressive scientism', represented by the Maudsley School. Britain amongst others during this period had witnessed a wider cultural upheaval and became noteworthy for a particular brand of anti-psychiatry. British anti-psychiatry was predicated on a variety of European traditions which were antithetical to naive empiricism: psychoanalysis; phenomenology; existentialism; Marxism; and post-structuralism. When Eastern mysticism is added to this list, it can be seen that this new and alternative form of eclecticism was at odds with older British intellectual currents.

Not only could methodological behaviourism not hold sway under these conditions of criticism and cultural turmoil, but the two-horse race between behaviour therapy and psychodynamic psychotherapy recruited new runners. While humanistic psychology associated in the USA since the 1940s with Maslow, May, Rogers, Kelly and others had found little place in British culture, the libertarian ethos of the 1960s (*c.* 1966–75) now allowed this third force in. Caution needs to be applied at this point about the impact of this American humanistic genre. To this day, derivatives of behaviourism and psychoanalysis have a greater presence in the statutory mental health services than do humanistic derivatives, which have been contained more in the voluntary sector (Samaritans, Marriage Guidance Council, now Relate, and so on) or in education (student and youth counselling). Moreover, as Neimeyer (1985) points out in his study of personal construct theory, British culture mainly incorporated the methodological prowess of the 'grid', rather than the therapeutic emphasis of Kelly.

The fourth critical factor needed to account for the eventual integration of discrepant therapeutic psychologies in economics. The sheer power of economics, at times, to shape ideological forms is evident when similarities are observed between different cultures in similar economic phases of development. For instance, notwithstanding any of the cultural differences acknowledged between the USA and Britain, integration of psychotherapeutic practices did take place at similar times on both sides of the Atlantic. (The former is associated with theoretical pluralism and a greater emphasis on the matrix of humanistic therapies than the latter, which is more associated with practical eclecticism.)

The aftermath of the Second World War for both countries was associated with welfare capitalism. The relationship between welfarism and therapy is summarized well here by Richards:

> The emergence of psychological practices is . . . coincident with welfare capital. By and large those practices have developed within the apparatuses of the welfare state, and we might therefore expect that they are deeply implicated in the principal business of those apparatuses, which is the containment and appropriate management of the economic and social tensions generated by the capitalist market. Amongst the main sites of psychological intervention are . . . the education and health services: through these vast and socially porous sectors permeate all the conflicts and tensions of society as a whole, along class, gender, ethnicity and party lines; between national and local government; between occupational groups and so on. They are above all scenes of contradiction and of

resolution attempted sometimes falteringly and sometimes with a confidence born of traditional authority and/or technological power. This is the modality of power which may be referred to as 'social democracy': a sociopolitical strategy for moderating market relations . . . through mitigatory provision and conciliatory practice. (Richards, 1986a: 115–16)

As Richards goes on to point out, this general process associated with post-war rebuilding culminated in an integrative ideology, manifested in consensus politics and 'social democracy'. Eclecticism within welfarism (including the psychological therapies) is one aspect for Richards, which, by the 1970s, is described as 'scientific humanism' (the integration of the opposing currents of scientism and humanism). Space was found now not only for the one-sided 'aggressive scientism' of Eysenck but also for the softer elements within psychotherapy derived from phenomenology, psychoanalysis and humanistic psychology. When, after 1979, Thatcherism disturbed the balance of social democracy by applying one side of the consensus equation (market forces) and attacking the other (individual dependence on the state for the amelioration of physical and psychological distress) the middle way, so characteristic of post-war welfarism, broke down, with consequences for the social organization of psychological practices.

As Offe (1984), a member of the Frankfurt School, points out, the welfare state is a 'de-commodifying' tendency. That is, publicly funded and owned welfare bureaucracies, though protecting (via conciliation and pacification of the population) the stability of the capitalist system, drain finance from the profit-making private sector. This eventually creates a fiscal crisis, one solution for which is the 're-commodification' of the welfare state. Welfare structures themselves are encouraged to fall victim to market forces and thus are relocated in the private profit-making area of the economy. All of this is now very familiar, since Thatcherism, although elements of it can be found in the policies of Labour administrations of the 1960s and 1970s. Offe notes that 'administrative re-commodification' is a solution for fiscal crisis in the capitalist state, which can be traced back to the 1960s. It is against this economic backdrop that certain aspects of mental health service reorganization impinging on psychotherapy can be appreciated.

Probably the most contentious aspect of mental health service reform since the Second World War is the run-down of mental hospital services. The fiscal crisis of the welfare state noted here is the major factor promoting this, though it is debatable precisely *when* this pressure led to dramatic hospital run-down consequences (Scull, 1977; cf. Busfield, 1986). What is certain is that the role and legitimacy of psychotherapy is altered according to where it is physically sited. Authoritarian hospitals sabotage psychotherapy (Pilgrim, 1988). By contrast, community facilities may at least come nearer to offering the architectural conditions of what Tuke called an 'ordinary household' (Donnelly, 1983; cf. Winnicott, 1958 in relation to the importance of setting in psychotherapy).

The fifth factor which needs to be borne in mind when considering the over-determination of eclecticism within therapeutic psychology, is that of professionalism. Because of its ambiguous epistemological status (is it a psychological practice or medical treatment?) as far as ownership is concerned, psychotherapy has been at the centre of important boundary disputes and conflicts between professional groups inside the mental health services over the past 20 years (Goldie, 1974; Baruch and Treacher, 1978). Moreover, because verbal psychotherapy ideologically offends both biological psychiatry and methodological behaviourism within clinical psychology, it has also been the focus at times of intra-professional conflicts (Pilgrim, 1986). During the 1970s before the full impact of the Trethowan Report (the DHSS review of the role of psychologists in the Health Service) psychotherapy often was the focus of disputes between psychologists and psychiatrists, along the lines noted earlier, when behaviour therapists strayed from their handmaiden, psychometric-tester role. Since then, even where NHS sites of work have an inter-professional consensus on the multidisciplinary delivery of psychotherapy, resentments accrue surrounding salary differentials, managerial authority and the rights of staff other than psychiatrists and psychologists to accept direct referrals from GPs (Pilgrim, 1986). (Note with reference to the maintenance of medical dominance in mental health services, that the Royal College of Psychiatrists, which was formed in 1971 out of the old Royal Medico-Psychological Association, advised the DHSS about the importance of medically managed NHS psychotherapy services: Royal College of Psychiatrists, 1975.)

In a context wider than the NHS, disputes also continue surrounding *which* professional groupings should be entrusted with the regulation of psychotherapeutic practice. This debate became formalized in the 1970s following government concern over Scientology (Foster, 1971). Subsequently, the British Psycho-Analytic Society contacted the Department of Health and Social Security to discuss the regulation of psychotherapy. The DHSS took no immediate action but encouraged the formation of a joint working party in 1975 by five analytically oriented groups plus representatives from the Royal College of Psychiatrists and the British Association of Behavioural Psychotherapy. They produced a report three years later (Seighart, 1978).

At that time, the British Psychological Society would send only an observer and subsequently the other main statutory representative bodies (the Royal College of Nurses, the Central Council for Education and Training in Social Work and the Royal College of Psychiatrists) disagreed with the need for a register of practitioners on the grounds that the standards of their profession provided any necessary protection for the public. Later, the Royal College of Psychiatrists changed its stance, taking a new interest in registration provided that it had a central role in establishing and policing the register. However, there was so much dissent amongst the mental health professions' groupings that by 1981 the Secretary of State for Health refused parliamentary time for the matter. Since then, the working group has continued to facilitate regular annual meetings on the topic (the Rugby Conference).

As with the parallel debates during this period concerning the registration of psychologists, effected in 1987, those arguing for the need for regulation emphasized the protection of the public and underplayed the issue of professional self-interest (protectionism, kudos, status, salary improvements, etc.). Such is the way of professionalization exemplified in the maturer professions like law and medicine, that public interest not self-interest tends to be the hallmark of official statements and rhetoric. These professional processes have tended to push psychological practices in a more eclectic direction with inter- and intra-professional compromises being worked out from faltering conflict resolution. The siting of multidisciplinary contact in smaller groupings outside hospitals has undoubtedly facilitated these compromises, as have the distractions of the consequences of attacks on welfare funding noted above.

Turning now to some tentative conclusions about the future of British psychotherapy based upon the discussion of the five factors above concerning the over-determination of eclecticism, the following implications arise:

1 In the near future, some new opportunities will be afforded to therapists to work in setting more conducive to their work than the old 'asylum' system. Moreover, the dominance of biological psychiatry associated with the territorial base of the hospital will break down to some degree, allowing alternative (psychological and social) interventions.

2 There will be some further relocation of psychiatric services to acute units within district general hospitals, which actually *amplifies* processes associated with the medicalization of personal problems (Baruch and Treacher, 1978).

3 Because of the wider deterioration of funding for the NHS and social services, positive opportunities will be offset by crises in staffing levels, and access to psychotherapy will be more and more limited to those able to pay privately. Consequently, morale is likely to deteriorate within state-funded groups of therapists.

4 Psychological distress will increase in the population and put greater pressure on existing resources. On this point it is important to note that monetarism and re-commodification have solved a problem at one level (by stabilizing the economy) but generated another problem at a second level (by amplifying distress and deviance due to higher levels of unemployment and its associated poverty, and greater levels of anxiety in those remaining in work).

5 Eclecticism in psychological therapy delivery will be strengthened as a result of practical questions of working in the community within cash limits taking precedence over finer points of dispute about particular models of intervention.

6 Eclecticism will be strengthened further by market forces generating pluralism in the private sector, where counsellors and therapists continue to proliferate, offering virtually any variant of therapy imaginable to those able to pay for the services on offer.

Discussion

I listed the six implications above in 1990 for the first edition of this book. The predictions they contain have been reasonably accurate. (Five or six years is not that long, of course.) The rundown and closure of the Victorian asylums has indeed meant that pressure has been placed on district general hospital psychiatry in response to people with mental health crises. However, what this has done is simply to reproduce the features of institutional biological psychiatry and left more psychotherapeutic-orientated work to find a place in the less developed range of community mental health facilities and the poorly accessible private sector (Pilgrim and Rogers, 1994).

. During the 1990s, the restructuring of the welfare state has been formalized in law by the passing of the 1990 NHS and Community Care Act. This represents the codification of a longer programme of reform by three terms of Conservative government, followed by a consolidating, if weakened, fourth term in 1992. The welfare state has not been dismantled but it has been converted into an engineered 'mixed economy of welfare', which emphasizes the role of the private and voluntary sectors, as well as the public sector, as service providers. As Offe (1984) noted, capitalism cannot live with the welfare state, but it cannot live without it. Even the most fervent, unbroken period of free-market-driven policies this century has not been capable of destroying the British welfare state. Instead, all public services, including the NHS and social services, have resonated with the impact of three processes of Conservative reform: privatization, quasi-marketization and consumerism.

Privatization has been direct for some parts of the NHS (such as ancillary workers) but for others, such as mental health workers, it has been indirect in two senses. First, some therapists have given up on the new business ideology of the NHS and opted to enjoy the freedom of working privately. This has depleted the public sector of therapists it has wholly or partially trained and developed. Second, as a result of quasi-marketization, some NHS patients requiring specialist care on the NHS have been referred to private facilities.

Quasi-marketization refers to the way in which public services, which used to provide services directly and be regulated directly by central government, have now been broken up into local purchasers and providers. These are not true markets (hence the notion of 'quasi-markets'), for a number of reasons. For example, in the NHS the functional separation of the old health authorities (now purchasers or commissioners) from their old employees seeing patients (now providers) has not created an open-ended system of consumers and retailers. In most localities the group of local provider professionals remain monopoly suppliers of their services, permitting only quite small opportunities for competition within these groups. Also, the public sector is (still) not profit making. Service commissioners work with earmarked budgets and, moreover, they buy services *on behalf of* their local population. In this sense they are not consumers of the services, even though they are their purchasers – they make proxy decisions for the public. This takes us to the third feature of the new mixed economy of welfare.

Consumerism has been central to government reforms of the past ten years. Given the managerial proxy, just noted, which has actually been put in place in the purchaser–provider split, within the public services containing psychotherapeutic practice, the importance of consumerism is more ideological than practical. None the less, the 1990 Act, plus its preceding White Papers *Caring for People* and *Working for Patients* (DH, 1989a, 1989b), stressed the need for services to be more responsive to user choice and expressed needs. The range of activities that occur within the ambit of psychotherapeutic practice would certainly to an extent be compatible with this ideology. Psychotherapy, particularly in its individual form, stresses a voluntary relationship and taking the consumer's view seriously. Indeed, many would argue that psychotherapy champions such an approach to helping interventions.

This has not gone unnoticed by service users. For example, the consumerism of the libertarian Right has provided opportunities for the users' movement from the libertarian Left to expand in recent years (Rogers and Pilgrim, 1991). People using mental health services want to prioritize talking treatments over biomedical interventions precisely because the former are more in sync with their own understanding of their problems. They see the sources of, and solutions to, their problems predominantly in a personal and social context (Rogers et al., 1993; Rogers and Pilgrim, 1993). It is not surprising that users' organizations, such as Survivors Speak Out, in their Charter of Needs put 'Provision of free counselling for all' as number three on their list of 15 demands.

However, this first-view compatibility between the expressed needs of people with mental health problems and the traditions of individual psychotherapy is not without its contradictions. For example, the drift (or scurry) of many therapists towards the private sector, as a solution to their own disaffection with a reformed NHS, has simply put personal help beyond the reach of those without the means to pay. And psychotherapists, as much as biological therapists, have shown a marked resistance to taking critical feedback from users seriously (Rogers et al., 1993: Ch. 1). Psychotherapists in particular have a tendency to discredit negative consumer feedback as being tainted by psychopathology or the distorting impact of transference. However, the recent debates about abuse at the hands of therapists highlights why practitioners cannot evade full and proper user accountability. This takes us to the question of the regulation of psychotherapy.

The regulation process, centred on the Rugby Conference, rolls on both unaffected and yet legitimized by consumerism (no user advisory group is yet evident). In early 1993 the UK Standing Conference on Psychotherapy became the UK Council for Psychotherapy and its development is mainly being determined by the predictable internecine disputes and jealousies which have always attended professionals squabbling for social status or religious groups posturing about their self-defined bit of moral high ground. The notion that registration can protect the public in a simple and direct way remains naive. Intimacy plus a power asymmetry will always bring with it the temptation and enactment of abuse in some cases. Registration may offer more chance of individual consumer redress for practitioner crimes and misdemeanours but it does not guarantee greater collective accountability, or greater utility of psychotherapy to people who need help in society. The most regulated of professions, medicine, continues to use that process as one of its many strategies for self-protection and social advancement in such a way that it actually *evades* public accountability (Stacey, 1992; Moran and Wood, 1993).

Psychotherapy will be no different. Indeed, with the slippery business of trying to claim that there are experts in human misery, and with a lack of consensus on theory and practice, it is difficult to see how psychotherapists will ever inspire public confidence, other than by recurrently behaving in a decent and civil way when encountering their clients. And will registration increase the probability of this happening? At present we do not know (though the example of medicine given above and the empirical evidence of deterioration in psychotherapy is not encouraging). An added problem for psychotherapists at present seems to be that ideological schisms are being codified in organizational splits even before state recognition appears on the horizon. For example, by 1995 both the UK Council for Psychotherapy and the British Confederation of Psychotherapists (a scrum of analytical therapists) are selling copies of their own separate registers.

Finally, how is psychotherapy looking as a force for progress in mental health services? For most of this dwindling century it has been a more or less successful brake on the well-oiled dehumanizing machine of biological psychiatry. It certainly continues in that role, as mental health services have both been dispersed and remained hospital centred. The fall of the asylum has unleashed some contradictory social forces. On the one hand the current emphasis on consumerism and community-based work (including crisis intervention) would suggest that psychotherapy will continue to play its progressive part. On the other hand the wider failure of social policy to create and sustain the citizenship of people with mental health problems, by providing them with affordable housing of their choice, employment and social transport, has actually determined their (poor) quality of life in recent years. In this light, even at its best, when untainted by collective professional self-interest or the individual financial considerations of its practitioners, psychotherapy can have a marginal impact (although this may still be worthy). At the population level, mental health in society will mainly improve as a result of poverty reduction and readjustments of power in favour of those social groups which are currently over-represented in mental health statistics (in Britain this means women, African-Caribbean and Irish people). The marginal but genuinely ameliorative role to be played by salaried psychotherapists lies in sites such as health centres, counselling services and voluntary groups in the community. Psychotherapy can be an alternative to biological treatments ('consumer choice'), although this does mean that psychotherapists would need to work with psychotic patients more than they have been inclined to do in the past. It can offer an ameliorative and secondary prevention role in working with people in predictable transitions, such as new adulthood, bereavement, divorce, pre-retirement and after birth. But the likely success of these interventions still has to be placed in the context of the wider forces which shape mental health in society.

References

Anderson, P. (1969) 'Components of the national culture', *New Left Review*, 50, July/ August.

Armstrong, D. (1980) 'Madness and coping', *Sociology of Health and Illness*, 2(3): 393–413.

Barham, P. (1984) 'Cultural forms and psychoanalysis: some problems', in B. Richards (ed.) *Capitalism and Infancy*. London: Free Association.

Baruch, G. and Treacher, A. (1978) *Psychiatry Observed*. London: Routledge & Kegan Paul.

Bion, W.R. (1959) *Experiences in Groups*. New York: Basic Books.

Blackman, D. (1979) 'Behaviour modification: control and counter-control', *Behaviour Analysis*, 1(2): 37–50.

Braverman, H. (1974) *Labour and Monopoly Capital*. London: Monthly Review Press.

Busfield, J. (1986) *Managing Madness*. London: Hutchinson.

Bynum, W.F. (1974) 'Rationales for therapy in British psychiatry', *Medical History*, 18: 39–45.

Castel, R. (1985) 'Moral treatment: mental therapy and social control in the nineteenth century', in S. Cohen and A. Scull (eds), *Social Control and the State*. Oxford: Basil Blackwell.

DH (Department of Health) (1989a) *Caring for People: Community Care in the Next Decade and Beyond*. London: HMSO.

DH (1989b) *Working for Patients*. London: HMSO.

DHSS (Department of Health and Social Security) (1977) *The Role of Psychologists in the Health Service* (Trethowan Report). London: HMSO.

Dicks, H. (1970) *Fifty Years of the Tavistock*. London: Routledge & Kegan Paul.

Digby, A. (1985) 'Moral treatment at the Retreat, 1796–1846', in W.F. Bynum, R. Porter and M. Shepherd (eds), *The Anatomy of Madness*, Vol. II, London: Tavistock.

Doerner, K. (1970) *Madmen and the Bourgeoisie*. Oxford: Basil Blackwell.

Donnelly, M. (1983) *Managing the Mind*. London: Tavistock.

Dryden, W. (ed.) (1984) *Individual Therapy in Britain*. London: Harper & Row.

Eysenck, H.J. (1952) 'The effects of psychotherapy: an evaluation', *Journal of Consulting Psychology*, 16: 319–24.

Eysenck, H.J. (1958) 'Learning theory and behaviour therapy'. Paper presented to the Royal Medico-Psychological Association, 3 July.

Foster, J.G. (1971) *Enquiry into the Practice and Effects of Scientology*. New York: Dodd Mead.

Freidson, E. (1970) *Profession of Medicine*. New York: Dodd Mead.

Gibson, H.B. (1981) *Hans Eysenck*. London: Peter Owen.

Goldie, N. (1974) 'Professional processes among three occupational groups within the mental health field'. PhD thesis, City University, London.

Hearnshaw, L.S. (1964) *A Short History of British Psychology 1840–1940*. London: Methuen.

Holland, R. (1977) *Self and Social Context*. London: Macmillan.

Holland, R. (1981) 'From perspectives to reflexivity', in J.C.J. Bonarius, R. Holland and S. Rosenberg (eds), *Personal Construct Psychology*. New York: Macmillan.

Ingleby, D. (1985) 'Mental health and social order', in S. Cohen and A. Scull (eds), *Social Control and the State*. Oxford: Basil Blackwell.

Jones, M. (1984) Interview in *Guardian*, 1 August.

Kelly, G.A. (1955) *The Psychology of Personal Constructs*. New York: Norton.

Mackay, D. (1984) 'Behavioural psychotherapy', in W. Dryden (ed.), *Individual Therapy in Britain*. London: Harper & Row.

Millenson, J.R. (1969) *Principles of Behavioural Analysis*. London: Macmillan.

Moran, M. and Wood, B. (1993) *States, Regulation and the Medical Profession*. Buckingham: Open University Press.

Neimeyer, R.A. (1985) *The Development of Personal Construct Theory*. London: University of Nebraska Press.

Offe, C. (1984) *Contradictions of the Welfare State*. London: Hutchinson.

Parry, N. and Parry, J. (1976) *The Rise of the Medical Profession*. London: Croom Helm.

Pilgrim, D. (1986) 'NHS psychotherapy: personal accounts'. PhD thesis, University of Nottingham.

Pilgrim, D. (1987) 'Psychologists and psychopathy', *Bulletin of the British Psychological Society*, 40: 168–71.

Pilgrim, D. (1988) 'Psychotherapy in special hospitals: a case of failure to thrive', *Free Associations*, 7: 11–26.

Pilgrim, D. and Rogers, A. (1994) 'Something old, something new: sociology and the organisation of psychiatry', *Sociology*, 28(2): 521–38.

Richards, B. (1983) 'Clinical psychology, the individual and the state'. PhD thesis, North East London Polytechnic.

Richards, B. (1986a) 'Psychological practice and social democracy', *Free Associations*, 5: 105–36.

Richards, B. (1986b) 'Military mobilisations and the unconscious', *Free Associations*, 7: 11–26.

Roazen, P. (1974) *Freud and his Followers*. London: Allen Lane.

Rogers, A. and Pilgrim, D. (1991) '"Pulling down churches": accounting for the British mental health users' movement', *Sociology of Health and Illness*, 13(2): 129–48.

Rogers, A. and Pilgrim, D. (1993) 'Service users' views of psychiatric treatments', *Sociology of Health and Illness*, 15(5): 612–31.

Rogers, A., Pilgrim, D. and Lacey, R. (1993) *Experiencing Psychiatry: Users' Views of Services*. London: Macmillan.

Royal College of Psychiatrists (1975) 'Norms for medical staffing of a psychotherapy service for a population of 200,000', *Bulletin of the Royal College of Psychiatrists*, October: 4–9.

Scull, A. (1977) *Decarceration*. Englewood Cliffs, NJ: Prentice-Hall.

Scull, A. (1979) *Museums of Madness*. London: Allen Lane.

Seighart, P. (1978) *Statutory Registration of Psychotherapists: A Report of a Profession's Joint Working Party*. Cambridge: Plumridge.

Smail, D. (1982) 'Clinical psychology – homogonised and sterilised', *Bulletin of the British Psychological Society*, 35: 345–6.

Stacey, M. (1992) *Regulating British Medicine*. London: Wiley.

Stone, M. (1985) 'Shellshock and the psychologists', in W.F. Bynum, R. Porter and M. Shepherd (eds), *The Anatomy of Madness*, Vol. II. London: Tavistock.

Winnicott, D.W. (1958) 'Metapsychological and clinical aspects of regression in the psychoanalytical set-up', in *Collected Works*. London: Hogarth.

Woodworth, R.S. and Sheehan, M.S. (1964) *Contemporary Schools of Psychology*. London: Methuen.

Yates, A. (1983) 'Behaviour therapy and psychodynamic psychotherapy: basic conflict or re-conciliation and integration?', *British Journal of Clinical Psychology*, 22(2): 107–26.

2

Psychodynamic Therapy: The Freudian Approach

David L. Smith

Historical context and development in Britain

Historical context

Freudian psychotherapy originated in the work of Sigmund Freud (1856–1939), who developed it as the psychotherapeutic application of the science of the human mind that he called *psychoanalysis*. Originally trained as a neuroscientist, Freud was deeply interested in the biological basis of the mental life of human beings. Neuroscience was a new discipline in the late 19th century, and there was a widespread sense that at last the mysteries of the human mind might at last be solved scientifically. It is not surprising, then, that some of the main influences on Freud's work came from this field. Ernst Brücke, Freud's teacher and one of the most prominent physiologists in Europe, was instrumental in replacing outmoded vitalistic ideas with a materialistic concept of physiology. John Hughlings Jackson, the British neurologist, introduced Freud to the idea of dynamic systems as well as the idea of regression to more primitive developmental organizations. Jackson also introduced Darwinian ideas into neurology and psychiatry. Darwin himself was an important influence on Freud's thinking. Other scientific influences included Gustav Fechner, the psychophysiologist, Freud's friend Wilhelm Fliess, a physician, and the psychiatrist Theodore Meynert. Freud was also deeply influenced by the mythology of Greece, Rome and the Middle East and by the writings of Goethe and Shakespeare.

Freud became interested in hypnosis and the psychological basis of mental illness as a result of his studies in Paris with Jean-Martin Charcot in 1885–86. Upon returning to Vienna, Freud initiated a professional collaboration with his friend and mentor Josef Breuer, a distinguished physician who had several years earlier stumbled upon the rudiments of a new form of psychotherapy that he and Freud came to call the *cathartic method*. In 1893 Breuer and Freud published their 'Preliminary communication' and in 1895 they released their groundbreaking *Studies on Hysteria*. Breuer and Freud argued that neurotic symptoms could be explained as the result of a *splitting of consciousness*, often to avoid emotional pain. In 1895 Freud abandoned this model in favour of the view that painful thoughts can be rendered *unconscious*. The new idea of the unconscious made its public début in 1896, in the context of Freud's *seduction theory*, the thesis that emotional disorders are caused by repressed traumatic memories of childhood sexual experiences. Freud gradually abandoned the seduction theory during the closing years of the 19th century.

Freud began to attract a serious following in 1902, and by 1910 psychoanalysis had become an international movement. The development of psychoanalysis was influenced by the rise of National Socialism, which branded psychoanalysis as *zersetzend* (corrosive) – a 'Jewish' as opposed to an 'Aryan' science of the mind. Most of the continental analysts fled to Britain and the Americas, including Freud who arrived in London in 1938. Freud died of cancer in London in 1939.

The diaspora of the continental analysts had the immediate effect of making Britain and the United States the main centres of psychoanalytic activity. After the war psychoanalysis gradually re-established itself throughout Europe and, indeed, all over the world.

Development in Britain

The British Psycho-Analytic Society was established in 1913 by Ernest Jones. Original members included David Eder, probably the first practising analyst in Britain. Jones dissolved and reconstituted the Society in 1919, and in the same year began publishing the *International Journal of Psycho-Analysis*, which remains the official organ of the International Psycho-Analytic Association.

By the time the Freuds arrived in London after the *Anschluss* of Austria, Freud's daughter Anna had become a distinguished practitioner and theorist. There was considerable tension between those analysts affiliated with Anna Freud and those surrounding Melanie Klein, who had developed a rival approach to psychoanalysis which had become firmly established in Britain. British psycho-analysis became split between the Freudians, the Kleinians and a heterogeneous group consisting mainly of indigenous British analysts who became known as the 'Independent Group'. This situation gave rise to a good deal of intellectual ferment which produced a distinctive, creative and influential British psycho-analytical culture.

It is possible although not easy to obtain Freudian therapy within the NHS. There are numerous groups all over Britain that offer therapy and/or training. Most of these organizations are members of the United Kingdom Council for Psychotherapy (UKCP). Those few that are not members of UKCP are members of the British Confederation of Psychotherapists (BCP). Both UKCP and BCP publish a register of accredited practitioners.

Theoretical assumptions

Image of the person

Psychoanalysis has been in existence for one hundred years (Freud first used the term in 1896) and has developed numerous models of the person and conceptions of human nature. Even within the strictly Freudian tradition there are many disagreements about fundamental matters. Given the relatively heterogeneous nature of contemporary Freudian theory, the reader should remember that the account to follow is but one description among many.

Influenced by the rising science of neuropsychology, Freud conceived of the human mind as a function of the human brain and therefore as a part of the natural world. As a part of nature, the mind is subject to natural law. It is part of the same causal web that governs the rest of the universe. Freud called this the principle of *psychical determinism*. Although we like to imagine that we are somehow above and beyond the natural world, and that we govern our lives through autonomous acts of choice, the doctrine of psychical determinism claims that this is a false view. Of course, Freud did not deny that we make real choices, but he asserted that these choices are part of the natural world in which we have our being and cannot in any way oppose or transcend natural law. The theory of psychical determinism suggests that the human mind can be studied scientifically.

The idea that the mind is a natural system opens up the possibility that we are not immediately aware of its inner workings. Certainly, we do not have a direct introspective insight into the way that our brains operate. All we are aware of is the 'output': the result of highly complex internal processes. Freud described this state of affairs by saying that a great deal of our mental activity is unconscious. Freud (1900, 1915) described three distinct types of mental state. *Unconscious* mental states are totally inaccessible to conscious awareness. In order for an unconscious thought to become conscious, it must first become *preconscious*. Preconscious thoughts also exist outside conscious awareness, but they have formed links with language and therefore can, in principle, enter awareness. A selection of our store of preconscious thoughts will, at any given time, be *conscious*. Preconscious thoughts are usually easily retrievable (e.g. memories of recent events). Some unconscious thoughts, however, are permanently inaccessible. According to Freud, such thoughts are inaccessible because they would produce intense distress if allowed to enter consciousness. He described the process of keeping thoughts out of the preconscious system as *censorship* or *defence*. Although such ideas are kept out of consciousness, they influence us indirectly through their offshoots or *derivatives*. Pressing for expression, unconscious ideas form associative links with other ideas that, because innocuous, are allowed to enter consciousness. So, for example, a man with an anxiety-laden unconscious wish to harm his father might express this attitude indirectly by means of an intense hatred of men in positions of authority. Other men are unconsciously treated as proxies for the man's father.

Freud believed that we repress those thoughts that are simultaneously highly exciting and riddled with guilt or shame. Chief among these are sexual and aggressive impulses. Freud believed that the pressures of socialization cause us to hide aspects of our sexuality that contravene social mores and to suppress our tendency to obtain pleasure through harming and exploiting others. We all, therefore, possess a store of highly charged unconscious sexual and aggressive fantasies. According to the Freudian view, then, human beings are inherently divided and alienated from themselves.

Freud grew dissatisfied with the division of the mind into unconscious, preconscious and conscious regions and, in 1923, proposed a new 'structural' model (Freud, 1923) dividing the mind into three force-fields that he called the 'id', 'ego' and 'superego'. The id (in German *das Es*, 'the it') is the biological bedrock of motivation, containing raw sexual and aggressive impulses. The id is heedless of external reality and blindly seeks its own gratifications. Of course, if we were totally governed by the id, we would have little capacity to survive. We would ignore the threats posed by the external world and would be unable to rationally pursue the satisfaction of our desires. The ego (in German *das Ich*, 'the I') is the part of the personality responsible for co-ordinating internal with external reality. Its main function is to secure the gratification of the drives of the id while keeping one out of danger. Because the ego is adapted to external reality, it must sometimes suppress the cravings of the id when the expression of these would be disadvantageous. The id is innate and present from the beginnings of psychological life; the ego gradually emerges during the early years of infancy. Later, as the child becomes socialized, the values and taboos of society become internalized as the superego (in German *das Über-Ich*, 'the over-I'). The superego can be imagined as that part of the mind that rewards one for being 'good' and reproaches one for being 'bad'. The feeling of guilt is evoked when the values of the superego have been contravened.

Because of its asocial and passionate nature, the id is in a state of incessant conflict with the superego. The ego, caught in the middle and attempting to adapt to external reality as well, must find ways of skilfully effecting compromises between these uncompromising contenders. When conflict is severe and intense, this may prove to be impossible, in which case the ego is forced to defend against conflict by rendering the conflict unconscious.

Conceptualization of psychological disturbance and health

In the Freudian scheme, psychological disturbance can be equated with states of unmanageably severe conflict: the personality is literally torn apart by its own contradictions. Through defending against inner conflict, the person treats a distressing internal state as though it were an external danger: he or she flees from it.

Defence is not useful as a long-term solution. The distressing ideas disappear only from *conscious* awareness: they do not go out of existence. Because they are rooted in the inextinguishable biological drives of the id, unconscious ideas exert continual pressure upon the mind, finding expression in dreams, irrational actions, moods and so on. When the ego becomes overloaded and is consequently unable to handle the pressures engendered by defence, unconscious ideas erupt in the form of psychological symptoms. The specific form that such symptoms take is determined by numerous factors such as the nature of the warded-off ideas and impulses, the method by which they are defended against and the unique hereditary strengths and vulnerabilities of the individual. Freudian writes such as Fenichel (1980) describe how these factors interact for each diagnostic category.

The Freudian approach understands psychological illness as an inability to rationally manage inner states of intense anguish, dread and longing. Psychological health is therefore equated with the ability to handle such intense inner states adaptively and creatively. It must be emphasized here that Freud was opposed to any fixed demarcation between 'health' and 'illness'. We are all 'ill'; we are all somewhat mad. This is seen as a consequence of the contradictions inherent in human existence.

Acquisition of psychological disturbance

Severe psychological conflict is a necessary but not a sufficient condition for the outbreak of psychological disturbance. A second necessary condition is the deployment of defence. We must examine both of these more carefully to understand the emergence of psychological symptoms.

Freud came to the conclusion, after years of psychotherapeutic work with adults, that the conflicts powerful enough to produce psychological symptoms invariably stem from infancy. They are conflicts that we come across in the course of our development, during the period when we are both physically and emotionally dependent upon others. Freud attempted to reconstruct important aspects of child psychology by means of his psychoanalytic investigation of adults. Eventually he settled on a constellation of emotions, aspirations and fantasies that he believed to be the root of most forms of psychological disturbance. He called this constellation the *Oedipus complex*.

The term 'Oedipus complex' derives from the ancient Greek legend of Oedipus. Oedipus was the son of King Laius and Queen Jocasta of Thebes. Because it had been foretold that Laius would spawn a son who would destroy him, Laius has Oedipus mutilated and sent away to be killed. Oedipus manages to escape this fate and is adopted by the King and Queen of Corinth. As an adult, Oedipus consults the Oracle of Delphi, who informs him that he is destined to kill his father and marry his mother. Mistakenly believing that the King and Queen of Corinth are his natural parents, Oedipus decides, in an effort to avert his fate, to leave Corinth. Travelling across Greece, he engages an older man in a dispute about right of way. The disputants come to blows and the older man, who is in fact King Laius, is killed by Oedipus. Proceeding to Thebes, Oedipus finds that the city is besieged by a monster called the Sphinx. Anyone unable to correctly answer the riddle posed by the Sphinx is devoured by her. Oedipus correctly answers the riddle, and thus frees Thebes from her grip. He is rewarded by being permitted to marry the recently widowed Queen Jocasta. Many years later Oedipus mounts an investigation into the death of Laius, only to discover that he himself was the murderer. Oedipus blinds himself and Jocasta takes her own life.

Freud termed his discovery the 'Oedipus complex' because of the twin themes of incest and parricide found in the myth. He believed that the sexual instinct has its origins in infancy. Children's sexuality is of a different order to adult sexuality. It does not aim at sexual *intercourse*; it is largely *incestuous*, and it is expressed in *bizarre fantasies and anxieties*. During babyhood, sexuality is largely concentrated on sensations in the mouth and lips, which is why Freud called it the *oral stage* of development. During the toddler or *anal stage* of development sexuality is focused on anal sensations as well as impulses to sadistically control others. The *phallic stage*, so named because it corresponds to a period of intense preoccupation with the phallus, lasts from about the age of three until about the age of seven. During the *latency period* sexuality becomes somewhat suppressed and undergoes no new developments. This continues until puberty, which inaugurates the *genital phase* of mature sexuality.

The Oedipus complex reaches its height during the phallic stage. This stage is often erroneously described as a period when children are sexually attracted to the parent of the opposite sex. Freud, however, explicitly proposed that this stage has a homosexual as well as a heterosexual character.

Freud believed that the little boy is usually most intensely focused on his mother during this stage. He wishes to posses her completely and is fiercely jealous of all rivals, especially his father, who has a special status. His most intense erotic sensations are localized in his penis. Attached to the excitation are impulsions which the child cannot account for – obscure urges to do something violent, to press in, to knock to pieces, to tear open a hole somewhere (Freud, 1908: 218).

Because of his passionate jealousy, the little boy wishes that his father was out of the way and consequently imagines that his father wishes to retaliate. A common fantasy during this period relates to the belief that the boy's father will remove or damage his genitals (*castration anxiety*), and observation that females do not possess a penis lends plausibility to this possibility. Under the pressure of castration anxiety, the boy renounces his incestuous claims and enters the latency period.

Freud was more tentative in his account of female sexuality, the nature and development of which has been debated by psychoanalysts for many decades. Freud describes the little girl as entering the phallic phase with an incestuous attachment directly primarily towards her mother. Like the boy, she feels that her father is a rival, wishes to be rid of him and fears his retaliation. Also like the boy, her observation of the anatomical distinction between the sexes takes on significance within this context. Freud believed that the little girl feels her clitoris to be a stunted or inferior penis, and begins to envy the male genitals (*penis envy*). He was puzzled why this should be the case, and suggested that the psychological importance of the penis in this connection may derive from its link with the desired mother (Freud, 1926). Paradoxically, penis envy is understood to be a force that usually propels the girl towards a heterosexual, feminine stance. Feeling that she cannot compete with her father, because of her lack of a penis, she blames her mother for not having provided her with a penis and despises her for lacking a penis herself. The original loving attachment between daughter and mother therefore becomes tainted with a degree of hostility. The girl simultaneously transforms her wish for a penis into a wish for a baby and finally into an incestuous wish for her father. She then enters a predominantly heterosexual Oedipal situation. Freud felt that girls have greater difficulty abandoning the yearning for their fathers because of the absence of castration anxiety as a motivating factor.

Freud did not mean to imply that the Oedipal drama invariably unfolds along the lines of these schematic descriptions. It is clear from his writings that he believed that the broad Oedipal themes could be realized in a great variety of ways.

According to Freudian theory, the collapse of the Oedipus complex coincides with the establishment of the superego, which opposes the now repressed incestuous and rivalrous impulses. The core of neurotic conflict is believed to lie in the tension between these unconscious desires and the watchful, punitive superego. Oedipal conflicts are thus regarded as a necessary condition for the occurrence of psychological disturbances. However, as these conflicts are universal they cannot be regarded as sufficient. Psychological disturbances arise when one can no longer *cope* with these conflicts. The ego becomes overloaded and breaks down – usually in response to a single precipitating trigger, and the anxiety-laden desires of the id surge towards expression. These are then desperately evaded, only to emerge in disguised form as psychological symptoms. Because such symptoms are disguised expressions of forbidden desires, there will be some symbolic or associative link between the symptom and the specific unconscious ideas that are at its source, although such links may be extremely convoluted and obscure.

Perpetuation of psychological disturbance

Freud (1926) believed that overt symptoms were an expression of underlying psychological disturbance: overt symptoms and inner disturbance are not the same thing, and it is possible to remove overt symptoms without alleviating the inner disturbance of which they are an expression.

Psychological symptoms are perpetuated because of the advantages that they provide. Freud (1926) used the terms *primary* and *secondary gain* to designate these advantages. Primary gain is the main 'reinforcer' of psychological symptoms and is entirely intrapsychic. As symptoms are substitutes for repressed conflicts, the perpetuation of a symptom enables us to avoid facing devastating personal truths. The pain and distress occasioned by the symptom is more tolerable than the pain of recognizing one's own forbidden wishes. Secondary gain is less causally significant. Once a symptom is established, it may be used to provide other advantages. It may be used, for example, as an excuse to avoid unpleasant responsibilities or as a means of obtaining special privileges.

Psychological disturbance, as contrasted with psychological symptoms, is maintained by one's evasion of frightening aspects of one's personality. According to Freudian theory, there are several ways that we keep emotional reality at bay and thereby perpetuate psychological disturbance. These are called the *mechanisms of defence*. Some of the main mechanisms of defence are:

- *Repression*. This is the process of dealing with distressing thoughts by forgetting them. When we repress something, we unconsciously put it out of mind. One might, for example, forget some incident bound up with a forbidden sexual wish.
- *Disavowal*. Sometimes called *denial*, this process bars a perception rather than a thought from consciousness (Dorpat, 1985). When we disavow, we reject the existence of distressing aspects of the external world. One might, for example, deal with a conflict with one's father by disavowing that one *has* a father.
- *Projection*. Projection is the process of attributing a distressing aspect of oneself to someone else. One might, for example, deal with sadistic wishes by projecting them on to others and developing the idea that others are conspiring to harm one.
- *Introjection*. Introjection is the process of unconsciously emulating aspects of others. For example, we often 'introject' aspects of our parents' personalities and value-systems. Parental disapproval is transformed into self-disapproval. Introjection is sometimes called *identification, internalization* or *incorporation*.
- *Reversal*. Reversal is the process of directing an attitude towards oneself rather than towards someone else. Resentment towards one's mother might, for example, be transformed into impulses towards self-harm.
- *Displacement*. In displacement one substitutes one person for another. For example, a man with unconscious anxieties about incestuous yearnings might be powerfully repelled (or intensely attracted) by women resembling his mother in some way.
- *Isolation*. Isolation is the process of detaching thought from feeling. One might, for instance, recollect an important childhood loss without any sense of grief or rage.

- *Reaction formation.* Reaction formation means replacing an attitude by its opposite. One might substitute an attitude of disgust for that of sexual excitement, veneration for contempt, and so on.
- *Negation.* Negation means forming a false belief that one does *not* hold some distressing attitude. For instance, it is possible to adamantly hold that one does not have any homosexual inclinations to avoid the homosexual side of one's nature.
- *Rationalization.* Rationalization means finding false reasons for one's attitudes or actions. For instance, a compelling sadistic desire to torture someone might be justified on the grounds that that person deserves to be punished.
- *Conversion.* Conversion is the process of turning a distressing idea into a physical disorder. For example, the sense of dependency (being unable to 'stand on one's own two feet') might lead to incapacitating leg pains.
- *Acting out.* Acting out means taking some impulsive action to pre-empt awareness of distressing inner states. One might, for example, go shopping to ward off a sense of grief or depression.

Defence mechanisms are essential for the perpetuation of psychological disturbance because they keep core conflicts outside awareness. They may operate singly or in combination. Specific defences are linked with specific psychological disorders: paranoia is said to involve the extensive use of projection, depression thrives on introjection while obsessional neurosis involves reaction formation, isolation and negation.

Apart from the idea of secondary gain, the Freudian approach has little to say about the role of interpersonal factors in the perpetuation of psychological disturbance. Interpersonal processes are mainly seen as important only in so far as they augment the underlying conflicts or reduce the ability of the ego to deal with them. Mounting sexual frustration caused by the lack of an ongoing sexual relationship might, for example, aggravate underlying sexual conflicts. Interpersonal events are seen as significant only in so far as they induce a shift in the purely intrapsychic sphere.

It is important to stress that Freud believed that innate, biological factors have a large part to play in the development of psychopathology. According to this view all of us are born with special strengths and vulnerabilities. These innate features interact with environmental factors to produce the personality. Some of us are *born* with a constitutionally powerful oral drive, a heightened propensity for homosexuality, a difficulty in inhibiting impulses, and so on. A facile environmentalism is therefore inconsistent with the Freudian approach.

Change

According to Freudian theory, the personality is the expression of a balance struck between various intrapsychic forces, many of which are at odds with one another. In some cases the price paid for this skilful intrapsychic compromise is the existence of psychological symptoms or characterological rigidity. It follows that anything capable of upsetting the intrapsychic balance might contribute to the process of change. In ordinary life, then, symptoms might be modified in two ways: the lessening of the intensity of unconscious urges pressing towards consciousness, or the strengthening of the defences against them. The lessening of unconscious urges might come about through the effects of ageing or through a change in life circumstances, for example leaving a job in which aggressive urges were continually being aroused by an oppressive boss. It is also possible to find channels for 'sublimating' unconscious urges – that is, expressing them symbolically in more adaptive ways. For example, an individual troubled by anal urges might find relief in a pastime like pottery that might represent faecal play. The reinforcement of defences might also come about through a change in circumstances. For example, one's ego might be taxed by fatigue stemming from overwork. A change to less demanding employment might free more energy that can be used for defence.

Practice

Goals of therapy

Freudian therapists do not strive to turn 'disturbed' people into 'normal' people. 'Normal' people are simply those who have been able to suppress their inner conflicts to such an extent that they are quite unaware of them. 'Disturbed' people are less psychologically complacent. They are unable to manage their inner turmoil and therefore cannot ignore its existence, but the real nature of these inner concerns remains unconscious. Disturbed people know that they are disturbed but do not know what, at bottom, is disturbing them. The normal person is not conscious of any disturbance. The Freudian psychotherapist seeks to help a person become more self-aware than those who are normal, and better able to cope with this awareness than those who are disturbed. Winnicott (1965: 43) puts this pithily: 'We are poor indeed if we are only sane.' Freudian therapists concentrate on helping their clients to come to an understanding of previously unconscious aspects of themselves. They accordingly do not attempt simply to eliminate symptoms, but rather attempt to transform symptoms into insights. The gap left by a successfully resolved symptom is filled by a deepened understanding of one's inner life. This goal is incompatible with irrational, manipulative or authoritarian modes of treatment.

Freud believed that all psychotherapy works through two incompatible modes of influence: insight and suggestion. In cures through suggestion, the client experiences his or her therapist as an idealized parental figure. Therapists, often without realizing it, manipulate the client by using the power thus invested in them, finding ways to intimidate or seduce clients into making desired changes. Freudian therapists strive to eliminate the element of suggestion as completely as possible, although Freud believed that a measure of suggestion is inevitable. Complete candour is expected of clients, who are invited to confront all of those things in themselves that they have spent a lifetime avoiding. Therapists are expected to refrain from all suggestive measures and to single-mindedly pursue their clients' inner truth wherever it may lead.

One further point ought to be made in this context. Because of the emphasis on insight and self-knowledge, many individuals enter Freudian therapy primarily to gain a deeper understanding of themselves and develop a richer inner life, rather than to resolve some particular psychological disturbance. The therapy of such individuals does not differ in any essential respect from those who complain of 'disturbances'.

Selection criteria

Freudian therapy is essentially a one-to-one modality. Although some therapists have attempted to use the Freudian approach in groups or with couples, this alteration of the fundamental rules of treatment (total privacy and confidentiality) sets such efforts apart from classical Freudian therapy. It is perhaps more accurate to speak of group and couple therapy that is psychoanalytically *informed* than it is to speak of the psychoanalytic therapy of groups or couples. The same reservation applies to brief or time-limited psychotherapy. Freudian therapy is by its very nature a protracted process. The exploration of the most intimate and anguish-ridden aspects of one's personal life cannot be forced into some set schedule. Brief psychotherapy can, however, be informed by aspects of psychoanalytic theory.

There is a second, somewhat contentious distinction to consider here: the distinction between 'psychoanalysis' and 'psychoanalytic therapy'. Of course, in the broad sense, psychoanalytic therapy is just the application of psychoanalysis (a theory of the mind) to psychotherapy. However, the term 'psychoanalysis' is also used to designate a special form of intensive psychotherapy that is said to be distinguishable from psychoanalytic therapy. It is difficult if not impossible to find very substantive distinctions between the two. Opinion has it that psychoanalytic psychotherapy is less intensive and rigorous. Psychoanalytic therapists are said to see their clients less frequently than their psychoanalyst colleagues, and are said to place their patients on a chair in preference to the traditional Freudian 'couch'. Such generalizations do not survive real scrutiny. Some psychoanalysts work in an undisciplined fashion quite out of line with Freudian principles, while some psychoanalytic therapists work in an exemplary manner. The designations 'psycho-analyst' and 'psychoanalytic' therapists' are more useful as guides to the type of training that a practitioner has received than as reliable indications of the type of therapy on offer. In the present chapter I shall describe psychoanalytic therapy as for all practical purposes equivalent to 'psychoanalysis'. The two terms will be used interchangeably. It should also be noted that not all psychoanalysts and psycho-analytic therapists work in the Freudian mode. Jungians, Kleinians, Lacanians and many others employ these labels.

Freud (1905) felt that psychoanalytic therapy worked best with people possess-ing a reasonable degree of education and having a reliable character. Later writers such as Karush (1960) and Kuiper (1968) claim that the ideal Freudian client is able to tolerate frustration, anxiety, passivity and depression, and possesses a capacity for insight, adequate reality resting, adequate interpersonal relations and positive motivation.

Bachrach and Leaf (1978) concluded after a careful study of the literature that the outcome of psychoanalytic treatment is positively correlated with the pre-treatment level of functioning.

Outcome research has cast considerable doubt on all of these claims by demonstrating that there is little relationship between how well people do in psychoanalysis and predictions made on the basis of pre-treatment assessments (Wallerstein, 1987). One important factor that has not been adequately studied is the 'fit' between client and therapist (ibid.). Chiefetz (1984) has pointed to the conditions of treatment (the provision of an adequate physical environment, privacy, confidentiality, and so on) as a more significant variable than the degree of education and cultural background of clients.

Freudian therapy is not indicated for persons suffering from psychotic disorders (Freud 1905), although forms of the approach have been used both in the treatment of psychosis and of the 'borderline syndrome' (Kernberg, 1980). The Freudian approach is believed to be best suited to the treatment of neurotic or perverse symptoms and character traits.

Qualities of effective therapists

Because Freudian therapists renounce any attempt to influence the client through force of personality or 'charisma', one of the most important qualities of the competent practitioner is the ability to subordinate his or her personality to the 'analytic attitude'. Adherence to the ethical commitment to healing through insight must suffuse every aspect of the therapist's work. This is expressed in the three main professional values of Freudian practice (Dorpat, 1979):

- a caring commitment to the client;
- a respect for the client's autonomy;
- a devotion to the pursuit of truth.

These attitudes are collectively named the *rule of neutrality*.

Because the Freudian approach is rooted in the attitude of 'finding out' about human beings rather than the attitude of 'already knowing', the therapist should be a naturally inquisitive person (Schafer, 1983). The arduous and often lengthy nature of psychoanalytic therapy demands patience as well as emotional stamina. As Freudian therapy focuses on the unknown (unconscious) dimensions of mental life, the therapist must be able to tolerate and perhaps even enjoy long periods during which he or she does not really understand what is going on. Finally, the Freudian therapist must be able to endure extended periods of outward passivity. Because this approach is rooted in understanding rather than manipulation, it eschews an active, conversational or interventionist approach. To understand something of another person's most intimate and hidden concerns it is necessary to spend long periods quietly listening to them.

Therapeutic relationship and style

Many aspects of Freudian therapeutic style are entailed by the rule of neutrality. The Freudian therapist is quite, reflective and primarily concerned with exploring the client's emotional concerns. The therapist does not offer advice on how clients should live their lives. The role of the therapist is to assist clients to understand themselves more fully. This attitude is surprisingly difficult to maintain. It is always tempting to play the role of expert or 'guru', particularly when clients yearn for this sort of guidance. However, such behaviour would be unrealistic and dishonest, as the attitude inspiring it would be based on an idealization of the therapist. Freudian therapists accordingly feel that it is important to counteract their own (inevitable) tendencies in this direction. Freudian therapy is therefore characterized by a strict, self-imposed discipline on the part of the therapist, which may give the approach a somewhat formal or mannered quality. In their efforts to pursue unconscious meaning, Freudian therapists must concentrate their attention fully on the client. They must avoid undermining the client's autonomy in any way. They must also abandon conventional social modes of interaction. Because of the exclusive focus on the client, therapists refrain from disclosing their own personal concerns (the *rule of anonymity*). As Freudian therapy is ultimately about helping people live satisfactory lives in the world outside, it is also important for the therapist to refrain from acting as a proxy friend or lover, even though clients may clamour for this sort of gratification (the *rule of abstinence*). Overall, then, the Freudian therapist works very hard at maintaining an appropriate relationship with his or her clients. This creates an atmosphere in which clients feel safe to reveal highly vulnerable, shameful and guilt-ridden aspects of themselves. The disciplined nature of the analytic attitude should not be confused with inhumanity or aloofness. It is rooted in an attitude of compassion towards fellow struggling, suffering human beings.

The basic Freudian skills are creating an atmosphere of safety and keeping out of the client's way. Therapists' silence is broken only infrequently, usually to share with clients their ideas about the clients' inner struggles (this is called *interpretation*). Even when the therapist is silent, he or she is intensely engaged with the client – listening carefully and respectfully. This attitude of silent attending is, from the client's point of view, very different from 'talking to a brick wall': it provides the whole process with a powerful sense of intimacy.

Freudian therapists attempt to maintain a non-judgmental attitude. They do not take sides in clients' intra- and interpersonal conflicts. They offer neither condemnation nor praise, and do not try to reassure clients, all of which are felt to detract from clients' autonomy and the quest for truth. Apart perhaps from an initial handshake, Freudian therapists do not engage their clients in any form of physical contact. The seeming austerity of these restrictions is offset by the fact that they are designed to create a situation in which clients can authentically be themselves without fear of censure or interference.

Major therapeutic strategies and techniques

According to Freudian theory, emotionally charged ideas are able to produce symptoms only in so far as they participate in *unconscious conflict*. For this reason, the main strategy deployed by Freudian therapists is to 'make the unconscious conscious'. Another way to formulate this is to say that Freudian therapists attempt to help their clients integrate disowned aspects of themselves. This process, if successfully implemented, does not *solve* a person's emotional dilemmas. It does not automatically render a person content or happy. Rather, it enables people to confront their own deepest concerns more directly, and undermines the tendency to handle these concerns non-insightfully. As Freud ironically put it, it is not the therapist's task to solve all the client's problems, but rather to replace neurotic misery with ordinary unhappiness (Breuer and Freud, 1895). Psychoanalytic therapy does not claim to produce happiness and fulfilment; it merely strives to remove some of the obstacles to such attainment. Freudian therapy attempts to relieve the surplus misery stemming from unconscious conflicts; it cannot remove the sources of pain and unhappiness that are intrinsic to human life.

Freudian therapists strive insightfully to remove psychological obstacles to the recognition of disturbing inner truths. The therapeutic environment is an important element of this process. Freudian therapists attempt to sustain an environment in which their clients can feel safely contained. They strive in a 'neutral' manner, secure total privacy and confidentiality, and ensure that sessions are of a set frequency and duration. Many therapists provide a 'couch' on which clients can recline, with the therapist seated unobtrusively outside the client's visual field, an arrangement that encourages unconscious expression.

Clients are expected to *free-associate* during sessions. 'Free association' means letting thoughts emerge into your mind without censoring them in any way, and describing these out loud to the therapist. People normally constrain their thoughts and hold many thoughts back from expression to others. Free association is a consciousness-expanding process. One is required simply to remain open to one's experience and be entirely honest with the therapist about what is going on. Freud described free association in an early publication as follows:

> He [Freud] asks the patient to 'let himself go' in what he says, 'as you would do in a conversation in which you were rambling on quite disconnectedly and at random'. . . . He insists that they must include in it whatever comes into their heads, even if they think it unimportant or irrelevant or nonsensical; he lays special stress on their not omitting any thought or idea . . . because to relate it would be embarrassing or distressing to them. (1904: 251)

Free association is intrinsically therapeutic because it encourages one to stop running away from oneself and hiding one's personal concerns from others. It is also important in relation to the Freudian belief in psychical determinism. Freud held that if the mind is part of nature it follows that mental events are not random, and that thoughts that seem to come into one's head from nowhere during the process of free association must be caused by other thoughts of which we are unaware. Free association thus makes the unconscious influences on mental life more apparent. Free association is described as the *fundamental rule* of psychoanalysis.

When one attempts to free-associate with complete candour, one finds that there are 'sticking points' when this becomes difficult. Freudian therapists call this phenomenon *resistance*. Sometimes this is because one feels ashamed or guilty about admitting certain things to another person. At other times, however, one just seems inwardly stuck. Even when free-associating on one's own, without the embarrassing presence of another, there are times when it becomes excruciatingly difficult to comply with the fundamental rule. Freud thought that this happens only when one has difficulty admitting something to *oneself*. This type of resistance is said to occur whenever disturbing unconscious ideas are close to consciousness. It is therefore an unconscious attempt to 'block' free association and shore-up defences against painful truths.

Resistance is not treated in an adversarial fashion. It is extremely important in the therapeutic process because it points to areas of emotional vulnerability – 'chinks' in clients' defensive armour. Resistance is a sign that something is unconsciously causing one anguish. Freudian therapists need to be good at detecting signs of resistance in their clients.

Freudian therapists listen to their clients in a special frame of mind that helps them to be aware of resistance. Freud called this attitude *gleichschwebende Aufmerksamkeit* which is usually translated as 'free floating', 'evenly suspended' or 'evenly hovering' attention. In my opinion 'evenly gliding attention' best captures the sense of Freud's term. Evenly gliding attention is in many respects similar to free association. Therapists silently let themselves go, refraining from conscious reflection on their client's discourse. Theoretical beliefs are allowed to sink into the background, and no attempt is made to fix information in memory. Therapists listen to their patients as though they were listening to music or poetry. When attending to another person whilst in this state of mind, sensitivity to emotional nuances is greatly heightened, and it becomes much easier to detect the operation of resistance.

Freudian therapy attempts to achieve its goals through the insightful dissolution of resistances. Instead of attempting forcibly to 'break down' a resistance (which would be antithetical to the Freudian ethic of neutrality), the therapist tries to help the client understand what is going on. Once the client has recognized what it is that he or she fears allowing into awareness, there is no longer any need to maintain the resistance.

There is much disagreement in the field about just what constitutes an appropriate psychoanalytic intervention. Some therapists believe that the ethic of neutrality is consistent with a wide variety of interventions, including questions and 'confrontations'. Others believe that neutral only licenses a limited range of interventions. Using the 'strict' interpretation there are only three types of intervention available to the Freudian therapist: silence, management and interpretation.

A Japanese riddle poses the question: 'What is the most important part of a rice bowl?' The correct answer is 'The space inside.' We are not accustomed to thinking of an empty space as an important part of anything. The riddle leads us to realize that an empty space, an apparent 'nothing', can perform important functions. In Freudian therapy the intervention of silence, seemingly a mere absence of speech, becomes highly important. Silence creates the 'space' within the therapeutic container: a space to be filled by the client's free associations and resistances. The Freudian therapist is silent to make room for the client. He or she is silent a great deal of the time to secure a great deal of room for the client. Silence is therefore an intervention of fundamental importance. It is regarded as something therapists actively *do*.

'Management' is a shorthand term for 'management of the environment' or 'frame management' ('frame' is a psychoanalytic term for the ground-rules and setting of the therapy). Management in therapy means creating and sustaining an environment that reliably encourages and safeguards the therapeutic process. It encompasses factors like warmth, comfort, privacy, confidentiality, regularity and so on. Like silence, management is non-verbal. These two non-verbal interventions are the most important activities for Freudian therapists. By creating an atmosphere of safety in which clients can communicate deeply, these interventions establish preconditions for the interpretation of unconscious meanings.

While listening to clients' free associations, Freudian therapists will at some point detect the presence of resistance. They will then move *out* of the state of evenly gliding attention and reflect upon this observation, attempting to reach an understanding of *how* the resistance is operating, *why* it is being deployed (i.e. its motive) and *what* it is that the resistance is barring from awareness. A hypothesis of this kind is called an *interpretation* (in German *Deutung*). Strictly speaking, interpretation is not an intervention: it is a cognitive process (Freud, 1913). At an appropriate moment the interpretation may be offered to the client. Properly speaking, this is called 'voicing an interpretation', but it has come to be called 'interpretation' for short. Not all resistances are interpreted. Much of the time the therapist simply does not understand enough to interpret a resistance. At other times, the therapist may feel that it is preferable to allow the client to come to grips with a resistance without interference.

To summarize, interpretation is nothing more than offering to clients ideas about the unconscious basis of a resistance that has come into play. Interpretations should be given in simple, straightforward and ordinary language. The therapist should explain in the interpretation just how he or she reached his/her conclusions. Interpretation should be presented as a rational process rather than the product of some mystical 'insight'. Interpretations can only be evaluated on the basis of clients' responses to them (Smith, 1987). An accurate and timely interpretation should diminish resistance and give deeper concerns freer play.

During the course of therapy, the relationship between client and therapist becomes quite intense and everything that happens in therapy becomes coloured by the emotional tone of the client's attitude towards his or her therapist. These deep, irrational emotional currents are attributed to a process called *transference*. Transference is a hypothetical process in which present-day figures are unconsciously used as surrogates for unconscious images of significant persons from the client's past. Transference is said to occur as a compromise between the forces of expression and the forces of defence. The client is afraid of remembering aspects of the past and yet the problematic memories press strenuously for discharge. In transference, the client lives out the past without realizing it as such. Because all the most urgent, repressed aspects of the client's past are believed to find expression in some aspect of the 'transference relationship', Freudian therapists attempt to interpret their clients' resistances within the context of transference. Clients may for example become inhibited while free-associating because they fear that the therapist will despise and ridicule them for mentioning certain topics, or they may only mention things calculated to please or titillate the therapist. In Freudian therapy the relationship between therapist and client quickly becomes and remains the central focus. Transference becomes the stage upon which the long-forgotten dramas of childhood are repeated and reintegrated.

The term 'counter-transference' is often mentioned in the same context as 'transference'. In spite of appearances, counter-transference is quite a different sort of concept. It can be defined most economically as any disruption of the analytic attitude of neutrality. Counter-transference is caused by therapists' own personal limitations, including their unresolved emotional difficulties and unconscious conflicts, although it can also be induced by pressures exerted by clients. For example, a client tells his therapist that he is refraining from mentioning something important, and goes on to talk about trivial matters. The client uses a great deal of body language while discussing these unimportant matters. Because the therapist is now in a heightened state of curiosity, she pays disproportionate attention to the client's body. The client has skilfully and unconsciously induced the therapist to gaze intensely at his body and thus enact with him an exhibitionistic sexual fantasy. Through recognizing and silently analysing her lapse, the therapist might draw accurate conclusions about this client's concealed wish to exhibit himself. So in some instances counter-transference can be used to reveal important information about clients.

The change process in therapy

Although they ultimately aim at relieving whatever presenting problems the client has brought to therapy, Freudian therapists attempt to do this by means of expanding clients' self-awareness. From beginning to end the process is characterized by the gradual, careful and systematic analysis of resistance, with an increasing focus on transference issues. The analysis of resistance alters the structure of patients' defences, bringing unconscious material to light and eliminating symptoms.

The course of 'treatment' can be divided into an opening, middle and end phase. The opening phase begins with the establishment of a verbal contract and includes the identification and beginning analysis of resistance. This phase may also include a 'honeymoon period' of rapid improvement that is, however, unstable and not rooted in real insight. The middle phase is marked by the deepening of transference and the intensive analysis of resistance. Gains achieved during the middle phase may be temporarily lost during the termination phase, and important issues concerning death and separation may be explored. Much work also goes on *after* termination, without the assistance of the therapist.

The elimination of symptoms is not the sole measure of therapeutic progress, as symptoms can be removed by means that leave the underlying disturbance untouched. Freudian therapy should in the end impel clients towards greater 'soulfulness', tolerance, passion and independence of spirit. Clients develop an acute awareness of the complexity and contradictoriness of human existence. They come to feel more at home with their own and others' bodily yearnings.

Failure to make therapeutic progress may be due to the therapist, the client or both. There is always a price to be paid in therapy, above and beyond the therapist's fee. In Freudian therapy, this price includes the experience of a great deal of previously buried anguish. For many, this price is too high: neurotic suffering is more tolerable to them than the suffering attendant upon making the unconscious conscious. This may be due to the sheer magnitude of a person's distress and/or the lack of consolations and compensations elsewhere in life. This is to some extent true of all of us. We can each tolerate only a certain degree of self-knowledge. No therapist has the right to presume that such natural barriers must be crossed. It is the client who draws the line.

The lack of progress can more frequently be attributed to the therapist's failings. Such is the complexity of the analytic process, and the depth of our ignorance about the working of the human mind, that even successful treatments may include errors of considerable magnitude. The opportunities for error are endless. The maintenance of strict self-discipline and ongoing supervision are the most extensively used safeguards against this. When confronted by an impasse, the therapist should first consider how he or she has contributed to it, and redouble efforts at understanding. As Freud was fond of saying, the best way to shorten an analysis is to do it correctly!

Limitations of the approach

The limitations of the Freudian approach are manifold. Freud believed that he had created a science of the human mind. With the benefit of hindsight it is obvious that he did not succeed in creating a science, although it is arguable that he created a *potential science*. Isolated from the scientific community, psycho-analysis since Freud has not made good its founder's dream. The upshot of this is that psychoanalytic therapy remains a rather vague, intuitive and invalidated procedure, an art or craft rather than an applied science. It is known that Freudian therapy sometimes works and sometimes does not work. Psychoanalysis lacks the clarity and intellectual resources to determine (non-speculatively) why this should be the case. There is no objective method for examining the basic problems of theory and technique and refining the approach. Psychoanalysis must achieve greater scientific and philosophical clarity to advance beyond its present situation. The work of Adolf Grünbaum (1984, 1993) has been especially important in demonstrating just how weak the scientific claims of psychoanalysis are. Writers like Cioffi (1974), Macmillan (1991) and Esterson (1993) have pointed to numerous incoherencies in Freudian theory. Attempts at quantitative study of the psychotherapeutic process have already undermined many of the ideas widely held by Freudian practitioners (Langs, 1992).

Some Freudians have attempted to deal with these objections by claiming that psychoanalysis is properly an interpretative art rather than a science. Even so, claims to knowledge must be backed up by evidence if they are to be taken seriously. Even an interpretative art needs some reliable method of distinguishing truth from illusion. It is precisely this that psychoanalysis (in common with virtually all other forms of therapy) lacks.

On a more prosaic note, Freudian therapy has a limited range of applicability. It is lengthy and uncertain, and is therefore not widely regarded as cost-effective. Although short-term 'psychodynamic' therapies have been developed, these are only marginally Freudian, departing from its spirit and technique in numerous respects. The vast majority of those seeking Freudian therapy must obtain it privately, which places it beyond the reach of those not sufficiently well off. (Although most training institutes offer low-cost therapy, these schemes are staffed by students in training rather than experienced practitioners.)

Case example

The client

The client whom I shall call Mr T., was 37 years old when he began once a week psychotherapy that was to continue for six years. He had been in therapy twice before: once with a Freudian psychoanalyst and at a later stage with a bio-energetic therapist. His presenting problem was psychosomatic: he suffered from severe neck pains which his physician attributed to 'stress'. Mr T. was an architect. He had been born and raised in the North of England and settled in London shortly after graduating from university.

The therapy

After a few weeks of therapy Mr T.'s neck pains disappeared. It was only then that he revealed his deeper reasons for coming to therapy. He suffered from uncontrollable outbursts of extreme rage and suspiciousness, often with racist overtones, which he feared would one day cause him to kill someone. He was also prone to periods of depression and profound despair. Besides all of this, Mr T. was sexually troubled. He was unhappily homosexual, and felt that there was something inauthentic about his attraction to swarthy boys.

During the first year of therapy most sessions were taken up with his two passionate interests: English literature and tennis. He was deeply interested in the personalities of the (male) authors and tennis champions. Very little significant interpretative work could be done during this period, but two crucially important themes emerged: the theme of admired men who have achieved immortality through their progeny and the theme of men locked in intense, heated competition.

During the first year of therapy Mr T. blamed virtually all of his problems on his mother, who was described as a sinister witch-like figure. His father was described enthusiastically as a friend and protector. In the years of therapy that followed, this picture was substantially revised. An important step in this direction came about when Mr T. noticed that he would invariably arrive at my office in a depressed mood if his previous session had been particularly productive. Free-associating to this, he hit upon a rich vein of images of male–male competition and memories of his father. He realized that the prospect of improvement led him to feel guilty. After many weeks of work it emerged that he was afraid of doing better than his father. His depression functioned as a prohibition. It took Mr T. much longer to realize that this guilt concealed a potent ambition to 'beat' his father. This was expressed in the transference by his depressively showing me that I was impotent to help him.

Mr T.'s relationship to his father came more into focus as we explored the complex nature of his sexuality. His attraction to swarthy boys was multiply determined. Mr T. wanted to love a boy because the boy in him wanted to be loved. Through identifying with the boy he could imagine that he was a boy being treated with tender sensuality. It became clear, eventually, that this expressed a longing for his mother's affection. The essential quality of 'darkness' that the attractive boy was required to possess was derived from Mr T.'s father, who had a Mediterranean complexion. The beloved boy therefore also seemed to represent the client's father. This remained a mystery until Mr T. began to work on understanding the quality of 'ungenuineness' which he attributed to his homosexual fantasies. Mr T.'s homosexual love also contained a powerful undercurrent of hatred. This love was partly a reaction-formation against aggression. His sexual preference thus contained two themes characteristic of the Oedipus complex: the wish for his mother's sensual affection and the hatred of his father.

As these matters gradually unravelled, Mr T. began to revise his portrayal of his parents. His mother now emerged as a caring but rather inhibited woman who lived in fear of her husband. His father appeared to be a very disturbed man who was prone to episodes of violent and paranoid jealousy, as well as hypochondriacal anxieties concerning his testicles. Mr T. began to feel that he had vilified his mother because of his terror of his father's jealousy, and recalled how his father attempted to turn him against his mother. These realizations coincided with the disappearance of his depressive and violent episodes, which had been based on an identification with his frightening father.

The client's fear and hatred of his father explained an important detail of his outbursts of rage and suspiciousness. When these occurred Mr T. would often form the idea that a Black male (e.g. a Black employee at his firm) was attempting to exploit him in some way. He would then feel a sense of hatred towards Black people in general. The theme of 'blackness' was derived from his father's black hair and dark complexion. When Mr T.'s hatred of his father was brought to light these episodes of racial hatred disappeared entirely.

During the fourth year of therapy Mr T. began to experience strong heterosexual desires, and his conscious homosexual yearnings correspondingly decreased. He had one brief affair with a man during this period, but was too terrified of rejection to approach women. During times of stress he would find himself again attracted to boys. At around this time the analysis of a dream triggered the memory of a disturbing childhood event. At the age of four, Mr T. visited a neighbour in the company of his mother, and witnessed her breastfeeding her baby. This produced an uncanny feeling in him and after this experience he began to be plagued by the fear that his head would explode. This feat persisted on and off for several years. When the dread came upon him he would run to his mother in a state of panic. Mr T.'s associations suggested that the observation of breastfeeding had stirred up desperate longings for his mother's affection which in turn stimulated fears of violent punishment by his father. The explosion of his head may have been a disguised portrayal of castration.

As we approached termination a new symptom emerged. Mr T. complained of losing all sexual desire and developed the conviction that his penis was shrinking away. This seemed to be related to his fear of the prospect of becoming more sexually potent than his father. The client unconsciously introjected his father, who had hypochondriacal ideas about his testicles, and suppressed his sexuality for fear of castration, which was expressed in the thought of his penis shrinking away.

Therapy was terminated at Mr T.'s behest. He was satisfied with the disappearance of his pains, rages and depressions and felt generally more self-confident, happy and socially at ease. He was not satisfied with his sexuality. He continued to long for and fear women, and the anxieties surrounding his penis had not entirely disappeared. He felt, however, that he could fully resolve these problems only when he no longer had me to fall back on.

From a Freudian perspective there are a number of obvious weaknesses in my work with Mr T. I did not, for example, consistently analyse his aggression towards his father in the context of our relationship. I also failed to explore his infantile fantasies about the female genitalia in any depth. I might also be justifiably taken to task for not having looked more closely into his pre-Oedipal psychotic anxieties. All of these issues could be seen as having a strong bearing on Mr T.'s fear of women, which remained unresolved.

Since my work with Mr T., I have grown very sceptical about much of Freudian theory. I have come to believe that the depth of our ignorance and the absence of objective means for investigating psychotherapeutic theories warrants a cautious and sceptical attitude towards all forms of psychotherapy. With the benefit of hindsight I am therefore much less confident about the value of my work with Mr T., although I would not dismiss it globally. As a psychotherapist, I now mainly use the communicative approach to psychoanalytic psychotherapy (Smith, 1991). In line with this approach I would no longer concentrate on Mr T.'s unconscious reading of the here-and-now rather than pursuing his infantile fantasies. I would also be much more alert to the destructive impact of my errors, and would be considerably more cautious about accepting the validity of my interventions.

References

SE refers to the *Standard Edition of the Complete Psychological Works of Sigmund Freud*, 24 vols. (1955–74) ed. and trans. J. Strachey, London: Hogarth Press and the Institute for Psycho-Analysis.

Bachrach, H.M. and Leaf, L.A. (1978) 'Analyzability: a systematic review of the clinical and quantitative literature', *Journal of the American Psychoanalytic Association*, 26: 881–920.

Breuer, J. and Freud, S. (1895) 'Studies on hysteria', in *SE 2*: 1–323.

Chiefetz, L.G. (1984) 'Framework violations in psychotherapy with clinic patients', in J. Raney (ed.), *Listening and Interpreting: The Challenge of the Work of Robert Langs*. New York: Jason Aronson.

Cioffi, F. (1974) 'Was Freud a liar?', *The Listener*, 91 (7 February): 172–4.

Dorpat, T. (1979) 'On neutrality', *International Journal of Psychoanalytic Psychotherapy*, 6: 39–55.

Dorpat, T. (1985) *Denial and Defense in the Therapeutic Situation*. New York: Jason Aronson.

Esterson, A. (1993) *Seductive Mirage: An Exploration of the Work of Sigmund Freud*. Chicago: Open Court.

Fenichel, O. (1980) *The Psychoanalytic Theory of Neurosis*. London: Routledge & Kegan Paul.

Freud, S. (1900) 'The interpretation of dreams', in *SE 4 and 5*: 1–626.

Freud, S. (1904) 'Freud's psycho-analytic procedure', in *SE 7*: 249–57.

Freud, S. (1905) 'On psychotherapy', in *SE 7*: 257–68.

Freud, S. (1908) 'On the sexual theories of children', in *SE 9*: 205–26.

Freud, S. (1913) 'On beginning the treatment: further recommendations on the technique of psycho-analysis', in *SE 12*: 121–45.
Freud, S. (1915) 'The unconscious', in *SE 14*: 159–209.
Freud, S. (1923) 'The ego and the id', in *SE 19*: 3–63.
Freud, S. (1926) 'Inhibitions, symptoms and anxiety', in *SE 20*: 77–175.
Grünbaum, A. (1984) *The Foundations of Psychoanalysis: A Philosophical Critique.* Berkeley, CA: University of California Press.
Grünbaum, A. (1993) *Validation in the Clinical Theory of Psychoanalysis: A Study in the Philosophy of Psychoanalysis.* Madison, CT: International Universities Press.
Karush, C.F. (1960) in S.A. Guttman (reporter), 'Criteria for analyzability: panel reports', *Journal of the American Psychoanalytic Association*, 8: 141–51.
Kernberg, O. (1980) *Internal World and External Reality: Object Relations Theory Applied.* New York: Jason Aronson.
Kuiper, P.C. (1968) 'Indications and contraindications for psychoanalytic treatment', *International Journal of Psycho-Analysis*, 49: 261–4.
Langs, R. (1992) *Science, Systems and Psychoanalysis.* London: Karnac.
Macmillan, M. (1991) *Freud Evaluated: The Completed Arc*, Amsterdam: Elsevier.
Schafer, R. (1983) *The Analytic Attitude.* London: Hogarth.
Smith, D.L. (1987) 'Formulating and evaluating hypotheses in psychoanalytic psychotherapy', *British Journal of Medical Psychology*, 60(4): 313–17.
Smith, D.L. (1991) *Hidden Conversations: An Introduction to Communicative Psychoanalysis.* London: Routledge.
Wallerstein, R.S. (1987) 'The assessment of analyzability and of analytic outcomes', *Yearbook of Psychoanalysis and Psychotherapy*, 2: 416–27.
Winnicott, D.W. (1965) 'The effect of psychosis on family life' (1960), in D.W. Winnicott *The Family and Individual Development.* London: Tavistock.

Suggested further reading

Bettelheim, B. (1982) *Freud and Man's Soul.* New York: Fontana.
Freud, S. (1915–17) *Introductory Lectures on Psycho-Analysis.* Harmondsworth: Penguin, 1979.
Greenson, R. (1967) *The Technique and Practice of Psycho-Analysis.* London: Hogarth.
Kaufmann, W. (1980) *Discovering the Mind, Vol. 3: Freud vs. Adler and Jung.* New York: Jason Aronson.
Schafer, R. (1983) *The Analytic Attitude.* London: Hogarth.

3

Psychodynamic Therapy: The Kleinian Approach

Cassie Cooper

Historical context and development in Britain

Historical context

Melanie Klein was born in Vienna in 1882, the youngest of four children. Her family, the Reizes, were well-known members of the local orthodox Jewish community. Libussa, her mother, was the daughter of a rabbi and her father Moriz, was a Talmud student. For the Jewish community in Europe this was the heady period of 'emancipation'. Age-old prejudices were receding, and professional barriers crumbling at the onset of new and radical political philosophies. Stimulated by these opportunities, Melanie's father (at the age of 37) left his religious studies to read for a medical career, and later still took up practice as a dentist.

Melanie Klein's published recollection of these early years was that her family was a warm, loving and united group. Both parents were intellectuals with an extensive knowledge of literature and the sciences. In particular Melanie had a strong attachment to her only brother Emmanuel, a medical student who was five years her senior. At the age of 14 Melanie expressed a wish to study medicine. Her brother recognized her creative potential and with his help and encouragement Melanie mastered the Latin and Greek necessary for entry to a *Gymnasium* (grammar school). However, a long list of deaths punctuated the history of the family. A sister, Sidonie, died in 1886 aged eight, and Emmanuel also became seriously ill and gave up his studies. These events affected Melanie and, in a surprising change of direction, she succumbed to the social and religious conventions of the day. At the age of 17 she became engaged to Arthur Klein, an industrial chemist and friend of her brother; seemingly choosing to abandon her plans for a medical career. A year before the marriage in 1903, her beloved brother died in tragic circumstances. He was 25 years old. Melanie was then 21.

Melanie always expressed regret at not having qualified as a doctor and continued her strong interest in the science of medicine. For this reason and others the marriage was not wholly successful, although in due course Melanie gave birth to three children, a daughter and two sons: Melitta (1904), Hans (1907) and Erich (1914).

In 1911, prior to the outbreak of the First World War, the Klein family moved to Budapest and it was here, in the course of her continued interest in medical matters, that Melanie was introduced to the writings of Sigmund Freud and in particular his work on dreams. She was both excited and intrigued, for she found in Freud's theories of human development some truths that she had always been seeking. Living in Budapest enabled her to meet Dr Sandor Ferenczi, the principal

Hungarian analyst of that time and a colleague and correspondent of Freud. She became his patient (1912–19) and her personal analysis facilitated her emerging ideas about the application of psychoanalysis to young children. Ferenczi helped her to develop her techniques, in which toys and play are used as the equivalent to dreams and free association which are part of the analytic process for adults.

Melanie was now able to return to her interrupted career, and before the end of the First World War had already begun to specialize in the analysis of children and to establish her own practice. Her first published paper, 'The development of a child', was read to the Hungarian Psychoanalytic Society in 1921. The analysis of small children was an unknown area, barely touched upon except by Freud in his work with 'Little Hans', and the paper received a mixed reception from the strictly Freudian group.

Dr Karl Abraham, President of the Berlin Psychoanalytic Society, showed considerable interest in this work, and extended an invitation to Melanie to settle in Berlin and devote herself to further psychoanalytic practice and research. Melanie accepted and went to Berlin taking the children with her, but this move precipitated the end of an unsuccessful marriage; her husband chose to live in Sweden, where he had extensive business interests. The end was rancorous, with both parties arguing bitterly about custody of the children until their eventual divorce in 1921.

In Berlin, Klein continued her personal development in analysis with Karl Abraham. She was strongly influenced by his ideas and formed a deep and lasting admiration for his work on the early stages of infantile development.

Like Ferenczi, Karl Abraham urged her to develop further her innovative techniques for working with children. Soon she was introducing new and startlingly bright ideas into the processes of child and adult analysis.

Abraham was her staunch supporter and advocate, but this remarkable relationship was a brief one. After only one year, Abraham developed a fatal illness and died in 1925. Following his death, Klein carried on regular daily self-analysis, a procedure which Freud had initiated. All her later works were based on this process, with daily analytic observations of her own and her patients' behaviour compared, examined and interpreted one against the other. Continuing to enlarge and report on new insights into the earliest years of a child's life, Klein's contributions to the Berlin Society evoked much controversy. In London, Ernest Jones, Freud's biographer, one of his original pupils and the doyen of psychoanalysts in Britain, gave support to her views by inviting her over to give a course of lectures to the British Society in 1925 and, incidentally, to analyse his own children. This was followed in 1926 by an invitation for her to stay and work permanently in London. Klein was pleased to do so. It was in London that her work flourished and her individual clinical and theoretical approach was eventually accepted by other British analysts. She continued to live in England writing, practising, arguing and teaching until the time of her death in 1960 aged 78.

Developments in Britain

Members of the British Psycho-Analytic Society are often referred to as the 'English School'. This differentiated the work that was developing in London (under the influence of Melanie Klein) from that of other centres of psychoanalytic learning, notably that of the so-called 'Viennese' School.

The differences I refer to were accentuated by the view of the British (Kleinian) analysts that the experiences of the first weeks of life were *significant* to the development of the individual.

They were also of the opinion that the anxieties, defences, unconscious fantasies, and the development in children of two years of age, and even younger, of a transference relationship, could be explored and understood, using the method of free association. In this case the word 'transference' relates to the development of an evaluative relationship between the therapist and patient. This emotional relationship can be interpreted as either 'positive' (good feelings) or 'negative' (rejection and hostility).

In the early 1930s, before the Nazis invaded Europe, an attempt was made in an exchange of lectures (Riviere, unpublished, 1936; Waelder, 1937) with the Berlin and Viennese Societies to clarify their different stance on this and other issues. In fact *they agreed to be different*. From 1933 to 1939 psychoanalysis (the so-called Jewish disease) was persecuted out of existence on the continent. In 1938 many German and Austrian analysts fled from the Nazi occupation in Europe to settle in London. At this point, theoretical and practical conflicts of opinion became emphasized, threatening to cause a split within the established British Society. Melanie Klein continued her work and there grew around her a large group of analysts and psychotherapists, with an increasing number of students who wished to apply to her for training analyses and supervision. Alix Strachey, Susan Isaacs, D.W. Winnicott, Joan Riviere, Ernest Jones, T.E. Money-Kyrle and Hanna Segal all supported and developed the theories of Melanie Klein. Unity was preserved in the British Society only by developing two separate streams of training within the main teaching course. The 'Continental' School of Anna Freud and the 'English' School of Melanie Klein, and later on the evolution of the current 'Independent' Group who are able to develop their own techniques and interpretations without rigid adherence to one 'school' or another.

In old Vienna psychoanalysis was considered a 'fringe' profession which guaranteed only an uncertain income and a distinct lack of the upmarket prestige enjoyed by others in the sphere of academic psychiatry. The larger number of psychoanalysts who left Germany and Austria chose to live in the USA where they are now firmly ensconced, and have become, financially and socially, members of the upper middle class.

In the years which followed, the American School still tended to be narrow and conservative in its approach to conflicting psychodynamic theories and this contrasted with the English School which in the early 1920s was substantially non-medical and somewhat amateurish. The English School was considered to be more daring and experimental in its approaches to Freud's original teaching. Psychoanalysis in England can never be regarded as intellectually complacent and this is due in part to the influence of Melanie Klein and her followers who, for a considerable time, were subjected to venomous anger, humiliation and malicious gossip and rumour. This anger contributed to the fact that Kleinian theory did not take off in the USA. There are very few women in the profession of psychoanalysis who have aroused such ire in the male establishment.

Melanie Klein can be truly described as one of the great innovators in dynamic psychotherapy but she nevertheless accepted as fundamental the common themes of psychoanalytic theory which Farrell (1981) simplified as follows:

- No item in mental life or in the way we behave is accidental. It is always the outcome of antecedent conditions.
- Mental activity and behaviour is purposeful or goal directed.
- Unconscious determinants mould and affect the way we perceive ourselves and others. These are thoughts of a primitive nature, shaped by impulses and feelings within the individual of which they are unaware.
- Early childhood experience is overwhelmingly important and pre-eminent over later experience.

In addition to these basic assumptions, Melanie Klein threw new light on the hitherto unexplored regions of the pre-Oedipal stage (i.e. the child's unconscious wish to be sexually united with a parent of the opposite sex and thus eliminate the other parent).

She went on to propose:

- that environmental factors are much less important than had previously been believed;
- that the beginnings of the superego can be identified within the first two years of life;
- that any analysis which does not investigate the stages of infantile anxiety and aggressiveness in order to confront and understand them is necessarily unfinished;
- that the most important drives of all are the aggressive ones.

Theoretical assumptions

Image of the person

The birth of a baby somewhere in the world during the next few years will signal that the population of the world has reached 10 billion. Every minute 150 babies push their way to or are pulled towards birth: 220,000 per day, nearly 80 million a year, are wrested supine and exhausted from the darkness of the birth canal into the glare of light. Some of these babies will go hungry and their families will starve, they will arrive unwanted, neglected, be abandoned, abused, used; life for them will be the 'days full of pain and work is vexation' (*Emek Habacha*) that is described in Ecclesiastes 2: 22. For some it would have been better not to have been born – only one in a thousand will be so lucky.

To some extent Kleinian theory shares this bleak point of view. Life is never portrayed as a bowl of cherries but rather as a series of events that have to be endured, experienced, overcome. Psychoanalytic theory holds the view, however, that each human being possesses a unique capacity to tap into resources that lie hidden deep within the psyche waiting to be utilized, which can make their own special contribution to the human condition.

The Kleinian psychoanalytic concepts that surround the mysterious processes of conception, pregnancy and birth endeavour to identify those elements of life which start to evolve in the foetus before it develops into a living person. The parents bring to this situation an already developed capacity for living their own lives in a certain way; whilst the baby's persona is split: at one moment a clear page waiting to be inscribed, at another a mass of powerful instinctual drives focused on one aim – survival.

We know that the foetal environment is rich with acoustic stimulation through the mother's eating, drinking, breathing and heartbeats and that a foetus eight weeks after conception can move its limbs and in a further eight weeks has gained sufficient strength to communicate these movements to its mother through the uterine walls. At approximately 26 weeks, this tiny being can change position at will and if poked or prodded by external examination will attempt to avoid this contact. The baby is sensitive to pain, it winces, opens its mouth in a silent cry and responds to cold and heat. The foetus has been observed drinking amniotic fluid and is able to distinguish the food eaten by its mother: sweetness which it likes and bitterness which is avoided. The foetus responds to stroking of the abdomen and gentle noise, turning its face, opening its mouth and moving its tongue. It can reach forward to obtain comfort by sucking its thumbs, fingers and toes. The ability to see, to hear, to feel are therefore not senses which are magically bestowed at birth, and the foetal heartbeat resonates rapidly to the external situation of its mother.

> Far from being a silent, dark, encapsulated environment, the inter-uterine world is dynamic, full of changes which respond to outside conditions and stimulations, therefore not only the environment of the uterus changes continuously during gestation but each foetus also inhabits a different though broadly speaking similar environment and thus is subject to different experiences and stimulations. (Piontelli, 1992: 37)

The human baby is born prematurely, its instincts are weak and it seems to have poor instinctual notions of how to avoid danger or to get satisfaction for its own needs. The human baby is more helpless and dependent upon others for the satisfaction of its vital needs than even those mammals most closely related to our species. When its caretaker (usually its mother) satisfies the baby's hunger, she is at one with it and hence not felt as separate.

When, however, she is unable to satisfy the baby's needs she (or her breast) is experienced as separate from the baby and thereby becomes its first distinct psychological object. When the mother removes her presence from the baby, two things happen. One is that the loss or removal of the means to satisfy its needs (the breast or its substitute) produces an anxiety in the baby. Anxiety is an affectual state that warns the baby of danger.

In order to cope with this anxiety, the baby has to re-create a mother for itself. The satisfaction she represented has to be fantasized so that the baby can conjure up in its mind the imagery and feeling of a good feed. This in turn becomes the ego: a separate area within oneself.

It is hard to believe that 'mothering' was not deemed relevant psychologically until the 1920s. In view of the emphasis in this direction by Bowlby, Winnicott and more recently in the popular writings of Miller, it is easy to forget that the processes of mothering appeared of little interest to psychoanalysis.

Freud's work, and the observations of those who followed him, concentrated upon the divisions that affect the human condition. Human beings are born under one law but bound unremittingly to another. Each individual at birth brings something unique with them, but the divisions of the mind are formed by a headlong incursion into a world which is the arena for the orders, wishes, desires, fantasies and commands of other people and which is racked by the tortured patterns of humankind's laws, prohibitions, aggression and culture.

It was left to Melanie Klein to emphasize the importance of the 'pre-Oedipal layers' of personality development. The connections between the ego and the impulses, the drives and the body feelings and their relationship to the outside world (represented by the touch and feel of a parent's hands), became the two poles of Klein's basic model of the neonate. She maintained that the baby brings into the world two main conflicting impulses, love and hate. Love is the manifestation of the life drive. Hate, destructiveness and envy are the emanations of the death drive. These innate feelings are constantly at war with each other. The neonate tries to deal with these conflicts.

A tiny body struggles to cope with various impulses, a body with sensations which are constantly endangered by the need to gratify overwhelming desires, and which has, in a very short space of time, to develop mature mechanisms for dealing with them. The baby meets a world which is both satisfying and frustrating. It exists from the moment it seeks and finds its mother's breast or its substitute, then gradually the world becomes more complicated and it seeks and finds again its father.

During the early months of life it must be supposed that the baby can make no distinction between itself as a personal entity and the bewildering world of light and darkness which surrounds it. The baby can only at this stage experience them as objects. Its mother's nipple, a good feed, a soft cot or the touch of a hand that gives it pleasure are easily regarded as good objects, while something that gives pain, like hunger, wet, cold, discomfort, can easily be converted into something that is bad.

To the baby, hunger is a frightening situation; it is not able to understand the meaning of time, of patience, of the tolerance of frustration. It cannot appreciate that these situations are of a temporary nature, and will soon be followed by a feeling of pleasurable relief as the warm milk goes down. A small change in the immediate situation can change feelings of anger and discomfort into blissful gratification. It follows then that the baby is able to love and hate one and the same object in rapid succession. There are no qualifications. It is all or nothing at all, black and white.

Conceptualization of psychological disturbance and health

Hanna Segal explains: 'In interpreting projection one indicates to the patient that he/she is attributing to another person a characteristic which is in fact their own' (1973: 121). In doing so the therapist endeavours to make the patient aware of the motives that lie behind the projective fantasy and the constricting distortions that this fantasy can produce on one's perception of the object in view and also of the self.

Take for example the projection of one's own aggressive sexuality on to the sexual relationship of one's parents. Sexual intercourse of parental figures could then be perceived as cruel and sexually dangerous, and the development of one's own sexual feelings could be inhibited in later life.

Introjection and projection In a paper 'Notes on some schizoid mechanisms' (1952a), which was read to the British Society in 1946, Melanie Klein introduced the concepts of ego splitting and projective identification and later she related these concepts to the onset of psychosis. It was her view that anxiety was a predominant factor in psychosis since our earliest anxieties (in infancy) are psychotic in content. 'The normal development of infants,' she wrote, 'can be regarded as a combination of processes by which anxieties of a psychotic nature are bound, worked through and modified' (Klein, 1952a: 81). This was more complicated than the theory of projection described by Freud. An understanding of the processes of introjection and projection are of major importance since in the therapeutic process we can find parallels for all these situations. Every human being will go through phases in life in which they return to or experience relationships which were unsatisfactory in their past.

For every human being the outer world and its impact, and the kind of experiences they live through, the objects they come into contact with, are not only dealt with externally but are taken into the self to become part of their inner world, an entity inside the body. As we *introject* these new experiences into our personalities, we take on the concept that we can truly *rely on ourselves*. An enduring self-image and increased self-esteem can be facilitated by this form of introjection.

Where this can go awry relates to the relative strength or weakness of a person's ego and the supportive nurturing processes which do or do not accompany one throughout life. If, for example, we admire someone else to such an extent that we endow this other person with abilities and characteristics (good or bad) that we would wish to emulate, and identify with them to such an extent that we endeavour to live as they do we take into ourselves and take over the image and behaviour of another being with the subsequent failure to take responsibility for our own future development.

Projection goes on simultaneously. It is a manifestation of a person's ability to project on to other people those aggressive and envious feelings (predominantly those of aggression) which by very nature of their 'badness' must be passed on either by projection or, alternatively, carefully repressed.

An example of this process is where the patient attempts to arouse in the therapist feelings that he or she finds impossible to tolerate within themselves but which the patient unconsciously wishes to express – using the therapist as a means of communication – evacuating unpleasant, dangerous and guilt-ridden thoughts and attempting to take over the mind of another.

It is important to understand that although projection is a general term used in other analytical theories, *projective identification* is a strictly Kleinian concept which is held, by Kleinian therapists, to be responsible for severe difficulties in both establishing one's own identity and feeling secure enough to establish other outward-looking relationships. The term 'projective identification' covers a complex clinical event: one person who does not wish to own his or her feelings of love and hate manipulatively induces another into experiencing them; with consequent visible changes of affect in behaviour of both people concerned, bringing pressure to bear on the therapist, sometimes subtly, sometimes powerfully causing them to act out in a manner which reflects the patient's own projections.

It is a difficult and complicated concept to understand as it deals – in the main – with the subjective experience of a therapist and the use to which the therapist is put in being unwittingly drawn into the patient's fantasy world. For example, a patient may deal with the deprived part of his or her own childhood by idealizing the parenting process in therapy. This can in turn deprive the patient of future resourcefulness, but may also trigger off in the therapist a mutual longing for the closeness and dependence of parenthood. Inevitably the therapist must respond to these pressures, however imperceptibly they intrude.

This process highlights the internal world built up in the child and adult alike, which is partially a reflection of the external one. This two-way process continues throughout every stage of our lives, zigging and zagging, interacting and modifying itself in the course of maturation but never losing its importance in relation to the world around us. The judgement of reality is never quite free from the influence of the boiling mercury of our internal world.

Meltzer (1979) considers the concept of projective identification to be one of Melanie Klein's greatest contributions to psychoanalysis: 'A concrete conception of the inner world . . . a theatre where meaning can be generated.' Bion (1988) has led the way to considerable developments in techniques in distinguishing between normal and pathological projective identification with his formulation of a container/contained model which illustrates how projective identification can be an essential expression of the kinds of experience that a patient cannot capture in the spoken word.

Melanie Klein did not really consider herself to be a theoretician; she saw herself as a face worker describing these phenomena as and when she observed them, with an awareness that one may get it wrong and an emphasis on the constant need for supervision to avoid the hazard of confusing one's personal feelings with that of a patient.

Basic ideas from Freud and Bion enter into Klein's theories. We can identify with our own hatred (at times) of reality and thinking, which are the precursor to the ego's loss of reality in psychosis. We can resonate to the psychotics' unmodified primitive anxieties and their use of the defences of projection and introjection in a desperate search for a cure. Bion in his 1957 paper 'The differentiation of the psychotic from the non-psychotic personalities' comments:

> The differentiation of the psychotic from the non-psychotic personalities depends on a minute splitting of all that part of the personality that is concerned with awareness of internal and external reality, and the expulsion of these fragments so that they enter *into* or *engulf* their objects. (Bion, 1988: 43)

Splitting In *Our Adult World and its Roots in Infancy* Melanie Klein (1960) described the situation which arose when the projected bad objects (representations of the child's own ferocious and aggressive impulses) rebound on it. The situation of a young mother who tries to please a baby who is literally biting the hand that feeds it, is a case in point.

Children may refuse food and scream even when they are desperately hungry, kick and push when they mostly long for a caress. These stages, which thankfully are largely outgrown in the process of normal development, can be identified with the delusional sense of persecution sometimes found in the paranoid adult. A residual persecutory element can always be found in the sense of guilt which is central to all civilizations. Since the infant continues to need a good mother – indeed its life depends upon it – by splitting the two aspects and clinging only to the good one like a rubber ring in a swimming pool, it has evolved for the time being a means of staying alive. Without this loving object to keep it buoyant the child would sink beneath the surface of a hostile world which would engulf it.

Melanie Klein's view was that in the early years of life the objects that surrounded the infant were not seen and understood in *visual terms*. This included a wide range of 'objects' – parents, siblings, blankets, food, bathing, cots, prams, toys, etc. These would be construed only as they were *experienced* as good or bad. Klein took this further and became concerned with the splitting of aspects of the ego itself into good and conversely bad parts. In later life, these split off parts could become more obsessional, leading to a fragmentation of the self. Klein linked this fragmentation to the onset of schizophrenia. Here the patient has carried this process of splitting to the extreme, splitting each split yet further into a multifarious and bewildering group of repressions and concessions that in the end become chaos.

Greed and envy In a paper 'Notes on some schizoid mechanisms' Klein (1952a) singled out greed and envy as two very disturbing factors, relating them first to the child's dominant relationship with the mother and later with relationships to other members of the family, and eventually she extended them to the individual's cycle of life.

Greed is exacerbated by anxiety, the anxiety of being deprived, the need to take all one can from the mother and from the family. A greedy infant may enjoy what it has for the time being, but this feeling is soon replaced by the feeling of being robbed by others of all that it needs in the way of food, love, attention or any other gratification. The baby who is greedy for love and attention is also afraid that it is unable to give these to others, and this in turn exacerbates its own situation. The baby needs everything, it can spare nothing and therefore what can it reasonably expect to receive from others? If an infant is relatively unable to tolerate frustration and anxiety on its own, serious difficulties can arise if the mother is unable, through depression or environmental problems, to provide consolation and mediation.

The infant can then experience murderous feelings towards this seemingly ungiving mother. In seeking to destroy that which is needed for its own survival, the infant is experiencing ambivalent feelings – one moment contemplating murder, the next, suicide. Caught up in a vicious cycle, the need to attack or withdraw produces panicky feelings of being trapped, unpleasant claustrophobic feelings which are replicated in later life.

Envy is a spoiling pursuit. If milk, love and attention are being withheld for one reason or another, then the loved object must be withholding it and keeping it for their own use. Suspicion is the basis of envy.

If the baby cannot have what it desires there is a strong urge to spoil the very object of desire so that no one can enjoy it. This spoiling quality can result in a disturbed relationship with the mother, who cannot now supply an unspoilt satisfaction. Envious attacks give rise to greater anxiety – particularly when these attacks are directed towards the mother. It is difficult to acknowledge what has been done – the baby's fear is that it has gone too far but it is resentful of attempts which may be offered to facilitate, to make reparation.

It is only when there is such a breakdown of the natural protective forces that one notices how distorted the relationship between mother and child can become, exacerbating the post-natal situation and leading to the depressive illness to which some women are liable.

Melanie Klein enlarged on these problems, stating quite firmly that the aggressive envy experienced in infancy can inhibit the development of good object relations, i.e. the child's ability to develop an intense and personal relationship with other objects (such as toys) which they may treat as alive, lovable, able to give love in return, needing sympathy or producing anger, and able to develop personalities which could be seen to be alive. This in its turn can affect the growth of the capacity to love. 'Throughout my work I have attributed fundamental importance to the infant's first object relations – the relation to the mother's breast and to the mother – and we have drawn the conclusion that, if this primal object which is introjected, takes root in the ego with relative security the basis for a satisfactory development can be laid' (Klein, 1957: 389).

Projective identification Projective identification illustrates most clearly the links between human instinct, fantasy, and the mechanisms of defence. Sexual desires, aggressive impulses, can be satiated by fantasy. Fantasy can be as pleasurable and as explicit as we wish to make it, and it is also a safety net – it contains and holds those bad parts of our inner self. The use of fantasy is obvious in literature, in science, in art and in all activities of everyday life.

One aspect of murderous fantasy is the rivalry which results from the male child's desire for the mother: his rivalry with his father and all the sexual fantasies which can be linked to this. The Oedipus complex, which is described in Chapter 2, on Freudian therapy, is rooted in the baby's suspicions of the father who takes the mother's love and attention away from him. The same applies to the female child, for whom the relationship to the mother and to all women is always of supreme importance.

Klein, however, placed her emphasis on earlier and more primitive stages as precursors of the Oedipus complex. She argued that these Oedipal feelings were identifiable in the baby at the age of six months and were the result of the projection of infantile fantasies of rage and aggression on to the parent. Whilst continuing to support Freud's tripartite differentiation of the psychic apparatus into ego, id and superego, she went on to claim that each of these areas of the psyche was identifiable almost from the day of birth.

The paranoid-schizoid position The paranoid-schizoid position is distinguished by the characteristic persecutory anxiety of threat to the *individual*. This is distinct from the threat to the object (the anxiety characteristic of the depressive position). The paranoid-schizoid position is easily identifiable in earliest infancy when at the beginning of life the child builds up its inner world of the self and others, but it is not constricted to early childhood development and continues throughout the life of an individual, fluctuating constantly with the depressive position.

Because of the strength of these early primitive feelings, an infant will initially experience two separate feelings about its primary object (i.e. its mother or caregiver). At one level there is the need to idealize this person and this conflicts with moments when the loved one is experienced as horrendous. So it is that the world is experienced as light and dark, good and bad, distorted by fluctuating moods of pleasure and pain and conflicting needs and desires.

The infant lives in a constricted world peopled by individuals who are experienced as good or bad. These are the early distortions which Klein described as the paranoid position. It is with difficulty and depression that the infant grows, realizing that life is a mixture of good and bad; that those we idealize are vulnerable and can let us down. The mother we idealize as the source of comfort, nourishment and support can at the same time be the one who is the centre of attack and hatred by the loving and hating ego: a split in which good experiences predominate over bad ones. In normal development, this process is a necessary precondition for true integration in childhood, adolescence and adult life.

If, however, for any reason this process is disturbed, many pathological changes can occur. When anxiety, hostility and envious feelings become overwhelming, projective identification takes on another dimension. If there is no tidy split between the good and the bad, fragmentation takes place. The object of anger is split into tiny fragments, each one containing a small but violently hostile part of the ego. This is damaging to the development of the ego and in its attempts to relieve itself of the pain of disintegration a vicious circle can be established in which the very painfulness of confronting reality brings with it increased feelings of persecution. Reality is then distorted by bizarre objects and enormous hostility, which frighten and threaten the depleted ego.

A successful negotiation of the paranoid-schizoid anxieties experienced in the early months of the infant's development leads to a gradual organization of its universe. Splitting, projection and introjection combine to help sort out perceptions and emotions and to separate the good from the bad. From the beginning the tendency is towards integration as well as splitting. When these integrative processes become more stable and continual, a new phase of development occurs. This is how Klein describes the move to the depressive position.

The depressive position The depressive position begins when the baby begins to recognize its mother. In the early months of life the baby is concerned with the integration of the sights and sounds and stimuli, both pleasant and unpleasant, with which it is surrounded. Out of this dreamlike world sufficient integration is achieved for the baby to experience its mother as a whole object – not a succession of parts. She is no longer breasts that can feed, hands that can hold, a voice that can soothe, facial grimaces that either please or frighten, but a complete entity on her own, separate, divided from the baby – someone who can choose to hold it close or stay away, can kiss or neglect or abuse her child. This gradual understanding of the separation process, this gradual awakening to the fact that it is one and the same person who is the container of both good and bad feelings, is then transposed internally to the baby. The infant is as separate from her as she is from it, and can both love and hate its mother.

Its previous fears of being the frail object of destruction extend subtly to an inner knowledge that it too can destroy the one person it loves and needs for survival. The anxiety has changed from a paranoid to a depressive one. In acknowledging the very existence of a separate being, the baby becomes exposed to the fear that it has made the cut. Aggression has destroyed the cord which linked the baby to the mother, leaving the child with feelings of unutterable guilt, sadness and deprivation, a hurt that can never be healed, a pain that can never be assuaged.

In the depressive situation the baby has not only to deal with a destroyed breast and mother but also with the influx of Oedipal envy and jealousy. These processes involve intense conflict, which is associated with the work of mourning and which always results in anxiety and mental pain. In the Kleinian view, mental pain *is* pain: it hurts, and mere gratification does not make it go away. Separation is painful, is experienced as a kind of death, the death of that which was and can never be again.

This process of separation and the depressive anxieties that it invokes was described in a 1948 paper, 'On the theory of anxiety and guilt' (Klein, 1952b). It emphasized that depressive anxieties are a part of everyone's normal development, and that the guilt feelings which have developed are understood as part of the *imagined* harm done to a child's love object.

When this is facilitated it can enable reparation to commence. A child can then show subtle tenderness to those around it and the anxieties and paranoid fears of early infancy can become modified during this period, although these anxieties may be painfully reawakened in the normal mourning processes of later life. Adult depression is known to involve a reactivation of this stage of infantile depression, so Kleinian psychotherapists consider the actual mourning situation a productive period in therapy. When an adult admits to feeling menaced and persecuted, the recriminations and self-reproaches of the depressed patient are interpreted and hopefully understood as a manifestation of the early persecutory impulses which were directed so savagely at the self.

In preceding paragraphs some developmental models have been explained, in particular those of the impulses of destruction, greed and envy, illustrating how the persecutory and sadistic anxieties of early life can disturb the child's emotional balance and inhibit its ability to acquire and maintain good social relationships.

Melanie Klein's understanding of what she was later to label 'the depressive position' highlighted the simple truth that human beings feel better when they are labelled as being 'good' than they do when they are made to feel bad.

The world in which we now live has taken its toll of childhood. Alongside the obvious signs of materialistic success comes the urgent need to be seen to be a good and successful parent. Whatever the criteria for this measure of success and in order to make sure of being loved, the child has to go along with this fantasy. If they feel unloved, it must be their fault. They are too slow at school, too ugly, naughty, unacademic, lacking in social graces, poor at sport, should have been a boy or should have been a girl. Their self-esteem is low. Their parents have suppressed any recollection of their own innocent and painful childhood experiences. We are terrified of the possibility that hatred can overpower the love we are expected to profess.

Twenty years on from the death of Melanie Klein, Dr Alice Miller wrote:

> Almost everywhere we find the effort, marked by various degrees of intensity and by the use of coercive measures, to rid ourselves as quickly as possible of the child within us – i.e. the weak, helpless, dependent creature – in order to become an independent competent adult deserving of respect. When we encounter this creature in our children we persecute it with the same measures once used on ourselves. And this is what we are accustomed to call child rearing . . . . The methods that can be used to suppress vital spontaneity in the child are: laying traps, lying, duplicity, subterfuge, manipulation, 'scare' tactics, withdrawal of love, isolation, distrust, humiliating and disgracing the child, scorn, ridicule and coercion even to the point of torture. (Miller, 1983: 105)

All human beings, wherever they live, exist only in relationship to other human beings. The physical processes of conception, pregnancy and birth are the same for us all. In the uterus all babies exist in comparative safety; it is only when the baby makes its post-natal appearance, head or feet first or precipitately by Caesarian section, that it learns about the reality of solitary existence.

Acquisition of psychological disturbance

Loss of the parent in any form – breast or hand – gives rise to a primary separation anxiety, which gives way to grief and then to the experience of mourning that which is lost. Aggression is also a major part of the mourning process.

If the normal processes of childhood are disrupted in some way, if fantasy becomes reality and the loved object dies, leaves, neglects, batters, sexually abuses, reacts too possessively, becomes obsessional, it follows that these disruptions of a normal interaction are likely to take a pathological course later in life. This leads not only to an aggressive stance towards society but to self-aggression and abuse. Pathological fragmentation and the onset of the depressive position can be delineated in this way:

Pathological fragmentation ⟷ Normal splitting ⟷ Depressive position

Dr John Bowlby gave the following examples:

> Many of those referred to psychiatrists are anxious, insecure individuals usually described as over-dependent or immature. Under stress they are apt to develop neurotic symptoms, depression or phobia. Research shows them to have been exposed to at least one, and usually more than one, of certain typical patterns of pathogenic parenting, which includes:
>
> a) one or both parents being persistently unresponsive to the child's care-eliciting behaviour and/or actively disparaging and rejecting him;

b) discontinuities of parenting, occurring more or less frequently, including periods in hospital or institution;

c) persistent threats by parents not to love a child, used as a means of controlling him;

d) threats by parents to abandon the family, used either as a method of disciplining the child or as a way of coercing a spouse;

e) threats by one parent either to desert or even kill the other or else to commit suicide (each of them more common than might be supposed);

f) inducing a child to feel guilt by claiming that his behaviour is or will be responsible for the parent's illness or death. (Bowlby, 1979: 136–7)

Cassie Cooper wrote:

To be a child and especially to be a 'good' child in today's world is not to be a child at all. Instead these children of the nineties, the children of projection, grow up too quickly to become in their turn mothers, friends, comforters, translators, advisers, support and sometimes lovers of their own parents.

In taking care of other siblings, throwing themselves between parents in order to save a marriage, attempting to provide academic kudos, high earnings, sexual titillation and satisfaction, masochistic or sadistic gratification, the child will do anything, anyhow, for parental love and approval. (Cooper, 1988: 12–13)

It is these anxieties which are the cause, if not confronted, of both childhood psychoses and mental illness in adult life.

Perpetuation of psychological disturbance

In Kleinian theory human development is postulated as a series of events: events that have to be endured, experienced and overcome. In particular the theory aims to understand the difficulties experienced in early childhood by both parents and child. It emphasizes that loss of closeness to a parent figure gives rise within the individual to separation anxiety. This feeling of anxiety is internalized by the child and changes as time passes to the experience of bewildered mourning for that which has been lost. Aggression and self-destructiveness become a major part of this mourning process as throughout life the child tries again and again to re-enter that fantasized place of safety to become one with its mother.

We now know (and the dissolution of family life in contemporary society proves the point) that if the normal processes of separation are disrupted in any way, if fantasy becomes reality and the love objects die, leave, reject, batter, disparage, react too possessively or obsessively, lose face, become depressed, unemployed, redundant, are forced to move home, these disruptions of a normal interaction are likely to take a pathological course later in life.

W.R. Bion postulated that when the infant was accosted by feelings that could not be managed, the fantasy developed that these feelings could be evacuated and then put on to their primary caregiver (i.e. the mother). Obviously if the mother is capable of understanding and accepting the child's anxiety and helplessness without her own balance of mind being disturbed, she can contain the feelings and comfort her child in a way that will make these feelings more acceptable.

The child would then feel reassured enough to live with these feelings in a way that is manageable. However, if this process goes wrong – and it can go wrong, particularly if the mother herself is distressed and cannot take the child's projections – the child is forced to internalize these anxieties, repress and bottle them up, empty them out of mind, so that he or she does not have to bear those unpleasant feelings. If this condition persists, the child is well on the way to psychotic behaviour later in life.

The psychoanalytic approach to all forms of psychological disturbance is based on the assumption that psychological trauma and symptoms, both verbal and non-verbal, of one's patients can be understood and can be examined with the intention of understanding.

There is no such thing as a person who does not have areas of psychological disturbance within their personality; equally, in every person there are areas of their personality which are neurotic and capable of forming good relationships, however ephemeral these relationships may seem to be. In psychoanalytic psychotherapy, provided this healthier part of a patient's ego is in evidence, it is possible to work with this patient with the professed aim of strengthening this healthy part and enabling it to become dominant in relation to the disturbed part of the personality.

In her work with small children Melanie Klein was of the opinion that infantile neurosis was the structure which defends the child against primitive anxieties of a paranoid and depressive nature. She subsequently maintained that it is this form of psychotic anxiety that in later years blocks off the growth of symbol formation and the development of the ego. It is the resolution of this anxiety that is the aim of therapy, in that this frees the ego to develop and re-establish its symbolic processes.

> It is our contention that psychotic illness is rooted in the pathology of early infancy where the basic matrix of mental function is formed . . . . In psychosis it is all these functions that are disturbed or destroyed. The confusion between the external and the internal, the fragmentation of relationships and the ego, the deterioration of perception, the breakdown of symbolic processes, the disturbance of thinking: all are features of psychosis. Understanding the genesis of the development of the ego and its object relationships and the kind of disturbance that can arise in the course of that development is essential to understanding the mechanisms of the psychotic. (Segal, 1986: 153)

The ability to contain the infant's anxiety by a mother or caregiver capable of understanding is the beginning of stability. If this does not happen, the anxiety is introjected and can grow and develop into the experience of an even greater terror, a nameless fear of excessive destructive omnipotence. In the psychotherapeutic setting these intolerable feelings can be projected on to the therapist, who is capable of tolerating and understanding these terrifying projections – this can be acknowledged and understood by the patient, who feels that the situation becomes more tolerable. With careful interpretation and thought this patient can identify and allow the growth of a part of their personality – the part which is capable of real commitment, caring and understanding.

Change

Kleinian psychotherapy adheres to the common principles which underlie psychoanalytic theory: that it is the unconscious mechanisms which operate within the human psyche which dominate the process of change for every human being. However, Klein had more to add to this original concept.

Let us take the well-used analogy that, at birth, every human being is a *tabula rasa* a white tablet, a clean slate. The circumstances of one's life are then written on the white surface. To this end the human being learns to live with their history and the alternating vicissitudes and pleasant episodes of life.

What is important here is the emphasis placed by Kleinian therapists on two factors:

1   There is no gain in life without a subsequent loss and the ambivalent feelings that temper any form of progress, i.e. the baby gains approval from its parents when it takes its first mouthful of solid food – but the breast is then lost to it for ever. The pride a baby will experience when learning to walk diminishes when it acknowledges that the intimacy of helplessness is relinquished.
2   Survival in a dangerous world depends on one's ability to reconcile oneself to the fact that every 'have' is balanced by a 'have not'.

The well-known game played by children, 'I'm the King of the Castle', is a case in point. The consciousness of the self and the feeling of enjoyment in winning are transient. As the child grows up it becomes more aware of the effect of its behaviour on other people and it learns to compromise and to understand the implications of frustration.

The process of change can never be viewed as a clear and shining goal; rather it is the development of a growing sense of wise detachment towards life. Developing from this detachment comes the sense of personal identity which enables us to go through life with a tolerant irony and strengthens our resistance to the temptations of fame, wealth and self-aggrandizement and enables us to take what comes.

Hinshelwood identifies the change processes within Kleinian theory as:

1   the development of the subject's awareness of psychic reality;
2   balancing the currents of love and hate which run within the self. (Hinshelwood, 1989: 19)

In our therapeutic work we may find that an adult has emerged from this therapeutic process, an adult whose ego can organize and substantiate its own defences against the anxieties that belong to primary separation and loss.

Practice

Goals of therapy

Melanie Klein never altered the technical principles which were the foundation of her early work, *The Psychoanalysis of Children* (1932a). This work continues to form the basis of the psychodynamic work undertaken by Kleinian psychotherapists and colours their distinctive concepts of mental functioning.

It is important to stress here that the theories of Melanie Klein have never been popular. Freudian and post-Freudian doctrines have had more appeal. It was perhaps easier to accept the hidden agenda of the Oedipal conflict and the 'tidy' process of oral, anal and later libidinal development than to take on board the confrontation with the life and death struggle which lies at the root of Kleinian thinking. To tilt at the precious idealization of the 'loving' mother and to confront instead the infantile struggle for 'survival' are unpleasant and uncomfortable. In Kleinian therapy we have to take a long, hard look at our fantasies of parental love: if these are removed what bleak prospect of life does the Kleinian therapist provide?

Patients who undertake this kind of psychotherapy are bound to come to the first session full of hopes and fears, with deep-rooted fantasies and phobias about themselves and about their therapist. They present material in the very first session which concerns anxieties that are central to them at that moment. Predominantly they want to feel 'better', to obtain relief from suffering (Colby, 1951), and are seeking, like an infant, immediate gratification of their needs. Wish-fulfilment is not confined to those who seek psychotherapy. Eavesdrop on any everyday conversation and you will conclude that people always hope to get what they feel they need to make them happy and want to obtain it in the shortest possible time and with a minimum of effort: powerful wishes for a magical solution rather than facing up to the realities that underline our complex psychological make-up.

In Kleinian psychotherapy it is maintained that anxiety can act as a spur to development and personal achievement, providing this anxiety is not excessive.

At the commencement of therapy it is important to work with the patient's unconscious fantasies about themselves and with others, and in particular how such fantasies relate to the reality of the outside world, in the way it has been experienced both in the past and in the present.

This may sound simplistic. When studying certain isolated aspects of human behaviour the reductive approach is very appealing. The plain facts are, however, that human beings are complex and that the very process of functioning as a person requires a conceptual level that does justice to what is revealed of these complex forces. Behaviour which is as thoughtless, demanding and extortionate as the infant's relationship with its mother reflects the need to exhaust and exploit the therapist and to experience yet again the feelings of guilt and anxiety which are associated with such behaviour.

A Kleinian therapist would have it that psychotherapy has more in common with an educational experience than a form of medical treatment. Successful psychotherapy should begin a process of learning and personal development which moves along at its own pace. The foundation stone of this process must be the relationship between therapist and patient. If this goal is similarly perceived and worked upon by both parties, the outcome will be the achievement of some mutual satisfaction.

Melanie Klein was quite clear about the efficiency of her method in the treatment of adults. Her primary goal was the reduction of immediate anxiety by encouraging patients to face their inhibitions and to facilitate a more positive relationship with their therapist. This in turn would enable patients to experience themselves as real people in a real world and to maintain a balance between the feelings of love and hate which alternate in every psyche.

By the end of therapy it is hoped that patients will feel able to form full and satisfactory personal relationships, that they will have gained insight into their personal situation and feel released from their early fixations and repressions. They will be less inhibited and better able to enjoy the good things of life while remaining sensitive, open and capable when problems arise. They will be able to assess their internal world, possess a quiet reassurance and ego strength which stems from the knowledge that even in times of great stress they will survive and, perhaps even more importantly, that they want to survive.

The means by which true reparation (i.e. growth, in the Kleinian sense) takes place are essentially mysterious. It is something which happens when the 'mental atmosphere is conducive to objects repairing one another. The frame of mind of tolerance, of pain, of remorse over one's destructiveness' (Meltzer, 1979: 18–19). These reparative mental conditions follow when there is an understanding of one's infantile dependency upon internal objects – one's idealized mother and father and the moment of one's own creation – so that one can in life accept oneself as a product of what was and is, in an atmosphere of tolerance and acceptance.

Melanie Klein stated:

> My criterion for termination of analysis is, therefore, as follows: have persecutory and depressive anxieties been sufficiently reduced in the course of analysis, and has the patient's relation to the external world been sufficiently strengthened to enable him to deal satisfactorily with the situation of mourning arising at this point? (Klein, 1950: 78–80)

Selection criteria

Only uncommonly aware and brave people wish to know about themselves and to face up to what psychotherapy can reveal. There are many patterns to therapy and many different approaches to the relief of psychic pain. Patients have a choice in the kind of treatment they would prefer, and can and do move from individual to group therapy, from group therapy to family therapy, if they so wish, and in whatever sequence seems beneficial to them at a particular time.

Initially the referral of a patient for psychotherapy would be made by a general practitioner. With luck, the would-be patient and their doctor have discussed a preference for one modality or another. There is a need for each patient to accept responsibility for their problem and, in seeking for some amelioration of their situation, to actively participate in making the decision, choosing to work on a one-to-one basis in individual therapy or deciding that they would gain greater motivation and strength from the support, modelling and challenge that can be offered in a therapy group or a family group setting.

In selecting patients for individual therapy there are criteria which the Kleinian psychotherapist would seek to fulfil:

- that the patient has problems which can be clearly defined in psychodynamic terms;
- that the patient appears motivated enough for change and insight into their previous behaviour;
- that the patient has enough internal strength to cope with the demands and tensions that are to be created by the process of interpretation and confrontation;
- that the patient produces evidence that they are able to accept and sustain a long-standing relationship with the therapist and with significant others in their immediate surroundings.

Patients will arrive with a little knowledge of how Kleinian therapy differs from other forms of treatment, how the procedure works, and even less knowledge about the outcome of psychotherapy. Initially the psychotherapist will indicate that therapy involves a detailed process of examining and discussing problems. Patients are told that it could be distressing and painful, that there are no guaranteed 'cures', but that they can be enabled to help themselves to identify the origin of their symptoms, the reaction to these symptoms and the ways in which these symptoms constrict their life.

The therapist must have the right to decide if he or she is prepared to work with a specific patient. Personal feelings will obviously affect the outcome of an initial diagnostic interview. Conversely, the patient may decide that he or she will be unable to work with the therapist. It is essential to respect the rights of both parties in such a delicate transaction. What is important is that the relationship between therapist and patient can be one in which there is mutual respect, the respect of one human being for another and hope for the potentialities of this other person. This is termed the 'therapeutic alliance'.

It is hoped that each patient has the capacity to come out of therapy with the opportunity to love well, to play well and to have some optimism for the future.

The Kleinian psychotherapist finds it most suitable to work with patients whose underlying conflicts are towards the narcissistic side, whose egos have undergone considerable deformation or weakening. These patients will come into therapy expressing inability to love or to be loved by others, with conflicts about dealing with other people in a social, sexual or work setting, general intellectual and academic underfunctioning and symptomatic phobias, anxiety states and minor perversions.

For some patients there may be a need to limit the period of treatment. It is useful anyway to indicate that the treatment will not go on indefinitely, that it will end at a certain time. A statement of this kind may not be indicated for all patients, but could be necessary in certain instances. In contrast to psychoanalysis, in Kleinian psychotherapy there is a realistic indication that the treatment will terminate some day. The therapist will point out that the therapeutic relationship will come to an end and this is an important and necessary factor in working through the attachment process, a process which is repeated throughout life when some aspect of a 'good object' is given up in this way.

Qualities of effective psychotherapists

Freudian and Jungian analysts continue to proliferate but Kleinian psychotherapists have been in short supply. As with other modalities, it is an expensive and prolonged training, in most cases a postgraduate training, and in every case a training which involves the student in an extensive commitment both of time and money over many years; they must tailor their lifestyle to personal therapy four or five times a week.

It is a training which centres on the personality of the would-be therapist, and this understanding of the self is tuned to perfect pitch like the finest violin. The therapist is encouraged to become an instrument which can interpret, colour and respond to the musical score, resonate and bend beneath the fingers of the musician, constantly changing and developing their diagnostic sensitivities in interpretation and technique. A Kleinian psychotherapist will have experienced this long-term period of personal analysis, followed by a shorter period of training analysis at one of the formal institutes, and long-term supervision of their work with individual clients.,

In *The Psychoanalysis of Children* Melanie Klein wrote:

> The analysis of children at puberty demands a thorough knowledge of the technique of adult analysis. I consider a regular training in the analysis of adults as a necessary foundation. . . . No one who has not gained experience adequately and done a fair amount of work on adults should enter upon the technically more difficult field of child analysis. In order to be able to preserve the fundamental principles of analytic treatment in the modified form necessitated by the child's (and the adult's) mechanisms at the various stages of development, the therapist must besides being fully versed in the technique of early analysis possess complete mastery of the technique employed in analysing adults. (Klein, 1932a: 342)

It is the Kleinian view that an analyst or a psychotherapist who dogmatically believes that they and only they, plus a few other chosen spirits who adhere rationally and rigidly to their particular school and their particular form of dogmatism, have not, in Kleinian terms, advanced beyond the paranoid-schizoid position to be capable of doubt as to whether they, or anyone else has the key to understanding the complexity of a human being.

The fundamental concepts of the paranoid-schizoid and depressive positions naturally affect the ways in which the Kleinian psychotherapist will view their patients' presentations.

In dealing with the early anxieties which arise from the relationship between the baby and the breast, faced by the harsher and more persecutory anxieties which lie in the deepest strata of the mind, the more primitive the processes that are aroused by this process, the more important it is for the Kleinian therapist to remain unaltered in a basic function, namely to refer the anxiety back to its source and resolve it by systemically analysing the transference situation.

The therapist will need to be sensitive to those embryonic features of emotional problems which are present in all human beings and which are clearly reflected in the patients. The therapist will be aware that possible events in one's life, both in reality and in imagination, which did occur and which could have developed, should not be denied and repressed.

The transition from childhood to adulthood requires an understanding of the fact that in every person lies the capacity to have been something and someone else. The therapist should be able to encourage the flowering of this inner self in the patient, while remaining for most of their professional life in a situation where their own self-expression is forbidden.

The steady, accepting but neutral attitude of the Kleinian psychotherapist differs from the manipulative and role-playing attitudes advocated by certain other strategies of intervention. Power is acknowledged and interpreted. In Kleinian psychotherapy the therapist allows himself or herself to be used as an *object*. In this way the psychotherapist actually intrudes but does not obtrude.

Making clear the transference manifestations which develop during this process is regarded as the primary means by which the patient is helped towards better health, to be able to maintain continuing psychic functioning. The personality of the therapist – calm, interested, helpful, giving full attention to each minute detail of the patient's behaviour and language – re-creates in the therapeutic alliance an opportunity to correct the infantile distorted view of object relationships that has constricted the patient's life. It provides incentive and reward in a benign relationship that encourages the patient to achieve the tasks that are imposed by the discipline of therapy and provides each patient with a model of strength and an identification with a reality: the real live person of the therapist.

At times the psychotherapist, guided by the ethical goals of treatment and the understanding obtained from their own training and personal psychotherapy, must safeguard against any interference with a professional attitude to the patient based on prior knowledge of their own difficulties and problems which stem from their own ethical values, attitudes and boundaries. For instance if the therapist is mourning the death of a parent or partner it may be difficult to work with a patient in a similar position.

Therapists are not empty husks; they have prejudices, fears, painful trigger spots. It is better for both therapist and patient to acknowledge and identify these feelings. This may mean that at times the therapist will decide not to take a particular patient into treatment. This is a serious decision for patient and therapist alike and must be handled in such a fashion that making a referral to another agency or individual does not further disturb the patient and cause more pain.

Therapeutic relationship and style

The Kleinian technique as adapted in psychotherapy is psychoanalytic and based – as are others – on classical Freudian analysis. This means that the setting for therapy is formal and the number of sessions will vary (an analysis offers five or six sessions each week), but in psychotherapy this is the exception rather than the rule. However, the session time is the same (50 minutes) and the patient can be offered a choice of either couch or chair.

The therapist uses the techniques of free association and interpretation and in all essentials other than the frequency of sessions psychoanalytic principles are strictly adhered to. The style of the therapist is confined to listening and in-terpreting the material brought by a patient. Criticism, encouragement, reassurance and advice-giving are avoided. However, the atmosphere is relaxed and facilitative.

To understand and appreciate the difference between the Kleinian relationship in therapy with the patient and other methodologies one must look at the nature of the interpretations given to the patient. Klein changed the emphasis in the analytic process from formal Freudian theories to aspects of material not seen before. She was impressed by the prevalence and power of the mechanisms of projection and introjection, and highlighted the fact that these introjections led to the building of the inner complex world, with its projections which colour the world and our perceptions of reality. Once verbalized and 'seen', as it were, these revelations of our primitive levels of experience can be understood and detected in the material provided by our adult patients.

A Kleinian therapist is aware that if a patient gains control in psychotherapy their difficulties will be perpetuated in later life. The patient will continue to live a life constricted by the paranoid-schizoid symptoms which caused them to seek therapy in the first place. It follows that however neutral and laid back the therapist may contrive to be, in successful therapy the therapist maintains control of the kind of relationship that will operate with this patient.

> In all forms of psychoanalytic psychotherapy, therapist and patient are confronted with a basic problem, the problem of object need. Every patient regards the psychotherapist as real, regards all the manifestations of the treatment situation as real and strives to regard the therapist as a real object. The therapist too wants to regard the patient as real and to respond to the patient as a real object. (Tarachow, 1970: 498–9)

The primary urge in this relationship is the temptation to turn back the clock, to regress, to restore the symbiotic parental relationship that initially occurred with the mother: to lose the boundaries and fuse, to re-create the past as it was, and return to the time of ultimate dependency replete, at one inside the mother.

It is important to point out here that in no way should the therapist confuse the therapeutic function with the parental function. The therapist may give over part of their mind to this experience, since they come so close to the patient's life experience, but in essence the therapist must also remain detached from it, holding on to professional anonymity. The therapist will be aware of the seductive danger of imagining him/herself (even for the briefest time) as the ideal parent figure for the patient. The therapist uses these skills of awareness and identification to assess and understand the complexities of the interaction of the patient with the parent parts of the therapist.

We may be deeply affected, feel involved, but paradoxically this affection and involvement is distilled, detached, separated in a way which is impossible in the true relationship between a parent and child.

The Kleinian psychotherapist works assiduously to develop this therapeutic alliance, the intimate, real and close working together of two minds. For this to come about both the therapist and the patient undertake a controlled ego splitting (where either good or bad parts of the self are split off from the ego and projected into love or hatred of external objects: i.e. parental figures or caregivers) in the service of the treatment. The therapist and the patient work together in constructing a barrier against the need for a constricted object relationship. The therapist is not a breast, a hand or a voice, but a human being who is complete in every way. The therapist as well as the patient has to struggle constantly against the array of temptations which lead them to believe that they can allow themselves to become closer to their patient, with consequent dissolution and camouflaging of the existing ego boundaries. These temptations are further compounded because certain aspects of the therapeutic alliance are real. The therapist behaves in a caring, concerned, real and human way to the patient, and the patient is able to glean over a period of time real things about the therapist: that the therapist may be single or married, the family is away on holiday, that the therapist smokes, prefers one colour to another, that there is a secretary, a family pet, small children and that the therapist may share accommodation with other psychotherapists, etc.

These realistic aspects of the treatment relationship must be understood by the Kleinian psychotherapist. Among other things they lead to identification with the reality aspects of the therapist, who uses them *wordlessly* to correct transference distortions and to supply the motivation necessary for the therapeutic work of transference interpretation. Close attention to what may be happening in the immediate present has many analogies with what could have been happening in the reconstructed past. What is important is the urgent need that the transference process serves in the here and now and should not be disregarded in the therapist's search for its meaning in the past.

It is important to stress that every interpretation made by a therapist results in a loss or a deprivation for the patient. It can frustrate, denying the patient an opportunity to gratify their fantasy wishes, often placing them in the position of relinquishing some infantile object: 'It is a paradox that the interpretation – the act of the therapist that deprives the patient of the infantile object – also provides him with an adult object in the form of the sympathetic therapist' (Tarachow, 1970: 498–9).

Despite many changes in current Kleinian practice and in how unresolved issues are being tackled by therapists, there is a strong continuity in the way in which fundamental principles have endured:

- the process – the overriding importance given to the responses to interpretation;
- the transference – the centrality of interpreting the transference;
- the emphasis on the patient's early childhood experiences and their level of functioning in this period;
- the belief that love and hate go side by side and that the turmoil caused by the sense of destructiveness is counterbalanced by love.

Major therapeutic strategies and techniques

The role of the psychotherapist is centred entirely on transference and its interpretation. The therapist listens intently to the patient's material, and endeavours not to be involved at all in giving practical advice, encouragement, reassurance or to offer any active participation in the life of the patient or the patient's family.

Transference interpretation The concept of transference relates not only to an understanding of the 'here and now', the situation which is actually evolving between the psychotherapist and the patient, but to an understanding of the way facts and fantasies which relate to past relationships, especially those of internal figures from the patient's inner world, are transferred on to the therapist. The transference is expanded as a total situation which includes the functioning of the patient as well as the symbolic meanings placed on to the therapist.

This lively process takes in current problems and relationships, which are again related to the transference as it develops. The Kleinian psychotherapist is aware of the transference at the very *beginning* of therapy, but in giving interpretations careful attention must be paid to the way they are handled, the timing, the order and the language used, and especially to the amount of interpretation.

Understanding of transference and counter-transference and their effect on therapy are the tools which are used to investigate both the positive and negative feelings directed towards the therapist. Counter-transference was first seen as a neurotic disturbance in the therapist which prevented him or her from obtaining a clear and objective view of the patient, but now it is understood to be an important source of information about the patient as well as a major component in understanding the interaction of the therapist and the patient.

In other words, we are deeply affected and involved but also paradoxically uninvolved with our patients. These feelings bring with them the pressure to identify with the counter-transference situation and to act it out in ways either unconsciously and subtly or obviously and aggressively.

Interpretation of these feelings should be sparse and succinct, using everyday language, avoiding technical and analytic terms which may give satisfaction to the therapist but are of little value to the patient. If your patients cannot understand you, they may as well go home. The best initial interpretations are simple restatements of the problem as presented by the client but relayed back in dynamic terms.

If it is difficult to teach psychotherapy, it is even more difficult to describe the techniques of psychotherapy. In an earlier paragraph I stressed that the Kleinian psychotherapist will have learned skills through long-term psychoanalysis or psychodynamic psychotherapy, a process not unlike the age-old system of apprenticeship to a master or skilled craftsman of some repute and proven worth. The technique of psychotherapy is not static, and psychotherapists regularly attend case discussion groups, supervision sessions, seminars and study groups to meet and compare experiences and to learn from each other in a lively fashion.

Contemporary Kleinian technique emphasizes:

- the immediate here and now situation;
- all aspects of the setting – i.e. the room where therapy takes place;
- the importance of understanding the content of the anxiety;
- 'the consequence of interpreting the anxiety rather than the defences only (so-called deep interpretation)' (Spillius, 1983: 321–2).

In ways that are comparable with other techniques, the therapist keeps expressions of personality and lifestyle out of the session. Maurice Winnicott humorously remarked, 'of course you can acknowledge that there is a war going on', but political statements or discussion of other issues do not belong in the consulting room. In this way the client is enabled to make contact with an expectation of *others* which related more closely to the emotions that are experienced as a result of therapy, than they do to what is happening at that moment in the external world.

It is important to stress that the past is connected to the present *gradually*. Interpretations are given in a certain sequence: preparatory interventions, interpreting resistances and defences, gauging the patient's readiness to accept the interpretation and wording it carefully.

In the Kleinian model, interpretations go from the surface to the depth; from what is known or imagined to occur in the present, to what exists in the past, which is less well known or unknown. The therapist layers slowly to the earliest mental processes of childhood, and to the later more specialized types of mental functioning, which are the unconscious infantile archaic wishes and fantasies – those which focus on the therapist as a possible source of gratification.

The change process in therapy

Atholl Hughes, in 'Contributions of Melanie Klein to psychoanalytic technique', gives a particularly clear definition of the change process in Kleinian therapy:

> As the patient is helped to distinguish good experiences they can identify with the analyst as a person who can care for their own insight and well being and the way is open for the patient to do the same. As the patients envy lessens it becomes possible to appreciate positive qualities in oneself and others, acknowledged along with destructive qualities. Integration of split off parts of oneself is comparable to a process in the development of the normal infant who begins, at about three months of age, to tolerate loving and hating the same object with less splitting and projection.
>
> On the basis of a repeated satisfying experience, the child is able to introject, that is to take into their own personality, ideas and feelings of a good mother with less hostility and idealisation. The child is then in a position to tolerate feelings of concern and responsibility towards the mother in whom the capacity to introject is crippled. (Hughes, 1974: 113–14)

During treatment, the patient comes to understand that feelings of aggression and love can be valuable, and so it is possible to value them. Early responses to interpretation which were felt by the patient to be prohibitive, unkind or unduly harsh, and which tended either to frustrate desire or to punish –permitting, even commanding, the patient to enter in fear and trepidation the forbidden areas of primitive and passionate feelings – these regressive infantile expectations are overcome and are replaced by a rationality that can be accepted and understood.

Melanie Klein opened the door to insights which enable us at least to attempt to contend with human behaviour. We are confronted in life with a view of ourselves in a succession of social relationships which are disrupted by hatred, jealousy, rivalry, greed and other destructive feelings. The process of change in therapy enables us at least to establish more constructive relationships. It is said that as Freud discovered the child in the adult, so Klein discovered the infant in the child.

Patients change as they become more open and free to acknowledge their constant struggle between love and hate. Facilitated by their therapy, knowledge of the destructive elements which are present in the psyche can lead to clearer judgement, increased tolerance of ourselves and others, with the ability to remain in control and to be less fearful.

This problem of change can be identified as a desire for reconciliation and reparation. The patient can begin to identify with other people in a caring and sensitive way. The patient can let go of the negative aspects of the painful frustrations and suffering of the past, believing once again in their own capacity to love and therefore expecting to be loved in return. In making this reparation for the past the patient can make good the imagined injuries both given and received in infancy and move on to relinquish their guilt.

Limitations of the approach

There is a proliferation of different methods of psychotherapy, many of which do not emphasize self-awareness, and which open wide the question of causation of therapeutic change. They postulate that change is not engendered by the growth of self-awareness. Questions are frequently asked about the extent to which the theories and concepts of Kleinian therapy affect the technique of psycho-analysis.

Scientific examination of the causes of therapeutic change must involve an examination and description of the variables which, in context, facilitate such change. Experimental methods can then be evolved to test the hypotheses which are formed.

Kleinian psychotherapy, as judged by these contemporary standards, is still unable to provide the scientific evidence necessary to meet the basic criteria of dis-conformability. Moreover it becomes increasingly evident that it is an over-simplification to look at psychopathology as if it can be isolated from the changing attitudes of the nuclear age.

But what of the Kleinian method both as a focus of inquiry and as a therapy? Some Kleinian therapists find it difficult to acknowledge there is an outside environment that their patients have created and in which they function. In seeking to re-create the patient's internal and fantasized world of childhood the Kleinian is perhaps too eager to divorce patients from their social and cultural background.

We have, after all, moved on considerably from the early 1900s and have come to realize (I hope) that our patients are a specific group of people who have reacted in a specific way to their problems and who come, specifically, to seek help from Kleinian psychotherapy. A human being cannot develop in a sterilized plastic bubble. A baby is conceived at the coming together of its parents, who contribute to this act of creation the essence of their own personalities at that given moment. The baby is born at a predicted time and season of the year, in a special place and in a particular way and significantly others become involved in its well-being. It depends throughout life on the availability and proximity of other human beings. In the wheatfields of America, a man will sow the wheat that provides bread for this child, and in the sweatshops of Hong Kong another child will labour to cut its clothes.

In the heat of the moment, focusing mainly on early childhood experiences and/ or recollections, the broader social context and subjective processes which brought these two human beings together can sometimes get left out of the consulting room, especially as the focus is on manoeuvrability and tactics. Kleinian psycho-therapy holds the view that external events are not of primary importance, but we know that these events can exacerbate or alleviate certain aspects of the personality.

Inevitably the decision on what process to use with the patient in effecting change is shaped by one's theoretical approach. However, if the therapist practises therapy all day and every day from only one viewpoint, then there is a real danger of the Kleinian therapist becoming subsumed and consumed by their own stance. The rigorous adherence to basic psychoanalytic methods should not become rigidity. This contrasts sharply with other strategies of intervention where the emphasis has shifted from the processes within an individual to those in the context of his or her relationships with others (i.e. family therapy and personal construct psychology).

B.J. Farrell (1981) reinforces the limitations imposed by strict adherence to one kind of analytic theory, and in response to Melanie Klein he makes the point that Kleinian theory was (and still is) innovative. In continuing to extemporize and to employ new forms of psychoanalytic method, the Kleinian therapist may be tempted to seek to obtain affirmation of any novel input from the patients themselves.

It was a technical invention – the technique of child analysis – which gave Melanie Klein the idea that the free play of young children can be interpreted psychoanalytically, giving access to the more primitive areas of the mind that still provides the Kleinian therapist with a wealth of new material and has continued to provoke considerable revision of analytic theory. This technique influenced theory.

But the question is: when the Kleinian therapist continues to report new case material and new findings, how is it possible to decide whether the therapist has, in fact, just misinterpreted basic Kleinian theory? If the therapist is hesitant about challenging results, does this imply that the original theory itself is 'shaky' and in need of amendment?

For the Kleinian therapist the nagging doubts must persist. The crucial question remains: what effect does the assumption of a Kleinian theoretical stance have on the behaviour of this therapist?

Do interpretations always dictate the therapist's goals for patients? Do Kleinian therapists only seek out what they expect to find? Do therapists, in order to fit their own expectations, distort what information patients provide? The deeper the analytic work, the more primitive the processes mobilized, the more essential it is to adhere to the basic psychodynamic model.

Kleinian therapists tend to forget that because they see their patients in such a strictly controlled analytic setting, they are immolated from a view of their patient in the external world. True, the patients report on their daily life, but these reports are highly selective and often only pertinent to the failures rather than the successes of life outside the consulting room. Anxious behaviour by one patient can be interpreted as a repression of unconscious ideas which are threatening to become conscious. The same anxious behaviour in another could be viewed externally as a way of appealing for a sympathetic approach from the therapist. These two interpretations of behaviour represent astonishingly different theoretical systems. In this way the therapist's viewpoint can be distorted.

The reader of this book will note that various theorists differ considerably on the postulation of central motives or goals for *all* human beings. Why do they differ so much? Is it not that the task of ferreting out the central motives of all human beings is impossible? Is it not an unattainable goal to poll every patient on their expectations of life and their private responses to the slings and arrows of outrageous fortune?

Would Kleinian psychotherapy suffer if each patient's motives were seen as unique? Psychoanalytical psychotherapy has been defined as a perspective which is essentially pre-theoretical in nature, but perspectives are often constricted by ideological underpinnings whether we are aware of them or not.

It was Huxley who wrote: 'Give me good mothers and I shall make a better world', but it is the converse which is true: 'Make me a good world and I shall give you good mothers.' It is hoped that Kleinian therapy can eventually be more explicit in stating that the amelioration of at least some areas of maternal deprivation and childhood abuse will only be possible when these intrinsic requirements can be met.

In looking forward to the future, R.D. Hinshelwood writes:

> Increasingly throughout the 20th century human beings have been understood as psychological beings. Their difficulties have therefore been increasingly seen as psychological and less as moral. The impetus for this change has comprised many elements, but psychoanalysis has figured prominently among them.
>
> In very large measure, across the whole of our culture, the general apperception of mental illness and disturbance has been moulded by psychoanalysis itself. As psychoanalytic ideas have spread, so the presentation of psychological difficulties has become permeated by a psychoanalytic sophistication.
>
> This has created a particular situation for psychoanalysts. They face a moving target. New kinds of patients mean new ideas which in turn mean new ways of working, but they also mean patients with new ways of presenting themselves and thus a new target for the psychoanalytic probe. (Hinshelwood, 1994: 240)

Case example

The client

Dean is a tall, slim, good-looking man, 30 years of age. He came into therapy on a once-a-week basis 22 months ago, having been referred by his GP. Dean also had a couple of sessions with an insightful practice nurse, who had reinforced the idea that psychotherapy could be helpful to him.

Dean had diagnosed himself as 'feeling depressed'. He presented in his first session with me a general feeling of loneliness, isolation and a lack of social functioning. At one time he had contemplated suicide but had made no real attempt, continuing to rely, initially, on the mild antidepressants prescribed by the GP. These thoughts were still prevalent.

Dean is the eldest son of six children. He alone was born before the parents married. His mother was only 17 years old. There are now two other brothers, David (26) and Don (24), plus three sisters, Pamela (28), Sarah (8) and Stacey (4). All three brothers were given first names which began with the letter D, a humorous whim of his mother.

Both parents are alive and well, father still working in London and mother at home looking after Stacey. They met whilst the father was in the Navy and married after a brief romance. Their first four children were born at regular intervals of two years but the two younger sisters came 16 years later. His parents have always had a difficult time – arguments and threats to leave, especially when his father's alcohol intake increased.

Apart from his mother and sisters there are two other significant women in Dean's life. His paternal grandmother (aged 75) of whom he is very fond, and an off-and-on girlfriend, Maureen (34) whom he met four years ago while backpacking in Australia. There are other grandparents, cousins, aunts, uncles in the extended family with whom there is little contact.

Dean has told me of his awkwardness and shyness whenever he meets new people. If they do seem to respond to him, he feels impelled at the outset to tell them about his father's alcohol dependency, a situation which has seriously affected his life and that of his mother. He is convinced that people label him as a 'misery', someone very difficult to talk to. His defence against these feelings is to insist that he is not actually interested in whether people like him or not.

Dean has been more involved in his parents' marital problems than his brothers, but his oldest sister, Pamela, has been very disturbed with symptoms which included anorexia nervosa and was herself in therapy following a suicide attempt. She has now married and become a devout Christian.

Before deciding to come into therapy Dean feared that he would follow in his father's footsteps and become a drunk. As a young man his social life had revolved around the pub and his father's drinking habits, as his father liked to have him around. He felt socially inept, tongue-tied and awkward in these places, but the *bonhomie* created by alcohol was attractive and helped him relax. As he grew older, however, he realized that the alcohol provided only a short-term solution for loneliness and shyness and helped his need to prove himself to his father as 'one of the boys'.

Dean is a hardworking and committed patient. He is a prolific writer and on his own initiative keeps a daily journal of his thoughts and feelings and about his therapy. Sometimes he reads short excerpts to me when illustrating a rethinking process. He has also provided written background material on childhood memories and experiences. (This is not engendered or encouraged by myself as therapist and is not part of the therapeutic technique.)

Dean's home was not a comfortable place. His parents argued continually and sometimes violently – throwing things at each other – but the children escaped physical punishment. Dean had his own small room to which he would retreat when the level of verbal abuse the parents hurled at each other reached a crescendo.

Dean's mother – 'a very beautiful woman' – was often threatening to leave and she would turn to Dean as the eldest son 'and the most sensible', appealing to him to speak to his father, to intervene in the situation and give her advice and support. But Dean was pulled in several directions; he was afraid of his father and wanted his father to think he was 'one of the boys'. His father liked taking him around and Dean recalls that although his father spent most of his nights and sometimes days in an orgy of drinking he was 'entertaining, lively and very much a showman'. It was not a good idea for him to complain to his father about his relationship with his wife. 'Several times I told my mother to leave him but after a while I could see that she wouldn't go. It could have been the house or money that kept her at home.'

Dean's father excelled in competitive sports like archery, golf and fishing; he liked to show off and would take Dean with him to these events, expecting him to compete. However, if at times Dean felt admiration for his father's larger than life character, these feelings would quickly evaporate when his father's drinking became excessive and he grew maudlin. Then the showing off, the boasting, became boring, repetitive and deeply shaming.

Money and the lack of it was a family problem. His father had skills as a plasterer and could always find work, but he had grandiose and way-out ideas for new business ventures, both legal and illegal, and when these went awry money became short and the arguments at home increased in vehemence. Sometimes there would be no money at all and his mother would shout, seeking material compensation for staying in such an unpredictable marriage. She longed for a large and beautiful home, for stability – a longing which was never fulfilled. The family house is still in need of repair and rebuilding and is still a low priority for his father.

At junior school there was no sense of relief or safety from the unhappy scenes at home. Dean was too quiet and bullied. His father advocated 'hit them back', but he was not too good at defending himself. He was neither popular nor unpopular but already a 'loner' both at school and at home. There were local gangs of boys with whom he could play and with whom he joined in sexual experimentation and mutual masturbation. He masturbated frequently both in the company of these boys and alone at home while looking at magazines. There was no need to fear admonishment from his parents – they were 'not involved'. His father did not make any effort to attend parents' evenings at school but his mother attended occasionally. Both appeared little interested in his school work or questioned him about progress at school. School teachers were aware of his father's alcohol problem but there was little they could do to help and their view of Dean's future progress was not optimistic, although he was quite good at mathematics and could have gone forward to GCSEs.

Sexual play and experimentation amongst the boys at school continued, followed by curiosity, excitement and embarrassment about girls. Dean was awkward and panicky when challenged to kiss girls or 'touch them up'. These panics occur frequently in his relationships with women. 'It's different when you are approached by men – you can retaliate with aggression if you don't like them or want them. Usually woman make me fearful.'

Against all odds Dean did well in junior school. It had taken him a long time to learn to read but when he finally did start, 'I would read non-stop'. At secondary school, studies continued to improve without any of the previous bullying by classmates. He was given the nickname 'Mr Serious' because of his solitariness and 'Bodger' because he was showing a clear practical bent and spent time in taking apart and mending mechanical objects.

Dean says: 'I was a follower and not a leader. I knew that my parents weren't really bothered about me so I spent a lot of time staying alone or in other friends' houses. There were no constraints, no one even asked where I was or what I was doing.' Father was now drinking heavily. His latest enterprise – a car showroom – became another financial disaster. Dean was drawn into working in all these ventures, some of which were enjoyable whilst 'risky'. Others made him nervous, especially those which were questionable and illegal.

'I could invite friends to come home with me If I wanted to but I was always tense when my father came home rolling drunk, talking incessantly about himself, often repeating himself. He would start telling them about the death of his mother, what hardship he had suffered in his childhood. I didn't mind him telling this to old friends but when they had to listen to his stories month in and month out, I used to cringe when I saw him open his mouth. It was at this time that I really understood that my father was a drunk and that his drinking had turned him into a moron. I was so ashamed of him.'

Dean has said little as yet about his mother. She was always at home with the children but constantly threatening to leave if her husband did not give up drinking. The question then was, where could she go? Dean added that if they had split he would have stayed with his father. 'He needed me more.' Later, Dean changed this into 'My father was more entertaining.'

After several bouts of very heavy drinking his father's health deteriorated and he became delusional. He was admitted to hospital and detoxified, after which he joined Alcoholics Anonymous and has since managed to stay abstinent, but even so the marriage situation remains unstable. Husband and wife are always at odds and still seemingly incompatible. There are always threats by his mother to move out but she makes no move to do so. Dean has moved away and does not get involved. In the family home brothers and sisters got on well together but, outside his home, at school or casually if Dean had to meet anyone new he would become panic-stricken. At times he had to force himself to walk past a group of strangers. He was sure that people felt uncomfortable with him. He was a 'strange' person.

Although he was interested in girls, any attempt at a relationship was 'a disaster'. To get closer to a girl he found attractive was a huge task. After a few failed attempts he would give up – his level of anxiety was too great. At 16 he was propositioned by a man offering him money for sex. He resisted volubly, drawing other people's attention to the man. Sexual experiences with boys at school did not recur but there were times even now (when drunk) that he experienced sexually exciting thoughts about men. He has had oral sex with men and still finds at times that he is attracted to men and has had dreams in which other men participated in oral sex and bondage.

In the therapy sessions Dean reflected on what it meant to be 'overshadowed' by his father, recalling that events that he had shared with his father – the golf, archery and fishing competitiveness – were always a battle for prowess between them. He questions why he had spent so much time with his father. Why did he regard himself as his father's ally? He didn't love his father or admire him; why did he allow his father to intimidate him? Even now he has to avoid him and keeps away.

Three months into therapy Dean handed me the following list. He had decided not to take any more antidepressant pills, he felt better and more able to think ahead.

- I have always been shy.
- I have always had daydreams of grandeur and heroics.
- I have always been in Dad's shadow.
- Until I started therapy I had bad dreams of violence being done to me.
- I am usually obedient (Mother's good boy) towards people I like and need.
- I can often be the reverse with people I no longer like and need.
- Am I looking to be mothered?

(It is not a requirement of therapy that clients produce written material and I think this is the first 'list' I have ever received. Dean obviously thought this list could convey more than his verbal communications.)

When Dean left school, he became apprenticed and later obtained several City and Guilds qualifications. He is now a professionally qualified service engineer with a speciality in air conditioning systems and has since worked in a nuclear power station and the Channel Tunnel. Dean earns a substantial salary in a responsible post and uses his money freely to indulge in a wide range of hobbies: travel, hill walking, photography and camping.

Dean is accompanied on these activities by his one girlfriend, Maureen whom he met while on holiday in Australia four years ago. Dean and Maureen live as neighbours on two houseboats, moored on a local canal. At the moment they are living apart but still see each other frequently, still have regular sex and share tastes in music, films and books, but they rarely stay together for long. Maureen is critical of Dean, complaining that he is depressed, cynical and has low self-esteem. Dean would not argue with this description, but he retaliates by describing Maureen as forceful and critical. 'She has more get-up and go than me. I don't know what is going to happen with Maureen and myself. She now seems to be getting more and more down, same problems, unhappy at work, not much social life except with each other. I don't know if our relationship is a "bad" one with a few problems or a "good" one with more than a few problems. I know I feel love for her at times but we don't seem to be helping each other. Living so near to each other is perhaps a big mistake but then again I keep thinking may be that things will sort themselves out, perhaps things will fall into place. I am also beginning to wonder if we're more different from each other than we realized. She says she behaves differently with other people when I'm not there; maybe I do too but I don't think to any extent. When I do think about all this and look at it coldly my reaction is to call it a day with her, but I also think that what we have in many ways is good and worth trying to sort out and I think it will probably be OK. Sex is always good with Maureen.'

Dean is forthright in his current view of his life situation. He feels that he is full of nervous energy, can't keep still for five minutes, filling his life with work. He describes himself as having a cynical, derogatory sense of humour but says that he can be reliable and knowledgeable when called upon. Dean is still apologetic about being too serious and quiet, keeping his personal thoughts to himself. Perhaps he has become too controlled in his behaviour towards Maureen, more fussy about what he will or won't do. In particular he relishes personal discomfort, living a fairly frugal existence on his boat and setting himself painful physical tasks in his leisure time.

Maureen has said that as she is getting older she would like to have children. Dean tells her that he could not envisage being a father and inflicting his 'negativity' on his children. They are still battling through.

The therapy

At a very early age children become acquainted with reality through the deprivations which it imposes on them. They defend themselves against reality by repudiating it. The fundamental thing however, and the criterion of all later capacity for adaptation to reality is the degree in which they are able to tolerate the deprivations that result from the Oedipal situation. (Klein, 1926: 128–9)

In Klein's view the Oedipal situation reaches its zenith at the age of four years. By the time Dean was four his mother had produced two other babies. The 'urge to know' of the four-year-old child was considerably influenced by the conflicting passages of passionate love and murderous hate which were stimulated by Dean's sense of frustration and ignorance in the face of the mystery of his parents' sexuality and aggression.

Dean's feelings of deprivation at being left out and abandoned were directed towards his mother, who had now become an integrated figure (love object) instead of a collection of parts. Oscillating feelings of love and hate were experienced with the added dimension of guilt which came from the fear that his feelings of hate and disappointment would damage his mother for ever.

The strong wish to make reparation to the person/object which he felt he had damaged became evident in his conflicting behaviour towards his mother: at one time her supporter and advice giver and at another ready to abandon her and go off with his father.

Dean's father was always a powerful and rivalrous figure. What child could compete with him? This rivalry marked the beginnings of the direct and inverted Oedipus complex.

When things go wrong within the family structure at this early level the developmental stages of infancy are impeded and the child has difficulty in progressing towards the capacity for rational thought and a sense of centring within the self. There are several possible abnormal reactions to this sense of imposed impotence and frustration. The individual may develop a desire for obsessional compulsive damaging acts to put right the imagined damage to his loved ones. This became overt during our later therapy sessions.

In therapy, Dean had bridled at the thought that his mother's attention was attracted elsewhere with the arrival of a sister and a brother within the first four years of his life, but at the time of writing he has told me that it was his intention to confront his mother to get at the truth of a 'number of things – I am fed up with lies and half-truths.'

During therapy we have returned time after time to Dean's presenting problem of loneliness and isolation. Kleinian therapy postulates that a sense of loneliness stems from feelings of regret and pain caused by having suffered an irreparable and irrecoverable loss of the passion and closeness of the basic relationship with the mother. Later this loneliness can diminish when in adult life we come to the conclusion that life is far from perfect and we cannot return to our childhood. Dean appears to accept that it is impossible to achieve permanent and complete integration (the resolution of the love–hate ambivalence that appears when the depressive position has been reached). He also knows that a debilitating and painful sense of loneliness is apt to reappear at any time.

During therapy we can see that an understanding of these mechanisms as they operate in Dean's daily life have taken place in two stages. First, his ability to recognize the similarity between his relationship with Maureen and the stop/go relationship his mother offered to his father. Analysing the transference situation in so far as it affects Maureen entails reduction of the splits and the love–hate ambivalence by which he controls their relationship. It is important to realize, however, that Dean operates a complex structure in his relationship with Maureen and with others. Two modes of response are juxtapositioned in differing measures and hover between projection and introjection. Dean has become adept at disavowal, denying, not owning to what material he has already produced, repressing his violence other than the violence he can fantasize as being done to himself.

In therapy Dean admits that at times I have come to stand for the internal figures in his life, so all the material that he has brought contains the dynamic element of transference: not necessarily just a transference directed to what is happening between us in the consulting room but also transferences which encompass the current external relationships in his life, his relationship to me (good mother some of the time and bad mother when I am ill or choose to go away on holiday). All these relationships link with his relationships with parental figures in the past.

In Dean's case the projection of his own inhibited and painful sexuality into his parents' relationship gave rise to the perception that his parents did not have the components for a sexually active marriage. Dean finds it uncomfortable to think about the arrival of his two sisters, 16 years after the birth of his brother. How could this have happened? Both of them must have been mistakes. 'I knew nothing about their arrival. I was not around when my mother was pregnant.' Not only can he fantasize that his father was demanding and sexually dangerous to his mother, but he also clings to the punitive perception of himself as devoid of aggression and sex.

Dean is still irrationally terrified of making contact with new people. He feels trapped in social situations and creates a distance between himself and others. Even a relatively healthy individual like Dean has failed to master his anxieties in relation to women and in certain situations he uses defences which are damaging and extreme in their effects and their offensiveness, for example recently getting drunk and making sexual overtures to the wife of a friend. The results of his persecutory anxieties (setting himself up for rejection) create bizarre thoughts in Dean (punishment in dreams) which intensify his feelings of intense fear and cause a sense of chaos and confusion which overwhelms him and results in these overt states of extreme panic and depression. This anxiety could result in an intolerable state. However, Dean's latest written effort is summarized below. (Again, this was volunteered by Dean and handed over at the end of a session.)

There are several things I think I should do to try and improve. Unfortunately I don't know the answers. When reading back through this it sounds very dismal and negative, yet I think things will improve. It will be interesting to see what happens. Things to try and do:

1. Go away by myself or with someone else. This should take a bit of the strain off us (although Maureen and I will probably have a terrible row if I go off walking by myself).
2. Fishing: try to find a crowd to go sea fishing with.
3. Socialize: the hardest one to crack. I need to change my outlook on life in general.

> One of the basic problems is that I am not interested in people unless I know them. How to know them if you are not prepared to be interested?

> A thing to remember. This can only be sorted out if I try. It will not happen by itself. It is a lot easier to waffle to people about this than to do anything about it.

This statement exhibits, I believe, the hallmark of a real development of the personality which a Kleinian psychotherapist would seek – Dean's internal object now understanding and contributing to an internal concept of his whole self. Dean is beginning to take more responsibility for himself and his impulses and to look at his sexual ambivalence, to think about the impulses which he has always labelled as negative and bad, to feel guilt and concern at times for others and to finally separate from his parental morass.

However, in relation to dealing with this process of separation, Brenman (1982) draws up an impressive list of the types of separation-related acting out in which a patient may engage during treatment: from time to time Dean resorts to this form of acting out.

1. Indulging in loveless sexuality
2. Hatred, criticisms and grievances to comfort himself
3. Become excessively intrusive or by virtue of projection feeling intruded on by others
4. Occupying himself with physical fitness and various kinds of masturbatory fantasy
5. Form compulsive attachments – exciting, hateful, idyllic etc. which require pathological attachment to replace what is felt to be missing.

What solution can psychotherapy offer to Dean, for whom at times this solitude is a nightmare?

> If solitude is experienced as a nightmare then it is life as a whole that is hereby wrecked . . . . Solitude is not the forgoing of relationship with others. On the contrary it allows each individual to define himself and the confrontation with originality of the other brings out the preciousness and irreplaceability of what each person alone can contribute. The worth of the object and the subject derives from the fact that each is unique, it is born of their solitude. (Quinodoz, 1993: 192–3)

After the usual summer break, Dean's return to regular weekly therapy was marked by long and painful 'confessions' about disturbing and violent thoughts that have occurred. On one occasion sitting behind a young girl at a pop concert he had fantasies of breaking her spine and he has thoughts of rape of both sexes, but these thoughts all remain in fantasy.

He is now re-experiencing the murderous anger and frustration he repressed as a child and hovers between the longing to act out these fantasies with strangers and the equally exciting fantasy of having acts of violence conducted against him.

We continue to work together. It is his intention that at some future time he can talk about himself and his difficulties in a therapy group.

References

Bion, W.R. (1988) 'The differentiation of the psychotic from the non-psychotic personalities' (1957), in E. Bott Spillius (ed.), *Melanie Klein Today*, Vol. I: *Mainly Theory*. London: Routledge. pp. 61–78.

Bowlby, J. (1979) *The Making and Breaking of Affectional Bonds*. London: Social Science Paperbacks, Tavistock.

Brenman, E. (1982) 'Separation – a clinical problem', *Bulletin of the British Psychoanalytical Society*, 1(2): 14–23.

Colby, K.M. (1951) *A Primer for Psychotherapists*. New York: Ronald Press.

Cooper, C. (1988) 'The Jewish mother', in H. Cooper (ed.), *Soul Searching*. London: SCM Press.

Farrell, B.J. (1981) *The Standing of Psycho-analysis*. London: Oxford University Press.

Hinshelwood, R.D. (1989) *A Dictionary of Kleinian Thought*. London: Free Association Books.

Hinshelwood, R.D. (1994) *Clinical Klein*. London: Free Association Books.

Hughes, A. (1974) 'Contributions of Melanie Klein to psycho-analytic technique', in V.J. Varma (ed.), *Psychotherapy Today*. London: Constable.

Isaacs, S. (1952) 'The nature and function of fantasy', in J. Rivière (ed.), *Developments in Psycho-analysis*. London: Hogarth.

Klein, M. (1926) 'The psychological principles of infant analysis', *International Journal of Psychoanalysis*, 8: 128–9.

Klein, M. (1932a) *The Psychoanalysis of Children*. London: Hogarth.

Klein, M. (1932b) 'Love, hate and reparation', in J. Rickman (ed.), *Psycho-analytic Epitomes*. London: Hogarth.

Klein, M. (1948a) 'The development of a child', in *Contributions to Psycho-analysis 1921–45*. London: Hogarth.

Klein, M. (1948b) 'A contribution to the psychogenesis of manic depressive states', in *Contributions to Psycho-analysis 1921–45*. London: Hogarth.

Klein, M. (1950) 'On the criteria for the termination of a psycho-analysis', *London International Journal of Psycho-analysis*.

Klein, M. (1952a) 'Notes on some schizoid mechanisms', in J. Riviere (ed.), *Developments in Psycho-analysis*. London: Hogarth.

Klein, M. (1952b) 'On the theory of anxiety and guilt', in J.Riviere (ed.), *Developments in Psycho-analysis*. London: Hogarth.

Klein, M. (1957) *Envy and Gratitude*. New York: Basic Books.

Klein, M. (1960) *Our Adult World and its Roots in Infancy*. London: Tavistock.

Meltzer, D. (1979) *The Kleinian Development*. London: The Clunie Press.

Miller, A. (1983) *For Your Own Good*. London: Virago Press.

Mollon, P.J. (1979) 'Transforming anxiety: a rationale for verbal psychotherapy', *New Forum Magazine*, Autumn/Winter, 5(4): 18–19.

Piontelli, A. (1992) *From Foetus to Child*. London: Routledge.

Quinodoz, J.M. (1993) *The Taming of Solitude* (New Library of Psychoanalysis 20). London: Routledge.

Segal, H. (1973) *Introduction to the Work of Melanie Klein*. London: Institute of Psychoanalysis Karnac Books.

Segal, H. (1986) *Delusion and Artistic Creativity and Other Psycho-analytic Essays*. London: Free Association Books.

Spillius, E.B. (1983) 'Some developments from the work of Melanie Klein', *International Journal of Psycho-analysis*, 64: 321–2.

Tarachow, S. (1970) *Introduction to Psychotherapy*. New York: International University Press.

Waelder, R. (1937) 'The problem of the genesis of psychical conflict in earliest infancy', *International Journal of Psycho-analysis*, 18: 406–73.

Suggested further reading

Anderson, R. (ed.) (1992) *Clinical Lectures on Klein and Bion* (New Library of Psychoanalysis 14). London: Routledge.

Grosskurth, P. (1986) *Melanie Klein. Her World and Her Work*. London: Hodder & Stoughton.

Klein, M. (1961) *Narrative of a Child Analysis*. London: Hogarth.

Piontelli, A. (1992) *From Foetus to Child* (New Library of Psychoanalysis 15). London: Routledge.

Quinodoz, J.M. (1992) *The Taming of Solitude* (New Library of Psychoanalysis 20). London: Routledge.

4

Psychodynamic Therapy: The Jungian Approach

Ann Casement

Historical context and development in Britain

Historical context

Analytical psychology is the term employed by the Swiss psychiatrist, Carl Gustav Jung (1875–1961), to depict his approach to depth psychology and psychotherapy. Though congruent with a psychodynamic perspective, Jung's approach to the human psyche and its drives displays several distinctive features, notably a marked stress on the interrelation of psyche and body.

Jung's childhood was marred by physical illness and emotional uncertainties. His relations with his pastor father and his mother were problematic (Jung, 1963). He happily asserted that his personal library and the cultural influences to which he was subjected were the formative factors in the evolution of his ideas, referring to the personal equation in saying that 'every psychology – my own included – has the character of a subjective confession' (Jung, 1961: 336).

Jung exemplified the anthropologist, Claude Lévi-Strauss's (1908–) term '*bricoleur*', an intellectual handyman who finds inspiration everywhere. The quest the two men shared was for universal structures underlying the mind/psyche, which led to borrowing a metaphorical screw from here, a figurative nut from there and, from elsewhere, an imaginative bolt. This 'bricolage' reflects Jung's view of the diversity and complexity of the psyche.

The first part of this chapter will present some of the main intellectual influences on Jung's work, which stretch as far back as the pre-Socratic thinkers like Heraclitus and include Plato's ideas. The latter are the forerunners of Jung's theory of archetypes, which concerns the inherited patterns in the psychosomatic unconscious. This is Jung's way of linking two sets of opposites: psyche and soma, and instinct and image, the concept of opposites being central to his psychology.

Western philosophy, particularly German Idealism and Romanticism, has had a general impact on analytical psychology. Kant's view of the 'moral order within' is echoed everywhere in Jung's work, while some would say that his 'starry heavens above' are more evident in Jung's ideas than in his own. Herder, the father of German Expressionism, also influenced Jung's populist and pluralistic approach to the psyche.

Given that Hegel synthesized Kantian reason and morality with Herder's ideas on desire and sensibility, he is a great, though largely unacknowledged influence on Jung. This lack of acknowledgement was perhaps due to Hegel's worldliness and his writings on the state, which were not to Jung's taste. Hegelian dialectics may be compared to the coming together of psychological qualities and elements hitherto seen as opposites. In Jungian therapy, these form into a new third position and the dialectic begins again.

Other strong influences on Jung were Schelling with his view that nature is a visible spirit; Rousseau's 'voice of nature within', and, crucially, the writings of Goethe, particularly *Faust*. Jung claimed to be distantly related to Goethe and therefore felt a strong affinity with him.

The 19th-century German Romantics Schopenhauer and Nietzsche, with their idea of the Will and the Superman, also contributed to what we would now call 'Jungian' psychology. The Vitalists such as Bergson and Driesch were the inspiration for ideas of the world as process rather than a static mechanistic view of the world. In such a world view, nature is animated by spirit as opposed to being regarded as inert matter. Monists such as the 3rd-century Neoplatonist, Plotinus, contributed their theory of the oneness of all things.

Jung sometimes compared his work to Gnosticism, which became the first heresy in early Christian times. One of its teachings is that initially there was a primordial oneness of all reality and existence and that there is an inherent longing for a return to this unity. The Gnostics also held that wisdom comes through direct experience leading to individual insight rather than through received dogma backed up by authority. Jung's attitude to Freud's intellectual leadership reflected these Gnostic values. Manichaeism, which has its origins in Gnosticism, held that there was an essential dualism to everything. Hence evil was not just an absence of good but a force in its own right, equal in power to good. The 'reality of evil' was a phrase Jung often used in relation to the sadistic and inhumane aspects of psyche and society alike.

Alchemy, another below-the-line phenomenon, was first brought to Jung's attention by the Sinologist, Richard Wilhelm. Knowing of Jung's long-term interest in oriental ideas, Wilhelm sent him a Chinese alchemical text, 'The Secret of the Golden Flower' (Jung, 1967). Following his study of this text, Jung joyfully announced that the alchemists – Eastern and Western – had discovered a way of exploring the path to what Jung later called individuation, meaning the realization or actualization of the potentials inherently existing in the self. The alchemical process by which base matter is transformed into gold may be compared to the corresponding 'stages' in a classical Jungian analysis in which the patient 'individuates', becoming a more or less whole person. Neurosis is transformed into selfhood. These analytical stages will be more fully described below.

At the turn of the century there was a proliferation of spiritualist groups and cultic nature movements, some of which centred around sun worship. Jung's fascination with mysticism and the occult drew him to these – and he often cites the vivid imagery, centred on the sun's phallus, of a psychotic patient of J.J. Honegger, one of his students at the Burgholzi mental hospital. Psychiatry was Jung's first profession and the major influences here were Pierre Janet, Theodore Flournoy and Eugen Bleuler.

The best-known influence of all on Jung was that of Freud, with whom Jung collaborated from 1907 to 1913. Their inherent personality, cultural and conceptual differences led to an irreparable split growing up between them. From today's standpoint, their theoretical views remain highly complementary and Jung's analytical psychology is, in part, a blend of Freud's psychoanalysis and Alfred Adler's individual psychology.

Development in Britain

A Jung club had existed in London since 1922 but the need and wish for increasing professionalization of analytical psychology led a group of analysts under the leadership of Michael Fordham to found the Society of Analytical Psychology (SAP) in 1946. This was the first Jungian training institute in the world and Jung was persuaded to be its first president in spite of the fact that he was always anti-institutional and once said: 'Thank God I am not a Jungian!'

A further development in the UK was Fordham's collaboration with Gerhard Adler, who was also a founder member of the SAP, and Sir Herbert Read to produce the English edition of Jung's *Collected Works*.

Fordham felt strongly that the split between Jung and Freud in 1913 had been a disaster and devoted himself to repairing this split. In the course of his pioneering work with infants and children, he began to bring together Jungian archetypal theory with Kleinian 'phantasies', which are the primary contents of unconscious mental processes. One of Fordham's most radical extensions of classical Jungian theory was to postulate that a 'primary self' is at work in infants from the beginning (Fordham, 1993). Instead of the psyche increasingly working towards synthesis, Fordham concluded from his work with infants and children that this 'primary self' 'de-integrates' from a state of inner wholeness to bring the infant into relation with the environment (ibid.). In this way the infant's expectation of feeding evokes the appropriate response from mother's breast in the external world. Following psychoanalytic object relations theorists, who also postulated the existence of an ego from the start, Fordham filled a gap in both classical psychoanalytic and analytical psychology theory in showing that a primary self exists from the beginning of life.

Classical theory had always seen the self (sometimes the Self) as an underlying unifying principle in the psyche–soma of the human organism which did not become directly important until the second half of life, say from a person's late thirties. 'The self is . . . as a rule in an unconscious condition to begin with. But it is a definite experience of later life, when the fact becomes conscious' (Jung, 1977: 725).

Fordham also introduced new ideas on the transference–countertransference into Jungian clinical practice. What happened in London, where analytical psychology was being blended with psychoanalytic theory and practice, came to be known as the developmental school of Jungians as it spread to other countries (see Samuels, 1985).

These and other departures from classical Jungian theory have replicated the original Jung/Freud split. Broadly speaking, there are now three groups of Jungian analysts internationally. Andrew Samuels (ibid.) has constructed a tripartite classification of analytical psychology into schools: the developmental school, which incorporates psychoanalytic theory and practice; the classical school, seeking to extend Jung's own ways of thinking and working; and the archetypal school, concentrating on the play of images in the psyche.

Analysts such as Gerhard Adler, the founder of the Association of Jungian Analysts, disagreed with Fordham about the Jung/Freud split being a disaster, regarding the work of the two men as incompatible (Adler, 1979). According to Adler, Jung was essentially a *homo religiosus* for whom the *meaning* of anyone's life was of paramount importance. This is in direct contrast to Freud's anti-religious stance. If we compare the work of the two men, we see that Freud's system is rational, logical and limited, whereas Jung's is non-rational, religious and aims at a wide but imprecise image of wholeness.

Theoretical assumptions

Image of the person

Theory of opposites   The last paragraph of the previous section attempted to give a brief picture of the differences that exists in the Jungian community. Some practitioners would be placed firmly at the archetypal end of a spectrum of concerns, others would be called Kleinian Jungians and there are many who have a syncretistic approach to their work. The present chapter is a pluralistic attempt (Samuels, 1989a) to hold a balance between the diversity of analytical psychology today and the unity it still possesses as having been inspired by Jung's own work. It is necessary to state Jung's premisses here before going on to indicate subsequent developments.

The theory of psychological opposites lies at the basis of Jung's own approach to the psyche. He said, for instance, that opposites are the indispensable pre-conditions of all psychic life (Jung, 1955–56). To give a simple example, when someone is murderously angry with another person, their desire to destroy the other competes with its opposite – concern for other people backed up by parental and religious teachings. How it words out depends on the individual's ego holding the tension between the opposites of anger and concern – he or she may shout, or bite the bullet, or seek the intercession of another, or engage in self-reflection that undermines the 'justification' felt in relation to the anger. On a cultural level, opposites such as spirituality and sexuality also have to be reconciled in some way. For Jung, on both the individual and cultural levels, neurosis consists of resolution of the tension and interplay of opposites by the neurotic taking up a position aligned with one extreme or another. These days, it is widely accepted that there are usually more than three positions (the two extremes and their resolution) and 'the opposites' are usually presented as a spectrum of possibilities.

Analytical psychology itself is a synthesis of two opposites: a spiritual quest for self-knowledge with a scientific approach to the workings of the psyche. However, the spiritual and religious elements in Jung's work have made it difficult for him to be found acceptable in academic and intellectual circles, and some Jungians eschew this aspect of Jung. On the other hand, the empirical psychologist is equally a part of him, for instance in his experimental work with the word association test. This discovered the existence of feeling-toned 'complexes', which are relatively autonomous aggregates of emotions and experiences in the psyche clustered around an archetypally patterned core. This method initially attracted

Freud's attention as he felt Jung was providing verification of the existence of the unconscious. However, Freud was repelled by the mystical and 'occult' Jung.

To do Jung's work full justice it is essential to maintain a balance between these two opposing forces. He pointed to the 'transcendent function' as the symbolical way of holding a balance between them and of withstanding the pull of one or the other, which would lead eventually to a rigid and rational psychology, or to its opposite: an equally rigid love of the irrational. To try to rationalize Jung by discarding the spiritual elements which speak of concerns for purpose and meaning is to reduce him to the status of a disciple of Freud. But to treat him only as a mystic leaves out the great body of work he contributed to empirical psychology.

Transcending that which presents itself to us as opposite is a chief dynamic running through Jung's work and the 'self' is a 'symbol' of this transcendence. In Jung's language, a symbol may be thought of as the intuitive way of knowing the as yet not fully knowable. 'The . . . central archetype of "self" . . . seems to be the point of reference for the unconscious psyche, just as the ego is the point of reference for consciousness. The symbolism associated with this archetype expresses itself on the one hand in circular, spherical, and quaternary forms, in the "squaring of the circle"; on the other hand in the image of the supraordinate personality' (Jung, 1977: 484).

The influences from the past on Jung's theory of opposites include Heraclitus' 'enantiodromia', which encompasses the idea that sooner or later everything turns into its opposite. An abrupt change from one strongly held position to an extreme other would be an example of this and is a time of great inner conflict for an individual. This is the Jungian equivalent of the object relations theory of 'splitting'. At this point there is a concentration of 'psychic energy', Jung's more neutral term for Freud's 'libido', which Jung saw as sexually loaded, in order to resolve the conflict by seeking for a new position. This method is also directly related to Hegel's dialectical scheme of thesis/antithesis/synthesis.

The object/subject dichotomy is another aspect of opposites exemplified, for instance, in what Jung terms the 'objective psyche'. This points to the 'reality of the psyche' as both a source of objective knowledge with its own autonomous way of functioning and as a container of more than personal of subjective contents. The latter aspect of the objective psyche Jung equated with the 'collective unconscious', the locus of universal motifs which are shared by all humans throughout time and space. One example is that of the personal mother of an individual, which has aspects in common with the universal image of the objective mother.

'Syzygy' is a term Jung applied to any set of yoked opposites, particularly sexually based ones like male/female, masculine/feminine, and yang/yin which he took from Chinese philosophy. Jung's own terms of 'animus/anima' denote the sexually opposite inner figures of a woman (animus) and a man (anima). This dichotomy has been modified by viewing anima/animus as interchangeable and as functioning equally in men and women to produce what might be seen as creative animation in both (Clark, 1987).

As stated above, the theory of archetypes concerns inherited patterns in the psychosomatic unconscious. It is Jung's way of linking two sets of opposites: psyche and soma and instinct and image. 'Synchronistic' experiences, which Jung claimed were acausal, underwrite this continuum, as the psychic can behave like the non-psychic and vice versa.

Synthesizing opposites is central to Jung's approach. It is also evidence of his personal pathology and points to an inner split that needed healing, which he attempted to do creatively through his work. Winnicott diagnosed Jung as having had a childhood psychosis, when he reviewed Jung's autobiographical work *Memories, Dreams, Reflections*, and saw Jung's lifelong quest as one in search of healing (Winnicott, 1964). The mercurial and paradoxical tone that runs through so much of Jung's work stems from his fascination with opposites and this is why his writings are often experienced as being elusive (as well as allusive) and difficult to pin down.

Metapsychology   As far as metapsychology is concerned, Jung owes much to Freud's model. For instance, they have in common a dynamic, economic and topographical interaction as their centre. The dynamic and economic attributes in Jung's model are articulated by the investment of 'psychic energy' in varying degrees of equivalence amongst the topographical spheres of 'consciousness', 'personal unconscious' and 'collective unconscious'.

Consciousness has the 'ego' as its centre, this being the agent in the psyche that an individual identifies with as 'I'. 'Persona' lies also in the conscious sphere and is the mask that the individual presents to the world. The 'shadow' lies in the personal unconscious and represents all those aspects that are seen to be undesirable by the ego and which are, therefore, repressed. 'Anima' and 'animus', like all 'archetypes', originate in the 'collective unconscious' and act unconsciously through projection when activated by an outer object, for example falling in love. The 'self' as the totality of the psyche is immanent throughout and functions both as the beginning and the end of all psychic activity. It mediates the opposites of good/evil, creativity/destruction, divine/human, etc., and offers the possibility of achieving wholeness or 'individuation' through the conjunction of opposites, or 'coniunctio'. Its presence is experienced as 'numinous', i.e. mysteriously powerful, and this is especially prevalent when there is a great deal of archetypal activity at work in an individual as, for instance, when collective unconscious contents are beginning to push through into consciousness.

Typology   Typology, the theory of innate personality differences, is an important, if highly problematic, part of Jung's work. Some time will be spent on its definition according to the Myers-Briggs model, one of the systems used to measure these differences (Myers, 1962).

One reason for Jung's interest in typology was the break with Freud, not only his own but also Alfred Adler's. By examining these and other 'personality clashes' throughout history, Jung sought to clarify his own position by showing how people with inbuilt differences can find it difficult to understand each other.

The two basic concepts here are those of orientation of attitude to the world and of ways of 'functioning' in it. Attitude is measured on a scale ranging from extroversion at one end to introversion at the other. Individuals who are extroverted tend to focus on the outer world of people and the external environment.

Extroverting in this way means that the individual is energized by what goes on in the outer world and that is where energy tends to be directed. Extroverts usually prefer to communicate more by talking than by writing and need to experience the world in order to understand it and thus tend to like action.

Introverts focus more on their own inner world and while introverting, energy is invested in that direction. Introverts tend to be more interested and comfortable when their work requires a good deal of their activity to take place quietly inside their heads. They like to understand the world before experiencing it, and so often think about what they are doing before acting.

The four functions concern ways of perceiving or acquiring information: sensation, intuition, thinking and feeling. Sensing is a way of perceiving through the senses of the eyes, ears, nose, touch and taste. These inform an individual of what is actually happening out there and keep one in touch with the realities of a situation. Sensing types tend to accept and work with what is given in the here-and-now, and have a realistic and practical approach to life. They are adept at working with facts.

Intuiting is the other way of perceiving and is directed to the meanings and possibilities that go beyond information given through the senses. Intuition takes in the whole picture and tries to grasp the essential patterns at work in any situation. Intuitives value imagination and inspiration and are expert at seeing new possibilities.

Once information is acquired through one of the two perceiving functions, it is necessary to make decisions or judgements about it. This is done through the two functions of thinking and feeling.

Thinking predicts the logical consequences of any particular choice or action. Decisions are made objectively on the basis of cause and effect and of analysing and weighing the evidence inherent in any situation. Individuals with a preference for thinking seek an objective standard of truth and are good at analysing what is wrong with something.

Feeling, on the other hand, considers what is important without requiring it to be logical. Values to do with the human domain are at the basis of this way of functioning and the emphasis is upon how much one cares about any situation. Individuals with a preference for feeling like dealing with people and tend to respond in a sympathetic, appreciative and tactful way to others. Feeling as used in Jung's typology is to be differentiated from actual feelings or emotions and is, instead, to do with a capacity for making judgements or decisions based on humane values.

The four functions are heavily modified by the two attitudes and an extroverted sensation type is quite different to an introverted sensation type in being orientated to the outer world. There is usually a primary and secondary way of functioning: for example an individual may have extroverted sensation as their primary function and introverted feeling as their secondary one. The two primary functions will be in the conscious part of the psyche and will be more differentiated. The two functions that are less developed will be unconscious, and when activated will bring forth unconscious material. This is why Jung stated that a great deal can be learned from the least differentiated function. This also applies to the attitudes; for instance, an extrovert will have introversion in the unconscious.

The final scale that applies to all this shows how a perceiving type orientates to life in a different way to a judging one. Perceiving through sensing and intuiting will lead to a flexible, spontaneous lifestyle. Individuals with this preference seek to understand life rather than control it. They prefer to stay open to experience, enjoying and trusting in their ability to adapt to the moment.

Individuals who have a judging approach through thinking and feeling tend to live in a planned and orderly way and want to regulate and control life. Decisions are taken which lead to closure and to a passing on to something else. Individuals with a preference for judging tend to be structured and organized in their approach. It is important to differentiate 'judging' used in the above context from judgmental; any of the types may be prone to the latter.

Conceptualization of psychological disturbance and health

The psychologically healthy individual is conceptualized as one who is free to interact with a degree of autonomy, in relation both to the environment and to the inner world of the psyche. The disturbed individual, on the other hand, is conceived as being the inverse of this in finding both inner and outer worlds too persecutory to relate to freely.

In analytical psychology, the unconscious is conceptualized as consisting of two realms: the 'personal unconscious' into which unacceptable contents are repressed; and the 'collective unconscious' which is the container of mankind's psychic inheritance and potential. Psychological disturbance may be associated with both realms. For instance, too much repression of personal material that is unacceptable to the individual's conscious mind will result in neurotic symptoms. These will also manifest if innate potential is denied existence and not integrated more consciously into the individual's life. To summarize, severe repression in relation to either of these unconscious realms will result in pathological functioning on the individual's part.

The inherent split in Jung between the empirical psychologist and his mythopoeic side are evident in his approach to psychopathology. It has already been stated that he began work as a psychiatrist. In the course of this work he was increasingly interested in schizophrenia and came to conceptualize it as a psychogenic disorder within a psychosomatic framework. This insight pointed to the possibility of using a psychological approach to the treatment of schizophrenia in particular, and psychosis in general. An example of this is given in the section below, 'Practice'. This was revolutionary at the time in relativizing the view that every psychosis was a purely neurological disorder. Instead, Jung suggested that schizophrenia resulted in part from the invasion of consciousness by contents from the collective unconscious which, in turn, pointed to the possibility that there was meaning in the utterances and behaviour of schizophrenics.

However, Jung's ambivalent attitude to psychopathology can be seen in the following: 'clinical diagnoses are important, since they give the doctor a certain orientation . . . they do not help the patient. The crucial thing is the story' (Jung, 1963: 145). This has led to a concentration in treatment by some Jungian therapists on the story or myth of the individual as a way of helping an individual to achieve psychological health. 'The general ambivalence in depth psychology concerning psychopathology is to be found *par excellence* in the Jungian world' (Samuels, 1989b).

As a result, analytical psychology was greatly lacking in clinical teaching and had to borrow heavily from psychoanalysis to fill this gap. In this way, concepts such as ego defences, transference–countertransference and acting-out have been introduced into Jungian practice. This, combined with the mythopoeic stance, can produce effective results in restoring health and potency to individuals.

Acquisition of psychological disturbance

Jung questioned Freud's theory of early traumatic experience as the cause of neurosis and eventually rejected it as being too deterministic. The former said that looking for causes in an individual's past kept the person tied forever to that past.

For Jung, on the other hand, there was an archetypal core at the centre of each neurotic symptom and he concentrated his attention on seeking this out. This is what is called the teleological approach in classical analytical psychology and is based on Aristotle's doctrine of final causes. This point of view looks at psychological phenomena to find out what they are for and where they are leading to, which, in turn, gives symptoms a purpose that results in them being experienced as not only pathological. Jung called his approach 'synthetic' in contrast to what he termed Freud's 'reductive' method. The synthetic approach puts the emphasis on what emerges from the starting point rather than on the starting point itself.

Depression seen from this viewpoint is both pathological as well as a manifestation of psychic energy being drawn from the conscious realm into the unconscious. This may arise when change is being signalled, for instance at the time of a major life event for an individual when the status quo has to be abandoned in favour of new life. If this is thwarted, the depression may well become chronic. There are many instances of this but a few will serve to illustrate the point: a young person who is unable to leave the parental home in order to take up the challenge of life; or an unhappily married person failing to deal with marital problems.

Perpetuation of psychological disturbance

A central feature for Jung in perpetuating psychological disturbance is the inability to separate from the mother, both personal and archetypal. He set out to demonstrate the failure to do so on the part of a young woman patient in his book *Symbols of Transformation* (Jung 1911–12). The patient's case history was sent to him by the psychiatrist, Flournoy and, although Jung himself never met her, he conducts a long-distance analysis from her notes, which ends with a negative prognosis of schizophrenia. However, a close reading of the book reveals that the real patient is Jung himself simultaneously working through his break with Freud and, at the same time, developing his own ideas through self-analysis.

The main theme of the book is to show that remaining in a state of what Jung thought of as psychological incest is a prime cause for the perpetuation of neurosis and even psychosis. This is in contrast with Freud's Oedipal theory of incest, which is a longing for actual coitus with the mother. Jung, on the other hand, splits the image of mother into a duality – the personal and the archetypal – and states that symbolic re-entry into or union with the mother is necessary in order to be reborn. Thus, the individuated person is 'twice-born', the first time physically from the personal mother and the second time symbolically from the objective mother. The book was an expression of Jung's own rebirth in his late thirties and its contents signalled the split between him and Freud.

Splitting is seen in Kleinian theory as an early defence used in controlling the object by dividing it into a good and bad part-object. In the above, Jung is referring to splitting the image of the mother into personal and archetypal and into good and bad. Another similarity with psychoanalytic pathology is Jung's theory of 'participation mystique' which he took from the anthropologist, Lévy-Bruhl. This entails an identification between subject and object so that the latter is experienced as being a part of the former, e.g. a spirit or a fetish object. Looked at psychologically, this represents a neurotic dependence on another object because it is experienced as being part of the self and in this way has tremendous influence over the individual. This theory of Jung's is the equivalent of projective identification where part of the self is projected into another person and is then experienced as the projected part.

In addition, there is the psychoanalytic concept of ego defences. These act to prevent unwanted personal and archetypal unconscious contents from breaking through into consciousness through the mechanisms of repression, denial and reaction-formation.

Another neurotic defence is that of extreme introversion which manifests in narcissistic feelings of grandiosity that act to keep an individual from being involved in interpersonal relationships. There is a place for healthy introversion as described above under 'Typology', but Western culture is identified with an extroverted thinking/sensation way of functioning so that many people feel forced to comply with this. If this compliance becomes pathological, they need to be helped to achieve a better balance between introversion and extroversion. In this way, it may be said that extreme extroversion can be as neurotic as extreme introversion.

Change

Change towards a healthier way of functioning is conceptualized in the Jungian canon as leaving a collective way of being and moving towards a more highly differentiated position as an individual. This is summed up in the Jungian concept of individuating. But as Kenneth Lambert has point out, Jung may have over-emphasized the beneficial effects of transformation 'so sharply as to suggest that normality equals false conformity' (Lambert, 1981: 33).

Although Jung tended to see individuating as relating to the Jungian path towards selfhood, Samuels states that Klein's view of healthy normality is very similar and may be summed up as 'emotional maturity, strength of character, capacity to deal with conflicting emotions, a reciprocal balance between internal and external worlds, and, finally, a welding of the parts of the personality leading to an integrated self concept' (Samuels, 1985: 132).

Certainly both Klein and Jung would agree with Freud in seeing psychic health as the outcome of the transformation of neurosis as a result of the change that occurs through the successful outcome of therapy. This change may be viewed positively by family and friends if the individual is experienced as being more flexible and spontaneous and less rigid in interacting with the environment. However, the reverse also arises, and the person may be experienced as having become more selfish and less compliant – in other words as having changed for the worse.

Practice

Goals of therapy

Goals of all kinds are of great importance in the classical Jungian approach to therapy, and its major concepts reflect this. These are based on a teleological or goal-directed view enshrined in a doctrine of final causes. This views the self as functioning essentially to push an individual towards the fulfilment of his or her destiny whether or not the ego concurs with it. This is what Jung means by the reality of the psyche. The classical approach has largely been orientated to therapy for individuals in the second half of life, i.e. in their late thirties and over, and the goal is that of individuation or attaining wholeness by the individual. This teleological view of the workings of the self points to an essentially religious attitude to life in its awareness of an immanent animated presence in all matters. Gerhard Adler's book, *The Living Symbol*, is an account of the individuating process at work in the analysis of a woman in the second half of life (Adler, 1961).

The first half of life was regarded by Jung as a period of extroversion where an individual is naturally orientated to worldly concerns such as marriage, children and career. It is in the late thirties that an individual's 'myth' challenges him or her to begin to separate from a collective worldly stance and to follow the quest for his or her own separate identity. Because of the heroic nature of this endeavour, Jung conceptualized it as a mythical confrontation with a dragon. This is, of course, a symbolic, inner dragon which is both the personal and the objective mother that seduces the individual into an attitude of inertia *vis-à-vis* life. The treasure which is hard to attain is that of the person's identity.

Both Jung's *Symbols of Transformation*, where the real 'patient' is Jung himself, and Adler's *The Living Symbol* are classical accounts about the goal of individuating in the second half of life. As previously mentioned, Fordham's reworking of the self as primary has resulted in his view that individuation as a goal is not confined to the second half of life. He cites Jung's claim that individuation is to be equated with achieving consciousness through differentiation of subject from object and shows that the child's gradual separation from the mother during its first two years of life is likewise a process of individuation (Fordham, 1976). In his synthesis of object relations theory and analytical psychology, Fordham demonstrated how, after birth, the infant's primary self de-integrates and, through increasing identification with the mother, begins to move towards early object-relating. Control over bodily functioning is increasingly mastered and the beginnings of a conscience and consciousness are set in train, which includes a synthesizing of opposites such as good/bad and from this there develops a capacity for concern. All these, combined with the start of the process of symbolization, are the prerequisites of the goal of individuation.

In this way, Fordham broadened Jung's goal-centred theory of individuation to include infancy and childhood and by doing so has established that it is a natural part of the goal of maturing rather than a work against nature, as Jung claims. The latter does allow for the fact that individuals individuate unconsciously but claims that this is not comparable with individuating through a long analysis. A further consequence of Fordham's revision of individuation is the modification of the first half/second half of life dichotomy.

Rosemary Gordon talks of a twofold goal in analysis: one is that of curing, which is to do with the expansion of ego through assimilation of contents from the personal and the collective unconscious; the other goal is that of healing, which is involved in the individuating process and the working towards a more complex wholeness of the individual (Gordon, 1979).

The above has largely concentrated on the positive aspects of the individuation process as a goal but there is a great deal of pathology involved in it as well. One danger is that of breakdown when archetypal activity is very strong and the patient may be overwhelmed with contents from the collective unconscious. Another danger is that of identifying with the mana-like power of these contents, which can lead to inflation of the ego. Jung points to Nietzsche's identification with the semi-legendary Persian prophet Zarathustra, which eventually contributed to his madness (Jarrett, 1988). Jung states that if Nietzsche had been more aware that Zarathustra was an archetypal figure calling him – Nietzsche – to explore his own inner world, he would not have seen himself as a prophet and broadcast his message of the Superman. This is an example of individuating but with a lack of the conscious integration which would have grounded Nietzsche.

Depression is another consequence of the individuating process: it becomes pathological when an individual elevates the unconscious to a position of moral supremacy over the conscious part of the personality. The latter then feels inferior and worthless and the result is that the individual becomes depressed. Nietzsche, on the other hand, identified with the mana personality and his ego became inflated (Jung, 1953).

A further complication of the goal of individuation concerns the behaviour of an individual intent on fulfilling his or her potential in respect to others. An extreme example of this would be a psychopath, but on a more mundane level every individual must to a greater or lesser extent curb potential fulfilment in relation to other people. Jung's awareness of these limitations is expressed in his saying: 'Certainly that consciousness, which would enable us to live the great Yea and Nay of our own free will and purpose, is an altogether superhuman ideal. Still, it is a goal' (Jung, 1953: 59).

To go back to Gordon's model of curing, one of the goals of Jungian therapy would be the enlargement of the ego, in other words an increase in consciousness of both outer and inner worlds. This in turn would lead to a greater balance of the two and a spontaneous flow of energy between them.

In short-term therapy, the goal would be to enable an individual to reach a better-adapted relationship to problems posed by the environment through supportive work by the therapist.

Selection criteria

Jungian therapists usually refer to individuals who come into therapy as 'patients' rather than 'clients', which has to do with the concept of suffering inherent in that word, the extension of this being the fact that every therapist has been through his or her own painful therapy. The term also expresses the patience that will be needed in a long therapy. Lastly, 'analysis' and 'therapy' are the terms used in the treatment of 'patients' who are being seen two or more times weekly. This is a simple way of differentiating this type of therapy from 'counselling', which applies to work with 'clients' on a once-weekly basis. However, it must be stressed that these are not hard and fast definitions as a patient seeing a therapist once a week may well be in analysis rather than counselling.

The terms 'analysis' and 'psychotherapy' are difficult to clearly differentiate. One way of doing so is to view analysis as working in greater depth and for longer duration than psychotherapy. In addition, Jungian psychotherapy may be understood as a method that employs *some* Jungian ideas.

There are no disorders that cannot be alleviated in some way by analysis or psychotherapy, and this will be demonstrated below. But there are a few caveats which it is important to bear in mind. Any persisting physical symptom must be treated by a medical practitioner and not viewed only as psychosomatic hysterical conversion which could justify analytical treatment. Another point that practitioners need to bear in mind is that the analytic process is primarily a relationship between two people and that a genuine rapport is necessary between them for any creative work to be made possible. If there is no 'fit' between analyst and patient from the start, it would be unwise to begin the treatment. It would be preferable to refer the patient to another practitioner.

At this point it would be useful to give an example of how a physical symptom may be treated both organically and analytically. A woman patient started analysis with me five years ago and her presenting problem was the messy breakdown of her marriage, combined with an increasingly problematic relationship with her teenage son. It was soon apparent that she was caught in a negative mother complex, which dominated all her relationships in a destructive way. A few months after starting therapy, she was diagnosed as having cancer of the breast and underwent major surgery. She needed many months of supportive therapy throughout this period but when she was ready to work on herself analytically, she began to see that the physical cutting out of 'mother' had been necessary in order to give her a chance to begin to separate herself from her complex and to find her own identity quite apart from that of 'mother'.

Traditionally, Jungian practitioners, in contrast to psychoanalysts, had a tendency to take on highly disturbed patients. Freud held to the view that psychoanalysis was really only suitable as a treatment for the neuroses but he looked to Jung's work with schizophrenic patients, initially as a psychiatrist, then as an analyst, to extend the frontiers of psychoanalysis to the treatment of the psychoses.

Winnicott's claim that Jung's quest for self-healing, rather than resolution through analysis, came from the latter's psychotic illness (Winnicott, 1964), is not borne out by early psychotherapeutic work done by Jung in the treatment of schizophrenia. In a paper he wrote in 1919 (Jung, 1960), Jung explores the possibility of psychotherapy for the psychoses. Initially he summarizes the difficulties of any such endeavour, e.g. that any apparent cure would be seen only as a remission of symptoms, and admits that he is not optimistic in this regard. He stresses the importance of searching out the psychological aetiology and course of psychosis and says that this is more easily done in comparatively simple cases.

He gave the example of a young girl who suddenly became schizophrenic. She was a peasant's daughter, who had trained as a teacher and who until that time had displayed no abnormal symptoms. One night she heard the voice of God and Jesus also appeared to her. When Jung saw her, she was calm but completely uninterested in her surroundings, and her answers to questions were given without any accompanying affect – as Jung comments, she might as well have been talking of the stove which she was standing next to, rocking gently back and forth all the while.

Jung asked her if she had kept any notes of her conversations with God and, saying yes, she handed him a piece of paper with a cross on it. Eventually, after a long period of questioning her, Jung discovered that the young woman felt herself to be in a state of sin because she had been attracted to a man she saw the day that her symptoms appeared. That night she experienced a religious conversion and God appeared to her.

Jung acknowledged that there must be a predisposition in someone who becomes schizophrenic but held that it is possible to discover the psychogenic causes of the disease and in this way to alleviate the symptoms. In Jung's view, psychosis was the result of a poorly differentiated consciousness and a sparsely stocked personal unconscious so that the subject is at risk of invasion by archetypal contents from the realm of the collective unconscious. This is why he advocated the identification of mythological motifs in the expressions of psychotics. He went on to associate psychosis with anima/animus and the neuroses with the workings of the ego (Jung, 1951).

All Jungian analysts have an internship in psychiatry as part of their training and work psychotherapeutically with psychotic and borderline patients, in circumstances where these patients are contained in a holding environment and are also on medication. Most of the work done with these patients would be psychotherapeutic rather than analytic, i.e. supportive and aimed at alleviating symptoms rather than the long and complicated inner journey that a full analysis involves. To summarize, as long as the practitioner is not over-optimistic about outcome and as long as the patient is contained in a holding environment, Jungian therapy can be applied effectively to psychosis.

Addiction is another complicated area that some Jungians have worked with therapeutically. The Italian, Luigi Zoja, has worked intensively in therapy with drug addicts and has come to see that the underlying motivation amongst young addicts is a need for the kind of initiation rituals that are so lacking in Western society (Zoja, 1985). He points to the need for treatment that is aimed at helping addicts to give up drugs and to heal damaged organs, also taking into account the underlying psychological needs that are expressed by addiction. He advocates bringing people together in a community which instils a common spirit and goal and in this way creates an atmosphere of being part of a mystical group. This gives meaning both to the addiction and to the process of treatment.

All of this echoes work done by anthropologists and sociologists; for instance the French anthropologist, Arnold van Gennep, in his writing about rites of passage described every ritual as having three distinct phases (van Gennep, 1960). The first is that of separation from the profane world; the second is being contained in the sacred world that exists outside normal social intercourse; the third is reincorporation into the world but with a new identity. The present writer works with the idea that a whole analysis or therapy is a rite of passage, as well as every session, with separation, containment and reincorporation being part of the process in each case.

To elaborate further the need for meaning and containment there is also the need for 'communitas', the term Victor Turner, the anthropologist applies to a mystical coming together for a joint purpose, in which individual identity is submerged in a meaningful way into community feeling as, for example, on a pilgrimage (Turner, 1969). The negative correlate of this is what the sociologist, Erving Goffman, calls the 'stripping process', which is to be seen at work in all total institutions, e.g. the Army, prison and hospitals (Goffman, 1961). This involves stripping the person of any individual identity in a brutal fashion by making them wear a uniform, by giving them a number instead of a name, etc. Many hospitals and psychiatric wards exemplify this negative stripping process at work rather than any positive group feeling of *communitas* and asylum. It is this dimension that psychotherapy can bring to bear on psychiatry.

Phobias are also amenable to analytical insight, although the symptoms may persist, e.g. fear of flying. When a patient is able to relate this fear to the anxiety that comes from being out of control – as in the sensation of being out of touch with the earth combined with not being at the controls of the plane – then the phobia may be able to be connected to its origins in infancy or childhood. One patient was able to recall being terrified every time her father threw her up in the air. Another managed to remember the fact that she had been dropped as an infant. Some behavioural therapy may also be required in working with phobic patients.

In addition, it may seem beneficial for a patient to have family or marital therapy when these sorts of problem begin to dominate the therapeutic work in each session. Another way of locating a major problem at any time is through working with dreams. These tend to throw up a constant stream of images related to a problem when it moves into the acute stage.

Where a patient is in both individual and another form of therapy at the same time, it is vital for the analyst to be aware of any signs of splitting between the two modalities, e.g. all the good being seen as belonging in one and all the bad in the other. An example of this is a patient I have who is also going to Alcoholics Anonymous, who began to split between the good analyst and the bad sponsor. By becoming aware of this in the analytic work, she was enabled to modify her projections on to both.

Some analytic patients come from GPs and psychiatry and are on medication such as antidepressants or psychotropic drugs. In these cases, it is important for the therapist not to become involved in the medical treatment, although the therapist may well have to liaise with the medical practitioner involved with the patient. This must be done with the consent of the patient at all times, the only exception being when a patient may be a danger to him/herself or to others, perhaps a child. Once again it is important for the therapist to be aware of possible splitting between, say, a GP and the therapist and to take steps to counteract this.

It is clear from all the above that therapy not only does not preclude treatment by other modalities but actively welcomes this as long as discrete boundaries are maintained and there is sufficient awareness of splitting and idealization.

Qualities of effective therapists

Therapy is a vocational profession and therapists may experience an inner calling which usually arises from their own deep psychic wounds. If these are left largely unhealed, there is a danger that a therapist will react to patients pathologically from neurotic counter-transference feelings, e.g. retaliating to or over-identifying with patients' disturbed behaviour. Where these wounds have been sufficiently healed, a therapist will be able to empathize with a patient's trauma and, in this way, be of service. Self-awareness on the therapist's part combined with empathy are the key to effective therapeutic intervention.

Every therapist has an extensive training analysis lasting for several years. This is preceded by pre-training analysis. For the duration of training, a trainee therapist also works under supervision by a senior analyst or therapist with clinical cases. The developmental school has started to require candidates to undertake a two-year infant observation with an attendant discussion group as part of training. However, it is important to pay attention here to Daniel Stern's recent writings on the difference between the psychoanalytic infant and the observed infant (Stern, 1985).

A trainee does not need to be medically qualified but has to have had some experience of working in a psychiatric unit. Candidates also need to have a background in the helping professions, for example as teachers, social workers or counsellors.

It was Jung who first pointed out in 1911 the necessity of a training analysis for all would-be analysts while he was president of the International Association of Psychoanalysts from 1910 to 1914 (Jung, 1961). The therapist's most important tool in therapeutic work is his or her own personality and character, which needs to be married to a capacity for awareness of limitations with regard to the level of disturbance that can be tolerated from patients. This capacity for self-awareness must be combined with what Gerhard Adler called the four 'Hs': honesty, humanity, humility and humour which, in turn, need to be linked to skills acquired during a long training lasting for several years. This includes personal therapy and supervision, theoretical seminars and scientific and clinical meetings which seek to build on an inherent psychological-mindedness in the trainee therapist. Continuous professional development is needed to ensure that a practitioner stays up to date with new theoretical and clinical ideas.

Therapeutic relationship and style

Above all a therapist needs to be able to combine spontaneity with an appropriate observance of boundaries. The first session is taken up with information-giving on the part of the patient and setting up of the therapeutic 'contract'. This includes agreeing between the therapist and patient the amount to be paid per session, the number of sessions that will be necessary per week across a spectrum that ranges from one session weekly to five, and whether the patient would benefit from being on the couch or in a chair. This 'contract' or therapeutic alliance is negotiated with what may be thought of as the functioning part of the patient's personality and will be needed throughout the work in relation to the more pragmatic side of analysis, as detailed above.

After establishing the contract, it is necessary to create a holding environment wherein the patient can feel safe to regress and to reflect on experiences that happen in therapy. There is no set plan for each session and this can often feel threatening for a patient, who will need to be able to endure not knowing what may happen. In order for this to happen, the therapist must communicate a feeling of security to the patient that he or she will not be let down. In this holding environment, the therapist must be sensitive to the feeling-tone of a session, for instance whether silence represents an angry withholding or resistance on the patient's part, or whether it is a creative silence which is allowing the patient to be truly in touch with his or her inner world.

The therapeutic approach is passive/receptive rather than active or directive. It is also somewhat formal and there is no physical contact between the two participants. Added to this, there is virtually no self-disclosure on the part of the majority of therapists apart from the minimum information required by the prospective patient to make an informed choice of therapist. It is always possible, even after years of experience, to be tempted into revealing personal details about oneself. In a recent session, a long-standing patient of mine recounted a dream which portrayed precisely an aspect of my personal life which she could not consciously know. I had to struggle momentarily with responding in a congratulatory manner about her wonderful intuition and with a desire on my part to show off, as it was a positive thing that she had intuited. Humour is a necessary quality for any therapist but so is the awareness that too much of it in a session may represent a manic defence.

In the final stages of a long therapy, a practitioner will begin to be more open in the interaction, perhaps at times admitting to liking something, or vice versa. But, on the whole, boundaries are all-important to this approach so that the analyst's stance will remain largely neutral and formal.

Major therapeutic strategies and techniques

Some Jungian analysts and therapists only use the couch, some only the chair, whereas others, like the writer, use either depending on the patient, or even both at different stages in the analytic work with the same patient. The couch is beneficial for a patient who is strongly resistant to regression, when this is necessary, to a more infantile stage. Resistance involves unconscious ego defences such as repression, denial, reaction-formation and 'acting-out' in various ways. The latter can include almost anything, but some examples would be flooding sessions with dream material, being consistently late or bringing an 'agenda' each time. The therapist needs to be sensitive to the timing of when it is safe to dismantle defences. This is most likely to be when the patient has sufficient ego strength to do so. To sum up, it may be said that the couch is appropriate to a more psychoanalytic approach.

The chair, on the other hand, is suited to the classical Jungian strategy which is based on a dialogue between therapist and patient.

Transference and counter-transference, as defined by psychoanalysis, are central to a developmental therapist's approach. In Freud's words, transferences are:

> new editions or facsimiles of the impulses and phantasies which are aroused and made conscious during the progress of the analysis; but they have this peculiarity, which is characteristic for their species, that they replace some earlier person by the person of the physician. (Freud, 1912).

Counter-transference applies to the therapist's unconscious reactions to the patient, particularly to the latter's transferences. Jung was alert to the utility of these reactions, referring to counter-transference as 'an important organ of information' in 1929 (Jung, 1954). Freud tended to depreciate counter-transference as residual neurosis on the part of the therapist but Jung's greater flexibility enabled Fordham to develop a detailed theory of there being two kinds of counter-transference. The first he calls 'syntonic', which is when an analyst may be so in tune with a patient's inner world that he finds himself feeling or behaving in a way that he comes to realize, on reflection, shows that there are aspects of his patient's inner workings projected into him (Fordham, 1957). This process puts at the disposal of the patient parts of the therapist that are spontaneously responding to the former in a way that is needed.

The other sort of counter-transference Fordham hit upon when he made a recording of a session of analysis he conducted with a boy of 11 who had problems with aggressive feelings. Later, on listening to the recording of this session, Fordham discovered that his own aggression had been in evidence, in that a reactivation of a past situation from his own childhood had replaced his relation to the patient. During that time, no analysis of the patient was possible. This phenomenon Fordham termed 'illusory' counter-transference.

A therapist working with these concepts of personal transference and counter-transference in mind would use interpretation both in and of the transference as a central strategy. All this is directed towards reparation of the patient's damaged inner object world and to an improved interaction with the environment. Working with the above kind of transference and counter-transference represented a major change of strategy to Jung's original one, the end-goal of which is individuation.

The change process in therapy

The change process in Jungian therapy has already been signalled (p. 86, above). Pathological symptoms are usually what bring an individual into therapy and may be seen as the opener of the way into a deeper awareness on the part of that individual. This chapter has already stated that if there are physical symptoms they need to be diagnosed by a medical practitioner in order to ascertain that medical treatment is not necessary alongside analysis. If the symptoms appear to be largely neurotic, i.e. originating in the psyche, then they can be treated analytically. In fact, symptoms may well persist as the therapy progresses.

The work of therapy, in this regard, is to identify what lies behind the symptom. For instance, repressed emotional disturbances will often manifest somatically if they are not attended to. Above all, therapy is an inner journey and the goal of this quest is the individual's true identity, which may have been hidden for a whole lifetime under a 'false self'. It is, in fact, in the patient's symptom or wound that his or her true identity lies hidden and here we see again the analogy with alchemy of the base metal being transformed into gold. Jung's depiction of an analyst as a 'wounded healer' stems from this 'telelogical' view of pathology.

Alchemy grew more important in Jung's work and he saw what he thought of as the archetypal transference reflected in the alchemical text, *Rosarium Philosophorum* (Jung, 1954). For his own purposes he used 10 of the woodcut prints that make up the *Rosarium*. These illustrate the story of an incestuous couple, sometimes depicted as king and queen, sometimes as brother and sister, and at others as sun and moon. The human figures are fully clothed in some of the pictures and naked in others. Jung thought that these 10 pictures contained the overall structure of an in-depth analysis culminating in individuation.

These pictures are for Jung a representation of the criss-crossing of both the conscious and unconscious relationship of analyst and patient. This is multi-faceted, i.e. on the personal as well as collective unconscious level, and involves the anima/animus of both individuals. As the analysis deepens beyond the persona and conventional level the couple are shown without clothes in the third picture called 'The naked truth' (Jung, 1954: Figure 3). Figure 4 shows the two still trying to hide their 'shadow' from each other: when it comes into the analysis it can lead to the termination of the work (Jung, 1954:).

If the analysis survives this stage a conjunction takes place between the two protagonists, who are then joined together in working towards greater consciousness. This is depicted in 'The conjunction' (Jung, 1954: Figure 5), which shows the couple having intercourse. However, as the whole of the analytic process is an 'as if' rather than a concrete endeavour, this is a symbolic conjunction and physical gratification between the two has to be forgone. This sacrifice leads to death-like feelings, which are depicted in the next picture. The two have to endure the difficulties that ensue from this stage of the analysis and the analyst needs to withstand the temptation to 'explain' what is happening and to give reassurances to the analysand.

If the analytic container can withstand all the difficult feelings up to this point, there will come a time when the analysand begins to be aware of experiencing the beginnings of 'new life'. This is the coming into being of the capacity for symbolization and is depicted in 'The new birth' (Jung, 1954: Figure 10) as an androgynous figure symbolizing the union of opposites. Eros is central to this kind of Jungian analysis, not just that which is sexually charged but also that which is to do with soul. In both meanings of the word, psyche needs eros.

The *Rosarium*, according to Jung, depicts the structure of a classical Jungian analysis, during the course of which dream analysis takes place through 'amplification' of dream images, which connects them to mythological and cultural motifs. 'Active imagination' may also be part of the work. Jung described this as dreaming with open eyes (Jung, 1921).

The developmental approach would look at change as reparation, through work in the transference, of damaged inner objects and an increased capacity for more real interaction with the environment. Compulsive behaviour will be modified, symptoms will be recognized as having inner meaning, and the capacity for tolerating anxiety and guilt will increase.

The lack of change is usually due to fear of relinquishing old patterns of behaviour even though they cause suffering. In this way, a patient may cling to a pathological way of functioning because it maintains fantasies of omnipotence, which are dependent on the pathology being experienced as the only thing the patient has in life. In some instances, the internalized parental voice is so strong that the person cannot go against it as doing so incurs unbearable feelings of guilt about getting better.

Ambivalence is common: patients often present with a compliant conscious wish to change and an unconscious defence against doing so. A male patient brought a dream early on in the analysis which showed him coming to the defence of a weak man who was losing a fencing match against an unknown but stronger opponent. We looked at this as his strong ego defending the vulnerable parts of himself that felt under attack from me in the sessions.

Limitations of the approach

Jung was an empiricist and his metapsychology evolved out of his phenomenological observations but he never aspired to be a scientific empiricist like Freud, who systemitized his observations into a quasi-scientific body of knowledge. There are Jungian hypotheses which could lend themselves to even more rigorous epidemiological research than has so far been done, e.g. the word association test and psychological types. There is much in the writings which is prospective and has potential for further elaboration.

There is also much that is faulty, as scholars are increasingly discovering. A recent example is Richard Noll's debunking of the Solar Phallus Man alluded to above (p. 78). In the book, Noll asserts that popular literature detailing myths about sun cults from antiquity was easily available at the time. This undermines Jung's claim that the patient's vision gave credence to his discovery of the 'collective unconscious' (Noll, 1994).

Deficiencies in Jungian clinical theory and practice were corrected by Michael Fordham's work in synthesizing analytical psychology and psychoanalysis. Apart from work in transference and counter-transference, Jungians have benefited from incorporating into their ethos insights on ego defences and resistance and from using the couch, where patients may be enabled to get in touch with persecutory anxiety and envy.

In recent years there has been an increase in the serious charges levelled at Jung and, by extension, at analytical psychology. Post-Jungians are becoming more rigorous in their efforts to face honesty Jung's failings in regard to his attitudes of racism, anti-Semitism and sexism. Andrew Samuels' work in this area has demonstrated that all of these charges have some foundation in fact and need to be taken seriously (Samuels, 1993).

The most damaging charge against Jung is that of anti-Semitism, and Samuels has explored this in his usual thoughtful way. He says that the short answer to it has to be 'yes' and cites the following quotations from Jung's 1934 paper, 'The state of psychotherapy today': 'The "Aryan" unconscious has a higher potential than the Jewish.' 'The Jew, who is something of a nomad, has never yet created a cultural form of his own and as far as we can see never will, since all his instincts and talents require a more or less civilized nation to act as host for their development', and 'the Jews have this peculiarity with women; being physically weaker, they have to aim at the chinks in the armour of their adversary' (Samuels, 1993: 292–3).

There are many instances of these sentiments on Jung's part, although Geoffrey Cocks offers in his defence that 'Jung conceded more to the Nazis by his words than his actions' (Cocks, 1985: 134).

The above quotations from Jung have much in common with the ideas of Otto Weininger, expressed in his book *Sex and Charter* (1903). Women are equated with Jews in being seen as inferior to the Aryan male: they share in common, amongst other qualities, inherent amorality, irreligion and hysteria. 'The organic untruthfulness of woman' cited in the book is very close to Freud's view on the subject of the female sex.

The concepts of 'self' (supraordinate personality) and 'numinosity' have tremendous potential for healing but, conversely, can be extremely hazardous when they lead to inflation of the ego. This arises when an individual becomes identified with the archetype of the Redeemer and loses touch with his or her common humanity. The danger then is that instead of using these concepts as a psychological tool, analytical psychology can be turned into a religious cult with all that that means in the impulse to convert, proselytize and to become a closed system.

Case example

The client

Frank is 41, unmarried and a research scientist. Although I have his full permission to use this material, for reasons of confidentiality I cannot disclose any more about his profession. He was referred to me from the psychiatric unit to which I was attached some years ago and has since been in twice-weekly therapy for four years. His presenting symptom was dependency on diazepam, of which he felt he needed increasingly large doses to enable him to relax. This had first been prescribed for tension when he was a teenager. His enormous unreleased rage makes it difficult for him to enter fully into life in any way. For instance, he cannot relax enough to urinate except in his own lavatory, which means that he can never drink anything at work or in a social setting because he becomes 'uncomfortable'. This, in turn, has led to increasing isolation and to his turning to marijuana for company.

Frank is the second of two sons of a colonial civil servant. The first eight years of his life were spend outside England. When he was coming up to eight years old, his brother, Lewis, who was four years older, died in a tragic accident. Lewis was the 'golden boy', attractive, outgoing and clever, in contrast to Frank, who is small, only averagely bright and very introverted. Lewis had been put down to go to one of the top public schools in England at 13 and his death put tremendous pressure on Frank to be a high achiever. Shortly after this tragedy, the family were posted back to England and Frank went to preparatory boarding-school and then to a second-rank public school until he was 18, both of which he hated.

The therapy

In the first session, we established the contract between us to do with fees, frequency of sessions and whether he would sit in a chair or use the couch. I quickly became aware of his huge resistance when we explored the possibility of him being on the couch and he was adamant that he would not even contemplate it. I began to feel that I was being controlling in trying to make him do something he clearly found completely unacceptable. I realized that this was my counter-transference and reflected back to him that he must have experienced boarding-school as very authoritarian. He became animated while he told me just how awful it had indeed been and that his only recourse was to be mulishly resistant on every occasion.

As the session progressed, I felt less than hopeful about how much creative work would be possible with him. He then asked me if he 'should' bring dreams. I asked if he ever remembered any and he said that he had always had vivid dreams. He proceeded to tell me one he had had the night before. 'I am working in the hospital laboratory and take a tray out of the fridge. When I look into it closely, I see a frozen little man but I cannot dislodge him. I put the tray back in the fridge.'

I did not interpret the dream but saw it as a sign from his unconscious that a true self is there, although in a frozen state, which he can only begin to look at in the laboratory or analytical container. This frozen figure seemed to me to represent the potential to develop as himself that had been traumatized by the death of Lewis, since when he had felt forced to develop in accordance with the wishes of others. The potential signalled by this dream made me decide to take him on as a patient.

In the course of therapy, he told me about his parents' marriage, which had lasted for 48 years. It had been unhappy, particularly after Lewis's death, and his mother had never recovered. She was the one with the money and had left Frank a considerable sum when she died two years before he started therapy. His father died a year after Frank started therapy.

Mother was sociable and outgoing and was frustrated by Father, who was an irascible introvert. As a consequence, they did little socializing and Mother increasingly took refuge in her relationship with Frank. Theirs was an idyllic relationship and resulted in his developing an idealized mother complex. He and Father, on the other hand, were distant with, even hostile to each other. In the course of therapy, Frank began to realize that he had internalized his parents' marriage and that their outer conflict was reflected in his inner world. This manifested in a longing for social contact and relating on the one hand, inhibited, on the other, by an incapacity to make small talk and relax in company. This forced him into isolation even while he was still at school.

Psychologically and emotionally he is immature and personifies what Jung calls the *Puer aeternus*, the archetypal eternal youth. The extreme opposite to this is the archetype of the *Senex*, the positive or negative old man, and this manifests in Frank's unconscious identification with his curmudgeonly father. Frank is tight-fisted with money and cynical about everyone and everything he encounters but can also be extremely naive and is sometimes taken advantage of by a more cunning acquaintance. This is especially true of women, of whom he has an unconscious expectation that they are going to dote on him as Mother did. When I am the empathic mothering therapist, he feels completely accepting of me but when he experiences me as the penetrating critical father, as, for instance, when I make an interpretation he does not like, he immediately becomes defensive and mulish.

His contributions in sessions are mostly about concrete 'out there' matters to do with his work or with what he is reading – his only real relationships being with books. Occasionally he brings a dream, relating it in an uninterested manner towards the end of a session. This is the only concession he makes to being a patient and from time to time he admits that he does not know why he is in therapy or whether it is helping him in any way. Two years ago, he brought the following dream:

'I am testing the serum of a patient for antibodies. There are hardly any and the prognosis is negative. I then test a sample of my own serum. It is extremely healthy and full of antibodies. For some reason I am dissatisfied with this.'

For the first time I felt that he was actually affected by a dream but initially we were both puzzled by it. As we explored it further in the session, I began to realize that it was showing his complete identification with the healthy part of himself, while at the same time his complete isolation from his own inner patient. When we looked at the dream this way, he displayed a genuine interest in it and agreed that it could be seen like that. For my part, this dream showed the beginnings of the Wounded Healer archetype being constellated in Frank.

Up to the time of this dream, he had managed to project everything that he felt was weak and frail and therefore unacceptable in him into his mother, his junior colleagues and, at times, into me in the transference. This dream showed that his 'shadow', i.e. all those parts of himself that he repressed and lived only through projection, was now becoming a little more acceptable as part of himself.

After this dream, the pressure of speech eased slightly and he began to feel less resistant in sessions. He has slowly come off the diazepam, although he is still using marijuana, and the beginning of some capacity for symbolizing has begun to manifest, along with a feel for his own inner reality. He sometimes even offers an insight into himself that he has come to realize on his own.

A recent dream showed him standing up to his knees in a bucket of water. He is looking down into it from a great height and sees small sharks and whales swimming about around the lower half of his legs. Suddenly, he is pulled further down into the water and wakes with a fright.

The dream shows that he has now been pulled deeper into the unconscious where he is confronted by both negative (sharks), as well as, positive (whales) aspects of Mother and of the anima. His idealization of Mother, which concealed her more devouring aspects *vis-à-vis* his sexuality, is beginning to transform in the transference into a more rounded picture of her as both the predatory as well as the nurturing mother.

Frank has only rarely been able to masturbate, which has its origins in feelings of guilt at boarding-school on the rare occasion when he did so. He remembers one night needing desperately to relieve his pent-up sexual tension by masturbating. He was so guilty about doing this with a picture of Mother overlooking his bed that he stuck drawing pins in her eyes to prevent her from seeing him and thus judging him harshly. We connected this with him sticking drawing pins in my eyes figuratively in the course of the therapy by keeping his sexual fantasies out of my sight for the same reason. Since this dream and the flood of material that it helped to release, he increasingly feels he can risk telling me about masturbating. His internalized mother and his religious beliefs – he is a practising Christian – have inhibited him from having any contact with his penis, which has taken on a dark numinous aspect for him. He is now beginning to relate to it increasingly as part of his body and can urinate in other people's lavatories, as well as his own, and recently managed to go on holiday to the Far East. However, he has never asked to use the lavatory in my consulting rooms and I feel it will be a real turning point in his development when he can do.

His *puer* defence against the internalized devouring saturnian father is also beginning to be modified in the transference. As a result, his creativity is starting to be released and some time ago he started to go to art therapy once a month. This is helping him to emerge from his extreme isolation and to express himself non-verbally. There is the beginning of some social life, although he is, as yet, a long way from forming any sort of intimate of sexual relationship, something for which he constantly yearns in his fantasies. I have discovered, in the course of my work as a therapist, that this is the usual consequence of unreleased libido which lives in a compensatory way as a highly active fantasy sex life. The equivalent is to be found in the fantasies of anorectic patients, which are obsessively focused on food.

The work with Frank proceeds slowly due to his huge resistance to change, and I feel that I could have been more assertive in the first session about him using the couch. In my experience, patients are often able to be less resistant when they are on the couch and can get to vulnerable feelings more easily. In retrospect, I have become aware of how his powerful scientist persona had controlled me, both in the first session and at times since then. Closely allied to this, my counter-transference feelings of being bullied by his saturnian father have given me an invaluable insight into his fear of authority, which is experienced only as negative. His rage against this negative authority, combined with the need to protect his own more vulnerable self, resulted in the need to be always in control. This had come to dominate his entire life even being directed at his bodily functions. The end result was a complete lack of spontaneity and of being trapped in persecutory anxiety feelings, which he needed ever increasing amounts of diazepam and marijuana to alleviate. As his rage slowly humanizes into anger which can increasingly be expressed against me, the need for suppressants is also gradually lifting.

The beginnings of creative play are happening for him both in the therapy and in his art group and it is in this playful space that he is making contact for the first time with his capacity for symbolization, which is the source of potential new life for Frank.

Epilogue

I would like to end this chapter by returning to Jung and to the intellectual historian, Henri Ellenberger's account of what he calls Jung's 'creative illness' during the period 1913–19 (Ellenberger, 1970). This followed the break with Freud (who had also undergone the experience of a 'creative illness') in 1913 when Jung felt deserted by all his friends and went through an emotional illness akin to a psychotic episode. He continued his work with patients and his relations with his family but spent a great deal of time alone brooding by Lake Zurich and relating to unconscious processes through 'active imagination'. This method of dreaming while still awake involves starting from an image, word or picture and allowing fantasies associated with it to evolve. This can create a new situation which allows unconscious contents to surface (Jung, 1955–56).

Ellenberger goes on to say that a 'creative illness' remits suddenly and is followed by a short period of euphoria and increased activity. The end result is a permanent change in personality evinced by feelings of being freed from the burden of social conventions and a move towards valuing one's own subjective feelings and ideas. This helps to throw light on the ideological battles that have taken place in the analytical world since the beginning of this century and that continue to take place up to the present time.

References

CW refers to *The Collected Works of C.G. Jung*. London: Routledge & Kegan Paul.

Adler, G. (1961) *The Living Symbol*. New York: Pantheon Books.
Adler, G. (1979) *Dynamics of the Self*. London: Conventure.
Clark, G. (1987) 'Animation through the analytical relationship: the embodiment of self in the transference and countertransference', *Harvest*, 13: 104–14.
Cocks, G. (1985) *Psychotherapy in the Third Reich: The Goering Institute*. London and New York: Oxford University Press.
Ellenberger, H.F. (1970) *The Discovery of the Unconscious*. New York: Basic Books.
Fordham, M. (1957) *New Developments in Analytical Psychology*. London: Routledge & Kegan Paul.
Fordham, M. (1993) *The Making of an Analyst*. London: Free Association Books.
Fordham, M. (1976) *The Self and Autism*. London: Heinemann.
Freud, S. (1955–74) *Standard Edition of the Complete Psychological Works of Sigmund Freud*, Vol. VII ed. and trans. J. Strachey. London: Hogarth Press.
Goffman, E. (1961) *Asylums*. New York: Anchor Books.
Gordon, R. (1979) 'Reflections on curing and healing', *Journal of Analytical Psychology*, 24(3).

Jarrett, J. (ed.) (1988) 'Nietzsches Zarathustra: notes of the seminar given in 1934–39 by C.G. Jung', *Bolingen Series XCIX*. Princeton, NJ: Princeton University Press.

Jung, C.G. (1911–12) *Symbols of Transformation*, in *CW*, Vol. V.

Jung, C.G. (1921) *Psychological Types*, in *CW*, Vol. VI.

Jung, C.G. (1951) *Aion*, in *CW*, Vol. IX(2).

Jung, C.G. (1953) *Two Essays on Analytical Psychology*, in *CW*, Vol. VII.

Jung, C.G. (1954) *The Practice of Psychotherapy*, in *CW*, Vol. XVI.

Jung, C.G. (1955–56) *Mysterium Coniunctionis*, in *CW*, Vol. XIV.

Jung, C.G. (1960) *The Psychogenesis of Mental Disease*, in *CW*, Vol. III.

Jung, C.G. (1961) *Freud and Psychoanalysis*, in *CW*, Vol. IV.

Jung, C.G. (1963) *Memories, Dreams, Reflections*. London: Collins/Routledge & Kegan Paul.

Jung, C.G. (1967) *Alchemical Studies*, in *CW*, Vol. XIII.

Jung, C.G. (1977) *The Symbolic Life*, in *CW*, Vol. XVIII.

Jung, C.G. (1988) *Nietzche's Zarathustra*, ed. James L. Jarrett. Princeton, NJ: Princeton University Press.

Lambert, K. (1981) *Analysis, Repair and Individuation*. London: Academic Press.

Myers, I. (1962) *The Myers-Briggs Type Indicator*. Palo Alto: Consulting Psychologists Press.

Noll, R. (1994) *The Jung Cult*. Princeton, NJ: Princeton University Press.

Samuels, A. (1985) *Jung and the Post-Jungians*. London: Routledge & Kegan Paul.

Samuels, A. (1989a) *The Plural Psyche: Personality, Morality and the Father*. London: Routledge.

Samuels, A. (1989b) *Psychopathology*. London: H. Karnac (Books).

Samuels, A. (1993) *The Political Psyche*. London: Routledge.

Stern, D. (1985) *The Internal World of the Infant*. New York: Basic Books.

Turner, V. (1969) *The Ritual Process: Structure and Anti-Structure*. London: Routledge & Kegan Paul.

Van Gennep, A. (1960) *Rites of Passage*. London: Routledge & Kegan Paul.

Winnicott, D.W. (1964) 'Book review: *Memories, Dreams, Reflections*, by C.G. Jung', *International Journal of Psychoanalysis*, 45.

Zoja, L. (1985) *Drugs, Addiction and Initiation: The Modern Search for Ritual*. London: Sigo Press.

Suggested further reading

Clarke, J.J. (1992) *In Search of Jung*. London: Routledge.

Fordham, M. (1978) *Jungian Psychotherapy*. London: H. Karnac.

Humbert, E. (1988) *C.G. Jung*. Wilmette, IL: Chiron.

Kerr, J. (1994) *A Most Dangerous Method*. London: Sinclair-Stevenson.

Zoja, L. (1995) *Growth & Guilt: Psychology and the Limits of Development*. London: Routledge.

5

Adlerian Therapy
Jenny Clifford

Historical context and development in Britain

Historical context

Alfred Adler (1870–1937) was a doctor in Vienna who became interested in functional disorders (*neuroses*) in which physically healthy patients complained of and genuinely suffered from physical symptoms which disrupted their lives. In 1911, he founded a new society which later became the Society for Individual Psychology. From 1902 to 1911 Adler attended the Wednesday evening meetings of the Viennese Psychoanalytical Society at Freud's invitation. Adler was the most active member of this group and Freud held him in high esteem. Adler's book *Study of Organ Inferiority and its Psychical Compensation: A Contribution to Clinical Medicine* (1917), first published in 1907, was well received by Freud and considered by him to complement psychoanalytical theory. In this book Adler described the relative weakness of an organ or a system in the body and the reaction of compensation either by the weak organ, another organ or the nervous system. In 1910 Adler became President and Stekel Vice-President of the Vienna Psychoanalytical Society; both men were joint editors, under Freud, of their new journal, *Centralblatt*. By 1911, however, it became obvious that Adler's views differed greatly from Freud's; Adler and Stekel resigned their positions and with a few others left to form a new society.

In 1912 Adler published *The Neurotic Constitution*, outlining his theory of neurosis, and laying down many of the basic tenets of Individual Psychology. Adler was now specializing in treating psychiatric patients, neurotic rather than psychotic. In 1914 the *Journal for Individual Psychology* was founded and Adler's ideas spread to Europe and the USA.

Adler was mobilized into the Austrian-Hungarian Army in 1916 and worked as an army physician in a military hospital in Cracow. On returning from the war to a destitute Vienna, Adler directed his energies towards educating people about Individual Psychology. His concept of *Gemeinschaftsgefühl* or 'social interest' fitted well into the new atmosphere of rebuilding a nation. (There is no direct translation in English of *Gemeinschaftsgefühl* and Adler was said to prefer the term social interest.) As well as a welfare programme and a housing and health programme, educational reforms were taking place in Vienna. Adler held open sessions with teachers and their problem children so that as many people as possible could learn about his ideas to enable children to grow up mentally healthy. He also lectured to teachers and at the teachers' request he was appointed professor at the Pedagogical Institute of Vienna in 1924.

In 1923 Adler lectured in England for the first time, at the International Congress of Psychology in Oxford, although he spoke very little English. In 1926 he was invited back to England by a few interested medical and psychological societies and by 1927 an Individual Psychology Club was founded in Gower Street, London; this club later became political and Adler dissociated himself from it. In 1927 Adler's book *Understanding Human Nature* was published. Based on a year's lectures given at the People's Institute in Vienna, it gives a complete description of Individual Psychology and its aim is to enable people to understand themselves and one another better. From 1926 to 1934 Adler spent the academic term in the USA and June to September in Vienna with his family. He went on lecture tours all over the USA; he was appointed lecturer at Columbia University from 1929 to 1931 and in 1932 a chair of medical psychology was established for him at Long Island Medical College. In 1933 he published *Social Interest: A Challenge to Mankind*, which described the concept of *Gemeinschaftsgefühl* (social interest) and placed it at the centre of his psychological theory. By 1934 Adler had settled permanently in the USA, where he was eventually joined by his family. A year later he founded the *International Journal of Individual Psychology* in Chicago. The theory of Individual Psychology and its application in medicine and education was now spreading throughout Europe and the USA. In 1937 Adler had planned a lecture tour in Holland and England and Scotland. In Holland, he gave over 40 lectures in three weeks, but suffered severe angina before he left for Britain. He and his daughter, Dr Alexandra Adler, herself a psychiatrist, had public and private lectures as well as university vacation courses booked at Aberdeen, York, Hull, Manchester, London, Edinburgh, Liverpool and Exeter. Sadly Adler died of a heart attack on the fourth day in Aberdeen while taking an early morning walk; he was 67 years old. Alexandra Adler arrived in Britain and fulfilled most of her father's and her own lecture commitments. She and her brother Kurt, also a psychiatrist, formed an Adlerian group in New York, which is still functioning today.

During the 1920s Rudolph Dreikurs, a young doctor, had worked with Adler's followers in their child guidance clinics in Vienna. In 1937 he went to the USA and soon established an open centre for family counselling in Chicago. From 1942 to 1948 he was professor of psychiatry at the Chicago Medical School where he exposed medical students to Adler's theories of personality, behaviour and psychopathology. By 1950, he was teaching a postgraduate course in child guidance at Northwestern University. Manford Sonstegard, who attended this course, afterwards went on to develop child guidance centres and parent education in Iowa and West Virginia and on his retirement as professor in counselling he went to Britain.

Development in Britain

A new Adlerian Society had been formed in London just before Adler's death, with Adler as its president. This stopped meeting during the Second World War but afterwards was reconstituted with Dr Alexandra Adler as its president. It was and still is called the Adlerian Society of Great Britain, and was affiliated to the Individual Psychological Medical Society which had been founded in the 1930s.

Dr Joshua Bierer who was personally trained by Adler emigrated to Britain and founded the first self-governed social therapeutic group for acute and chronic

inpatients at Runwell Hospital, Wickford, Essex. He also set up a social psychotherapy centre – now a day hospital – and clubs for outpatients and discharged
patients. Group therapy and community psychiatry are legitimate offspring of
Alfred Adler's thought and work, according to Ellenberger (1970).

In 1958, Rudolph Dreikurs visited England and Scotland and lectured at
Edinburgh, Aberdeen, Liverpool and London Universities at Dr Joshua Bierer's
invitation. Dreikurs found that Adlerian psychologists in England were engaged in
private practice but were not training parents, teachers, other psychologists or
psychiatrists. Adler, during the last 20 years of his life, had emphasized the need to
educate teachers, who have influence over large numbers of children so that the
ideas of Individual Psychology could benefit future generations and prevent mental
illness. Dreikurs too concentrated his efforts on teaching parents and teachers so
that children could be enabled to grow up mentally healthy and psychologically
able to participate in a democratic society. In 1976 Sonstegard came to England
and trained a group of health professionals in Buckinghamshire. These people
joined the Adlerian Society of Great Britain, some of whose members had worked
with Adler in Vienna. Sonstegard visited England annually and started to train
people to do family counselling, lifestyle assessment, group counselling, self-
awareness and psychotherapy. He was particularly interested in training lay
counsellors and encouraging parents to form study groups and family education
centres.

There are no formal Adlerian psychotherapy training courses in Britain
recognized by the Institute for Individual Psychology, which is the training
division of the Adlerian Society of Great Britain. In Europe Adlerian therapists
undergo many years of training. British Adlerian therapists have travelled to
America, Israel and Europe to continue their training as well as attending the
International Committee for Adlerian Summer Schools and Institutes (ICASSI)
which takes place annually in different countries.

Theoretical assumptions

Image of the person

The *holistic socio-teleological* approach of Adlerian therapy based on Adler's
Individual Psychology, maintains that people should be viewed in their social
contexts in order that their goals can be identified. People choose their own goals
based on their subjective perceptions of themselves and their world, their bodies,
minds and feelings in harmony with their consistent movement towards these
goals. Adlerians consider that people are creative, responsible, self-determined and
unique. The holistic socio-teleological approach can be defined as having three
parts.

Holistic   The term, 'individual', of Individual Psychology was used by Adler to
describe the indivisibility of a person: as such it is a holistic approach to psychotherapy. Adler wanted to stress the self-consistent unity of a person as opposed to
other theories which described conflicting divisions of the personality.

Social Human beings are socially embedded and their actions can be understood only when observed within a group.

Teleological All behaviour has a purpose and consequently it is possible to identify people's short- and long-term goals, which are of a social nature and reveal the total personality. Individual Psychology emphasizes that people are unaware of their goals and the private logic which underpins their movement towards the goals.

People can always choose how to respond to their inherited qualities and to the environment in which they grow up. People's basic concept of themselves and of life provides a guiding line, a fixed pattern; this is called the lifestyle. The ideas and beliefs according to which a person operates are called *private logic*. They are not common sense but *biased apperception*. Common sense is shared and understood by all people; private logic is owned and understood by one individual and characterizes his or her own biased perceptions of his or her experiences. A person's private logic is created in childhood and contains generalizations and oversimplifications. Individuals create their own unique lifestyle and are therefore responsible for their own personality and behaviour; they are creative actors rather than passive reactors.

People will have developed their own characteristic lifestyle by the time they are five years old, based on their own creative and unique perceptions of their situation in their family. Parents and their values and the atmosphere they create in the family will set the scene for each child to begin to make some assumptions about themselves, their world and their chosen direction of movement. Siblings and their choices of direction will have a major effect on the individual child.

The Adlerian view is that everyone is born with a desire to belong – to the family, to larger groups, to society and to the whole human race. Everyone is born in an inferior position and strives to overcome this position. If this striving for superiority takes place in the context of social interest, the whole group, all society and the future human race benefit. The feeling of belonging (or *Gemeinschafts-gefühl*) is an innate potentiality in every human being. If this potentiality develops in a person he or she feels an equal member of the human race, with a useful part to play, willing to contribute and co-operate; this potentiality can become severely limited or be non-existent when individuals feel inferior to their fellows, unsure of their place and unable to make a useful contribution.

The meaning we attribute to life will determine our behaviour so that we will behave as if our perceptions were true. Life will turn out as we expected and people will respond as we expected; this is a self-fulfilling prophecy.

Conceptualization of psychological disturbance and health

Mental health can be measured by the amount of *social interest* a person has. Mentally healthy people are assured of their place and contribute to the tasks of the groups to which they belong; they co-operate with their fellow human beings and are part of a community. The human race, when looked at from an evolutionary point of view, is always moving towards an improved position from a minus to a plus. The word *courage* is used by Adlerians to describe activity plus social interest, and a person who is said to be acting with social interest is *encouraged*. The encouraged individual has a positive attitude towards him or herself and has self-confidence and self-respect. The goal of mentally healthy people is to belong as *social equals* in the family, in larger groups and in the whole of humanity, making their unique and useful contribution to these groups. Social equality was a concept that Rudolph Dreikurs developed and wrote about: '[Social equality] implies that each individual is entitled to respect and dignity, to full and equal status, regardless of any personal quality or deficiency' (Dreikurs, 1967: 39).

A person who has social interest will feel equal to other people and will treat others as social equals. The mentally healthy person is moving on a *horizontal plane* towards others and is *task orientated*. Their behaviour is useful and is determined solely by the demands of the situation and by *common sense*. Their feeling of belonging enables them to identify with all human beings and to empathize with them.

Adler considered there were three major *life tasks* required of each member of the human race – work (or occupation), friendship and love. Dreikurs added two more – getting on with oneself and relationship to the cosmos. In Adler's time the way that people could fulfil the life tasks was seen as getting a job, having a social life and friendships, getting married and having children. Successful completion of these life tasks was seen as essential to the healthy perpetuation of the human race. More recently Adlerians have given a broader definition of the three life tasks to take account of unemployment and homosexual relationships. Of the three life tasks the intimate relationships with one partner are considered to be the most testing of a person's social interest and willingness to co-operate.

Psychological disturbance occurs when an individual *feels inferior* and unworthy of an equal place amongst his or her fellows. Social interest, which is an innate potentiality in every human being, does not grow in the presence of strong feelings of inferiority. The inferiority feelings are substituted by a *compensatory striving for personal superiority*. People who feel inferior and act superior cannot adequately fulfil the life tasks of occupation, friendship, and marriage because they are concerned with preserving their own prestige rather than responding to the needs of the situation and making their contribution to these tasks. Their movement is on a vertical plane away from the group, withdrawing from some or all of the life tasks. An unrealistic, unattainable goal of personal superiority is set by the individual and in the *neurotic individual* alibis then have to be found to explain why the goal is never reached. Neurotic symptoms or behaviours serve as such excuses and the mistaken ideas and attitudes that justify the useless behaviour are called *private logic*. An example of private logic might be 'I am the best at everything I do – unfortunately, I get bad headaches when I am under stress so I am never able to perform at my best.' The goal of being best at everything is unrealistic and unattainable, and the headaches are a neurotic symptom which safeguards the individual from having to admit that he is not as superior as he thinks he is. He likes to think he is superior because he feels inferior; the reality of the situation is that he is socially equal to all human beings. If his feelings of equality and social interest could be developed, he could divert his attention from his own self-esteem, personal security and prestige and concentrate on making his contribution to the tasks of living. His private logic could then be replaced by common sense – Adler's 'ironclad logic of social living' (Terner and Pew, 1978).

Psychotic individuals in the presence of certain predisposing conditions escape totally from the logic of social living and assume a reality of delusions and hallucinations that conforms to their own private logic. *Psychopaths* openly reject common sense and, like neurotics and psychotics, are motivated only by self-interest but, unlike the other two, have no conscience; they do not need the neurotic's excuses and symptoms nor the psychotic's distorted reality.

Acquisition and perpetuation of psychological disturbance

All human problems are essentially social in nature. (Dreikurs, 1967: 104).

We do not develop neurotic symptoms or behaviour as long as we feel we can function adequately. Neurosis will develop as soon as we feel unable to fulfil our obligations in one of the life tasks – at work, in friendships, in an intimate relationship. The symptoms and behaviour will be the excuse for not fulfilling the tasks adequately, not engaging in them at all, or retreating from them. Rather than facing failure and being found to be inadequate the symptom enables the discouraged individual to hesitate or evade and yet not lose face. Neurotics may not appear to have any difficulties until they meet a crisis for which they feel unprepared. For example a crisis for one individual might be having to find a job when she feels incapable of fulfilling the demands of employment. Facing the demanding task of marriage might become a crisis situation for another individual, so forcing her to break off an engagement. Rather than developing a symptom, an individual may choose safeguarding behaviour such as being totally absorbed in one life task, so leaving no time or energy to engage in the other two life tasks in which they feel inadequate.

Individuals feel unable to find their place due to varying degrees of inferiority feelings. As children they learned to feel inferior. Their parents may have spoiled them and given in to their demands, in which case they would have developed the mistaken idea that they were very special people who should be served by others. They may have learned to use displays of emotion to get this service – temper tantrums, tears or sulks. Adler uses spoiling and pampering synonymously in his writings. Sonstegard makes a distinction between the two: spoiling is giving in to a child's demands whereas pampering is doing for the child those things that the child can do for himself. Pampering is regarded by Sonstegard as the most disabling form of parenting. Pampered children feel unable to accomplish many tasks and constantly seek help from others. They lack self-confidence when they grow into adulthood, because they have such limited experience of learning and doing for themselves. Their parents' over-protection stunts their growth, so they doubt their ability to be independent or to make choices or to take risks and face hardships. Spoilt children in adult life will still be expecting others to serve them and let them have their own way. Pampered and spoilt people feel that the world is their enemy because it does not respond in the same way as did their parents. Adler pointed out that children play an active part in enlisting help in the case of pampering, or in demanding service in the case of spoiling. Criticized children grow up afraid of taking risks and making mistakes. Neglect is far less common than papering and spoiling but was acknowledged by Adler to produce discouraged children. Dreikurs was convinced that the parenting methods and education of our competitive society did not encourage mental health. Mistake-centred education and 'you could do better' parenting discourage children.

People's perception of their position in their family constellation forms the basis of their lifestyle. The parents set family values and create a family atmosphere and the children decide their place in the family. A competitive family will produce discouragement, the children competing against each other and eventually channelling themselves into separate spheres of success. They each choose something they can be best at, even if that is being naughty. As each child strives for superiority this necessitates putting the other siblings down. An eldest child is an only child for a while, possibly the centre of attention until the second child arrives and dethrones the first child. The first child has several options, one of which is to strive to retain her superiority. The second child may want to catch up with the first child and may succeed, in which case the first child will feel discouraged. The second child may give up because the first child is too capable and too far ahead. The youngest child may remain a baby for a long time, the other children acting as pampering parents; they have a vested interest in keeping the youngest a baby, as it enhances their superiority. However, some youngest children can become the most accomplished members of their families; they are never dethroned and strive to overcome all the other children. Individual children make their choice and choose their goals supported by mistaken ideas or private logic, interpreting their position in the family constellation. Neither the child nor the adult is aware of these goals or their private logic.

Even though people may not be co-operating and may not be fulfilling all of the life tasks, as long as their lifestyle is in harmony with their environment, there will be no disturbing behaviour or distressing symptoms. An adult, spoilt as a child, may find partners, relatives, children, friends who are willing to give in to her demands. An adult, pampered as a child, may find sufficient rescuers, helpers and advisers to take over responsibility for his life. If these individuals should lose their slaves or supports a crisis would ensue and disturbing behaviour might emerge in order to attract more applicants for the vacant posts. People may consciously regret their symptoms and seek treatment for them. They may convince themselves and others of their good intentions to get rid of their symptoms or their disturbing behaviour. Their efforts to fight the symptoms merely aggravate and perpetuate them. People's private logic maintains their mistaken and unrealistic life goals. Adler referred to this as a 'yes-but' personality where the individual is aware of their social obligations (yes) – (but) due to their private logic they have to continue with their useless behaviour. The feared situation is still avoided, the task or duty is evaded and the obligations of a relationship are sidestepped. Sometimes the symptom is *cured* but it recurs or is replaced by another symptom if its safeguarding tendency is still needed.

Change

Any occurrence in people's lives may become an encouraging experience, so causing them to change their perceptions. New behaviours which challenge the old premisses of the lifestyle may cause a revision in social interest with a consequent decrease in inferiority feelings. The new behaviour may be embarked upon as a result of encouragement from another person or, less often, due to an independent decision on the part of the individual. Changed circumstances – e.g. leaving home, partners or parents, or being left by partners or parents, leaving school, passing exams or failing exams, getting a job or losing a job – can start the changed behaviour. If the new behaviour has encouraging results then the private logic which underpinned the old behaviour is challenged and possibly revised.

As mentioned in the previous section, people may change their overt behaviour without any change in their motivation. Adlerians would consider that a behavioural change is superficial if not accompanied by an alteration of perception and an increase in social interest. People need to gain some insight into their mistaken ideas after changing their behaviour. Substituting acceptable behaviour for unacceptable behaviour is not a change in lifestyle if people still do not feel equal to their fellows. People who feel they must always be the centre of attention, and who change from unacceptable behaviour to acceptable behaviour, are still focused on their own superiority and sense of being special; they are not concentrating on what they can contribute to the task and the needs of the situation.

Practice

Goals of therapy

Adlerian psychotherapy is a learning process where there is re-education of clients' faulty perceptions and social values, and modification of their motivation. It is intended that clients should gain insight into their mistaken ideas and unrealistic goals, both of which are a source of discouragement. After insight there is a stage of reorientation of short- and long-term goals and readjustment of personal concepts and attitudes. The clients' original feelings of inferiority are superseded by a growing social interest. They feel encouraged as they recognize their equality with their fellow human beings. They concentrate on making their contribution and co-operating instead of looking at their personal status within groups.

There are four phases, each with its own goal in the Adlerian psychotherapy process:

1 establishing and maintaining a relationship with the client;
2 uncovering the dynamics of the client;
3 giving insight;
4 encouraging reorientation.

Selection criteria

There are no rigid guidelines for selecting individual therapy rather than couples therapy or group therapy. Individual choice on the part of both the therapist and the client is respected, although clients' rights to choose their kind of therapy are limited by what is available. Some therapists prefer to work with people in a group, acknowledging that each individual's problems are of a social nature, the group acting as an important agent in the psychotherapeutic process. Some therapists are reluctant to work with married individuals unless their partner is aware of the implications of psychotherapy and the changes it may encourage. When working with children, Adlerian therapists work with the whole family, parents and siblings, as they realize that if one child makes changes then the whole family will need to change too. Dreikurs, Mosak and Shulman (1952, 1982) introduced multiple psychotherapy: several therapists working with one client. This provides an ideal training opportunity. The client enjoys the attention of more than one therapist, and since the atmosphere is educational, discussion of interpretation of the clients' lifestyle, including disagreements between therapists, is enlightening and encouraging to the client. The client participates as an equal in explaining and understanding his or her private logic. It does happen that clients move from individual to group therapy or from a group to individual therapy and this move is mutually agreed between clients and therapists. Some clients receiving group therapy may have additional individual sessions from the group therapist. If a couple have a relationship problem the therapist may want to work with them as a couple; however, it may emerge that one or both partners need to do some individual work, in which case they would have some individual therapy. Clients who feel ridiculous if they share feelings and personal ideas tend to prefer individual therapy, one therapist being less threatening than a group of people.

Qualities of effective therapists

The effective Adlerian therapist feels truly equal to all human beings, and this includes clients and children. The therapist shows respect to the client, but this does not necessarily mean that the therapist is always nice and kind and accepting of all the client's behaviours. The relationship with the client is one of mutual respect, so the therapist shows herself respect by not tolerating unacceptable behaviour from the client and by giving honest feedback. The therapist shows respect towards the client by genuinely acting as if he had full responsibility for his decisions and actions. The therapist is warm and accepting of the person *as he is* and sincerely interested in understanding without judgement his lifestyle, his unique perception of life and his chosen life goals. The Adlerian therapist models social interest and shows herself to be a fallible human being who is making her own contribution, unafraid of making mistakes. The Adlerian approach is based on a clear philosophy of life and the therapist will espouse social values that enable all human beings to live together in harmony as equals now and in the future. The relationship with the therapist may be the first one where the client experiences a democratic, co-operative partnership between equals. The therapist needs to have the skills to win people over as well as the personal maturity to model social interest. Many clients resist entering a partnership between equals because this gives them too much responsibility. The therapist must resist the temptation to dominate, rescue, manipulate or fight with the client; all these therapist behaviours are disrespectful and belong to an authoritarian relationship rather than a democratic one.

There are many varied, creative and adaptable Adlerian therapists who use different modes of gaining insight and encouraging reorientation. Art therapy, psychodrama, non-verbal exercises, group exercises and dream analysis are some of the major approaches that Adlerian therapists use.

Therapeutic relationship and style

There is no prescribed style for Adlerian therapists but the relationship is one of equality. Initially, the therapist will respond sensitively to the client in order to quickly establish an atmosphere of trust and acceptance. The setting is usually relaxed and comfortable with the therapist and client facing each other in chairs of equal height. After the presenting problem has been briefly described by the client, some Adlerian therapists will want to move on to gathering information in order to be able to understand the client's lifestyle. The client may be surprised to be moved away from the *problem* and although the therapist's style is directive at this point it is respectful, so that an explanation is given as to why the therapist wishes to move on and the client's agreement is sought. Other therapists gather lifestyle information in a more informal way during the course of therapy. Both client and therapist embark upon this educational voyage of discovery actively as partners, the client providing the information and the therapist giving interpretations. The therapist's style will vary according to each client's needs, so that *empathy* is established. For instance, the therapist might use the client's vocabulary, seeking clarification if she is not sure what the client is saying; the therapist might give time and space for clients to express their feelings or might use humour during the sessions, and some therapists may self-disclose in order to give the client feedback on their behaviour in the session. Gradually the private logic will be uncovered and understood by the therapist. Interpretations need to be put to the client as they are merely hypothesized by guessing on the part of the therapist. The therapist will wish to see whether the client acknowledges if the therapist has made a true interpretation. The whole educational process will not take place unless therapist and client are co-operating and sharing mutually agreed goals. It is in the last phase – reorientation – that it becomes clear if both therapist and client share the same therapy goals. Clients have the right to gain insight and then decide not to make any changes. If the client does wish to make some changes, the therapist is there to guide him. Task-setting and completing the assignments also require a co-operative relationship. There will be difficult times, there may be strong emotions to work through, disagreements between therapist and client, but their resilient relationship endures these tests. The time-scale for the last phase (reorientation) will vary with each client. Some clients spend useful time with their therapist when they want to make some changes; others may need to be away from the therapist, having decided to stick to old familiar patterns. The door is always open for them to return when they feel ready to work on themselves again. The therapist demonstrates complete faith in the client by giving him total responsibility for his own reorientation.

Major therapeutic strategies and techniques

Adlerian psychotherapy can be described as a co-operative educational enterprise between equals – the therapist and client. The first stage of therapy is to *establish a co-operative relationship*, one between equals that is recognized by the presence of mutual respect. A co-operative relationship requires mutually agreed goals. An open approach towards stating goals will prevent ineffectual therapy between a therapist and a client who have different goals. If it is not possible to find mutually agreed goals psychotherapy will be ineffectual and may as well be terminated. Mutual respect is established by the therapist showing herself respect by refusing to play any *games* with the client, by only working towards agreed therapy goals and by openly commenting about behaviour towards herself that she finds un-acceptable; the therapist shows respect for clients by listening and accepting and acknowledging clients' rights to make their own decisions and take responsibility for their lives. The client needs to feel that the therapist cares but will not manipulate, dominate nor rescue. Dictatorial prescription and rescuing are equally disrespectful behaviours on the part of the therapist. This democratic relationship becomes part of the client's retraining; it is an action experience.

The second stage of the therapy is to *gather information* and *understand clients' lifestyles* and then to show clients how the presenting problem fits into their overall characteristic pattern of movement. From the first minutes of meeting clients, information will be available to the therapist from non-verbal clues – how clients enter the room, where they choose to sit, their posture, how they speak, etc. Adler was reportedly very clever at picking up information from this non-verbal behaviour. Verbal information is also available in the client's short description of the presenting problem, the subjective situation. The Adlerian therapist will not want to spend too long initially on the presenting problem, as she will need to discover the client's lifestyle before the significance of the problem can be under-stood. The objective situation of the client is also explored as the therapist finds out how the client is functioning in the three life tasks: work, friendships and intimate relationships. Some therapists may also enquire about relationships to God and moral-ethical beliefs. Clients are then asked, 'the question', i.e. what would be different if you were well/if you did not have this symptom? Client's answers will reveal the particular area of difficulty for them and their unrealistic goals.

The therapist will then move on to *lifestyle assessment*, which consists of understanding the client's family constellation and interpreting his early memories. A child creates his own unique lifestyle in the context of his family and in relation to his siblings. The therapist, therefore, asks the client to describe himself and his siblings as children. Family constellation is not just a reflection of birth order. Adlerians might describe typical eldest, second, youngest, middle and only chil-dren but as Adler said, 'Everything can also be different', and children may interpret their positions in the family constellation quite differently. An eldest child chooses how to respond to family values and to the experience of being dethroned by a younger child; all elder children experience being only children for a time. A second child chooses whether to compete with the eldest by overtaking them or by doing something or being something entirely different. A youngest may decide to remain the baby of the family or to surpass all the siblings in achievement. Family values will determine whether the competition takes place in academic achievements or in being an acceptable person or in some other realm of behaviour important to that family. Many children will decide to rebel against family values, either silently or openly. Most families are competitive; very few are democratic.

The therapist will want additional information, in order to verify the hypothesis that she is beginning to form about the client's lifestyle. Dreikurs said that you needed two points on a line before you could make a hypothesis about a person's lifestyle. The therapist asks the client for some of his early memories. Adler found that people remembered incidents, often innocuous and ordinary, that fitted in with their lifestyle. Clients are asked to think back as far as they can and tell the therapist the first thing they think of, if possible something that happened to them before they were five years old. People select, out of all their life experiences, those memories that depict a certain aspect of their lifestyle. It may be their view of themselves, their view of their world and the people in it, their view of how life should be or how they have to behave. The therapist has to interpret the early memories and align this information with that already gleaned from the description of the family constellation. The therapist wants to find out client's life goals and their underlying mistaken assumptions, i.e. their private logic. The overall movement of the client needs to be recognized. The presenting problem and future problems will fit into this basic pattern of living.

The third phase of *interpretation* and *giving insight* is now entered. The therapist's approach is to find enough points on a line to begin to make a hypothesis. This informed guess is then put to the client, so that it can be verified. The therapist is looking for the client's recognition. Previously, clients were unaware of their goals and private logic, so this phase of the therapy is where the therapist particularly needs to demonstrate her empathy; she needs to be able to describe the client's goals and mistaken ideas in words that the client understands, recognizes and owns. This disclosure does not have to be perfect at the first attempt. The therapist shows her fallibility and encourages the client to help her shape the lifestyle summary, so that it feels right for the client. The summary usually takes the form of: 'Life is . . .'; 'Others are . . .'; and 'I am . . .' themes. The therapist explains how clients chose their particular goals, so that there is no mystique in the interpretation of the lifestyle. Private logic once it is verbalized begins to lose its strength. The overgeneralizations, oversimplifications and unrealistic ideas can be challenged. 'Is it reasonable to expect . . .?' 'Is this really how people are?' 'Is it realistic for you to expect to always be . . .?'

Dreams may also be analysed. Adler said dreams were the 'factory of the emotions'; they set the mood that fuels people's actions. Remembered dreams that clients produce always fit within a person's lifestyle and never contradict it.

The therapist places the client's concerns and problems in the context of the lifestyle and shows how certain situations, relationships or demands can cause a crisis because they challenge the client's lifestyle. Neurotic symptoms can be understood as alibis which were necessary because the client was pursuing unattainable goals. Making clients aware of the purpose of their neurotic symptoms was described by Adler as 'spitting in the patient's soup'. The patient can persist with the symptoms but they will not give the same satisfaction as before.

The *re-orientation phase* follows on from gaining insight. The Adlerian therapist will use a mirror technique to show clients familiar patterns of movement towards consistent goals in all their behaviour. Attainable assignments will be set for clients that challenge their private logic. If the assignments are completed successfully then there is a weakening of client's private logic. Clients will begin to catch themselves pursuing the same goals and making the same justifications for their behaviour. Clients will catch themselves after, during, and then before they engage in the useless behaviour. Each 'aha' experience increases clients' new learning and growing understanding of their own personality. Each individual, once they have some insight, will decide whether or not to change and if to change, over how long a period. The old patterns are well tried and tested, automatic and to some extent feel comfortable. New patterns are scary. One method that Adler used when a client was fighting against a symptom or behaviour and actually increasing both was to encourage the client to increase the symptom or behaviour; this is known as paradoxical intention.

The change process in therapy

Once people's mistaken goals are revealed to them they can no longer pursue them with such conviction. Once their mistaken ideas are revealed to them they can choose to change. Gaining insight and choosing to change is one choice; gaining insight and choosing not to change is another. Insight will develop as individuals begin to recognize their patterns of behaviour. New behaviours which challenge the old assumptions are then tested out. New behaviours or assignments may be successful – the old private logic is then challenged and weakened and replaced by common sense. New behaviours may have disastrous outcomes, in which case clients may be tempted to retreat to old ways and to feel comfortable with familiar private logic. As their private logic decreases and common sense grows they will display increased social interest in all spheres of their lives and they will take on responsibility for their own life goals, perceptions and behaviours. As soon as they accept full responsibility for their own behaviour they enable themselves to make changes. Their increased sense of belonging and feeling of equal worth will be a source of encouragement to them. Inferiority feelings will diminish; their focus of interest will be on their personal contribution to the task in hand. They will feel content with themselves. Their unattainable goals will be replaced by the courage to be imperfect, an acknowledgement that all active, co-operating human beings make mistakes. The new behaviours and new goals will be followed by new assumptions. This process can be instant in a child, as when one of the Four Mistaken Goals of Misbehaviour (Dreikurs and Soltz, 1995) is revealed to them, very quick in a teenager and increasingly slower in a mature adult. It is harder for adults in established relationships to make changes as these changes will inevitably have an effect on partners in intimate relationships, and on close friends. The therapist, who has always treated the client as an equal, encourages the client to contribute as an equal. Clients may make a partial or complete change of personality, their private logic replaced by common sense, their inferiority feelings replaced by social interest and a feeling of belonging. The correction of one mistaken concept will enable growth and release further courage to tackle new behaviours and additional mistakes. The therapist will respect the client's right to choose when and how much to change. Behaviour change can occur years after initially gaining insight. It is best for the therapist not to fight with the client during times of inactivity; the therapist can be available when the client wants to make some changes but does not know how to. Each person, if they choose to change, will do so in their own unique and creative way.

Limitations of the approach

Adler's theory of personality provides Adlerian therapists with a complete understanding of all human behaviour. The practice of Adlerian therapists is very varied but always based on the foundation of a holistic socio-teleological view of people. Much of Adler's Individual Psychology has permeated other approaches in psychotherapy and counselling; many of his ideas are incorporated into other people's theories without acknowledgement. Adlerian theory appears to have widespread acceptance and relevance to students of human behaviour.

The psychotherapeutic procedures practised by Adler himself and by Rudolph Dreikurs are used today by therapists and any technique which a therapist finds helpful is added to the basic approach. The insight and the skills are only part of Adlerian psychotherapy. Psychotherapists need to have social interest and need to use their skills 'for the purpose of establishing an ideal community' (Dreikurs, 1953: v). The Adlerian approach can give a great deal of insight; to use the insight and understanding of people with social interest is an exacting demand on every therapist. Many people, including therapists, have grown up in families where power was used either openly in the form of control by anger or disguised in the form of manipulation. Therapists have to work on understanding their own skills in the arena of power before they can work with clients in a truly equal co-operative relationship. Many clients will find the idea of being responsible for their own behaviour distasteful and unacceptable.

The client may leave therapy with insight but unwilling to change. If therapy outcomes are looked at over too short a time the long-term effects of the insight may not be recorded. Changes have been seen several years after a lifestyle assessment was done. It is always worthwhile enabling a person to gain insight. It is never worthwhile fighting with them afterwards in order to force or persuade or shame them into change.

There are limitations to using Adlerian psychotherapy only in a one-to-one situation. So much information can be gained by observing clients in groups. So much can be gained by clients when trying out new behaviours in a safe group. So much can be gained by clients experiencing equal membership of a group with a shared goal of mutual growth.

Case example

The client

Martin was a 23-year-old engineering graduate working on a training scheme for a well-known engineering firm. He lived in a house with three other engineers and was an active sportsman. He felt unfulfilled in his life, bored with his job, indecisive and lacking in direction. He had an ambition to be a test pilot and had applied for a job which would involve a lot of travelling. Although he met many people at work and in his leisure pursuits he felt lonely.

It was explained that in order to understand Martin's difficulties we would need to understand him as a whole person. This would entail returning to look at his childhood, finding out about him as a child and then connecting that information to him as he was now; he agreed to do this and we arranged ten weekly sessions.

The therapy

We acknowledged that the concerns he was presenting were a general lack of fulfilment in his life, loneliness, and an inability to make decisions that would change his present situation. We then started on gathering the information needed to assess his lifestyle and started with his family constellation.

He was the second child, his sister being five years older than him. He described his sister, as a child, as a tearaway, always in trouble, and a tomboy; she had asthma, particularly when she was a teenager, and got a lot of attention from her mother for this. She had an alliance with her mother and was rather maternal herself. She could take offence easily. Martin was quiet and 'good' as a child; he did as he was told. However, when his sister was ill he was naughty. He was shy and seen as the baby of the family. He got on well with his father. Like his father, he liked making things and was easygoing. He liked sports but said he was not as good as his father. He said both he and his sister worked hard at school, his sister's best subjects being maths, social arts and psychology, while his best subjects were sciences and technical studies. He said they were both sensitive. When asked to describe his mother, he said she fussed quite a bit, was fairly nervous and sensitive and protective. She was in charge of the day-to-day running of the family. His father he described as very close to Martin – easygoing, silent, strong and very sporty. He was very firm when he felt strongly about something. His father died in a car crash when Martin was 12 years old. The family motto was to be honest and straightforward and not to upset people.

Here we have a competitive family where in order for children to feel they have a place they choose to be different. Martin and his sister were opposites in many respects. Martin's sister was an only child for five years and must have been very threatened by the arrival of a younger brother. She chose to be a rebel and kept her mother busy, either with her naughty behaviour or with her asthma. All that was left for Martin was to be good and quiet. Being shy would have got him some attention, and being the baby of the family meant that his mother would have given him extra help and attention. By being quiet and easygoing he gained his father's time and closeness. The family were living in Zambia when his father was killed and he was in boarding-school in Rhodesia. Martin said he had time to come to terms with his father's death slowly as he was away from home so much. A year after his father's death the family returned to Lincolnshire.

As we looked at Martin's family constellation he was surprised at how *competitive* his family was. Being exact opposites meant that he and his sister were competitors; by choosing different arenas they could both be winners. Martin even compared himself with his father by saying he liked sports but was not as good as his father, who won trophies. We looked at the narrowing effect of competition; if you have to be a winner in what you do then you will probably only engage in those activities where you think you will win. Martin had to consider if he had narrowed himself down. He had to look at the effects of competition in his life now. Did he engage in his numerous sporting activities only in order to compete? Did he move from one activity to another when he felt he was not going to be the winner? Where there are winners there have to be losers; that is the inevitable result of competition. Being a loser is discouraging; did his striving to be the winner and not always achieving this discourage him and contribute to his feeling of being unfulfilled? Martin had a lot to think about after looking at his childhood decisions.

The next source of information was Martin's early memories. In the first one he was sitting in a beach hut drinking lemonade. The beach hut was tall and pillarbox shaped. His parents and grandparents were there. He said there was no feeling attached to the memory. The second memory was of a time when he was three or four years old and he had a fight with someone and ended up hiding in a recess behind his front door; the other child came and rang the doorbell with his friends. He was worried that his mother would find out and there was no way out of it. His third memory was of starting school. He went with his sister on the first day, feeling excited and nervous. He felt good because his sister was there. Martin's fourth memory was when he was a bit older and he and another boy had a race. The boy beat him, and he felt very annoyed.

Together we looked at what these memories meant to Martin. The first memory is a memory of how life should be. He is safe and inactive with protective people around him drinking a sweet pleasant drink and there are no challengers. Martin confirmed that is how he would like life to be. The second memory shows the inevitable conflict arising for him in that he was a good boy who would want to follow the family motto, which was to be honest and straightforward and not to upset people, but the family motto was impossible to achieve. If Martin was to be straightforward and honest then he would at times upset people. This memory portrays the tension he places himself under as he tries to conform with this motto and please his parents. The motto itself also says he must please others and at the same time be true to himself. Martin acknowledged that this gives him a feeling of being trapped, which he dislikes. The third memory shows his view of the world, which is that it is exciting and a bit frightening. He feels reassured by the presence of other people who are more capable than him and feels confident to tackle the world with their help. He likes people to help him. This is the legacy of someone who was the baby of the family; he would always need help. Martin acknowledged this and although he was a very active person, when he had to make major decisions he found it very difficult to do so on his own. The fourth memory ties in with the information we gathered from his family constellation. He is competitive and hates losing; however, he has an expectation that he will lose and that other people will be better than him. Again he has a dilemma – he must please people and yet they do not please him; in fact they irritate him. None of his memories give him any solutions to these dilemmas, indicating that that is how he sees life and that is his lot. He said that he always likes to have a choice in order to avoid feeling trapped. Avoidance is probably the way he escapes entrapment. In order to summarize his lifestyle we came up with the following: *I am better than everyone else but I cannot win. The world is an exciting and frightening place and people make impossible demands upon me so I am hesitant and remain indecisive.*

At the next session we looked at the relationship with his father, which was cut short when Martin was 12. He enjoyed being with his easygoing father; he could be easygoing too – no competition – as his father was the winner anyway. They could be very close. Because of his father's death he was unable to develop this idyllic relationship into a more realistic one. He never learned how to maintain this closeness while growing into a man. He only experienced being an easygoing, quiet, good little boy being close to his silent, strong, easygoing father. This meant he was not prepared for adult relationships. He said that he got on with his housemates, but was perhaps too easygoing. He described how they were planning a party at his house and the others assumed they could use his hi-fi equipment without asking him. He was very annoyed and made excuses instead of giving them the real reason why they could not use it. We looked at ways he could have tackled that situation. He does like to have things just so; his parents used to say he was too fussy. This indicates a need to control what was happening to him and what he was doing. He told me that as a child he was shy; this is very controlling behaviour – a shy child makes other people be active and try to make contact with him. This tied in with a tendency not to do things unless he was sure of the end result. His outward behaviour would be indecision. Martin was discouraged to think of himself as indecisive and recognized that when he had to make a decision he maintained a middle position and was inactive. We discussed motivations behind his inactivity; one was his need to please people and at the same time be true to himself. He also showed a need to control himself and others, and inactivity gave him the possibility of almost perfect control. He was ambitious and set himself unrealistic goals, such as wanting to be a test pilot. He was unsure if he would achieve the goals so he hesitated about even trying. He controlled his behaviour because he did not think he would win, as his fourth memory tells him.

When asked to choose an animal that he would like to be he chose an eagle because it has no predators and is king of the birds, free to roam about and do what it wants. Here Martin shows us again his fear of other people and his wish for supreme power and his idea that given that power he would have complete freedom. I suggested to him that he still felt like a fledgling – dependent, weak and helpless. We talked about when he would leave the nest. We also talked about complete freedom being an unrealistic goal and how real life requires that we co-operate with others, make a contribution and take life as it comes. We talked about mistakes; that they are a basic part of human life and that he could learn from them. We talked about his unrealistic goal of supreme power and how he made himself feel inadequate when he did not live up to his expectations. He revealed how angry he was with himself.

By the end of the ten weeks Martin was more relaxed and accepting of himself. He was satisfied with his progress at work and had a more realistic view of his strengths and weaknesses. I had contact with him for three years, during which he moved to a more interesting department at work. This culminated in his going part-time at work and setting up in business with two other young men, making and designing fitted kitchens. This was a major life decision and he had been able to make plans that were realistic and had involved co-operation with workmates. He was enjoying his sporting activities instead of driving himself to compete. He was now engaged in two of the life tasks – occupation and friendships – with increased social interest; he only needed to embark upon the third life task of love and intimacy.

References

Adler, A. (1912) *The Neurotic Constitution*. London: Kegan Paul, Trench, Trubner & Co.

Adler, A. (1917) *Study of Organ Inferiority and its Psychical Compensation: A Contribution to Clinical Medicine*. New York: Nervous and Mental Diseases Publishing.

Adler, A. (1933) *Social Interest: A Challenge to Mankind*. London: Faber & Faber.

Adler, A. (1992) *Understanding Human Nature* (1927), trans. Colin Brett. Oxford: Oneworld Publications.

Dreikurs, R. (1953) *Fundamentals of Adlerian Psychology*. Chicago, IL: Adler School of Professional Psychology.

Dreikurs, R. (1967) *Psychodynamics, Psychotherapy and Counselling: Collected Papers*. Chicago, IL: Adler School of Professional Psychology.

Dreikurs, R. and Soltz, V. (1995) *Happy Children* (1964). Melbourne: Australian Council for Educational Research.

Dreikurs, R., Mosak, H.H. and Shulman, B.H. (1952) 'Patient–therapist relationship in multiple psychotherapy. II: its advantages for the patient', *Psychiatric Quarterly*, 26: 590–6.

Dreikurs, R., Mosak, H.H. and Shulman, B.H. (1982) *Multiple Psychotherapy: Use of Two Therapists with One Patient*. Chicago, IL: Adler School of Professional Psychology.

Ellenberger, H.F. (1970) 'Alfred Adler and individual psychology', Ch. 8 in *The Discovery of the Unconscious*. New York: Basic Books.

Terner, J. and Pew, W.L. (1978) *The Courage to be Imperfect: The Life and Work of Rudolf Dreikurs*. New York: Hawthorn Books.

Suggested further reading

Adler, A. (1964) *Superiority and Social Interest: A Collection of Later Writings*, ed. H.L. Ansbacher and R.R. Ansbacher. New York: Norton.

Adler, A. (1992) *What Life Could Mean to You* (1931), trans. Colin Brett. Oxford: Oneworld Publications.

Ansbacher, H.L. and Ansbacher, R.R. (eds) (1967) *The Individual Psychology of Alfred Adler*. New York: Harper & Row.

Corsini, R.J. (1984) 'Adlerian psychotherapy', Ch. 3 in *Current Psychotherapies*. Itasca, IL: Peacock.

Dreikurs, R. (1971) *Social Equality: The Challenge of Today*. Chicago, IL: Henry Regnery.

6

Person-Centred Therapy
Brian Thorne

Historical context and development in Britain

Historical context

Dr Carl Rogers (1902–87), the American psychologist and founder of what has now become known as person-centred counselling or psychotherapy, always claimed to be grateful that he never had one particular mentor. He was influenced by many significant figures, often holding widely differing viewpoints, but above all he claimed to be the student of his own experience and of that of his clients and colleagues.

While accepting Rogers's undoubtedly honest claim about his primary sources of learning there is much about his thought and practice which places him within a recognizable tradition. Oatley has described this as

> the distinguished American tradition exemplified by John Dewey: the tradition of no nonsense, of vigorous self-reliance, of exposing oneself thoughtfully to experience, practical innovation, and of careful concern for others. (Oatley, 1981: 192)

In fact in 1925, while still a student at Teachers College, Columbia, New York, Rogers was directly exposed to Dewey's thought and to progressive education through his attendance at a course led by the famous William Heard Kilpatrick, a student of Dewey and himself a teacher of extraordinary magnetism. Not that Dewey and Kilpatrick formed the mainstream of the ideas to which Rogers was introduced during his professional training and early clinical experience. Indeed when he took up his first appointment in 1928 as a member of the Child Study Department of the Society for the Prevention of Cruelty to Children in Rochester, New York, he joined an institution where the three fields of psychology, psychiatry and social work were combining forces in diagnosing and treating problems. This context appealed to Rogers's essentially pragmatic temperament.

Rogers's biographer, Kirschenbaum (1979), while acknowledging the variety of influences to which Rogers was subjected at the outset of his professional career, suggests nevertheless that when Rogers went to Rochester he saw himself essentially as a diagnostician and as an interpretative therapist whose goal, very much in the analytical tradition, was to help a child or a parent gain insight into their own behaviour and motivation. Diagnosis and interpretation are far removed from the primary concerns of a contemporary person-centred therapist and in an important sense Rogers's progressive disillusionment with both these activities during his time at Rochester marks the beginning of his own unique approach. He tells the story of how, near the end of his time at Rochester, he had been working with a highly intelligent mother whose son was presenting serious behavioural problems. Rogers was convinced that the root of the trouble lay in the mother's early rejection of the boy but no amount of gentle strategy on his part could bring her to this insight. In the end he gave up and they were about to part when she asked if adults were taken for counselling on their own account. When Rogers assured her that they were she immediately requested help for herself and launched into an impassioned outpouring of her own despair, her marital difficulties and her confusion and sense of failure. Real therapy, it seems, began at that moment and was ultimately successful. Rogers commented:

> This incident was one of a number which helped me to experience the fact – only fully realized later – that it is the client who knows what hurts, what direction to go, what problems are crucial, what experiences have been deeply buried. It began to occur to me that unless I had a need to demonstrate my own cleverness and learning, I would do better to rely upon the client for the direction of movement in the process. (cited in Kirschenbaum, 1979: 89)

The essential step from diagnosis and interpretation to listening had been taken and from that point onwards Rogers was launched on his own path.

By 1940 Rogers was a professor of psychology at Ohio State University and his first book, *Counseling and Psychotherapy*, appeared two years later. From 1945 to 1957 he was professor of psychology at Chicago and executive secretary (his own term) of the university counselling centre. This was a period of intense activity, not least in the research field. Rogers's pragmatic nature has led to much research being carried out on person-centred therapy. With the publication of *Client-Centred Therapy* in 1951 Rogers became a major force in the world of psychotherapy and established his position as a practitioner, theorist and researcher who warranted respect. In an address to the American Psychological Association in 1973 Rogers maintained that during this Chicago period he was for the first time giving clear expression to an idea whose time had come. The idea was

> the gradually formed and tested hypothesis that the individual has within himself vast resources for self-understanding, for altering his self-concept, his attitudes and his self-directed behaviour – and that these resources can be tapped if only a definable climate of facilitative psychological attitudes can be provided. (Rogers, 1974: 116)

From this 'gradually formed and tested hypothesis' non-directive therapy was born as a protest against the diagnostic, prescriptive point of view prevalent at the time. Emphasis was placed on a relationship between counsellor and client based upon acceptance and clarification. This was a period, too, of excitement generated by the use of recorded interviews for research and training purposes and there was a focus on 'non-directive techniques'. Those coming for help were no longer referred to as patients but as clients, with the inference that they were self-responsible human beings, not objects for treatment. As experience grew and both theory-building and research developed, the term 'client-centred therapy' was adopted which put the emphasis on the internal world of the client and focused attention on the attitudes of therapists towards their clients rather than on particular techniques. The term 'person-centred' won Rogers's approval in the decade before his death, because it could be applied to the many fields outside therapy where his ideas were becoming increasingly accepted and valued and because in the therapy context itself it underlined the person-to-person nature of the interaction where not only the phenomenological world of the client but also the therapist's state of being are of crucial significance. This 'I–Thou' quality of the therapeutic relationship indicates a certain kinship with the existential philosophy of Kierkegaard and Buber and the stress on personal experience recalls the work of the British philosopher/scientist Michael Polanyi (whom Rogers knew and admired). In the years before his death, Rogers also reported his own deepening respect for certain aspects of Zen teaching and became fond of quoting sayings of Lao-Tse, especially those that stress the undesirability of imposing on people instead of allowing them the space in which to find themselves.

Development in Britain

Although the influence of Rogers percolated spasmodically into Britain in the post-war years – mainly through the work of the Marriage Guidance Council (now known as Relate) and then often in an unacknowledged form – it was not until the mid-1960s that he came to be studied in British universities. Interestingly enough the reason for this development was the establishment of the first training courses in Britain for school counsellors. These programmes (initially at the Universities of Keele and Reading) were largely dependent in their first years on American Fulbright professors of psychology or counselling, many of whom were steeped in the client-centred tradition and introduced their British students to both the theory and practice of client-centred therapy. It is with the growth of counselling in Britain that the work of Rogers has become more widely known; it is probably true to say that during the 1970s the largest recognizable group of person-centred practitioners working in Britain was counsellors operating within the educational sector. It is also significant that when Rogers started working in the 1920s psychologists in the USA were not permitted to practise psychotherapy so he called his activity 'counselling'. British practitioners of person-centred therapy have tended to use the word 'counsellor' and to eschew the word 'psychotherapist' for perhaps different reasons. They have seen the word 'psychotherapist' as somehow conducive to an aura of mystification and expertise which runs counter to the egalitarian relationship which the person-centred approach seeks to establish between the therapist and client.

In the last 20 years the person-centred approach has moved decisively beyond the educational arena and has made its impact felt more widely. The Association for Humanistic Psychology in Britain has introduced many practitioners to Rogers's ideas and its journal *Self and Society* has featured many articles on his work. Indeed, he himself was a contributor to the journal. The work of the Facilitator Development Institute (FDI) founded in 1974 on the initiative of Rogers's close associate, Dr Charles Devonshire, has through its annual workshops introduced person-centred ideas to a wide variety of psychologists, social workers, psychiatrists and others. In 1985 the Institute began its first extensive training programme for person-centred counsellors, work now continued by Person-Centred Therapy (Britain) under the direction of three of FDI's original co-directors (Dave Mearns, Elke Lambers and Brian Thorne). Training courses are also offered in Britain by the Person-Centred Approach Institute International headed by Charles Devonshire which runs a number of training programmes throughout Europe. The Institute for Person-Centred Learning is a third independent training organization which has more recently established itself in Britain. In 1980 the Norwich Centre for personal and professional development gave Britain its first independent therapy agency committed to the person-centred approach and this centre has since 1992 significantly extended its work by establishing a nationwide workplace counselling service for the employees of one of Britain's largest insurance groups.

The influence of the person-centred approach in Britain was further enhanced by the publication in 1988 of *Person-Centred Counselling in Action* co-authored by Dave Mearns and Brian Thorne. This milestone book has now been reprinted on numerous occasions and has sold more than 45,000 copies (Mearns and Thorne, 1988). Significantly, too, the development of the Counselling Unit at the University of Strathclyde (directed by Mearns) and of the Centre for Counselling Studies at the University of East Anglia (directed by Thorne) has marked a resurgence of person-centred scholarship and training in British universities. These two units, together with the Centre for Counselling Studies at the University of Keele (under the direction of John McLeod) should do much to ensure that the person-centred approach is well represented in British academia in the years ahead.

Theoretical assumptions

Image of the person

Person-centred therapists start from the assumption that both they and their clients are trustworthy. This trust resides in the belief that every organism – the human being included – has an underlying and instinctive movement towards the constructive accomplishment of its inherent potential. Rogers (1979) often recalled a boyhood memory of his parents' potato bin in which they stored the winter supply of potatoes. This bin was placed in the basement several feel below a small window, yet despite the highly unfavourable conditions the potatoes would begin to send out spindly shoots groping towards the distant light of the window. Rogers compared these pathetic potatoes in their desperate struggle to develop with clients whose lives have been warped by circumstances and experience but who continue against all the odds to strive towards growth, towards becoming. This directional, or actualizing, tendency in the human being can be trusted and the therapist's task is to help create the best possible conditions for its fulfilment.

The elevated view of human nature which person-centred therapists hold is paralleled by their insistence on individual uniqueness. They believe that no two persons are ever alike and that the human personality is so complex that no diagnostic labelling of persons can ever be fully justified. Indeed, person-centred therapists know that they cannot hope to uncover fully the subjective perceptual world of the client and that clients themselves can do this only with great effort. Furthermore clients' perceptual worlds will be determined by the experiences they have rejected or assimilated into the self-concept.

Conceptualization of psychological disturbance and health

The self-concept is of crucial importance in person-centred therapy and needs to be distinguished from the self. Nelson-Jones (1982, 1995) has made the helpful distinction of regarding the self as the real, underlying, unique self – that is the essentially trustworthy human organism which is discernible in the physiological processes of the entire body and through the growth process by which potentialities and capacities are brought to realization – and contrasting this with the self-concept which is a person's conceptual construction of him or herself (however poorly articulated) and which does not by any means always correspond with the direct and untrammelled experiencing of the real self.

The self-concept develops over time and is heavily dependent on the attitudes of those who constitute the individual's significant others. It follows that where a person is surrounded by those who are quick to condemn or punish (however subtly) the behaviour which emanates from the experiencing of the real self, he or she will become rapidly confused. The need for positive regard or approval from others is overwhelming and is present from earliest infancy. If behaviour arising from what is actually experienced by the individual fails to win approval an immediate conflict is established. A baby, for example, may gain considerable satisfaction or relief from howling full-throatedly but may then quickly learn that such behaviour is condemned or punished by the mother. At this point the need to win the mother's approval is in immediate conflict with the promptings of the real self which wishes to howl. In the person-centred tradition disturbance is conceptualized in terms of the degree of success or failure experienced by the individual in resolving such conflicts. The badly disturbed person on this criterion will have lost almost complete contact with the experiencing of his or her organism, for the basic need for self-regard can in the most adverse circumstances lead to behaviour which is totally geared to the desperate search for acceptance and approval. The voice of the real self in such cases is silenced and a self-concept is developed which bears little relationship to people's deepest promptings, from which they are essentially cut off. Not surprisingly, perhaps, such attempts to create a self-concept which denies the nature of the real self cannot in the long run be successful. In most cases individuals, whatever face they may present to the world, hold themselves in low esteem and a negative self-concept is usually a further sign of disturbance at some level. In those rarer instances where the self-deception is more extreme the self-concept may at a conscious level appear largely positive but it will be quickly evident to others that such self-affirmation has been won at the cost of a deliberate and sustained refusal to allow adverse judgements into awareness, whether these threaten from within or from outside sources. Disturbed people can seldom trust their own judgement and for the person-centred therapist another sure mark of disturbance is the absence of an internalized locus of evaluation. This somewhat cumbersome term describes the faculty which determines individuals' capacity to trust their own thoughts and feelings when making decisions or choosing courses of action. Disturbed people show little sign of possessing such a faculty: instead they constantly turn to external authorities or find themselves caught in a paralysis of indecision. In summary, then, disturbance may be conceptualized as a greater or lesser degree of alienation from the real self prompted

by the fundamental need for self-regard. The resulting self-concept, usually negative and always falsely based, is linked to a defective capacity to make decisions
which in turn indicates the absence of an internalized locus of evaluation.

If individuals are unfortunate enough to be brought up amongst a number of
significant others who are highly censorious or judgmental, a self-concept can
develop which may serve to estrange them almost totally from their organismic
experiencing. In such cases the self-concept, often developed after years of
oppression of the real self, becomes the fiercest enemy of the person's true and
unique identity and must undergo radical transformation if the actualizing
tendency is to reassert itself.

The person-centred therapist is constantly working with clients who have all but
lost touch with the actualizing tendency within themselves and who have been
surrounded by others who have no confidence in the innate capacity of human
beings to move towards the fulfilment of their potential. Psychologically healthy
persons on the other hand are men and women who have been lucky enough to
live in contexts which have been conducive to the development of self-concepts
which allow them to be in touch for at least some of the time with their deepest
experiences and feelings without having to censure them or distort them. Such
people are well placed to achieve a level of psychological freedom which will
enable them to move in the direction of becoming more fully functioning persons.
'Fully functioning' is a term used by Rogers to denote individuals who are using
their talents and abilities, realizing their potential and moving towards a more
complete knowledge of themselves. They are demonstrating what it means to have
attained a high level of psychological health and Rogers has outlined some of the
major personality characteristics which they seem to share. The first and most
striking characteristic is *openness to experience*. Individuals who are open to
experience are able to listen to themselves and to others and to experience what is
happening without feeling threatened. They demonstrate a high level of awareness,
especially in the world of the feelings. Second, allied to this characteristic, is the
ability to live fully in each moment of one's existence. Experience is trusted rather
than feared and is the moulding force for the emerging personality rather than
being twisted or manipulated to fit some preconceived structure of reality or some
rigidly safeguarded self-concept. The third characteristic is the *organismic trusting*
which is so clearly lacking in those who have constantly fallen victim to the
adverse judgements of others. Such trusting is best displayed in the process of
decision-making. Whereas many people defer continually to outside sources of
influence when making decisions, fully functioning persons regard their organismic
experiences as the most valid sources of information for deciding what to do in
any given situation. Rogers put it succinctly when he said 'doing what "feels right"
proves to be a . . . trustworthy guide to behaviour' (1961: 190).

Further characteristics of the fully functioning person are concerned with the
issues of personal freedom and creativity. For Rogers a mark of psychological
health is the sense of responsibility for determining one's own actions and their
consequences based on a feeling of freedom and power to choose from the many
options that life presents. There is no feeling within the individual of being
imprisoned by circumstances, or fate or genetic inheritance, although this is not to
suggest that Rogers denies the powerful influences of biological make-up, social

forces or past experience. Subjectively, however, people experience themselves as free agents. Finally, the fully functioning person is typically creative in the sense that he or she can adjust to changing conditions and is likely to produce creative ideas or initiate creative projects and actions. Such people are unlikely to be conformists, although they will relate to society in a way which permits them to be fully involved without being imprisoned by convention or tradition.

Acquisition of psychological disturbance

In person-centred terminology the mother's requirement that the baby cease to howl constitutes a *condition of worth*: 'I shall love you if you do not howl.' The concept of conditions of worth bears a striking similarity to the British therapist George Lyward's notion of contractual living. Lyward believed that most of his disturbed adolescent clients had had no chance to contact their real selves because they were too busy attempting – usually in vain – to fulfil contracts, in order to win approval (Burn, 1956). Lyward used to speak of usurped lives and Rogers in similar vein sees many individuals as the victims of countless internalized conditions of worth which have almost totally estranged them from their organismic experiencing. Such people will be preoccupied with a sense of strain at having to come up to the mark or with feelings of worthlessness at having failed to do so. They will be the victims of countless introjected conditions of worth so that they no longer have any sense of their inherent value as unique persons. The proliferation of introjections is an inevitable outcome of the desperate need for positive regard. Introjection is the process whereby the beliefs, judgements, attitudes or values of another person (most often the parent) are taken into the individual and become part of his or her armamentarium for coping with experience, however alien they may have been initially. The child, it seems, will do almost anything to satisfy the need for positive regard even if this means taking on board (introjecting) attitudes and beliefs which run quite counter to its own organismic reaction to experience. Once such attitudes and beliefs have become thoroughly absorbed into the personality they are said to have become internalized. Thus it is that introjection and internalization of conditions of worth imposed by significant others whose approval is desperately desired often constitute the gloomy road to a deeply negative self-concept as individuals discover that they can never come up to the high demands and expectations which such conditions inevitably imply.

Once this negative self-concept has taken root in an individual the likelihood is that the separation from the real self of the organism will become increasingly complete. It is as if individuals become cut off from their own inner resources and their own sense of value and are governed by a secondary and treacherous valuing process which is based on the internalization of other people's judgements and evaluations. Once caught in this trap the person is likely to grow more disturbed, for the negative self-concept induces behaviour which reinforces the image of inadequacy and worthlessness. It is a fundamental thesis of the person-centred point of view that behaviour is not only the result of what happens to us from the external world but also a function of how we feel about ourselves on the inside. In other words, we are likely to behave in accordance with our perception of ourselves. What we do is often an accurate reflection of how we evaluate ourselves and if this evaluation is low our behaviour will be correspondingly unacceptable to ourselves and in all probability to others as well. It is likely, too, that we shall be highly conscious of a sense of inadequacy and although we may conceal this from others the awareness that all is not well will usually be with us.

The person-centred therapist recognizes, however, that psychological disturbance is not always available to awareness. It is possible for a person to establish a self-concept which, because of the overriding need to win the approval of others, cannot permit highly significant sensory or visceral (a favourite word with Rogers) experience into consciousness. Such people cannot be open to the full range of their organismic experiencing because to be so would threaten the self-concept which must be maintained in order to win continuing favour. An example of such a person might be the man who has established a picture of himself as honourable, virtuous, responsible and loving. Such a man may be progressively divorced from those feelings which would threaten to undermine such a self-concept. He may arrive at a point where he no longer knows, for example, that he is angry or hostile or sexually hungry, for to admit to such feelings would be to throw his whole picture of himself into question. Disturbed people are by no means always aware of their disturbance, nor will they necessarily be perceived as disturbed by others who may have a vested interest in maintaining what is in effect a tragic but often rigorous act of self-deception.

Perpetuation of psychological disturbance

It follows from the person-centred view of psychological disturbance that it will be perpetuated if an individual continues to be dependent to a high degree on the judgement of others for a sense of self-worth. Such persons will be at pains to preserve and defend at all costs the self-concept which wins approval and esteem and will be thrown into anxiety and confusion whenever incongruity arises between the self-concept and actual experience, an incongruity which may sometimes uncomfortably be 'subceived' (to use another person-centred term) below the level of conscious awareness while remaining unacknowledged in accurate symbolization. In the example above the 'virtuous' man would be fully subject to conscious feelings of threat and confusion if he directly experienced his hostility or sexual hunger, although to do so would, of course, be a first step towards the recovery of contact with the real self. He will be likely, however, to avoid the threat and confusion by resorting to one or other of two basic mechanisms of defence – perceptual distortion or denial. In this way he avoids or stifles confusion and anxiety and thereby perpetuates his disturbance while mistakenly believing that he is maintaining his integrity. Perceptual distortion takes place whenever an incongruent experience is allowed into conscious awareness but only in a form that is in harmony with the person's current self-concept. The virtuous man, for instance, might permit himself to experience hostility but would distort this as a justifiable reaction to wickedness in others: for him his hostility would be rationalized into righteous indignation. Denial is a less common defence but is in some ways the more impregnable. In this case individuals preserve their self-concept by completely avoiding any conscious recognition of experiences or feelings that threaten them. The virtuous man would therefore be totally unaware of his constantly angry attitudes in a committee meeting and might perceive himself as simply speaking with truth and sincerity. Distortion and denial can have formidable psychological consequences and can sometimes protect a person for a lifetime from the confusion and anxiety which could herald the recovery of contact with the alienated self.

Change

For people who are trapped by a negative self-concept and by behaviour which tends to demonstrate and even reinforce the validity of such a self-assessment, there is little hope of positive change unless there is movement in the psychological environment which surrounds them. Most commonly this will be the advent of a new person on the scene or a marked change in attitude of someone who is already closely involved. A child, for example, may be abused and ignored at home but may discover, to her initial bewilderment, that her teachers respect and like her. If she gradually acquires the courage to trust this unexpected acceptance she may be fortunate enough to gain further reassurance through the discovery that her teachers' respect for her is not dependent on her 'being a good girl'. For the young adult a love relationship can often revolutionize the self-concept. A girl who has come to think of herself as both stupid and ugly will find such a self-concept severely challenged by a young man who both enjoys her conversation and finds her physically desirable. There are, of course, dangers in this situation, for if the man's ardour rapidly cools and he abandons her the young woman's negative self-concept may be mightily reinforced by this painful episode. Where love runs deep, however, the beloved may be enabled to rediscover contact with the organismic core of her being and to experience her own essential worth. For clients beginning therapy the most important fact initially is the entry of a new person (the therapist) into their psychological environment. As we shall see, it is the quality of this new person and the nature of the relationship which the therapist offers that will ultimately determine whether or not change will ensue.

Practice

Goals of therapy

The person-centred therapist seeks to establish a relationship with a client in which the latter can gradually dare to face the anxiety and confusion which inevitably arise once the self-concept is challenged by the movement into awareness of experiences which do not fit its current configuration. If such a relationship can be achieved the client can then hope to move beyond the confusion and gradually to experience the freedom to choose a way of being which approximates more closely to his or her deepest feelings and values. The therapist will therefore focus not on problems and solutions but on communion, or on what has been described as a person-in-person relationship (Boy and Pine, 1982: 129). Person-centred therapists do not hesitate to invest themselves freely and fully in the relationship with their clients. They believe that they will gain entrance into the world of the client through an emotional commitment in which they are willing to involve themselves as people and to reveal themselves, if appropriate, with their own strengths and weaknesses. For the person-centred therapist a primary goal is to see, feel and experience the world as the client sees, feels and experiences it and this is not possible if the therapist stands aloof and maintains a psychological distance in the interests of a quasi-scientific objectivity.

The theoretical end-point of person-centred therapy must be the fully func-tioning person who is the embodiment of psychological health and whose primary characteristics were outlined above. It would be fairly safe to assert that no client has achieved such an end-point and that no therapist has been in a position to model such perfection. On the other hand there is abundant evidence, not only from the USA but also, for example, from the extensive research activities of Reinhard Tausch and his colleagues at Hamburg University (Tausch, 1975) and of Germain Lietaer at the University of Leuven in Belgium (e.g. Lietaer, 1984), that clients undergoing person-centred therapy frequently demonstrate similar changes. From my own experience I can readily confirm the perception of client movement that Rogers and other person-centred practitioners have repeatedly noted. A listing of these perceptions will show that for many clients the achievement of any one of the developments recorded could well constitute a 'goal' of therapy and might for the time being at least constitute a valid and satisfactory reason for terminating therapy. Clients in person-centred therapy are often perceived to move, then, in the following directions:

1 away from façades and the constant preoccupation with keeping up appearances
2 away from 'oughts' and an internalized sense of duty springing from externally imposed obligations
3 away from living up to the expectations of others
4 towards valuing honesty and 'realness' in oneself and others
5 towards valuing the capacity to direct one's own life
6 towards accepting and valuing one's self and one's feelings whether they are positive or negative
7 towards valuing the experience of the moment and the process of growth rather than continually striving for objectives
8 towards a greater respect and understanding of others
9 towards a cherishing of close relationships and a longing for more intimacy
10 towards a valuing of all forms of experience and a willingness to risk being open to all inner and outer experiences however uncongenial or unexpected. (Frick, 1971: 179)

Selection criteria

Person-centred therapy has proved its effectiveness with clients of many kinds presenting a wide range of difficulties and concerns. Its usefulness even with psychotics was established many years ago when Rogers and his associates par-ticipated in an elaborate investigation of the effect of psychotherapy on schizo-phrenics. More recently the innovative work of Garry Prouty (1995) has extended the application of person-centred theory to what he calls pre-therapy with hospitalized patients many of whom are severely dysfunctional. Rogers himself, however, offered the opinion that psychotherapy of any kind, including person-centred therapy, is probably the greatest help to the people who are closest to a reasonable adjustment to life. It is my own belief that the limitations of person-centred therapy reside not in the approach itself but in the limitations of particular therapists and in their ability or lack of it to offer their clients the necessary conditions for change and development. Having said this I freely admit that in my own experience there are certain kinds of clients who are unlikely to be much helped by the approach. Such people are usually somewhat rigid and authoritarian in their attitude to life. They look for certainties, for secure structures and often for experts to direct them in how they should be and what they should do. Their craving for such direction often makes it difficult for them to relate to the person-centred therapist in such a way that they can begin to get in touch with their own inner resources. Overly intellectual or logically rational people may also find it difficult to engage in the kind of relationship encouraged by person-centred therapy, where often the greatest changes result from a preparedness to face painful and confusing feelings which cannot initially be clearly articulated. Clients falling into these categories often turn out to be poorly motivated in any case and not infrequently they have been referred in desperation by an overworked medical practitioner, priest or social worker. Inarticulacy is in itself no barrier to effective therapeutic work, for inarticulate people are often brimming over with un-expressed feeling which begins to pour out once a relationship of trust has been established.

Clients who perhaps have most to gain from person-centred therapy are those who are strongly motivated to face painful feelings and who are deeply committed to change. They are prepared to take emotional risks and they want to trust even if they are fearful of intimacy. In my own work I often ask myself three questions as I consider working with a prospective client:

- Is the client really desirous of change?
- Is the client prepared to share responsibility for our work together?
- Is the client willing to get in touch with his or her feelings, however difficult that may be?

Reassuring answers to these three questions are usually reliable indicators that person-centred therapy is likely to be beneficial.

The person-centred approach has made significant contributions to small group and large group work and the person-centred therapy group (with two therapists or 'facilitators') is a common modality. Clients who give evidence of at least some degree of self-acceptance and whose self-concept is not entirely negative may well be encouraged (but never obliged) to join a group from the outset. More commonly, however, membership of a counselling group will occur at the point when a client in individual therapy is beginning to experience a measure of self-affirmation and is keen to take further risks in relating. At such a stage membership of a group may replace individual therapy or may be undertaken concurrently. In all cases it is the client who will decide whether to seek group membership and whether or not this should replace or complement individual therapy.

The person-centred therapist will be at pains to ensure that a client whose self-concept is very low is not plunged into a group setting prematurely. Such an experience could have the disastrous outcome of reinforcing the client's sense of worthlessness. In such cases individual therapy is almost invariably indicated.

Person-centred therapists can work successfully with couples and with family groups but in these contexts much will depend on the therapist's ability to create the environment in which the couple or the family members can interact with each other without fear. In order for this to be possible it is likely that the therapist will undertake extensive preparatory work with each individual in a one-to-one relationship. Ultimately the principal criterion for embarking on couple or family therapy (apart, of course, from the willingness of all members to participate) is the therapist's confidence in his or her own ability to relate authentically to each member. (For further discussion of this issue see Mearns, 1994: 56–60.) Such confidence is unlikely to be achieved in the absence of in-depth preliminary meetings with each person involved. Indeed, in couple therapy it is common for the therapist to agree to work for a negotiated period with each partner separately before all three come together in order to tackle the relationship directly. With a family the process is clearly more complex and the preparatory work even more time-consuming. Perhaps this is the main reason why person-centred family therapy remains comparatively rare. In a sense it is therapists who select themselves for such work and not the clients who are selected.

Qualities of effective therapists

It has often been suggested that of all the various 'schools' of psychotherapy the person-centred approach makes the heaviest demands upon the therapist. Whether this is so or not I have no way of knowing. What I do know is that unless person-centred therapists can relate in such a way that their clients perceive them as trustworthy and dependable *as people*, therapy cannot take place. Person-centred therapists can have no recourse to diagnostic labelling nor can they find security in a complex and detailed theory of personality which will allow them to foster 'insight' in their clients through interpretation, however gently offered. In brief, they cannot win their clients' confidence by demonstrating their psychological expertise for to do so would be to place yet another obstacle in the way of clients' movement towards trusting their own innate resources. To be a trustworthy person is not something which can be simulated for long and in a very real sense person-centred therapists can only be as trustworthy for another as they are for themselves. Therapists' attitudes to themselves thus become of cardinal importance. If I am to be acceptant of another's feelings and experiences and to be open to the possible expression of material long since blocked off from awareness I must feel a deep level of acceptance for myself. If I cannot trust myself to acknowledge and accept my own feelings without adverse judgement or incapacitating self-recrimination it is unlikely that I shall appear sufficiently trustworthy to a client who may have much deeper cause to feel ashamed or worthless. If, too, I am in constant fear that I shall be overwhelmed by an upsurging of unacceptable data into my own awareness then I am unlikely to convey to my client that I am genuinely open to the full exploration of his or her own doubts and fears.

The ability of the therapist to be congruent, accepting and empathic (fundamental attitudes in person-centred therapy which will be explored more fully later) is not developed overnight. It is unlikely, too, that such an ability will be present in people who are not continually seeking to broaden their own life experience.

Therapists cannot confidently invite their clients to travel further than they have journeyed themselves, but for person-centred therapists the quality, depth and continuity of their own experiencing becomes the very cornerstone of the competence they bring to their professional activity. Unless I have a sense of my own continuing development as a person I shall lose faith in the process of becoming and shall be tempted to relate to my clients in a way which may well reinforce them in a past self-concept. What is more, I shall myself become stuck in a past image of myself and will no longer be in contact with the part of my organism which challenges me to go on growing as a person even if my body is beginning to show every sign of wearing out. It follows, too, that an excessive reliance on particular skills for relating or communicating can present a subtle trap because such skills may lead to a professional behavioural pattern which is itself resistant to change because it becomes set or stylized.

Therapeutic relationship and style

Person-centred therapists differ widely in therapeutic style. They have in common, however, a desire to create a relationship characterized by a climate in which clients begin to get in touch with their own wisdom and their capacity for self-understanding and for altering their self-concept and self-defeating behaviours. Person-centred therapists' ability to establish this climate is crucial to the whole therapeutic enterprise, since if they fail to do so there is no hope of forming the kind of relationship with their clients which will bring about the desired therapeutic movement. It will become apparent, however, that the way in which they attempt to create and convey the necessary climate will depend very much on the nature of their own personality.

The first element in the creation of the climate has to do with what has variously been called the therapist's *congruence*, realness, authenticity or genuineness. In essence this congruence depends on therapists' capacities for being properly in touch with the complexity of feelings, thoughts and attitudes which will be flowing through them as they seek to track their client's thoughts and feelings. The more they can do this the more they will be perceived by their clients as people of real flesh and blood who are willing to be seen and known and not as clinical professionals intent on concealing themselves behind a metaphorical white coat. The issue of the therapist's congruence is more complex than might initially appear. Although clients need to experience their therapists' essential humanity and to feel their emotional involvement they certainly do not need to have all the therapist's feelings and thoughts thrust down their throats. Therapists must not only attempt to remain firmly in touch with the flow of their own experience but must also have the discrimination to know how and when to communicate what they are experiencing. It is here that to the objective observer person-centred therapists might well appear to differ widely in style. In my own attempts to be congruent, for example, I find that verbally I often communicate little. I am aware, however, that my bodily posture does convey a deep willingness to be involved with my client and that my eyes are highly expressive of a wide range of feeling – often to the point of tears. It would seem that in my own case there is frequently little need for me to communicate my feelings verbally: I am transparent enough already and I know from experience that my clients are sensitive to this transparency. Another therapist might well behave in a manner far removed from mine but with the same concern to be congruent. Therapists are just as much unique human beings as their clients and the way in which they make their humanity available by following the flow of their own experiencing and communicating it when appropriate will be an expression of their own uniqueness. Whatever the precise form of their behaviour, however, person-centred therapists will be exercising their skill in order to communicate to their clients an attitude expressive of their desire to be deeply and fully involved in the relationship without pretence and without the protection of professional impersonality.

For many clients entering therapy, the second attitude of importance in creating a facilitative climate for change – *unconditional acceptance* – may seem to be the most critical. The conditions of worth which have in so many cases warped and undermined the self-concept of the client so that it bears little relation to the actualizing organism are the outcome of the judgmental and conditional attitudes of those close to the client, which have often been reinforced by societal or cultural norms. In contrast, the therapist seeks to offer the client an unconditional acceptance, a positive regard or caring, a non-possessive love. This acceptance is not of the person as she might become, a respect for her as yet unfulfilled potential, but a total and unconditional acceptance of the client as she seems to herself *in the present*. Such an attitude on the part of the therapist cannot be simulated and cannot be offered by someone who remains largely frightened or threatened by feelings in himself. Nor again can such acceptance be offered by someone who is disturbed when confronted by a person who possesses values, attitudes and feelings different from his own. Genuine acceptance is totally unaffected by differences of background or belief system between client and therapist, for it is in no way dependent on moral, ethical or social criteria. As with genuineness, however, the attitude of acceptance requires great skill on the part of the therapist if it is to be communicated at the depth which will enable clients to feel safe to be whatever they are currently experiencing. After what may well be a lifetime of highly conditional acceptance clients will not recognize unconditionality easily. When they do they will tend to regard it as an unlikely miracle which will demand continual checking out before it can be fully trusted. The way in which a therapist conveys unconditional acceptance will again be dependent to a large extent on the nature of his or her personality. For my own part I have found increasingly that the non-verbal aspects of my responsiveness are powerfully effective. A smile can often convey more acceptance than a statement which, however sensitive, may still run the risk of seeming patronizing. I have discovered, too, that the gentle pressing of the hand or the light touch on the knee will enable clients to realize that all is well and that there will be no judgement, however confused or negative they are or however silent and hostile.

The third facilitative attitude is that of *empathic understanding*. Rogers (1975) himself wrote extensively about empathy and suggested that of the three 'core conditions' (as genuineness, acceptance and empathy are often known), empathy is the most trainable. The crucial importance of empathic understanding springs from the person-centred therapist's overriding concern with the client's subjective perceptual world. Only through as full an understanding as possible of the way in which clients view themselves and the world can the therapist hope to encourage the subtle changes in self-concept which make for growth. Such understanding involves on the therapist's part a willingness to enter the private perceptual world of the client and to become thoroughly conversant with it. This demands a high degree of sensitivity to the moment-to-moment experiencing of the client so that the therapist is recognized as a reliable companion even when contradictory feelings follow on each other in rapid succession. In a certain sense therapists must lay themselves aside for the time being with all their prejudices and values if they are to enter into the perceptual world of the other. Such an undertaking would be foolhardy if the therapist feels insecure in the presence of a particular client for there would be the danger of getting lost in a perhaps frightening or confusing world. The task of empathic understanding can be accomplished only by people who are secure enough in their own identity to move into another's world without the fear of being overwhelmed by it. Once there, therapists have to move around with extreme delicacy and with an utter absence of judgement. They will probably sense meanings of which the client is scarcely aware and might even become dimly aware of feelings of which there is no consciousness on the part of the client at all. Such moments call for extreme caution for there is the danger that the therapist could express understanding at too deep a level and frighten the client away from therapy altogether. Rogers, on a recording made for *Psychology Today* in the 1970s, described such a blunder as 'blitz therapy' and contrasted this with an empathic response which is constructive because it conveys an understanding of what is currently going on in the client and of meanings that are just below the level of awareness but does not slip over into unconscious motivations which frighten the client.

If the communication of congruence and acceptance presents difficulties, the communication of empathic understanding is even more challenging. Often a client's inner world is complex and confusing as well as a source of pain and guilt. Sometimes clients have little understanding of their own feelings. Therapists often need to marshal the full range of their emotional and cognitive abilities if they are to convey their understanding thoroughly. On the other hand, if they do not succeed there is ample evidence to suggest that their very attempt to do so, however bumbling and incomplete, will be experienced by the client as supportive and validating. What is always essential is the therapist's willingness to check out the accuracy of his or her understanding. I find that my own struggles at communicating empathic understanding are littered with such questions as 'Am I getting it right? Is that what you mean?' When I do get a complex feeling right the effect is often electrifying and the sense of wonder and thankfulness in the client can be one of the most moving experiences in therapy. There can be little doubt that the rarity of empathic understanding of this kind is what endows it with such power and makes it the most reliable force for creative change in the whole of the therapeutic process.

It was Rogers's contention – and he held firm to it for over 40 years – that if the therapist proves able to offer a relationship where congruence, acceptance and empathy are all present, then therapeutic movement will almost invariably occur. Towards the end of his life, however, he pointed to another quality which he saw not as additional to the core conditions but as sometimes resulting from their consistent application. This he called 'presence' and having first called attention to it in *A Way of Being* (Rogers, 1980: 129) he returned to it in an article published shortly before his death (Rogers, 1986). He talks of 'presence' in terms which seem somewhat at variance with the pragmatic, hard-headed tone of the scientific scholar of earlier years but I have come to see this later statement as capturing the essence of the therapeutic relationship when it is functioning at its most effective level.

Rogers wrote:

> When I am at my best, as a group facilitator or a therapist, I discover another characteristic. I find that when I am closest to my inner, intuitive self, when I am somehow in touch with the unknown in me, when perhaps I am in a slightly altered state of consciousness in the relationship, then whatever I do seems to be full of healing. Then simply my *presence* is releasing and helpful. There is nothing I can do to force this experience, but when I can relax and be close to the transcendental core of me, then I may behave in strange and impulsive ways in the relationship, ways which I cannot justify rationally, which have nothing to do with my thought processes. But these strange behaviours turn out to be *right*, in some odd way. At those moments it seems that my inner spirit has reached out and touched the inner spirit of the other. (Rogers, 1986: 199)

It is my own belief that the therapist's ability to be 'present' in this way is dependent on his or her capacity to be fearlessly alongside the client's experience even to the extent of being willing on occasions *not* to understand what is occurring in the client's world (Mearns, 1994: 5–9). Such a capacity is likely to develop in a relationship where counsellor and client have established a deep level of trust and where mutuality is increasingly possible (see following section). It explains, too, why the most fruitful relationships will be characterized by a developing ability on the part of both counsellor and client to move between different levels of experiencing with ease and confidence. As therapy proceeds, seriousness and humour, for example, will alternate and the pattern of interactivity will shift frequently as client and counsellor adopt, by turns, more active or passive roles. Furthermore a therapist's way of being fully present to his or her client is again likely to be indicative of the particular and unique personality of the therapist. I find that when I am able to be totally present in the moment this releases in me a quality which I have defined as 'tenderness' (Thorne, 1985, 1991). This in turn enables me to live with paradoxes and gives me the will to wait in hope when I am feeling powerless. With Rogers, who later in the same article acknowledges that his account 'partakes of the mystical' and goes on to speak of 'this mystical, spiritual dimension', I am persuaded that the relationship in person-centred therapy is at its most liberating and transforming when it 'transcends itself and becomes part of something larger' (Rogers, 1986: 199).

Major therapeutic strategies and techniques

There are no strategies or techniques which are integral to person-centred therapy. The approach is essentially based on the experiencing and communication of attitudes, and these attitudes cannot be packaged up in techniques. At an earlier point in the history of the approach there was an understandable emphasis on the ebb and flow of the therapeutic interview and much was gained from the microscopic study of client–therapist exchanges. To Rogers's horror, however, the tendency to focus on the therapist's responses had the effect of so debasing the approach that it became known as a technique. Even nowadays it is possible to meet people who believe that person-centred therapy is simply the technique of reflecting the client's feelings or, worse still, that it is primarily a matter of repeating the last words spoken by the client. I hope I have shown that nothing could be further from the truth. The attitudes required of the therapist demand the highest level of self-knowledge and self-acceptance and the translation of them into communicable form requires of each therapist the most delicate skill, which for the most part must spring from his or her unique personality and cannot be learned through pale imitations of Carl Rogers or anyone else.

In *Person-Centred Counselling in Action* (Mearns and Thorne, 1988) attention is drawn to the fact that the most productive outcomes seem to result from therapeutic relationships which move through three distinct phases. The first stage is characterized by the establishing of *trust* on the part of the client. This may happen very rapidly or it can take months. The second stage sees the development of *intimacy*: during this stage the client is enabled to reveal some of the deepest levels of his or her experiencing. The third stage is characterized by an increasing *mutuality* between therapist and client. When such a stage is reached it is likely that therapists will be increasingly self-disclosing and will be challenged to risk more of themselves in the relationship. When it occurs this three-stage process becomes so deeply rewarding for the therapist that a cynical critic might view it as the outcome of an unconscious strategizing on the therapist's part. So insidious is this accusation that I am now deeply concerned to monitor my own behaviour with the utmost vigilance in order to ensure that I am *not* embarked on a manipulatory plot aimed at achieving a spurious mutuality which may be deeply satisfying for me but quite irrelevant to the client's needs. Furthermore, the realization that person-centred therapy at its best may give access to a quality of relating which embraces the spiritual raises important questions about the counsellor's fitness for such a task and the personal discipline that this implies (Thorne, 1994). In an approach which explicitly turns its back on strategies and techniques as being contrived and potentially abusive of a client's autonomy, it becomes of the utmost importance that the therapist is preserved from self-deception, not only by the challenge of rigorous supervision but also by the willing acceptance of a discipline which has as its aim the most thorough integration of belief and practice. Without such integration the person-centred therapist runs the risk of mouthing and peddling the core conditions as if they were little more than behavioural conditions to be applied mechanically by a psychological technician after a few hours' 'skills training'. Such a travesty of the approach has led in the past to the ill-informed notion that person-centred therapy is 'easy' or that it can be useful *as a technique* in the early stages of therapy before more sophisticated and effective methods are introduced (Mearns and Thorne, 1988: 5).

The change process in therapy

When person-centred therapy goes well clients will move from a position where their self-concept, typically poor at the entry into therapy and finding expression in behaviour which is reinforcing of the negative evaluation of self, will shift to a position where it more closely reflects the essential worth of the self. As the self-concept moves towards a more positive view so, too, clients' behaviour begins to mirror the improvement and to enhance their perception of themselves. The therapist's ability to create a relationship in which the three facilitative attitudes are consistently present will to a large extent determine the extent to which clients are able to move towards a more positive contact with the promptings of the actualizing tendency.

If therapy has been successful clients will also have learned how to be their own therapist. It seems that when people experience the genuineness of another and a real attentive caring and valuing by that other person they begin to adopt the same attitude towards themselves. In short, a person who is cared for begins to feel at a deep level that perhaps she is after all *worth* caring for. In a similar way, the experience of being on the receiving end of the concentrated listening and the empathic understanding which characterize the therapist's response tends to develop a listening attitude in the client towards herself. It is as if she gradually becomes less afraid to get in touch with what is going on inside her and dares to listen attentively to her own feelings. With this growing attentiveness comes increased self-understanding and a tentative grasp of some of her most central personal meanings. Many clients have told me that after person-centred therapy they never lose this ability to treat themselves with respect and to take the risk of listening to what they are experiencing. If they do lose it temporarily or find themselves becoming hopelessly confused they will not hesitate to return to therapy to engage once more in a process which is in many ways an education for living.

In Rogers and Dymond (1954) one of Rogers's chapters explores in detail a client's successful process through therapy. The case of Mrs Oak has become a rich source of learning for person-centred therapists ever since, and towards the end of the chapter Rogers attempts a summary of the therapeutic process which Mrs Oak has experienced with such obvious benefits to herself. What is described there seems to me to be so characteristic of the person-centred experience of therapy that I make no apology for providing a further summary of some of Rogers's findings.

The process begins with the therapist providing an atmosphere of warm caring and acceptance which over the first few sessions is gradually experienced by the client, Mrs Oak, as genuinely *safe*. With this realization the client finds that she changes the emphasis of her sessions from dealing with reality problems to experiencing herself. The effect of this change of emphasis is that she begins to experience her feelings in the immediate present without inhibition. She can be angry, hurt, childish, joyful, self-deprecating, self-appreciative and as she allows this to occur she discovers many feelings bubbling through into awareness of which she was not previously conscious. With new feelings there come new thoughts and the admission of all this fresh material to awareness leads to a *breakdown of the previously held self-concept*. There then follows a period of disorganization and confusion although there remains a feeling that the path is the right one and that reorganization will ultimately take place. What is being learned during this process is that it pays to recognize an experience for what it is rather than denying it or distorting it. In this way the client becomes more open to experience and begins to realize that it is healthy to accept feelings whether they be positive or negative, for this permits a movement towards greater completeness. At this stage the client gradually comes to realize that *she can begin to define herself and does not have to accept the definition and judgements of others*. There is, too, a more conscious appreciation of the nature of the relationship with the therapist and the value of a love which is not possessive and makes no demands. At about this stage the client finds that she can make relationships outside of therapy which enable others to be self-experiencing and self-directing and she becomes progressively aware that at the core of her being she is not destructive but genuinely desires the well-being of others. Self-responsibility continues to increase to the point where the client feels able to make her own choices – although this is not always pleasant – and to trust herself in a world which, although it may often seem to be disintegrating, yet offers many opportunities for creative activity and relating (Rogers, 1954). I would add that for those clients who repeatedly experience those moments in therapy where 'inner spirit touches inner spirit' there is a strong likelihood that their sense of the numinous will be awakened or rekindled and that the search for meaning will be strengthened. Not infrequently clients towards the end of therapy report a new acknowledgement of spiritual reality which in some cases leads to a re-engagement with previously rejected religious observances or, more often, to the exploration of hitherto uncharted spiritual terrain.

Person-centred therapy is essentially an approach to the human condition based on trust. There is trust in the innate resourcefulness of human beings, given the right conditions, to find their own way through life. There is trust that the direction thus found will be positive and creative. There is trust, too, that the process of relating between counsellor and client will in itself provide the primary context of safety and nurture in which the client can face the pain of alienation from his or her own true self and move towards a more integrated way of being. Where blocks occur in therapeutic process they can almost invariably be traced back to a lack or loss of trust on the part of client or counsellor or both in the basic premises of the approach, and more particularly in the essentially healing process of the thera-peutic relationship. In many instances where the lack of trust is firmly lodged in the client, the person-centred therapist has the unenviable but clear task of learning to wait, of exercising patience while committing himself or herself to the consistent offering of the core conditions in the face of the client's fear, hostility or increasing pain. The situation is potentially more grave when the lack of trust resides in the therapist. He or she doubts his or her capacity to offer the core conditions to this particular client and is consumed with a fear of mounting failure. In such a situation, where supervision fails to resolve the stuckness, the therapist has no option but to address the issues with the client, not knowing whether this will herald movement forward or the end of the relationship. An ebbing of trust in the relationship itself can often be guarded against by an agreement at the outset between therapist and client to review their process periodically *as a matter of course*. Such 'stocktaking' facilitates an openness between counsellor and client which ensures that difficulties and doubts are not allowed to fester but can be faced squarely and in this way serve to strengthen rather than undermine the therapeutic relationship. This practice also reinforces the essentially shared nature of the therapeutic work. It offers the client the opportunity, as therapy proceeds, to invite the therapist to respond in new ways. Not infrequently, for example, clients wish to enlist the therapist's support in implementing new behaviours which are more in keeping with their changing self-concept and greater confidence. Progress can be unnecessarily impeded if in such instances clients believe that the therapist is interested solely in their state of being and is not concerned to help initiate action or to involve others in their development. Regular stocktaking will ensure that such misconceptions are rapidly dispelled. Would that such a practice was commonly adopted by married couples and others in close relationships!

Limitations of the approach

After 27 years as a person-centred therapist I am drawn to the conclusion, as I stated earlier, that the limitations of the approach are a reflection of the personal limitations of the therapist. As these will clearly vary from individual to individual and are unlikely to be constant over time I am sceptical about the usefulness of exploring the limitations of the approach in any generalized fashion. None the less I am intrigued by the question with respect to two particular issues. I believe that person-centred therapy has been in danger of selling itself short because of its traditional emphasis on the 'here and now' and because of what is seen as its heavy reliance on verbal interaction. Both these tendencies are likely to be reinforced when the therapist's congruence remains at a relatively superficial level.

In my own practice I have discovered that the more I am able to be fully present to myself in the therapeutic relationship the more likely it is that I shall come to trust the promptings of a deeper and more intuitive level within myself. Cautiously and with constant safeguards against self-deception I have come to value this intuitive part of my being and to discover its efficacy in the therapeutic relationship (for a further discussion of this issue see Thorne, 1991: 82–106). What is more, when I have risked articulating a thought or feeling which emanates from this deeper level I have done so in the knowledge that it may appear unconnected to what is currently happening in the relationship or even bizarre to my client. More often than not, however, the client's response has been immediate and sometimes dramatic. It is as if the quality of the relationship which has been established, thanks to the consistent offering of the core conditions, goes a long way towards ensuring that my own intuitive promptings are deeply and immediately significant for the client. Often, too, the significance lies in the triggering of past experience for the client – not in the sense simply of locating memories of past events but in releasing a veritable flow of feeling whose origin lies in past experience which is then vividly relived. Commonly, too, the therapist's intuitive response seems to touch a part of the client's being which cannot find immediate expression in words. I am astonished how often at such moments the client reaches out for physical reassurance or plunges into deep but overflowing silence in which new movement is mysteriously generated.

There are many in the person-centred tradition whose frustration with the essentially verbal nature of the therapy has led them to supplement the approach with methods culled from other disciplines (e.g. Tausch, 1990). Rogers's own daughter, Natalie, has pioneered an approach she calls person-centred expressive therapy (Rogers, 1993) which incorporates movement, art, music, pottery and creative writing as well as other essentially non-verbal channels of expression. Eugene Gendlin has developed the method of focusing for deepening inner experience (Gendlin, 1981). I do not myself believe that the future of the approach lies in these directions, fascinating and impressive as they are, especially the work of Gendlin which has evolved into what is now known as experiential psychotherapy. I am increasingly convinced that it is in the area of therapist congruence that the greatest advances can and should be made. The person-centred tradition's most precious gift to the world of therapy is its tested belief in the capacity of one human being to offer another a relationship of such quality that transformation can occur – and this without recourse to techniques, the imposition of behavioural or cognitive programmes or the exploration of complex unconscious processes. My hope is that person-centred practitioners will be emboldened to explore ever more deeply the implications of this transformative capacity of a relationship which derives its power from the therapist's ability to be accepting, empathic and congruent. Rogers discovered towards the end of his life that simply his presence could have an impact on others which he had not previously conceptualized. He found, in effect, that to be congruent was a continuing challenge to his own integrity and trust in life. It is on the future response to that challenge that the further development of person-centred therapy must ultimately depend.

Case example

The client

Peter, a student in his late twenties, first presented himself to me in the early autumn. He had just begun his training as a youth worker and as soon as he entered the room it was evident that he was in considerable distress. He told me that he had little faith in counselling, having had a previous bad experience, but that he had come at the insistence of one of his course colleagues who was concerned about him. His eyes filled with tears as he acknowledged that he was feeling desperate. He was growing convinced that he had made a disastrous mistake in coming into higher education and embarking upon youth work training. He felt academically inadequate and, unlike many of his colleagues, he had no faith in his capacity to respond to others in distress. He also appeared angry with the course tutors for having admitted him to the course in the first place. He believed that they had been fooled at interview and had been too readily convinced that his previous experience as a volunteer part-time youth worker was adequate preparation for a career in professional youth work. He seemed to be saying that they should have realized that he was both stupid and emotionally inadequate.

The therapy

During the opening minutes I was powerfully struck by Peter's almost total self-denigration. His physical appearance mirrored his words. He was wearing tattered jeans and a rumpled shirt and jacket. His hair and short beard looked unkempt and he was painfully thin. He rolled himself a straggly cigarette after the first couple of minutes and did not look me in the eye. Within myself I experienced deep compassion for him and felt an immediate engagement. Somewhat to my own surprise I found myself saying 'I'm glad you've come.' This congruent remark – for it reflected the strong feeling uppermost within me – had the effect of making Peter burst into tears. He wept uncontrollably for five minutes while I plied him tactfully with tissues. In the presence of another's distress it is not easy to stay in touch with the flow of one's own experiencing but the person-centred counsellor has an obligation to do this to the best of his or her ability. While Peter wept, I was all but overwhelmed by visions of young people (with gaunt faces and tattered clothes) sleeping rough under viaducts in London. They were the abandoned ones, the outcasts who had lost all self-respect. For me in those moments Peter had joined them: the potential youth worker had, in my imagination, become one of his future clients. The sense of Peter, the outcast, remained powerfully with me and yet it is difficult to trust such metaphors when they may be no more than the fantasies of a fevered imagination. I waited for Peter's tears to subside and then remembered that he had had a bad experience of counselling before: it seemed imperative that I did not promise more than I could deliver and yet I wanted to offer my commitment: 'I don't know how I can be of help but I want you to know that I will do my best to be alongside you in all this. It seems very dark and lonely for you at the moment.' I do not know if these were my exact words but I remember seeking to convey my understanding of his dereliction while at the same time making a clear statement about my preparedness not to abandon him. I suppose if I had been thinking in theoretical terms – which I was not – I would have been intent on establishing the core conditions as rapidly as possible so that Peter could experience at least a modicum of safety in my presence.

In the remainder of this first session and in the second a few days later Peter was able to tell me much of his story. He was a 'self-made man' who, having been thrown out of his parental home as an adolescent, ostensibly for playing truant and smoking cannabis, had eventually found a job in a neighbouring town with a company of sports outfitters. He had proved himself to be exceptionally talented at the work and quickly developed not only an encyclopaedic knowledge of sports equipment of all kinds but considerable financial and managerial acumen. A couple of years later he was appointed manager of a store in the West Country, fell in love with a local girl, married her and within a year they had their first child, a girl called Beth. The birth of the child seemed, in retrospect, to mark a change in his fortunes. He remembered difficulties with the staff in the store, an escalation of responsibilities and the slide into workaholism. At home he felt displaced by his daughter and became increasingly short tempered and uncooperative. One night his wife could bear it no longer and told him that she wanted to leave him. He went berserk and physically attacked her. Full of remorse, he pleaded with her in the weeks that followed and they sought help from a marriage guidance counsellor. For Peter this was a disastrous experience as he was made to feel guilty and inadequate. One night when he arrived home he found the house deserted. From that moment Peter's life disintegrated. He resigned from his job before he was sacked and for many months he was unemployed and desperate. Gradually, however, with a supreme effort of will, he began to rebuild his life while his wife instituted divorce proceedings. It was during this period that he began to assist at the local youth club and although he eventually found another job managing a jewellery shop he knew that he wished to do something different with his life. Although he had right of access to his daughter he had not seen her for many years because of his former wife's violent objection to the court order.

Peter's recounting of the story was articulate enough although there were times when he could scarcely bear to hear his own words. The initial sessions were much concerned, however, with his feelings about the course and whether or not he could survive. These were real issues because he was finding great difficulty writing essays and had already panicked about going for an interview with the man who was to be his first placement supervisor. So pressing were these concerns that two whole sessions were taken up with discussing an essay topic and rehearsing the dreaded interview. For the person-centred counsellor there is no incongruency in accompanying the client in this way. To avoid pressing issues in the interests of 'deeper' matters is to deny the client's right to determine the agenda. In fact, Peter's successful meeting with his placement supervisor was followed by the first glimmer of self-respect in his demeanour. I noticed that his clothes had been ironed and that he was wearing what looked like a new tie. With this 'self-made' man it seemed important, too, that I did not withhold companionship from him in the working out of strategies to deal with the urgent realities of his current existence.

As Peter experienced the beginnings of self-confidence in his academic work he was able to revisit the past which he had sketched out initially. He showed an increasing preparedness to face feelings inside himself and to give them full expression. This capacity to experience past feelings in the present moment is characteristic of the client in person-centred therapy once the therapeutic climate has been established, and the level of Peter's motivation was such that he plunged into both intolerable pain and, at times, incandescent anger. This 'reliving' of the past made work with him at this stage exceptionally demanding. I found myself caught up on an emotional rollercoaster and the unpredictability of Peter's inner exploration was at times frightening. His anger blinded him to the present reality and I was often the target for his rage as he accused me of despising him for his weakness or stupidity or even of mocking his tears.

I was as aware as any psychodynamic therapist that so-called transference phenomena were in play and that I was to some extent 'doubling' for his parents, his wife and other judgmental figures from the past. Such 'knowledge', however, can serve to distance me from a client and this I was determined to avoid. I did my best to receive Peter's outbursts and unjust accusations non-defensively, but without accepting their validity. In such a situation my acceptance, empathy and congruence were involved in a complex dance as I stayed alongside Peter without succumbing to his anger but without at the same time ducking behind the protective shield of 'the transference'. There were times when I felt exceptionally vulnerable and even feared for my physical safety. I was strengthened by my unshakeable belief that it is through relationship that past wounds are healed and that those who are temporarily blinded by pain or anger can only achieve clear vision by the refusal of the other to withdraw or diminish the quality of their presence. With Peter I was rewarded towards the end of the third month of our work together. One day, as he spoke of the terrible pain of separation from his daughter, he caught sight of the tears in my eyes. It was a moment when 'spirit touched spirit'. He stopped in mid-sentence and reached out for my hand: 'You really care, don't you?' he said. I nodded and we sat in silence for what must have been a good ten minutes. I knew after that deep silence that all was well and all would be well.

A few weeks later I made a monumental mistake. Peter was going away on his placement and would be in a town some 50 miles distant. Clearly our sessions could not continue during this time and I was much exercised about how best he could be supported during what was to be a two-month period. Foolishly, instead of voicing my anxiety and exploring the situation with Peter, I announced that I could arrange support from another counsellor in the placement town if he would like that. As soon as I had uttered the words I knew I had blundered. The mistake was serious, for Peter's self-concept was in a precarious state of change. Throughout his life he had seen himself as essentially stupid, unlovable and doomed to rejection. In the previous weeks this self-concept had been thrown into disarray by my commitment to him, my evident regard for his intelligence and most importantly, my manifest caring for and about him. For a minute or two after my offer of another counsellor, Peter was silent but then it became obvious that he was angry. Fortunately I was able to catch the feeling as it emerged. 'Peter, you're angry with me. I'm so very sorry. I realize I've made a dreadful mistake.' He visibly relaxed and his anger subsided to be replaced by a sad smile. By failing to respect Peter's capacity to order his own life, my proposal, born of genuine concern for him, had conveyed rejection, a vote of no confidence in him and had in addition all but undermined his confidence in my commitment to him. The incident reinforced for me the fragility of a self-concept in transition and how carefully it needs to be cherished.

Peter's placement was largely successful although there were several moments of self-doubt about which he poured himself out in letters to me. On his return, there gradually took place a shift in the power dynamic between us. I noticed that he no longer referred much to the past but was more concerned to see me as the person I am. He confessed that he had been reading some of my books and on one occasion we spent a whole hour exploring theological issues which had been triggered for him by something I had written. I found myself looking forward to our sessions as they progressively became a source of stimulation for me. The development of mutuality was clearly proceeding apace and I began to fear that I was in danger of spinning out Peter's therapy because I was enjoying it rather than because it was any longer necessary for his well-being. It struck me one day, however, as Peter was discussing his work with a particularly deprived client, that it was perhaps important for him that I should know that he now possessed the inner strength to offer others what initially he had required of me. He, too, needed to experience the mutuality and to live within this newly crafted relationship for a while. In fact it was several weeks later before he eventually raised the issue of terminating and then he did so with great clarity and precision: 'I should like to go on for a further six weeks,' he said. 'By then I shall be well into my final placement and I reckon I'll have got the message that I don't have to do everything on my own.' Six weeks later we met for the last time. He was studying Winnicott in preparation for his dissertation. He thanked me for being a *good enough* counsellor and gave me a hug as he left.

References

Boy, A.V. and Pine, G.J. (1982) *Client-centered Counseling: A Renewal*. Boston, MA: Allyn & Bacon.

Burn, M. (1956) *Mr Lyward's Answer*. London: Hamish Hamilton.

Frick, W.B. (1971) *Humanistic Psychology: Interviews with Maslow, Murphy and Rogers*. Columbus, OH: Charles E. Merrill.

Gendlin, E. (1981) *Focusing*. New York: Bantam Books.

Kirschenbaum, H. (1979) *On Becoming Carl Rogers*. New York: Delacorte Press.

Lietaer, G. (1984) 'Unconditional positive regard: a controversial basic attitude in client-centred therapy', in R. Levant and J. Shlien (eds), *Client-Centred Therapy and the Person-Centred Approach*. New York: Praeger. pp. 41–58.

Mearns, D. (1994) *Developing Person-Centred Counselling*. London: Sage.

Mearns, D. and Thorne, B.J. (1988) *Person-Centred Counselling in Action*. London: Sage.

Nelson-Jones, R. (1982) *The Theory and Practice of Counseling Psychology*. London: Holt, Rinehart & Winston.

Nelson-Jones, R. (1995) *The Theory and Practice of Counselling Psychology*, 2nd edition. London: Cassell.

Oatley, K. (1981) 'The self with others: the person and the interpersonal context in the approaches of C.R. Rogers and R.D. Laing', in F. Fransella (ed.), *Personality*. London: Methuen.

Prouty, G.F. (1995) *Theoretical Evolutions in Person-centered/Experiential Therapy*. Westport, CT: Praeger.

Rogers, C.R. (1954) 'The case of Mrs Oak: a research analysis', in C.R. Rogers and R.F. Dymond (eds), *Psychology and Personality Change*. Chicago, IL: University of Chicago Press.

Rogers, C.R. (1961) *On Becoming a Person*. Boston, MA: Houghton-Mifflin.

Rogers, C.R. (1974) 'In retrospect: forty-six years', *American Psychologist* 29(2): 115–23.

Rogers, C.R. (1975) 'Empathic: an unappreciated way of being', *The Counseling Psychologist*, 2: 2–10.

Rogers, C.R. (1979) 'The foundations of the person-centred approach', unpublished manuscript. La Jolla, CA.

Rogers, C.R. (1980) *A Way of Being*. Boston, MA: Houghton-Mifflin.

Rogers, C.R. (1986) 'A client-centered/person-centered approach to therapy', in I. Kutash and A. Wolf (eds), *Psychotherapist's Casebook*. San Francisco: Jossey-Bass. pp. 197–208.

Rogers, C.R. and Dymond, R.F. (eds) (1954) *Psychology and Personality Change*. Chicago, IL: University of Chicago Press.

Rogers, N. (1993) *The Creative Connection*. San Francisco: Science and Behavior Books.

Tausch, R. (1975) 'Ergebnisse und Prozesse der klienten-zentrierten Gesprächspsychotherapie bei 500 Klienten und 115 Psychotherapeuten. Eine Zusammenfassung des Hamburger Forschungsprojektes', *Zeitschrift für praktische Psychologie*, 13: 293–307.

Tausch, R. (1990) 'The supplementation of client-centred communication therapy with other validated therapeutic methods: a client centered necessity', in G. Lietaer, J. Rombauts and R. van Balen (eds), *Client-Centered and Experiential Psychotherapy in the Nineties*. Leuven: Leuven University Press. pp. 448–55.

Thorne, B.J. (1985) *The Quality of Tenderness*. Norwich: Norwich Centre Occasional Publications.

Thorne, B.J. (1991) *Person-centred Counselling: Therapeutic and Spiritual Dimensions*. London: Whurr.

Thorne, B.J. (1994) 'Developing a spiritual discipline', in D. Mearns, *Developing Person-centred Counselling*. London: Sage. pp. 44–7.

Suggested further reading

Kirschenbaum, H. and Henderson, V.L. (eds) (1990) *The Carl Rogers Reader*. London: Constable.

Mearns, D. and Thorne, B.J. (1988) *Person-centred Counselling in Action*. London: Sage.

Rogers, C.R. (1951) *Client-centred Therapy*. Boston, MA: Houghton-Mifflin.

Rogers, C.R. (1961) *On Becoming a Person*. Boston, MA: Houghton-Mifflin.

Thorne, B.J. (1992) *Carl Rogers*. London: Sage.

7

Personal Construct Therapy
Fay Fransella and Peggy Dalton

Historical context and development in Britain

Historical context

George A. Kelly, the creator of the psychology of personal constructs (1955, 1991), was not a man of his time. He was a revolutionary thinker who had dreams of what the psychological study of human beings should be like. These dreams were in direct contrast with the current psychological ethos of behaviourism. His ideas expressed in the philosophy of *constructive alternativism* can be traced back to the dim distant past, as can those of his contemporary, Jean Piaget. It was largely the approach of these two men that triggered off the interest, starting in the 1980s, in the philosophical approach of 'constructivism'.

This approach to the study of human beings is in direct conflict with the science of the past. No longer are there facts to be found and truths to be gleaned. All we can hope to do is come to a 'best guess' that what we now know will be superseded by a better 'best guess' in due course. One important philosopher who elaborated this view was Immanuel Kant (1724–1804). He said there was no way in which we could see the 'true' event (the noumena); the best we could do was to see things through our 'mind's eye' (the phenomena). In Kelly's terms, 'there are always alternative ways of looking at any event'. We each live in our own personal world although we may, of course, share many of our perceptions of events if we come from the same culture or the same family.

Another important aspect of Kelly's theory that stems from earlier philosophers is that we act upon our world rather than respond to it as the behaviourists would have us do. We are actors, we create our lives and can therefore re-create them if we find ourselves not to our own liking. We are also forms of motion. We are alive, and one aspect of living matter is that it is always on the move. What needs explaining is why we behave as we do. Here Kelly took behaviour, described by the behaviourists as a response *to* something, and made it into a question. That is, we make sense of our world by applying to it the personal constructs we have created in the past. These personal constructs are our mini-theories about how things are. In this way we can predict what may happen as the result of some action. Having made a prediction that, say, this client has normal hearing, we put this prediction to the test *by behaving* 'as if' this client could hear what was being said. Now, that prediction may be correct or incorrect, but the behaviour was asking the question, 'Am I right in thinking this person can hear well enough?'

Kelly received his PhD in psychology – with particular emphasis on physiology – in the early 1930s. He became professor and director of clinical psychology at Ohio State University in 1946. In order to gain a fuller insight into the context in which his ideas developed it is important to know something of his earlier studies:

in 1926 he obtained a BA degree in physics and mathematics, later a Master's degree in educational sociology, and in 1930 a Bachelor of Education degree at Edinburgh University.

His university courses in physics and mathematics took place around the time when Einstein's ideas were shaking the world of science, as were those of quantum mechanics. With this early training, it comes as no surprise to find that Kelly's model of the person is couched in the language of science, as is his whole theory (see Fransella, 1984, for a more detailed discussion of how training in physics may have influenced Kelly's theorizing). But Kelly's is a science based on the philosophy of constructive alternativism: a science in which there are no 'facts', only support for current hypotheses. These hypotheses may lead to others, which encompass new events, and so on. At some infinite moment in time we may learn all there is to know about the universe, for there *is* a reality 'out there'; but this is unlikely since the universe, like the person, is in a constant state of motion.

Development in Britain

George Kelly, an American, found receptive readers first and foremost in Britain. He thought that the amount of attention given to his theory by British psychologists would determine whether his work would stand or fall. Only in the 1980s has there been a quickening of interest in his work in its country of origin. Neimeyer (1983) has described its development in the context of the sociology of science. He uses Mullins's (1973) model of the sociohistorical development of new theory groups, which focuses on the changing patterns of communication.

The development of personal construct theory goes, according to Neimeyer, something like this. Before and for some time after the publication of Kelly's *magnum opus, The Psychology of Personal Constructs*, in 1955, he and others worked largely in isolation, However, by 1966 workers in Britain had attained a 'cluster' status; that is, local groups with a minimum of seven people had developed and there had been a publication explosion. The major force behind the development of interest in the theory in Britain was the lecturing and publications of Don Bannister.

Neimeyer finds that by 1972 the major clusters in Britain were beginning to dissolve and that personal construct theory was steadily establishing itself as a mature speciality; by contrast, America and the rest of Europe only started to enter the cluster stage of development in the 1980s.

Up to 1978 there was surprisingly little work published on the application of personal construct psychology (PCP) to psychotherapy – surprising since this is its 'focus of convenience'. But things have changed, and the quantity of publications in the therapy field is now considerable. Interest in Kelly's theory and philosophy is worldwide. National conferences take place in Australia, the United States, Germany and Britain independently of the biennial international congresses that were started in 1975. The first centre devoted solely to teaching, therapy and the general application of personal construct theory was set up in London in 1982 by Fay Fransella.

Theoretical assumptions

Image of the person

Kelly suggests we might look at the person 'as if' you and I were scientists. By this he meant that we could all be seen as doing the same sorts of things that scientists traditionally do. We have theories about why things happen; erect hypotheses derived from these theories; and put these hypotheses to the test to see whether the predictions arising from them are validated or invalidated. We test our predictions by behaving. Viewing all behaviour 'as if' it were an experiment is one of Kelly's unique contributions to our understanding of the person.

We approach the world not as it *is* but as it appears to us to be; we gaze at our world through our construing *goggles*. We make predictions about events constantly and continually – there is no let-up. We are active beings, 'forms of motion'.

Kelly suggests that we might come to understand ourselves and others, in psychological terms, by studying the personal constructs we have each evolved to discriminate between events and to help us predict those events in the future. Construing is not all going on in the head, though; we construe just as much with our bodies as with our minds. Kelly gives as an example our digestive system. Our stomach anticipates food, secretes gastric juices, behaves toward what it receives in an accepting manner if the food is in line with expectation, or rejects the food if it is not up to expectation, and so forth. Kelly considered dualistic thinking a hindrance to our understanding of the person. At any given moment it is just as appropriate to ask what a person is feeling as what he is thinking, for many constructs (discriminations between events) have either been formed before we have formulated the words to express them or have never acquired verbal labels. Personal construct theory is thus very much a theory of human experiencing.

For example, a young child may discriminate between types of voice – a harsh, grating voice and a soft, smooth one. The harsh, grating voice is related to feelings of reassurance, a large body to snuggle up to, and is there before the child goes to bed. The soft, smooth one gives conflicting messages: sometimes it is comforting like the harsh, grating one, but at other times – often when it is *particularly* soft and smooth – there are feelings of unease, of all not being well. Later, as an adult, that person may never be able to put into words exactly why he cannot abide women who have soft, smooth voices and why he himself has developed a harsh, grating one. His pre-verbal construing is being applied in adult life.

Conceptualization of psychological disturbance and health

Kelly argued fiercely against the use of the medical model in the field of psychological disorder. Like many others, he felt that those with psychological problems were not 'ill' and therefore did not need to be 'treated' by medical doctors. He believed that the use of the medical model hampers our attempts to understand people and to help them deal with whatever it is that is troubling them. If there is no 'illness' there can be no 'health'. For Kelly, all personal constructs are bi-polar.

Instead, he suggests that we might use the concept of *functioning*. A person who is functioning fully is one who is able to construe the world in such a way that predictions are, for the most part, validated. When invalidation *does* occur, the person deals with it by reconstruing. For example, you are at a party and go up to a stranger whom you construe as likely to be friendly. You start a general conversation and, before a few moments have passed, that 'friendly' person is arguing fiercely with you and being quite unpleasant. He is certainly not being 'friendly'. You have been invalidated in your prediction that this was a friendly person. If you are a well-functioning person, you will accept this invalidation and reconstrue the person, perhaps as someone who has a very deceptive façade and that you were stupid not to have seen through the veneer. You leave the incident behind you and put it down to experience.

But someone else, who is incapable of dealing with such invalidation, may not come out so unscathed. She may become more and more embarrassed, flustered and bereft of words. She would then become increasingly anxious since she has been confronted by an event which she now has difficulty in construing at all. Not only is she unable to predict the outcome of this event, but she finds she is increasingly unable to predict herself. The situation is a traumatic one. Hopefully, either someone will soon come to her rescue, or the stranger will move off. The person who experiences a considerable number of such predictive failures will often consider herself to 'have a problem'.

Another way of dealing with invalidation is to 'make' things work out the way we have predicted. When we do this we are being 'hostile' (we are extorting validational evidence for a social prediction that we have already seen to be a failure). For example, having construed the stranger as friendly, you might behave as if you were going to faint. He then puts his arm under your elbow to support you and guides you towards a chair. Now you can say to yourself: 'There you are! I knew he was really a friendly person!' Such hostility as this is well known in counselling and therapy. Yet there is nothing essentially 'bad' about hostility; it is a way of dealing with events when our construing lets us down.

Nevertheless, the person who functions reasonably well is one who does not use too much hostility to deal with invalidation and does not find himself too often confronted by events he cannot construe (and thus be overwhelmed with anxiety). The well-functioning person has been able to 'update' those potentially troublesome pre-verbal constructs. That is, he has been able to explore, at some level of awareness, those early childhood discriminations. For instance, is it really valid, in adult life, to take an instant dislike to people who have soft, smooth voices? Perhaps the construction does not now lead to useful predictions.

Acquisition of psychological disturbance

It makes no theoretical sense to ask how a disturbance in construing is acquired. Personal construct theory takes the position that we act upon the world and construe (predict) events in the world; we cannot 'acquire' something as if we were buying it in a shop or having it imposed upon us, like measles.

A client may construe his incapacitating headaches as a 'bodily symptom' which he 'acquired' as a result of some stressful psychological event. It is the client's construing that the therapist has to understand. However, to the therapist, the headaches are as much to do with construing as is the way the client describes them. *There is no body/mind dichotomy in Kelly's theory.* As the therapist examines the client's construing system (in verbal and non-verbal terms) she may examine the context within which the headaches arose. She will be asking herself such questions as: 'What experiment is my client conducting when he has these headaches?' 'What answers is he seeking from himself or others around him by behaving in that way?'

It is important always to remember that *behaviour is the experiment*. So we look at the event as if the child's first headache (or the way the client remembers it) was his way of asking a question of his world. It may have gone something like this: 'My mother does not cuddle me as much as I need. But when I have a headache she does. She is ignoring me again now. I feel a headache coming on. Yes, she is coming towards me.' Has he 'acquired a disturbance'? We think not. He has tried an experiment which, according to the way in which he construes the world, works. He gets his love.

We need to stress that, although we have spelled out a possible process in words, this does not mean that the thought goes consciously through the child's head in this way. A great deal of our experimenting goes on at a non-verbal level.

Perpetuation of psychological disturbance

The headaches are perpetuated because 'they work'. The child's predictions are validated. He may have started the process whereby whenever he feels unloved, he gets stressed and develops headaches.

Invalidation of our important notions of our selves comes most often, of course, from other people in our lives. Our experiments in life succeed or fail in relation to our understanding of others' understandings of us. But it can also come from within.

Problems may persist until the person is able to find acceptable alternative ways of dealing with the world. Many long-standing problems, such as stuttering, become enmeshed in the person's core-role construing. The person comes to see himself or herself as 'a stutterer', 'a headache sufferer', 'an unlovable person'.

The reasons for problems persisting must be sought within a person's construing of herself and her world. She behaves in a particular way because that is most meaningful to her; in that way she is able to achieve maximal control over events – and over herself. The problem becomes enmeshed in her core-role superordinate construing system. The longer the problem persists, the more difficulty the person is likely to have in changing – to change the construing of one's self is no easy undertaking.

Change

Since part of the model of the person in personal construct psychology is that we are a form of motion, the process of change is built into the theory. Kelly wrote his theory at two levels. There is the structure in the form of postulate, corollaries and other theoretical constructs. There is also the theory of human experiencing in the form of cycles of movement and transition.

The *fundamental postulate* states that ' a person's processes are psychologically channelized by the ways in which he anticipates events' (Kelly, 1991, Vol. I: 32). Three of the elaborative corollaries are specifically concerned with change.

The *experience corollary* states that 'a person's construction system varies as he successively construes the replication of events' (Kelly, 1991, Vol. I: 50). Merely being in a situation does not, of itself, mean that one has had experience. An agoraphobic woman placed in a specific situation at some point in her behaviour therapy hierarchy will only have experience of that situation if her construing of the world is in some way different after it from what it was before. Kelly equates experience with learning:

> The burden of our assumption is that learning is not a special class of psychological process; it is synonymous with any and all psychological processes. It is not something that happens to a person on occasion; it is what makes him a person in the first place. (Kelly, 1991: Vol. I, p. 53)

The *choice corollary* states that 'a person chooses for himself that alternative in a dichotomized construct through which he anticipates the greater possibility for extension and definition of his system' (Kelly, 1991, Vol. I: 45). This is a basic motivation construct. As living beings we strive to make our world a more predictable and personally meaningful place. We may not like the world in which we are living, but it is preferable to live in it than to launch ourselves into a vast sea of uncertainty.

In a certain sense, the client is 'choosing' to remain as he is rather than change. The person who has stuttered since early childhood sees no alternative but to continue stuttering in adulthood; that is the way he can make sense of himself interpersonally. If he were to suddenly become a fluent speaker, he would be launched into chaos (Fransella, 1972). In much the same way, smoking becomes personally meaningful for the smoker, obesity for the obese and depression for the depressed.

A personal construct approach involves helping the client construe what he or she is going to become and not simply eliminating the undesired behaviour.

The *modulation corollary* discusses a third aspect of change. It states that any variation within a construing system 'is limited by the permeability of the constructs within whose range of convenience the variants lie' (Kelly, 1991, Vol. I: 54). Construing new events is difficult if many of a person's constructs are not open to receive them; they are pumice rather than sponge. Someone who stutters and knows too precisely how people respond to his attempts at communication will find it difficult to employ new constructions of those interactions. He will not 'see' different responses.

While the corollaries of personal construct theory describe the theoretical structure underpinning change, the cycles of movement describe the change process. These are the cycles of experience, creativity and decision-making (CPC cycle).

The cycle of experience is about the process of reconstruing itself. The whole of psychotherapy therefore is seen in terms of human experiencing rather than as treatment. Kelly puts it like this:

> Psychotherapy needs to be understood as an experience, and experience, in turn, understood as a process that reflects human vitality. Thus to define psychotherapy as a form of treatment – something that one person does to another – is misleading. (Kelly, 1980: 21)

In the first place we have to have *anticipation*. Behaving is our experimentation to test out our anticipations about what confronts us. But we also have to be committed to these anticipations. We have to care about what happens. We have to invest something of ourselves in our experiments. The problem with problems is that we continue to conduct the same old experiments again and again without adding the final, essential component – reconstruing. As reconstruing completes one cycle of experience, so others start.

The creativity cycle starts with loosening up our construing of events and then tightening them again, hopefully in a different pattern. We have a problem in life. We go for a long walk and 'mull it over'. We allow ideas to come and go as they please (we are construing loosely). Then suddenly we have a flash of inspiration. Quickly, before it can slip away, we tighten things up again so we can look to see whether or not we have indeed found a solution. This cycle of creativity, like that of experience, repeats itself again and again:

> The loosening releases facts, long taken as self-evident, from their rigid conceptual moorings. Once so freed, they may be seen in new aspects hitherto unsuspected, and the creativity cycle may get under way. (Kelly, 1991: Vol. II, p. 301)

The ability to loosen the construing of events is often one of the first lessons the client has to be taught. Problems very often result in our tightening our construing so as to make it more manageable, more predictable. It can be quite threatening to a client to be asked to let go the anchors that hold the construing together, even for a short time.

The decision-making or CPC cycle is independent of tightened or loosened construing. We have a decision to make. First of all we look at the alternatives available to us (we Circumspect). Eventually we focus on the way that makes the most sense (we Pre-empt the issue). Now we are in position to be in Control of the situation and are precipitated into action.

Practice

Goals of therapy

The person with a psychological problem is seen as being 'stuck' – she keeps repeating her behavioural experiments over and over again. Since personal construct psychology views the person (amongst other things) as a form of motion, enabling the person to 'get on the move again' becomes the goal of therapy:

> The task of psychotherapy is to get the human process going again so that life may go on and on from where psychotherapy left off. There is no particular kind of psychotherapeutic relationship – no particular kind of feelings – no particular kind of interaction that is in itself a psychotherapeutic panacea. (Kelly, 1969: 223)

Selection criteria

Since everyone is seen as a construing process, no one person would be deemed unsuitable for personal construct psychotherapy. What usually provides the limiting factor is the context in which the therapy will take place. Not all places can deal with the overactive, the catatonic, the violent. There is also another limiting factor, but one less easy to define – the psychotherapist him or herself. There are very few therapists who would wish to say they are equally successful with any client with any type of problem. The limitations are thus in the physical therapy context and in the therapist, not in the client.

There are a few criteria which help the therapist decide whether or not the client is likely to benefit from personal construct psychotherapy. But none would automatically lead to a rejection of the client. One is that the client should be willing to go along with the idea that the therapist does not have the answers – the client does. All the therapist has is a theory about how people may go about the business of making sense of themselves and the world around them. If the client is basically looking for psychological 'pills', then they are not likely to take to the idea that psychotherapy means work.

A good prognostic sign is that the client has some existing construct to do with psychological change: not only that it is possible to change, but that they, themselves, may find it possible to change.

In choosing whether the client is most likely to be able to contemplate change in the one-to-one situation or in the presence of others, a number of factors have to be considered. For instance, a very withdrawn adult would rarely be seen without any contact being made with those caring for that person. The choice is then between only seeing the client in the company of one or two relatives; seeing client and relatives on different occasions; or seeing the client alone for part of the session with the relative(s) joining later. The choice will depend on the problem as seen by all parties. If the problem seems to be very definitely one that focuses on interactions and the withdrawn client not seeming to want to communicate more, then the emphasis would probably be on seeing client and relative(s) together. If the client is clearly withdrawn and experiencing some internal turmoil, most work would be done with the client alone.

However, the die is not cast for ever. As the withdrawn client becomes less so, the relatives may gradually be brought into the sessions; as they come to understand what their interactions with their client are all about *from the client's point of view* and vice versa, the client may increasingly be seen alone.

Clients are referred for group therapy if their problem is clearly related to interpersonal issues, for instance if they feel poorly understood by others or that others are something of a mystery to them. It is of interest to note that for Kelly group work was the preferred method, certainly within a hospital setting.

It is not uncommon for a client to be seen both individually and in a group. Here it is important that the same therapist is not involved in both. The client needs to be able to separate out the two experiences. There are experiments which the client may wish to conduct with or upon the therapist individually which would not be appropriate in a group. This requires very close collaboration between the therapists, for it is they who must ensure that the client moves along a single path toward reconstruing and does not get mixed messages. For instance, it would be counter-therapeutic for one therapist to be working with the client on the basis that the client needs to be helped to 'tighten' aspects of their construing while the other therapist is focusing on 'loosening'.

Qualities of effective therapists

Although no one has yet tried to relate the qualities of personal construct therapists to success or failure with clients, Kelly specifies a number of skills that they need to acquire.

A subsuming system of constructs   Above all, therapists must have a 'subsuming construct system' and be skilled in its use. Every therapist needs a set of professional constructs within which to subsume the client's own personal system of constructs. For the analyst, it is spelled out in psychoanalytic terms; for the cognitive therapist, in cognitive terms; for the personal construct therapist it is spelt out in terms of the theoretical constructs stated in the psychology of personal constructs. Kelly describes it thus:

> Since all clients have their own personal systems my system should be *a system of approach* by means of which I can quickly come to understand and subsume the widely varying systems which my clients can be expected to present. (Kelly, 1991: Vol. II, p. 28)

A therapist should be able to specify precisely what constructs are being used whenever a therapeutic decision is made. For example, if he systematically uses the writing of a self-characterization (see 'Fixed role therapy', p. 159) with clients, he should be able to state precisely what this procedure is designed to do.

In personal construct therapy, the subsuming system is that which defines the theory itself. Those constructs most commonly used in psychotherapy are referred to as 'professional constructs'. One already mentioned is *loose* versus *tight*: is the client using constructs in a way that leads to varying predictions (loosened construing) or to predictions which state that events will definitely be one way or another (unvarying or tight construing)? Bannister (1962) based his theory of the origins and maintenance of schizophrenic thought disorder on this construct.

To be effective the personal construct therapist must be able to 'work within' a client's construing system whether it be overly tight or overly loose. She has to understand these process differences both experientially and theoretically. Therapists who lack an adequate knowledge of the professional constructs or who lack the skill of suspending their own value system in order to subsume that of the client, may fail to help a client change. Once the therapist allows her *own* construing to intervene between herself and the client, she not only fails to be of use to the client but may also find herself being used by that client and have difficulty extricating herself.

Creativity, versatility and aggression   Given the focus on the client and therapist as personal scientists, the therapist needs to be creative, versatile and aggressive. Kelly comments that 'Every case a psychotherapist handles requires him to devise techniques and formulate constructs he has never used before' (1991,

Vol. II: 32). Such creativity means the readiness to try out unverbalized hunches, and a willingness to look at things in new ways:

> Creation is therefore an act of daring, an act of daring through which the creator abandons those literal defences behind which he might hide if his act is questioned or its results proven invalid. The psychotherapist who dares not try anything he cannot verbally defend is likely to be sterile in a psychotherapeutic relationship. (Kelly, 1991: Vol. II, p. 32)

To be creative the therapist must be able to adopt a variety of roles and be aggressive in testing out hypotheses (personal construct aggression being the active elaboration of one's construing). In psychotherapy, both client and therapist must be prepared to be aggressive and to take risks.

It must be borne in mind that an unwritten basic tenet of personal construct psychology is that we have created ourselves and can therefore re-create ourselves if we so wish.

Verbal ability   The therapist must be skilled both verbally and in observation. A therapist must be able to embrace the client's view in addition to having a wide-ranging vocabulary. By understanding the meanings that word-symbols have for the client the therapist can minimize the risk of misunderstandings.

Therapeutic relationship and style

The personal construct therapist's relationship and style can best be understood by looking once again at the model of the 'person as scientist'. Client and therapist are partners in the struggle to understand and so find a solution to the same problem. The therapist, like a research supervisor, knows something about designing experiments, has experience of some of the pitfalls involved in any type of research and knows that, ultimately, only the research student can carry out the research.

This supervisory/research student model may sound cold and calculating, but it is not. Anyone who has ever been in one or both of those positions know only too well how totally involving and challenging is the task. One important aspect of such a relationship is that both client and therapist must have a personal commitment to solving the problem and to the necessary work and experimentation that this involves.

A central feature of the therapeutic relationship is spelled out in the *sociality corollary*. This says that we may be seen as playing a role in relation to another if we try to see the world through the eyes of the other. The personal construct therapist, above all else, is struggling to see things as the client sees them. Only by being successful in this can any meaningful therapeutic strategy be undertaken.

To start with the therapist adopts the *credulous approach*: all personal evaluation is suspended; there are no judgements. Everything the client says is accepted as 'true'. This cannot, of course, go on, but it is essential to the establishment of the initial role relationship. As the therapist gains increasing access to the client's world and begins to formulate hypotheses about the nature of the problem, the therapist begins to put these to the test. However, being active in therapy does not mean that the therapist necessarily adopts a directive role; she may, in fact, be very quiet and give the client absolute freedom to do, say or think whatever he wishes. Nevertheless, the role is decided on by the therapist. Her construing of the client's constructions leads her to consider that this 'quiet' role is something the client can use *at this stage of the therapy*.

This all means that the personal construct therapist will change style according to what is most likely to help the client's reconstruing process. A therapist may be humorous at one time and serious at another; active and then passive, or formal and then informal. Self-disclosure, as with all these other styles, will only be used *if the client can make use of the disclosure*, otherwise it is self-indulgence on the part of the therapist. The personal construct therapist, therefore, is a *validator or invalidator of the client's construing*.

One implication of construing the therapist as validator of the client's construing is that she uses the relationship as another valuable 'tool' for helping the client's reconstructions. For instance, 'transference' or 'dependency' is not a general problem to be 'dealt with'. At a specific stage in therapy it may be useful, such as when attempts are being made to verbalize pre-verbal constructs; at another time or with other clients, dependence on the therapist may prevent the client from conducting useful experiments outside the therapy consulting room.

The therapeutic style is thus dictated by the ways in which the therapist construes the needs of the client, always remembering that client and therapist are *both* in the experimenting and reconstruing business and work as partners.

Major therapeutic strategies and techniques

The therapist hopes that all interactions with the client will aid the client in reconstruing. The therapist's principal goal is to help the client find alternative ways of looking at himself, life, and the problem. But before the therapist can be reasonably sure about these possible alternative ways, she has to have a moderately clear idea of what it is that is holding the client back from doing this on his own.

Most of the techniques stemming directly from personal construct psychology are concerned with providing the therapist as well as the client with information on how the client views the world at the present time. In that sense the methods can be called 'diagnostic'. Only fixed role therapy is a therapeutic tool in its own right – designed specifically to bring about reconstruing (alternative constructions). However, the diagnostic techniques do themselves bring about reconstruing in many instances, although this is not their prime aim.

Kelly talks about techniques thus:

Personal construct psychotherapy is a way of getting on with the human enterprise and it may embody and mobilize all of the techniques for doing this that man has yet devised. Certainly there is no one psychotherapeutic technique and certainly no one kind of interpersonal compatibility between psychotherapist and client. The techniques employed are the techniques for living and the task of the skillful psychotherapist is the proper orchestration of all of these varieties of techniques. Hence one may find a personal construct psychotherapist employing a huge variety of procedures – not helter-skelter, but always as part of a plan for helping himself and his client get on with the job of human exploration and checking out the appropriateness of the constructions they have devised for placing upon the world around them. (Kelly, 1969: 221–2)

A few specific methods that have arisen from Kelly's work are outlined below.

Repertory grid technique   This technique has been modified a number of times since Kelly first described it in 1955 (see Fransella and Bannister, 1977). Its uses are many and, although the raw data can give rise to many useful insights, there is a variety of methods of statistical analysis. It is basically a technique which enables the therapist to obtain some degree of quantification of the relationships between constructs and how these relate to individuals who are being construed. Though it has a place in the psychotherapy setting, it is not essential to it. It is only useful if the therapist sees it as such. It can be used to validate therapists' hunches, for monitoring change over time, or in helping clients explore their construing of events more fully. In all cases grids are a part of the therapy as the results are fed back to the client.

Laddering, pyramiding and the ABC model   These are all methods for exploring construct relationships without getting into the complexities of statistical analyses that are often necessary with repertory grids.

Laddering helps the client explore the relationships between constructs at more and more abstract levels (Hinkle, 1965). For instance, if the client uses the construct 'dominant' versus 'submissive', the client would be asked which he would prefer to be. If the answer was 'submissive', the therapist would ask 'Why do you prefer to be that? What are the advantages of being a submissive rather than a dominant person?' The client might answer that submissive people do not get attacked, whereas dominant people do. The client is again asked why he prefers not to be attacked. The reply might be that he would not know how to respond if he were attacked, he would not know what to do. And so the questioning goes on, until the construing has reached such a superordinate level that it has nowhere else to go (in this example it might be something to do with self-preservation).

Laddering is not easy to learn. It can go round in circles or produce answers that block all further enquiry. But having learned how to make it work, most people find it an invaluable tool for gaining insight very quickly into the most important values the client holds about himself and others. Not only does it enable the therapist to learn about the client, but frequently it also enables the client to gain considerable insight into his own construing.

Pyramiding (Landfield, 1971) aims at identifying the more concrete levels of the construing system of the client. Instead of asking 'Why?', the client is asked: 'What?' or 'How?': 'What sort of person is a submissive person? How would you know that a person is being submissive?' This method can be very useful when planning behavioural experiments.

The ABC model involves finding out the advantages and disadvantages to the client of each pole of a construct (Tschudi, 1977). This can be used to advantage with constructs connected with 'the problem'. A woman whose 'problem' is being overweight might be asked for an advantage of being the desired weight (perhaps she would be able to wear nice clothes); then for a disadvantage of being over-weight (perhaps she gets out of breath when going upstairs). Next, she is asked for a disadvantage of being the normal weight (perhaps she would find there was too much choice around and so get confused), and finally for an advantage of being overweight (perhaps men do not bother her). These answers are regarded not as 'truths' but as guidelines for understanding and further exploration.

The self-characterization Kelly says that if he were to be remembered for one thing only, he would like it to be his first principle: 'If you do not know what is wrong with a person, ask him, he may tell you' (Kelly, 1991: Vol. I, p. 241). A working model for this is the self-characterization he described. The instructions are carefully worded, as follows:

> I want you to write a character sketch of (e.g. Harry Brown) just as if he were the principal character in a play. Write it as it might be written by a friend who knew him very *intimately* and very *sympathetically*, perhaps better than anyone ever really could know him. Be sure to write it in the third person. For example, start out by saying 'Harry Brown is . . .'. (Kelly, 1991: Vol. I, p. 242)

There is no formal method of analysis. However, one might look at the first sentence as if it were a statement of where the person is now and at the last as a statement of where the person is going. One might look for themes running through the whole piece. What one tries to do is go beyond the words and glimpse inside where the person lives. These character sketches can be written from a variety of standpoints: 'Harry as he will be in ten years' time'; '. . . as he will be when his problem has disappeared', or any other form which seems to offer the person a way of exploring and communicating his constructions of the world. An example of the use of the self-characterization as the main therapeutic instrument can be found in Fransella (1981). Jackson (1988) has developed ways of using the self-characterization with children and adolescents. It also plays an important part in the case study at the end of this chapter.

Techniques from other therapies The choice of technique is always deter-mined by the current formulation of the problem, which is couched in the language of the professional theoretical constructs. Personal construct therapists find the use of dream material, guided fantasy, systematic desensitization and many other techniques of great value for specific purposes, but it must be emphasized that the choice of technique is guided by theory.

Fixed role therapy This is the only method that is offered by Kelly as a therapeutic tool in its own right. He gave it as an example of the theory in action and based it on the self-characterization. In his description of fixed role therapy, he also gives an implicit account of the way we invent and create ourselves. Kelly acknowledges his indebtedness to Moreno and his methods of psychodrama (1964) here.

The therapist writes a second version of the client's original self-charac-terization. This is not a replica of the first, since that would only lead back to where the client is now; nor should it be a complete opposite, since no one will readily turn their life on its head. Instead, the client's *fixed role sketch* is written so as to be 'orthogonal' to the first. For instance, if the client is using the construct 'aggressive' versus 'submissive' in relation to her boss, the sketch might talk of being 'respectful'.

When the sketch has been written, client and therapist pore over it together. They modify it until it describes a person the client feels it would be possible for her to be. The client now lives the life of that person for a few weeks; she eats what her new person eats, dresses as she would dress and relates to others as this person would relate. During this period of fixed role enactment the therapist has to see the client fairly frequently. The sessions focus on what the client sees as going on, which ventures were successful and which were not, what messages she is getting from others and so forth.

The purpose of this fixed role enactment is to get over the idea that we can, indeed, change ourselves; that even the client can change, though he seems so stuck at the moment. He learns about self-inventiveness; he learns what happens when he alters a particular item of behaviour, and whether it is useful to explore this line of enquiry further or whether he should try something else. He discovers how the way we construe others and behave towards them influences how they behave towards us. He learns to read new messages from others. This is especially important since the person we have invented is, in large part, the result of the way we have construed the reactions of others to us.

Fixed role therapy is certainly not suitable for everyone, but it can be very useful in modified form. For instance, the client and the therapist may choose to work out just one experiment for the former to carry out during the period before the next appointment. This might be to experiment with being respectful to her boss on just one occasion and see what difference it makes to how the boss reacts, and to how the client feels about herself. These 'mini' fixed roles need to be worked out carefully with the client, but can give useful insights into the direction in which both client and therapist think she might profitably travel. This procedure was used with the client discussed at the end of this chapter.

The change process in therapy

There are no clear stages in the change process that are applicable to all clients. We have to ask questions derived from the theory. How permeable is the client's construing in the problem area? What is at stake for her if she were to contemplate changing in some radical way? How loosely or tightly knit is her construing in areas relating to anticipated change? And so on. In other words, the change process will be determined by the 'diagnosis' the therapist makes of why the client is unable to move forward on her own.

Diagnosis is the planning stage of treatment for the therapist. This does *not* imply that the therapist is placing the client in some medical pigeonhole such as 'depression', 'schizophrenia' or 'psychopathic'. Personal construct diagnosis does not imply any illness or disturbance. It is couched in the language of the theory to provide guidance for the therapist as to a possible way forward for the client. There is no one way forward for all-comers.

There are some specific factors that may impede the reconstruction process by the client. These factors are often to be found in the constructs to do with transition. The change process can involve anxiety, threat or hostility. All can impede movement if not dealt with sensitively by the therapist.

Any change is accompanied by anxiety as we move into areas we find it difficult or impossible to construe for a while. But this is rarely a problem if the client moves forward in moderate steps. Threat can bring the client up short as she perceives that, if things go on as they are at the moment, she will have to change how she construes some essential aspect of her 'self'. As one client put it:

Writing the self characterisation focused on something which I suppose has been associated with panic – although not consciously associated with panic – the feeling that I was going to have to change more drastically – in a sense either remain more or less the same or the change would have to be more drastic than I had thought. Writing the self characterisation focused my attention on *not wanting to change*. Not wanting to change because I felt that if I was going to have to change as dramatically as I was feeling was necessary, I'd lose 'me'. (Fransella, 1981: 228)

If a client is able to put the threat into words like that, it is usually possible to move forward from there. The client had to elaborate precisely what the 'me' was that was in danger of being lost and whether, on close examination, that was necessarily true. But some clients are not able to put the threat into words. Often the client realizes, at some level of awareness, that these radical changes are just too much to be contemplated. She relapses. She has made a positive choice – in her terms – and has signalled that an alternative therapeutic strategy is required. Relapse is not a negative event, but the client's safety-net.

The problem becomes more difficult if the client defends her position by becoming hostile. That is, by extorting evidence to prove that she really should be the sort of person she always knew herself to be. She can 'make' the therapy fail. It is really the therapist's fault, not the client's. She can produce evidence that there has really been no great change at all by pointing out that the experience indicating psychological movement to the therapist was really 'a chance event – that combination of circumstances will never happen again!'

Hostility is dealt with by discovering what it is that is so important for the client to retain and then by exploring areas of construing that will help elaborate the sort of self the client wants to become. Exploration with the client just mentioned revealed that the 'me' he was afraid of losing was 'the child me'. This was to do with a rich fantasy life and a world of deep experiencing. He evolved for himself a way in which he could change to becoming 'an adult' and yet retain areas of living in which he could still experience the valued childlike qualities.

Limitations of the approach

A major undeveloped area for personal construct therapy is group work. Although Kelly advocated its use and devoted a chapter to working with groups of people, little use has been made of it. The focus of this therapy has always been on the one-to-one situation.

Apart from this, limitations lie with the therapist rather than with personal construct therapy. The therapist finds it easier if she has the full co-operation of the client – at least implicitly. She finds it easier to work with those who are verbally fluent, but that is not essential. She finds it easier to work with those from a culture similar to her own but, again, this is by no means essential. If all human beings are seen as experiencing, construing beings, then personal construct therapy should be able to be used by all.

Case example

The client

Cathy was 32 years old. Her initial contact on the telephone gave me [P.D.] a vivid first impression of what was to come: could she see me *immediately*, everything was falling apart and she was *panicking*.

When she arrived the following day her distress showed itself in extreme physical tension and breathlessness and she seemed on the verge of tears for much of the session. She had been deeply anxious for some weeks, was unable to concentrate on her job and felt that she was destroying relationships all round.

The story she told was wide-ranging and complicated but the most important factors seemed to be the death of her mother two years before and her subsequent assumption of responsibility for her younger sister and her depressed father; her agonizing doubts about moving in with her boyfriend; and her frustration with most of the people she worked with in a highly pressurized television company. When I put these points to her as a summary of the main issues she agreed and said towards the end of our time that she would like to work with me if I didn't think that she was a hopeless case.

We agreed on four initial sessions to explore things, which would hopefully give us some idea of what might be needed in terms of time and frequency of further sessions. She had been referred to me by someone who had lent her a book on PCP and she saw it as having an 'active' quality which she needed. I asked her to write a self-characterization, as I felt that she could not begin to change *how* she was without looking at *who* she was at the moment.

The therapy

This writing formed one important source of data for my attempt to subsume aspects of Cathy's construing system. It began 'Cathy is a person of extremes. She is either in the depths of despair or over the moon.' The final sentence read: 'What she would really like to find is some peace within herself.' This notion of extremes pervades the whole of her writing: in the drama of her descriptions of events, the themes of dazzling success and abject failure, intense love and hatred towards people. Constructs recurred to do with being 'hyped up' vs. 'comatose', 'lonely' vs. 'oppressed by people', 'domineering' vs. 'a whimpering child'. As it seemed clear that neither pole of any such construct was acceptable to her, my initial formulation of her problem was that she must experience constant invalidation with no viable alternatives. Even the things she longed for had a sting in the tail: would 'domestic bliss' with her boyfriend Sam inevitably lead to 'mind-numbing boredom'?

The sharpest swing of all seemed to come in relation to dependency. She had had a loving but stormy relationship with her mother, alternating between desperation for her approval and rebellion against her control. She worried constantly about her sister, who seemed to drift along in her life as an unmarried mother 'shacking up' with one feckless man after another, and Cathy deeply resented the pain it caused her. She longed to comfort her unhappy father but was angry at being unable to get near him. Her relationship with Sam consisted of periods of 'pathetic reliance' on him and fierce rejection of his unshakeable support and affection. Though she longed for friendship, her difficulty with seeing things from another's point of view made her intensely critical and prickly.

After going through the self-characterization with her and exploring some of these themes and constructs a number of areas for possible reconstruction emerged. First, in order to free herself from the crippling intensity of see-sawing from one extreme to another she needed to loosen her construing of herself and her experiences in such a way that she had other paths to go down. Every setback need not be a disaster, every delay need not mean the end of a desired outcome. An early sign of loosening came when, describing an incident at work, she started to say 'I failed miserably', laughed and substituted 'I made a bit of a mess of it'. She was able, gradually, to recognize when an event had truly core implications for her and when she could step back and let things be.

I asked her to experiment with her reactions; in particular, to disagreements with Sam. Typically she would immediately defend her view if he ventured to differ from her. The only alternative to her would be 'giving in – having no opinions of my own'. Instead, using an aspect of fixed role therapy, she agreed to try a new approach: to hear him out, even ask him to elaborate to be sure she understood and only then affirm her opinion or be prepared to concede to his point of view. She came to realize how little she listened to others but how useful it could be!

Discriminating what was important from what need not matter was not easy and held some threat for her in terms of loss of the clarity which her extreme construing gave her, but she worked at it for the sake of the inner peace she genuinely sought.

The dependency issue was of course more complex, since it involved pre-verbal experience at its root. We explored her relationship with her mother in some depth. The not uncommon ambivalence towards her in terms of needing her and rejecting her control had been compounded by her mother's dependence on her during her last two years when she suffered from cancer. At the time of her mother's death Cathy felt that she had been too caught up with 'mothering' her sister and trying to help her father to face her own feelings of grief. She found herself crying for her now as she had not done then. I suggested that she use a photograph of her mother to 'tell' her all the things she had not been able to before. She felt that though she began talking to her as a child she came to speak to her as a woman.

It was very hard for Cathy to find a right balance in her relationship with her sister. She could accept intellectually that she was not responsible for her and that Mary had to lead her own life, but still she worried. Clarifying the differences between her sister's views of things and her own and trying to allow them their own validity helped a little, I believe. For example, we looked at the advantages and disadvantages of feeling 'responsible' vs. 'not caring about people' (the ABC model) and found that although there were no advantages in not caring about people, feeling responsible for them could lead to 'intrusion' and 'alienation' from Mary's point of view, as well as genuine concern and practical help. But Cathy changed more in behaviour towards her than she did in her heart, interfering less, criticizing less but often 'boiling'.

Communication with her father became no easier but here Cathy did reconstrue her relationship with him to a large extent. She recognized his constriction after her mother's death as a choice which made sense to him, made his life manageable. It was not for her to try to persuade him to 'do more, see more people'. Hardest of all – he did not need her.

The greatest change in Cathy's relationship with Sam came with our joint recognition that it could actually work as it stood. When we explored it in more depth it emerged that although Sam seemed able to take anything Cathy threw at him he was by no means a doormat. His love was indeed unshakeable, but he made it quite clear when he took exception to how she was behaving. Also, she had not looked at all at what she might be giving him. He had some difficulty with his career, also in television, and she was a tremendous support to him. A close friend of his had died recently and he had been able to share his grief with Cathy in a way that his other reserved male friends had not allowed. The effect on her of acknowledging her own value in the relationship was an important step in coming to like herself more.

In parallel with working on these closer relationships we attempted some movement on how she was with work colleagues in particular, as this was causing her (and them) some grief. The main difficulty seemed to be with sociality. She had very little skill in putting herself in another's shoes and no inclination to see things through their eyes. I asked her to write character sketches of various key people as if she were them. She made some progress in transferring the way she listened to Sam. She became more discriminating about what she could expect from whom. But, although she developed more understanding of why people did what they did or said what they said, she grew scarcely more tolerant. Her hostility in this area undoubtedly stemmed from her conviction that they neither liked nor understood her. If she were to concede to them as she could to Sam, the threat was that they would simply take advantage of her. It seemed to me that all this was linked to her problems with her sister, who had no love for her, and it would take very long and hard work on Cathy's part to make any profound difference.

We had 15 sessions in all, and although Cathy recognized that there were areas where further change would be beneficial she felt that she had 'done enough for the moment'. For my part I felt that in some areas at least she was on the move. She was better able to discriminate between what were truly superordinate issues and what could be let go as unimportant. Although still volatile she could more often experience that peace within herself. My prediction was that the relationship with Sam would flourish but I was concerned that she had too many eggs in one basket. I hoped that at some time in the future she would address the dependency issue further and come to value a wider range of people and trust them with her vulnerability.

References

Bannister, D. (1962) 'The nature and measurement of schizophrenic thought disorder', *Journal of Mental Science*, 108: 825–42.

Fransella, F. (1972) *Personal Change and Reconstruction: Research on a Treatment of Stuttering*. London: Academic Press.

Fransella, F. (1981) 'Nature babbling to herself: the self characterisation as a therapeutic tool', in H. Bonarius, R. Holland and S. Rosenberg (eds), *Personal Construct Psychology: Recent Advances in Theory and Practice*. London: Macmillan.

Fransella, F. (1984) 'What sort of scientist is the person-as-scientist?', in J.R. Adams-Webber and J.C. Mancuso (eds), *Applications of Personal Construct Theory*. Ontario: Academic Press.

Fransella, F. and Bannister, D. (1977) *A Manual for Repertory Grid Technique*. London: Academic Press.

Hinkle, D. (1965) 'The change of personal constructs from the viewpoint of a theory of construct implications'. PhD thesis, Ohio State University.

Jackson, S. (1988) 'A self-characterisation: development and deviance in adolescent construing', in P. Maitland and D. Brennan (eds), *Personal Construct Theory: Deviancy and Social Work*. London: Inner London Probation Service and Centre for Personal Construct Psychology.

Kelly, G.A. (1969) 'The psychotherapeutic relationship', in B. Maher (ed.), *Clinical Psychology and Personality: The Selected Papers of George Kelly*. New York: Krieger.

Kelly, G.A. (1980) 'A psychology of optimal man', in A.W. Landfield and L.M. Leitner (eds), *Personal Construct Psychology: Psychotherapy and Personality*. New York: Wiley.

Kelly, G.A. (1991) *The Psychology of Personal Constructs*, Vols I and II. London: Routledge. First published in 1955.

Landfield, A.W. (1971) *Personal Construct Systems in Psychotherapy*. New York: Rand McNally.

Moreno, J.L. (1964) *Psychodrama*. New York: Beacon. First published in 1946.

Mullins, N. (1973) *Theories and Theory Groups in Contemporary American Sociology*. New York: Harper & Row.

Neimeyer, R.A. (1983) 'Uneven growth of personal construct theory', *Constructs*, 2(5): 5–6. London: Centre for Personal Construct Psychology.

Tschudi, F. (1977) 'Loaded and honest questions: a personal construct theory view of symptoms and therapy', in D. Bannister (ed.), *New Perspectives in Personal Construct Theory*. London: Academic Press.

Suggested further reading

Bannister, D. and Fransella, F. (1985) *Inquiring Man*, 3rd edition. London: Routledge.

Dalton, P. and Dunnett, G. (1992) *Psychology of Living*. Chichester: Wiley.

Dunnett, G. (ed.) (1988) *Working with People: Clinical Uses of Personal Construct Therapy*. London: Routledge.

Fransella, F. (1995) *George Kelly*. London: Sage Publications.

Fransella, F. and Dalton, P. (1990) *Personal Construct Counselling in Action*. London: Sage Publications.

8

Existential Therapy

Emmy van Deurzen-Smith

Historical context and development in Britain

Historical context

The existential approach is first and foremost philosophical. It is concerned with the understanding of people's position in the world and with the clarification of what it means to be alive. It is also committed to exploring these questions with a receptive attitude, rather than with a dogmatic one. The aim is to search for truth with an open mind and an attitude of wonder rather than fitting the client into pre-established frameworks of interpretation.

The historical background to this approach is that of 3,000 years of philosophy. Throughout the history of mankind people have tried to make sense of human existence in general and of their personal predicaments in particular. Much of the philosophical tradition is relevant and can help us to understand an individual's position in the world. The philosophers who are especially pertinent are those whose work is directly aimed at making sense of human existence. But the philosophical movements that are of most importance and that have been directly responsible for the generation of existential therapy are phenomenology and existential philosophy.

The starting point of existential philosophy (see Warnock, 1970; Macquarrie, 1972) can be traced back to the last century and the work of Kierkegaard and Nietzsche. Both were in conflict with the predominant ideologies of their time and committed to the exploration of reality as it can be experienced in a passionate and personal manner. Kierkegaard (1813–55) protested vigorously against Christian dogma and the so-called 'objectivity' of science (Kierkegaard, 1941, 1944). He thought that both were ways of avoiding the anxiety inherent in human existence. He had great contempt for the way in which life was being lived by those around him and believed that truth could ultimately only be discovered by the individual in action. What was most lacking was people's courage to take the leap of faith and live with passion and commitment from the inward depth of existence. As Kierkegaard lived by his own word he was lonely and much ridiculed during his lifetime.

Nietzsche (1844–1900) took this philosophy of life a step further. His starting point was the notion that God was dead (Nietzsche, 1961, 1974, 1986) and that it is up to us to re-evaluate existence in light of this. He invited people to shake off the shackles of moral constraint and to discover their free will in order to soar to unknown heights and learn to live with new intensity. He encouraged people not to remain part of the herd, but to dare stand out. The important existential themes of freedom, choice, responsibility and courage are thus introduced.

While Kierkegaard and Nietzsche drew attention to the issues that needed to be addressed, Husserl's phenomenology (Husserl, 1960, 1962) provided the method to address them in a rigorous manner. Husserl (1859–1938) contended that natural sciences are based on the assumption that subject and object are separate and that this kind of dualism can only lead to error. He proposed a whole new mode of investigation and understanding of the world and our experience of it. Prejudice has to be put aside or bracketed, in order to meet the world afresh and discover what is absolutely fundamental and only directly available to us through intuition. If we want to grasp the essence of things, instead of explaining and analysing them we have to learn to describe and understand them.

Heidegger (1889–1976) applied the phenomenological method to understanding the meaning of being (Heidegger, 1962, 1968). He argued that poetry and deep philosophical thinking can bring greater insight into what it means to be in the world than can be achieved through scientific knowledge. He also favoured hermeneutics, an old philosophical method of investigation which is the art of interpretation. Unlike interpretation as practised in psychoanalysis (which consists of referring a person's experience to a pre-established theoretical framework) this kind of interpretation seeks to understand how something is subjectively experienced by the person herself.

Most recent contributions to existential exploration are based on Heidegger's work. There is a vast literature on the subject by authors such as Jaspers (1951, 1963), Tillich and Gadamer within the Germanic tradition and Sartre, Camus, Marcel, Ricoeur, Merleau-Ponty and Levinas within the French tradition (see for instance Spiegelberg, 1972, or Kearney, 1986). Few psychotherapists are aware of this literature, or interested in making use of it. Psychotherapy has traditionally grown within a medical rather than a philosophical milieu and it has to a large extent yet to discover the possibility of a radical philosophical approach.

From the beginning of this century some psychotherapists were, however, inspired by phenomenology and its possibilities for working with people. Binswanger, in Switzerland, was the first to attempt to bring existential insights to his work with patients, in the Kreuzlingen sanatorium where he was a psychiatrist. Much of his work was translated into English during the 1940s and 1950s and, together with the immigration to the USA of Tillich and others, this had a considerable impact on the popularization of existential ideas as a basis for therapy (Valle and King, 1978). Rollo May played an important role in this, and his writing (1969, 1983; May et al., 1958) kept the existential influence alive in America, leading eventually to a specific formulation of therapy (May and Yalom, 1985; Yalom, 1980). Much of humanistic psychology was influenced by these ideas, but it invariably diluted and sometimes distorted their original meanings.

In Europe existential ideas were combined with some psychoanalytic principles and a method of existential analysis was developed by Boss (1957a, 1957b, 1979) in close co-operation with Heidegger. In Austria Frankl developed an existential therapy called logotherapy (Frankl, 1964, 1967), which focused particularly on finding meaning. In France the ideas of Sartre (1956, 1962) and Merleau-Ponty (1962) and of a number of practitioners (Minkowski,

1970) were important and influential but no specific therapeutic method was developed from them.

Development in Britain

Britain became a fertile ground for the further development of the existential approach when Laing and Cooper took Sartre's existential ideas as the basis for some of their writing (Laing, 1960, 1961; Cooper, 1967; Laing and Cooper, 1964). Without developing a concrete method of therapy they critically reconsidered the notion of mental illness and its treatment. In the late 1960s they established an experimental therapeutic community at Kingsley Hall in the East End of London, where people could come to live through their madness without the usual medical treatment. They also founded the Philadelphia Association, an organization providing alternative living, therapy and therapeutic training from this perspective. The Philadelphia Association is still in existence today and is now committed to the exploration of the works of philosophers such as Wittgenstein, Derrida, Levinas and Foucault as well as the work of the French psychoanalyst Lacan. It also runs a number of small therapeutic households along these lines. The Arbours Association is another group that grew out of the Kingsley Hall experiment. Founded by Berke and Schatzman in the 1970s, it now runs a training programme in psychotherapy, a crisis centre and several therapeutic communities. The existential input in the Arbours has gradually diminished and has been replaced with a Kleinian emphasis. The impetus for further development of the existential approach in Britain has largely come from the School of Psychotherapy and Counselling at Regent's College, London, which is a large centre of training in psychotherapy and counselling that offers existentially oriented academic programmes at all levels, from certificate and diploma, through BA and MA to PhD. It also offers an advanced training in Existential Psychotherapy, which is the only training in Britain leading to registration as an Existential Psychotherapist with the United Kingdom Council for Psychotherapy. Regent's College has attracted many senior existential practitioners and authors.

Major British publications dealing with existential therapy include contributions by Jenner (de Koning and Jenner, 1982), Heaton (1968, 1988), Stadlen (1989), Cohn (1994), Spinelli (1989, 1994), Cooper (1989), Eleftheriadou (1994), Lemma-Wright (1994) and van Deurzen-Smith (1988, 1992, 1996). Other writers such as Lomas (1981), Smail (1978, 1987, 1993) and Smith (1991) have published work relevant to the approach although not explicitly 'existential' in orientation. The journal of the British Society for Phenomenology regularly publishes work on existential and phenomenological psychotherapy.

An important development was that of the founding of the Society for Existential Analysis in 1988. This society brings together psychotherapists, psychologists, psychiatrists, counsellors and philosophers working from an existential perspective. It offers regular fora for discussion and debate as well as major annual conferences, and publishes the *Journal of the Society for Existential Analysis* twice a year. It is also a member of the International Federation for Daseinsanalysis, which stimulates international exchange between representatives of the approach from around the world.

Theoretical Assumptions

Image of the person

The existential approach considers human nature to be open-minded, flexible and capable of an enormous range of experience. The person is in a constant process of becoming. I create myself as I exist and have to reinvent myself daily. There is no essential self, as I define my personality and abilities in action. This impermanence and uncertainty give rise to a deep sense of anxiety (Angst), in response to the realization of one's insignificance, and simultaneously responsibility to have to create something in place of that emptiness. Everything passes and nothing lasts. One finds oneself somewhere in the middle of this passing of time, grappling with the givens of the past and the possibilities of the future, without any sure knowledge of what it all means.

Existential thinkers seek to avoid restrictive models that categorize or label people. Instead they look for the universals that can be observed cross-culturally. There is no existential personality theory which divides humanity into types or reduces people to part components. Instead there is a description of the different levels of experience and existence with which people are inevitably confronted.

The way in which a person is in the world at a particular stage can be charted on this general map of human existence (Binswanger, 1963; Yalom, 1980; van Deurzen-Smith, 1984). One can distinguish four basic dimensions of human existence: the physical, the social, the psychological and the spiritual. On each of these dimensions people encounter the world and shape their attitude out of their experience.

Physical dimension On the physical dimension (*Umwelt*) we relate to our environment and to the givens of the natural world around us. This includes our attitude to the body we have, to the concrete surroundings we find ourselves in, to the climate and the weather, to objects and material possessions, to health and illness and to our own mortality. The struggle on this dimension is, in general terms, between the search for domination over the elements and natural law (as in technology, or in sports) and the need to accept the limitations of natural boundaries (as in ecology or old age). While people generally aim for security on this dimension (through health and wealth), much of life brings a gradual disillusionment and realization that such security can only be temporary.

Social dimension On the social dimension (*Mitwelt*) we relate to others as we interact with the public world around us. This dimension includes our response to the culture we live in, as well as to the class and race we belong to (and also those we do not belong to). Attitudes here range from love to hate and from co-operation to competition. The contradictions can be understood in terms of acceptance versus rejection or belonging versus isolation. Some people prefer to withdraw from the world of others as much as possible. Others blindly chase public acceptance by going along with the rules and fashions of the moment. Otherwise they try to rise above these by becoming trendsetters themselves. By acquiring fame or other forms of power, we can attain dominance over others temporarily. Sooner or later we are, however, all confronted with both failure and aloneness.

Psychological dimension On the psychological dimension (*Eigenwelt*) we relate to ourselves and in this way create a personal world. This dimension includes views about our character, our past experience and our future possibilities. Contradictions here are often experienced in terms of personal strengths and weaknesses. People search for a sense of identity, a feeling of being substantial and having a self. But inevitably many events will confront us with evidence to the contrary and plunge us into a state of confusion or disintegration. Activity and passivity are an important polarity here. Self-affirmation and resolution go with the former and surrender and yielding with the latter. Facing the final dissolution of self with death brings anxiety and confusion to many who haven't yet given up their sense of self-importance.

Spiritual dimension On the spiritual dimension (*Ueberwelt*) we relate to the unknown and thus create a sense of an ideal world, an ideology and a philosophical outlook. It is here that we find meaning by putting all the pieces of the puzzle together for ourselves. For some people this is done through adhering to the dogma of a religion or some other prescriptive world view, for others it is about discovering or attributing meaning in a more secular or personal way. The contradictions that have to be faced on this dimension are often related to the tension between purpose and absurdity, hope and despair. People create their values in search of something that matters enough to live or die for, something that may even be ultimate and universally valid. Usually the aim is the conquest of a soul, or something that will substantially surpass human mortality (as for instance in having contributed something valuable to mankind). Facing the void and the possibility of nothingness are the indispensable counterparts of this quest for the eternal.

Conceptualization of psychological disturbance and health

Disturbance and health are two sides of the same coin. Living creatively means welcoming both. Well-being coincides with the ability to be transparent and open to what life can bring: both good and bad. In trying to evade the negative side of existence we get stuck as surely as we do when we cannot see the positive side. It is only in facing both positive and negative poles of existence that we generate the necessary power to move ahead. Thus well-being is not the naive enjoyment of a state of total balance given to one by mother nature and perfect parents. It can only be negotiated gradually by coming to terms with life, the world and oneself. It doesn't require a clean record of childhood experience, nor a total devotion to the cult of body and mind. It simply requires an openness to being and to increasing understanding of what the business of living is all about. From an existential perspective psychological well-being is seen to be synonymous with wisdom. This results from being equal to the task of life when it is faced honestly and squarely. Psychological disturbance is seen as a consequence of either avoidance of truth or an inability to cope with it. Discontent is generated for many people through self-deception in a blind following of popular opinions, habits, beliefs, rules and reasons. Others are at a loss to make sense of the paradoxes of life that they are forcefully confronted with and that overwhelm them.

To be authentic is to be true to oneself. Finding one's inner authority and learning to create an increasingly comfortable space inside and around oneself, no matter what the circumstances, is a considerable challenge. As the self is defined by its vital links to the world around it, being true to oneself has to be understood as being true to life. This is not about setting one's own rules or living without regard for others. It is about recognizing the necessities, givens and limitations of the human condition as much as about affirming freedom and insisting on one's basic rights.

Many people avoid authentic living, because it is terrifying to face the reality of the constant challenge, failures, crises and doubts that existence exposes us to. Living authentically begins with the recognition of one's personal vulnerability and mortality and with the acknowledgement of the ultimate uncertainty of all that is known. It is superficially far more rewarding to play at being certain, role-defined and self-important. Even the self-image of sickness or madness can seem more attractive than having to struggle with yourself and face your vulnerability in an uncertain world.

Ultimately it is the essential human longing for truth that redeems. One is reminded of truth by the pangs of one's conscience, which may expose one's evasion of reality. A sense of courage and possibility can be found by stopping the dialogue with the internalized voices of other people's laws and expectations. In the quietude of being with myself I can sense where truth lies and where lies have obscured the truth. The call of conscience reaches me through a feeling of guilt, that is, existential guilt, which tells me that something is lacking, something is being owed to life by me: I am in debt to myself.

The call of conscience comes through an attitude of openness to possibilities and limitations. This openness leads to Angst as it exposes me to my responsibilities and possible failure, but when I accept this anxiety it becomes the source of energy that allows me to be ready for whatever the future holds in store. And so, in facing the worst, I prepare myself for the best. I can live resolutely only when I can also surrender and release myself. I can be free only when I know what is necessary. I can be fully alive only when I face up to the possibility of my death.

Acquisition of psychological disturbance

When well-being is defined as the ability to face up to the disturbing facts of life, the notion of disturbance takes on a whole new meaning. Problems and obstacles are not necessarily an impediment to living well, for any potentially distressing situation can be seen as a challenge that can be faced. Problems are first of all problems in living and will occur at any stage in human development. In fact the only thing you can be sure of is that life will inevitably confront you with new situations that are a challenge to your established ways and evasions of the human paradox. When people are shocked out of their ordinary routine into a sudden awareness of their inability to face the realities of living, the clouds start to gather. Even though we may think of ourselves as well-adjusted people who have had a moderately acceptable upbringing, unexpected events, such as the death of a loved one, the loss of a job or another significant sudden exposure of our vulnerability, may still trigger a sense of failure, despair or extreme anxiety. Everything around us suddenly seems absurd or impossible and our own and other people's motives are questioned. The value of what used to be taken for granted becomes uncertain and life loses its appeal. The basic vulnerability of being human has emerged from behind the well-guarded self-deception of social adaptation. Sometimes a similar disenchantment and profound disturbance arise not out of an external catastrophe but out of a sense of the futility of everyday routines. Boredom can be just as important a factor in generating disturbance as losses or other forms of crisis.

No matter how securely a person is established in the world some events will shake the foundations of that security and transform the appearance of existence. For some people, however, such false security is not at first available. They never achieve 'ontological security' (Laing, 1960), which consists of having a firm sense of one's own and other people's reality and identity. Genetic predisposition obviously makes some of us capable of greater sensory awareness and psychological susceptibility than others. People who have such extraordinary sensitivity may easily get caught up in the conflicts that others are trying to avoid. If they are exposed to particularly intense contradictions (as in certain family conflicts) they may fall into a state of extreme confusion and despair and withdraw into the relative security of a world of their own creation.

Both the ontologically secure person who is disturbed by a crisis (or boredom) and the ontologically insecure person who is overwhelmed by the less pleasant sides of ordinary human existence are struggling with an absence of the usual protective armour of self-deception. Life is suddenly seen in all its harshness and paradoxical reality. Without the redeeming factor of some of the more positive aspects of life such realism can be distressing.

This does not mean that this kind of crisis or generation of anxiety should be avoided. It can be faced and integrated by making sense of it. The existential view of disturbance is that it is an inevitable and even welcome event that everyone will sooner or later encounter. The question is not how to avoid it, but on the contrary how to approach it with determination and curiosity.

Perpetuation of psychological disturbance

Problems start to become more serious when the challenge of disturbance is not faced but evaded. Then a self-perpetuating negative spiralling downwards can happen which leads to confusion and chaos. This is most likely to occur if we are not linked to a vital support system. As long as our family or other intimate networks of reference are strong and open enough to absorb the contradictions in which we get caught up, distress can be eased and overcome: the balance can be redressed. But if we find ourselves in isolation, without the understanding and challenge of a relative, a partner or a close friend, it is easy to get lost in our problems. Society's rituals for safeguarding the individual are these days less and less powerful and secure. Few people gain a sense of ultimate meaning or direction from their relationship to God or from other essential beliefs. Many feel at the mercy of temporary, ever-changing, but incessant demands, needs and desires.

In time of distress there seems all too often to be nowhere to turn. Relatives and friends, who themselves are barely holding their heads above water, may be unavailable. If they are available, they may want to soothe distress instead of tackling it at the root. Spiritual authority has gradually been eroded and has been replaced with scientific authority, which is unable to address moral or spiritual dilemmas. It is hardly surprising that people turn increasingly to psychotherapists or counsellors. Unfortunately, there is little evidence that psychotherapy and counselling are able to lessen distress. To some extent a reliance on therapeutic cure may present another perpetuation of disturbance, as long as the basic existential issues are not dealt with and the client is kept in a passive role.

Paradoxically, the institutions in our society often seem to encourage the very opposite of what they are supposed to be about. When the family becomes a place of loneliness and alienation instead of one that fosters togetherness and intimacy, when schools become places of boredom and reluctance instead of inspiring curiosity and learning and when doctors' surgeries become places of dependence and addiction instead of centres of healing and renewal of strength, it is time for essentials to be reconsidered. Much disturbance is not only generated but also maintained by a society that is out of touch with the essential principles of life.

Often it is in the distress of those who face a crisis that the disturbance of society is expressed. It is therefore hardly surprising that we are inclined to want to obliterate this reminder of failings at the heart of our own existence. If we are willing to attend to the message of such distress we give ourselves a chance to be reminded of the ways in which we perpetuate our own misunderstanding and avoidance of life.

Change

Life is one long process of change and transformation. Although people often think they want to change, more often than not their lives reflect their attempts at maintaining the status quo. As a person becomes convinced of the inevitability of change she may also become aware of the many ways in which she has kept such change at bay. Almost every minute of the day people make small choices that together determine the direction of their life. Often that direction is embarked upon passively: people just conform to their own negative or mediocre predictions of the future. But once insight is gained into the possibility of reinterpreting a situation and opting for more constructive predictions a change for the better may come about. This requires the person to learn to live deliberately instead of by default, and it can only be achieved by first becoming aware of how one's daily attitude and frame of mind is set to a form of automatic functioning that keeps one repeating the same mistakes.

It is not easy to break the force of habit, but there are always times when habits are broken by force. Crises are times when old patterns have to be revised and when changes for the better can be initiated. This is why existential therapists often talk about a breakdown as a possible breakthrough and why people often note with astonishment that the disaster they tried so hard to avoid was a blessing in disguise. In times of crisis the attention is refocused on where priorities lie so that choices can be made with more understanding than previously.

Whether such an event is self-imposed (as in emigration or marriage) or not (as in natural disasters or bereavement) it has the effect of removing previously taken for granted securities. When this happens it becomes more difficult for us to obscure the aspects of existence that we would rather not think about, and we are compelled to reassess our own attitudes and values. In the ensuing chaos we must make choices about how to proceed and how to bring new order into our lives. If we can tolerate the uncertainty of such situations instead of fleeing towards a new routine, such times can be an opportunity for rectifying life's direction.

Once a crisis has been faced in such a constructive manner it becomes easier to be open to change at other times as well. People can learn to re-evaluate their values and reassess their priorities continually, thus achieving a flexibility and vitality that allows them to make the most of life's naturally transformative character. Many people dread change and hide from it but they have to face it at a time of crisis. Existential therapy can be particularly helpful in those circumstances.

Practice

Goals of therapy

The goals of existential therapy are (1) to enable people to become more truthful with themselves; (2) to widen their perspective on themselves and the world around them; and (3) to find clarity on how to proceed into the future while taking lessons from the past and creating something valuable to live for in the present.

The word 'authenticity' is often used to indicate this goal of becoming true to oneself and therefore more real. This is a much abused term, which misleadingly suggests that there is a true self, whereas the existential view is that self is relationship and process – not an entity or substance. It can also become an excuse for people who want to have their cake and eat it. Under the aegis of authenticity anything can be licensed: crude egoism may very well be the consequence.

In fact, authenticity can never be fully achieved. It is a gradual process of self-understanding. It means getting to know the self as it is created in one's relationships to the world on all levels. Helping people to become authentic means assisting them in gaining a greater understanding of the human condition, so that they can respond to it with a sense of mastery, instead of being at its mercy.

The task of the therapist is to have attained sufficient clarity and openness to be able to venture along with any client into murky waters and explore (without getting lost) how this person's experience fits into a wider map of existence. Clients are guided through the disturbances in which they are caught and are helped to examine their assumptions, values and aspirations, so that a new direction can be taken. The therapist is fully available to this exploration and will often be changed in the process. The poignancy of each new adventure over the dangerous ground of life requires the therapist to become aware of previously unrecognized aspects of life. Therapy is an adventure that client and therapist embark upon together. Both will be transformed, as they let themselves be touched by life.

Selection criteria

Clients who come specifically for existential therapy usually already have the idea that their problems are about living, and are not a form of pathology. This basic assumption must be acceptable to clients if they are to benefit from the approach. A genuine commitment to an intense and very personal philosophical investigation is therefore a requirement. A critical mind and a desire to think for oneself are an advantage. People who want another's opinion on what ails them and who would prefer symptom relief to a search for meaning should be referred to other forms of therapy.

The approach is especially suitable for people who feel alienated from the expectations of society or for those seeking to clarify their personal ideology. The approach is relevant to people living in a foreign culture, class or race, as it does not dictate a specific way of looking at reality. It also works well with people confronting adversity in their lives or who are trying to cope with changes of personal circumstances (or want to bring those about). Bereavement, job loss or biological changes (in adolescence or middle age) are a prime time for the reconsideration of the rules and values one has hitherto lived by.

Generally speaking the existential approach is more helpful to those who question the state of affairs in the world, than to those who prefer the status quo. This approach seems to be most right for those at the edge of existence: people who are dying or contemplating suicide, people who are just starting on a new phase of life, people in crisis, or people who feel they no longer belong in their surroundings. It is less relevant for people who do not want to examine their assumptions and who would rather not explore the foundation of human existence.

Even though existential work consists in gaining understanding through talking, the client's level of verbal ability is not important. Very young children or people who speak a foreign language will often find that the simpler their way of expressing things, the easier it becomes to grasp the essence of their world view and experience. The approach is not about intellectualizing, but about verbalizing the basic impressions, ideas, intuitions and feelings a person has about life.

The existential approach can be applied in many different settings: individual, couple, family or group. When it involves more than one person at a time, the emphasis will be on clarifying the participants' perceptions of the world and their place in it, in order to encourage communication and mutual understanding between them. The focus is always on the individual's experiences and relationships.

A dimension of existential exploration can easily be added to almost any other approach to psychotherapy, but it will soon be found that this makes a re-evaluation of one's method necessary. Many of the more directive and manipulative forms of therapy are in flagrant contradiction of existential principles. Interpretative methods such as psychoanalysis or analytical psychology betray the existential rule of openness to the different meanings that emerge for individuals. In the final analysis existential work requires a commitment to a philosophical investigation, which necessitates its own guidelines and parameters.

Qualities of effective therapists

Good existential therapists combine personal qualities with accomplishment in method, but on balance it is more important that they are the right sort of people than that they have a high level of skill. Qualities can be described as falling into four categories: (a) life experience, (b) attitude and personality, (c) theoretical knowledge, (d) professional training.

Life experience The existential therapist will characteristically be mature as a human being. This maturity will manifest itself in an ability to make room in oneself for all sorts of, even contradictory, opinions, attitudes, feelings, thoughts and experiences. Rather than clinging to one point of view, existential therapists will be capable of overseeing reality from a wide range of perspectives. They will also be able to tolerate the tension that such awareness of contradictions generates. There are a number of life experiences that appear to be particularly helpful in preparing people for such maturation. Cross-cultural experience is an excellent way to stretch the mind and one's views on what it means to be human. People who have permanently had to adjust their whole way of perceiving and dealing with the world (especially when this includes a change of language) have had the all-important experience of questioning previous assumptions and opening up to a new culture and perspective.

Raising a family, or caring for dependants in a close relationship, is another invaluable source of life experience relevant to creating an open attitude. Many women have little academic schooling but great practical experience in this area. Their life experience can become one of the building blocks of the kind of maturity needed to become an existential therapist.

The experience of having been immersed in society from several angles, in different jobs, different academic studies, different social classes and so on, is a definite advantage. The existential therapist is likely to be someone who has lived seriously and intensely in a number of ways and not just through the caring professions. People opting for psychotherapy as a second career are often especially suitable.

Finally, the *sine qua non* of becoming an existential therapist is to have negotiated a number of significant crossroads in one's personal life. Existential therapists will have had their share of existential crises. Of course they will also have had to develop their ability to deal with these satisfactorily, so that their own lives were enriched rather than impoverished by the experience. Although all this maturity conjures up the image of someone advanced in age, it must be noted that maturity is not always commensurate with years. Some young people may have weathered greater storms than their elders and, what is more, may have lived their relatively shorter lives with greater intensity, maturing into fuller human beings.

Attitude and personality Existential therapists should be capable of critical consideration of situations, people and ideas. They are serious, but not heavy-handed, downtrodden or cynical. They can be lighthearted, hopeful and humorous about the human condition, whilst intensely aware of the tragic poignancy of much of existence.

They should be capable of self-reflection, recognizing the manner in which they themselves represent the paradoxes, ups and downs, strengths and weaknesses that people are capable of. They should have a genuine sense of curiosity and a strong urge to find out what it means to be human. They should be capable of sustaining an attitude of wonder. Existential therapists will now and then abandon psychological theory altogether and reach for poetry, art or religion instead.

Theoretical knowledge   A basic working knowledge of philosophy, that is of the controversies and perspectives that the human race has produced over the centuries, is more useful to this approach than any other kind of knowledge. Included in this would be a familiarity with the history of psychology and psychoanalysis and a wide study of the many different approaches to psychotherapy that have been developed over the years. This will provide a map of different views on human nature, health and illness, happiness and unhappiness, which again will train and broaden the mind and personal outlook of the therapist.

Professional training   The existential therapist needs the kind of training that an eclectic therapist needs: a generic one. But instead of borrowing bits and pieces of technique from each to produce a complex amalgam, essentials are distilled and applied within a consistent philosophical framework. Specific skills of dialectical interaction can then be developed. Training should consist of a significant amount of clinical work under supervision and of self-reflection and analysis. Here again it is the quality that will be judged instead of the quantity. Numbers of hours of individual and group therapy are irrelevant. Some people will not reach the necessary perspective and depth with any amount of therapy. Others will be well ahead by having engaged in a discipline of self-reflection for years. The degree of readiness usually becomes obvious in supervision sessions, for one's response to other people's troubles is an excellent test of one's own attitude to life and level of self-knowledge.

Therapeutic relationship and style

It is important for the existential therapist to have a flexible attitude towards therapeutic style. Not only do different therapists interpret the approach in diverse ways, but clients also have their own individual requirements which may vary over time. The existential therapist is ready and willing to shift her stance when the situation requires this. In a sense this variability is characteristic of the existential therapeutic style.

There are, of course, common features running through all of this. All existential therapists, for example, strive to recognize and question their preconceptions and prejudices as much as possible in their work. There is also a consistent appreciation of the unique situation of the client. The existential therapist strives to take the dilemmas of the client seriously – eschewing recourse to diagnoses and solutions. This seriousness includes openness and wonder as essential attributes of the existential attitude and does not preclude humour when appropriate.

Existential therapists are fundamentally concerned with what matters most to the client. He or she avoids making normative judgements, and renounces any ambition to, even implicitly, push the client in any particular direction. The attitude is non-directive, but not directionless. The client is assisted in finding his or her own perspective and position in the world in relation to the parameters and limits of human existence.

At times the therapist might facilitate the client's investigations through an attitude of relative passivity and silent intervention. At other times active dialogue and debate are required. On such occasions the therapist intervenes to point out contradictions in or implications of the client's avowed point of view. The use of confrontation to offer opinions or moral evaluations of the client is not consistent with the existential attitude.

The existential therapist resists the temptation to try and change the client. The therapy is an opportunity for the client to take stock of his life and ways of being in the world. Nothing is gained from interfering with these. The client is simply given the space, time and understanding to help him come to terms with what is true for him. What he wants to do with this afterwards is up to him. The therapist does not teach or preach about how life should be lived, but lets the client's personal taste in the art of living evolve naturally within the context of existential and social constructions.

The only times when the therapist does follow a didactic line is when she reminds the client of aspects of a problem that have been overlooked. She gently encourages the client to notice a lack of perspective, think through consequences and struggle with contradictions. She puts forward missing links and underlying principles. The therapist never does the work for the client but makes sure that the work gets done. The client's inevitable attempts to shirk and flee from the task in hand are reflected on and used as concrete evidence of the client's attitude to life. The same can be said of the actual encounter between the client and the therapist, which is also reflected on and seen as evidence of the client's usual ways of relating.

Generally speaking the therapeutic style follows a conversational pattern. Issues are considered and explored in dialogue. The rhythm of the sessions will follow that of the client's preoccupations – faster when emotions are expressed and slower when complex ideas are disentangled. Existential therapists need to learn to allow clients to take the amount of space and time in this conversation that they need in order to proceed at their own pace. Existential therapists create sufficient room for the client to feel that it is possible to unfold their troubles.

Existential sessions are usually quite intense, since deep and significant issues often emerge. Moreover, the therapist is personally engaged with the work and is willing to be touched and moved by the client's conflicts and questions. The human dilemmas expressed in the therapeutic encounter have as much relevance to the therapist as to the client. This commonality of experience makes it possible for client and therapist to work together as a team, in a co-operative effort to throw light on human existence. Every new challenge in the client's experience is grist for the mill. The therapeutic relationship itself brings many opportunities to grasp something of the nature of human interaction. The therapist, in principle, is ready to consider any past, present or future matter that is relevant to the client.

Major therapeutic strategies and techniques

The existential approach is well known for its anti-technique orientation. It prefers description, understanding and exploration of reality to diagnosis, treatment and prognosis. Existential therapists will not generally use particular techniques, strategies or skills, but they will follow a specific philosophical method of enquiry which requires a consistent professional attitude. This method and attitude may be interpreted in various ways, but it usually includes some or all of the following ingredients.

Cultivating a naive attitude By consistently meeting the client with an open mind and in the spirit of exploration and discovery a fresh perspective on the world will emerge. This requires a great deal of intellectual discipline on the part of the therapist, who continuously has to observe and question her own prejudice.

Themes: clear themes will run through the apparently confused discourse of the client. The therapist listens for the unspoken links that are implicit in what is said. When the theme is obvious and has been confirmed several times the client's attention can be drawn to it.

Assumptions: much of what the client says will be based on a number of basic assumptions about the world. Generally people are unaware of these. Clarifying implicit assumptions can be very revealing and may throw new light on a dilemma.

Vicious circles: many people are caught up in self-fulfilling prophecies of doom and destruction without realizing that they set their own low standards and goals. Making such vicious circles explicit can be a crucial step forward.

Meaning: often people assume that they know what they mean when they talk about something. But the words they use can hide, even from themselves, the significance of what they mean. By questioning the superficial meaning of the client's words and asking her to think again of what she wants to express, a new awareness may be brought about.

Values: people live their lives by standards and principles that establish values which they often take for granted and of which they are only dimly aware. Getting clarity about what makes life worth living and which aspects of life are most important and deserve making sacrifices for is an important step towards finding one's sense of direction.

Facing limitations As the existential approach is essentially concerned with the need to face the limitations of the human condition, the therapist will be alert for opportunities to help the client identify these.

Self-deception: much of the time we pretend that life has determined our situation and character so much that we have no choices left. Crises may provide us with proof to the contrary. The safe crisis of the therapeutic interaction is a suitable place for rediscovering opportunities and challenges that had been forgotten.

Existential anxiety: the anxiety that indicates one's awareness of inevitable limitations and death is also a dizziness in the face of freedom and a summoning of life energy. Existential anxiety is the *sine qua non* of individual awareness and full aliveness. Some people have dulled their sensitivity so as to avoid the basic challenges of life, others are overwhelmed by them and yet others have found ways of disguising them. Optimal use of anxiety is one of the goals of existential work. The therapist will recognize the client's existential anxiety and will assist in finding ways of living with it constructively.

Existential guilt: the sense of being in debt to life and owing it to oneself to do or not do something is another source of insight into one's limitations and priorities. Therapists watch for existential guilt hidden in various disguises (such as anxiety, boredom, depression or even apparent self-confidence).

Consequences: clients are sometimes challenged to think through the consequences of choices, both past and future. In facing the implications of one's actions it becomes necessary to recognize limitations as well as possibilities. Some choices become easier to make; others become less attractive. Existential therapy does not condone the clients' tendency to want only support and acceptance and wallow in a sense of their own suffering; it encourages clients to confront their own responsibilities in relation to the world, other people and themselves.

Paradoxes: in helping the client to become more authentic the concept of paradox can be of great help. If clients are inclined to evade the basic human dilemma of life and death and contradictions that flow from it, their self-affirmation may look more like egocentricity. Checking that a person is aware of her capacity for both life and death, success and failure, freedom and necessity, certainty and doubts, allows one to remain in touch with a fundamental search for truth.

Exploring personal world view The existential approach is open to all of life's dimensions, tasks and problems and the therapist will in principle explore together with the client all information that the latter brings along.

The fourfold world: using the model of four dimensions of existence discussed earlier it becomes possible to listen to the client's account of herself as revealing her preoccupations with particular levels of her existence.

A systematic analysis of how the client expresses her relationship to the physical, social, psychological and spiritual dimensions of her world can provide much insight into imbalance, priorities and impasses. An impression can be formed of where on the whole territory of human existence the client is struggling for clarity.

Dreams: listening to dreams with this model in mind can be extremely enlightening. The dream is seen as a message of the dreamer to himself. The dream experience reflects the dreamer's attitudes on the various dimensions of existence and the client's dream existence and world relations in it are as concrete as those of waking life.

Of course the same applies to the fantasies or stories that the client reports. Each of these is a miniature picture of the way in which he relates to the world and much can be learned from examining them carefully.

Questions: exploring the client's world view is an ongoing enterprise and it is best done with an observation-orientated attitude. Questions are often asked in order to check whether a certain event or situation is seen in a particular light. Existential therapists will often make observations and inferences and elicit further material that will either confirm or disconfirm hypotheses. The therapist draws the client's attention to what seems to be the case. Sometimes an enquiry might be made in order to clarify a perception, along the lines of an exploration: 'What makes this so important to you?', or 'What is this like for you?' or 'What does it mean to you?' The question never suggests a solution nor judges right or wrong, but investigates the client's personal opinion and inclination.

Enquiring into meaning   All investigations eventually lead to gaining a greater understanding of what makes the world meaningful to the client. The idea is to assist the client in finding purpose and motivation, direction and vitality. In the process a number of irrelevant and misleading motivations may be encountered and eliminated. Quite often new interpretations of past or present events are arrived at, altering the client's orientation to life and the future.

Emotions: feelings are of great help in this process. Understanding the meaning of one's emotions and the message they contain in terms of what one aspires to or is afraid to lose is of crucial help in finding the pattern of purpose currently at work. Each emotion has its own significance (van Deurzen-Smith, 1988) and the whole range of the emotional spectrum can be used as a compass in indicating one's direction in life. Emotions like shame, envy and hope are indicators of values that are still missing but implicitly longed for. Love, joy and pride are within the range of emotions that indicate a sense of ownership of what is valued. Whereas jealousy and anger express an active response to the threat that what is valued may be lost, fear and sorrow come with the giving up and eventual loss of what really mattered.

Beliefs: all observations on the client's preoccupations lead to a picture of her opinions, beliefs and values. It is important to extract these respectfully. Nothing can be gained from opposing the client's values with an alternative set of values. It is the client's conscience that has to be uncovered and revitalized. If deeply held values are contested or criticized conformity will be encouraged rather than reliance on an inner sense of purpose. Light is thrown on the ways in which personal beliefs may fail to take into account wider implications for others. This will expand the system of beliefs into something that can encompass the facts of life and a broader frame of reference.

Talents: many talents, abilities and assets will have been hidden by the client's preoccupation with what is wrong with her. The therapist will attend to these and strive to draw attention to the wisdom and strength that are lying fallow. Often it is useful for the therapist to build on the example of the client's abilities as they come to the fore and use them as the point of reference for further understanding.

Recollection: memories will be seen as malleable and open to new interpretation. While clients often set out with fixed views of their past they discover the possibility of reconsidering the same events and experiences in different ways. It is essential to encourage clients to discover how they influence their future with their own version of the past and how it is within their power to recollect themselves in new ways, thereby opening new vistas. In addition to this the absolutely determining factors from the past will be moderated by a knowledge of the possibility for positive or negative transformation. When the client realizes that he is the ultimate source of the meaning of his life, past, present and future, living is experienced as an art rather than a duty.

The change process in therapy

The aim of existential therapy is not to change people but to help them to come to terms with the transformative process of life. The assumption is that when people do face reality they are likely to find a satisfactory way forward. People are often hurried and under the impression that they can speed life up and force great rewards out of it with relatively little effort. One of the aims of existential therapy is to enable people to stop deceiving themselves about both their lack of responsibility for what is happening to them and their excessive demands on life and themselves. Learning to measure one's distress by the standards of the human condition relieves pressure and at the same time provides a clearer ideological basis for making sense of personal preoccupations and aspirations. Clients change through existential therapy by gradually taking more and more of life's ups and downs in their stride. They can become more steadfast in facing death, crises, personal shortcomings, losses and failures if they accept the reality of constant transformation that we are all part of. They can find ways of tuning into these changes, instead of fighting them or trying to speed them up.

In other words they can acquire a measure of wisdom in learning to distinguish between the things they can change and those they cannot change. They can come to terms with the givens and find the courage to tackle the uncertainties. They can find out what matters enough to them to be committed to it, live for it and ultimately perhaps even die for it.

As they are constantly reminded to do their own thinking on these issues, people can learn to monitor their own actions, attitudes and moods. The therapy gives clients an opportunity to rediscover the importance of relating to themselves and taking time for contemplation and recreation. Existential therapy teaches a discipline for living which consists of a frequent process of checking what one's attitude, inclination, mood and frame of mind are, bringing them back in line with reality and personal aspirations.

Change is initiated in the sessions, but not accomplished in them. The process of change takes place in between the sessions and after therapy has terminated. The therapeutic hour itself can never be more than a small contribution to a person's renewed engagement with life. It is only a kind of rehearsal for life. The change process is never-ending. As long as there is life there will be change. There is no place for complacency or self-congratulatory belief in cure.

As existential therapy has no criterion for cure, it could in theory be an endless process. To make sure it does not become this, the criterion for finishing a series of sessions is simply to stop when the client feels ready to manage alone again. To encourage such self-reliance, relatively short-term therapy is encouraged (three months to two years).

Limitations of the approach

The emphasis that the existential approach places on self-reflection and under-standing can lead to certain limitations. The approach often attracts clients who feel disinclined to trust other human beings because they perceive the existential approach as leaving them in total control. This limitation can only be overcome by a therapist who neither fights the need nor leaves it unchallenged, but who assists the client in turning such self-reliance to a positive end.

The approach is also often misconstrued as 'intellectual'. Some existential therapists tend to emphasize the cognitive aspect of their clients' preoccupations and some clients are attracted to the approach with the hope of avoiding senses, feeling and intuition. A good existential therapist would heed all these different levels of experience, as full self-understanding can be achieved only through openness to all different aspects of being. Nevertheless the emphasis on self-reflection remains central and the criticism is therefore a valid one to some degree.

The practical limitations of the approach have already been referred to in the section on selection criteria. As the approach does not stress the illness–health dimension, people who directly want to relieve specific symptoms will generally find the existential approach unhelpful.

The existential therapist neither encourages the client to regress to a deep level of dependency nor seeks to become a significant other in the client's life and nurture the client back to health. The therapist is a consultant who can provide the client with a method for and systematic support in facing the truth, and in this sense is there to allow the client to relate to herself more than to the therapist. This might be considered a limitation of the approach by clients who wish to regress and rely on the therapist as a substitute parental figure. Good existential therapists obviously enable the client to confront that issue just as bravely as any other issue and come through with greater self-understanding.

Perhaps the most absolute limitation is that of the level of maturity, life experience and intensive training that is required of practitioners in this field. It should be clear from the above that existential therapists are required to be wise and capable of profound and wide-ranging understanding of what it means to be human. The criteria of what makes for a good existential therapist are so high that the chances of finding bad existential therapists must be considerable.

One can imagine the danger of therapists pretending to be capable of this kind of wisdom without actual substance or inner authority. Little would be gained by replacing technological or medical models of therapy, which can be concretely learned and applied by practitioners, with a range of would-be existential advisers who are incapable of facing life's problems with dignity and creativity themselves. The only way around this is to create training organizations that select candidates extremely carefully on personal qualities and experience before putting them through a thorough training and a long period of intensively supervised work.

Case example

The client

Peter is a professional man of around 30. He is tall and thin and covers a basic shyness with a self-mocking attitude. As he speaks he emerges as intelligent and highly articulate. He excels in verbal expression to such an extent that one would expect him to have cultivated his ability to a more academic level. From the start he relishes arguing with me and yet most of what Peter says during our first meeting is tentative. He strikes me as a young man who knows he has effectively played his way through life so far, but who has begun to realize that it is time to grow up.

There is a hint of defeatism in his voice, a suggestion of oppressive doubt. He is inclined to dismiss the therapeutic relationship out of hand as non-viable, yet there is also a curiosity and genuine vulnerability. I note that Peter would be unlikely to tolerate any directive attempts to control him. Existential therapy is therefore an appropriate choice, although I have some doubt whether he wants to be helped at all.

The main issue that he puts forward is that of his relationships. He has a girlfriend for whom he cares. Their relationship is long-standing, but it has been made difficult by his desire to be free and have other relationships. Now he has become aware of the hurt this has caused his girlfriend. He has somewhat reluctantly reached the conclusion that the relationship is worth committing to. His girlfriend wants to settle down and have children. He is not at all sure that he is ready for this.

He also feels incompetent at expressing his tender feelings, especially to his girlfriend, and he is worried about the times when he gets into a rage with her. He openly admits to having considerable misgivings about psychotherapy. He worries that it is self-indulgent. Peter cannot remember much about his childhood and does not think there is any point in trying to.

Hearing all of this I am aware of his status of reluctant client and I realize that working with him will be difficult. I suspect that short-term therapy appeals to him because it will allow him to get his feet wet and prove to himself and others that he can do this, without actually having to plunge in. We agree to a 10-week contract.

The therapy

Peter misses the first session and at the second says that it is not very easy for him to concentrate because he keeps getting distracted by other ideas: everything leads to so many other avenues. Most of all he is afraid of confabulation. He might be pinning things down in one way when they were actually much more complex. It is always like this with him, he says: he always seen many aspects to things and this makes it difficult to take sides. He is afraid of committing some sort of injustice.

He says that while other people, for instance, tell loads of stories about their adolescence he has none to tell. His preoccupation with getting things wrong and writing the story of his life in an unfaithful way is a serious one. The idea of being fair and just to reality as well as to other people emerges as a guiding principle for him. One could say this is one of his central values.

From here he moves on to contemplate the contradictions between his relationship to his girlfriend and the time he spends with his friends, smoking, drinking and arguing. He is dissatisfied with the long nights talking for he always ends up worrying about the things he has said in anger, which leave him with an emotional hangover. I remark that smoking, drinking and arguing with his friends could be considered self-indulgence. He agrees and says that he believes that the time has come to commit himself to his girlfriend and that he has now decided to move in with her and away from the gang who keep him within the old culture. He feels the need to assure me and him that this is for real. At the same time he is worried about what he might miss. We talk about his current way of life and he wonders why it is not satisfactory to him. I suggest that much of what comes easily takes one on a downward spiral, which is ultimately self-destructive. He then contrasts it with the possibility of devoting oneself to a career, a relationship, or even to raising children. I point out how these things involve effort rather than ease, but that they build something constructive.

Peter is driven to question anything that reeks to him of 'establishment' values and he talks of things turning around in vicious circles and not leading anywhere. 'Don't they lead anywhere, are you sure?' I ask and this makes Peter question whether it is of any use for things to lead somewhere. Every intervention I make evokes his reaction. 'Why,' he says with a dismissive gesture, 'should one build these things if life is meaningless anyway? Why should I bother?' 'Maybe,' I query back in return, 'life only seems meaningless when one lives on the downward spiral in self-indulgence. Perhaps it becomes meaningful only when you put in the effort to build something up and move into an upward spiral.'

The next session Peter arrives in a bad mood. Everything has gone wrong. He has had a row with his girlfriend. He has been rushing around doing various things that he describes and each in turn has led him to lose his temper with people and then get worried about what they will think of him. He tells me how he used to have a real temper problem until he decided at some point in his early twenties that he should not lose his temper so often. Lately however he has begun to fear that suppressing the anger might be bad for him and he lets his temper flare up again now. He goes off into generalizations and after a minute I stop him and ask him to recount the concrete events that triggered his anger.

He tells me of his frustration with his girlfriend, who after having a good time out with her own friends, overwhelmed him with her stories about it and then resented him not going to bed at the same time as her, because he wanted to write. When he finally did go to bed, she woke up 'only to have the last word'. The next day when she stopped him again when he was writing he shouted at her that she was not respecting his needs.

We talk about what is required when two people have just moved in together and need to find ways to accommodate each other. Peter concludes abruptly that the cause of all the trouble is his busy social life. He decides to withdraw from these social relationships completely. He looks wounded and martyred as he makes this announcement and I enquire what that decision will do to him. He admits that no social relationships will mean boredom. I point out how the extreme positions of total immersion in these social relationships on the one hand or total withdrawal from them on the other hand both seem unsatisfactory. It sounds as if there must be a better solution somewhere nearer the middle of that continuum. It would be important to understand what these relationships offer him. Peter then begins to consider what they actually involve and describes how he tends to use them for getting into arguments over trivia. It is as if he picks fights to prove himself worthy. I note that it looks as if he seeks to test his intelligence but does this in a way that seems wasteful.

Peter is despondent and fears he is going around in circles again. I suggest that the trick is to find a way to make these circles turn into upward spirals instead of downward ones.

A week later Peter is looking relaxed when he comes in and says that things have been better. He has not gone out so much, has worked hard and is getting some results. This is largely because he had deadlines to meet. Later on it transpires that he does the same thing in many different guises: using other people's deadlines or commitments as parameters for his own activity. He is, for instance, getting his girlfriend to persuade him to have children. I remark how he seems to be waiting for other people to push him into action, while keeping himself smugly at a distance from the decision-making.

Peter responds strongly to my use of the word 'smug'. Other people have called him smug and he does not like it. He thinks it is a bad thing to be smug and asks me if I think it is a bad thing. Suddenly he sounds small and dependent, wanting guidance. We begin to examine what smugness means to him and how it might apply to him. Yes, he does have a basic ease with life and a sense of having sorted things quite nicely. He does not really want to look into himself, and because he avoids doing so he has not discovered what is inside him. I say: 'You have not really been broken by life, you have not ever been truly challenged and in a way you long for it and in another way you want to keep things as they are.' He says he has never even been to a funeral. He has never had his heart broken. I say: 'You have never suffered real loss and it is through loss that people get more challenged, is it?'

He is not sure, but he wants to know how he can find something that will challenge him. He says he worries that he is too egotistical. He starts arguments for the sake of the argument and for his own pleasure. He pushes people until they give in or give up. 'So you always win?' 'Yes,' he says, self-satisfied and embarrassed at the same time. 'It sounds as if you are arguing with the wrong people then – you have not met your match.' This strikes another chord. He has apparently become so confident that he argues on other people's points, rather than pursuing his own line of thinking. He does not believe strongly enough in anything to want to argue it for its own sake. It is as if he has become bored with arguing itself for lack of commitment. 'You don't let yourself be challenged and stretched there either,' I comment. He sighs and talks about how he sometimes wonders about taking up some strict discipline, like Islam. Fundamentalism has a fascination for him, because of his yearning for boundaries and rules: his longing for something to come up against, be challenged by. He yearns for something greater than himself that will both stretch him and provide him with an outside parameter to grow up against, or towards. I note that it is not so much a boundary as a goal that he lacks.

At one point he says that our work together has given him plenty of new retorts for arguments although he has not found opportunities to apply them. I feel under pressure to match him and stretch him, but also to spare him and leave him the illusion that he can win. It would be all right if he were fighting his hardest, but Peter seems to play in a noncommittal manner. It is as if he fears that if he commits himself to something he might lose. He is not prepared to really hazard himself, but this withdrawal dissatisfies him as much as it does me.

I confront him with this, saying how he seems to use all his energy and considerable abilities to play around instead of getting on with life. I am now convinced that he has taken the therapy in the same way as he takes life: passively and seeing it as something he wants to win, but without wanting to put in the labour that is required or take a risk. I put it to him at the end of the session that underneath his smugness he has a sense of falling short and of wasting his abilities. He sits up and takes notice; there is a sense of poignancy. Then Peter claims to have little or no ambition and a very unclear sense of his own possible contribution in life. Although I can challenge his smugness, I cannot provide anything to fill the emptiness until he has learned his own lessons through an actual experience of loss and subsequent discovery of what matters to him.

At the next session there is a long silence to start with. At last he hesitantly ventures: 'I am not sure I want to be thinking about the meaning of life. I work all week and this hour is the most demanding of the week. I don't know that I want to be making this effort. There is nothing really wrong with my life. I am making changes anyway. I used to be into short-term happiness of the moment and that seems to be fading, but it is too much of an effort to plan anything else.'

He speaks of his work, sitting at the computer and knowing that he is not producing things that are as good as he is capable of producing. He knows he could do better, but he doesn't. I remark that he sounds like a school teacher giving himself a bad report. He says that is frequently what teachers used to say about him and it is true. He knows that he can do better, but it just doesn't seem worth the effort.

I point out how sceptical he seems to be of almost everything that might be of value. 'I am cynical,' he says. 'Yes and proud of it,' I reply. He blushes and grins. He asks me if it is wrong to be cynical and if he should change. I tell him I don't think that is the relevant question as long as he clearly does not want to change. I also note that someone who has a lively mind and who is used to questioning things cannot just stop doing so.

After a further exchange I say: 'It seems to me that it all depends on how you use that ability to question, whether you use it to take you forward or whether you let it get you stuck.' He is not quite sure he understands this. I give the example of someone who questions that two and two equal four. I say that such questioning might lead you to discover new mathematical principles if you acted on your scepticism and moved into some new form of mathematical investigation. However if you did not act on your scepticism in order to discover some new truth, if instead you merely continued to question that two and two is four, without any further action, you would in effect be stopping both your own progress and your ability ever to make any useful ordinary calculations in your life. Scepticism is only the first step. If you don't move beyond it it might cripple you rather than serve you. I add: 'In your case your cynicism may be an essential asset, if you know what to do with it, but right now it looks like it often stops you from living.'

He is quiet for a while. Then he says, almost to himself: 'I think I may have a problem after all – for nothing really seems meaningful or possible to me. There is no purpose; not even looking for a purpose seems meaningful.' I remain quiet. The silence seems to weigh on him. 'It is so intense here,' he complains and he looks pained. 'Life just does not seem meaningful. It is not perfectible, only manage-able.' 'And sometimes not even that,' I add. He immediately bounces back. 'I have never felt I could not manage,' he says confidently and with some surprise at his own certainty on this point. I say: 'Yes, your issue is not that you are stressed or distressed, but rather understressed: there is not enough creative tension. You have found a great way of keeping tension at bay.' He agrees and instantly reverts to blaming this on his laziness. I point out how dismissive it is to brush off a coping strategy as mere laziness. He says that he has accepted that life does not bring happiness or satisfaction since he was in his early twenties. I see him suppressing a sigh. I ask: 'What were the dreams you abandoned?' He replies shyly: 'Oh, I sang and I wrote, but I could never achieve that perfection, that bliss, that you sometimes, rarely, feel when you listen to certain music or read a novel. Take Nabokov for instance. He brings together so much detail: it is like seeing all the knots – then he flips it over and suddenly you are faced with the perfection of a well-knotted carpet. Sometimes in a film as well, you feel so transported, it is bliss, but it is short-lived. I've accepted that I can't share that with people. I've tried maybe once or twice, when I was drunk, but they can't understand.' He has suddenly come to life as momentarily he allows himself to resonate with this dimension of deep yearning inside of him. He is poised to dismiss it.

I gently remark how he cuts himself off – from others, from his aspirations, from his own future, from his ability to create such moments. He protests that that is not his doing, but life. He says life is basically pretty meaningless. I say, 'Yes to those who expect it to carry intrinsic meaning.' 'Maybe I am just more passive than active,' he ponders mournfully. Then he asks me whether I think that he would get meaning out of having children. I point out to him how he reverts to asking me to give him guidance instead of following his own. He contends that it makes no difference if life is intrinsically meaningless anyway. 'That is the way of talking of someone who doesn't see meaning in life. You conclude that there can't be any meaning, because it is not there intrinsically. You are ruling out the possibility that if there is no meaning to start with, it is up to you to create some, like Nabokov creates carpet magic.'

Peter looks puzzled. He says he does not understand. I sense that he is on the verge of discovering his own power to create, works of art in his job, constructive relationships and possibly children. The creativity is within his grasp and he knows it on some level, but he has made it taboo for himself and I sense that he wants me to guide him towards it so that he can discard and dismiss it again. I realize that he will have to understand why he has made his creative power so taboo before he can reach out for it again. I do not think he is willing or able to do so through my intervention.

Peter comes to the next session in a rebellious mood. He announces that he has moved and then maintains a heavy silence, which I allow to unfold. He tells me that there are three things that bothered him in the last session. The first is that he is cynical, the second that he cuts himself off emotionally and the third that he makes me feel as if he is asking me to give him guidance. He also realizes that all three are connected. The first two things he can accept, but it really bothers him that I think that he wants guidance. His cynicism wouldn't even let him, he explains, for how can you ever tell anyone how to live their life?

I point out to him that far from thinking that he wants advice in order to act on it, I have the impression that he wants me to give him guidance so that he can reject it. In the same way in which he keeps his past out of his field of vision, he is also good at keeping others at a safe fighting distance.

He rises to my implied challenge by saying that there is nothing worth going over in his past and that he learned not to show his emotions when living in the East End. In the working-class atmosphere in which he grew up you just had to keep yourself from others emotionally and not give anything away. 'What's the point in saying I have had a difficult childhood and that is why I am who I am,' he says rather scornfully. Then he goes on to recount a number of events in his past that throw new light on the way in which he conducts himself. He realizes that his memories are there to be retrieved if he wants them. He can also see that most of what he talks about today is full of sadness and resentment.

I wonder if he will have the courage to take the work a stage further, but as it happens he goes off on a two-week holiday with a group of friends at this point. On his return it is clear that he has withdrawn from the work we have begun. He is more cynical and aloof than before and I wonder why he bothers to continue to see me. As soon as we get anywhere near serious he reverts to scepticism or mockery. I observe how it seems as if he runs into the sea, dips his toes in, then sees the waves and runs back. He does not plunge in and he does not try to swim. I decide to pressure him less; my interventions become more succinct and are often paradoxical in nature. If he asks 'How can I be more self-reflective?' I reply: 'Why should you want to be?' When he talks of being lazy, I retort: 'Why not be lazy?'

This works well to a certain extent, for it fires him into showing his potential for creativity. Peter is definitely at his best when challenged to deploy his strength. In the end, however, he tends to disengage from the exchange, determined to stay in control of his own destiny, afraid to respond positively to external influences. A pattern develops whereby he starts out with a half-hearted effort to work on something, then rises to the challenge that I offer, taking a considerable step forward, only to take two steps back a little later, undoing anything that could be seen as having come from me.

When we come to the end of our contract and it is time to evaluate our work together I suggest that he is good at actively protecting his own living space but that he pays an important price of lack of stimulation, challenge and creativity for that. He has kept me out successfully, in the same way in which he keeps others at bay. He does not let his past or his future impinge on the present. I contend that the way in which he treats the therapy says a lot about his attitude towards life. 'Yes, how do I do that?' He sounds anxious. 'You can blame it on me if you want to,' I suggest, half jokingly.

For the first time in our work together he is the one who insists on being serious. 'I don't want to blame it on you,' he says. 'How do I run away from therapy?' he insists. 'You flee by withdrawing into cynicism or into abstractions. You keep things on a narrow base by not bringing things like dreams, memories, fantasies, and rarely even real events, concrete interactions, feelings, preoccupations. You keep things on an even keel by going over well-rehearsed arguments, keeping me out of your internal life and proving me wrong all the time. You have rarely talked about your parents, or your sisters and brother or concrete things that happen between you and others. You have never even mentioned your girlfriend's name.' There is a thoughtful silence. He avoids my eyes. Then he lifts his head and says: 'I would like to try.' At that moment the clock that indicates that our time is up begins to strike. 'Saved by the bell, Peter,' I say. He gets up slowly. The next session will be the last.

In the last session he again brings me the issue of not being able to concentrate. He tells me that it is related to him having had to learn to skim-read for his job. 'Ah,' I say, 'this is wonderful. You have just summed up in one image the pattern that you have been struggling to describe and understand for the past month. It is a pattern that we have seen at play in many different aspects of your life, including in the way you have approached therapy. There are too many books, too many friends, too many possibilities, too many avenues to quickly explore, resulting in a lack of depth and purpose. But not only do you show how it is that you operate in those moments – skimming the surface and gathering quantity rather than quality – you also tell me why you do it. It is possible for you to do this, you say, because you have taught yourself to do so for practical purposes. You need to get through a lot and fast. So you have adapted and learned to do it.'

He beams, but states dismissively: 'Well, that is what comes easy to a lazy person.' He is persistent and determined in holding on to this negative self-image. I am not playing ball. 'Nah,' I say, 'that is a very personal view of the matter. What you refer to as the easy result of laziness would seem like something quite difficult to achieve to some other people. You find it easy to spread yourself thinly and skim the surface, whilst there are others who have the greatest difficulty in emerging from self-absorbed depth. Some people find it hard even to get through one book for instance, let alone skim-read so many.' He accepts the credit for this particular talent.

After some further discussion Peter begins to wonder whether he might also be capable of a more profound approach at times. 'You think that I have that in me?' he asks. 'I know that you have that in you from the evidence you have given me over the past weeks and months.' 'How do I bring that out?' he asks and I reply that life will do that sooner or later, if he is willing to learn from what happens to him. Now he moves on to wondering why life has spared him so much to date. We have been there before, but he is now able to find some answers for himself. He comes to the conclusion that it is two sided. In the first place he has been spared major tragedies up to now, but in the second place when difficulties have hit him he has been able to keep them under control. He acknowledges both his ability to keep things safe and avoid trouble in that way and the risk of losing out on letting himself be touched by life.

I reflect on the 10 sessions we have had, saying that these too seemed for him a time to try to get through relatively unscathed and that he did so successfully. He remarks, tongue in cheek, that he came to me with honourable intentions but that he will walk away from these sessions to go right back to where he was, untouched. 'And that was just the point you wanted to prove,' I reply: 'that you could do that and that you were emotionally independent.' 'Yes, in a way, but that would be just what you would say.' 'Not necessarily. There are other possible interpretations. For instance that you feel like a failure for not having been able to get more deeply involved.' He nods. 'Or that you had to postpone it, so that you could come to the end and recognize that all the work in a way is yet to be done, so that these 10 sessions were just a way to test the ground so that you could start proper therapy after that.' 'I have wondered about that,' he says. 'You think I ought to do that?' 'Not until you feel ready for it,' I reply.

I am not surprised when Peter responds to a very detailed written account of our work together with comments that are thoughtful but largely dismissive. His tone is jokey and sometimes sarcastic. Though it hurts to see my work rejected in this way, I recognize that Peter is confirming his ability to be in control of his own life and his therapy, claiming his right not to be reduced to the status of client. It would be easy to pathologize Peter and to see his response as evidence of a deep-seated problem for which he urgently requires more therapy.

Nothing would be gained from such an approach and I prefer to respect Peter's determination to protect his independence of thinking about himself and to confirm his ability to come out victorious from what could have been a fairly threatening situation. This is the gain from therapy that he claimed for himself, to some extent at my expense. It is not what I would have planned for him or what gratifies me the most, but it is not for me to plan my clients' learning and my gratification comes from being able to do a professional job with integrity.

I am convinced that life will confront Peter with his refusal to learn from others until he eventually finds a way to do so. It was not within my gift to teach him that in 10 sessions. It remains noteworthy that Peter made some significant changes in his life at the same time and very much despite of his work with me. This indicates that his commitment to improving himself is real and that he needs to do it under his own steam and in his own time. I conclude that he has ample personal resources to draw on and that our work together played some small part in focusing his considerable strengths, paradoxically by bringing into awareness some of his current limitations in using them.

References

Binswanger, L. (1963) *Being-in-the-World*, trans. J. Needleman. New York: Basic Books.

Boss, M. (1957a) *Psychoanalysis and Daseinsanalysis*, trans. J.B. Lefebre. New York: Basic Books.

Boss, M. (1957b) *The Analysis of Dreams*. London: Rider.

Boss, M. (1979) *Existential Foundations of Medicine and Psychology*. New York: Jason Aronson.

Cohn, H.W. (1994) 'What is existential psychotherapy?', *British Journal of Psychiatry*, 165(8): 669–701.

Cooper, D. (1967) *Psychiatry and Anti-psychiatry*. New York: Barnes & Noble.

Cooper, R. (ed.) (1989) *Thresholds between Philosophy and Psycho-analysis*. London: Free Association Books.

De Koning, A.J.J. and Jenner, F.A. (1982) *Phenomenology and Psychiatry*. New York: Academic Press.

Deurzen-Smith, E. van (1984) 'Existential therapy', in W. Dryden (ed.), *Individual Therapy in Britain*. London: Harper & Row.

Deurzen-Smith, E. van (1988) *Existential Counselling in Practice*. London: Sage Publications.

Deurzen-Smith, E. van (1992) 'Deurzen-Smith, E. van', in *Hard Earned Lessons from Counselling in Action*. London: Sage.

Deurzen-Smith, E. van (1994) *If Truth Were a Woman. . . .* London: Regent's College.
Deurzen-Smith, E. van (1996) *Everyday Mysteries: Existential Dimensions of Psychotherapy.* London: Routledge.
Eleftheriadou, Z. (1994) *Transcultural Counselling.* London: Central Book Publishing.
Frankl, V.E. (1964) *Man's Search for Meaning.* London: Hodder & Stoughton.
Frankl, V.E. (1967) *Psychotherapy and Existentialism.* Harmondsworth: Penguin.
Heaton, J. (1968) *The Eye: Phenomenology and Psychology of Functions and Disorders.* London: Tavistock.
Heaton, J.M. (1988) *The Provocation of Levinas.* Routledge: London.
Heaton, J.M. (1994) *Wittgenstein for Beginners.* Cambridge: Icon.
Heidegger, M. (1962) *Being and Time*, trans. J. Macquarrie and E.S. Robinson. New York: Harper & Row.
Heidegger, M. (1968) *What is Called Thinking?* New York: Harper & Row.
Husserl, E. (1960) *Cartesian Meditations.* The Hague: Nijhoff.
Husserl, E. (1962) *Ideas.* New York: Collier.
Jaspers, K. (1951) *The Way to Wisdom*, trans. R. Manheim. New Haven and London: Yale University Press.
Jaspers, K. (1963) *General Psychopathology.* Chicago: University of Chicago Press.
Kearney, R. (1986) *Modern Movements in European Philosophy.* Manchester: Manchester University Press.
Kierkegaard, S. (1941) *Concluding Unscientific Postscript*, trans. D.F. Swenson and W. Lowrie. Princeton, NJ: Princeton University Press.
Kierkegaard, S. (1944) *The Concept of Dread*, trans. W. Lowrie. Princeton, NJ: Princeton University Press.
Laing, R.D. (1960) *The Divided Self.* Harmondsworth: Penguin.
Laing, R.D. (1961) *Self and Others.* Harmondsworth: Penguin.
Laing, R.D. and Cooper, D. (1964) *Reason and Violence.* London: Tavistock.
Lemma-Wright, A. (1994) *Starving to Live: The Paradox of Anorexia Nervosa.* London: Central Books Publishing.
Lomas, P. (1981) *The Case for a Personal Psychotherapy.* Oxford: Oxford University Press.
Macquarrie, J. (1972) *Existentialism, an Introduction, Guide and Assessment.* Harmondsworth: Penguin.
May, R. (1969) *Love and Will.* New York: Norton.
May, R. (1983) *The Discovery of Being.* New York: Norton.
May, R. and Yalom, I. (1985) 'Existential psychotherapy', in R.J. Corsini (ed.), *Current Psychotherapies.* Itasca, IL: Peacock.
May, R., Angel, E. and Ellenberger, H.F. (1958) *Existence.* New York: Basic Books.
Merleau Ponty, M. (1962) *Phenomenology of Perception*, trans. C. Smith. London: Routledge & Kegan Paul.
Minkowski, E. (1970) *Lived Time.* Evanston, IL: Northwestern University Press.
Nietzsche, F. (1961) *Thus Spoke Zarathustra*, trans. R.J. Hollingdale. Harmondsworth: Penguin.
Nietzsche, F. (1974) *The Gay Science*, trans. W. Kaufmann. New York: Random House.
Nietzsche, F. (1986) *Human, All Too Human: A Book for Free Spirits*, trans. R.J. Hollingdale. Cambridge: Cambridge University Press.
Sartre, J.-P. (1956) *Being and Nothingness: An Essay on Phenomenological Ontology*, trans. H. Barnes. New York: New York Philosophical Library.
Sartre, J.-P. (1962) *Sketch for a Theory of the Emotions.* London: Methuen.
Smail, D.J. (1978) *Psychotherapy, a Personal Approach.* London: Dent.
Smail, D.J. (1987) *Taking Care.* London: Dent.
Smail, D.J. (1993) *The Origins of Unhappiness: A New Understanding of Personal Distress.* London: HarperCollins.
Smith, D.L. (1991) *Hidden Conversations: An Introduction to Communicative Psychoanalysis.* London: Routledge.
Spiegelberg, H. (1972) *Phenomenology in Psychology and Psychiatry.* Evanston, IL: Northwestern University Press.

Spinelli, E. (1989) *The Interpreted World: an Introduction to Phenomenological Psychology*. London: Sage Publications.

Spinelli, E. (1994) *Demystifying Therapy*. London: Constable.

Stadlen, A. (1989) 'Was Dora "ill"?', in L. Spurling (ed.), *Sigmund Freud: Critical Assessments*. London: Routledge.

Valle, R.S. and King, M. (1978) *Existential Phenomenological Alternatives for Psychology*. New York: Oxford University Press.

Warnock, M. (1970) *Existentialism*. Oxford: Oxford University Press.

Yalom, I. (1980) *Existential Psychotherapy*. New York: Basic Books.

Suggestions for further reading

Deurzen-Smith, E. van (1988) *Existential Counselling in Practice*. London: Sage Publications.

Macquarrie, J. (1972) *Existentialism: an Introduction, Guide and Assessment*. Harmondsworth: Penguin.

May, R., Angel, E. and Ellenberger, H.F. (1958) *Existence*. New York: Basic Books.

Sartre, J.-P. (1962) *Existential Psycholanalysis*. Chicago: Henri Regnery Co.

Yalom, I. (1980) *Existential Psychotherapy*. New York: Basic Books.

9

Gestalt Therapy

Malcolm Parlett and Judith Hemming

Historical context and development in Britain

Historical context

Gestalt therapy did not appear in a flash. As is usual with any movement, there were preceding ideas forming a fertile substratum, out of which grew this radical revision of psychoanalysis.

The two primary founders of the approach were Frederick (Fritz) Perls (1893–1970) and his wife and collaborator, Laura Perls (1905–92). The prehistory of Gestalt therapy begins in Germany, where they were born and educated and where, throughout the 1920s, they were exposed to the ideas and experimental culture that flowered at that time. Philosophy, education, the arts, politics, and psychology were all in creative upheaval. The young couple were of the radical avant-garde.

Fritz Perls, after active service in the First World War, trained and practised as a neuropsychiatrist and had analysis with several orthodox Freudians and then with Wilhelm Reich. Laura Perls was taught by leading members of the then popular Gestalt school of psychology. An accomplished musician, she also studied with Paul Tillich and Martin Buber. Some of the 'ancestors' of Gestalt therapy can be identified: Freud, with his instinct theories; Reich, with his emphasis on the body; Buber, with his passionate views on the need for human 'meeting'; the Gestalt psychologists (Wertheimer, Kohler, Koffka and Lewin) with their criticism of reductionist psychology and their view of perception and thinking being organized in coherent patterns, or *gestalts*.

Then there was the Institute where Laura and then Fritz worked; directed by Kurt Goldstein, whose views of 'self-actualization' and 'organismic self-regulation' (he coined the terms) also fed into the eventual synthesis.

The Perls were also exposed to the radical philosophy of existentialism and phenomenology which became major foundations of the Gestalt approach. Fritz was involved in theatre with the director Max Reinhardt – his love of dramatization was later reflected in his training workshops; Laura was involved in dance, movement, and Eastern philosophy.

This extraordinary cultural epoch did not, of course, survive. By 1933, Fritz and Laura Perls were on the Nazi blacklist as left-wing radicals. They fled to Holland, and then to South Africa, where they remained working as psychoanalysts till 1946. They continued to lap up other ideas and influences, for example holism, as first written about by Smuts, the South African philosopher and prime minister. Perls's first major statement, *Ego, Hunger and Aggression* (Perls, 1969a) criticized psychoanalysis and suggested a new approach to therapy. After the war they emigrated to the USA.

Post-war New York was another place and time marked by great cultural stimulus. The Perls became a focus for a group of writers, political activists and therapists, including the poet, educator and social critic Paul Goodman, who was to write a major part of the book published in 1951: *Gestalt Therapy* (Perls et al., 1974). The first Institute of Gestalt Therapy was set up in New York in 1952 and Laura Perls continued to be a key figure until her death in 1992. In contrast, Fritz Perls began moving restlessly between different locations. He was not successful until he turned up at the famed Esalen Institute in California. Then, at the height of the 1960s counterculture, he became widely known and Gestalt therapy became linked to the human potential movement, encounter, and the development of humanistic psychology generally.

Numerous stereotypes and misconceptions about Gestalt stem from this time. Many would-be Gestalt practitioners imitated Perls and his personal style of work, taking the techniques he was experimenting with at the time to be the essence of the whole approach. Gestalt became equated with what Fritz Perls did, and the full depth and substance of the Gestalt philosophy and practice was not communicated. The history of Gestalt therapy since that time has been about reclaiming what he appeared to throw away, about returning to European philosophical roots, and building on other founding influences and teachers.

But alarming misinformation still persists – e.g. that Gestalt is confrontational, has little theory, and is mainly techniques which any therapist can borrow without specific Gestalt training. These stereotypes have slowly given way to appreciation of Gestalt therapy for its practical philosophy and links to psychoanalysis, and for its compatibility with holistic, relativistic, and postmodern trends of thought (see Parlett, 1991; Clarkson, 1993).

The practice, as well as the theory, of Gestalt therapy has matured, with less emphasis on episodic, group activities and more on longer-term individual work, acknowledgement of group process and the importance of the surrounding social and professional context. Today there is recognition that to practise Gestalt therapy requires a demanding period of training in order to offer what once looked deceptively simple.

Development in Britain

There have been three distinct phases of Gestalt activity in Britain. In the 1970s, there were two growth centres in London, Quaesitor and Community, which offered Gestalt workshops along with other kinds of humanistic and alternative approaches. It was the era of American visitors presenting weekends and therapy 'marathons'. Gestalt training was offered by Owen and Joan O'Leary, Roger Dalton, Ischa Bloomberg, and others.

The second phase, from 1981 to 1992, was a period of expansion. Landmarks included the founding of the Gestalt Centre, London by Ursula Fausset, and the setting up of the Gestalt Psychotherapy Training Institute (GPTI). The Metanoia Institute, Gestalt SouthWest, Cambridge GATE, the Sherwood Institute, Manchester Gestalt Centre, and centres in Edinburgh and elsewhere, all began training courses specifically in Gestalt therapy.

The third phase, growing from the second, has involved greater professionalization, national and international contacts, with well attended biannual British

Gestalt conferences, attempts to build a national association, and increased attention to accreditation. GPTI and the Gestalt Centre, London became founding member organizations of the (now) UK Council for Psychotherapy. The third phase has been marked by a steady flow of new British publications (e.g. Clarkson, 1989; Houston, 1993; Clarkson and Mackewn, 1993). Another major development was the publication of the *British Gestalt Journal* from 1991.

Alongside the setting up of these organizations and systems of accreditation, there has been an undertow of disquiet. Gestalt began as a questioning approach, radical and innovative, with an anti-establishment ethos. Some now believe that the pendulum has swung too far – that the sparkle of Gestalt has been dulled by respectability. Others say it has matured and consolidated, and is a strong candidate for being the centre of a more integrated psychotherapy in the future (Resnick and Parlett, 1995).

Theoretical assumptions

Image of the person

Gestalt therapy, a powerful synthesis of differing ideas and outlooks, has a central idea that human beings are in constant development. Our life situations are always evolving and we do not exist independently from the surrounding 'field' (Parlett, 1993; Yontef, 1993). The person is not regarded as a fixed, categorizable entity but as an exploring, adapting, self-reflecting, interacting social and physical being in a process of continuous change, evolving throughout life towards greater maturity.

The person is seen holistically, both in biological and in social terms. The human being is a complex organism, a primate, with inbuilt patterns of reacting (for instance to shock), with physical needs which underlie much of daily life, and a bodily, visceral reality which cannot be ignored. All experience is embodied. Psychological life is grounded in the physical realities of feeling states, the emotions, and the life of the body – e.g. health and sickness, fluctuations of energy, ageing, sensual satisfactions, pain, and the quality of sleep. A 'life of the mind' or a 'psyche' without a 'soma' is an impossibility, a fiction arising from Descartes's dualistic outlook (Damasio, 1995).

The holistic vision of the person includes his or her being socially formed, a 'carrier' of cultural values and language, and reflecting attitudes and behaviours derived from family and society. Inevitably he or she is affected by, and necessarily a participant in, a political climate, social trends and fashions, language conventions, and an economic system.

Altogether, in the Gestalt outlook, the intrinsic connectedness of each person as an 'open system' to other levels of system is acknowledged as central. The person can only exist in relation: exchanges occur between breather and air breathed, lovers require a beloved, a person is not an 'employer' without others who are employed. The whole of life is relationship, acknowledged or not, and the exchanges – occurring across the 'contact boundary' (Perls et al., 1974) between person and situation – constitute life itself, in which the person is responding to, and also necessarily acting upon, the environment in order to live.

The Gestalt approach rests on each person being necessarily 'self-organizing' and 'self-actualizing'. To survive, let alone flourish in the world, the person is managing and adjusting to opportunities as well as they are able to, seeking ways to obtain what they regard as necessary and satisfying.

Existence calls for versatility, for 'creative adjustment' (Perls et al., 1974) a capacity to learn from experience, and self-orienting principles by which to live and to exercise choice and self-responsibility. Obviously some people are far more advantaged or skilful than others, even if the same impulse is always there: to improve on one's life or to evolve. Some people can retain a capacity to operate creatively even in unfavourable conditions (e.g. as hostages or in situations of grinding poverty): they make choices and are not overwhelmed, whereas others have insufficient 'self-support' (or inner strength) to adjust creatively in the face of obstacles and require a more benign and supportive environment before they can act 'with good form' (Zinker, 1994). The Gestalt approach rests on the belief that anyone can, if they want to and have sufficient support, learn how to function in life with greater skill and satisfaction.

Conceptualization of psychological disturbance and health

Gestalt therapists are wary of language and assumptions that seem to 'fix' a person or pattern of experience as 'disturbed'. The health of a person does not relate only to intrapsychic phenomena. As suggested above, any human being, given adverse enough circumstances, might operate in a way that could be seen as 'disturbed' if regarded in isolation. Equally, given conditions that suit them, most people tend to be naturally adaptable and to function adequately.

However, human beings are creatures of habit and in situations where we are not comfortable and are not managing, we are likely to fall back on repertoires and responses that were once creative solutions but that do not relate to present circumstances. In 'healthy' mode we are capable of the necessary involvement with what is actually in front of us; in 'disturbed' mode we can seem victims of inappropriate habitual patterns of thinking, feeling and reacting which get in the way of functioning well with the actual circumstances of the present. Life calls for us continuously to extend our abilities to maintain ourselves in changing conditions, rather than perpetuating obselete responses, or 'fixed gestalts', which are self-limiting. We can recognize what Gestaltists call a 'freer functioning system' using aesthetic criteria – is there poise, balance, flow and equilibrium? In times of personal or collective chaos, graceful and creative qualities are often among the first casualties.

Disturbance is conceptualized as loss of the ability to adjust creatively in particular situations. The exact ways in which individuals act stereotypically, do not 'flow', and experience themselves adrift, become the foci for Gestalt investigation (as do their creative opposites).

Recognition of needs Orientating oneself in life rests on the capacity to recognize needs. In a given situation one particular need will stand out from others. For example, if I meet an old friend in the street, how exactly I relate to him will be a function of my needs at the time (perhaps I am feeling isolated and I have a need for human contact; or I may be rushing to an appointment and my dominant need may be to avoid being late). The total situation may include constraints (e.g. the lack of privacy, and perhaps a residue of parental prohibitions about 'hanging about gossiping').

Life is full of these processes – these temporary configurations of a person's experience, the *gestalts* of a life, which form and, when completed, dissolve. Creative adjustment is another way of saying that gestalts are well formed, graceful and fulfilling, and when complete or finished they disappear. Of course, it is not just episodes that interest us, but also the relationship between the various different gestalts that constitute a person's 'lifespace'. Some gestalts are short lived, others of long duration, and creative adjustment involves balancing of many, often competing, needs.

We can think of each gestalt having a life-cycle of its own. Whether it is a street encounter, or having a baby, or taking an exam, or making a complaint, there are discernible phases in how the cycle unfolds; and they relate to both energy and time. Typically, there is a build-up of interest and vital energy as we become more focused and more involved – say, in preparing for an exam. There is usually a discernible high point in the cycle, when 'something happens' which is significant (in this case, writing the exam paper), and thereafter the energy slowly or rapidly dissipates: the examinee becomes less involved, and becomes more easily distracted by other priorities or new needs emerging. The gestalt is dissolved as a temporary organization of present experience by a new one (e.g. after the exam, going on holiday). The process of an individual cycle can be depicted diagrammatically (Figure 9.1).

Recognition of the dominant need or imbalance rests on the person's being able to sense and feel (Stage One) and then to allow these feelings and sensations into awareness (Stage Two). For instance a woman may experience sensations of tension in her legs and realize that she feels like moving around. She may not be able to *explain why* she has the tension and the need to move around, but that may be less important than *noticing and acting on* the need, the somatic truth, of her experience. Many people need to be invited to recognize such bodily sensations – they do not naturally notice them or attend to them 'consciously'.

Stage Three occurs when the person mobilizes herself, using physical energy in this case to stand up. At this point she is in a state of readiness to take action (Stage Four); in the example, the action may be to start moving and to experience doing so. The next stage (Five) is when the person is fully engaged in whatever she needs to do – say, to move around the room; at this point she will be sensorily, emotionally and physically involved in moving around; she will be concentrating on what she is doing and be involved in it. At some point (Stage Six) engagement may reach a high point of 'final contact' – say she stamps the floor with emphasis – after which she stops. The need (to move around) has dissipated. Then follows a crucial stage (Seven) of integrating, or taking in fully, what has happened. This is often the time when there are cognitive insights: the person may realize how much she needs 'to put her foot down' in other ways or she may simply be noticing with

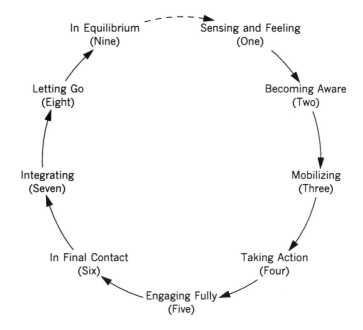

Figure 9.1   *The cycle of awareness*

relief the loss of felt tension in her legs: she may say something like 'I've needed to do this for some time.'

Stage Eight involves letting go; it is marked by loss of interest and concentration, the end of the cycle of this gestalt, and a return to equilibrium (Stage Nine) in which temporarily no need or imbalance is registered. The person is clearly satisfied and her attention is no longer on her legs or on wishing to move; she may experience a temporary 'void', a time of natural quietness and lack of particular focus at this point in the cycle.

The 'Gestalt (or needs or experience or contact) cycle' is portrayed in a variety of different forms (e.g. Zinker, 1977; Hall, 1976; Clarkson, 1989) and represents an idealized sequence of forming a gestalt (becoming involved), moving through several stages (of engaging with the project or experience), and self-destructing after completion.

The emerging and receding of different gestalts is a continuous process. If interrupted, the gestalt may not complete its life-cycle. (If, exceptionally, the exam were cancelled, the examinee 'would be left hanging'.) Unfulfilled states of being result from such interruptions, many of which are self-induced and repetitive. For some individuals, the satisfaction of *completing gestalts* and moving on is rarely achievable.

Some interruptions to the natural flow of experience are environmental (e.g. the phone goes as I am about to say goodnight to my child). Other interruptions are consciously chosen, and wisely so – if I have an urge to hit a traffic warden, interrupting that cycle before the stage of taking action is a wise and mature choice. More often, however, interruptions come from fixed assumptions (e.g.

'people are not interested in what I have to say') or lack of awareness, either of self or the environment (e.g. I do not register my dissatisfaction with a conversation till it is over).

Awareness Limiting our awareness is a major impediment to managing ourselves effectively in the world. Awareness is noticing, recognizing, being in touch with. . . . Its opposites include being distracted, oblivious, or out of touch. Part of being aware relates to the five senses and our capacity to take in information from our surroundings. It also involves recognizing our feeling states and bodily sensations. By accurately attuning to reality – whether internal or external (and Gestalt therapy downplays the distinction) – the individual can orientate him/ herself appropriately.

Awareness of self and of the world involves direct experience rather than talking about or conceptual understanding. We all engage in self-talk – e.g. planning, remembering, futurizing and arguing with oneself, and these are essential for human living; but they can displace our capacity to hear, see, smell, and to tune into bodily reactions and emotional feelings. The person with a rich, sensation-filled somatic and emotional life feels generally more alive than someone who identifies him/herself only with what is going on 'in the mind'.

The issues are philosophically difficult, but there is, in Gestalt therapy, a conviction that despite the importance of thinking and rationality, a person is limited if out of touch with his or her primary experience. Knowing what one feels 'in one's bones', or recognizing one's 'heart's desire', is essential for the refining of values. To know that something does not 'feel right' is a human sensibility which collectively and individually needs cultivating if we are to assume full personal responsibility. In Gestalt therapy the body is regarded as a source of wisdom, a provider of organismic truth.

Contact styles Gestalt therapists also attend to the 'contact boundary', the relationship between person and situation, noticing the exact patterns of how people connect (or fail to connect) to their surroundings and circumstances. Particular attention has been given in Gestalt therapy to four kinds of transaction at the contact boundary.

The first relates to the way in which the contact boundary is subjected to overload or potential invasion from the outside. For instance, suppose a man receives a repeated message from his boss (e.g. that he is 'careless'). The man may take on the message without question, as an automatic given, so that it becomes a part of his outlook. He has *introjected* it. Alternatively, the man may incline to the opposite response of rejecting utterly any message from 'authority'.

If he is adjusting creatively – i.e. responding flexibly and appropriately – there will be times when he introjects to good effect (introjecting instructions might be life-saving in a particular setting); and other times when he sensibly rejects, say a gratuitous insult, out of hand. The contact boundary here operates like a membrane with different degrees of permeability – sometimes letting information in, sometimes keeping it out. The more situations that evoke disturbed reactions, the less likely he/she is to operate flexibly: a fixed pattern of managing contact at the boundary results. And *always* or *never* rejecting what is said to one are both self-defeating contact styles. In most circumstances, operating semi-permeably allows us to be influenced to a degree by what impinges on us, neither 'swallowing it whole' nor 'spitting it out entirely', but instead 'chewing it over' before assimilating it and digesting it (or not).

A second kind of contact boundary transaction relates to containment or expression of feelings, responses or energy. Again a failure of adaptability is evident if, say, a man has grown into adulthood rarely able to contain his angry feelings, so he flies into uncontrollable rages when frustrated. Another may have the opposite tendency, repeatedly to hold in or hold back (*retroflect*) all his angry feelings, so that he becomes held in muscularly, in his voice, and with some possible accompanying somatic problems. A profoundly unbalanced life could follow from either habitual submergence of angry energy or from its repeated expression.

Again, most situations call for some combination of expression and control, with the contact boundary operating flexibly. We recognize that in some contexts release and full-bodied expression of feelings, or of our opinions, is appropriate and safe, whilst in other settings the consequences of expressing them might be serious. If, however, we are 'stuck' in either habitually retroflecting or alternatively expressing ourselves in extreme fashion, *irrespective of the circumstances*, we are likely to suffer unpleasant consequences of one kind or another.

A third contact boundary disturbance of particular interest in Gestalt therapy is where 'what belongs to self' is inaccurately located as 'belonging to the environment'. Thus, a woman who is not owning her intelligence may be delighted by how intelligent her colleague seems: she *projects* her own qualities on to the other. When she learns to acknowledge that she herself is intelligent, the fascination with the other person's qualities may be less.

Projection is present universally, and is by no means always dysfunctional. Indeed, empathy and identifying with others' experience depend upon it, and in certain situations the complete absence of an ability to project would suggest a profoundly insensitive or even psychopathic response. Much projection, however, is limiting and the basis for much intractable human conflict in relationships and communities.

A fourth focus of interest in contact styles relates to the extent to which the contact boundary separates 'self' from 'other'. If a boy joins a gang and his identity is altogether submerged, his separateness is temporarily put aside: he has become *confluent* with his environment. If, by contrast, he cannot fit in, feels altogether different and regards the situation as completely alien, he leans in the opposite direction of extreme differentiation or isolation.

If the contact boundary is operating flexibly, we can experience times both of 'losing ourselves in' and 'of not going along with' something in our environment. Both are functional. If, however, we habitually and without awareness lean towards one or the other pole, regardless of circumstances, then there are bound to be occasions when the result interrupts creative living.

There are a number of other contact transactions which form part of what Gestalt therapists notice, e.g. relating to how attention is sustained or deflected; and the degree to which individuals 'watch themselves' as they engage in an activity or, alternatively, 'surrender' to the experience. Since the Gestalt therapist is focusing on the ongoing act of living, the focus on contact styles is inevitably central. (Fuller descriptions are available elsewhere, e.g. Polster and Polster, 1973.)

Acquisition of psychological disturbance

As noted, 'health' is thought of as involving flexible self-maintenance in a changing environment; 'disturbance' as the opposite. The ongoing flow of forming gestalts, completing them, and their dissolving back into the background of life is an idealized picture. Gestalts are often incomplete: since all of life is relational, a satisfactory meeting of 'self' with 'other' can never be assured.

When a person experiences herself at odds with her situation – e.g. she feels misunderstood by a teacher – there is a 'rupture' in the relational field (Wheeler, 1995). This person, for instance, may well feel awkward or embarrassed (which are varieties of the experience of shame), and – not feeling supported or 'met' by the environment – she adapts as best she can. She may retroflect her tears, recognizing that she may be further shamed if she cries; and/or she may decide to conform exactly to the teacher's wishes. Her spontaneous response is replaced with a newly learned deliberate response. The gestalt is not fully resolved and the response is one of a 'false self' (Tobin, 1982).

At the moment of trauma, of loss of feeling secure, there will be certain feeling states, body positions, thoughts and sensory experiences occurring all together in the situation which has become dangerous or distressing. These form a specific gestalt which, *if appropriate support were promptly reinstated*, might well 'run its course' (e.g. the child is physically held, is able to tell her parent and recovers equanimity). When, however, the loss of support is perpetuated, this gestalt remains unresolved as a 'frozen phenomenological formula' (Resnick and Parlett, 1995). Such times of shame, humiliation and loss of sense of well-being and of being 'received by' the environment supportively, occur in almost every young person's life. They are likely to have greater developmental impact the more intense the experience and the younger the person who suffers them.

What happens is that this painful, perhaps consciously forgotten, traumatic time can be easily restimulated subsequently, with a concurrent re-emergence of the feelings (or environmental conditions, or thoughts) which constituted aspects of the frozen or unresolved gestalt. When this occurs, the immediate response is to avoid further re-entry to this state of being; the learned adaptive response (e.g. the conformity to the powerful other) then appears as the known way to avoid its being reawakened, and is replayed.

To fall back on previously established habits of perceiving, feeling, thinking and acting is another way of saying that the person is no longer reacting experimentally and creatively to a newly emerging unique situation, but responding with an obselete response to a different (past) situation. Instead of responding to the actual circumstances of here and now existence, the person is projecting the past into the present, and responding with yesterday's attempted solution. Obviously, the more that a person does this, the more 'out of touch' he or she will be. Behaviour, thinking and feeling will become stereotypic, and adaptability to real-life circumstances becomes more and more difficult.

Other features of disturbance inevitably follow, including further shaming experiences because the person is now behaving 'oddly', and changes in self-image. They begin to suppress (or even blot out) feelings; they stop discriminating between their own needs and what they are expected to do (or feel); and they learn to function 'intentionally' and require – in order to act spontaneously and autonomously – more favourable and supportive conditions than before. Inevitably, their capacity to make and complete gestalts – wholes of experience – has been eroded. This in turn limits their capacity to self-manage and live experimentally. Their habitual contact styles are essentially adaptive and self-protective for the time being, but as they get older and move to new environments, these styles are not related at all to the actual situations they encounter. Yet they remain as hangovers from the past, played out in the present.

Perpetuation of psychological disturbance

It is central to Gestalt thinking that even though a person's pattern of disturbed functioning may have originated in the past, the manifestation of the disturbance is played out and witnessed in the present, and can only be undone (deconstructed) by first *living it* in the present and *changing it* in the present. Individuals' fixed patterns (of adapting, getting by, manipulating, etc.) are often so habitual and taken for granted that they are not easily accessible to the person's present awareness. Indeed, he or she may not realize at all how much he/she is 'operating on automatic', and that alternative choices might be possible that would be more life-enhancing or creative.

As we have seen, these automatic patterns of thinking, moving, feeling arise as a result of some form of re-enactment of a previously unresolved, frozen, or fixed gestalt. If, for instance, someone has to confront an abusive person in a work setting, and this evokes or triggers the memory (in or out of awareness) of an earlier traumatic situation (like being shouted at by an angry teacher), then the old reactions, feeling state, and sense of powerlessness are likely to be at least partially reawakened. An up-to-date, more mature or 'healthy' response may be possible, provided that the individual has enough self-support (a feeling of inner strength) or has additional environmental support (in the form, say, of an assertive colleague being present when she confronts the abusive person). However, if the total situation contains no more support than was present at the time of the original trauma, then the old response is likely to be experienced similarly to how it was in the past.

The undoing or deconstructing of a fixed gestalt requires experimenting with a novel solution, and is usually felt as a dangerous enterprise. The experience of being unable to deal 'healthily' with the present situation may well lead to anxiety, a sense of confusion, and experiences of shame – which include 'feeling awkward', embarrassed and shy as well as, in more extreme form, feeling ashamed and severely 'not OK' in a situation. To make a change, and to update oneself, requires existentially entering the unknown, and catastrophizing is common – e.g. 'If I allow myself to feel sad, I'll fall apart altogether', or 'If I say "no" to him, he will walk out.' Only by changing the field of forces, as it were, so that there is sufficient backing and encouragement, will the person be able to take the risk of doing something new. The provision of adequate support is therefore crucial.

Given that it is so unsettling to deconstruct a fixed way of being – even if the person recognizes that the pattern is self-damaging or self-limiting – it is not surprising that disturbed patterns of behaviour and feeling are very difficult to shift. Moreover, in cases of more severe disturbance there often has to be extensive initial work of becoming more aware and finding out about sources of support in the field, before these experiments can be countenanced. So the familiar, if unwelcome, patterns are likely to remain in place, even after therapy is well under way.

Two further factors help to keep the fixed gestalt intact. The version of the self which forms a part of that gestalt (e.g. my 'frightened self') is only one of many selves, including perhaps my 'self-critical self'. What often happens is that when one self appears the other soon follows, and an internal debate is set up between different selves: 'Part of me wants to do X, but another part of me knows that it will be hopeless if I try' is a very frequent kind of confusion. So part of how 'disturbance' is maintained is by the endless circulating through these contradictory versions of self, without integration or their 'working together'.

Second, the person, existing in a relational world, does not create a version of himself in isolation, but always with a 'self–other' referent (Beaumont, 1993). If he creates himself as 'a failure' he is probably creating others in his field as 'condemning of his failure' or as 'success', and then he acts towards these projected versions of the other *as if these fantasies were true*. In the co-created field of people interacting, such expectations are well known to be often self-fulfilling. Thus, the person feeling abandoned may act in a way that drives others away; and when they become alienated by how she is behaving, she finds additional confirmation for her belief system that she is being abandoned. This often unaware manipulation of other people or of groups reflects another common way in which disturbed patterns are maintained.

Change

Gestalt therapy can be thought of as a potent means for speeding up the evolution of a person, yet development occurs anyway. People 'grow up', 'take on a new lease of life', 'come to their senses', or 'are forced to come to terms with things', as a result of changes in their life situation – like promotion at work, meeting a new partner, coping with accidents, becoming a grandparent, or enforced redundancy.

A person who is fixed in their relating to human situations has a reduced capacity for dealing with novel or stressful situations. Yet Gestalt therapists operate with the belief that the human being has an inbuilt urge to complete gestalts and to find an inner sense of balance and good form. They see themselves as assisting a natural life process of human creativity, potential resourcefulness and a desire to grow. A man, say, has a pattern of retreating from social contacts; it does not mean he will retain this as a fixed personal characteristic throughout life. He may find himself in a new work group where he is stimulated and encouraged to break his habit of withdrawal, and then finds that he 'is taken out of himself'. The next time he may be a little less reluctant to take part. Such growth experiences occur for all of us, throughout life, and many people change, mature and mellow as a result of unlearning patterns of avoidance and stereotyped reactions they acquired earlier in life, and do so without therapy.

Gestalt therapy is based on a model of the change process that builds on these normal ways in which people develop and mature, and extends them. In offering a supportive relationship and context Gestalt therapists provide opportunities for personal exploration of how the client limits and distorts life experience in some or many ways. The process of therapy becomes itself one of life's new situations: it offers an opportunity to experience life differently and to extend the range of ways in which a person can operate in the world with greater satisfaction.

Incremental change through assimilating new life (or therapy-generated) experiences is quite different from intentional self-reform or 'improvement' according to rules (as in diets or some religious teachings). This difference is reflected in Gestalt therapy in what is called the 'Paradoxical Theory of Change' (Beisser, 1970). This says that change occurs when a person 'becomes what he is, not when he tries to become what he is not'. In other words, deliberate attempts to change by conscious control or acts of will are usually doomed. Instead, for individuals to 'move on' in life they need to begin with accepting what they are already doing. They may realize how they have left gestalts incomplete (e.g. by mourning a loss or expressing a resentment). They may risk trying a new adaptation or response. Ordinary life situations call for these personal innovations, which are usually accompanied by fear reactions (from 'stage fright' to intense anxiety) but which, once achieved and practised, become part of the person's natural repertoire.

Practice

Goals of therapy

Much psychotherapy, deliberately or unwittingly, subscribes to a model in which the expertise of the specialist helper fosters dependency in the patient. The emphasis of Gestalt therapy is on encouraging the person to recognize his or her own expert status – that we are the authors of our own lives (our own 'authority'). At the beginning of the therapy the person may be unable to assimilate this, in which case *empowerment* will be one focus of therapy. The goal is to promote self-support sufficient for the person to live a life of freedom and choice (thus increasing his or her 'response-ability'), so that he or she is not automatically dependent on favourable aspects of the environment in order to function creatively.

The work of therapy is to foster conditions in which individuals, at whatever level of awareness they start from, become active participants in developing awareness, self-support, integration and the ability to interact authentically with others. These interrelate closely. As aspects of our personal evolution they are never attained once and for all: Perls noted that 'there is always the possibility of richer maturation – of taking more and more responsibility for yourself' (1969b: 65). The therapeutic journey, as conceived in Gestalt therapy, is therefore potentially lifelong and for many people can turn into a meditative discipline or path. Of course, not everyone engaged in Gestalt therapy as a patient, client or customer goes this far; many will stop when they have restored, or learned, more satisfying ways of functioning in the world.

Concerned with supporting personal development, Gestalt therapy is not a normative approach designed to foster 'well-adjusted behaviour' as conventionally defined. It values individuals finding unique solutions to unique situations – recognizing the special nature of each person's history, circumstances, values, needs and preferences. The emphasis is on people finding their own goals within their own lives and discovering their potential to meet these goals.

Selection criteria

The Gestalt therapy system orientates the work of its practitioners, but each applies Gestalt principles in individual ways and uses different methods according to her/his training, professional background and personal style.

It follows from this that each therapist–client pairing is also individual and that to argue that certain individuals are 'suitable' for Gestalt therapy as such, while others are unsuitable, does not make sense. A clinical psychologist working, say, in a hospital setting and from a Gestalt therapy base, may work therapeutically with severely fragmented and disoriented individuals, applying Gestalt principles appropriately and effectively. A school counsellor, on the other hand, though trained in Gestalt, would almost certainly not work with such individuals, although she might be well qualified to apply Gestalt thinking and practice to working with the children referred to her.

The most likely course of action for a practitioner, faced with an enquirer, will be to have an introductory meeting in order to assess what the individual might benefit from most – perhaps once- or twice-weekly individual sessions, joining an ongoing therapy group, or participating in a weekend workshop.

Practitioners of Gestalt therapy give emphasis to the unique nature of each person's therapeutic needs. Suppose, for instance, that the extent of disturbance is such that a client has little contact with reality, so that he has been labelled 'psychotic' or 'borderline'. A high degree of environmental support and time, commitment and attention on the part of the therapist may be called for. This might entail residential care, with the therapist seeing the client every day for a specified period of time. Such conditions, even in hospital settings, are often not available, and it would be highly irresponsible to engage the client in intensive exploration without the necessary environmental support.

Obviously, then, initial meetings and contacts are very significant. The person's presenting problem may indicate one form of intervention rather than another – a relationship problem might best be explored with the partner in couples therapy, and someone cut off and lonely might benefit most from a group. But the stress is on the special nature of each enquiry, not on any rule.

In weighing up what the person might benefit from most, the Gestalt therapist does not ignore the usual psychiatric diagnostic categories (Delisle, 1991). However, she will want most to observe how aware the person is of his own process – i.e. of the current direction of his interest, bodily state, physical and social needs, feeling sense, and how capable he is of externalizing his inner experience. She will also note how he communicates with her (the client's contact style or functions), and how he interrupts or blocks his experience (in terms of the Gestalt cycle). The therapist may also think in terms of polarities, and be influenced by what strikes her as 'missing' with this person: e.g. he may manifest no assertiveness or, though married, fail to mention his wife or children. All of this may suggest to the therapist the appropriateness of a specific course of action. At this stage, one-to-one therapy might be suggested for someone who was unaware of, or unable to externalize, his inner experience. Joining a group might be thought desirable at a later stage, when the person has become more familiar with the Gestalt method – i.e. has acquired facility with its self-investigative procedures (which constitute both a demand for, as well as a means to, greater awareness).

Qualities of effective therapists

Basic to all training of Gestalt psychotherapists is that all trainees have prolonged individual and group therapy themselves. Gestalt therapy is not an approach which can be applied by people who are themselves largely unaware of their own contact style or bodily experience; it is not based on acquiring techniques or on theoretical understanding from books. The approach has to be known from the inside, experienced as a powerful means of self-enquiry and progressively incorporated into one's own personal life and work as a therapist.

Effective Gestalt therapists vary greatly in their personal and professional qualities. Aside from their diversity, and their having achieved an adequate level of integration themselves, such therapists are distinguished by their authenticity and openness about their feelings and reactions, as well as (hopefully) by their competence in handling a broad spectrum of interpersonal transactions (including intimacy, conflict, appropriate physical contact, emotional expression, separation and endings, and maintaining clear boundaries). In addition, they need to have acquired the ability to 'bracket off' (set aside for the time being, not forget or suppress) their own preoccupations and problems in order to be fully present (or 'all there') for the client and, even more, to recognize those occasions when they are unable to do this and are therefore not competent to practise for the time being. Finally, they need to have a strong ethical base, to be non-exploitative, and to have a fundamental respect for the integrity of the therapy process.

Therapeutic relationship and style

Although there are wide differences between Gestalt therapists, most would conceptualize what they do along the following (or similar) lines.

They aim to provide a relationship and setting which supports and provokes the person's exploring her 'here and now' experience – that is, what she is aware of in the actual, present context of being in the therapy room, relating to the therapist (or, in a group, with the other members).

The emphasis given to exploring present reality in Gestalt therapy can easily be misunderstood: it does not mean that references to past and future are banned – that would be absurd. But when dwelling on past or future events, what the person is currently and actually doing is *remembering* or *anticipating*, both of which involve constructing an imagined reality in the present. Exactly *how* the person reconstructs her or his past, or formulates a vision of the future, is part of what she is doing at the moment. It is an essential part of the investigation of what the person *actually does*, which is often more significant than what she says or reports about another time or place.

Open-ended enquiry, which characterizes Gestalt therapy in practice, can flourish only within a relationship based on dialogue (see, for instance, Yontef, 1993). This emphasis derives from the work of Martin Buber (1970) and involves each party meeting the other as a person, not as a role. Gestalt therapists let themselves be themselves and encourage those they work with to do the same. Thus, they may communicate (obviously selectively) some of their own life experience and express their own feelings, with respect and a sense of timing, honouring the validity of the other's reality and not imposing their own views and values. Relating dialogically also calls for the therapist to 'show his caring by his honesty more than by his constant softness' (Yontef, 1984: 47).

Along with the emphasis on reporting present awareness – which derives from the phenomenological tradition (Spinelli, 1989) – and on offering the possibility of a person-to-person relationship, Gestalt therapy is also characterized by its emphasis on experimentation ('try it rather than talk about it') (Zinker, 1977). 'All therapy is play,' said Fritz Perls, and the effective Gestalt therapist is skilled in creating experimental situations and methods to provide learning experiences which extend a person's repertoire.

When it comes to individual style it is difficult to generalize. The competent Gestalt therapist employs different styles according to person, situation and stage of therapy. His choices are based on skills and experience; his response to a particular instance depends on his creativeness (e.g. in finding ways to heighten the person's awareness of their surroundings). The therapist may at times be challenging, pointing out how he feels manipulated by a certain response of the client; at another time he may extend a hand, literally, to establish a channel of support when the client momentarily falters before taking a risk. He may listen intently and sympathetically to an emotionally laden account of an early trauma now being recounted for the first time. In contrast, with another person at another time, he may report his sense of being bored by the repeated recital of well-known facts. He is, after all, attending to individuals' unfolding realities, to their unique experiences; and this demands authentic, spontaneous and creative responses – not rehearsed reactions and 'therapy techniques', which demean the relationship.

In his response at a given moment, the experienced therapist is affected by many different factors: the person's severity of disturbance, her prior experience and the stage of the therapeutic relationship, her confusions at the contact boundary, the degree of essential support available to her, and 'procedural' concerns such as the time available. It is therefore appropriate that each practitioner has a range of styles.

Gestalt therapists also diverge from one another considerably in their overall style and disposition to therapy. Each is enjoined to find his or her own way of integrating and applying the philosophy and methodology of Gestalt therapy in a creative, intelligent, sensitive and ethical fashion that does justice to their talents, personality, and background.

Major therapeutic strategies and techniques

Awareness training An important priority in Gestalt therapy is the focus on awareness training. The approach offers an equivalent (some say) to Zen training or other forms of meditation. Awareness is the key to personal experiment and change. If a man has suppressed his feelings, say, of love for his father, the process of becoming aware of his having done so is the first and necessary stage of allowing the feelings to be acknowledged and perhaps expressed to his father in person.

Awareness work involves cultivating the practice of attending to the bodily 'felt sense'. Through education in heightened awareness, individuals are effectively acquiring a 'biofeedback' system: by more accurately attuning themselves to their actual physical and emotional experience, moment by moment, they can recognize more accurately when they are tensing up, withdrawing, suppressing a feeling and, with this additional information, can choose to relax, breathe differently, speak out or withdraw, or whatever they need to do in order to feel more balanced or satisfied. The more awareness a person has, the more he or she can influence his or her life choices and destiny.

Working with polarities The Gestalt therapist reacts not only to what is presented – the client's behaviour and experience in the session itself – but is also interested in 'what is missing'. It is a central tenet of Gestalt therapy that all of us have within us the potential for acting and experiencing differently from how we usually do. Each 'quality' has its polarized opposite, and the more fixed a characteristic, the more there may be avoidance of the opposite quality, at least in the present situation. Thus, if a man is always tidy and organized, he may be missing out on the experience of letting a little disorder and unpredictability into his life. That he has 'chosen' extreme order may be out of fear of allowing any disorder at all, which he may well represent to himself as 'chaos and catastrophe'.

Gestalt therapy involves attending to such polarities, often renaming them in less pejorative language, exploring the associated feeling reactions to them, and uncovering gently the potentialities latent in the hitherto rejected behaviours and experiences.

Recognizing interruptions and avoidances There are numerous ways in which human beings stop the flow of their naturally unfolding experience. We may attempt to avoid painful or unpleasant memories, emotions or realizations. We interrupt our awareness or restrict our feelings by holding the breath, at the same time as tensing the musculature in certain parts of the body. Inhibition (wholesale avoidance of certain impulses), intellectualizing (often in the form of 'explaining away'), and displacement (e.g. instead of dealing with his wife he takes it out on his employee), are among other common patterns of avoidance.

By 'tracking' – or following closely what is happening for a person who is attending to and reporting his moment-by-moment thoughts, percepts and feelings – the therapist is able to spot points of 'interruption of flow' in this ongoing process: e.g. shifts in vitality, changes in eye contact, movements in body position, a sentence left unfinished. All may indicate something withheld, glossed over, blotted out or diverged from. The therapist may on occasion draw attention frequently to such interruptions, at other times she may not intervene for long periods, perhaps letting the person tell his story (Polster, 1987) or leaving him to struggle to articulate some hitherto undefinable feeling. All depends on the total situation and the moment.

The skilled Gestalt therapist focuses with precision on two aspects of interruption or avoidance. First, she notices at what point in the gestalt cycle the interruption occurs: is the client not *recognizing his need*? Is he stopping from *mobilizing* his energy? Is he accomplishing these but holding back from *engaging fully* – i.e. is he not making contact with what will meet his need? Is he doing all these but not *integrating* (taking in or learning from) his experience? Or is he unable to *let go*?

Second, the therapist identifies the contact styles that have become habitual for the individual, and how these might be explored – e.g. does he retroflect his sadness or does he express it? Does he project his own unacknowledged feelings on to others? Becoming aware of interrupted gestalts and avoidances of engagement with others is the first step to relearning.

Working with 'resistance'   It is easy to fall into imagining that if a client refuses a suggestion the therapist makes, she is 'resistant'. Gestalt therapists have a different view. Resistance is not always to be fought and 'overcome'. Rather (like the French Resistance), it can be celebrated for the fighting spirit it betokens. Identifying a theme of a specific session usually includes a statement of something the individual needs (wants, craves, is determined to have) and something stopping the person getting what he/she wants (fears of retribution, unwillingness to take a risk, etc.). The therapist signals that she has no investment in a particular outcome, and invites the client to explore both the desire and the reluctance, the need and resistance, often amplifying the latter.

Working with transference   Gestalt therapists are continuously seeking a real as opposed to a transferential relationship. This does not mean that clients' reactions are free of transference but that the therapist is challenging these, inviting clients to use their eyes and ears to see and listen to the actual person behind their projections. The process of dissolving the transference is probably never fully completed but the whole tenor of the work is to test fantasies that the individual may have, not to allow them to continue unchallenged.

Experimentation and techniques   Gestalt therapy provides experiential learning and the experiment is central: 'It transforms talking about doing into doing, stale reminiscing and theorizing into being fully here with all one's imagination, energy and excitement' (Zinker, 1977). It is the pursuit of greater awareness through active behavioural expression, entailing senses, skeletal muscles and full bodily and emotional involvement.

Experiments grow out of themes emerging during the tracking of ongoing awareness and are ways of 'thinking out loud, (concretizing) one's imagination' (Zinker, 1977). There are no set structures or techniques, though necessary preconditions for a successful experiment include ensuring that the person is 'grounded' and has sufficient self-support; that the experiment is pitched at the right level of risk for the individual at the time; that he/she understands what he or she is doing and has agreed to it; and that it incorporates the person's own language and images. The therapist's creativity in noticing and expanding these ideas is also important.

Experiments can be simply minor additions to 'tracking' – i.e. following the awareness reporting of the client. Thus, a man reporting that he is 'fed up with doing Y' may be hunching his shoulders as he says it. The therapist might invite him to exaggerate the posture of his body, or to stay in the hunched position to explore what it may represent. Alternatively the experiment might be exploring an 'opposite' body position. All of these would be designed to heighten awareness and fill out the experience, which is always more than its verbal description.

Other experiments may involve deliberate rearrangements of the field to provide an opportunity to try out a risky-seeming 'first try' at a new behaviour which the client wishes to explore – perhaps a woman asking fellow members of a group for feedback about her appearance or their reactions to something she has done. The task of the therapist is to help design and focus the experiment, to check that there is sufficient support in the field (e.g. enough encouragement, time, freedom from interruptions) to enable the person to try out what she wants – without making the conditions so safe that the client finds the experiment 'too easy' and therefore not extending her experience.

Experimentation can employ any of a whole variety of media, from dramatizations, dance or other physical movement, to dialogues between parts of the self, sculpting, artwork, working with dreams, fantasy trips, trying out specific language or behavioural changes. Often the therapist will encourage metaphorical and intuitive thinking, which in the majority of people is less developed than their capacity to be verbal and explanatory.

Some experiments have become classics – for instance the 'empty chair', in which a person speaks to someone with whom he has unfinished business, or to another part of himself, a polar opposite (the 'weak' him may speak to the 'strong' him). He may then move to the other chair and react from that position – either being the other person or the other aspect of self.

'Two-chair work' has been widely copied and used by therapists from other schools, so we shall say more about it. As a means of exploring communication between different selves (or between 'self' and 'other'), physical shifts – such as moving from seat to seat – can assist in symbolizing profound changes in field conditions, i.e. how a life scene is seen from one position or from another. However, many Gestalt therapists use other ways of differentiating the field, perhaps inviting the client to take two particular body positions or turning the lights down or up, and do not rely on chairs. If they do set up this particular experiment they are likely to adapt it according to circumstances – which can never be anticipated. What is important is to attend to what is needed at the time: perhaps turning the experiment into moving between three places, or the therapist taking one of the parts herself, or upturning or reversing or elevating one chair to make a point. The precise 'technique' is irrelevant, because the focus is actually upon, say, heightening differentiation and exploring possible integration of selves, and there are any number of ways in which this can be done, once the principle has been understood.

Gestalt therapy experimentation needs to be perpetually innovative to accord with exactly what is required in a unique situation. Although Gestalt techniques have been widely copied, their use in isolation from the rest of the Gestalt therapy system is highly questionable. They are not recipes. As Yontef has remarked: 'There is no Gestalt therapy cookbook . . . therapy is an art [requiring] all of the therapist's creativity and love' (1988: 32).

Support A crucial therapeutic skill required in Gestalt therapy has to do with provision of support. Considering the fact that shame reactions (as discussed earlier) are prevalent features when working with issues where clients feel vulnerable – which is the case in most therapeutic situations at times, and especially before the relationship has reached a trusting stage – the therapist needs to be acutely aware of the possibility of heightening feelings of exposure, embarrassment or shame, often inadvertently or without recognizing that he or she is doing so. Gestalt experiments may, by asking someone to do something highly unusual, themselves be shaming. For some clients, even asking questions or making statements that are experienced as 'personal' can be shaming.

Some degree of experiencing shame may be inevitable, given the nature of the therapeutic process, and the intention of experimenting with novel behaviour. But the calibration of what is possible requires acute sensitivity on the part of the therapist. The development of a therapeutic relationship in which shame reactions can be safely addressed is of the first importance. Any inauthenticity or lack of presence can be deleterious to the establishment of the degree of trust required to create the necessary safety and sense of security, in which the most risky changes can be attempted. Taking 'a professional stance', including the making of psychological interpretations by the therapist, is another way of subtly diminishing the client to the status of an object. Successful Gestalt therapy requires achieving a 'subject–subject' relationship, rather than a 'subject–object' form of association between therapist and client (Wheeler, 1995).

The achievement of a supportive relationship is perhaps the most important single feature of the approach in practical terms. It is also basic to the fundamental view of the person which lies at the core of the approach – namely, that we exist, and grow, in relationship. The establishment of a sufficiently supportive context for therapy is arguably the basis of the approach, and all the rest – the phenomenological awareness work, the attention to contact styles, the experimentation – simply contributes to establishing the relationship as a real one based on a level of respectfulness equivalent to love, and therefore as intrinsically healing (Latner, 1995).

The change process in therapy

Work with awareness lies at the heart of Gestalt therapy: attending to present experience, noticing what the person is doing, and recognizing her processes of contact and avoidance. Yontef (1988) has suggested a developmental sequence within therapy in which initially the client may talk about her problem but may have little awareness of what she is actually doing. In the course of therapy she recognizes how unaware she was previously; she begins to notice her characteristic style of avoidance; in time, she learns to recognize the ways she has been interrupting the natural process of gestalt formation and completion. She becomes aware of being aware and (paradoxically) of being unaware. The next stage is when the person 'becomes aware of [her] overall character structure', her general patterns and the conditions which give rise to her being less aware. Finally, the high level of awareness reached in therapy 'permeates the person's ordinary life' (Yontef, 1988).

Another way that Gestalt therapists think of change is in terms of the awareness cycle. Later stages of the cycle depend on earlier stages being undergone. Movement in therapy is signalled by the person being more skilful in completing unfinished situations from the past and also with new gestalts arising in the present. She learns to avoid her avoidance; she interrupts more of her interruptions as they occur. In the process she acquires greater facility in forming and completing gestalts, and experiences more fulfilment and less dissatisfaction.

Limitations of the approach

The major limitation of Gestalt therapy is the reverse side of one of its strengths. Because it requires a high level of personal responsiveness on the part of the therapist, an ability to work in numerous different ways according to the special circumstances of a particular therapist–client pairing, and because the 'Gestalt outlook' has to be grasped and known before the theory can be fully understood, there are real difficulties in teaching the approach, in communicating its essence to those who have not directly experienced it, and in codifying its methods and concepts in ways which are helpful to practitioners and trainees while not oversimplifying it.

Additionally, there is wide acknowledgement that until recently Gestalt therapists have paid little attention to infant development. Developmental theories have tended to be borrowed from psychoanalytic sources. Daniel Stern's (1985) book presents a model of infant development which is congruent with Gestalt theory and the development of the self.

More generally, certain criticisms of therapy (see, for instance, Hillman and Ventura, 1992) strike home hard for Gestalt therapists. Gestalt therapy – acknowledging the environment or situation as a major co-determinant of the person's mental health – has an obvious responsibility for linking therapy with activity directed at social, community-orientated or political change. And by and large, Gestalt therapists have done little in this regard, working with individuals and couple systems without attending to the wider field of society and the times we live within. They are not alone in this among therapists, but the model of Gestalt therapy offers no comfortable justification for avoiding such involvement.

Case example

The client

Sheila is a freelance professional in her early forties, living alone. When she first came to see me (JH) she felt unhappy and isolated. Despite appreciating her independence and having a network of friends, she did not know how to take these friendships into any kind of personal or intimate realm. Spurred on by having recently agreed to voluntary redundancy at work and by experiencing back pain that her osteopath could not alleviate, she decided to seek therapy.

Sheila was the middle child of three, born to a Jewish family where the father had left to work in another city when she was six and then died soon after returning, three years later. She described her parents as undemonstrative; there had been a minimum of physical contact. Feelings were rarely expressed, neither warmth, grief or need.

Apart from going away as a student, she continued to live with her mother until the age of 30 and even after that time she remained as an actively dutiful daughter. Although she had known for many years she was a lesbian it was not until she had left home in her early thirties that she 'came out'. Except for one fleeting relationship with a woman, when I met Sheila she had allowed herself virtually no intimate contact with anyone, friend or lover, during all her adult life. She felt unknown.

The therapy

Because she was so unused to speaking personally, and because she felt so much shame, it took many weeks and was acutely painful for Sheila to tell her life story – its emptiness and her deep loneliness as a child; her fears of both intimacy and rejection. She also told me of her many but muted complaints about the people in her current life who took her co-operative behaviour for granted.

I was immediately struck by how controlled Sheila was, how powerfully she held in (retroflected) all her energy. For example, she barely breathed or looked at me, paused lengthily before each utterance, and spoke with a low, throttled voice. Her body seemed rooted to the ground. As she spoke she reminded me of a brave student trembling to speak up for herself against hopeless odds.

An important part of our early work was discovering and mapping together her whole belief system (her introjects) that kept her so isolated. She told me that expressing feelings, especially sadness or anger, were signs of weakness, to be kept secret in the presence of others, or translated into thoughts, more under her control. 'Being right' was also essential, and she would correct me if my tracking or describing what I saw or understood did not meet her standards of accuracy. She even disagreed that she often disagreed with me! While I was not judgmental about how she had acquired these beliefs, I challenged them in our relationship. I made it clear that I valued hearing about her true feelings. And I shared my feelings with her too. I told her when I felt touched, outraged, even when I felt sleepy. It was novel, even shocking, for her to hear how she had an impact on anyone else.

Although Sheila sometimes understood that she had encased herself in this bubble of isolation, more usually she tended to project the withdrawal on to others and experience them as withholding and insensitive. Our relationship was no exception. I noticed that she often treated me as if I were both demanding and withholding, which was not how I felt at all. As we explored this she became clearer that she was projecting on to me an image of her mother. Whenever she had denied her mother, she felt overwhelmed with guilt. If she yielded she was resentful. She recognized feeling the same ambivalence towards me. I felt as if I was unpleasant medicine she was taking for her own good.

No matter how kind and gentle I was to Sheila, that was not how I was experienced. Yet she would make herself attend to my every intervention with the utmost conscientiousness, even when she clearly had no real personal energy for the topic or activity. I would notice the energy in our conversation fade out, tell her, and then hear how she had withdrawn. I told her I wanted to know if she was not interested, or upset. I also pointed out how she would push me to take charge and then would feel constrained or disappointed in me if I did.

It took meeting once a week for five or six months to establish any real trust; speaking of all these personal matters broke her strongest taboo. She wanted me to listen to her without interruption, following her agenda without letting her know what I noticed about how she was as she spoke. Stiffly, she told me that she felt resentful when I interrupted her own ways of distracting or distancing herself. I was respectful of her desire for more space and gave less feedback for a while. As our relationship developed I increased my interventions again; she was better able to make use of them.

Being actively encouraged to tell the truth and to be in charge herself was a completely new experience for Sheila. She had longings for close contact, fantasies of being touched and held by me. I recognized the poignancy of these longings without trying to meet them. She was resentful. In these ways, honest and open interchange between us was slow to build.

Initially Sheila did not have strong feelings, other than complaint, of which she was aware. Having desensitized herself, any time a feeling such as grief or love broke through she would feel overwhelmed, and shut down feeling to get control again. I spent many sessions helping her increase her tolerance of such feelings, showing her how to breathe more fully, reassuring her that what she felt would not affect my acceptance of her, and that she had the power to stop and restart whenever she needed. She found she had to get to know feelings in small increments so that she had time to study them, and also so that she was not too frightened. Learning to stay with bodily sensations and gather support to face their experienced message was at the heart of our early work.

We began to explore how her body revealed what she wanted to ignore. When I felt she could tolerate having it pointed out to her, I would ask her to notice how, when she began to experience a feeling, she would press one foot into the floor with the other, or squeeze one hand with the other. She often stroked her throat as if to send the sensations back down again. I suggested, as an experiment, that she dialogue between the part of her that wanted to shut down and the part that wanted to express itself. Often she would experience severe back pain. It was, she began to feel, a message to herself to bear a feeling stoically.

Our first moments of relaxed contact began as she was arriving and settling in, or when she was just about to leave. At these times she might smile or let slip a little remark which showed that what was happening was important for her. I was warmed when she lit up and told her so, highlighting rather than ignoring her 'just-outside-therapy' self. We compared it to the 'therapy self' she aimed to present, and she began to let more of herself be available in our meetings, once she had my reassurance that her humour and other interests, her less troubled ways of being, were a valuable and necessary resource in our relationship.

As Sheila progressively reclaimed a fuller sense of herself, initially her unhappiness deepened. As I challenged her to let me meet her, she was triggered to connect to key periods of her childhood: when her father left, when he died, and when Sheila tried to manage school and home in the years that followed. That was the time in her life when she had made decisions about how to manage herself in the face of great difficulties, storing up the grief and complaint which she was now in a safe enough environment to begin to release.

But the releasing of this stored-up energy was deliberately unspectacular. The first time she cried, after nearly a year of therapy, was when I briefly left the room during a two-hour session. Because for decades she had controlled the tissues and muscles around her eyes to prevent herself from crying she burst some blood vessels during her first big outburst of fury and tears, and scared herself for a day or two before they healed. In exploring how freeing it had been for her to cry when I was not watching her, Sheila saw again how she had configured me as her mother, into someone who would not want to know her feelings.

The next time she was tearful she could tolerate having me with her without inhibiting herself so much. I encouraged her to keep in steady contact with me and not explode 'privately' – to no one in particular. Now it was possible for her to complete some of her long-stored communications to her mother. After one session, where she had expressed her passionately felt needs to me as I experimentally 'stood in for' her mother, she reached out to let me comfort her, and I experienced none of her original ambivalence or projection; it was a moment of real and present contact.

After this she also spent many sessions reconnecting to her father, dialoguing with her inner image of him, expressing appreciation and resentments, saying goodbye more fully. She gradually found that she could reach out to me. This affected not only her relationship with me but with others; her friendships deepened, and she made new boundaries between herself and her mother without losing contact. Significantly also, her voice became less throttled.

After two years Sheila also joined my weekly therapy group, ready to explore wider contacts. The group members were early witnesses of her greater daring in emotional exchange. She 'came out', telling of her experience as a lesbian. She found that she could befriend and be befriended by people to whom she could also say no when she wanted. Initially she brought self-contained issues to explore; dreams and difficult moments at work. Later she interacted more with the group members. She allowed herself to feel more warmly and easily in their presence. I offered her many experiments that enabled her to build bridges out of her habitually isolated way of being. She became more playful, even mischievous, allowing moments of flow and uninterrupted exchange.

Sheila also experienced several periods of deep unhappiness during those years, sometimes triggered by my holiday absences. They were valuable in that she and I could use them to explore feelings of love and longing in her original family and also in our own relationship. I encouraged her to give voice to her loving feelings, which deepened her feelings of loneliness but also created greater awareness of how she could develop closer relationships. She discovered that she did figure in other people's lives, and that this did not mean she had to be burdened by their expectations (her archaic projection) – she could negotiate and choose how much contact was comfortable for her. I was the first person with whom she practised these skills.

Gradually I increased my robustness of response and also affirmed her when she let herself be more robust. We began to tease each other with good humour. She could recognize more quickly when she was sulking or felt punitive and 'came back' more quickly. Instead of feeling overlooked she took responsibility for not overlooking herself. In one session she adopted a little soft toy to be her 'overlooked heart', held it, acknowledged its pain and apologised for all the lost years. She began to release herself from her old self-image as a person whom nobody knew.

The impact of Sheila's therapy is evident yet hard to specify. Initially her relationship with me enriched her life; later, her changing life enriched our relationship. She still lives alone and, apart from a brief love affair, she has not yet entered into a long-term intimate contact with anyone. But her contact with others continues to deepen. She continues to use the therapy as a laboratory to create more open exchange. We tell each other when we do and do not feel accurately seen and met by the other, and both of us are committed to this task. This experience of good contact fuels her capacity to take risks in the rest of her life. As her self-support is increasing, and she feels less dependent on me to create the conditions of safe meeting between us, I anticipate that we will be ready to part.

References

Beaumont, H. (1993) 'Martin Buber's "I–Thou" and fragile self-organization: Gestalt couples therapy', *British Gestalt Journal*, 2(2): 85–95.

Beisser, A. (1970) 'The paradoxical theory of change', in J. Fagan and I. Shepherd (eds), *Gestalt Therapy Now*. New York: Harper & Row.

Buber, M. (1970) *I and Thou*. New York: Scribner's.

Clarkson, P. (1989) *Gestalt Counselling in Action*, 2nd edition. London: Sage Publications.

Clarkson, P. (1993) '2,500 years of Gestalt: from Heraclitus to the big bang', *British Gestalt Journal*, 2(1): 4–9.

Clarkson, P. and Mackewn, J. (1993) *Fritz Perls*. London: Sage Publications.

Damasio, A.R. (1995) *Descartes's Error: Emotion, Reason, and the Human Brain*. London: Picador.

Delisle, G. (1991) 'A Gestalt perspective of personality disorders', *British Gestalt Journal*, 1(1): 42–50.

Hall, R.A. (1976) 'A schema of the Gestalt concept of the organismic flow and its disturbance', in E.W.L. Smith (ed.), *The Growing Edge of Gestalt Therapy*. New York: Brunner Mazel.

Hillman, J. and Ventura, M. (1992) *We've Had a Hundred Years of Psychotherapy and the World's Getting Worse*. New York: Harper.

Houston, G. (1993) *Being and Belonging*. Chichester: John Wiley.

Hycner, R.H. (1985) 'Dialogical Gestalt therapy: an initial proposal', *Gestalt Journal*, 8(1): 23–49.

Hycner, R.H. (1991) 'The I–Thou relationship and Gestalt therapy', *Gestalt Journal*, 13(1): 41–54.

Jacobs, L. (1989) 'Dialogue in Gestalt theory and therapy', *Gestalt Journal*, 12(1): 25–67.

Kepner, J. (1987) *Body Process: A Gestalt Approach to Working with the Body in Psycho-therapy*. New York: Gardner Press (Gestalt Institute of Cleveland Press).

Latner, J. (1995) Letter in *British Gestalt Journal*, 4(1): 49–50.

Parlett, M. (1991) 'Reflections on field theory', *British Gestalt Journal*, 1(2): 69–81.

Parlett, M. (1993) 'Towards a more Lewinian Gestalt therapy', *British Gestalt Journal*, 2(2): 115–20.

Perls, F.S. (1969a) *Ego, Hunger and Aggression: The Beginning of Gestalt Therapy* (1944) New York: Vintage Books.

Perls, F.S. (1969b) *Gestalt Therapy Verbatim*. Lafayette, CA: Real People Press.

Perls, F.S., Hefferline, R.F. and Goodman, P. (1974) *Gestalt Therapy Excitement and Growth in Human Personality* (1951). Harmondsworth: Penguin.

Polster, E. (1987) *Every Person's Life is Worth a Novel*. New York: Norton.

Polster, E. (1993) 'Individuality and communality', *British Gestalt Journal*, 2(1).

Polster, E. and Polster, M. (1973) *Gestalt Therapy Integrated*. New York: Brunner Mazel.

Resnick, R. and Parlett, M. (1995) 'Gestalt therapy: principles, prisms and perspectives', *British Gestalt Journal*, 4(1): 3–13.

Rosenblatt, D. (1995) Letter in *British Gestalt Journal*, 4(1): 47–9.

Spinelli, E. (1989) *The Interpreted World*. London: Sage Publications.

Stern, D.N. (1985) *The Interpersonal World of the Infant*. New York: Basic Books.

Tobin, S.A. (1982) 'Self-disorders, Gestalt therapy, and self-psychology', *The Gestalt Journal*, 5(2): 4–45.

Wheeler, G. (1995) 'Shame in two paradigms of therapy', *British Gestalt Journal*, 4(2).

Yontef, G. (1984) 'Modes of thinking in Gestalt therapy', *The Gestalt Journal*, 7(1): 33–74.

Yontef, G. (1988) 'Assimilating diagnostic and psychoanalytical perspectives into Gestalt therapy', *The Gestalt Journal*, 11(1): 5–32.

Yontef, G.L. (1993) *Awareness, Dialogue and Process*. New York: The Gestalt Journal Press.

Zinker, J. (1977) *Creative Process in Gestalt Therapy*. New York: Brunner Mazel.

Zinker, J. (1994) *In Search of Good Form*. San Francisco: Jossey Bass.

Suggested further reading

Clarkson, P. (1989) *Gestalt Counselling in Action*. London: Sage Publications.

Clarkson, P. and Mackewn, J. (1993) *Fritz Perls*. London: Sage Publications.

Passons, W.R. (1975) *Gestalt Approaches in Counseling*. New York: Holt, Rinehart & Winston.

Perls, F.S. (1973) *The Gestalt Approach and Eye Witness to Therapy*. Ben Lomond, CA: Science and Behavior Books.

Polster, E. and Polster, M. (1973) *Gestalt Therapy Integrated*. New York: Brunner Mazel.

Yontef, G. (1993) *Awareness, Dialogue and Process*. New York: The Gestalt Journal Press.

Zinker, J. (1977) *Creative Process in Gestalt Therapy*. New York: Brunner Mazel.

10

Transactional Analysis

Petrūska Clarkson, Maria Gilbert and Keith Tudor

Historical context and development in Britain

Historical context

Transactional Analysis as first developed by Eric Berne (1958) is a multifaceted system of psychotherapy. Berne's emphasis on the interactional aspect of communication is reflected in the name *Transactional* Analysis. He saw this as an extension to the in-depth emphasis of psychoanalysis with its focus on intrapsychic dynamics. Transactional Analysis as a theory of psychotherapy integrates intrapsychic dynamics with interpersonal behaviours in an original and creative manner and is based on the ego state psychology of Federn (1953).

Berne saw Transactional Analysis as a 'systematic phenomenology' which could usefully fill a gap in psychological theory (Berne, 1975b: 244). Phenomenology as a philosophical approach values the importance of the person's subjective experience above any interpretation, prejudgement or preconceived theories or ideas. Throughout his life, Berne adhered to his belief in the person's inner drive to health and growth, which places him firmly in the humanistic tradition. However, he was far from being optimistic in a simplistic way. As is demonstrated throughout his writings, he had a vivid respect for the power of people's destructive potential, both as individuals and as nations.

Eric Berne, born Eric Leonard Bernstein (1910–70), was a Canadian psychiatrist who originally trained as a psychoanalyst at the New York Psychoanalytic Institute. Although he never officially qualified as a psychoanalyst, the influence of his training analysts is manifest in his theory. The intrapsychic phenomenological interests of Federn combined with the social-developmental emphasis of Erikson is reflected in Berne's integrative approach.

Berne's first interest in research was in the field of intuition. He sharpened his skills personally and professionally during his work at an army induction centre where he recognized the continuing existence of the person's 'inner Child'. He saw such 'ego images' persisting through adult life as reproductions of the person's earlier experiences. These observations led to the development of ego state theory.

In 1958 Berne began a series of meetings of mental health professionals interested in Transactional Analysis under the name the San Francisco Social Psychiatry Seminar. On 6 May 1960 the group was granted a charter by the State of California as a non-profit educational corporation offering alternative approaches to earlier types of psychotherapy. This period was also notable for the incorporation of a strong behaviourist influence into Transactional Analysis.

Later, as theory developed, the group took the name of the San Francisco Transactional Analysis Seminars. The year 1965 saw the establishment of the International Transactional Analysis Association (ITAA), which now has over 5,000 members in 50 countries throughout the world.

Berne wrote prolifically about Transactional Analysis (TA) in a creative and original style with enormous popular appeal. Along with his wit, accessibility, humour and common sense, there is also a depth of wisdom and clinical experience that lends an impressive character to his written work. He made a genuine contribution to 20th-century psychology which is often unacknowledged. Nevertheless, his influence is manifested in the ubiquitous references, for example, to 'the Child' in the person, psychological 'games' and other TA concepts which have been absorbed into popular vocabulary and other approaches to psychotherapy. Recently Miller (1994) has acknowledged that the 'inner child', a term associated with and frequently ascribed to her, is taken from TA.

Eric Berne was an imaginative thinker, widely read and with an insatiable curiosity and intellectual courage. He had a great capacity for self-reflection, experimentation and innovation. He was both as iconoclast and keenly aware of the social responsibilities of psychologists and psychotherapists. He had the courage to cut loose from what did not work and to risk the disapproval of establishment psychiatry by, for example, introducing the radical practice of having patients present at hospital case conferences. Such departures marked him as a radical humanist committed to a basic value system which recognized the worth of every person.

Development in Britain

According to the best information available (Allaway, 1983), John Allaway and Joe Richards created the first evening courses in Transactional Analysis for mature students of the University of Leicester in the early 1960s, both in Leicester and in Northampton. Laurence Collinson and David Porter started the first TA discussion group in London in April 1972. In November 1972 Warren Cheney, a psychotherapist from Berkeley, California, and a teaching Member of ITAA, led the first official TA Introductory Course (101) in Sheffield organized by Dr Alan Byron.

From 1975 onwards Dr Margaret Turpin and Dr Michael Reddy were teaching official TA training programmes as provisional teaching members under supervision from sponsors in the USA. Michael Reddy subsequently became Britain's first teaching member, followed by Margaret Turpin. From this evolved a series of official TA training programmes in Britain and the Institute for Transactional Analysis (ITA) as the country's official link with the ITAA. David Porter, followed by Laurence Collinson, were the first editors of the *ITA Bulletin*. Michael Reddy played a key role in the establishment of TA in the rest of Europe and in the formation of the European Association for Transactional Analysis (EATA). The ITA's first annual conference was at Heythrop College in London in October 1974. Since then an ITA conference has been held annually, reflecting a corresponding growth in the organization in Britain.

The Institute for Transactional Analysis is the professional body which defines and safeguards standards of competence, professional guidelines and ethical practice for all practitioners, psychotherapists and teachers and supervisors of Transactional Analysis in Britain. The Institute holds a register of members (1) who are in contractual supervised training; (2) who have qualified as Transactional Analysts; (3) who are provisionally endorsed supervisors and trainers; and (4) who have qualified as trainers and supervisors of Transactional Analysis (by virtue of rigorous international examination of their theoretical knowledge and demonstrated competence in teaching and supervision).

The Level 1 TA clinical examination is an internationally accredited and standardized qualification which is awarded on completion of stringent written and oral requirements. This externally assessed competency-based examination certifies an individual psychotherapist to practise Transactional Analysis.

Currently TA, with its emphasis on professionalism and international standards of accreditation, is taking its place alongside other psychotherapies in Britain. The ITA is a member of the United Kingdom Council for Psychotherapy.

Theoretical assumptions

Image of the person

Basic to TA theory and philosophy is Berne's concept of the fundamental worth of the human being, for which his shorthand was 'OK-ness'. This concept embraces valuing and respecting human beings and is not to be confused with blatant approval of all of their behaviour. It is, however, predicated upon an assumption that the infant is born with a basic drive for health and growth and a need for loving recognition (in Berne's terminology 'OK'). In his discussion of child development, Berne (1975b) had already adopted an object relations approach which he used within an existential framework. Berne took from Melanie Klein the term 'position' to indicate an internal psychological condition, formed in early childhood and always potentially present in the personality. However, he did not see this as necessarily defensive or negative.

The three not-OK positions that Berne identified are: I'm OK – You're not OK (paranoid); I'm not OK – You're OK (depressive) and I'm not OK – You're not OK (schizoid). Berne's unique contribution was the addition of position number one, I'm OK – You're OK, which Klein omitted. He regarded this position as intrinsically constructive and existentially possible. In this way he envisaged the nature of the person as having an inborn potential available from birth, for fulfilment and self-actualization. Transactional Analysts believe that it is possible to maintain an existential position of OK-ness.

Berne postulated the existence of three drives: mortido (the death instinct), libido (the sexual instinct) and physis (a general creative force which eternally strives to make things grow and to make growing things more perfect). The first two correspond to the Freudian ideas of thanatos and eros, whereas physis is Berne's addition which he defines as 'the creative force of Nature which makes all things grow in an orderly and "progressive" way' (Berne, 1957: 68). TA recognizes the constraints of heredity, specifically the relationship of temperament or basic limitations of intellect and physique to psychological health (James, 1981: 24–7) but considers that the drive towards psychological health in the person can modify, adapt to or overcome many apparent limitations.

Berne's central contribution is his elaboration of ego states and his development of therapeutic techniques to directly influence and change these. An ego state is the subjectively experienced reality of a person's mental and bodily ego with the original contents of the time period it represents. Clarkson and Gilbert (1988: 21) describe ego states as '"chunks of psychic time" – complete and discrete units of psychological reality' or 'natural psychological epochs'.

Berne integrated the neurosurgical findings of Penfield (1952), which demonstrated that human beings can *relive* earlier experiences in their lives given the appropriate stimulation. To quote Penfield: 'The subject feels again the emotion which the situation originally produced in him and he is aware of the same interpretation, true or false, which he himself gave to the experience in the first place' (Penfield, 1952: 178). This experiential difference between remembering an earlier experience and *reliving* a past event as if it were happening in the present occurs as age regression in hypnosis and also occasionally occurs in more or less complete forms in everyday life. Berne used this as validation for the existence of ego states together with the clinical evidence he was gathering from his patients.

In his contact with patients Berne observed three different *categories* among the multitude of ego states which constitute the personality. One category is concerned with here-and-now reality (the Adult), one with the person's past experience (the Child) and one with the introjects or internalizations of significant authority figures (the Parent).

An 'Adult ego state is characterized by an autonomous set of feelings, attitudes, and behavior patterns which are adapted to current reality' (Berne, 1975b: 76). The integrated Adult ego state therefore represents the biologically mature person with full emotional responsivity (pathos) a guiding set of considered values (ethos) and the capacity to think clearly and to deal effectively with need-fulfilment in the here-and-now (logos).

A 'Child ego state is a set of feelings, attitudes and behavior patterns which are relics of the individual's own childhood' (Berne, 1975b: 77). When Berne writes about the Child ego state he is often referring to a multitude of such Child ego states which represent the entire earlier developmental history of an individual. These are accessible to being relived as such, in the present, by the adult person. This phenomenon is of particular value in psychotherapy.

A Parent ego state 'is a set of feelings, attitudes, and behavior patterns which resemble those of a parental figure' (Berne, 1975b: 75). The person whose Parent predominates habitually, or at a given moment is not acting 'like her mother', she is actually reproducing, without editing, her mother's total behaviour, including her mother's inhibitions, her mother's reasoning and her mother's impulses, as well as her mother's Child ego states. The Parent ego state may be actively reproduced as when the person is behaving like an historical patent towards another person or may be active internally as in the person's own mental dialogue, for example in self-criticism.

Figure 10.1 is a diagrammatic representation of these three categories of ego states. The diagnosis of ego states is at the heart of Berne's psychotherapeutic

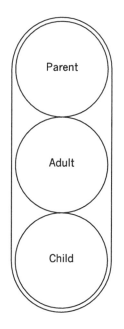

Figure 10.1 *Structural diagram of a personality (Berne, 1978: 12)*

approach. He outlines four different methods of ego state diagnosis (Berne, 1975b), all of which are essential for the complete identification of an ego state:

1 *Behavioural* diagnosis of any ego state is based on the observable words, voice tone, gestures, expressions, posture and attitudes of a person.
2 *Social* diagnosis of any ego state is made by observing the kinds of reactions which the person elicits from other people.
3 *Historical* diagnosis of any ego state is based on historical validation – that a past experience actually did occur in a particular ego-state.
4 *Phenomenological* diagnosis of any ego state is confirmed on the basis of subjective self-examination, particularly of intense experiences.

In normal life people may find themselves in different ego states at different times. In everyday life people experience themselves for longer or shorter periods as younger than they are, for example when going for job interviews, or when ill, or when going through customs. This is the everyday appearance of Child ego states. Equally people may find themselves responding to their children exactly as one of their parents reacted to them, for example by admonishing them not to stare rudely at people, or to be brave at the dentist, or to respect their elders. This is the everyday experience of Parent ego states.

Functional Analysis is the subdivision of Transactional Analysis which relates primarily to the behavioural and social components of ego state diagnosis. In this model, which is most useful for communication training and behavioural change, *behaviours* are classified under the following *descriptive* headings: Controlling Parent, Nurturing Parent, Adult, Free Child and Adapted Child. Figure 10.2 represents the functional description of these observable behaviours.

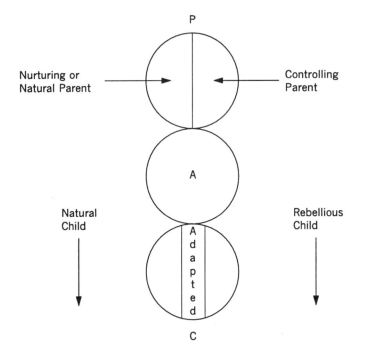

Figure 10.2 *Descriptive aspects of the personality (personality functions) (Berne, 1978: 13)*

Conceptualization of psychological disturbance and health

There are three different ways of conceptualizing psychological disturbance: through affective and cognitive interference in the functioning of the integrated ego (confusion model), through the existence of internal conflict between different parts of the ego (conflict model), and through developmental deficits and inadequate parenting (deficit model).

Confusion model In the confusion model, psychological health can be structurally defined as the strengthening of integrated Adult functioning. The efficiency of the Adult ego state is dependent on the quality of its information and problem-solving abilities as these are integrated into the personality. The concept of *contamination* describes the way in which effective Adult functioning is impeded by limiting beliefs, traumatic experiences and learned emotional and physiological responses.

Contaminations can occur when the Parent ego state intrudes upon the Adult (e.g. prejudices) or when the Child ego state intrudes upon the Adult (e.g. phobias). Figure 10.3 shows a double contamination of the Adult ego state by both Parent and Child contaminations, which can severely impede reality testing and effective functioning. In terms of Berne's original structural model of ego states, the psychotherapeutic goal would be the achievement of a fully integrated Adult ego state without interference from unresolved experiences from a person's

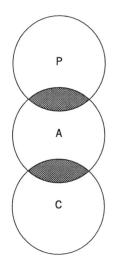

Figure 10.3   *Double contamination of the Adult ego state (Berne, 1975b: 48)*

past (Child ego states) or from the influence of internalized significant others (Parent ego states).

Conflict model   In the conflict model, best represented in TA by impasse theory, psychological disturbance is conceptualized in terms of intrapsychic 'stuck points' between different ego states. For example, the Parent may be 'driving' the person to work harder and harder, while the Child may need to play more. If the early decision in the Child ego state has involved shutting down on the expression of feelings, then a conflict or 'impasse' will arise when such a person starts wanting to assert herself, for example in an abusive marital relationship. Health represents the ability to resolve such impasses within the personality and to function smoothly without blocking needs, values or emotions.

Developmental deficit model   In the developmental deficit model, psychological disturbance results from inadequate, pathological or neglectful parenting at critical development stages in a child's life. For example, children of alcoholics may need the corrective experience of a relationship where consistency of response is provided in the context of a reparative therapeutic relationship. As an additional example, people with narcissistic personality disorders have often lacked the mirroring or reflecting essential for a healthy sense of self – this can be supplied in the therapeutic relationship. In radical reparenting (such as developed by Schiff et al., 1975) schizophrenics have the opportunity to regress and then to move through important child developmental stages while introjecting a new Parent ego state. As a result of this process the healthy person has at his or her disposal a supportive and challenging set of guiding values which he or she has autonomously integrated as the end result of good parenting.

A developmental perspective Although this tripartate conceptual model is essentially a metatheoretical framework for diagnosis and treatment planning, it can also be viewed and often used developmentally in the sequence: confusion, conflict and deficit. Much of the initial work with clients comprises Parent or Child *decontamination* of the Adult ego state (confusion model). This is followed by the clarification and resolution of impasses at various levels (conflict model), usually conceptualized as between the Parent and Child with redecisions made in the Adult (Goulding and Goulding, 1976; Mellor, 1980) – although Clarkson (1992a) diagrams the Type III impasse as between the Adult and Child in the Child. Reparative therapeutic responses to developmental needs (deficit model) usually take place after the client has worked through initial confusion and conflict. Thus, Eamon, who had a history of diagnosed psychiatric illnesses, treated predominantly through medication, presented in therapy alternatively as aggressive and apologetic (confusion). Gradually he expressed his inner conflict, initially through the vehicle of a negative transferential relationship with his male psychotherapist before internalizing and then externalizing this as a conflict with his father. This was followed by 'spot reparenting' work (Osnes, 1974), undertaken on a contractual basis and designed to reconstruct part of Eamon's Parent ego state and to give new, positive messages for his Child.

Obviously, this confusion–conflict–deficit sequence is not a strict or inevitable one, and, to a certain extent, depends on the individual's personality. Nevertheless it is a coherent and practical application of this conceptual model.

Acquisition of psychological disturbance Berne introduced the concept of *scripting* to describe the process by which a person, usually in early childhood, makes far-reaching decisions that influence and shape her or his subsequent life experiences. A *script* is formed out of the child's response to the environment, particularly to her or his interaction with her or his parents and/or significant others. The combination of inherited limitations and/or predispositions interact with trauma (e.g. shock) or cumulative conditioning events (e.g. frequent criticism) so that the infant makes survival conclusions (pre-verbal and physiological) or script decisions (e.g. never to depend on others again). Such conclusions or decisions are fundamentally aimed at survival in the particular set of circumstances in which the child finds herself. The result may be any one or more of the kinds of psychological disturbance described above. Woollams and Brown (1978) speak about the *vulnerability quotient* of the young child and list five factors that play a determining role in a person's script decisions: lack of power, inability to handle stress, immature thinking capacity, lack of information, and lack of options.

The script matrix is a simplified diagrammatic representation of the origin of the script messages/influences and prohibitions from the parents or significant others in the child's life (see Figure 10.4). S (Script) refers to the negative inhibiting messages (e.g. Do not have satisfactory intimate relationships). C (Counterscript) refers to the precepts or positive instructions about how to live (e.g. Work hard). R (Release) refers to an outside intervention or condition by which the individual is released from the script (e.g. a heart attack in a young stockbroker). A (Aspiration) refers to the individual's autonomous aspirations (e.g. the drive to health and intimacy). P (Pattern) refers to the modelling of

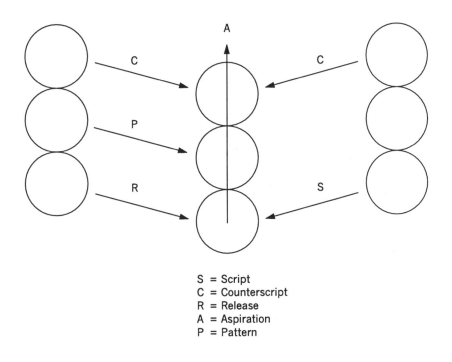

S = Script
C = Counterscript
R = Release
A = Aspiration
P = Pattern

Figure 10.4   *Script matrix (Berne, 1978: 128)*

significant figures (e.g. a father who never stopped working at the cost of his family life).

Scripting is the process by which the growing person limits her own capacity for spontaneity, awareness and intimacy in the interests of survival. This is usually practically and psychologically equated with acceptance from the caretaking figures. The premature and far-reaching script decisions, based on inadequate information and immature undeveloped mental capacities, hamper the normal developmental processes. Script decisions may also occur in response to trauma or a repeated series of sub-acute injurious events or psychological strain. Psychological disturbance, often acquired in childhood, can also be acquired in adulthood through similar damaging experiences (e.g. torture of political prisoners).

Berne stressed the importance of the human infant's capacity to love and his need for love and recognition as basic to human psychological development. His concept of *stroking* grew from his appreciation of the enormous power which the provision or withdrawal of recognition can have on human behaviour, and particularly on infants and children. He drew on studies (e.g. Spitz, 1945) which found that human infants, even though adequately cared for physiologically, fail to thrive, or may even die in the absence of genuine interpersonal recognition. Giving or withholding *strokes* is, therefore, intimately related to the scripting process, since that which gets stroked will tend to develop (repeat) even to the child's detriment. A child whose parents applaud restraint and stoicism may never feel free to show emotion even in intimate relationships. Both learning theory and the common human response to solitary confinement attest to the power of stroking (negative or positive reinforcement) to modify behaviour.

Perpetuation of psychological disturbance

The major way in which psychological disturbance is perpetuated is in the person's seeking out the same strokes to which he or she became habituated in childhood (motivation) or in the person's construing current situations in a way that fits the preconceived requirements of the script (cognitive mediation). Erskine and Zalcman (1979) in their *racket system* provide a visual model for viewing the script in action with a particular focus of the self-reinforcing nature of the script process as it is played out in the person's current life. It presents a combination of intrapsychic and interpersonal factors as well as the interface between them (see Figure 10.5). The *script beliefs* refer to the self-limiting beliefs about self, others and quality of life related to early decisions. The *repressed feelings* are the feelings repressed at the time of such script decisions. The *rackety displays* are the behaviours which a person engages in as a result of such script beliefs. The *reinforcing memories* refer to all the memories a person collects to reinforce their basic script position. People in the environment will either reinforce the basic script beliefs by repetition of earlier patterns or the individual may construe even positive or ambiguous events in the environment to support the basic script beliefs. In this way, intrapersonal and interpersonal mechanisms interact within the environment to perpetuate the script. Figure 10.5 shows an individual's racket system.

Dana's intrapsychic cognitive beliefs about herself, others and the world influence her behaviours, internal experiences and fantasies. Behaving then in the ways described (e.g. charming or tantrumming to get her needs met), she enacts the external manifestations of her intrapersonal process in the interpersonal field. People then react to her manifest behaviours in ways which repeat earlier trauma (e.g. being hurt by her behaviour, or acting in destructive or unhelpful ways towards her). This creates further reinforcing memories which fuel her original script beliefs while the underlying feelings related to the original trauma remain suppressed. In this way, a self-reinforcing system is created and maintained until an intervention in the system changes its functioning.

The racket system is useful to show how a person constantly seeks the approval that he or she did not get as a child, but he or she does it in such a way that it guarantees a repetition of the earlier traumatic outcome or deficit. The person may become increasingly desperate and escalate his or her behaviour to the point of the most tragic outcome, for example suicide.

Berne's concept of the *script pay-off* refers to the destructive outcome of self-limiting script decisions in a person's life. Unless the person changes his or her self-chosen destiny, psychological disturbance is maintained by the person's continuing to behave in self-destructive ways. This is the unconscious operation of mortido (the death instinct) in the person's life.

The smallest unit in which human beings recreate the original stimulus–response sequences which maintain the racket system is the *transaction*. This is the central component in TA theory which makes it possible to analyse in a moment-to-moment way the manner in which people repeat their relationships with important

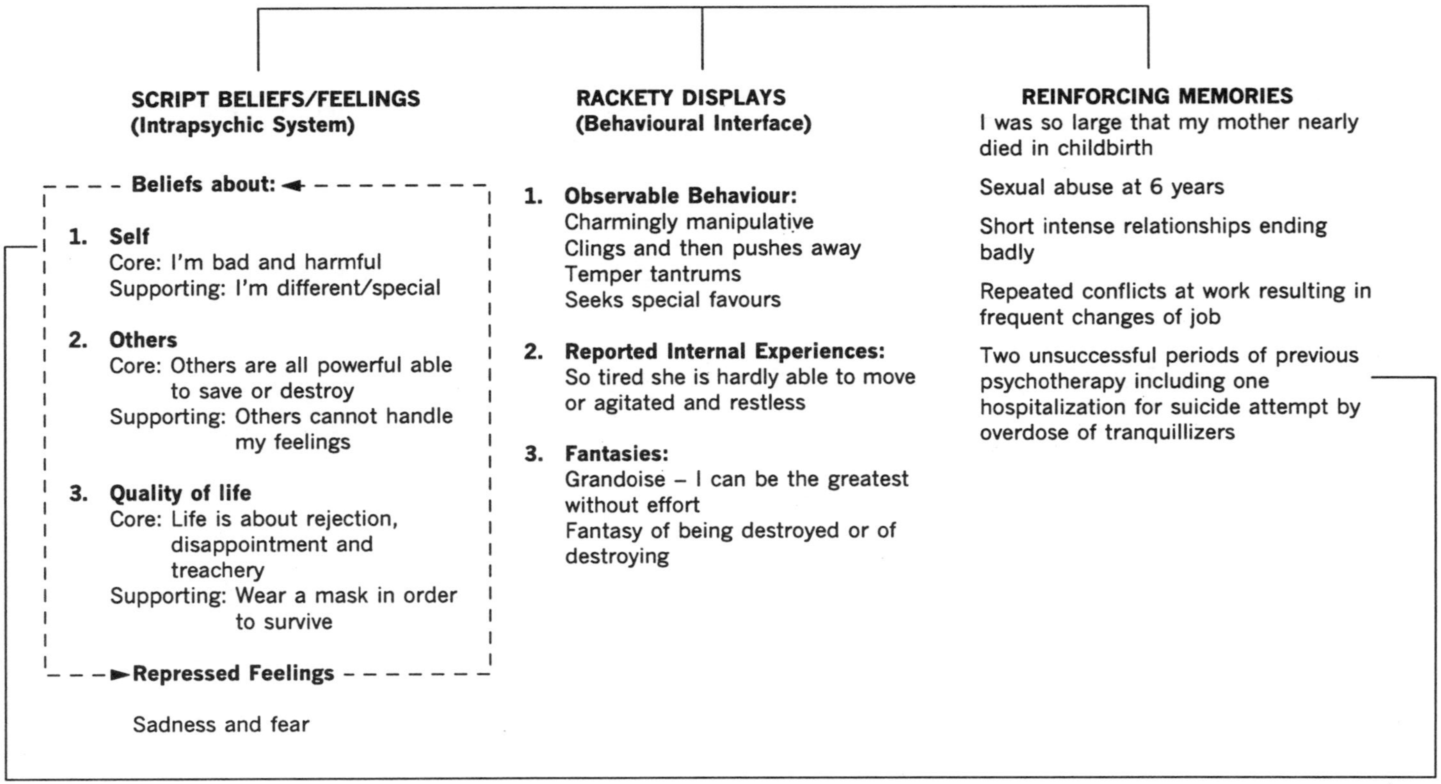

SCRIPT BELIEFS/FEELINGS
(Intrapsychic System)

- - - **Beliefs about:** ← - - - - -

1. **Self**
   Core: I'm bad and harmful
   Supporting: I'm different/special

2. **Others**
   Core: Others are all powerful able
   to save or destroy
   Supporting: Others cannot handle
   my feelings

3. **Quality of life**
   Core: Life is about rejection,
   disappointment and
   treachery
   Supporting: Wear a mask in order
   to survive

- - ▶**Repressed Feelings** - - - -

   Sadness and fear

RACKETY DISPLAYS
(Behavioural Interface)

1. **Observable Behaviour:**
   Charmingly manipulative
   Clings and then pushes away
   Temper tantrums
   Seeks special favours

2. **Reported Internal Experiences:**
   So tired she is hardly able to move
   or agitated and restless

3. **Fantasies:**
   Grandoise – I can be the greatest
   without effort
   Fantasy of being destroyed or of
   destroying

REINFORCING MEMORIES
I was so large that my mother nearly
died in childbirth

Sexual abuse at 6 years

Short intense relationships ending
badly

Repeated conflicts at work resulting in
frequent changes of job

Two unsuccessful periods of previous
psychotherapy including one
hospitalization for suicide attempt by
overdose of tranquillizers

Figure 10.5 *Dana's racket system*

figures in their early childhood. For example, if a child is continually victimized by parents, this process may manifest as a tendency to apologize for everything she does (e.g. 'I'm sorry . . .', 'I didn't mean to do that . . .'). In subsequent relationships she may tend to repeat transactions with people in which she overtly or covertly takes the 'victim' position. So any sequence of communication between her and others may be analysed minutely into its covert and overt transactional components so that she may be helped out of these self-defeating patterns.

Berne categorized transactions into three types: complementary (predictable), crossed (unpredictable), and ulterior (with hidden or covert agenda). These divisions facilitate the easy analysis of functional and dysfunctional communication between people, so enabling people to identify those transactions that further the script and to practise new options.

Transactional Analysis of this type also forms the basis of *games analysis*. The psychological game forms the interactional sequence by which a person perpetuates the script in his communication with others and ensures a negative, though familiar, outcome. A game is defined as a series of transactions with an ulterior purpose that proceeds to a well-defined predictable pay-off. Such games are played outside of Adult ego state awareness and promote the script through the patterned repetition of negative outcomes. A great deal of Berne's fame arose from his book *Games People Play* (Berne, 1975a); with its unprecedented popularity it made useful psychological information accessible to vast numbers of ordinary people.

Change

Change from psychological disturbance to psychological health can be conceptualized in Transactional Analysis as a manifestation of physis – the drive towards psychological health and growth in every human being towards autonomy.

Berne saw autonomy as the aim of the well-functioning person. Autonomy is manifested by three qualities: awareness, spontaneity and intimacy.

1 *Awareness* refers to a freshness of perception freed from archaic conditioning, related to the current reality and an appreciation of the sensory richness of the environment.
2 *Spontaneity* means the option to choose and express one's feelings freely and the liberation from the compulsion to play psychological games.
3 *Intimacy* means spontaneous, game-free, honest quality of relationship which is not an adaptation to parental influences.

> For certain fortunate people there is something which transcends all classifications of behaviour, and that is awareness; something which rises above the programming of the past, and that is spontaneity; and something that is more rewarding than games, and that is intimacy. (Berne, 1975a: 162)

Since the force for growth and change is a basic human drive, it can occur in a variety of settings of which the psychotherapeutic relationship is one. In the course of the normal developmental phases of childhood and adulthood, the person continues to develop and grow under the influence of physis. But when this natural self-actualizing process has been damaged and the person has become locked in a self-reinforcing destructive life pattern, *force majeure* may be required to effect a shift. Clarkson (1989) has identified religious conversion, crisis, love, and education, along with psychotherapy, as circumstances which can facilitate sudden and long-lasting fundamental changes in human beings. All of these may involve a profound change in the person's frame of reference (or beliefs), physiology, behaviour, emotions and interpersonal transactions.

Practice

Goals of therapy

The goal of TA is twofold: symptom relief (social control) and/or script release (autonomy). The ultimate aim is for the person to become self-actualizing and take responsibility for his or her own life choices and personal development.

TA sets very specific therapeutic goals (the contract system) which allows for precision in meeting well-defined psychotherapeutic goals (for example to have regular orgasms with a partner). The contract system is one of the chief hallmarks of TA psychotherapy. In this way, a Transactional Analyst can work in brief, focused ways towards verifiable outcomes. This approach within TA is well suited to short-term psychotherapy with circumscribed goals, as well as marking accomplished stage-posts in the course of long-term psychotherapy.

Some Transactional Analysts (who have the required knowledge of theory and experience of personal psychotherapy) are also interested in depth psychotherapy, frequently of a long-term nature, which has 'script cure' as a goal. Script cure is achieved when the person breaks out of his script and becomes autonomous. The metaphor Berne repeatedly used was to change princes and princesses (who had become 'frogs' through social and parental influences) back into princes and princesses so that they could continue their development as autonomous, spontaneous and aware individuals.

Transactional Analysts continue to investigate the concept of cure and its meanings in clinical practice (Clarkson, 1988; Erskine, 1980; Goulding and Goulding, 1979). Berne also gave many warnings against claiming 'cure' without checking out very carefully the nature and stability of the psychotherapeutic change that has apparently taken place.

Selection criteria

Transactional Analysis has been successfully used with a very wide range of clients, for example people who are mentally handicapped, schizophrenic, anti-social, alcoholic, as well as those with the full spectrum of adjustment disorders, personality disorders and clinical syndromes such as anxiety, phobias and compulsions (Harris, 1973; Goulding and Goulding, 1979; Schiff et al., 1975; Woods and Woods, 1982; Loomis and Landsman, 1980, 1981; Thomson, 1986; Steiner, 1971a; and Groder, cited in Barnes, 1977). So the method *per se* is adaptable to almost any client population in the hands of skilled and experienced practitioners. The theoretical scope and the methodological diversity of Transactional Analysis lends itself to applications limited only by the personality, preferences and training of the individual psychotherapist. Because of this diversity, there is practically no category of client that has not been treated by a Transactional Analyst.

Because Transactional Analysis works with the whole system, whether intra-psychically or interpersonally, any component/s of the client system may be the focus of psychotherapeutic intervention at any one time. It is not unusual for a combination of individual and group or family/couples therapy to be considered appropriate.

A detailed discussion of the criteria for such decisions is beyond the scope of an introductory chapter. It would depend on the developmental needs of the client. For example, a client who was very traumatized shortly after birth might need to have a long period of individual psychotherapy in order to build and test a relationship of trust. The nature of the transference relationship would also influence choice of individual psychotherapy as the preferred modality. For example, this may be appropriate with a person who has an intense need to develop a strong transference relationship with the psychotherapist integrating a split between good and bad to the exclusion of others (dyadic transference), as is the case in some people with borderline traits.

Many people prefer individual psychotherapy because it can provide a repara-tive experience for difficulties experienced in childhood with the earliest caretaker. Some people, who have never had the experience of being in a caring affirmative relationship with a significant other, may need and deserve the exclusive attention of the psychotherapist in an individual setting. Individual psychotherapy is also the modality of choice when individuals are so damaged or fragmented that they may be unable to benefit from the healing culture of a group or when they behave in anti-social, offensive ways or engage in provocative games likely to lead to scapegoating or undermining of the effectiveness of the group for other members.

Equally, others may prefer group therapy – or group 'treatment' as Berne (1966) referred to it – if they are particularly interested in resolving interpersonal issues. Clients who are only children or who isolate themselves may benefit from being in a group. Some Transactional Analysts (e.g. Berne, 1963, 1966; Peck, 1978, 1981; Steiner, 1971a) emphasize group therapy/treatment as the preferred mode of therapy, since working in groups provides opportunities for the analysis of transactions (or 'transactional analysis proper'). Berne reflects this perspective when discussing the patient's side of the contract as far as their contribution to the group is concerned: 'that he [*sic*] will offer from time to time for the therapist's consideration samples of his behavior toward other people' (Berne, 1966: 92).

Qualities of effective therapists

TA is a psychotherapeutic approach which lends itself to interpretation by a wide variety of personalities. In the study of effectiveness of different group leaders, Lieberman et al. (1973) found Transactional Analysts among the most effective as well as among the least effective. However, there are certain common criteria which are evaluated in the clinical training and by written and oral examination in qualifying as a Transactional Analyst (see, for instance EATA, 1993).

These are:

- a sound theoretical background in Transactional Analysis;
- an ability to explain and apply different TA approaches;
- clarity of contracts and treatment direction;
- awareness of discounts (Mellor and Sigmund, 1975; Schiff et al., 1975) and incongruities;
- perceptual and cognitive clarity of client assessment;
- the therapist's potency or personal authority and protection or ability to create a safe environment for the client;
- effectiveness of interventions;
- professionalism, defined as an awareness of the privileges and limitations of training by clearly relating to ethical principles;
- intuition and creativity, demonstrating a range of options for therapeutic interventions; and
- an overall rating.

Berne himself stressed the need for the clinician to use all five senses in observing and listening to clients, stating that 'observation is the basis of all good clinical work, and takes precedent even over technique' (1966: 65–6).

Ideally the TA therapist will model healthy living and psychological well-being most of the time. This does not mean that therapists have to be perfect, but that they must be willing and able to engage in mutually satisfactory intimate relationships, and an emotionally rich and varied psychological life. This transparency can be demanding on the therapist but is also a most powerful tool for change.

The TA therapist assumes that the client can become an equal partner in the therapy process, and in fact expects that clients will assume responsibility for contributing to their own healing process. Integrated Adult functioning on the part of the therapist is facilitated by both personal therapy and regular supervision.

Therapeutic relationship and style

Berne's model of self-reflection in therapy with his clients is a valuable tradition within TA and has encouraged therapists to be alert to their own process (counter-transference) and potential for playing games. Berne provided a detailed method for analysing games which enables therapists to identify the points at which they may be invited to participate in a potential game. Games analysis can be helpful to both psychotherapist and client in focusing on both the psychotherapeutic relationship and the client's wider network of interaction. This calls for therapists who are willing to be active and interventionist, as well as clients who are informed, questioning and active on their own behalf.

The adoption of any one attitude, such as neutrality towards a client, is anathema to an approach which values uniqueness and difference, and requires from therapists range and flexibility. Sometimes the therapist may be substantially more active, for example in crisis intervention or in the treatment of serious clinical depression. At other times the therapist may indeed take a position of objective neutrality, such as in working with some people who have borderline symptomatology. The involvement of the person of the therapist will vary from client to client, and depend on the stage of psychotherapy. This may range from using humour and personal experiences to giving information, confrontation or a determined neutrality.

There are several levels of relationship which therapists may use depending on their training, their own individual psychotherapy, their personal preferences or the appropriateness of a particular level of relationship to a particular client or client group.

The core foundation stone in Transactional Analysis is respect for yourself and the other person. This forms the basis of the *contractual therapeutic relationship* (the I'm OK – You're OK position). This kind of working alliance is exemplified by involving clients in their own goal setting and treatment planning, and encouraging their reading and acquiring psychological knowledge where appropriate.

The *transference relationship* is the externalization of the original intrapsychic relationship on to the therapist. If a therapist has both personal experience and training in working with transference, it can form the fulcrum for most in-depth long-term psychotherapy in Transactional Analysis.

The reparative or *developmentally needed relationship* is the relationship which the therapist may assume to help the client to correct developmental deficiencies, overcome trauma and provide what was lacking in the original situation. For example, for a person who was hospitalized at the exploratory period of child development and over-protected by nervous parents, the psychotherapist may need to provide support and encouragement for risk-taking and experimentation.

The *core relationship* as described by Barr (1987: 137) refers to the integrated Adult to Adult relationship between the psychotherapist and the client. The core relationship, in this sense, is based on the therapist's willingness to be available as a genuine and authentic person in an I–Thou encounter with another human being.

In addition to the core or real relationship there is also the transpersonal relationship in TA.

> The deepest part of the self is traditionally described by words such as heart, soul, spirit, spiritual core, essence, substance, and so forth. Some simply add an adjective to the word 'self' and describe this inner essence as the 'real self' the 'undivided self', the 'integrated self', the 'transpersonal self', or the 'fully-human self'. (James and Savary, 1983: 3)

Clarkson (1992a) sees this transpersonal relationship as the relationship of both the client and the therapist to physis – the life force within, between and beyond them which 'makes things grow and . . . growing things more perfect' (Berne, 1957: 89).

Transactional Analysts range from counsellors with a very specific focus and narrow range of educational/behavioural skills who work with short-term contracts to psychotherapists who engage *inter alia* in long-term in-depth work with their clients involving a radical restructuring of personality within the context of a transferential relationship. It is a tribute to the International Transactional Analysis Association that practitioners from such diverse orientations can find an identity within this approach.

Major therapeutic strategies and techniques

All the strategies and techniques used by the therapist will be determined by his or her assessment (or diagnosis) of the particular client's developmental needs. We shall briefly outline some general strategies and indicate related techniques.

Contracting   The treatment contract is an integral part of TA therapy and defines the responsibility of both parties involved in the therapeutic relationship. A contract worded in specific terms, for which the outcome can be observed and measured, not only avoids disappointment and misunderstanding about goals but also gives clarity to the therapeutic process. A well-defined or 'hard' contract is to be distinguished from a 'soft' contract which is vague and may lead to confusion or deliberate or accidental misunderstandings. The contract is a primary vehicle for emphasizing the client's responsibility for his or her own treatment process. It maximizes co-operation and facilitates positive motivation on the part of the client.

The contract establishes a working alliance between therapist and client, based on the belief that the client has an active drive for health, contrasted with approaches where dealing with the client's resistance to change is a core feature of therapeutic technique. The skill of the therapist resides in finding creative ways to actualize the client's positive forces for growth, while both people take into account the important 'survival' functions of the client's defences which have been built up over many years and under considerable pressure. The contractual nature of TA psychotherapy is one of its distinctive features which Berne saw as a prime vehicle for minimizing the destructive effects of psychological games in the therapeutic relationship.

Decontamination   The strategy of decontamination involves the strengthening of the integrated Adult ego state. The therapist deals with unintegrated material from Parent ego states that may be impeding effective functioning by techniques which highlight the nature of Parental beliefs and assumptions that are out of date and no longer apply in the person's current situation. For example, a man who has an 'ingrained belief' that women cannot be trusted, incorporated from a paranoid father, may engage in a lifetime of repetitive, destructive sexual relationships. Such contaminations from the Parent ego state are by definition outside of the person's conscious awareness. What parents believe often appears to the child to be inviolate truths. The therapist also deals with unresolved childhood fears and traumatic archaic Child ego states as they currently interfere with effective reality testing in the Adult ego state. For example, an unreasonable fear that people in authority will cause damage may result from a childhood blighted by abusive parenting. By separating the contents of the different ego states, through techniques ranging from transference interpretation to symbolic enactment, the therapist can facilitate the client's awareness of untested automatic assumptions about themselves, others or the nature of reality. In this sense, all transference interpretations can be said to be decontamination interventions since they are designed to separate out current reality from archaic experiences.

Berne describes the eight major categories of therapeutic operations which are particularly effective for decontamination. Swede (1977) summarizes these therapeutic operations as follows:

1 *Interrogation* Asking questions to document and elicit important information
2 *Specification* Categorizing and clearly stating certain relevant information
3 *Confrontation* Using information previously obtained to point out inconsistencies [to a client]
4 *Explanation* Stating what the therapist's Adult thinks is going on
5 *Illustration* Using an anecdote, simile or comparison to reinforce a confrontation or explanation
6 *Confirmation* Using new confrontations to confirm the same issues (previously confronted)
7 *Interpretation* Stating ways of understanding a situation, thereby correcting distortions and regrouping past experiences
8 *Crystallization* Making summary statements of a patient's position to facilitate decision-making.

(Swede, 1977: 25)

Impasse resolution in the conflict model TA is based on the concept of script decisions made in early childhood, which determine the person's subsequent behaviour. These original decisions were made as a protective measure by the child under parental and/or environmental pressure and persist into Adult life. As long as there is no desire to contest such a limitation, the person may be unhappy, disturbed or psychologically ill, and unaware of any possibility of change. As the person mobilizes energy (or the urge to healthy growth asserts itself) different parts of the ego come into conflict with one another. As this conflict intensifies, the person moves into an 'impasse' or 'stuck point'. This is often the time when they seek the help of the therapist and are well motivated for change although they are experiencing quite intensely the counter-pull of the script.

Redecision therapy (Goulding and Goulding, 1979) is a set of therapeutic procedures aimed at resolving impasses between Child ego states and Parent ego states, and different aspects of Child ego states. The purpose of redecision is for the client to reverse the earlier script decisions which maintain a self-defeating and unsatisfactory life so that they can reclaim their intrinsic health, effectiveness and autonomy.

The fact that historical Child ego states can be relived in the present in their full original vividness as if the person were experiencing them now makes it possible to access these intentionally in the course of psychotherapy. Of course, there are also spontaneous regressions to Child ego states (e.g. experiencing the therapist as a 'withholding father'), which the therapist can use to facilitate redecision.

Redecision *techniques* include allowing the client to re-experience past traumatic events with full affective, cognitive and physiological expression. This *reliving*, in the present, of the original experience, allows the client fully to cathect the particular Child ego state of that time when the script decision was made and to express earlier unmet needs or hurts emotionally.

The client is then encouraged to explore and experience the advantages and disadvantages of perpetuating the particular decision in the present time. Then the client can take the opportunity to replace the self-defeating decisions of the past with fresh decisions in that particular Child ego state, witnessed by the Parent and the decontaminated Adult ego state. An important aspect of this technique is to validate the client for constructive decisions (made in the interest of survival) in their childhood. The final steps in this process involve practising the redecisions in and outside of the therapy sessions through rehearsal, experimentation and self-monitoring until the new behaviours and related feelings are firmly grounded in the personality (Pulleybank and McCormick, 1985). Such redecisions involve significant restructuring of the Child ego state. Redecisions made at sufficient depth, intensity and at the appropriate state of treatment for that particular individual, can result in lasting personality changes.

Parenting and reparenting techniques in the deficit model Generally the paradigm for all parenting and reparenting types of strategies is providing the 'inner child' of the patient with the kinds of parenting experience that were lacking in the individual's childhood. Such corrective emotional experiences are contractually provided by the psychotherapist in the context of the therapeutic relationship.

Radical reparenting involves a wide range of techniques for providing adequate Parent ego states often for psychotic patients. This treatment is usually provided in a therapeutic community setting in which the patients are provided with parenting by the new 'therapist' parents. The new parenting experience is provided while fostering a complete regression which allows the patient's Child to move through the developmental cycle once again in a healthier way. This involves the decathexis (withdrawal of energy) of the original pathological Parent ego state and the voluntary contractual incorporation of a complete new Parent ego state, usually that of the psychotherapist. Further psychotherapy is usually still necessary to integrate the replaced Parent ego state structure fully into integrated Adult functioning. The originators of this approach were Schiff and her collaborators (Schiff et al., 1975).

Time-limited reparenting involves providing the reparative experiences related to a particular deficit in a past Child ego state which is contributing to the person's current psychopathology. For example, a child may have been unsupported when involved in an accident, so the therapist provides the support that was missing at the time during a symbolic enactment in the consulting room.

Self-reparenting is a technique developed by James (1981, 1985) and James and Savary (1983). Individuals provide themselves with new parent messages without necessarily introjecting or incorporating from the therapist. This is possible with non-psychotic clients because of the relative integrity of their personality, in contrast with the fragmentation and the destructiveness of the Parent ego states found in psychotic patients. This technique presupposes a healthy level of Adult ego state functioning.

Clearly these techniques need to be used with extreme care, under intensive supervision, taking into consideration the needs of an individual client, their diagnosis and the nature of the therapeutic contract.

Working with the Parent ego state One of the most fruitful developments in Transactional Analysis was the discovery that clinicians can contact a client's Parent ego states as vividly real phenomena. In the same way that a Child ego state can be accessed and relived in the present in the psychotherapy, Parent ego states can also be made available for any of the therapeutic strategies and techniques discussed above (Dashiell, 1978; Mellor and Andrewartha, 1980). Changes can be effected in the Parent ego state through decontamination, redecision or varieties of parenting techniques. Since these incorporated parental figures from a person's past can be interviewed or treated 'as if' they were real people, significant changes in the structure in the Parent ego states can be achieved. Although integrated Adult functioning would still be the major therapeutic goal, more benign internal Parent ego states can support psychotherapeutic changes more effectively. For example, a person can replace hypercritical self-commentary with encouraging interior messages.

The change process in therapy

Berne was interested in the kind of cure which meant that a person could break out of script entirely and put 'his [sic] own show on the road, with new characters, new roles, and a new plot and payoff' (Berne, 1978: 362). A script cure involves a basic redecision about the course of a person's life which is accompanied by changes in thoughts, feelings and behaviours. 'Such a script cure, which changes his character and his destiny, is also a clinical cure, since most of his symptoms will be relieved by his redecision' (ibid.).

The process of moving out of script can be achieved by Transactional Analysis treatment. A number of TA theorists and practitioners since Berne have formulated descriptions of the phases of treatment planning in TA psychotherapy. These are summarized and compared in Table 10.1. Following Clarkson's (1992b) summary, Table 10.1 also includes a description of the nature and steps of each phase of treatment planning, together with principal TA concepts and interventions predominantly used within each phase. Below we give a brief outline of these phases; this is followed by their application to a case example. Although these are discrete and recognizable phases, there may be movement between them and a return to earlier phases when new or particular issues are addressed.

Phases of treatment planning

Establishing a working relationship   As clients grow aware of unhappiness or discomfort they become motivated to seek help. Following an initial assessment, which will include the exchange of information about TA psychotherapy and the nature of the change process, many TA therapists agree to work with a client for an initial, short period in order to establish a working relationship. This forms the basis on which both client and therapist may agree to continue to meet.

(Initial) contracting   Initial contracting sets the focus for initial therapeutic treatment, which may be to gain 'social control' as regards the presenting problem, and which will almost inevitably be made 'in script'. This is why we include a further treatment contracting stage after decontamination.

Table 10.1 *Comparative phases of TA treatment planning*

Berne	Woollams and Brown (1978)	Clarkson (1992b)	Nature and steps of the phases	Diagnoses, concepts and interventions
Establishing a working alliance	Motivation	Establishing a working relationship	This stage develops from the administrative and professional levels of contract (Berne, 1966)	Contracting (Steiner, 1971b)
		(Initial) contracting	Setting the focus for treatment (rather than a contract for cure)	Distinguishing between social control contracts and autonomy contracts (Holloway, 1974)
Decontamination	Awareness	Decontamination	Strengthening the Adult	Structural ego state diagnosis; script and racket analysis; escape hatch closure (Holloway, 1973)
	Treatment contract	(Treatment contract)	Establishing an autonomy contract (Holloway, 1974)	
Deconfusion	Deconfusing the Child	Deconfusion	Working principally with the Child ego state	Empathic transactions (Clark, 1991)
		Establishing an internal Nurturing Parent	Working principally with the Parent ego state	Functional ego state analysis; egograms (Dusay, 1972); stroke economy (Steiner, 1971b)
		Emotional fluency	Facilitating emotional release	Emotional literacy (Steiner, 1984)

continued overleaf

Table 10.1 (cont.)

Berne	Woollams and Brown (1978)	Clarkson (1992b)	Nature and steps of the phases	Diagnoses, concepts and interventions
	Redecision	Redecision work	Resolving impasses; changing early decisions	Impasse clarification; redecision work (Goulding and Goulding, 1979)
		Parent ego-state work	Releasing the client from the toxic power and influence of their Parent ego states	Parent interview (McNeel, 1976); Parent resolution process (Dashiell, 1978)
		Rechilding	Regression; reparenting	Regression workshops; reparenting
		Reorientation	Reorienting in the world	Time structuring (Berne, 1966, 1973); options (Karpman, 1971); confronting games (Dusay, 1966)
Relearning	Relearning	Relearning	Knowing and (re)learning within the client's new frame of reference	
	Termination	Termination	Ending appropriately	Script cure and therapy checklist (Berne, 1975b); ending (Lankford, 1980; Tudor, 1995)

Decontamination At this stage clients who want to change clarify for them-selves what they want to change. This process involves the decontamination of the Adult ego state so that clients become aware of unresolved archaic issues in the Child ego state and of unassimilated Parental ego state material.

Treatment contract From their decontaminated Adult ego state, clients are now in a position to make a treatment contact. A TA treatment contract is operationally verifiable and stated in specific terms so that both the client and the therapist can assess the psychotherapeutic goals. Reviewing the treatment contract is done regularly during the course of treatment on the path to autonomy.

Deconfusion of the Child ego state At this stage clients are helped to identify and express the unmet needs and feelings in the Child ego state which were supressed at the time of the script decision in the interests of psychological and/or physical survival. It is important in this phase for clients to develop a sense of internal safety in order to support redecisions when they make them.

Establishing an internal Nurturing Parent The focus of therapy moves from the Child ego state to the Parent ego state in order to confront internal Critical Parental messages and to establish a supportive and strong internal Nurturing Parent, offering permission, protection and potency, prior to any redecision work.

Emotional fluency This is a phase in which the client builds up emotional fluency, or emotional literacy (Steiner, 1984), and an ability to cathect or energize their Child ego state as a result of which they experience emotional release and relief from, for example, introjected Parent influences.

Redecision work The redecision stage of therapy involves clients in changing earlier decisions which gave rise to the script. Redecision is usually a process that takes place over time, rather than a one-off statement of change (and indeed may take place outside the immediate therapeutic environment). As stated above (p. 226) different authors within TA have different conceptualizations as to the ego state in which the redecision is made.

Parent ego state work Parent ego state work at this stage aims to decathect the toxic power and influence of the client's Parent ego states. At times this involves the therapist talking with the client's parent/s through the client role-playing their parent/s. Transactional Analysts have developed a number of techniques for working with the Parent ego state (noted in Table 10.1). At other times it may be necessary for clients to make redecisions in the Parent ego state.

Rechilding Rechilding 'is the creation of new ego states on psychophysio-logically developmentally earlier sub-strata' (Clarkson and Fish, 1988: 52). As such, rechilding is an adjunct to the other and previous Adult, Child and Parent ego state interventions. It always involves regression, although not necessarily reparenting, and is usually and most effectively done in groups led by two or more psychotherapists.

Reorientation Clarkson (1992b) suggests that clients' experience of the reorientation phase is one in which they are often disoriented, confused and 'not knowing', whereas the next, relearning phase is more about 'knowing'. Having completed most of their therapeutic work, this is a phase in which clients are adjusting to the changes in their frame of reference (Schiff et al., 1975).

Relearning For a redecision to be lasting and meaningful it must be integrated into the client's life and functioning. At this stage the client practices the new unfamiliar behaviours with the support of the therapist, who is there to provide information and feedback on the client's progress to assess whether the client is 'stable under stress' (Clarkson and Fish, 1988), and to provide any necessary relearning.

Termination Termination follows the reorientation and reintegration phase of psychotherapy. In TA terms termination is appropriate when a client has met his or her contract: the psychotherapeutic goals have been met and the client is ready to leave psychotherapy. Both the client and the psychotherapist take part in the process of assessing the fulfilment of contract and goals. It is our view that this termination phase has been insufficiently studied; Tudor (1995) develops TA perspectives on ending psychotherapy.

Lack of therapeutic progress may be due to inadequate diagnosis and chaotic treatment planning. We believe that one of the major reasons for lack of progress is the therapist's inability or unwillingness to enter into the phenomenological world of the client.

Limitations of the approach

Although Transactional Analysis benefits from a rich repertoire of diverse techniques, there is considerable scope for the development of more theoretical and applied approaches to dealing with bodily awareness, affective work and transpersonal perspectives. A major strength of Transactional Analysis is its accessibility in that concepts can be translated into simple language which can be understood and used by lay people. The disadvantage of this virtue is the unwise popularization of misconceived notions which are based on an inadequate study of the primary sources of Transactional Analysis literature or ignorance of the more recent theoretical developments as represented, for instance, in the *Transactional Analysis Journal*. In a recent theoretical biography of Eric Berne, Stewart (1992) reviews popular criticisms of TA and offers rebuttals of these criticisms.

Clinical practice in Transactional Analysis far outstrips in complexity, sophistication and subtlety the available written material on the subject. It is hoped that in the future the accumulated experience of veteran clinicians will become more freely available in the professional literature to the benefit of colleagues of other approaches as well as beginning clinicians in Transactional Analysis.

In practice, then, the limitations of the approach are the limitations of the individual practitioner. Clients or referring colleagues need to question the nature and duration of an individual practitioner's own psychotherapy; for example, whether or not they have had experience of long-term individual psychotherapy on a weekly or twice-weekly basis and their previous professional background (e.g. psychiatry or teaching) for suitability for the work to be undertaken.

The future hope and development of Transactional Analysis as a psychotherapy depends on increasing standards of professionalism in practice; an integration into Transactional Analysis theory of major trends from mainstream psychology and developments in other approaches to psychotherapy; and a return to understanding the historical conceptual framework from which Berne evolved his thought and work.

Case example

The client

Establishing a working relationship: referral and initial assessment/ diagnosis Liam is a nurse; he is single; in his spare time he paints and, when he first came to psychotherapy, wanted to change his working week so as to give more time and expression to his artistic talents. His immediate motivation for coming to psychotherapy comprised various concerns about his sexuality and, specifically, about feeling guilty as regards sex; difficulties in attachment and closeness in relationships; and his fear of others' anger as well as of his own unexpressed anger. Liam's predominant mental condition was one of confusion and guilt. His physical condition reflected this: he had a concave chest, his neck jutted forward, his upper body looked collapsed, and he looked and sounded apologetic.

During an initial agreed period of six weeks the therapist established a working relationship with Liam during which he learned more of Liam's family, developmental, sexual and relationship history.

Liam's parents were both working-class people with, according to Liam, strong aspirations and strong opinions. They worried about appearances and what the neighbours thought (or were thought to think) and at the same time believed themselves to be superior to others. This formed the origins of Liam's (apparently contradictory) life positions. His parents were strict Roman Catholics and the notion of evil and original sin was a very strong influence on Liam, although he stopped attending church when he was 16. Berne's (1978) three-handed life positions provide a comprehensive summary of Liam's family history and psychological positions. The I − You + They − combination, that is: I − (because I'm sinful), You + (because others know best), They − (the neighbours, because they are working class), describes the servile position Liam inherited; whilst the I − You + They + (because 'they', the Church and other authorities are right) describes Liam's presented combination: 'the self-punishing . . . masochist, the melancholic position in pure form' (Berne, 1978: 90). Both these positions, however, covered Liam's I + You - They - 'solitary, self-righteous critic' (ibid.).

As a child Liam experienced the focus of his parents' – especially his mother's – attention. He remembered being told from an early age not to do what he wanted either because it was 'wrong' or for fear of what the neighbours would think. He also had to 'get it right' according to the strict moral code of his parents and the Church. He adapted to these messages by becoming a 'Good Child': a syndrome

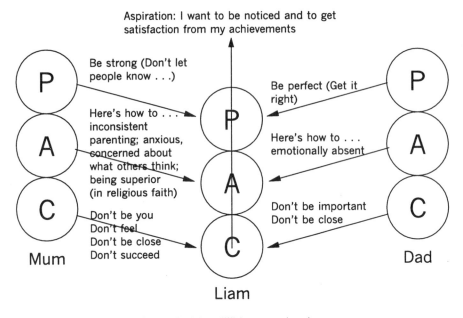

Figure 10.6 *Liam's script matrix showing Berne's (1978) aspiration arrow and Liam's script decisions*

in which 'the dynamic is expressed behaviourally as failure to ask for what one wants and failure to initiate negotiation if the request is denied' (Weiss and Weiss, 1984: 119).

Prior to coming into therapy Liam had had an active sexual history with a number of partners as well as one long-term sexual relationship which he described as having been 'quite traditional', in which his partner was less interested in sex and sexual experimentation than was Liam. This led him to retreat from negotiating what he wanted, assuming disapproval and, instead, putting his sexual energies into practices about which he felt – and feels – guilty.

TA diagnosis is a process of information-gathering, assessing that information and reflecting on that assessment. Through contracting it can be used to facilitate treatment planning. The diagnoses the therapist develops are the result of his interactive work with Liam, rather than a fixed and rigid diagnostic starting point. For instance the therapist derives a script matrix (Figure 10.6) from the information Liam gives about his background as well as his current life.

Liam's script matrix is seen to be consistent with other TA diagnoses such as Ware's (1983) work on personality adaptation. Liam's grandiosity and rigidity of thought; his unrealistic expectations of himself, covering a deep-seated insecurity; his projection of negative and hostile thoughts on to others; and his hyper-sensitivity all led the therapist to a diagnosis of a paranoid personality adaptation, consistent with the counterscript messages 'Be Strong' and 'Be Perfect'.

Other TA diagnoses were used, such as Levin's (1988) work on developmental cycles; structural ego state, game and racket analysis. These are generally complemented by comparative diagnoses, such as the American Psychiatric Association's (1994) multi-axial *Diagnostic and Statistical Manual IV* (*DSM IV*) – and, in Liam's case, neo-Reichian character analysis.

Initial contracting During the initial six sessions Liam said he wanted to get away from rigid structure. He described himself as having a computer-like mental filing system which was reflected in his over-concern for detail (Levin's, 1988, functional metaphor for this developmental age is 'computer'). Liam qualified a lot of what he said by putting it in context and talking in extended sentences with numerous sub-clauses. Having identified this in the first sessions, initially Liam asked for little structure to the therapy. This appeared different (i.e. out of script), but it became apparent that, although thinking was his 'contact door' (Ware, 1983), in fact Liam's thinking was highly contaminated (in the TA sense), rigid and over-structured in a way which Liam himself experienced as confusing. What he needed in therapy was both clear thinking *and* a clear structure, which would support rather than limit his self-development; whilst, developmentally (Levin, 1988), his therapist was aware of Liam's needs for time and information, reasons, and limits as well as affection. Following this shared realization, Liam's initial contract was to ask questions of his therapist about the process of therapy and to ask for structure to his psychotherapeutic work. As he agreed this contract, he visibly sighed as if he was letting go of some weight of responsibility. For his part, the therapist agreed to answer Liam's questions. In the context of Liam's issues about trust, the therapist viewed Liam's request for more structure in the therapy process as 'making process', perhaps even 'counterscript cure' (Clarkson, 1992b), although not a contract for 'script cure'.

Decontamination Although these three initial phases are distinct, in practice they are often interchangeable. With Liam, decontamination work was part of establishing a working relationship in which he did not believe that his therapist was out to 'get him' or criticize him. Also, by strengthening Liam's Adult through decontamination work, he and his psychotherapist identified a treatment contract.

Liam's ego state contaminations were of both varieties: the Parent contaminated Adult *prejudice* ('You can't do that') and the Child contaminated Adult *fantasy*, mainly taking the form of grandiose, paranoid delusions:

> *Liam*: It would take everyone who is affected by my behaviour to tell me that it doesn't matter, it was not a problem.
> *Therapist*: If they told you, would you believe them?
> *Liam*: Yes.
> *Therapist*: Yes?
> *Liam*: Yes, but it's impossible that they'd all tell me . . . (tape extract from session).

This reflects Zechnich's (1968) identification of two kinds of two distinct paranoia phenomenon: paranoia in the Child ('Am I OK?', 'Am I doing it right?') and paranoia in the Parent of the Child ('They're not OK'). Further decontamination work with Liam involved ego-state diagnosis; drawing up his script matrix, following which he enacted a two-chair, internal Parent–Child dialogue;

and drawing up his racket system. As a result of this, Liam identified a cultural and family script (Roberts, 1975) to 'know your place' which Liam experienced as holding him back, confirming the injunction 'Don't succeed'. Liam recognized the impact of these two script messages: he described himself as only being able to understand two modes of being; 'one is to be frightened of people, and the other is to tell them to "fuck off". I don't have anything in between those two extremes' (quote from tape transcript).

Treatment contract Having understood the nature of the influences from his parents and his own archaic childhood experiences, Liam was ready to make a treatment contract with his therapist. That this is a *phase* of treatment planning is reflected by the reformulation of the following contracts over time. Together with his therapist Liam formulated the following TA treatment contracts:

1   To challenge (and have challenged) my beliefs about my ability to change and ability to solve problems (levels of discounting on the discount matrix, Schiff et al., 1975);
2   To restructure my time and to renegotiate my employment so that I have and make time for my art;
3   To learn to say what I want at work and with friends;
4   To take care of myself by getting seven hours' sleep every night, by not drinking caffeine after midday, by limiting my alcohol consumption to no more than three pints in any one day, and to limit my smoking (from an unlimited intake to not more than five cigarettes when I am drinking socially).
5   To make a new decision (a redecision) about the influence I allow my mother to have in my life.

In these formulations the therapist is engaging with Liam largely on a cognitive level which is consistent with his personality adaptation (Ware, 1983) and 'open door' of thinking.

Liam also developed what he and his therapist referred to as his 'process contract':

6   I will act autonomously, by evaluating myself accurately, and by being and staying in Adult whilst getting accurate feedback from others. And I will be and stay in Adult by holding and valuing my own truth; by assuming rational goodwill (on the part of others); and by checking out others' assumptions firstly with myself and only then with others. (quote from tape transcript)

This elaborated both Liam's internal shift and his external (behavioural) manifestation in making his treatment contract.

Deconfusion Clarkson makes the general point that approaches in treatment planning are 'a kind of treatment loop that needs to be followed whereby the client may need to recycle to the decontamination phase from the confusion phase and vice versa' (1992b: 106) and, specifically, links the 'treatment loop' between decontamination and deconfusion to the client's personality adaptation. In working with Liam his therapist generally did decontamination work first followed by deconfusion, although there was some 'recycling', which took the form of further decontamination work particularly concerning Liam's beliefs about the 'right way' to do therapy.

Having built a therapeutic relationship with Liam by making contact through thinking, the therapist was then able to engage with him in affective work about his concerns about his sexuality, his generalized guilty feelings, and his fear of anger. In this phase of giving attention to and working with the Child ego state, the therapist was confronting Liam's discounting, and using empathic transactions (Clark, 1991), e.g.:

> *Therapist*: When you joke about (and against) yourself, I feel sad for this little, lost two-year-old who had to be so adult and responsive . . .
>
> *Liam*: . . . I am beginning to learn . . . that is a process that I do to myself, it's something that I enact all the time. I am beginning to understand more fully how I am actually doing that because every time you say something like I am denigrating myself, it becomes apparent to me how much you are seeing the things that I take for granted as being the way that everyday life is for everyone . . . you keep describing those things back to me as something I am doing to myself as if it's unduly harsh for one thing; as if it is coming from me and therefore I have the choice not to do it; and as if you're not taking it for granted that everyone behaves that way towards themselves all the time – which I've always assumed that was just like the way life is . . . I feel very sad . . . I feel upset by that. (quote from tape transcript)

Establishing an internal Nurturing Parent Following this work, Liam's therapist introduced the concept of functional ego states and egograms to Liam, identifying his egogram (his external, behavioural functioning, in relation to others) (Figure 10.7, above the line) as well as his psychogram (Dusay, 1977), i.e. his own, internal analysis of how he experiences his functioning (Figure 10.7, below the line.

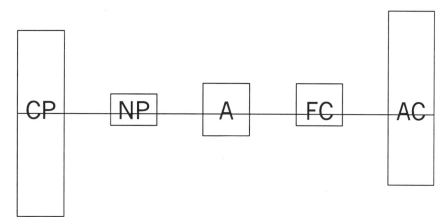

Figure 10.7 *Liam's egogram and psychogram*

As his therapist introduced this material, Liam experienced a number of strong reactions. He doubled up, holding his stomach in pain. Liam said he was frightened about the idea of establishing and promoting his internal Nurturing Parent (NP) and Free Child (FC). During the exploration of his strong physiological and emotional reactions, he realized that when he considers expanding his internal NP he rubberbands back into an archaic Child ego state in which he expected (and still expects) to get hurt. Similarly, his external reactions reflected an archaic defensive response to a harsh and unfriendly world. On a cognitive level he was aware of identified internal introjects e.g. 'You shouldn't be doing this . . . You're not allowed to be happy.' Liam realized that he had a vast catalogue of things he was (and still believed he was) not allowed to do. Following this, working on the basis of the constancy hypothesis (Dusay, 1972), Liam drew up a strategy to separate the process of establishing his internal NP and FC from any backlash from his internal Critical Parent. Liam agreed:

- to catalogue things I want to have or do;
- to then write down any internal negative introjects I identify, i.e. 'the objections' and to discuss their impact in therapy;
- to identify NP responses to wanting, having and doing things;
- to then do some of these 'things', activities, etc. anyway;
- to discuss this process in therapy.

Emotional fluency This exercise represented a breakthrough for Liam and, although he experienced some 'script backlash', particularly from his Influencing Parent (Edwards, 1968) in the form of his parents' Catholicism and passivity, Liam became more emotionally fluent and able to acknowledge the conflict he experienced. A year later in therapy Liam drew his egogram and psychogram and compared it with his previous one.

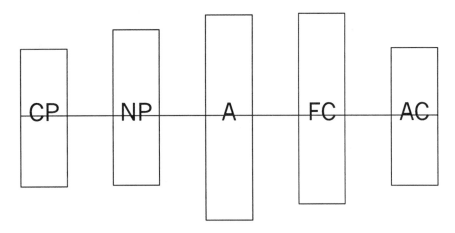

Figure 10.8 *Liam's egogram and psychogram*

Redecision work Akin to the recycling of earlier phases of treatment planning, there is in the TA psychotherapeutic process – and was in Liam's therapy – some alternating between the phases of emotional fluency, redecision and Parent ego state work. Thus Liam's increased emotional literacy (Steiner, 1984) led him to some redecisions, for example about acknowledging what he was doing well – and, given his personality adaptation, it was significant that this was about *doing*. Following the identification and establishing of his internal NP, Liam developed a dialogue: when he was self-critical, he was now conscious of this and came up with nurturing, self-caring responses, e.g.:

> *Liam*: Here's something that I'm doing well, at this very moment, in accepting that there's no right answer to [my] question . . . so there's no ideal model of the right way of doing it which I'm failing to live up to . . . I'm managing to let go of stuff about rules and regulations. (quote from tape transcript)

Parent ego state work   However, despite a new emotional fluency and expression of feeling, Liam still experienced the negative, restructuring influence of his Catholic background. On looking through some texts, he quoted from the Bible, 'The Lord shall fight for you, and ye shall hold your peace' (Exodus 14: 14). Liam understood 'holding his peace' to mean to stay still, to be passive. He also remembered part of the catechism:

> 'Jesus Christ has given us another great rule with these words: "If any man will come after me, let him deny himself . . ." . . . We are to deny ourselves by giving up our own will, and by going against our own humours, inclinations and passions . . . We are bound to deny ourselves because our natural inclinations are prone to evil from our very childhood; and, if not corrected by self-denial, they will certainly carry us to Hell'. (*A Catechism of Christian Doctrine*, 1898/1985, paras 342–4)

Reading this, Liam commented that it rendered the idea of going out and getting what he wanted utterly meaningless – which threatened to undermine the agreements on which he was working. Following this the therapist decided with Liam to conduct a Parent interview (McNeel, 1976) with the local Roman Catholic priest of his childhood since Liam had identified the priest as a significant Parent figure when drawing up his script matrix. The purpose of the Parent interview was first to get some minimum release for Liam to decide what was right for himself, specifically in terms of gaining release and relief from psychotherapy; and, secondly, to reparent the Parent (Mellor and Andrewartha, 1980). The therapist conducted a Parent interview with the priest and, later, with Liam's mother – with Liam playing the respective roles – as a result of which Liam got the minimal release he needed.

Following this, Liam clarified a number of contaminations, for instance one regarding his ability to paint. When he explored this further, he realized that he was dependent on external acknowledgement of a piece of art for acceptance; as he clarified this he said: 'I know it's not true but I *feel* it is'. After an art summer school he reported having had a difficult time, feeling paranoid, excluded and judged negatively by others at the school. Prior to the subsequent summer school Liam's therapist facilitated him to do some two-chair work (Goulding and Goulding, 1976), experiencing, confronting and breaking through his (Type II) impasse in response to three powerful Parental injunctions 'Don't be important', 'Don't expect or ask for what you want', and 'Don't succeed'. On his return from the summer school, Liam reported that he had had a successful time both artistically and socially.

Rechilding Liam had not done regressive, rechilding work as a specific phase of his individual treatment and, indeed, it is not recommended in individual therapy. Liam's therapist originally chose to work with Liam individually for two reasons: because that was the mode in which he presented; and because Liam specifically said that he did not want to be in a group as he had previously been in a therapy group for six months in which he had felt intimidated and frightened by what he perceived to be the 'therapy culture' of cathartic expression. Having worked in individual therapy for over two years, Liam took up the offer of a place in one of the therapist's psychotherapy groups in order both to consolidate the changes he had made – this time in a supportive group environment – and, indeed, to have and to internalize a reparative experience of a group.

Reorientation and relearning Liam's reorientation (unknowing), and especially relearning (knowing), took place predominantly in group psychotherapy, initially supported by the continuation of his individual therapy on a less frequent basis and, later, by his participation in the group as his only form of therapy. Given the issues he presented with, his growing connection with and genuine caring (as distinct from a rackety caring) for others was an important (re)learning for Liam.

At one stage Liam missed a number of group sessions – an echo of an earlier ambivalence about committing himself to therapy – about which he felt guilty and was highly critical of himself. The therapist knew that towards the end of therapy there is frequently a recycling of earlier issues. He confronted Liam and reminded him of his ability to be self-nurturing and compassionate: accepting the vicissitudes of life (stability under stress) on the road to autonomy.

Termination In the last phase of therapy Liam reviewed his achievements in a process of evaluating his progress in therapy. He acknowledged and celebrated that he had met all the contracts he originally made and allowed himself time to celebrate this with others in the group.

The criteria by which the TA therapist determines whether and to what extent goals have been achieved is based on Berne's (1975b) diagnostic criteria for ego states, i.e. behavioural, social or operational, historical and phenomenological (see p. 233). Thus, with Liam, the therapist looks for behavioural changes, in terms of 'demeanors, gestures, voices, vocabularies, and other characteristics' (Berne, 1975b: 75–6) which reflect Liam's autonomy; Liam holds himself differently, appearing upright, facing the world and, in therapy, sits differently, leaning back and getting more support for himself. On a social or operational level the therapist is interested in how Liam reports his reactions, particularly to the behaviour of others; another gain of being in a group. Historically, he has developed a more sophisticated awareness of the influence of Parental figures involved in the prototype for his behaviours. In phenomenological terms, Liam has re-experienced 'in full intensity, with a little weathering, the moment of epoch when he assimilated the parental ego state' (ibid.: 76).

This case example is inevitably a condensed version of a much longer and more complex psychotherapeutic process, with certain phases representing months of regular work with Liam – and, for other clients, even years. In presenting this case study we have highlighted some of the ways in which a TA practitioner thinks about and applies TA to the psychotherapeutic process.

References

Allaway, J. (1983) 'Transactional Analysis in Britain: the beginnings', *Transactions: Journal of the Institute of Transactional Analysis*, 1: 5–10.

American Psychiatric Association (1994) *Diagnostic and Statistical Manual of Mental Disorders*, 4th edition, revised. Washington, DC: APA.

Barnes, G. (ed.) (1977) *Transactional Analysis after Eric Berne: Teachings and Practices of Three TA Schools*. New York: Harper & Row.

Barr, J. (1987) 'The Therapeutic Relationship model: perspectives on the core of the healing process', *Transactional Analysis Journal*, 17(4): 134–40.

Berne, E. (1957) *A Layman's Guide to Psychiatry and Psychoanalysis*. New York: Grove Press (first published in 1947 as *The Mind in Action*).

Berne, E. (1958) 'Transactional Analysis: a new and effective method of group therapy', *American Journal of Psychotherapy*, 12: 735–43.

Berne, E. (1963) *The Structure and Dynamics of Organizations and Groups*. New York: Grove Press.

Berne, E. (1966) *Principles of Group Treatment*. New York: Grove Press.

Berne, E. (1973) *Sex in Human Loving* (1970). Harmondsworth: Penguin.

Berne, E. (1975a) *Games People Play* (1964). Harmondsworth: Penguin (first published in 1964).

Berne, E. (1975b) *Transactional Analysis in Psychotherapy* (1961). London: Souvenir Press.

Berne, E. (1978) *What Do You Say After You Say Hello: The Psychology of Human Destiny* (1972). London: Corgi.

A Catechism of Christian Doctrine (1898), revised edition. London: Catholic Truth Society.

Clark, B.D. (1991) 'Empathy transactions in the deconfusion of Child ego states', *Transactional Analysis Journal*, 21: 92–8.

Clarkson, P. (1988) 'Script cure? A diagnostic pentagon of types of therapeutic change', *Transactional Analysis Journal*, 18(3): 211–19.

Clarkson, P. (1989) 'Metanoia', *ITS News*, 23: 5–14.

Clarkson, P. (1992a) 'Physis in Transactional Analysis', *Transactional Analysis Journal*, 22: 202–9.

Clarkson, P. (1992b) *Transactional Analysis Psychotherapy*. London: Routledge.

Clarkson, P. and Fish, S. (1988) 'Rechilding: creating a new past in the present as a support for the future', *Transactional Analysis Journal*, 18: 51–9.

Clarkson, P. and Gilbert, M. (1988) 'Berne's original model of ego states: some theoretical considerations', *Transactional Analysis Journal*, 18(1): 20–9.

Dashiell, S.R. (1978) 'The parent resolution process: reprogramming psychic incorporations in the parent', *Transactional Analysis Journal*, 8(4): 289–94.

Dusay, J. (1966) 'Response to games in therapy', *Transactional Analysis Bulletin*, 5(18): 136–7.

Dusay, J. (1972) 'Egograms and the constancy hypothesis', *Transactional Analysis Journal*, 2: 37.

Dusay, J. (1977) *Egograms*. New York: Harper & Row.

Edwards, M. (1968) 'The two parents', *Transactional Analysis Bulletin*, 7(26): 37–8.

English, F. (1975) 'The three-cornered contract', *Transactional Analysis Journal*, 5: 383–4.

Erskine, R.G. (1980) 'Script cure: behavioural, intrapsychic and physiological', *Transactional Analysis Journal*, 19(2): 102–3.

Erskine, R.G. and Zalcman, M.J. (1979) 'The racket system: a model for racket analysis', *Transactional Analysis Journal*, 9(1): 51–9.

European Association for Transactional Analysis Professional Training and Standards

Committee (1993) *Training and Examination Handbook*, 2nd edition. Nottingham: EATATSC.

Federn, P. (1953) *Ego Psychology and the Psychoses*. London: Maresfield Reprints.

Goulding, R. and Goulding, M. (1976) 'Injunctions, decisions, and redecisions', *Transactional Analysis Journal*, 6: 212–19.

Goulding, M.M. and Goulding, R.L. (1979) *Changing Lives through Redecision Therapy*. New York: Brunner Mazel.

Harris, T.A. (1973) *I'm OK – You're OK* (1967). London: Pan.

Holloway, W.H. (1973) 'Shut the escape hatch', Monograph IV in *The Monograph Series I–X*. Medina, OH: Midwest Institute for Human Understanding. pp. 15–18.

Holloway, W.H. (1974) 'Beyond permission', *Transactional Analysis Journal*, 4(2): 15–16.

James, M. (1981) *Breaking Free: Self-Reparenting for a New Life*. Reading, MA: Addison-Wesley.

James, M. (1985) *It's Never Too Late to Be Happy: The Psychology of Self-Reparenting*. Reading, MA: Addison-Wesley.

James, M. and Savary, L. (1983) *A New Self-Therapy with Transactional Analysis*. Reading, MA: Addison-Wesley.

Karpman, S. (1971) 'Options', *Transactional Analysis Journal*, 1: 79.

Lankford, V. (1980) 'Termination: how to enrich the process', *Transactional Analysis Journal*, 10: 175–7.

Levin, P. (1988) *Becoming the Way We Are* (1974), 3rd edition. Deerfield Beach, FL: Health Communications.

Lieberman, M.A., Yalom, I.D. and Miles, M.B. (1973) *Encounter Groups: First Facts*. New York: Basic Books.

Loomis, M.E. and Landsman, S.G. (1980) 'Manic-depressive structure: assessment and development', *Transactional Analysis Journal*, 10(4): 284–90.

Loomis, M.E. and Landsman, S.G. (1981) 'Manic depressive structure: treatment strategies', *Transactional Analysis Journal*, 11(4): 346–51.

McNeel, J. (1976) 'The Parent interview', *Transactional Analysis Journal*, 6: 61–8.

Mellor, K. (1980) 'Impasses: a developmental and structural understanding', *Transactional Analysis Journal*, 10: 213–20.

Mellor, K. and Andrewartha, G. (1980) 'Reparenting the parent in support of redecisions', *Transactional Analysis Journal*, 10: 197–203.

Mellor, K. and Sigmund, E. (1975) 'Discounting', *Transactional Analysis Journal*, 5: 295–302.

Miller, A. (1994) *The Drama of the Gifted Child*, revised edition. New York: Basic Books.

Osnes, R.E. (1974) 'Spot reparenting', *Transactional Analysis Journal*, 4: 40–6.

Peck, H. (1978) 'Integrating Transactional Analysis and group process approaches in treatment', *Transactional Analysis Journal*, 8: 328–31.

Peck, H. (1981) 'Some applications of Transactional Analysis in groups to general systems theory', in J.E. Durkin (ed.), *Living Groups: Group Psychotherapy and General Systems Theory*. New York: Brunner/Mazel. pp. 158–71.

Penfield, W. (1952) 'Memory mechanisms', *Archives of Neurology and Psychiatry*, 67: 178–98.

Pulleybank, E. and McCormick, P. (1985) 'The stages of redecision therapy', in L.B. Kadis (ed.), *Redecision Therapy: Expanded Perspectives*. Watsonville, CA: Western Institute for Group and Family Therapy.

Roberts, D. (1975) 'Treatment of cultural scripts', *Transactional Analysis Journal*, 5: 29–35.

Schiff, J.L., Schiff, A.W., Mellor, K., Schiff, E., Schiff, S., Richman, D., Fishman, J., Wolz, L., Fishman, C. and Momb, D. (1975) *Cathexis Reader: Transactional Analysis Treatment of Psychosis*. New York: Harper & Row.

Spitz, R. (1945) 'Hospitalism: genesis of psychiatric conditions in early childhood', *Psychoanalytic Study of the Child*, 1: 53–74.

Steiner, C.M. (1971a) *Games Alcoholics Play*. New York: Grove Press.

Steiner, C.M. (1971b) 'The stroke economy', *Transactional Analysis Journal*, 1: 9–15.

Steiner, C.M. (1984) 'Emotional literacy', *Transactional Analysis Journal*, 14: 162–73.

Stewart, I. (1992) *Eric Berne*. London: Sage.

Swede, S. (1977) *How to Cure: How Eric Berne Practiced Transactional Analysis*. Corte Madera, CA: Boyce Productions.

Thomson, G. (1986) 'Agoraphobia: the etiology and treatment of an attachment/separation disorder', *Transactional Analysis Journal*, 16(1): 11–17.

Tudor, K. (1995) 'What do you say about saying goodbye?: Ending psychotherapy', *Transactional Analysis Journal*, 25: 228–33.

Ware, P. (1983) 'Personality adaptations (doors to therapy)', *Transactional Analysis Journal*, 13(1): 11–19.

Weiss, L. and Weiss, J. (1984) 'The good child syndrome', in E. Stern (ed.), *TA: The State of the Art*. Dordrecht: Foris. pp. 119–26.

Woods, K. and Woods, M. (1982) 'Treatment of borderline conditions', *Transactional Analysis Journal*, 12(4): 288–300.

Woollams, S. and Brown, M. (1978) *TA: The Total Handbook of Transactional Analysis*, Englewood Cliffs, NJ: Prentice-Hall.

Zechnich, R. (1968) 'Two kinds of paranoia', *Transactional Analysis Bulletin*, 7(26): 44.

Suggested further reading

Berne, E. (1975) *Transactional Analysis in Psychotherapy: A Systematic Individual and Social Psychiatry* (1961). London: Souvenir Press.

Berne, E. (1978) *What Do You Say After You Say Hello: The Psychology of Human Destiny* (1972). London: Corgi.

Clarkson, P. (1992) *Transactional Analysis Psychotherapy – An Integrative Approach*. London: Routledge.

Goulding, M.M. and Goulding, R.L. (1979) *Changing Lives through Redecision Therapy*. New York: Brunner Mazel.

Stewart, I. and Joines, V. (1987) *TA Today: A New Introduction to Transactional Analysis*. Nottingham: Lifespace Publishing.

11

Cognitive Therapy

Stirling Moorey

Historical context and development in Britain

Historical context

During the middle years of this century psychology was dominated by the twin edifices of behaviourism and psychoanalysis. For one the individual's internal world was unimportant and his or her actions were determined by environmental events. For the other the internal world was all important, but its workings were unconscious and accessible only with the help of a trained guide. The thoughts which most people regarded as central to their experience of everyday life were seen by both schools as peripheral. There were, however, some lone voices which defended the individual as a conscious agent. Kelly (1955) emphasized the way in which the person seeks to give meaning to the world, and suggested that each of us constructs our own view of reality through a process of experimentation. Ellis (1962) drew attention to the role of irrational beliefs in neurotic disorders, and developed rational-emotive therapy (RET) to change these beliefs systematically. The study of the mental processes which intervene between stimulus and response is termed 'cognitive psychology'. This includes a wide range of activities such as thinking, remembering and perceiving. It was not until the 1970s that psychology began to undergo a 'cognitive revolution' (see Mahoney and Arnkoff, 1978) which led to a greater interest in the relevance of cognitive processes to therapy.

This revolution came in part from within behaviourism. Starting from a learning theory perspective, some behavioural psychologists began to investigate how cognitions could be treated as behaviours in their own right, and so might be conditioned or deconditioned (Cautela, 1973). Others considered the person's contribution to the management of his or her own behaviour (Kanfer and Karoly, 1972); this led to a theory of self-regulation known as self-control theory.

Cognitive theory started to break away from Skinnerian and Pavlovian learning theory with the work of Bandura. He showed that it was possible to understand the phenomenon of modelling from a cognitive rather than strictly behaviourist perspective (Bandura, 1977; Rosenthal and Bandura, 1978). An even more radical step was taken when Mahoney drew attention to the significance of cognitive processes such as expectation and attribution in conditioning (Mahoney and Arnkoff, 1978). Clinical psychology now pays considerable attention to factors that in the past would have been considered far too mentalistic (Brewin, 1988).

This increasing interest in cognition has led to the development of various cognitive-behavioural therapies. Although they all have slightly different theoretical perspectives they share common assumptions and it is often difficult to distinguish them in terms of the techniques used in clinical practice. Mahoney (1987) listed 17 current cognitive therapies. Of these the most influential are Ellis's rational-emotive therapy (now known as rational emotive behaviour therapy – see Chapter 13), Meichenbaum's cognitive-behaviour modification and Beck's cognitive therapy. Ellis aims through therapy to make the client aware of his or her irrational beliefs and the way in which they lead to maladaptive emotional states. His emphasis is on cognitive processes that are evaluative rather than inferential. If, for example, a client reported that she felt depressed when a friend ignored her in the street, rather than asking her if there were any alternative explanation (e.g. her friend was preoccupied and did not notice her) Ellis would initially home in on the evaluative belief underlying her reaction ('I must be liked by people'). Meichenbaum's approach differs from Ellis in the emphasis it places on the role of cognitive processes in coping. Meichenbaum (1985) has studied the use of self-instructions as a means of coping with stressful situations. This has led to a therapy which he has called 'Stress Inoculation Training'. This model has had considerable influence on cognitive-behaviour therapy in general and on stress management in particular, but few therapists in Britain would use Meichenbaum's approach exclusively.

There would, however, be a larger number of clinicians in Britain who see their practice as a form of Beck's cognitive therapy. This is the most researched form of cognitive-behaviour therapy (Beck et al., 1979; Beck and Emery, 1985). Beck, like Ellis, was originally an analyst who became disillusioned with the orthodox Freudian tradition of the 1950s. His research into depression led him to believe that this condition was associated with a form of 'thought disorder' (Beck, 1963, 1964), in which the depressed person distorted incoming information in a negative way. The therapy that arose from Beck's cognitive model focused on teaching patients to learn to identify and modify their dysfunctional thought processes. Underlying these negative thoughts are beliefs or assumptions which need to be restructured to prevent further depression. In 1977 Beck's group published the first outcome study comparing cognitive therapy with pharmacotherapy in depressed patients (Rush et al., 1977). This generated great interest, first, because previous studies had shown psychotherapy to be less effective than drug treatment with this group of patients, and second, because psychologists were already becoming interested in cognitive approaches. From its origins in the USA cognitive therapy has become increasingly popular in Europe, especially in Britain and Scandinavia. The approaches of Beck and Ellis are 'rationalist' since they assume that psychological disturbance results from irrational or distorted ways of seeing the world. 'Constructivist' cognitive therapy (Guidano and Liotti, 1983; Liotti, 1986) stresses the person's active role in constructing reality, and is in a sense relativist: we each construct our own world. Therapy then becomes a journey that therapist and client embark on together, neither sure of where they will finally disembark. This form of cognitive therapy, which includes a more developmental interest than that of Beck and Ellis, has become influential in Italy and other parts of Europe.

Development in Britain

Cognitive therapy became known in Britain largely through the pioneering work of British researchers who sought to evaluate Beck's treatment in the British Isles. Dr Ivy Blackburn carried out an outcome study in Edinburgh (Blackburn et al.,

1981), while Dr John Teasdale and Dr Melanie Fennell carried out similar work in Oxford (Teasdale et al., 1984). These studies showed cognitive therapy to be as effective as antidepressants with depressed patients, and also proved that the treatment could be applied outside American private practice in a National Health Service setting. In keeping with the empirical nature of the therapy (see p. 266 below) British cognitive therapists have been committed to research. From the work carried out with depression in the early 1980s cognitive therapy in Britain has broadened to encompass generalized anxiety (Butler et al., 1991), panic disorders (Clark, 1986), eating disorders (Fairburn, 1985), hypochondriasis (Salkovskis and Warwick, 1986), patients with life-threatening illness (Moorey and Greer, 1989) and even schizophrenia (Chadwick and Lowe, 1991).

Theoretical assumptions

Image of the person

This chapter will concern itself with Beck's cognitive therapy, but many of the theoretical and clinical points described are shared with other forms of cognitive-behaviour therapy. Cognitive therapy makes a number of assumptions about the nature of the human individual:

1   The person is seen as an active agent who interacts with his or her world.
2   This interaction takes place through the interpretations, inferences and evaluations the person makes about his or her environment.
3   The results of the 'cognitive' processes are thought to be accessible to consciousness in the form of thoughts and images, and so the person has the potential to change them.

Emotions and behaviour are mediated by cognitive processes. This distinguishes cognitive therapy from strict behaviour therapy which sees the organism as a black box: what goes on inside the box is of little consequence. It also distinguishes it from psychoanalysis, which gives prime importance to unconscious rather than conscious meanings. According to Beck

> The specific content of the interpretation of an event leads to a specific emotional response . . . depending on the kind of interpretation a person makes, he will feel glad, sad, scared, or angry – or he may have no particular emotional reaction at all. (Beck, 1976: 51–2)

The behavioural response will also depend upon the interpretation made: if a situation is perceived as threatening the person may try to escape, if it is perceived as an insult the person may take aggressive action. An important concept in Beck's view of normal and abnormal behaviour is the idea of the 'personal domain'. The personal domain is the conglomeration of real and abstract things which are important to us: our family, possessions, health, status, values and goals. Each of us has a different set of items in our personal domain; the more an event impinges on our domain the stronger our emotional reaction is likely to be.

The meaning we give to a situation will be determined by the mental set we bring to it. Life is too short to work out what each event means to us afresh. We need rules or guidelines to allow us to make educated guesses about what is likely to happen next. If we did not have an internalized rule that we should stop at red traffic lights, our insurance bills would be considerably higher. Some of these assumptions about the world are shared, but others are intensely personal and idiosyncratic. Cognitive theorists call the hypothetical cognitive structures which guide and direct our thought processes 'schemata'. A schema is like a template which allows us to filter out unwanted information, attend to important aspects of the environment and relate new information to previous knowledge and memories (Kovacs and Beck, 1978). In areas we know well we have well-developed schemata (e.g. schemata for driving a car, or how to behave at a social gathering), whereas in new situations schemata will be less well developed.

Conceptualization of psychological disturbance and health

In the cognitive model, psychological disturbance is seen as a result of some malfunction in the process of interpreting and evaluating experience. In psychological health our schemata are sufficiently consistent to allow us to predict likely occurrences, but also flexible enough to allow changes on the basis of new information. Most of the time we are capable of processing information in an accurate or even a slightly positively biased fashion (as evidenced by studies demonstrating that non-depressed subjects make internal attributions for success but external attributions for failure: Alloy and Ahrens, 1987; Bradley, 1978). In emotional disturbance information-processing is biased, usually in a negative distorted way.

Beck suggests that we are all capable of functioning as rational problem-solvers at least some of the time. Psychological health requires us to be able to use the skills of reality-testing to solve personal problems as they occur. For instance, an adaptive way of dealing with a failure experience such as being turned down for a job would involve thinking about the interview, assessing one's performance, taking responsibility for any faults or weaknesses that might have contributed to the failure and looking for ways to prevent it happening in the future. In psychological disturbance people revert to more primitive thinking which prevents them functioning as effective problem-solvers (Beck et al., 1979: 15). This thinking tends to be global, absolute and judgmental. So a depressed person who is not successful at a job interview would label herself as a total failure, would conclude that it was entirely her own fault that she did not get the job, and would ruminate about the interview, focusing on all the things that went wrong without thinking about any of the positive factors.

Faulty and adaptive information-processing When this primitive thinking is in operation information-processing is biased or distorted. Beck (1976) identifies 'logical errors' which characterize the thinking in psychological disorders. Table 11.1 summarizes some of the common logical errors. The tendency to distort information repeatedly in a maladaptive way is one of the factors which distinguishes psychologically healthy from psychological disturbed individuals. Psychological health is seen as a state where the individual is able to make relatively accurate interpretations and evaluations of events, but this does not imply that

Table 11.1 *Cognitive distortions*

1	*Arbitrary inference* refers to the process of drawing a specific conclusion in the absence of evidence to support the conclusion or when the evidence is contrary to the conclusion.
2	*Selective abstraction* consists of focusing on a detail taken out of context, ignoring other more salient features of the situation and conceptualizing the whole experience on the basis of this fragment.
3	*Overgeneralization* refers to the pattern of drawing a general rule or conclusion on the basis of one or more isolated incidents and applying the concept across the board to related and unrelated situations.
4	*Magnification and minimization* are reflected in errors in evaluating the significance or magnitude of an event that are so gross as to constitute a distortion.
5	*Personalization* refers to the patient's proclivity to relate external events to himself when there is no basis for making such a connection.
6	*Absolutistic, dichotomous thinking* is manifested in the tendency to place all experiences in one of two opposite categories; i.e. flawless or defective, immaculate of filthy, saint or sinner. In describing himself, the patient selects the extreme negative categorization.

Source: Beck et al., 1979

psychologically healthy people will always think and act rationally. Taylor and Brown (1988) argue persuasively from research evidence that a degree of self-deception may be necessary for mental health. This is no clear definition of mental health in the cognitive model because it was developed to explain emotional disorder and so an absolute definition of adaptive information-processing is not possible. Beck and other cognitive therapists have adopted the standard psychiatric classifications of mental disorders (*DSM IV*). A distinction is made between 'Axis I' disorders such as anxiety, depression, anorexia, etc. and 'Axis II' disorders, which are essentially disorders of personality. Beck has always stressed the importance of having a good theory to describe the condition you are studying or treating. Starting with his pioneering work on depression, cognitive therapists have been mapping the cognitive abnormalities seen in the various psychiatric disorders. Beck (1976) suggests that in depression there is a negative view of the self, the world and the future. In anxiety the cognitive distortions involve a perception of major physical or social threat together with an underestimation of the individual's ability to cope with the threat. There is evidence that anxious patients selectively attend to cues which represent threat.

Williams et al (1988) describe some of the tests of cognitive models of emotional disorders. More specific models of certain types of anxiety disorder have been proposed by researchers in Oxford. Clark (1986) presented a cognitive model of panic, which emphasizes the way in which catastrophic misinterpretations of bodily symptoms create a vicious circle of anxiety leading to more bodily sensations and more panic. Salkovskis and Warwick (1986) adapted this model for hypochondriasis: the hypochondriac misinterprets innocuous bodily sensations such as headache, twinges, etc. as signs of chronic life-threatening illness. Each of these diagnostic groups therefore filters information in a slightly different way.

Negative automatic thoughts People with psychological disorders differ from the non-distressed in the content as well as the form of their thinking. They are prone to frequent, disruptive thoughts known as 'negative automatic thoughts'.

These are spontaneous thoughts or images which are plausible when the patient experiences them, but are in fact unrealistic. For instance, an anxious person may repeatedly think 'I can't cope. There's nothing I can do about my problems. Something terrible is going to happen. What if I'm going mad?' and may have images of collapsing, or going berserk. A depressed person may ruminate about his failures, thinking 'I'm useless, I never do anything right, I'm just a fraud.' We all experience these thoughts at times, but they are much more frequent and distressing in people with emotional disorders.

Cognitive schemata   We have already seen how cognitive schemata are necessary for effective functioning in the world. Healthy schemata are reasonably flexible whereas unhealthy ones tend to be more rigid, absolute and overgeneralized. For instance, a belief that 'I must *always* be nice to *everyone*' is inflexible and irrationally universal. A more healthy rule might be 'It is generally better to be pleasant to people, but in certain circumstances it is OK to be unpleasant.' The person with the more rigid rule will tend to criticize themselves heavily if they fall short of their excessively high standard. Schemata may vary in the extent to which they are active at a given time. When they are latent they are not involved in information-processing, but when activated they channel all stages of processing (Beck et al., 1990). In a psychological disorder like depression, the negative schemata tend to become more active. Beliefs such as 'If you are not successful you are worthless' seem more plausible if you are depressed and unconditional beliefs like 'I am stupid and unlovable' may generate negative self-referent thoughts.

In personality disorders these schemata may be active more pervasively. Someone with a dependent personality disorder may believe they are helpless and unable to survive alone even when they are not depressed. The core belief 'I am helpless' is associated with various conditional beliefs like 'If I find someone to rely on I can survive', and behavioural strategies consistent with the schema (i.e. finding and cultivating relationships where a strong person will look after you). Just as cognitive therapy has identified cognitive disturbances for emotional disorders, the different personality disorders have their own cognitive styles. The paranoid person believes that anyone is a potential enemy and so acts with suspicion and wariness; the narcissistic person believes that he is very special and so acts in a grandiose fashion. These schemata are more difficult to shift than in disorders such as depression because they are so pervasive and deeply embedded in the individual's belief system.

Acquisition of psychological disturbance

Beck considers that there are many factors which predispose an individual to emotional disturbance. He has considered these factors in relation to various conditions, including depression (Beck, 1987), anxiety (Beck and Emery, 1985) and personality disorders (Beck et al., 1990). He attempts to integrate cognitive factors with other factors to develop a multifactorial theory of psychological disorder. Table 11.2 shows some of the long-term (predisposing) and short-term (precipitating) factors which may be associated with anxiety or depression in adult life.

Table 11.2 *Long-term and short-term vulnerability factors*

Predisposing factors

1 Genetic predisposition.
2 Physical disease (e.g. hypothyroidism and depression, hypothyroidism and anxiety).
3 Developmental traumas which lead to specific vulnerabilities (e.g. loss of a parent in childhood may be associated with depression in adult life).
4 Personal experiences too inadequate to provide adequate coping mechanisms (e.g. parents who provide poor models of how to cope with rejection).
5 Counterproductive cognitive patterns, unrealistic goals, unreasonable values and assumptions learned from significant others.

Precipitating factors

1 Physical disease.
2 Severe external stress (e.g. exposure to physical danger may precipitate anxiety, loss of a partner may induce depression).
3 Chronic insidious external stress (e.g. continuous subtle disapproval from significant others).
4 Specific external stress (which acts on a psychological vulnerability).

Source: Adapted from Beck and Emery, 1985: 83

This suggests a much more complex aetiology for emotional disorders than the simplistic notion that cognitions cause emotions. Beck very clearly asserts that

> the primary pathology or dysfunction during a depression or an anxiety disorder is in the cognitive apparatus. However, it is quite different from the notion that cognition causes these syndromes – a notion that is just as illogical as an assertion that hallucinations cause schizophrenia. (Beck and Emery, 1985: 85)

The aetiological factors described above can all be seen as operating on the 'cognitive apparatus' in one way or another.

Underlying assumptions We have already begun to consider the vital role that beliefs play in psychological health and disturbance. Early learning experiences, traumas and chronic stresses can all lead to idiosyncratic beliefs and attitudes which make a person vulnerable to psychological disturbance. For instance, someone who endures long periods of illness as a child and is overprotected by his parents may develop a belief that he is frail and vulnerable and needs to be supported by others in order to survive. Someone who is continually criticized for making even small mistakes may elaborate the belief that she *must* get everything she does completely right. Continuing our view of the person as an active construing agent, we can conceptualize these beliefs as a way the person makes sense of the world by developing ideas about how the world does, or should, operate. The more rigid, judgmental and absolute these beliefs become, the more likely they are to cause problems. Examples of beliefs which predispose to anxiety include the following:

- 'Any strange situation should be regarded as dangerous.'
- 'My safety depends on always being prepared for possible danger.'
- 'I have to be in control of myself at all times.'

Examples of beliefs which predispose to depression include the following:

- 'I can only be happy if I am totally successful.'
- 'I need to be loved in order to be happy.'
- 'I must never make a mistake.'

One of the features of cognitive therapy in recent years has been an interest in developmental factors. Young (1990, 1994) has mapped out various ways in which family experiences can create maladaptive schemata. These assumptions may remain relatively quiescent until an event occurs which is of particular relevance to them. This causes them to be activated and to become the primary mode for construing situations. For instance, because of early childhood experiences a woman may believe that she needs to be loved in order to survive. While she is in a relationship this belief will not be salient, unless she thinks that she might lose the love of the person concerned. But if she is rejected by her lover it is likely to be activated. It acts as a premiss to a syllogism:

- 'I need to be loved in order to survive.'
- 'X has left me.'
- 'Therefore I cannot survive.'

These underlying assumptions become less obvious again when the person recovers from the depression. But they remain dormant as a potential source of vulnerability. Cognitive therapy aims not only to correct faulty information-processing but also to modify assumptions and so reduce vulnerability to further psychological disturbance.

Perpetuation of psychological disturbance

The concept of biased information-processing readily explains how information which is contrary to the client's cognitive schema is filtered out or manipulated in such a way that it is made consistent with her belief system. This is commonly seen in depression, where positive information (e.g. past achievement) is repeatedly disqualified. The depressed person will say that past successes do not count because they were due to luck, or to people helping. As Beck remarks,

> even though the depressive may be reasonably accurate in a cognitive appraisal (for example, 'They seem to like me'), the overall meaning is still a negative one: 'If they knew how worthless I was, they would not like me'. (Beck, 1987: 12)

Behaving in a manner that is consistent with dysfunctional beliefs can also help to maintain negative emotions. A simple example of this can be seen in a phobia, like a dog phobia, where avoidance of a feared stimulus (dogs) prevents the person from acquiring information that contradicts the negative belief (that dogs are dangerous). A more subtle form of avoidance is seen in panic disorder. A patient who fears she will collapse while having a panic attack because she feels dizzy, may hold on to chairs or railings to keep herself from falling. This safety behaviour prevents the patient from discovering that she will not collapse.

In personality disorders 'schema maintenance' (Young, 1990) takes place when cognitive distortions or behavioural strategies lead the individual to think or act in ways that perpetuate the problem. Someone with an abandonment schema believes that she is doomed to be rejected in any close relationship (often as the result of key experiences of rejection, loss or separation in childhood). If her partner is late for a meeting or rings up to cancel, her automatic thought is 'It's happening again. He's just like all the rest. He'll leave me soon.' She may try to prevent rejection by constantly looking for reassurance from her partner and this clinging behaviour may actually have the effect of alienating him and bringing about every abandonment she fears. An alternative strategy which many people who fear abandonment employ is to keep away from relationships altogether and so escape the pain of rejection. This strategy has been termed 'schema avoidance' (Young, 1990).

External factors can also help to perpetuate psychological disturbance. Real-life problems such as unemployment or bereavement make it difficult for depressed people to believe that there is a future, or to believe that they are of value. Similarly, chronic stress or social rejection can contribute to the continuation of anxiety states. The influence of close personal relationships can be very important in this respect. Hooley et al. (1986) have shown that a relationship in which the partner makes frequent negative comments predicts relapse in depression. The more negative the external environment the more difficult it is to challenge negative thinking.

Change

At present the cognitive model has not been developed to explain changes in emotional state that are not due to psychological intervention. It is possible to accept that the special techniques which will be described later can help a person out of a profound depression or anxiety state, but if the schema shuts out information that is inconsistent with the negative self-image how can spontaneous remission occur? This is a question which the cognitive model has not yet been able to answer. It may be that over time a succession of positive experiences slowly break down the depressive style. In some instances it seems that a single important event can produce cognitive change. For instance, a woman who believes that she can be happy only if she is in a relationship might experience an improvement in mood if she finds a new boyfriend. Alternatively it may be that other factors, perhaps even biological ones, are responsible for recovery.

Practice

Goals of therapy

Cognitive therapy has three main goals:

1 to relieve symptoms and to resolve problems;
2 to help the client to acquire coping strategies;
3 to help the client to modify underlying cognitive structures in order to prevent relapse.

Unlike other forms of psychotherapy which sometimes lose sight of the patient's presenting complaint, cognitive therapy is problem oriented. Whether the complaints are symptoms of psychiatric illness like anxiety and depression, behavioural problems like addiction or bulimia, or interpersonal ones like social anxiety, the primary goal is always to help clients solve the problems which they have targeted for change. In the first session the therapist helps to clarify the problems as the patient sees them and to establish priorities. The therapist tries to target symptoms or problems which are both important to the client and amenable to therapeutic intervention.

The whole course of cognitive therapy can be seen as a learning exercise in which the client acquires and practises coping skills. The aim is to teach skills which can be used to deal with the current episode of distress, but can also be employed if problems recur. Many clients find that the methods of cognitive therapy can be generalized to other situations beyond the initial focus of therapy. This goal of therapy is 'to help patients uncover their dysfunctional and irrational thinking, reality test their thinking and behaviour, and build more adaptive and functional techniques for responding both inter- and intrapersonally' (Freeman, 1983: 2). While cognitive therapy seeks to relieve distress it does not set out to change the personality completely. Learning how to navigate the squalls of life in our own battered vessel is often a more realistic objective than trying to rebuild it to someone else's specification as an ocean liner.

The final goal of therapy is the modification of maladaptive underlying assumptions. The intention is not to restructure all of a person's irrational beliefs, but only those which are causing problems. Beliefs that are rigid, global and self-referent (e.g. I can be happy only if I'm successful at everything I do; I need a close relationship to survive) predispose the individual to future emotional disturbance. If these beliefs can be made more flexible, specific vulnerability to psychological disturbance will be reduced.

Selection criteria

Which patients? Psychotherapy research is showing that a variety of therapies are effective with people in emotional distress; research has not yet determined which clients respond best to which type of treatment. The criteria therapists employ in the selection of clients for therapy are usually based on clinical experience rather than scientific evidence. The possible exception to this is in the field of depression, where some data are available from outcome studies to guide the clinician (see Moorey, 1988 for a review of factors predicting outcome in cognitive therapy of depression). Cognitive therapy has been found to be as effective or more effective than antidepressants in the treatment of depressed outpatients (Rush et al., 1977; Blackburn et al., 1981; Murphy et al., 1984). One can predict that patients who fit the criteria used in these studies will be good candidates for cognitive therapy. Thus depressed outpatients who do not show symptoms such as delusions and hallucinations or psychomotor retardation are likely to respond well. As with most treatments, the more chronic the problem the more difficult it is to produce change. What does seem clear from these studies is that within the normal range the level of intelligence does not correlate with outcome; neither does education or social class, so this therapy does not have to be restricted to socially privileged groups. Less severe forms of depression, as encountered in patients attending a general practitioner, may respond even better (Blackburn et al., 1981; Teasdale et al., 1984). Insufficient studies exist to make judgements about cognitive therapy with depressed patients, but a cognitive-behavioural approach seems promising.

Clinical experience suggests that what applies to depression also applies to other disorders. Cognitive therapy is limited by the client's capacity to engage in self-help strategies. The more severe the disorder – whether it is severe anxiety, depression, obsessive compulsive disorder, and so on – the more difficult it is to carry out homework assignments and challenge dysfunctional thinking. Another factor which may interfere with this self-directed component of therapy is the personality of the client. People with major difficulties in the way they relate to others often brings these difficulties into the therapy session, so a dependent person may want to rely too much on the therapist or an obsessional person may get so bogged down in recording thoughts that he or she makes no progress.

Another factor which seems to affect outcome is the extent to which the client understands and accepts the cognitive model. Fennell and Teasdale (1987) have suggested that those who accept the rationale for therapy and find their first homework assignment a success are more likely to do well. The implications are that if the clients do not respond to the idea that their thoughts might have some relevance to the problem during the initial sessions then cognitive therapy may not be the right approach. There are some people who are just not 'psychologically minded', and who find it extremely difficult to introspect even to the extent that cognitive therapy requires.

Moorey (1996) looks at some of the factors to consider when making a referral for cognitive behaviour therapy.

Individual or group therapy?   Studies have shown that group cognitive therapy is effective in depression, but the effects are not as strong as with individual therapy (e.g. Rush and Watkins, 1981). For this reason therapists reserve group work for the less severely disturbed patient. Some problems, however, do lend themselves to a group approach.

Social anxiety and other problems which contain a significant interpersonal element may be well suited to group therapy, since it allows a degree of in-session testing out of maladaptive beliefs about other people. Another consideration in choosing clients for group therapy is the extent to which the group can help in modelling appropriate coping behaviour. Simon Jakes, working with people with tinnitus at the Royal Throat, Nose and Ear Hospital in London, has (personal communication) successfully used a group cognitive therapy approach, and here it seems that one of the important components is the opportunity to share the experience of the illness with others who are in a similar situation.

Behavioural marital therapists are becoming more cognitive in their approach (Epstein, 1983), and techniques exist for treating couples with cognitive behaviour therapy. Although therapists using Beck's model have usually worked in an individual or group format cognitive therapy for couples is now developing in its own right (Beck, 1989).

Some patients may initially require individual therapy when they are most distressed but can then go on to a group as their mood improves. This can be especially helpful if interpersonal factors (e.g. lack of assertiveness or fear of disapproval) are considered to be relevant to future relapse. Young (1990) describes a combination of group and individual therapy in the treatment of patients with personality disorders. The group provides a 'laboratory' where the client can test out maladaptive beliefs in relative safety.

A rather different use of groups is the utilization of more than one therapist (Moorey and Burns, 1983). This is an effective training procedure and can also be of help to the patient. When therapy gets stuck it may be helpful to bring another therapist into the session, who will then provide a new perspective on the case. Burns (personal communication) is using multiple therapy with difficult clients at his clinic in Philadelphia.

Qualities of effective therapists

First and foremost, cognitive therapists need to have good general interpersonal skills. Although the therapy sometimes appears to place a strong emphasis on cognitive and behavioural techniques these are deemed to be effective only if they are used within the context of a good therapeutic relationship. Warmth, genuineness and empathy are vital components of this relationship:

> We believe that these characteristics in themselves are necessary but not sufficient to produce an optimum therapeutic effect. However, to the degree that the therapist is able to demonstrate these qualities, he is helping to develop a milieu in which the specific cognitive change techniques can be applied most efficiently. (Beck et al., 1979: 45–6)

Cognitive therapists need to have good listening skills, to be able to reflect accurately the cognitive and emotional components of the client's communication, and to demonstrate an active and warm interest in the client. If this is not done there is a real danger that attempts to challenge distorted thinking will be perceived by the client as insensitive or even persecutory. Good therapists seem to be able to get inside the client's cognitive world and empathize while at the same time retaining objectivity.

Many would see the qualities described above as essential to any form of psychotherapy. It is more difficult to specify qualities which make someone a good cognitive therapist rather than a good psychotherapist in general. Perhaps one of the most important factors is the extent to which the therapist can accept the cognitive model. The therapist has to be prepared to work in a problem-oriented way without continually looking for unconscious motives in the patient's self-defeating thinking and behaviour. He or she must be able to blend the interpersonal skills described in the last paragraph with a directive approach which involves a great deal of structure and focus. While specific cognitive therapy skills can be learned the therapist still needs to accept the basic rationale for doing therapy in this way.

No published data exist on factors which predict how well someone will function as a cognitive therapist, although it has been shown that competency in the therapy improves with training (Shaw, 1984). The impression from my own experience of training cognitive therapists is that people with more clinical experience do better than those without, people with a background in behaviour therapy do better than those with a psychodynamic background, and people who take to the model enthusiastically do better than those who are less committed.

Therapeutic relationship and style

The aim of cognitive therapy is to teach the client to monitor thought processes and to reality-test them. Rather than assume that the client's view of the situation is distorted or correct, the cognitive therapist treats every statement about the problem as a hypothesis. Therapy is *empirical* in the sense that it is continually setting up and testing out hypotheses. Client and therapist *collaborate* like scientists testing a theory. For instance, a depressed person may believe that there is no point in doing anything because there is no pleasure in life any more.

Hypothesis
If I visit my friend tomorrow I will get no pleasure from it.

Experiment
Arrange to visit from 3 p.m. to 4 p.m., and immediately afterwards rate the amount of pleasure I get on a 0–10 scale.

Most depressed people find they get at least some enjoyment out of activities they used to find pleasurable. Experiments like this can gradually erode the belief that it is not worth doing anything by providing evidence that there is still pleasure open to them and so increase the person's motivation.

Teaching the client to be a 'personal scientist' is done through *collaboration* rather than prescription. Wherever possible the therapist will encourage the client to choose problems, set priorities and think of experiments. This collaboration is the hallmark of cognitive therapy and there are a number of reasons for including the client in the problem-solving process as much as possible.

- Collaboration gives the client a say in the therapy process and so reduces conflict.
- Collaboration fosters a sense of self-efficacy by giving the client an active role.
- Collaboration encourages the learning of self-help techniques which can be continued when therapy is ended.
- Collaboration allows an active input from the person who knows most about the problem.

This collaboration serves to reduce the sorts of misinterpretation that can sometimes affect the therapeutic relationship. In non-directive therapies, the impassive stance of the therapist means that the patient has to construct an image of the therapist based on her own predictions and rules about people. The resulting misinterpretation (transference) can be used therapeutically. Cognitive therapy wants to reduce this and does not use the relationship as the focus of therapy. It sees the therapist and client as partners in the process of problem-solving. This does not prevent the therapist being very active and directive at times, but it always gives space for the client to contribute and give feedback on what the therapist is doing. With more severely depressed clients there is often a need for a lot of direction at first, but as the mood improves and the client learns the principles of cognitive therapy the relationship becomes more collaborative. Ideally by the end of therapy the client is doing most of the work and thinking up his or her own strategies for change. When the therapist is most directive at the beginning of treatment he or she must also be most empathic in order to establish rapport.

Another characteristic feature of cognitive therapy is the way in which the session is structured. At the beginning of each session an agenda is set, with both client and therapist contributing to this. Usually the agenda will include a brief review of the last session, developments in the last week and the results of homework assignments. The work then goes on to the major topic for the session. Anyone listening to a cognitive therapy session will also be struck by two further features: the use of summaries and feedback. Two or three times during a session the client or therapist will summarize what has been going on so far. This helps to keep the client on track, which is particularly important if anxiety or depression impairs concentration. Asking the client to summarize also reveals whether or not the therapist has got a point across clearly. The therapist regularly asks for feedback about his or her behaviour, the effects of cognitive interventions, and so on.

Major therapeutic strategies and techniques

Emery (in Beck and Emery, 1985) describes a four-step process of problem-solving in cognitive therapy:

1 Conceptualize the patient's problems.
2 Choose a strategy.
3 Choose a tactic or technique.
4 Assess the effectiveness of the technique.

Conceptualization Cognitive therapy is based on a coherent theory of emotional disturbance, and this theory can be used to conceptualize the patient's problems. The clearer the conceptualization, the easier it becomes to develop strategies (i.e. general methods for solving the patient's problems) and techniques (specific interventions). For instance, a woman presented with complaints of fatigue and memory problems, but did not have any physical cause for these symptoms. The initial formulation was that the symptoms were stress related, and over the course of two assessment interviews the therapist was able to construct a clearer picture of the problem using the cognitive model. The client had a very poor self-image and was in a difficult marriage where her husband was very critical. She described a constant stream of thoughts criticizing herself which occurred whenever she needed to make decisions. She was also able to identify negative thoughts about the marriage ('It's hopeless, I'm trapped'). The cognitive formulation explained her memory problems as a natural result of only partly attending to anything: she was distracted by the running commentary she gave on her actions. Her fatigue probably resulted from the frequent negative thoughts she was having about herself and her marriage.

Because she had a belief that there was nothing she could do about her marital problems she tended to put these thoughts to the back of her mind using 'cognitive avoidance', and selectively focused on the physical symptoms. This in turn led to a further set of negative thoughts – 'Is there something wrong with my brain? Am I going senile?' This formulation allowed the therapist to develop a comprehensive treatment strategy.

Therapeutic strategies　Each therapist has a particular way of formulating a case, and strategies are tailored to the individual personality of the client. The following list tries to cover the strategies most commonly used in cognitive therapy. For different coverage of this issue see Beck and Emery (1985: 180–6) and Guidano and Liotti (1983).

Distancing and distraction: These strategies are aimed at helping the client to get some distance from the constant flow of maladaptive thinking. Distancing the client from the automatic thoughts helps to reduce the strength of the negative emotional response. Techniques that help the client to act as a more objective observer of his or her own thoughts are usually helpful here. Counting negative thoughts, explaining the rationale and defining problems all help to achieve some distance and perspective. Distraction reduces the frequency of automatic thoughts. This can be done by getting the client to engage in mental or physical activity which moves the attention from the negative thoughts to something else.

Challenging automatic thoughts: This strategy aims to change the client's thinking by challenging the validity of the cognitions. Techniques can be behavioural, e.g. setting up an experiment, or cognitive, e.g. looking for the evidence in favour, and against a maladaptive belief.

Challenging underlying assumptions: This strategy challenges the rules that guide the client's maladaptive behaviour. A broad range of cognitive and behavioural techniques are needed to achieve this. For instance, the advantages and disadvantages of an assumption can be explored, reasoning used to challenge the assumption and a behavioural experiment arranged to test it out.

Building skills: Not all problems are caused by inappropriate thoughts. Some of the difficulties the client experiences will be due to real problems, and cognitive therapy then employs problem-solving techniques. This often requires the teaching of specific skills, e.g. through assertiveness training, social skills training and time management.

Major cognitive techniques　In this section I will describe some of the cognitive and behavioural techniques that are commonly used in cognitive therapy. There is considerable overlap between all of these methods and the distinctions made here are somewhat arbitrary. In challenging a particular cognition a therapist might employ several cognitive and behavioural techniques.

Socratic questioning: Cognitive therapy helps clients to identify and then modify their maladaptive thoughts. This is achieved by using the approach of collaborative empiricism described earlier. The client and therapist are co-investigators trying to uncover the interpretations and evaluations that might be contributing to the client's problems. This is an inductive process of guided discovery. Wherever possible the therapist asks questions to elicit the idiosyncratic meanings which give rise to the client's distress and to look for the evidence supporting or refuting the client's beliefs. This use of questioning to reveal the self-defeating nature of the client's automatic thoughts has been termed 'Socratic questioning'.

Identifying negative automatic thoughts: The therapist teaches the client to observe and record negative automatic thoughts. Initially the concept of an automatic thought is explained: it is a thought or image that comes to mind automatically and seems plausible, but on inspection is often distorted or unrealistic. Thoughts the client has during the session can be used to illustrate this, e.g. in the first session a depressed client may be thinking 'I don't know why I've come, there's nothing anyone can do for me.' Written material such as the leaflet *Coping with Depression* (Beck and Greenberg, 1974) is also used to explain the basic features of therapy. The client is then given the homework task of collecting and recording negative automatic thoughts. The exact format of this will depend on the problem. A depressed client will be asked to monitor depressed mood, recording the situation which triggered a worsening of depression, and the thoughts associated with it. Someone with an alcohol problem would monitor cravings for drink, and again record the situations in which they occurred and the thoughts that precipitated them. This phase of identifying thoughts help clients to start making the link:

Event $\longrightarrow$ negative automatic thought $\longrightarrow$ disturbed emotion or behaviour

Identifying thoughts may also be therapeutic in its own right, since just recording negative thoughts sometimes reduces their frequency. Clients should try to record their thoughts as soon after the stressful event as possible, when it is fresh in their mind.

Modifying negative automatic thoughts: When the client has learned to identify the maladaptive thinking the next step is to learn how to challenge the negative thoughts. Through Socratic questioning the therapist shows the client how to change his or her thinking. This cognitive restructuring by the therapist usually brings relief in the session, but it takes longer for the client to practise challenging thoughts outside the therapy session, which becomes a situation where the therapist models the process of cognitive restructuring and gives the client feedback on his or her success at the task. Clients are encouraged to use a form to record and challenge their automatic thoughts (see p. 276) to help them internalize the process of identifying and modifying negative automatic thoughts.

There is a number of methods the therapist can use to help a client modify negative thinking:

Reality testing: This is probably the most common method of cognitive restructuring. The client is taught to question the evidence for the automatic thoughts. For example, you hear that your five-year-old son has hit another child at school. You immediately think 'He's a bully. I'm a useless parent', and feel depressed. What is the evidence that your son is a bully? Has he done this sort of thing before? Is this unusual behaviour for a five-year-old child? Bullying implies an unprovoked attack. Could he have been provoked? What is the evidence that you are a useless parent? Have you been told by anyone in your family that you are doing a bad job? Is a single instance of bad behaviour in a five-year-old child proof that you are a bad parent?

Looking for alternatives: People who are in emotional crisis, especially if they are depressed, find it difficult to examine the options that are open to them. They get into a blinkered view of their situation. Looking for alternatives is a way of helping them out of this mental set. The therapist gently asks for alternative explanations or solutions and continues until as many as possible are generated. At first these will probably all be negative but after a while the client will start to come up with more constructive alternatives.

Reattribution: A more specialized form of the search for alternatives involves reattributing the cause of, or responsibility for, an event. A client who experiences panic attacks may believe that the physical sensations of dizziness and a pounding heart are signs of an impending heart attack. The therapist, through education, questioning and experimentation, helps the client to reattribute the cause of these experiences to the natural bodily sensations of extreme anxiety. For example, the client who attributes her son's behaviour to her failure as a mother can be taught to change the focus of responsibility; many factors contribute to a child's behaviour, and a parent does not have control of all of them.

Decatastrophizing: This has been termed the 'What if' technique (Freeman, 1987). The client is taught to ask what would be the worst thing that could happen. In many cases when the fear is confronted it becomes clear that it is not so terrible after all. For example, you are preparing to visit a friend for the weekend and do not have much time to pack. You think, 'I can't decide what to pack. I mustn't forget anything.' You get into more and more of a panic trying to remember everything in time. Why would it be so awful if you did forget something? Would it be the end of the world if you turned up without a toothbrush?

Advantages and disadvantages: This is a very helpful technique to enable clients to get things into perspective. If a difficult decision has to be made or if it seems difficult to give up a habitual maladaptive behaviour, the client can list the advantages and disadvantages of a certain course of action.

Behavioural techniques   Freeman (1987) considers the behavioural techniques in cognitive therapy to serve two purposes: they work to change behaviour through a broad range of methods; and they serve as short-term interventions in the service of longer-term cognitive change. This second goal differentiates the behavioural tasks used in cognitive therapy from those used in more conventional behaviour therapy. These tasks are set within a cognitive conceptualization of the problem and are used to produce cognitive change. Seen in its simplest form, behavioural work changes cognitions by distracting clients from automatic thoughts; and challenging maladaptive beliefs through experimentation.

Behavioural methods are often used at the beginning of therapy when the client is most distressed and so less able to use cognitive techniques.

Activity scheduling This is a technique which is particularly useful with depressed clients but can be applied with other problems too. The rationale for scheduling time centres on the proposition that when they are depressed, clients reduce their level of activity and spend more time ruminating on negative thoughts. The schedule is an hour-by-hour plan of what the client will do. As with all the procedures in cognitive therapy, this needs to be explained in some detail and a clear rationale given. It is often set up as an experiment to see if certain activities will improve mood. The therapist stresses that few people accomplish everything they plan, and the aim is not to get all the items done but to find out if planning and structuring time can be helpful. Initially the aim may just be to monitor tasks together with the thoughts and feelings that accompany them. The emphasis is usually on engaging in specific behaviours during a certain period rather than the amount achieved. For instance, a client would be encouraged to decide to do some decorating between 10 a.m. and 11 a.m. on a certain day, rather than plan to decorate a whole room over a weekend. These tasks are set up as homework assignments and the results discussed at the beginning of the next session.

Mastery and pleasure ratings This technique can be used in conjunction with activity scheduling. Clients rate how much mastery (feelings of success, achievement or control) or pleasure they get out of a task (on a 0–10 scale). Since depressed clients often avoid engaging in pleasant activities, this method allows the therapist to establish which activities might be enjoyable for clients and to encourage them to engage in them with greater frequency. It also challenges all-or-nothing thinking, by showing that there is a continuum of pleasure and mastery rather than experiences which (1) are totally enjoyable or unenjoyable and (2) yield complete success or failure.

Graded task assignments All-or-nothing thinking can also be challenged using graded task assignments. Many clients think, 'I have to be able to do everything I set myself, or I have failed.' The therapist begins by setting small homework tasks which gradually build up in complexity and difficulty. The client is encouraged to set goals that can realistically be achieved, so that he or she completes a series of successful assignments.

Behavioural experiments We have already seen how behavioural experiments are an important component of cognitive therapy. Hypotheses are continually generated and put to the test. This usually involves a negative prediction of some form. For instance, an anxious client may state that he is too anxious even to read. An experiment can be set up in the therapy session where the client reads a short paragraph from a newspaper, thus disproving the absolutism of this statement. The client can then go on to read articles of increasing length over the following week. Experiments are often set as homework. For instance, a depressed client who firmly believes that she is unable to go shopping could be asked to go shopping with her husband. Even if the client is not able to carry out the assignment the experiment is not a failure because it provides valuable information about what might be the blocks to the activity.

Relaxation   Relaxation is useful for clients with anxiety-related problems. Several methods of relaxation training can be used successfully – graded muscle relaxation, breath control, visualization of pleasant scenes, meditation, etc. These can be taught in the session or the client can take away a relaxation tape. Relaxation serves the following purposes in cognitive therapy:

- promoting self-awareness and monitoring of bodily states;
- providing a coping technique for reducing anxiety;
- providing a coping technique to facilitate the execution of behavioural experiments;
- promoting a feeling of mastery over symptoms.

Other behavioural techniques   Cognitive therapy employs a variety of other behavioural techniques where appropriate. Cognitive and behavioural rehearsal is frequently used during the session in preparation for a difficult homework assignment. Role-play can be a very effective cognitive change technique. When clients have practical problems that need to be solved, behavioural techniques based on a skills training model are especially useful. This will usually involve forms of assertiveness training or social skills training for people who have deficits in interpersonal skills.

Treating patients with personality disorders   There is not room in this chapter to describe the treatment of personality disorders in detail (see Beck et al., 1990; Young, 1990; Linehan, 1993 for useful guidelines). Because it can be difficult to establish a therapeutic alliance, and because of the strength with which the dysfunctional beliefs are held, treatment is usually longer than with emotional disorders. Clients often find it difficult to identify automatic thoughts and so much of the work has to be done at the schematic level. Repeated recognition of core beliefs and the behavioural strategies stemming from them is often necessary before change can occur, and sometimes a much more confrontational style is needed to overcome schema avoidance (Young, 1990). This can include the use of emotive techniques to activate schemas. For instance, a schema may be activated by reconstructing a traumatic scene from childhood in role play. This is often associated with powerful feelings of fear, hurt and anger. Initially the client is unable to think rationally and is overwhelmed by the feelings, but a skilful therapist can help the client get some distance from the affect without getting caught up in it. Cognitive restructuring can then be used to challenge guilt or blame the person feels for the trauma or abuse, and to challenge beliefs that the past must always poison the present. More active techniques like imagery rescripting can help to change the sense of powerlessness which is often part of the memory. The conceptualization is even more important in this work than in standard cognitive therapy. To guide the interventions the therapist needs a clear picture of how core beliefs were developed as a result of childhood experiences, how compensatory beliefs and coping strategies emerged, and how these schemata operate in the clients' present to maintain the maladaptive interpersonal patterns. Sharing this conceptualization with the client can help give meaning to a seemingly chaotic and meaningless present.

The change process in therapy

It is difficult to summarize a typical course of cognitive therapy since strategy and technique depend on the individual client and the problems being treated. There is, however, generally a progression through therapy. At the beginning of therapy the emphasis is on conceptualizing the client's problems, teaching the cognitive model and producing early symptom relief. Techniques aimed at symptom relief in the early stages of therapy tend to be more behavioural. As therapy progresses the client learns to monitor and challenge automatic thoughts and this forms the major focus in therapy. As the client's problems reach some resolution the emphasis shifts to identifying and challenging underlying assumptions, and to work on relapse prevention. Change occurs through the modification of cognitive structures as evidence accumulates to refute the distorted view of the world which the client holds. This process is not always smooth. The client may come with very different expectations of treatment than the therapist. For instance, a client with a hypochondriacal preoccupation will believe that there is a physical cause for his or her problems and will be reluctant to accept the cognitive model. In the early sessions with this type of client the therapist tries to engage the client in the therapy, perhaps examining the evidence for the client's explanation of the symptoms, and getting his or her agreement to try the new approach on an experimental basis. For people who find it difficult to understand the concept of negative automatic thoughts it may take longer to explain and demonstrate their nature. Others are frightened to record such thoughts because they make them feel worse.

This may require that more time be spent in examining possible gains from exposing themselves to short-term distress in order to achieve long-term benefit. With clients who have personality problems maladaptive patterns of relating to others will be brought into the session and these need to be addressed as part of therapy: for example dependent clients may fail to carry out homework assignments because they hope that the therapist will support and help them without the difficult learning of self-reliance. These patterns often act as blocks to therapy and must be openly discussed with the client.

Limitations of the approach

Many of the limitations of cognitive therapy are the same as those that apply to any form of psychotherapy. People with very severe mental disturbances are not readily treated with talking treatments. This applies particularly to those who suffer from delusions and hallucinations, although experimental cognitive approaches may have something to offer even these clients (Birchwood and Tarrier, 1992; Kingdon and Turkington, 1994). Motivation to change is an important construct that is not always assessable until therapy is under way. The emphasis placed on homework and self-help can be a limitation for some clients. One study of cognitive therapy for depression found that people who endorsed ideas about self-control did well with cognitive therapy, whereas those who did not responded better to drugs (Simons et al., 1986). Subsequent studies have not all supported this finding. As we have seen, the question of acceptance of the theoretical model, and the ability and willingness to carry out self-help assignments, must be taken into account when considering clients for therapy. The more clearly difficulties can be defined as problems the easier it is to do cognitive therapy. With vague characterological flaws which manifest themselves as problems in interpersonal relationships it is sometimes very hard to find a focus. With such clients the form of therapy described here may not be adequate. One major advantage that cognitive therapy has over some forms of therapy is its commitment to the scientific method. It is being applied to a widening field of disorders, and as long as its practitioners continue to evaluate its efficacy the next 10 years should provide answers to the question: what are the areas of application and the limits of this approach?

Case example

The client

Peter was a 35-year-old policeman who sought help for symptoms of depression and post-traumatic stress disorder. Having worked hard and successfully for many years, he was given more and more responsibility and he began to find the stress of police work increasingly difficult to handle. To his surprise he started to remember traumatic incidents that he had believed he handled perfectly well at the time, and had forgotten. These included memories of a psychiatric patient who died in police custody, a policeman friend who died of myocardial infarction, a cot death where he witnessed a post-mortem on the baby, his niece dying from cot death, and his mother's death. A black and white picture was running through his mind like a cine film where all of the images rushed from one to another. This lasted for about 10 minutes at a time. With each memory he thought 'I should have done better', and blamed himself for not saving the people. He found it difficult to do anything with these repetitive intrusive thoughts, and got frustrated when he failed to stop them.

Although his symptoms had improved with an antidepressant prescribed by a psychiatrist he still experienced 'flashbacks' every day; he had a pervasive low mood, was unable to get much pleasure out of things, and could not concentrate. Sleep and appetite were reasonably normal and he had put on weight on the antidepressant.

Peter was the eldest of three children. His mother had died from a heart attack eight years earlier. He could not remember much about his early childhood, but felt it was basically a happy time. At school he did not do well academically, but was given lots of responsible jobs such as being on the School Council. He left school after taking A levels and had worked as a policeman ever since. Peter had not had a sexual partner for two years: he felt that his relationships suffered because he devoted all his time and energy to work.

A diagnosis of post-traumatic stress disorder (PTSD) and depression was made and he was placed on the waiting list for cognitive therapy.

The therapy

The first session   The first therapy session started three months later. Peter had improved a little in his mood, but the PTSD symptoms were unchanged. The therapist and client identified three problems:

- low self-esteem
- intrusive traumatic images
- acting defensively when under criticism

The goals deriving from these target problems were:

- to be able to make a mistake without being excessively self-critical;
- to reduce the frequency of the images to less than once a week, and the discomfort by 50 per cent;
- to act less defensively if he•made a mistake.

The problems were discussed in more detail and the cognitive model for depression and PTSD was explained. The therapist conceptualized the case as follows:

Peter had a set of underlying assumptions that he must be in control at all times, must be strong, responsible for others and never make a mistake. These had allowed him to do well in his career at the expense of his private life. But with increasing pressure at work and more responsibility he began to doubt his own abilities. He began to remember occasions when he had not been able to control events, and became anxious about his coping abilities. As he remembered more past traumas that he labelled as mistakes he became depressed. His belief that his worth depended on making no mistakes meant that he saw himself as a failure. Peter's underlying assumptions were of the sort that made it difficult to work through his traumatic memories.

This conceptualization helped with planning treatment. Target problems were depressed mood and anxiety, which were treated with cognitive restructuring, and intrusive memories, which indicated unfinished processing of the traumatic incidents, and were treated through exposure. From the conceptualization it was clear that work on beliefs would need to be an integral part of therapy from session 1: Peter needed to learn that it was safe to trust the therapist and to reveal weaknesses.

Sessions 2–4 Peter was given *Coping with Depression* by Ivy Blackburn. He took well to the cognitive model and soon became adept at monitoring and challenging automatic thoughts using the methods described above. Most of his negative automatic thoughts were related to incidents where he felt he had made mistakes. He quickly became adept at replacing his self-critical thoughts with more self-accepting ones. Table 11.3 shows some of the negative automatic thoughts and rational responses Peter completed as homework. Using the downward arrow technique (Burns, 1980) the therapist identified one of his underlying assumptions as: 'If I make a mistake, I'm useless.'

Sessions 5–11 By the fifth session Peter was feeling considerably better. His Beck Depression Inventory score had dropped from 27 to 15, and he felt he was being much less self-critical. The symptoms of PTSD, however, remained much the same. The focus of therapy then changed to these symptoms. The most troubling of these seemed to be high arousal and hypervigilance. There were numerous situations in which he felt on edge and feared that he would be attacked. On examining the situations further, he was able to see that he was reacting to them all as if they

Table 11.3 *Daily Record of Dysfunctional Thoughts*

SITUATION	EMOTION	AUTOMATIC THOUGHTS	RATIONAL RESPONSE	OUTCOME
What were you doing or thinking about?	What did you feel? How bad was it (0–100%)?	What were your thoughts? How far did you believe each of them (0–100%)?	What are your rational answers to the automatic thoughts? How far do you believe each of them. (0–100%)?	1. How far do you now believe the thoughts (0–100%)? 2. How did you feel (0–100%)? 3. What can you do now?
Vehicle behind flashing lights	Guilty 75%	What have I done wrong? Maybe my lights are defective. 90%	There was no evidence I'd done anything wrong. He could have an electrical defect or be signalling to another vehicle. Nothing happened that was worth worrying about.	1. 5% 2. Slightly irritated 10% 3. Forget it.
Car repairs cost more than expected	Guilty 80%	It's my fault. I might get hassle from the insurance company. 70%	A qualified engineer did the estimate – it had nothing to do with me. 90%	1. 5% 2. Guilty 0% 3. Try to forget it.
Asked Chief inspector if I could speak. He said he was busy	Guilty 90%	I've done something wrong. He doesn't want to speak to me. 80%	The exchange was very short. There's no evidence to support my conclusion. 90%	1. 10% 2. Uneasy 80% 3. Leave it.

were 90 per cent dangerous. In fact, most of the incidents associated with anxiety over the week were only 10 per cent dangerous. Identifying this distortion (jumping to conclusions or arbitrary inference) proved helpful. Peter then spontaneously remembered that he had been trained to use coping self-talk and breathing exercises when facing danger, and he decided to put these into practice in his everyday life as if he were facing a violent incident. This proved very effective.

Focusing on the intrusive images, Peter created a hierarchy:

1 Memory of friend's suicide
2 Sudden death of a friend from a heart attack
3 Cot death of niece
4 Images of post-mortem of a baby

A common theme across these images was the concept of responsibility. He believed that he ought to have done something to prevent the deaths. This was obviously linked to his belief that he must never make a mistake. As the therapist helped him examine the degree of responsibility he had for these situations and also the degree of control he had over them, Peter began to realize that he was expecting the impossible of himself. He had assumed that he was the only factor in determining the outcome of these incidents, forgetting how other people and external circumstances played a part. The first two items on the hierarchy became much less problematic as a result of this intervention alone. The next two were more difficult because he did not feel so responsible, but was filled with an overwhelming sense of sadness and impotence at thinking about the deaths of the babies. The therapist set him the task of writing down the experiences as home-work and then reading it out in the session. This produced a great wave of affect. He was also encouraged to listen to tapes of the sessions in which he described the scenes. This exposure work helped to reduce the frequency and severity of the intrusive memories. At this point the general psychiatrist who had been seeing him took him off the medication at his request.

Session 12 The Christmas holiday came before the 12th session. Peter came back after the break feeling more depressed and disheartened. He said that he should be coping better now after all the effort people had put into helping him, but when the nature of this setback was examined, it became clear that the PTSD symptoms had improved by 90 per cent. It was only the depression that had worsened. The therapist helped him to list the possible reasons for the mood change: stopping medication, external stresses such as a shoulder injury and his approaching return to work after several months off sick. The therapist also helped him to look at his 'depression about depression' and the beliefs that had produced it:

• 'I should be able to deal with any situation with my own resources.'
• 'I must do whatever I do perfectly.'
• 'I must take 100 per cent responsibility for any situation in which I find myself.'

Peter was able to see how his thinking about the setback derived from his perfectionistic assumptions. His beliefs that he alone was responsible for what

> I have a rule that I should always act responsibly and in accordance with all rules.
> This is understandable because, historically, I've taken responsibility for family issues.
> For as long as I can remember I have always held positions of responsibility. The legal
> and moral responsibilities of the job have increased my sense of duty and responsibility.
> I get a strong sense of being able to make things better. This makes me feel useful.
> However by sticking to 'The Rule' I have taken responsibility for things that weren't my
> jobs.
> The disadvantages of applying 'The Rule' are that I have little or no time for myself or
> my friends. I am always short of time and under pressure.
> The consequences of the pressure are that I am rarely at my best. I don't play any more.
> At work I frequently come across to my colleagues as a 'Hard Ass'.
> When I find myself sticking to 'The Rule' now my options could be:
>
> 1. To question 'The Rule'.
> 2. Ask what the 'Play' option could be.
> 3. Ask what other options there could be.
> 4. Test whether 'The Rule' could be applied more flexibly.

Figure 11.1 *Flashcard for challenging assumptions*

happened had led him to blame himself for what seemed a natural depressive reaction. The therapist suggested that his self-criticism might actually be making the depression worse. He felt less depressed at the end of the session and continued to monitor and challenge negative automatic thoughts about depression, determining to blame himself less.

Sessions 13–15 Having challenged his belief that he must not be depressed, his depression lifted. The last sessions were spent working on the advantages and disadvantages of his perfectionistic assumptions, challenging their logic and usefulness and finding more flexible alternative beliefs. He created a flashcard for challenging these assumptions (Figure 11.1).

The BDI score had dropped from 27 to 2 over the 15 sessions. The Beck Anxiety Inventory score fell from 12 to 2. Intrusive images and the high physiological arousal he experienced when anxious disappeared completely, while his avoidance of situations and memories associated with the traumatic events also reduced considerably.

Follow-up Peter was able to return to work at the end of therapy, but was on special placement, rather than in the high-pressure setting of active police work. This temporary administrative post suited him well. He remained free from symptoms for over a year. As the possibility of a return to the beat approached he again became anxious and depressed, but there was no recurrence of any of the symptoms of PTSD. However, Peter feared that if he returned to his old job, he would be unable to resist falling into his old pattern of excessive responsibility and overwork. He knew that his new, more flexible set of rules was still fragile. He came back into therapy to work further on 'The Rule' and also decided to leave the police for a job where he was not at risk of becoming 'rulebound'.

Acknowledgement

I should like to thank my colleague Mrs Ruth Williams for her helpful advice in the preparation of an earlier version of this chapter.

References

Alloy, L.B. and Ahrens, A.H. (1987) 'Depression and pessimism for the future: biased use of statistically relevant information in predictions for self versus others', *Journal of Personality and Social Psychology*, 53: 366–78.

Bandura, A. (1977) *Social Learning Theory*. Englewood Cliffs, NJ: Prentice-Hall.

Beck, A.T. (1963) 'Thinking and depression: 1. Idiosyncratic content and cognitive distortions', *Archives of General Psychiatry*, 9: 324–33.

Beck, A.T. (1964) 'Thinking and depression: 2. Theory and therapy', *Archives of General Psychiatry*, 10: 561–71.

Beck, A.T. (1976) *Cognitive Therapy and the Emotional Disorders*. New York: International Universities Press.

Beck, A.T. (1987) 'Cognitive models of depression', *Journal of Cognitive Psychotherapy: An International Quarterly*, 1: 5–39.

Beck, A.T. (1989) *Love is Never Enough*. London: Penguin.

Beck, A.T. and Emery, G. with Greenberg, R.L. (1985) *Anxiety Disorders and Phobias: A Cognitive Perspective*. New York: Basic Books.

Beck, A.T. and Greenberg, R.L. (1974) *Coping with Depression*. New York: Institute for Rational Living.

Beck, A.T., Rush, A.J., Shaw, B.E. and Emery, G. (1979) *The Cognitive Therapy of Depression*. New York: Guilford Press.

Beck, A.T., Freeman, A. and Associates (1990) *Cognitive Therapy of Personality Disorders*. New York: Guilford Press.

Birchwood, M. and Tarrier, N. (1992) *Innovations in the Psychological Management of Schizophrenia*. Chichester: John Wiley.

Blackburn, I.M. (1984) *Coping with Depression*. London: Chambers.

Blackburn, I.M., Bishop, S., Glen, A.I.M., Whalley, L.J. and Christie, J.E. (1981) 'The efficacy of cognitive therapy in depression: a treatment trial using cognitive therapy and pharmacotherapy, each alone and in combination', *British Journal of Psychiatry*, 139: 181–9.

Bradley, G.W. (1978) 'Self-serving biases in the attribution process: a re-examination of the fact or fiction question', *Journal of Personality and Social Psychology*, 36: 56–71.

Brewin, C.R. (1988) *Cognitive Foundations of Clinical Psychology*. Hove and London: Lawrence Erlbaum Associates.

Burns, D.D. (1980) *Feeling Good*. New York: William Morrow & Co. Inc.

Butler, G., Fennell, M., Robson, P. and Gelder, M. (1991) 'Comparison of behaviour therapy and cognitive behaviour therapy in the treatment of generalised anxiety disorder', *Journal of Consulting and Clinical Psychology*, 59: 167–75.

Cautela, J.R. (1973) 'Covert processes and behaviour modification', *Journal of Nervous and Mental Diseases*, 157: 27–36.

Chadwick, P.D.J. and Lowe, C.F. (1991) 'Measurement and modification of delusional beliefs', *Journal of Consulting and Clinical Psychology*, 58: 225–32.

Clark, D.M. (1986) 'A cognitive approach to panic', *Behaviour Research and Therapy*, 24: 461–70.

Ellis, A. (1962) *Reason and Emotion in Psychotherapy*. Secaucus, NJ: Lyle Stuart.

Epstein, N. (1983) 'Cognitive therapy with couples', in A. Freeman (ed.), *Cognitive Therapy with Couples and Groups*. New York: Plenum Press.

Fairburn, C.G. (1985) 'Cognitive-behavioural treatment for bulimia', in D.M. Garner and

P.L. Garfinkel (eds), *Handbook of Psychotherapy for Anorexia Nervosa and Bulimia*. New York: Guilford Press.

Fennell, M.J.V. and Teasdale, J.D. (1987) 'Cognitive therapy for depression: individual differences and the process of change', *Cognitive Therapy and Research*, 11: 253–71.

Freeman, A. (1983) 'Cognitive therapy: an overview', in A. Freeman (ed.), *Cognitive Therapy with Couples and Groups*. New York: Plenum Press.

Freeman, A. (1987) 'Cognitive therapy: an overview', in A. Freeman and V. Greenwood (eds), *Cognitive Therapy: Application in Psychiatric and Medical Settings*. New York: Human Sciences Press.

Guidano, V.F. and Liotti, G. (1983) *Cognitive Processes and Emotional Disorders: A Structural Approach to Psychotherapy*. New York: Guilford.

Hooley, J.M., Orley, J. and Teasdale, J.D. (1986) 'Levels of expressed emotion and relapse in depressed patients', *British Journal of Psychiatry*, 148: 642–7.

Kanfer, F.H. and Karoly, P. (1972) 'Self-control: a behaviouristic excursion into the lion's den', *Behaviour Therapy*, 3: 378–416.

Kelly, G. (1955) *The Psychology of Personal Constructs*, Vols I and II. New York: Norton.

Kingdon, D.G. and Turkington, D. (1994) *Cognitive Behaviour Therapy of Schizophrenia*. Lawrence Erlbaum Associates.

Kovacs, M. and Beck, A.T. (1978) 'Maladaptive cognitive structures in depression', *American Journal of Psychiatry*, 135: 525–7.

Linehan, M.M. (1993) *Cognitive-behavioural Treatment of Borderline Personality Disorder*. London: The Guilford Press.

Liotti, G. (1986) 'Structural cognitive therapy', in W. Dryden and W. Golden (eds), *Cognitive Behavioural Approaches to Psychotherapy*. London: Harper & Row.

Mahoney, M.J. (1987) 'Psychotherapy and the cognitive sciences: an evolving alliance', *Journal of Cognitive Psychotherapy: An International Quarterly*, 1: 39–59.

Mahoney, M.J. and Arnkoff, D.B. (1978) 'Cognitive and self-control therapies', in S.L. Garfield and A.E. Bergin (eds), *Handbook of Psychotherapy and Behaviour Change*, 2nd edition. New York: Wiley.

Matthews, A. and MacLeod, C. (1985) 'Selective processing of threat cues in anxiety states', *Behaviour Research Therapy*, 23: 563–9.

Meichenbaum, D. (1985) *Stress Inoculation Training*. New York: Pergamon Press.

Moorey, S. (1988) 'Cognitive therapy with depressed outpatients factors associated with outcome', in W. Dryden and P. Trower (eds), *Cognitive Psychotherapy: Stasis and Change*. London: Cassell.

Moorey, S. (1996) 'Cognitive behaviour therapy for whom?', *Advances in Psychiatric Treatment*, 2: 17–23.

Moorey, S. and Burns, D.D. (1983) 'The apprenticeship model: training in cognitive therapy by participation', in A. Freeman (ed.), *Cognitive Therapy with Couples and Groups*. New York: Plenum Press.

Moorey, S. and Greer, S., (1989) *Psychological Therapy for Patients with Cancer: A New Approach*. Oxford: Heinemann Medical Books.

Murphy, G.E., Simons, A.D., Wetzel, R.D. and Lustman, P.J. (1984) 'Cognitive therapy and pharmacotherapy singly and together in the treatment of depression', *Archives of General Psychiatry*, 41: 33–41.

Rosenthal, T.L. and Bandura, A. (1978) 'Psychological modelling: theory and practice', in S.L. Garfield and A.E. Bergin (eds), *Handbook of Psychotherapy and Behaviour Change*, 2nd edition. New York: Wiley.

Rush, A.J. and Watkins, J.T. (1981) 'Group versus individual cognitive therapy: a pilot study', *Cognitive Therapy and Research*, 5: 95–103.

Rush, A.J., Beck, A.T., Kovacs, M. and Hollon, S. (1977) 'Comparative efficacy of cognitive therapy and imipramine in the treatment of depressed outpatients', *Cognitive Therapy and Research*, 1: 17–37.

Salkovskis, P.M. and Warwick, N.M.C. (1986) 'Morbid preoccupations, health anxiety and reassurance: a cognitive-behavioural approach to hypochondriasis', *Behaviour Research and Therapy*, 24: 597–602.

Shaw, B.F. (1984) 'Specification of the training and evaluation of cognitive therapists for outcome studies', in J. Williams and R.L. Spitzer (eds), *Psychotherapy Research: Where Are We and Where Should We Go?* New York: Guilford Press.

Simons, A.D., Murphy, G.E., Levine, J.L. and Wetzel, R.D. (1986) 'Cognitive therapy and pharmacotherapy for depression', *Archives of General Psychiatry*, 43: 43–8.

Taylor, S.E. and Brown, J.D. (1988) 'Illusion and well-being: a social psychological perspective on mental health', *Psychological Bulletin*, 103: 193–210.

Teasdale, J.D., Fennell, M.J.V., Hibbert, G.A. and Amies, P.L. (1984) 'Cognitive therapy for major depressive disorder in primary care', *British Journal of Psychiatry*, 144: 400–6.

Williams, J.M.G., Watts, F., Macleod, C. and Matthews, A. (1988) *Cognitive Psychology and Emotional Disorders*. Chichester: John Wiley.

Young, J.E. (1990) *Cognitive Therapy for Personality Disorders: a Schema-focused Approach*. Sarasota: Professional Resource Exchange.

Young, J.E. and Klosko, J.S. (1994) *Reinventing Your Life*. New York: Plume Books.

Suggested further reading

Beck, A.T. (1976) *Cognitive Therapy and the Emotional Disorders*. New York: International Universities Press.

Beck, J.D. (1995) *Cognitive Therapy: Basics and Beyond*. New York: Guilford Press.

Hawton, K., Salkovskis, P.M., Kirk, J. and Clarke, D.M. (eds) (1989) *Cognitive Behaviour Therapy for Psychiatric Problems*. Oxford: Oxford Medical Publications.

Scott, J., Williams, J.M.G. and Beck, A.T. (eds) (1989) *Cognitive Therapy in Clinical Practice*. London: Croom Helm.

Williams, J.M.G. (1992) *The Psychological Treatment of Depression: a Guide to the Theory and Practice of Cognitive Behaviour Therapy*, 2nd edition. London: Routledge.

Young, J.E. and Klosco, J.S. (1994) *Reinventing Your Life*. New York: Plume Books.

12

Behaviour Therapy
Geraldine O'Sullivan

Historical context and developments in Britain

Historical context

The term 'behaviour therapy' was coined by Skinner in the early 1950s and was reintroduced and made popular by Lazarus in 1958. Under the term is included a variety of techniques which bring about observable and measurable changes in human behaviour. The basic therapeutic principles have been in use for centuries, as shown by examples of its application in literature spanning the ages. Locke (1693) outlined the exposure principle which now forms the basis of a behavioural intervention for decreasing anxiety. He advised that 'if your child shrieks and runs away at the sight of a frog, let another catch it and lay it down at a good distance from him; at first accustom him to look upon it; when he can do that to come nearer to it and see it leap without emotion; then to touch it lightly, when it is held fast in another's hand; and so on, until he can come to handle it as confidently as a butterfly or sparrow' (Locke, 1693: 481–2). Even Freud (1919: 165–6) acknowledged the importance of exposure to the feared situation. He wrote: 'One can hardly master a phobia if one waits till the patient lets the analysis influence him to give it up . . . . One succeeds only when one can induce them by the influence of the analysis to go and to struggle with the anxiety while they make the attempts.' In the 1800s a captain in the Royal Navy controlled the behaviour of prisoners on an island in the Pacific by using the technique of contingency rewards (Pitts, 1976). In the early 1900s Janet (1925) observed that ritualizers who entered certain institutions (the Army or the Church) often improved with the discipline imposed by institutional practices. This is reminiscent of the technique of response prevention which is now used in combination with exposure in treating obsessive-compulsive disorder. The variety of early literature reports indicate that in many respects behaviour therapy is based on common sense but its routine application in clinical practice has only been developed and systematized within the last 25 years.

Originally, behaviour was viewed as being explicable in terms of the principles of learning theory. During the early 1900s learning theory was undergoing development. The concept of classical conditioning was formulated by Pavlov (1927), based on experiments with animals. In his famous experiment, Pavlov paired presentation of food with the sound of a bell. After a series of such presentations, eventually the bell alone elicited salivation. The essential feature of classical conditioning is that an unconditioned stimulus (food), which leads automatically to an unconditioned response (salivation), when presented repeatedly with a conditioned stimulus (bell), causes the conditioned stimulus to be sufficient in itself to produce a conditioned response (salivation). About that time operant conditioning was also undergoing development. Thorndike (1911) studied animals using a wooden box with a door which could be opened by pulling a loop. When a cat was placed within the box generally it made a number of ineffectual movements but eventually it accidentally pulled the loop and escaped. Gradually the animal decreased the length of time it took to pull the loop and escape. Instrumental or operant conditioning states that behaviour is largely determined by its consequences. Favourable consequences (escape) reinforce a particular piece of behaviour (pulling the loop) and if reinforcement is discontinued, then that piece of behaviour is likely to gradually cease (extinction).

A series of applications of these new learning models followed in human case experiments. Maladaptive behaviour was produced and abolished in humans (usually children) using learning principles. The most famous case was that of little Albert who was subjected to repeated presentations of a white rat paired with a loud noise (Watson and Rayner, 1920). After a number of such pairings the infant reacted with fear to the white rat. This fearful response generalized to other similar stimuli, e.g. a fur coat. On the basis of this experiment Watson and Rayner concluded that phobias are conditioned emotional responses. Watson's conviction of the power of learning theory to explain human behaviour was so great that he claimed that through conditioning he could make an infant into a thief, a lawyer or a doctor.

Wolpe (1958) proposed a hypothesis of neurosis in terms of Pavlovian learning principles. Within this theory, behaviour was viewed as being under direct stimulus control. Wolpe attempted to incorporate learning principles in the treatment of neurotic disorders. He advocated the pairing of relaxation, which is antagonistic to anxiety, with contact with the conditioned stimuli. The client was trained to relax and the relaxation was paired with imaginal contact with the feared object or situation, the assumption being that relaxation reciprocally inhibits the anxiety response, leading to a weakening of the association between the stimuli and anxiety. This technique was termed systematic desensitization and was used for many years in the treatment of phobic and obsessive-compulsive disorders.

Development in Britain

Wolpe spent some time at the Maudsley Hospital working with British psychologists such as Hans Eysenck and Jack Rachman, and psychiatrists such as Isaac Marks and Michael Gelder became interested in behaviour therapy. They played significant roles in the development and the systematic therapeutic application of behavioural techniques. Eysenck and Rachman (1965) wrote an influential book entitled *Causes and Cures of Neurosis*. Since that time the Maudsley has continued to play a significant role in the development and refinement of behaviour therapy. In 1971 the British Association for Behavioural Psychotherapy was formed by the Maudsley group to foster basic research and exchange of information and to promote behaviour therapy in Britain. Emergence of behaviour therapy as a major therapeutic approach occurred in the 1970s, with numerous techniques being developed, refined and experimentally validated.

Over the years modifications have arisen including incorporation of cognitive components in an attempt to improve outcome further. Cognitive therapies focus on modifying distorted thoughts and then using the new cognitive skills to aid exposure to feared situations. In addition, cognitive therapies focus on internal cues such as somatic manifestations of autonomic arousal and catastrophic thoughts. This represents a change from the external cues which behaviour therapy has traditionally dealt with. However, all cognitive approaches also include exposure to external cues.

Within Britain two schools have developed, one adhering primarily to the behavioural approach and not focusing directly on cognitions in therapy and the other cognitive-behavioural group focusing on cognitions first and then behaviour. Clearly, there is a lot of overlap between these approaches. A disadvantage of cognitive therapy is that it can be more time-consuming than behaviour therapy. In the latter, the role of the therapist is reduced to that of assessor, monitor and coach as the majority of patients carry out between-session homework. In addition, it has been shown that attitude change automatically arises as a result of change in behaviour (Watson et al., 1972) and cognitions do not need to be formally addressed in therapy. On the other hand, the cognitive-behavioural group argue that outcome is improved in the long term as a result of changing the way the individual responds on encountering stressful situations, so breaking the vicious circle in which symptoms cause worry and worry leads to more symptoms (Gelder, 1986). So far, there is no convincing evidence showing that the systematic incorporation of the cognitive approach reliably improves outcome. A study an agoraphobics found no additional benefit when cognitive restructuring was added to (exposure) behaviour therapy (De Ruiter et al., 1989). Similarly, in obsessive-compulsive disorder, no advantage was found in combining cognitive therapy with behaviour therapy (Emmelkamp and Beens, 1991).

Behaviour therapy has evolved into the study of the application of therapeutic interventions in clinical phenomena. Accompanying this empirical investigation has been a growth in behavioural literature. A substantial number of journals on the treatment of anxiety disorders has arisen both in the States and in Britain over the last two decades.

In Britain the clinical demand for treatment has led to the training of many other mental health professionals in behavioural psychotherapy. Today, behaviour therapy is a well-established treatment modality and is a safe, effective intervention in many disorders that were previously untreatable (Stern and Drummond, 1991). However, advances in treating anxiety disorders have not been accompanied by a corresponding understanding of the mechanisms of treatment.

Theoretical assumptions

Image of the person

An individual's behaviour is a reflection of his or her overall state of well-being. Human functioning can be enhanced by influencing behaviour. Self-control and mastery of the environment allow people to achieve their goals.

Learning theory According to the traditional behavioural model all human behaviour, both normal and abnormal, is determined by learning, i.e. classical and operant conditioning. Symptoms are viewed as discrete pieces of behaviour which have arisen through faulty learning. A distorted stimulus–response link leads to an inappropriate response to neutral stimulus, this response being maintained by its consequences. There are individual variations in conditionability, with some individuals showing greater arousal and autonomic fluctuation. However, just as normal behaviour can be modified, maladaptive behaviour can be altered by means of unlearning.

Objectivity This is a central theme of behaviourism. It focuses on overt behaviour and the environment rather than subjective experiences or the internal forces that are assumed to underlie the problem. It has emphasized the empirical approach and insists that alteration of human behaviour is quantifiable.

Cognitive theory Dissatisfaction with the stimulus–response explanations of behaviour led Lazarus (1971) to appeal for a more eclectic view of human behaviour in *Behavior Therapy and Beyond*. As traditional behaviour therapy neglected internal mediating concepts, the cognitive-based approach emphasizes the causal role of private thoughts, beliefs, irrational ideas and assumptions in the production and maintenance of abnormal behaviour. It stresses the importance of each individual's perception of external events rather than the direct influences of the environment itself. Modification of these abnormal assumptions and perceptions can aid alterations of problematic behaviour.

Conceptualization of psychological disturbance and health

Maladjusted vs. well-adjusted The pattern of behaviour which predominates in a society determines the norms. Behaviour that violates social norms is deemed pathological and is labelled 'deviant' and maladjusted. One's ability to behave competently, sometimes even in the face of adversity, influences one's general adjustment in many aspects of one's life. Many anxious individuals are maladjusted in important areas such as social, interpersonal work, sexual and leisure activities. Their abnormal behaviour precludes achievement of 'mastery' in these areas. In contrast the well-adjusted individual moves competently in these areas, which leads to more positive social reinforcements.

Fear of fear vs. stoicism Fear of anxiety, panic and even the somatic manifestations of these is a common theme amongst anxious individuals. Avoidance can rapidly ensue after just one panic. The somatic manifestations of anxiety (e.g. increased heart rate) are selectively attended to and sometimes normal activities which elicit these can also be avoided (e.g. exercise). All of us experience stress, anxiety and fear regularly, but despite this we continue to face the situations associated with these: i.e. there is an acceptance and ability to cope with stress and anxiety.

Passivity-avoidance vs. assertion   The individual who continuously retires in the face of discomfort will not recognize a relationship between his/her actions and environmental circumstances which are amenable to change. In contrast, the individual who manipulates the environment will elicit favourable responses leading to a high rate of positive reinforcement.

Learned helplessness vs. self-efficacy   An individual's behaviour is an index of his/her perception of self-competence and self-efficacy (Bandura, 1977). The healthy individual perceives her/himself as having the ability to cope with daily stress, and even with threatening situations. This is closely related to the individual perception of control over his or her life. In learned helplessness (Seligman, 1975) the individual perceives his/her responses as futile, leading to failure to initiate coping responses: i.e. there is a perceived lack of personal competence.

Psychological health   The behavioural model views psychological well-being in terms of control over one's environment and good adjustment in social, interpersonal, work, sexual and leisure activities. The healthy individual elicits a high rate of positive reinforcement from the environment and has the ability to evaluate events and situations appropriately based on a realistic appraisal of the evidence.

Acquisition of psychological disturbance

There is a tendency to make inferences about the aetiology of a disorder based on effective interventions, but this can lead to incorrect conclusions. A variety of different causes can lead to the same end result. It is now known that depression may be caused by a number of factors, including an inherited biological pre-disposition, endocrine abnormalities and adverse life events. Within an individual factors interact in complicated ways to produce illness. Similarly, behavioural disorders are not explicable as a result of one specific aetiological factor; it is likely that they are the end results of a series of complicated interactions involving many factors. Some factors implicated in causation and perpetuation will be considered. It should be noted that these interact in complicated ways within the individual sufferer.

First, our predisposition to experience fear/anxiety in specific ways and to react to these with predictable patterns of behaviour are partly determined by inherited biological factors. In evolutionary terms, defensive adaptations against threat were necessary to ensure survival and have been incorporated into our genetic make-up (Marks, 1987). Survival requires a search for hostile factors within the environment so that evasive action can be taken. Evolutionary factors may be invoked to explain the limited range of phobias that commonly arise in people. Because of evolutionary pressures, certain aspects of the environment may be attended to more readily and therefore are more likely to produce fear/anxiety responses.

In addition, specific responses may be associated with certain environmental cues. There are certain fears which can be considered as being innate, as they are observed prior to any sensitizing contact with these stimuli. Examples include heights (as shown by avoidance of a 'visual cliff' by young children: Gibson and Walk, 1960), loud noises, sudden movements (e.g. writhing movements of snakes) and the separation anxiety observed in children when contact with a familiar figure is threatened. Being in an unfamiliar environment automatically leads to increased vigilance. Agoraphobia (fear of public places) can be viewed as venturing beyond one's familiar home territory to a more threatening and hostile one, where greater vigilance is necessary. However, after continued contact with that unfamiliar environment the appraisal of it as threatening wanes. This is equivalent to the way *exposure therapy* improves phobias that are seen in clinical practice. Phobias and rituals commonly involve situations (snakes, spiders, open spaces, checking) that were potentially threatening or protective to pre-technological man (De Silva et al., 1976).

Genetic studies have shown that anxiety neuroses occur more frequently among relatives of sufferers. Family studies have found a prevalence of approximately 20 per cent among relatives, with females being at twice the risk compared with males (Cloninger et al., 1981). To date, adoption studies are lacking so the existing studies have failed to separate hereditary from environmental factors. Such studies are necessary to determine the extent of the contribution of vicarious factors i.e. children observing the behaviour of neurotic parents and using this as a model for their own future behaviour, as opposed to a genetic contribution.

Sociocultural factors are also important in the neuroses. In our society it is easier for women to show fear and be fearful. In Western countries the majority of agoraphobics are female (75 per cent) as opposed to India, where the reverse applies with a preponderance of male agoraphobics. It is possible that agoraphobia in Indian women may simply not be identified because their role is centred around the family home.

The feminist view is that in the traditional model, 'a woman's place is in the home' and in a patriarchal society with sex-role stereotyping promotes the display of fear and the development of phobias in women. On the other hand, typically men are supposed to be fearless, macho and traditionally the breadwinners. They are more likely to be coerced by social pressure to face up to and endure their anxiety, which is the basic component of exposure therapy. An interaction of genetic and social factors can be postulated leading to the likelihood of women showing neurotic disorder at a lower genetic loading than men because of sex-role stereotyping.

An organic-biological theory of anxiety has been advocated (Klein, 1987). It is claimed that panic is caused by a biological dysfunction, independent of psychological and situational factors, leading eventually to agoraphobia. Such a narrow, circumscribed hypothesis is insufficient to explain the origin of such a complex disorder. Moreover, proponents of this theory infer that because of the biological aetiology, only a physical method of treatment is indicated. Empirical evaluation of panic disorder/agoraphobia suggests that avoidance can sometimes precede panic (Lelliott et al., 1989). In addition, results of numerous controlled trials of exposure therapy and pharmacotherapy individually and in combination indicate that exposure therapy is superior to drugs and leads to more lasting improvement (Marks and O'Sullivan, 1988). There is no doubt that at some stage anxiety/panic is mediated at a biological level but so far the evidence suggests that this may be a manifestation of anxiety rather than a cause.

Most people develop fears and rituals at some time, but in the majority these do not develop into major handicaps. Phobias and rituals may be caused by failed extinction rather than by acquisition (Marks, 1982). This may be part of a generalized failure in coping. Goldstein and Chambless (1978) found that agoraphobics lacked assertiveness compared with other groups. Perhaps those who develop major disorders are the ones who tend to retreat in the face of discomfort and are less likely to face their fears. During exposure therapy they are taught to face their fears, leading to a general increase in self-mastery. Results of many follow-up studies in phobics and obsessive-compulsives demonstrate that there tends to be a generalization of gains from the main problem to other areas over the months and years after treatment.

In summary, the aetiology of anxiety disorders is a complex one embracing several factors interacting in different ways and modifying the expression of emotion within each individual sufferer. These include evolutionary, genetic, cognitive, sociocultural, past experience and vicarious factors.

Similar aetiological factors apply with regard to 'appetitive' disorders. All forms of behaviour can be viewed as being on a continuum, with abnormal behaviour at one end, differing quantitatively rather than qualitatively. This variation may be of constitutional and genetic origin, or may be acquired through faulty learning. Whatever the precise cause of 'deviations' from the norms, there is no doubt that sociological factors largely determine the criteria used to define 'deviance'. Behaviour that falls outside the normal pattern is considered 'deviant'. The sociological concept of deviance is related to laws, mores and behaviour (Bancroft, 1974). Most forms of deviance violate these factors.

In eating disorders, social factors have again been implicated in causation. Pressure on females to be thin in order to be considered attractive has led to the rigorous pursuit of thinness. Reports of anorexia nervosa are rare in the early literature, when being thin was regarded as the norm. Cases are unusual in developing countries where to be fat is regarded favourably as it symbolizes wealth.

Perpetuation of psychological disturbance

Once a fear of a particular object or situation has not been extinguished but has become established, the thought of approaching or coming into contact with the feared stimulus elicits intense anxiety: approaching the stimulus becomes very difficult and avoidance often ensues. The reduction in anxiety that results from the avoidance promotes further avoidance. A vicious cycle of fear and avoidance ensues, each perpetuating the other. Catastrophic thoughts about the situation or the associated physical consequences of anxiety are common. Examples include a fear of dying or doing something uncontrolled when anxious and panicky. Others focus on the physical components and may fear vomiting, shaking or blushing in public. In effect, fear of fear and a spiral of anticipatory anxiety occur and avoidance of fear-evoking situations perpetuates the problem. At the time of presentation for treatment, the mean duration of the problem is on average eight to ten years for most phobic and obsessive-compulsive patients. A central argument of operant conditioning is that unreinforced conditioned reactions extinguish fairly rapidly so learning theory fails to explain the perpetuation of neurosis. Mowrer wrote:

> Common sense holds that a normal, sensible man or even a beast will weigh and balance the consequences of his acts; if the net effect is favourable, the action producing it will be perpetuated, and if the net effect is unfavourable, the action producing it will be inhibited, abandoned. In neurosis, however, one sees actions which are predominantly unfavourable consequences, yet they persist over a period of months, years or a lifetime. (1950: 127)

Conditioning theory of neurosis does not explain the chronic course of such disorders. However, operant conditioning is useful in explaining the continuation of 'appetitive' behaviour. The positive reinforcement obtained from engaging in the behaviour leads to its perpetuation.

Certain aspects of the environment may promote perpetuation of the problem. Alcohol and minor tranquillizers may be used as a means of reducing anxiety, but once their effect begins to wear off, more need to be taken to reinstate the effect, leading to the risk of dependence. Indeed, many male phobics may be presenting at alcohol dependence units rather than seeking help for their phobias. Interpersonal factors may facilitate continuation of the problem. The phobic individual, in particular the agoraphobic, often has impaired ability to work and socialize and to carry out everyday tasks. Some may be so incapacitated that they become housebound, leading to dependence on others to fulfil their basic needs. It has been speculated that spouses of agoraphobics have chosen timid, dependent partners because this fulfils a need in themselves and they may resist changes in their partner, thereby perpetuating the problem. In turn, spouses have difficulty adjusting to and accepting a more independent, self-sufficient partner once the sufferer has been successfully treated. In general, this pattern does not overtly apply but occasionally a morbidly jealous spouse may welcome a housebound partner and may resist any attempts towards change.

In the eating disorders, characteristically subjects have cognitive distortions with regard to food, weight and body image. These distortions serve to maintain the problem. In the behavioural excesses the positive reinforcement obtained by engaging in the behaviour maintains it.

Change

Some individuals naturally overcome their phobias and fears in the early stages of their development because avoidance of the fear-eliciting object or situation may not be feasible. They are thus exposed to the phobic object/situation, leading to habituation. Social circumstances can sometimes alter so that approaching one's fears becomes inevitable. For those who engage in behavioural excess, the environmental contingencies associated with it can occasionally change so that the negative consequences of the behaviour increase and the rewards diminish, i.e. positive reinforcement decreases leading to a reduction in the behaviour. An example is the transvestite who marries and whose spouse threatens to leave if the behaviour persists.

It is likely that individuals lacking specific skills may acquire them through vicarious factors. Timid individuals may model the behaviour of those who are more assertive and thereby increase their own assertive skills. These examples of change are naturally occurring applications of the techniques used in behaviour therapy.

Practice

Goals of therapy

Behavioural psychotherapy consists of a range of therapeutic methods whose goal is to change behaviour directly. It focuses on the main problem without attempting to uncover unconscious processes. It is problem oriented, structured, directive, empirically based and short term. The problem may be a behavioural deficit (phobic avoidance, social skills deficit, erectile failure, etc.) or excess (compulsive rituals, sexual deviation, habit disorders, etc.) which lead to severe handicap. Initially the principal goal is to *alter behaviour* which restricts the client's day-to-day activities, thus improving the quality of life early; later in the treatment process, other areas can be focused on. The aim is *not* to abolish anxiety totally, as this is generally impossible, but to help individuals to put their anxiety in perspective so that incapacitation is reduced. Individuals are taught to face the situations that lead to anxiety and learn to deal with this.

Selection criteria

Certain criteria aid the identification of patients likely to benefit from behaviour therapy. First, the problem should be defined in terms of observable behaviour, for example the persistent avoidance of certain situations that trigger discomfort. The problem needs to be current and predictable i.e. there are consistently identifiable triggers. Anxiety is situational as opposed to free-floating or generalized. The patient, with the aid of the therapist, should be able to specify clearly definable behavioural goals. This is crucial to treatment. Nebulous statements like 'I want to live a normal life' are not adequately precise.

Patient and therapist must agree on specific goals. Patient cooperation is essential. The patient cannot be treated against his/her wishes and must be willing to invest a lot of time and effort to overcome the problem. The individual must set aside adequate time each day for several weeks to carry out homework tasks. In addition, patients often have to ensure considerable discomfort during the programme, so motivation to overcome the problem in order to achieve worthwhile change is essential. A family member who acts as a co-therapist is helpful in the treatment process in that he or she can readily provide encouragement to carry out tasks and praise for achievements made. This can be valuable in maintaining motivation and co-operation. Major physical or mental complications are contra-indications to behaviour therapy. Serious physical diseases such as cardiac, respiratory and gastrointestinal disorders make high levels of anxiety undesirable. In these conditions rapid exposure is not advisable and if behaviour therapy is to be carried out at all, it needs to be graded to avoid extreme anxiety. Major psychiatric disorders such as acute psychotic illnesses, severe depression and mania are contra-indications. Otherwise suitable patients who take quantities of alcohol to the point of being drunk or large doses of sedative drugs (e.g. benzodiazepines) daily are unlikely to benefit from exposure therapy. These substances produce state-dependent learning leading to loss of any treatment gains once the effect of alcohol or drugs wears off. Sometimes patients are willing to reduce alcohol or drugs and a withdrawal regime may have to be worked out with them. During the treatment the maximum permissible amount of alcohol is two units daily (or diazepam 10 milligrammes) daily (or the equivalent thereof). Antidepressants do not interfere with behaviour therapy and indeed can be indicated in those obsessive-compulsive and agoraphobic patients who intermittently develop depressive episodes.

Definite clinical indications for behaviour therapy include phobic, obsessive-compulsive and sexual disorders (including sexual dysfunctions and deviations), social skill deficits, habit disorders such as hair-pulling, stammering, certain childhood problems such as enuresis, school phobia and conduct disorders. Behavioural intervention has been shown to be beneficial and can be used as an adjunct to treatment in eating disorders (anorexia nervosa, bulimia, obesity), morbid grief, hypochondriasis, nightmares, psychosomatic disorders and mental subnormality. The majority of patients fulfilling these selection criteria respond well to exposure therapy provided they comply with treatment. A small percentage fail to habituate despite compliance. Attempts have been made to identify these but to date no reliable pre-treatment markers have been identified to pinpoint non-responders. After treatment has begun, those who fail to make gains within a few weeks of adequate exposure have a less favourable prognosis. In addition, those who tend to remain demoralized and depressed despite some improvement in main phobic or obsessive-compulsive handicap are more likely to do less in the long run (O'Sullivan and Marks, 1990). The whole area of non-responders to exposure therapy needs further examination.

As behaviour therapy is tailored for each individual patient, it is usually carried out on an individual basis. However, it can also be carried out in groups. There are no specific indicators for individual as opposed to group therapy. The approach is the same in both. Behavioural group therapy can be used for patients who have similar problems. In general, outcome is similar for both but behavioural group therapy is particularly helpful in patients with social skills deficits where they can use the group setting for role-play, modelling and furthermore can obtain feedback from the other group members. There is no evidence to suggest that those who fail to respond to individual behaviour therapy are likely to respond to group-based treatment.

Qualities of effective therapists

It is a misconception that special expertise is required to be a behaviour therapist; nor is profound background knowledge of learning theory required. Originally, behaviour therapy fell within the realm of psychologists and doctors, but now many nurses and other mental health professionals have been trained as behaviour therapists and are successfully treating a large number of sufferers. The important initial step is to acquire the skills necessary for the analysis of behavioural problems and this requires good interviewing skills and the ability to elicit detailed information about the patient's behaviour. These skills can be developed and improved by interviewing many patients, formulating their problems and discussing these with a skilled therapist. The behaviour therapist needs to acquire certain specific techniques and has to be able to adapt these to different clinical problems. The techniques can be learned easily under the supervision of a skilled therapist.

The degree of therapist input required varies from patient to patient. Some patients need basic assessment and instructions and are largely self-sufficient, while others require much therapist guidance and coaching including modelling, pacing and encouragement. It is important for therapists to be flexible and respond to individual patients' needs. In behavioural psychotherapy, it is the systematic application of intervention techniques which is viewed as being responsible for change. It is a doing and not just a talking process. It analyses discrete behaviours provided they can be specified in quantifiable terms, and empirically validated techniques are applied to these. Attention to detail is an important quality of effective therapists. Traditionally, less scientific approaches have been shunned and little attention has been paid to non-specific aspects of the treatment process including the patient–therapist relationship. More recently, the patient–therapist relationship is being viewed as an important component in the treatment process.

Therapeutic relationship and style

In behaviour therapy, the relationship between therapist and patient is not developed for specific therapeutic purposes as it is in some forms of psychotherapy. However, a good therapeutic relationship is advantageous for many reasons. Therapist and patient need to agree on the aims and goals of therapy. Targets have to be set and altered at regular intervals. A good therapeutic relationship may hinder patient dropout, especially during the early phases, when discomfort is often at its greatest. It may also aid patient co-operation and compliance and so improve the outcome. A good therapeutic relationship forms part of the important motivating factors which encourage the patient to carry out therapeutic tasks that can sometimes be difficult and uncomfortable. Although it has been shown that behaviour therapy can be carried out with written instructions and self-help manuals when it is applied to the more minor disorders of behaviour, the treatment of more serious disorders requires a therapist with the ability to strike up a good relationship with the patient.

As in any therapeutic interaction, a warm empathic therapist is desirable. In behaviour therapy, the therapist must also be active and directive, with a determination to obtain detailed descriptions of the actual behaviour in addition to setting targets and pacing the rate of treatment. The combination of warmth and the ability to be directive is often found in the most effective therapists.

Even though the therapeutic relationship tends to be formal, the patient often discloses personal details which they may not have discussed previously. Clearly in any therapeutic relationship there is a danger that dependency may develop. Behavioural therapy is no exception but generally the risks tend to be less than in other forms of psychotherapy. The reduced likelihood of dependency is likely to be related to the therapist encouraging the patient to be self-reliant from the start and the number of treatment sessions is also discussed early in the treatment process. Provided that dependency has not developed there should be few difficulties in terminating a course of behaviour therapy. Generally the last treatment sessions are spaced out and follow-up sessions are also given.

In summary, in behavioural psychotherapy the patient–therapist relationship is not viewed as central to the treatment process as ultimately it is the methodology which is essential. However, it is not a mechanistic treatment into which relationship factors do not enter; on the contrary, a good therapeutic relationship aids treatment and improves the outcome.

Major therapeutic strategies and techniques

Behavioural analysis   When a patient who fulfils the selection criteria presents for treatment the first step is the behavioural analysis. This allows the therapist to gain a detailed picture of the problem and to formulate therapeutic strategies that are individually tailored. This involves obtaining precise information about the nature, predictability and impact of the problem. First, the *nature* of the problem needs to be ascertained in detail. This has several components. The behavioural consequences of the occurrence of the fear need to be determined; does fear lead to avoidance, escape, reassurance, seeking, engaging in excesses (checking), etc.? The physical/autonomic manifestations of the fear should be enquired about; what happens physically in the feared situation?: palpitations, sweating, diarrhoea, trembling, etc. Some patients are very frightened by certain physical components. This is particularly true with regard to panics, which are sudden surges in level of anxiety accompanied by a variety of somatic symptoms. Some patients fear they may die during one of these panic attacks. Explanation that panic is a variant of anxiety and that people don't die during panics often brings immense relief. What precise feelings and thoughts are evoked by the fear – 'I will make a fool of myself', or 'Everybody is watching me', or 'I am going to lose control'. What were the antecedents of the episode? Was there anticipatory anxiety and were there catastrophic thoughts? It is important to determine the precise nature of all the situations that elicit fear, and each should be rated for the degree of distress aroused, allowing the formation of a hierarchy of the various fear-evoking situations. The aftermath is also important: is there immediate relief or discomfort for several hours? Information about the onset of the problem can sometimes be obtained by asking the patient to describe the first episode, since many can recall this accurately. Some report adverse life events or interpersonal problems preceding onset.

The course since onset can vary considerably with some patients describing some fluctuations in the course of the condition, including exacerbations and temporary remissions, while others report a gradual, continuous deterioration. Aggravation of symptoms is sometimes reported by female patients premenstrually. In these circumstances attempts to ameliorate pre-menstrual tension can be helpful. The presence of modifying factors should also be enquired about.

Some patients' distress is temporarily reduced by alcohol or the presence of a trusted companion. Some agoraphobics use a pushchair when venturing out of home, which acts as a 'safety signal'. Careful questioning along these lines provides information about the behavioural, psychological, cognitive and physical components of the problem, along with its onset and course. The next step in the behavioural analysis is to determine the current *predictability* of the problem. This incorporates the frequency, duration, severity and all the situational features of the episodes. Lastly, the *impact* of the problem on the individual's life is important. In what ways and to what degree is the individual's lifestyle impaired? Are work, social and leisure activities affected and if so, to what extent? What effect does it have on other family members? Careful collection of this information will give the therapist a comprehensive picture of the patient's avoidance profile and an appropriate treatment plan can be drawn up.

The precise behavioural strategy used to treat an individual patient depends on the presenting problem. Therapeutic approaches can be divided into three main categories. First, a reduction in *anxiety-linked behaviour* (phobias, rituals, ruminations, sexual dysfunction) may be the goal of therapy. The techniques used in this case will be different from those required to reduce *appetitive behaviour* (obesity, bulimia, sexual deviation) and from those which are useful in the *development of new behaviour* (social skills deficits). Each of these categories will be discussed.

The central component in achieving anxiety reduction for a fear-eliciting stimulus is *exposure* to that situation and endurance of the resultant discomfort until it diminishes. Most techniques used to overcome anxiety-linked behaviour contain the exposure ingredient. The principal techniques include exposure *in vivo* (real-life exposure) and occasionally imaginal exposure (fantasized exposure). Others include audiotape techniques, which is the repeated listening to a taped distressing ruminative thought. Response prevention is the obstruction of discrete neutralizing behaviours that diminish discomfort following exposure to the eliciting cue, e.g. preventing handwashing following contact with a door handle. The deliberate exaggeration of fears is occasionally used and this is termed paradoxical intention. It is sometimes claimed that relaxation therapy effectively improves situational anxiety, but this has not been shown in controlled studies. Relaxation techniques applied as coping tactics during exposure may be beneficial in some patients but the systematic use of reciprocal inhibition, i.e. alternating relaxation with exposure, does not yield optimal results and may retard the rate at which gains are made.

The exposure principle In clinical practice the majority of patients who present for treatment suffer from phobic or obsessive-compulsive disorders. Exposure therapy is now the most widely used behavioural intervention in both types of disorder. Exposure is better when carried out with *real* rather than fantasized fear cues. Real-life exposure leads to more discomfort in the course of treatment than imaginal but generally results in greater improvement and more rapid gains. The latter can be resorted to when exposure *in vivo* is difficult to arrange, as for example in flight phobias. In planning an exposure programme it should be remembered that long periods of exposure reduce fear more than shorter ones. Stern and Marks (1973) found that two hours of continuous exposure was more effective than four half-hour sessions. With continued exposure to the frightening situation panic commonly begins to reduce within 30 to 40 minutes of the start of exposure, even in phobias that have been present for many years. Occasionally, several hours may be needed before anxiety begins to fall. The crucial factor is to continue exposure until this happens. Exposure treatment can be *therapist aided*, in which case the therapist accompanies the patient into the phobic situation, or *self-exposure*, when the patient enters the phobic situations alone. The rate at which exposure is carried out can vary, but more rapid exposure yields faster clinical gains. Ultimately the pace is governed by what the sufferer is able to do. Rapid real-life exposure to the most feared stimulus in the fear hierarchy is termed *flooding*. In clinical practice a more graded approach is generally used, beginning with the less fearful cues and gradually working up the hierarchy. Exposure can vary from being an easy task in some cases to being complicated in others and the amount of therapist input necessary varies considerably from patient to patient. Some execute their own programme with the aid of self-help manuals and homework diaries while others require much therapist input, involving grading and alteration of tasks, attention to all fear cues, pacing and therapist-aided exposure.

Discomfort may be particularly high during the early stages of treatment and the urge to escape will be strong, but gradually as treatment progresses the level of anxiety will fall and eventually situations which were previously avoided can be approached without undue discomfort. In between therapist sessions homework exposure activities will be required, with the patient setting aside at least two hours daily for homework. All activities should be recorded in a homework diary. A self-help manual such as *Living with Fear* (Marks, 1978) which sets out guidelines for an exposure programme can be used by the patient. Each week targets are set, which are reviewed and altered as treatment progresses. Targets are specific pieces of behaviour which are currently absent from the individual's behavioural repertoire but would be of value to the individual and are frequently repeatable within the individual's daily lifestyle. An inherent part of behavioural treatment is the repeated measurement of levels of anxiety and avoidance. This will provide objective information about progress. Relatives can reduce therapist input by acting as co-therapists, accompanying the patient into phobic situation. They can also monitor the homework programme and provide praise for gains that are made.

Illness phobics, hypochondriacs and obsessive-compulsive patients seek reassurance repeatedly, usually from family members. It is counterproductive to reassure those who ritualistically seek reassurance. The illness phobic and hypochondriac will seek reassurance that they don't have a specific illness or are not ill. The provision of reassurance leads to a temporary reduction in anxiety, but anxiety quickly returns. Similarly, obsessional patients may seek reassurance that they have not harmed someone or become contaminated. The family members must be taught not to respond to requests for reassurance. The therapist may need to get them to rehearse an appropriate response to requests for reassurance such as 'Hospital instructions are that I don't answer that question.' Illness phobics and hypochondriacs may seek reassurance behaviourally from their general practitioners by requesting frequent physical examinations and blood tests. In these circumstances the primary care physician needs to be accurately informed about the treatment process and requested not to provide any further reassurance in the form of unnecessary investigations and examinations.

An aspect of obsessive-compulsive disorder which has proven resistant to behavioural interventions is the obsessional rumination. Techniques such as thought-stopping and prolonged exposure have not been very effective. More recently, case reports indicate that listening to an audiotape of the ruminative thoughts and the unfavourable consequences of this can be effective (Lovell et al., 1994).

An exposure approach is helpful in some cases of morbid grief. In guided mourning it is assumed that avoidance of feelings and situations associated with a deceased loved one maintains the morbid grief (Sireling et al., 1988). The subject is exposed to memories and situations, both in real life and in imagination, which are associated with the deceased.

Reduction in appetitive behaviour   To achieve control over appetitive behaviour any combination of techniques can be applied. Self-monitoring and self-regulation involve diary-keeping and the recording of both internal and external cues that induce the problematic behaviour. These aid the therapist and the patient to examine the problem and the circumstances in which it occurs. Substitution of a normal behaviour pattern is attempted by prescribing the normal behaviour at regular set intervals along with the use of stimulus-control measures. This approach is useful in obesity and bulimia. Confining eating to one room; eating food prepared and placed on a plate; limiting 'danger' foods; drawing up and adhering to a shopping list are examples of stimulus control measures. Alternative activities are also encouraged as these can substitute for the problematic behaviour and thereby reduce the likelihood of its occurrence. These behavioural techniques are frequently used in conjunction with a cognitive approach during which the individual's attitudes and thoughts about the problematic behaviour are explored (Schmidt and Treasure, 1994).

In sexual deviations aversion therapy was originally used. This is the pairing of a noxious stimulus such as an electric shock or an emetic with the overt or imagined deviant act. A series of such pairings leads to reduction and eventual extinction of the problem. But despite the efficacy of aversion therapy it remained unpopular because of its unpleasantness. Today 'covert sensitization', devised by Cautela (1966), is the technique applied most regularly in the sexual deviations. Instead of using physical aversions, unpleasant mental images (appropriately chosen for each individual) are employed and are paired with the deviant behaviour. This is practised regularly. The next stage is to increase arousal to an individually chosen normal scene by pairing arousal by masturbation with a normal fantasy.

Other techniques which can be employed to reduce appetitive behaviours include response cost (engaging in the activity carries a negative consequence, e.g. contributing a fixed sum of money to one's most hated organization); and satiation (the repeated practising of the behaviour for hours until the individual becomes fed up with it).

Development of new behaviour   Social skills training is a stepwise training in how to show appropriate emotional expression in social circumstances by the use of voice, eyes, posture, gesture and key phrases. It aims to teach new forms of social behaviour, beginning with the simplest. Active components are goal-setting, role-play, modelling rehearsal, problem-solving, feedback, graded real-life practice, homework, assignments and evaluation. It is often conducted in groups because of the opportunity they provide for modelling, peer feedback and real-life practice. It is usually considered important for all group members to have roughly similar levels of skills to avoid the danger of some being left behind. Social skills training groups are generally closed and time limited, usually comprising 6–10 members who meet weekly for approximately 10–12 sessions. Often training begins with simple behaviours, such as exchange greetings and maintaining eye contact, and gradually moves on to more complex situations such as conversing with strangers. Between sessions, individuals are asked to record performance and feelings.

In sexual skills training, education, improving communication, regular graded practice allowing adequate time and privacy for sex, and diary-keeping are used. Contingent reward may be particularly useful in children or mentally handicapped individuals, the basic principle being that positive consequences depend on the individual engaging in the appropriate activity. Response cost and time out may be helpful in reducing undesirable, discrete behaviours.

Depression   With the advent of behavioural/cognitive models of depression, psychological interventions using behavioural/cognitive strategies have been developed and used either independently or as adjuncts to physical methods of treatment. One view advocated by Lewinsohn (1974) was that depressives did not engage, or engaged less often, in positively reinforcing activities: i.e. he viewed depression along the stimulus–response paradigm. In treatment, the aim is to improve social skills and to reinstate reinforcing activities which have decreased. This involves identifying events that were enjoyed in the past and then setting goals of increased involvement in these activities. Seligman (1975) proposed that the depressed-prone individual has a lifelong history of failure in exercising control over reinforcers in the environment and is characterized by passivity, helplessness and inability to be assertive. In treatment various techniques such as self-control therapy, self-monitoring, self-evaluation, self-reinforcement, assertiveness training and pleasant event therapy (getting the patient to engage in pleasurable activities) can be used. While not formally addressing distorted cognitions, the behavioural approach utilizes some cognitive techniques, including self-observation, self-monitoring and self-control. In this respect there is a lot of overlap between the behavioural and cognitive approaches in the management of depression.

Beck's cognitive model not only emphasizes the depressed individual's feelings of helplessness and hopelessness but also focuses on cognitive distortions involving negative view of self, current circumstances and the future (Beck, 1963). In cognitive therapy, the aim is to identify these negative thoughts by getting the individual to keep a written record of moods and associated thoughts during everyday life. These negative thoughts are then answered by examining the evidence for and against each belief, so that the individual becomes aware of cognitive errors and thereby corrects them, leading ultimately to altered cognitions. As well as these verbal tests, 'behavioural tasks' are assigned between sessions to aid 'learning from experience'.

In summary, the majority of patients requiring behavioural treatment can be managed on an outpatient basis. A majority, approximately 5 per cent, require admission. Certain individuals may need admission to withdraw from alcohol or drugs, or because of distances involved. In these circumstances, a relative may also need to be admitted so that co-therapy can proceed following discharge.

The change process in therapy

To achieve habituation the individual must experience fear while attending to fear-relevant information. With continued contact with the fear-evoking stimulus a new 'non-fear structure' is formed, leading to emotional change. Patients who improve with treatment first show physiological responses which correspond with their self-reports of anxiety. These two responses both change with continued contact with the feared object or situation. After repeated exposures the original fear response decreases. Habituation of autonomic responses with continued exposure may aid attitudinal change in the individual regarding the persistence of anxiety. In this way, behaviour therapy leads to modification of attitude. Overall, three stages are observable in the modification of fear: the activation of anxiety, its diminution during sessions, and its waning across sessions. These stages correspond with treatment outcome (Foa and Kozak, 1985). The length of exposure required for habituation differs; the more intense the fear is, the longer the duration of exposure is required. Habituation occurs more quickly in simple phobics than in agoraphobics and obsessive-compulsives (Foa and Kozak, 1985). In appetitive disorders the individual's behaviour is controlled first in the therapeutic setting; with homework, this generalizes to the individual's natural environment. A reduction in the unwanted behaviour is usually accompanied by an increase in alternative, more appropriate behaviours: i.e. there is a change in the probability of performing a certain response. Observational learning may aid the acquisition of these new skills. The modelled behaviour is encoded imaginally, and the individual draws on this later to perform the appropriate response, which becomes incorporated as part of the normal behavioural repertoire within the natural environment.

In summary, in anxiety disorders change involves activation of fear and the formation of a new set of items of information to modify it; in behavioural deficits, new skills are observed and practised and then incorporated; in the behavioural excesses, appropriate behaviours replace inappropriate ones. In the long term, modification in general beliefs and attitudes occurs, leading to general changes in self-efficacy and improved coping abilities.

Limitations of the approach

Behavioural psychotherapy is beneficial for approximately 25 per cent of all neurotic patients and for 10 per cent of adult psychiatric patients as the main therapeutic intervention (Marks, 1982). One of the drawbacks of exposure is the discomfort the individual must endure to overcome the problem. Approximately

25 per cent of patients either refuse the offer of treatment or drop out soon after it has begun. Of those who comply with the treatment programme the majority make substantial gains but few lose all traces of anxiety. Many experience a sufficient amelioration in anxiety or rituals in the presence of provoking stimuli to allow them to lead a normal life. A minority of patients fail to respond despite compliance, and these need to be studied further in the future. These non-responders to exposure are generally also resistant to other interventions such as antidepressants. As noted earlier, behaviour therapy has focused on external cues, but with increasing attention to internal cues, the exposure principle is being successfully applied to other anxiety disorders which do not possess specific external triggering factors. This usually occurs in association with cognitive techniques.

Case example

The client

Mr B., a milkman, married with three children, presented complaining of uncontrollable shakes and a fear that he might swallow his tongue. These problems had begun six months previously and he had become increasingly incapacitated. He had passed out on a few occasions and had been referred to a neurologist, who ruled out epilepsy. Mr B. had not worked for two months at the time of presentation. Pre-morbidly, he had been an active man who loved sports and used to play squash and football several times a week.

Because of his fear of swallowing his tongue, which had generalized to a fear of swallowing fluids and food, he had developed a number of avoidances. These included avoidance of swallowing his spittle, and rolling his tongue around his mouth. He also ate and drank as little as possible and when he did eat or drink he did so as quickly as possible. He restricted his food intake to soups and pasta and avoided meats, etc. As a result he had lost two stones in weight. He had stopped playing squash and football. He was concerned that there was an underlying physical cause for his problem.

A number of rituals had arisen to reduce his fear, including holding his tongue between his teeth and sometimes with his hand, and repeatedly wiping his spittle away using his hand. He also recurrently sought reassurance from various family members that he was not going to swallow his tongue, e.g.: 'It is not possible to swallow your tongue, is it?' Mr B. was extremely anxious and was afraid he might stop breathing. As a result he was hyperventilating. In summary, the problem was that of an obsessional rumination that he was going to swallow his tongue, causing anxiety and hyperventilation. He had developed a number of avoidances and rituals in an attempt to reduce his fear.

The problem first began seven years earlier. It was not as severe at that point and Mr B. had been given diazepam for a few months. The fear had gradually disappeared, but it recurred following a party six months prior to presentation. In his past history he reported that he disliked school and had symptoms of school phobia after he changed schools in his early teens. He was very close to his children and recently there had been marital discord because of his anxiety.

The therapy

When the patient was assessed, he was agitated, restless and was repeatedly wiping spittle from his mouth. He was also concerned about his physical health and was experiencing a number of unpleasant bodily sensations including light-headedness, tingling and numbness in his arms, as well as the sensation that he was unable to breathe. He believed that these unpleasant bodily symptoms resulted from a physical illness, which in turn made him feel more anxious. During the assessment, Mr B. sighed several times and at other times appeared to be gasping for breath. To ascertain whether these were related to hyperventilation he was asked to stand upright and to breathe as quickly and deeply as possible for three minutes. He was instructed to raise his right index finger when he experienced bodily sensations similar to his recurrent physical problems. After 1.5 minutes he raised his finger and indicated that he was feeling light-headed and after a further half-minute he began to experience tingling in his arms. The role of hyperventilation in producing unpleasant bodily sensations was explained. We discussed the unpleasant effects that resulted and how similar these were to his usual physical symptoms. This was followed by breathing retraining.

The patient was asked to sit comfortably in his chair and place a hand on his stomach. He was instructed that when he inhaled, his abdomen should move rather than his chest. He was asked to breathe out slowly, pause and then inhale deeply and count one, two, three, before exhaling slowly. He was instructed to do this 10 to 15 times each minute and to practise this twice each day for periods of up to 10 minutes. The exposure rationale was explained to him and the import- ance of not engaging in neutralizing ritualistic activities was stressed. He was advised to read a self-help book (Marks, 1978). He was willing to undergo treat- ment and seemed very motivated. His wife would act as co-therapist, if necessary. At the outset the following goals were set: swallow all his spittle and roll his tongue around his mouth; drink adequate quantities of fluids slowly and eat all types of food including meat and fruit; resume his previous sports, such as football and squash.

He was seen one week later, after he had read the self-help book. His anxiety had already decreased as he had realized that his physical symptoms were related to anxiety and hyperventilation and did not signify an underlying physical illness. We agreed that he would need about eight sessions. He was asked to bring his wife to the next session. The exposure rationale was again stressed, which in his case involved letting the thought that he might swallow his tongue come and not fighting it.

During session 2, Mr B. was asked to swallow his spittle and not to remove it from the side of his mouth with his hand. This caused a lot of discomfort initially, but his anxiety fell during the session. As his homework he was asked to continue with this. For the remainder of the session we concentrated on his fluid and food intake as this area was deemed to be most pressing in view of his weight loss. He had prepared a list of a range of food items and rated the anxiety associated with eating each type of food. Meats, fruits and hard chewy sweets caused the highest anxiety, followed by bread and cheese. He was given homework of drinking fluids *slowly* and not gulping them: he was requested to drink fluids slowly over 30 minutes and to do this four times daily. Further homework involved eating foods such as yoghurts and puddings which he was avoiding; he felt he could begin eating these. His wife was asked to stop providing reassurance that he would not swallow his tongue. She was advised to give a set reply: 'Instructions from the doctor are that I don't answer that question.' She agreed to ensure that other members of the family responded similarly.

By session 3, Mr B. was swallowing spittle without difficulty. Taking fluids had become easier and he was also eating more. He had gained 3 kilograms in weight. Homework for the third, fourth and fifth weeks concentrated on his food intake. He was instructed to eat an increasing range of foods *slowly* over 30 minutes and asked to stop mashing all his food. In addition, rituals such as holding his tongue between his teeth were banned and he was told to increase his anxiety by rolling his tongue around his mouth for as long as possible. The original rumination that he might swallow his tongue caused only mild anxiety by week 5.

Graded exposure to exercise was started. The homework initially involved brisk walks and by session 6 it included light training and playing squash. By session 8, the original goals had been achieved. Mr B. was eating and drinking normally, swallowing his spittle and had resumed sporting activities. He felt ready to return to work and a follow-up review was arranged.

Four weeks later, he telephoned requesting an early appointment. When seen, he reported that he felt more anxious again and that the ruminations were more troublesome. On further questioning it emerged that his ruminations had recurred during a two-week period when his mood felt low. During that phase he had many symptoms of a mild depressive illness, including poor energy and loss of interest and the feeling that everything seemed an effort. This phase of depressed mood had spontaneously lifted but afterwards he felt more anxious and was again ruminating. A fear of swallowing his spittle had recurred but despite this he had continued to resist the impulse not to swallow. He was reminded that setbacks can occur especially in the context of depression and it was re-emphasized that the important factor was to let the ruminations come, face his fear and not engage in anxiety-reducing behaviours. He was seen two weeks later, by which time he had improved again. Improvement was maintained at three- and six-month follow-ups.

References

Bancroft, J. (1974) *Deviant Sexual Behaviour: Modification and Assessment*. Oxford: Clarendon Press.

Bandura, A. (1977) 'Self-efficacy toward a unifying theory of behavioural change', *Psychological Review*, 84: 191–215.

Beck, A.T. (1963) 'Thinking and depression', *Archives of General Psychiatry*, 9: 324–33.

Cautela, J.R. (1966) 'Treatment of compulsive behavior by covert sensitization', *Psychological Research*, 16: 33–41.

Cloninger, C.R., Martin, R.L., Clayton, P. and Gaze, S.B. (1981) 'Follow up and family study of anxiety neurosis', in D.F. Klein and J. Rabkin (eds), *Anxiety: New Research and Changing Concepts*. New York: Raven. pp. 137–50.

De Ruiter, C., Ritken, H., Garssen, B. and Kraaimaat, F. (1989) 'Breathing retraining, exposure and a combination of both in the treatment of panic disorder with agoraphobia', *Behaviour Research & Therapy*, 27: 637–56.

De Silva, P., Rachman, S. and Seligman M. (1976) 'Prepared phobias and obsessions', *Behaviour Research & Therapy*, 15: 65–77.

Emmelkamp, P.M.G. and Beens, H. (1991) 'Cognitive therapy with obsessive-compulsive disorders: a comparative evaluation', *Behaviour Research & Therapy*, 29: 293–300.

Eysenck, H.J. and Rachman, S. (1965) *Causes and Cures of Neurosis*. London: Routledge & Kegan Paul.

Foa, E.B. and Kozak, M.J. (1985) 'Treatment of anxiety disorders: implications for psychopathology', in A.H. Tuma and J.D. Maser (eds), *Anxiety and the Anxiety Disorders*. Hillsdale, NJ: Lawrence Erlbaum Associates.

Freud, S. (1919) 'Turning in the ways of psychoanalytic therapy', in *Collected Papers*, Vol. II. London: Hogarth Press/Institute of Psycho-Analysis.

Gelder, M.G. (1986) 'Psychological treatment for anxiety disorders: a review', *Journal of the Royal Society of Medicine*, 79: 230–3.

Gibson, E.J. and Walk, R.D. (1960) 'The "visual cliff"', *Scientific American*, 202: 64–71.

Goldstein, A.J. and Chambless, D.L. (1978) 'A reanalysis of agoraphobia', *Behavior Therapy*, 9: 47–59.

Janet, P. (1925) *Psychological Healing*. New York: Macmillan.

Klein, D.F. (1987) 'Anxiety reconceptualized. Gleaning from pharmacological dissection early experience with imipramine and anxiety', in D.F. Klein (ed.), *Anxiety*. Basle: Kerger.

Lazarus, A.A. (1971) *Behavior Therapy and Beyond*. New York: McGraw-Hill.

Lelliott, P., Marks, I.M., McNamee, G. and Toberna, A. (1989) 'Onset of panic disorder with agoraphobia', *Archives of General Psychiatry*, 46: 1000–5.

Lewinsohn, P.M. (1974) 'A behavioural approach to depression', in R.M. Friedman and M.M. Katz (eds), *Psychology of Depression: Contemporary Theory and Research*. New York: Wiley.

Locke, J. (1693) *Some Thoughts concerning Education*. London: Ward Lock.

Lovell, K., Marks, I.M., Nashivani, H. and O'Sullivan, G. (1994) 'Should treatment distinguish anxiogenic from anxiolytic obsessive-compulsive ruminations? Results of a pilot controlled study and of a clinical audit', *Psychotherapy and Psychosomatics*, 61: 150–5.

Marks, I.M. (1978) *Living with Fear*. New York: McGraw-Hill.

Marks, I.M. (1982) *Cure and Care of Neuroses: Theory and Practice of Behavioural Psychotherapy*. New York: Wiley.

Marks, I.M. (1987) *Fear, Phobias and Rituals*. New York: Oxford University Press.

Marks, I.M. and O'Sullivan, G. (1988) 'Drugs and psychological treatments for agoraphobia/panic and obsessive-compulsive disorders: a review', *British Journal of Psychiatry*, 15: 650–8.

Mowrer, O.H. (1950) *Learning Theory and Personality Dynamics*. New York: Arnold.

O'Sullivan, G. and Marks, I. (1990) 'Long-term outcome of phobic and obsessive-compulsive disorders after treatment', in R. Noyes, M. Roth and G.D. Burrows (eds), *Handbook of Anxiety Disorders*, Vol. IV. Amsterdam: Elsevier.

Pavlov, I.P. (1927) *Conditional Reflexes*. London: Oxford University Press.

Pitts, C.E. (1976) 'Behaviour modifications', *Journal of Applied Behavior Analysis*, 9: 146.

Schmidt, U. and Treasure, J. (1994) *Getting Better Bit(e) by Bit(e). A Survival Kit for Sufferers of Bulimia Nervosa and Binge Eating Disorders*. Hove: Lawrence Erlbaum Associates.

Seligman, M.E.P. (1975) *Helplessness*. San Francisco: Freeman.

Sireling, S., Cohen, D. and Marks, I. (1988) 'Guided mourning for morbid grief', *Behavior Therapy*, 19: 121–32.

Stern, R.S. and Drummond, L.M. (1991) *The Practice of Behavioural and Cognitive Psychotherapy*. Cambridge: Cambridge University Press.

Stern, R.S. and Marks, I.M. (1973) 'Brief and prolonged flooding: a comparison in agoraphobic patients', *Archives of General Psychiatry*, 28: 270–6.

Thorndike, E.L. (1911) *Animal Intelligence*. New York: Macmillan.

Watson, J.B. and Rayner, R. (1920) 'Conditioned emotional reactions', *Journal of Experimental Psychology*, 3: 1–14.

Watson, J.P., Gaind, R. and Marks, I.M. (1972) 'Physiological habituation to continuous phobic stimulation', *Behaviour Research & Therapy*, 10: 269–78.

Wolpe, J. (1958) *Psychotherapy by Reciprocal Inhibition*. Stanford, CA: Stanford University Press.

Suggested further reading

France, R. and Robson, M. (1986) *Behaviour Therapy in Primary Care*. London: Chapman and Hall.

Kazdin, A.E. (1978) *History of Behavior Modification, Experimental Foundations of Contemporary Research*. Baltimore, MD: University Park Press.

Marks, I.M. (1982) *Cure and Care of Neuroses, Theory and Practice of Behavioural-Psychotherapy*. New York: Wiley.

Rehm, L.P. (1981) *Behavior Therapy for Depression*. New York: Academic Press.

Stern, R.S. and Drummond, L.M. (1991) *The Practice of Behavioural and Cognitive Psychotherapy*. Cambridge: Cambridge University Press.

13

Rational Emotive Behaviour Therapy

Windy Dryden

Historical context and development in Britain

Historical context

Rational emotive behaviour therapy (REBT) was established in 1955 by Albert Ellis, a clinical psychologist in New York, who originally called the approach rational therapy (RT). Ellis received his original training in psychotherapy in the 1940s in the field of marriage, family and sex counselling. In the course of his practice he realized that this kind of counselling was limited because 'disturbed marriages (or premarital relationships) were a product of disturbed spouses; and that if people were truly to be helped to live happily with each other they would first have to be shown how they could live peacefully with themselves' (Ellis, 1962: 3). He thus embarked on a course of intensive psychoanalytic training and received his training analysis from a training analyst of the Karen Horney group whose technique was primarily Freudian. In 1949 Ellis began to practise orthodox psychoanalysis with his patients, but was disappointed with the results he obtained. His patients appeared to improve, claimed to feel better, but Ellis could see that their improvement was not necessarily sustained. He then began to experiment with various forms of face-to-face, psychoanalytically oriented psychotherapy. Although he claimed that these methods brought better results and within a shorter period of time than orthodox psychoanalysis, he was still dissatisfied with the outcome of the treatment. In 1953 he began to research a monograph and a long article on new techniques in psychotherapy (Ellis, 1955a, 1955b) which influenced him to practise a unique brand of psychoanalytic-eclectic therapy; still, Ellis remained dissatisfied.

Throughout his career as a psychoanalytically inspired therapist from the late 1940s and 1955, Ellis had become increasingly disenchanted with psychoanalytic theory, claiming that it tended to be unscientific, devout and dogmatic. He had always maintained his early interest in philosophy and enjoyed thinking about how this field could be applied to the realm of psychotherapy. He used his knowledge of philosophy to help him answer his most puzzling question: 'Why do highly intelligent human beings, including those with considerable psychological insight, desperately hold on to their irrational ideas about themselves and others?' (Ellis, 1962: 14). The writings of Greek and Roman Stoic philosophers (especially Epictetus and Marcus Aurelius) were particularly influential in this respect. These philosophers stressed that people are disturbed not by things but by their view of things. Ellis began to realize that he had made the error of stressing a psychodynamic causation of psychological problems (namely that we are disturbed as a result of what happens to us in our early childhood); instead, he started to emphasize the philosophic causation of psychological problems (namely that we remain disturbed because we actively and in the present reindoctrinate ourselves with our disturbance-creating philosophies).

From this point he began to stress the importance that thoughts and philosophies (cognition) have in creating and maintaining psychological disturbance. In his early presentations and writings on what has become known as rational emotive behaviour therapy, Ellis (1958) tended to overemphasize the role that cognitive factors play in human disturbance and consequently de-emphasized the place of emotive and behavioural factors. This was reflected in the original name that he gave to his approach: rational psychotherapy. In 1962 Ellis published his pioneering volume, *Reason and Emotion in Psychotherapy*. In this he stressed two important points: that cognitions, emotions and behaviours are interactive and often overlapping processes; and that 'human thinking and emotions are, in some of their essences, the same thing, and that by changing the former one does change the latter' (Ellis, 1962: 122). He concluded that the label rational-emotive therapy (RET) more accurately described his therapeutic approach. In 1993, Ellis decided to change the name of the therapy once more to rational emotive behaviour therapy (REBT). This was in response to critics who claimed that RET neglected behaviour and was purely cognitive and emotive in nature.

As noted above, the theory of rational emotive behaviour therapy has from its inception stressed the importance of the interaction of cognitive, emotive and behavioural factors both in human functioning and dysfunctioning and in the practice of psychotherapy. Ellis has acknowledged, in particular, his debts to theorists and practitioners who have advocated the role of action in helping clients to overcome their problems (Herzberg, 1945; Salter, 1949; Wolpe, 1958). Indeed, Ellis employed a number of *in vivo* behavioural methods to overcome his own fears of speaking in public and approaching women (Ellis, 1973).

Initially, rational emotive behaviour therapy received unfavourable and even hostile responses from the field of American psychotherapy. Despite this, Ellis persisted in his efforts to make his ideas more widely known; and as a result REBT is now flourishing. Its popularity in the United States increased markedly in the 1970s, when behaviour therapists became interested in cognitive factors, and the present impact of cognitive-behaviour therapy has helped REBT to become more widely known there. Currently, REBT is practised by literally thousands of mental health professionals in North America. It is taught and practised in Holland, Germany, Italy, France, India, Pakistan, Australia, Israel and other parts of the world, including, of course, Britain.

Development in Britain

Until the early 1990s, training in REBT was available on an *ad hoc* basis from myself or Dr Al Raitt. Since training opportunities in REBT were limited, there were few therapists properly trained in REBT. Then, under the auspices of the Centre for Stress Management in Blackheath, London, I began a programme of certificate, diploma and advanced diploma courses in REBT. These courses, which are now run under the auspices of the Centre for Rational Emotive Behaviour Therapy, attracted and continue to attract people from a range of helping professions, and the number of REBT therapists has increased to the extent that an Association of Rational Emotive Behaviour Therapists was formed in 1993. The association, which publishes twice a year a journal entitled the *Rational Emotive Behaviour Therapist*, is at present seeking to join the Behavioural and Cognitive Section of the United Kingdom Council for Psychotherapy (UKCP). If successful, this application will lead to REBT therapists being listed as such on the UKCP's voluntary register.

A recent development is the establishment (in September 1995) of an MSc in Rational Emotive Behaviour Therapy at Goldsmiths' College, University of London under my directorship. This course is the first Master's course in REBT in Europe and the second in the world (the first being in Mexico). These developments are being underpinned by empirical research carried out on various REBT hypotheses by myself and Frank Bond at the University of London and by Duncan Cramer at the University of Loughborough.

Theoretical assumptions

Image of the person

Rational emotive behaviour therapy holds that humans are essentially hedonistic (Ellis, 1976): their major goals are to stay alive and to pursue happiness efficiently, that is, in a non-compulsive but self-interested manner enlightened by the fact that they live in a social world. It is stressed that people differ enormously in terms of what will bring them happiness, so rational emotive behaviour therapists show clients not what will lead to their happiness but how they prevent themselves from pursuing it and how they can overcome these obstacles. Other basic concepts implicit in REBT's image of the person include those listed below.

Rationality In REBT, 'rational' means primarily that which helps people to achieve their basic goals and purposes; 'irrational' means primarily that which prevents them from achieving these goals and purposes. However, 'rational' also means that which is flexible, logical and consistent with reality, whereas 'irrational' also means that which is rigid, illogical and inconsistent with reality.

Human fallibility Humans are deemed to be by nature fallible and not perfectible. They naturally make errors and defeat themselves in the pursuit of their basic goals and purposes.

Human complexity and fluidity Humans are seen as enormously complex organisms constantly in flux, and are encouraged to view themselves as such.

Biological emphasis Ellis (1976) argues that humans have two basic biological tendencies. First, they have a tendency towards irrationality; they naturally tend to make themselves disturbed. Ellis (1976) makes a number of points in support of his 'biological hypothesis'. These include the following:

(a) Virtually all humans show evidence of major human irrationalities.
(b) Many human irrationalities actually go counter to the teachings of parents,

peers and the mass media (for example, people are rarely taught that it is good to procrastinate, yet countless do so).

(c) Humans often adopt other irrationalities after giving up former ones.

(d) Humans often go back to irrational activity even though they may have worked hard to overcome it. (Ellis, 1976)

Second, and more optimistically, humans are considered to have great potential to work to change their biologically-based irrationalities.

Human activity Humans can best achieve their basic goals by pursuing them actively. They are less likely to be successful if they are passive or half-hearted in their endeavours.

Cognitive emphasis Although emotions overlap with other psychological processes such as cognitions, sensations and behaviours, cognitions are given special emphasis in REBT theory. The most efficient way of effecting lasting emotional and behaviour change is for humans to change their philosophies. Two types of cognition are distinguished in Ellis's (1962) ABC model of the emotional/behavioural episode. The first type refers to the person's inferences about events and includes such cognitive activities as making forecasts, guessing the intentions of others and assessing the implications of one's behaviour for self and others. Inferences are hunches about reality and need to be tested out. As such they may be accurate or inaccurate. They are placed under 'A' of the ABCs of REBT[1] since they do not fully account for the person's emotions and/or behaviours at C. The second type of cognition – beliefs – is evaluative in nature and indicates the personal significance of the event for the person concerned; such cognitions, which are placed under 'B' of the ABCs of REBT, do account for the person's emotions and/or behaviours at C.

Constructivistic focus (Ellis, 1994) has recently argued that REBT is best seen as one of the constructivistic cognitive therapies. In REBT, the constructivistic focus is seen in the emphasis that REBT places on the active role that humans play in constructing their irrational beliefs and the distorted inferences which they frequently bring to emotional episodes.

Concepts of psychological disturbance and health

Rational and irrational beliefs Ellis (1962) has distinguished between two types of evaluations of personal significance: rational and irrational beliefs. Rational beliefs are evaluations of personal significance which are non-absolute in nature, logical, consistent with reality and self- and other- enhancing. They indicate desires, preferences and wishes. Feelings of pleasure result when humans get what they desire, whereas feelings of displeasure (sadness, annoyance and concern) result when they fail to get what they want. Such negative emotions are deemed to be healthy responses to negative events since they do not significantly interfere with the pursuit of established or new goals.

Irrational beliefs are evaluations of personal significance stated in absolute terms such as 'must', 'should', 'ought' and 'have to'. They are rigid, illogical, inconsistent with reality and self- and other- defeating. It is noted that people often change their desires into demands: negative emotions such as depression, anger, anxiety and guilt occur when people make demands on themselves, on other people and/or the world. Ellis (1994) regards these negative emotions as unhealthy responses to negative events since they generally impede the pursuit of established or new goals. Ellis (1982) claims that rational beliefs underlie functional behaviours, whereas irrational beliefs underpin dysfunctional behaviours such as withdrawal, procrastination, alcoholism, substance abuse and so on.

The process of making absolute demands on reality is called 'musturbation'. It is linked to a process called 'awfulizing'. 'Awfulizing' is the process of making grossly exaggerated negative conclusions when one does not get what one 'must' or when one gets what one 'must not'. Ellis considers awful to mean 'more than 100% bad' and to stem from the demand 'It should not be as bad as it is.'

Self-damnation vs. self-acceptance Self-damnation occurs when I either fail to do what I must, or do what I must not. It involves: (a) the process of giving my 'self' a global negative rating; and (b) 'devil-ifying' myself as being bad or less worthy. This second process rests on a theological concept, and implies either that I am undeserving of pleasure on earth or that I should rot in hell as a subhuman (devil). The REBT alternative to global negative self-rating and self-damnation is unconditional self-acceptance: unconditional acceptance of oneself as a fallible human being who is constantly in flux and too complex to be given a single legitimate rating. REBT theory advocates that it is legitimate, and often helpful, to rate one's traits, behaviours, etc., but that it is not legitimate to rate one's self at all, even in a global positive manner, since positive self-rating tends to be conditional on doing good things, being loved and approved, and so on.

Discomfort disturbance vs. discomfort tolerance According to REBT there are two types of fundamental human disturbance. These are ego disturbance (as outlined in the previous section) where demands are made on one's self; and discomfort disturbance, which stems from the irrational belief: 'I must feel comfortable and have comfortable life conditions.' Conclusions that stem from this premiss are (a) 'It's awful' and (b) 'I can't stand it when these life conditions do not exist.' Discomfort disturbance occurs in different forms and is central to a full understanding of a number of emotional and behavioural disturbances such as anger, agoraphobia, depression, procrastination and alcoholism. Demands made on other people either involve ego disturbance (for example 'You must approve of me or I'll be less worthy') or discomfort disturbance ('You must approve of me and give me what I must have'), and thus do not represent a fundamental human disturbance.

Discomfort disturbance usually impedes people from working persistently hard to effect productive psychological change. The ability to tolerate discomfort and frustration, not for its own sake but in order to facilitate constructive psychological change, is a primary criterion of psychological health in REBT theory. It forms the basis of a philosophy of long-range hedonism: the pursuit of meaningful long-term goals while tolerating the deprivation of attractive short-term goals which are self-defeating in the longer term.

Psychological health Ellis (1983a) shows how 'musturbation' is involved in dogmatism, devout belief (religious and secular) and religiosity, since these are all based on absolute demands on reality. He equates much emotional disturbance with these processes, advocating a scepticism which is based on a non-absolute view of reality as the emotionally healthy alternative. Non-absolutism is at the core of the REBT view of psychological health, as can be seen in the following list of criteria of positive mental health outlined by Ellis (1979b): self-interest; social interest; self-direction; tolerance; acceptance of ambiguity and uncertainty; flexibility; and scientific thinking (employing the rules of logic and scientific analysis in solving emotional and behavioural problems). In this respect, psychologically healthy people are not cold and detached, as those with a scientific approach to life are commonly but erroneously assumed to be; indeed, they experience the full range of healthy emotions, positive and negative. Other criteria of psychological health emphasized in REBT include commitment, calculated risk-taking, self-acceptance and acceptance of reality.

Acquisition of psychological disturbance

Rational emotive behaviour therapy does not posit an elaborate theory concerning how psychological disturbance is acquired. This follows logically from Ellis's (1976, 1979b) hypothesis that humans have a strong biological tendency to think and act irrationally. While Ellis is clear that humans' tendency to make absolute commands and demands on themselves, others and the world is biologically rooted, he does acknowledge that environmental factors contribute to emotional disturbance and thus encourage humans to make their biologically-based demands (Ellis, 1979a). He argues that because humans are particularly open to influence as young children they tend to let themselves be over-influenced by societal teachings such as those offered by parents, peers, teachers and the mass media (Ellis, 1979b). One major reason why environmental control continues to wield a powerful influence over most people most of the time is because they tend not to be critical of the socialization messages they receive. Individual differences play a part here also. Humans vary in their suggestibility: while some humans emerge relatively unscathed emotionally from harsh and severe childhood regimes, others emerge emotionally damaged from more benign regimes (Werner and Smith, 1982). Ellis strongly believes that we, as humans, are not disturbed simply by our experiences; rather, we bring our ability to disturb ourselves to our experiences.

In doing this we can be said to play a large role in constructing our disturbances (as noted on p. 307). We construct our demands out of our strong preferences and from these demands we construct our overly distorted negative inferences about reality. Having constructed such inferences we then focus on them and construct a further set of demands: that these inferred As should not be as bad as they are, for example. As a result we deepen the intensity of our already constructed disturbance. As will be seen, this is a far cry from models of psychotherapy which place negative life events at the centre of an explanation of how psychological disturbance is acquired.

Perpetuation of psychological disturbance

While REBT does not put forward elaborate theories to explain the acquisition of psychological disturbance, it does deal more extensively with how such disturbance is perpetuated. First, most people perpetuate their psychological disturbance precisely because of their own theories concerning the 'cause' of their problems. They do not have what Ellis (1979b) calls 'REBT Insight 1': that psychological disturbance is 'caused' mainly by the beliefs that people hold about the negative events in their lives. They tend to attribute the 'cause' of their problems to situations, rather than to their beliefs about these situations. Lacking 'Insight 1', people are ignorant of the major determinants of their disturbance; consequently they do not know what to change in order to overcome their difficulties. Even when individuals see clearly that their beliefs determine their disturbance, they may lack 'REBT Insight 2': that they remain upset by reindoctrinating themselves in the present with these beliefs. People who do see that their beliefs determine their disturbance tend to perpetuate such disturbance by devoting their energy to attempting to find out why and how they first adopted such beliefs instead of using such energy to change the currently held beliefs. Some people who have both insights still perpetuate their disturbance because they lack 'REBT Insight 3': only if we consistently work and practise in the present as well as in the future to think, feel and act against these irrational beliefs are we likely to surrender them and make ourselves significantly less disturbed (Ellis, 1979b). People who have all three insights see clearly that just acknowledging that a belief is irrational is insufficient for change to take place.

Ellis (1979b) stresses that the major reason why people fail to change is due to their philosophy of 'low frustration tolerance' (LFT). By believing that they must be comfortable, people will tend to avoid the discomfort that working to effect psychological change very often involves, even though facing and enduring such short-term discomfort will probably result in long-term benefit. As Wessler (1978) has noted, such people are operating hedonistically from within their own frames of reference. They evaluate the tasks associated with change as 'too uncomfortable to bear' – certainly more painful than the psychological disturbance to which they have achieved a fair measure of habituation. They prefer to opt for the comfortable but disturbance-perpetuating discomfort of their problems rather than face the 'change-related' discomfort which they rate as 'dire'. Clearly, therapists have to intervene in this closed system of beliefs if psychological change is to be effected. This philosophy of low frustration tolerance which impedes change can take many different forms. One prevalent form of LFT is 'anxiety about anxiety'. Here, individuals may not expose themselves to anxiety-provoking situations because they are afraid that they might become anxious if they did so: a prospect which they would rate as 'terrible' because they believe 'I must not be anxious'.

'Anxiety about anxiety' is an example of a phenomenon that explains further why people perpetuate their psychological disturbances. Ellis (1979b) has noted that people often make themselves disturbed about their disturbances; thus they block themselves from working to overcome their original psychological disturb-ance because they upset themselves about having the original disturbance. Humans are often inventive in this respect – they can make themselves anxious about their anxiety, depressed about being depressed, guilty concerning their anger, and so on. Consequently, people often have to overcome their secondary disturbances before embarking on effecting change in their original problems.

Ellis (1979b) has observed that people sometimes experience some kind of perceived pay-off for their psychological disturbance other than the gaining of immediate obvious ease. Here such disturbance may be perpetuated until the perceived pay-off is dealt with, in order to minimize its impact. For example, a woman who claims to want to lose weight may not take the necessary steps because she fears that losing weight would make her more attractive to men: a situation which she would view as 'awful'. Remaining fat protects her (in her mind) from a 'terrible' state of affairs. It is to be emphasized that the REBT therapists stress the phenomenological nature of these pay-offs: in other words, it is the person's view of the pay-off that is important in determining its impact, not the events delineated in the person's description.

A final major way that people tend to perpetuate their psychological disturbance is explained by the 'self-fulfilling prophecy' phenomenon (Jones, 1977; Wachtel, 1977): by acting according to their predictions, people often elicit from themselves or from others reactions which they then interpret in such a way as to confirm their initial self-defeating forecasts. In conclusion, Ellis (1979c) believes that humans tend naturally to perpetuate their problems and have a strong innate tendency to cling to self-defeating, habitual patterns, thereby resisting basic change.

Change

REBT theory argues that humans can and do change without psychotherapy. First people can change their disturbance-creating philosophies by reading rational self-help material or talking to people who teach them sound rational principles. I personally derived much benefit in the 1970s from reading and acting on the principles described in Ellis and Harper's (1975) *A New Guide to Rational Living* and helped myself to overcome feelings of inferiority which I experienced from my early teens. Well before that time, I heard Michael Bentine talk on the radio about how he overcame his fear of talking in public due in large part to his stammer. He said that he helped himself by telling himself: 'If I stammer, I stammer. Too bad.' I thought this was excellent advice and because I was scared in my teens to speak in public because I had a stammer, I undertook a similar programme of speaking in public (behavioural exposure) while telling myself: 'If I stammer, I stammer. Fuck it!' (cognitive restructuring). The conjoint use of behavioural and cognitive techniques is frequently the hallmark of change when people (whether they are in therapy or not) alter their disturbance-creating philosophies.

People can help themselves overcome or gain relief from their problems in a number of ways other than changing the philosophies that underpin their psychological problems. They may succeed at changing their distorted inferences about negative events at A or they may put their situation into a more positive frame. They may help themselves by learning new skills like assertion or study skills and thereby improve their relationships with people and their performance at college. They may leave a situation in which they experience their psychological problems and find a new, much more favourable situation. Similarly, they may find a job or a relationship which may help them to transform their problems into strengths. Thus, a very obsessive person may flourish in a job environment that values his obsessiveness.

Finally, people may help themselves by telling themselves obvious irrationalities. I might help myself enormously if I tell myself and believe that I have a fairy godmother who will protect me from trouble and strife or if I think that I am a wonderful person because I write books and articles on rational emotive behaviour therapy!

As this chapter shows, the most enduring psychological changes are deemed to occur when someone changes their irrational beliefs to rational beliefs. All the other changes mentioned tend to be more transient and dependent on the existence of favourable life conditions.

Practice

Goals of therapy

In trying to help clients to overcome their emotional difficulties and achieve their self-enhancing goals, rational emotive behaviour therapists have clear and well-defined aims.

In this discussion it is important to distinguish between outcome goals and process goals. Outcome goals are those benefits which clients hope to derive from the therapeutic process. Ideally, rational emotive behaviour therapists try to assist clients to make profound philosophic changes. These would involve clients (a) giving up their demands on themselves, others and the world, while sticking with their preferences; (b) refusing to rate themselves, a process which would help them to accept themselves unconditionally; (c) refusing to rate anything as 'awful'; and (d) increasing their tolerance of frustration while striving to achieve their basic goals and purposes. If therapists are successful in this basic objective, clients will be minimally prone to future ego disturbance or discomfort disturbance. They will still experience healthy negative emotions such as sadness, annoyance, concern and disappointment, since they would clearly retain their desires, wishes and wants; however, they will rarely experience unhealthy negative emotions such as depression, anger, anxiety and guilt since they would have largely surrendered the absolutistic 'musts' 'shoulds' and 'oughts' which underlie such dysfunctional emotional experiences. In achieving such profound philosophic changes, clients would clearly score highly on the 11 criteria of positive mental health mentioned earlier (see p. 309). If such ideal client goals are not possible, rational emotive behaviour therapists settle for less pervasive changes in their clients. Here clients may well achieve considerable symptomatic relief and overcome the psychological disturbance that brought them to therapy, but will not have achieved such profound philosophic changes as to prevent the development of future psychological disturbance. In this case, clients benefit from therapy either (a) by making productive behavioural changes which lead to improved environmental circumstances at A in Ellis's ABC model; or (b) by correcting distorted inferences at A. In reality most clients achieve some measure of philosophic change, while only a few achieve a profound philosophic change.

Process goals involve therapists engaging clients effectively in the process of therapy so that they can be helped to achieve their outcome goals. Here Bordin's (1979) concept of the therapeutic alliance is helpful. There are three major components of the therapeutic alliance: bonds, goals and tasks.

Effective bonds These refer to the quality of the relationship between therapist and client that is necessary to help clients achieve their outcome goals. Rational emotive behaviour therapists consider that there is no one way of developing effective bonds with clients: flexibility is the key concept here.

Agreement on goals Effective REBT is usually characterized by therapists and clients working together towards clients' realistic and self-enhancing outcome goals. The role of therapists in this process is to help clients distinguish between (a) realistic and unrealistic goals; and (b) self-enhancing and self-defeating goals. Moreover, REBT therapists help clients see that they can usually achieve their ultimate outcome goals only by means of reaching a series of mediating goals. In addition, some REBT therapists like to set goals for each therapy session, although Ellis (1989) is against this practice because, he argues, it forces clients to identify goals that they do not really have. Client goals can be negotiated at three levels: ultimate outcome goals, mediating goals, and session goals. Effective REBT therapists help their clients explicitly to see the links between these different goals and thus help to demystify the process of therapy.

Agreement on tasks REBT is most effective when therapist and client clearly acknowledge that each has tasks to carry out in the process of therapy, clearly understand the nature of these tasks and agree to execute their own tasks. The major tasks of rational emotive behaviour therapy are: (a) to help clients see that their emotional and behavioural problems have cognitive antecedents; (b) to train clients to identify and change their irrational beliefs and distorted inferences; and (c) to teach clients that such change is best effected by the persistent application of cognitive, imagery, emotive and behavioural methods. The major tasks of clients are: (a) to observe their emotional and behavioural disturbances; (b) to relate these to their cognitive determinants; and (c) to work continually at changing their irrational beliefs and distorted inferences by employing cognitive, imagery, emotive and behavioural methods.

Selection criteria

In response to a question that I asked Albert Ellis concerning selection criteria, he said the following:

> In regard to your question about placing people in individual, marital, family, or group therapy, I usually let them select the form of therapy they personally want to begin with. If one tries to push clients into a form of therapy they do not want or are afraid of, this

frequently will not work out. So I generally start them where they want to start. If they begin in individual therapy and they are the kind of individuals who I think would benefit from group, I recommend this either quickly after we begin or sometime later. People who benefit most from group are generally those who are shy, retiring, and afraid to take risks. And if I can induce them to go into a group, they will likely benefit more from that than the less risky situation of individual therapy. On the other hand, a few people who want to start with group but seem to be too disorganized or too disruptive, are recommended for individual sessions until they become sufficiently organized to benefit from a group.

Most people who come for marital or family therapy actually come alone and I frequently have a few sessions with them and then strongly recommend their mates also be included. On the other hand, some people who come together are not able to benefit from joint sessions, since they mainly argue during these sessions and we get nowhere. Therefore sometimes I recommend that they have individual sessions in addition to or instead of the conjoint sessions. There are many factors, some of them unique, which would induce me to recommend that people have individual rather than joint sessions. For example, one of the partners in a marriage may seem to be having an affair on the side and will not be able to talk about this in conjoint sessions and therefore I would try and see this partner individually. Or one of the partners may very much want to continue with the marriage while the other very much wants to stop it. Again, I would then recommend they be seen individually. I usually try to see the people I see in conjoint sessions at least for one or a few individual sessions to discover if there are things they will say during the individual sessions that they would refuse to bring out during the conjoint sessions.

On the whole, however, I am usually able to go along with the basic desire of any clients who want individual, marital, family or group psychotherapy. It is only in relatively few cases that I talk them into taking a form of therapy they are at first loath to try. (Ellis in Dryden, 1984: 14–15)

While I cannot say whether or not other REBT therapists would agree with Ellis on these points, his views do indicate the importance that REBT theory places an individual choice.

Within individual therapy, it is important to distinguish between those who may benefit from brief REBT and those who may require a longer period of therapy. I have recently published an 11-session protocol for the practice of brief REBT (Dryden, 1995a). In it I outline the following seven indications that a person seeking help might benefit from brief REBT:

1 The person is able and willing to present her problems in a specific form and set goals that are concrete and achievable.
2 The person's problems are of the type that can be dealt with in 11 sessions.
3 The person is able and willing to target two problems that she wants to work on during therapy.
4 The person has understood the ABCDEs of REBT[2] and has indicated that this way of conceptualizing and dealing with her problems makes sense and is potentially helpful to her.
5 The person has understood the therapist's tasks and her own tasks in brief REBT, has indicated that REBT seems potentially useful to her and is willing to carry out her tasks.
6 The person's level of functioning in her everyday life is sufficiently high to enable her to carry out her tasks both inside and outside therapy sessions.
7 There is early evidence that a good working bond can be developed between the therapist and the person seeking help.

The more a person meets such inclusive criteria, the more suitable she is for brief REBT.

On the other hand if one or more of the following six contra-indications for brief REBT are present, it should not be offered as a treatment modality.

1   The person is antagonistic to the REBT view of psychological disturbance and its remediation.
2   The person disagrees with the therapeutic tasks that REBT outlines for both therapist and client.
      [These two points are contra-indications for REBT (whether brief or longer-term) as a treatment modality and the person should be referred to a different therapeutic approach that matches her views on these two issues.]
3   The person is unable to carry out the tasks of a client in brief REBT.
4   The person is at present seriously disturbed and has a long history of such disturbance.
      [The above two points do not mean that the person is not a good candidate for longer-term REBT.]
5   The person seeking help and the therapist are clearly a poor therapeutic match.
      [In this case referral to a different REBT therapist is in order. Brief REBT cannot yet be ruled out.]
6   The person's problems are vague and cannot be specified even with therapist's help.
      [While in this case the person is clearly not suitable for brief REBT, she may be suitable for longer-term REBT if she can be helped to be more concrete. If she cannot, then REBT may not be helpful for her.]

It should be stressed that Ellis's and my views on selection criteria are only suggestions and need to be tested empirically before firm guidelines can be issued on selection criteria for REBT in general and as an approach to individual therapy in particular.

Qualities of effective therapists

Unfortunately, no research studies have been carried out to determine the personal qualities of effective rational emotive behaviour therapists. REBT theory does, however, put forward a number of hypotheses on this topic (Ellis, 1978), but it is important to regard these as both tentative and awaiting empirical study.

Since REBT is a fairly structured form of therapy, its effective practitioners are usually comfortable with structure, but flexible enough to work in a less structured manner when the situation arises.

REBT practitioners tend to be intellectually, cognitively or philosophically inclined and are attracted to REBT because the approach provides them with opportunities to fully express this tendency.

Ellis argues that REBT should often be conducted in a strong active-directive manner; thus, effective REBT practitioners are usually comfortable operating in this mode. Nevertheless, they have the flexibility to modify their interpersonal style with clients so that they provide the optimum conditions to facilitate client change.

REBT emphasizes that it is important for clients to put their therapy-derived insights into practice in their everyday lives. As a result, effective practitioners of REBT are usually comfortable with behavioural instruction and teaching and with providing the active prompting that clients often require if they are to follow through on homework assignments.

Effective rational emotive behaviour therapists tend to have little fear of failure themselves. Their personal worth is not invested in their clients' improvement. They do not need their clients' love and/or approval and are so not afraid of taking calculated risks if therapeutic impasses occur. They tend to accept both themselves and their clients as fallible human beings and are tolerant of their own mistakes and the irresponsible acts of their clients. They tend to have, or persistently work towards acquiring, a philosophy of high frustration tolerance, and do not get discouraged when clients improve at a slower rate than they desire. Effective practitioners tend to score highly on most of the criteria of positive mental health outlined earlier in this chapter and serve as healthy role models for their clients.

REBT strives to be scientific, empirical, anti-absolutistic and undevout in its approach to people's selecting and achieving their own goals (Ellis, 1978). Effective practitioners of REBT tend to show similar traits and are definitely not mystical, anti-intellectual and magical in their beliefs.

REBT advocates the use of techniques in a number of different modalities (cognitive, imagery, emotive, behavioural and interpersonal). Its effective practitioners are comfortable with a multi-modal approach to treatment and tend not to be people who like to stick rigidly to any one modality.

Finally, Ellis (1978) notes that some rational emotive behaviour therapists often modify the preferred practice of REBT according to their own natural personality characteristics. For example, some practise REBT in a slow-moving passive manner, do little disputing and focus therapy on the relationship between them and their clients. Whether such modification of the preferred practice of REBT is effective is a question awaiting empirical enquiry.

Therapeutic relationship and style

Taking their lead from Ellis (1979d), most rational emotive therapists tend to adopt an active-directive style in therapy. They are active in directing their clients' attention to the cognitive determinants of their emotional and behavioural problems. While they often adopt a collaborative style of interaction with clients who are relatively non-disturbed and non-resistant to the therapeutic process, Ellis (personal communication) argues that they ought to be forceful and persuasive with more disturbed and highly resistant clients. Whichever style they adopt, they strive to show that they unconditionally accept their clients as fallible human beings and to be empathic and genuine in the therapeutic encounter.

They strive to establish the same 'core conditions' as their person-centred colleagues, albeit in a different style (see Chapter 6, by Thorne). They, however, do not regard such 'core conditions' as necessary and sufficient for therapeutic change to occur. Rather, they regard them as often desirable for the presence of such change. While research in the more relationship-oriented aspects of REBT is sparse, DiGiuseppe et al. (1993) did find in one study that REBT therapists were rated highly on the core conditions by their clients.

Ellis (in Dryden, 1985) has argued that it is important for REBT therapists not to be unduly warm towards their clients, since he believes that this is counterproductive from a long-term perspective, in that it may inappropriately reinforce clients' approval and dependency needs. However, other REBT therapists do try to develop a warm relationship with their clients. Consistent with this, DiGiuseppe et al. (1993) found that Ellis was rated as being less warm than other REBT therapists in their study.

While an active-directive style of interaction is often preferred, this is not absolutely favoured (Eschenroeder, 1979). What is important is for therapists to convey to clients that they are trustworthy and knowledgeable individuals who are prepared to commit themselves fully to the task of helping clients reach their goals. Therapists must develop the kind of relationship with clients that the latter will, according to their idiosyncratic positions, find helpful. This might mean that, with some clients, therapists emphasize their expertise and portray themselves as well-qualified individuals whose knowledge and expertise form the basis of what social psychologists call communicator credibility. Such credibility is important to the extent that certain clients will be more likely to listen to therapists if they stress these characteristics. Other clients, however, will be more likely to listen to therapists who portray themselves as likeable individuals. In such cases, therapists might de-emphasize their expertise but emphasize their humanity by being prepared to disclose certain aspects of their lives which are both relevant to clients' problems and which stress liking as a powerful source of communicator credibility.

I once saw two clients on the same day with whom I emphasized different aspects of communicator credibility. I decided to interact with Jim, a 30-year-old bricklayer, in a casual, 'laid-back' style. I encouraged him to use my first name and was prepared to disclose some personal details because I believed, from what he had told me in an assessment interview, that he strongly disliked 'stuffy mind doctors who treat me as another case rather than as a human being'. However, in the next hour with Jane, a 42-year-old unmarried fashion editor, I portrayed myself as 'Dr Dryden' and stressed my long training and qualifications because she had indicated, again in an assessment interview, that she strongly disliked therapists who were too warm and friendly towards her; she wanted a therapist who 'knew what he was doing'. REBT therapists should be flexible with regard to changing their style of interaction with different clients. They should come to a therapeutic decision about what style of interaction is going to be helpful in both the short and long term with a particular client. Furthermore, they need to recognize that the style of interaction that they adopt may in fact be counterproductive (Beutler, 1979); for instance, they should be wary of adopting an overly friendly style of interaction with 'histrionic' clients, or an overly directive style with clients whose sense of autonomy is easily threatened. No matter what style of interaction REBT therapists may adopt with individual clients, the former should be concerned, genuine and empathic in the therapeutic encounter.

Major therapeutic strategies and techniques

The primary purpose of the major therapeutic strategies and techniques of REBT is to help clients give up their absolute philosophies and adhere to more relative ones. However, before change procedures can be used, REBT therapists need to make an adequate assessment of clients' problems.

Assessment of client problems   Clients often begin to talk in therapy about the troublesome events in their lives (A) or their dysfunctional emotional and/or behavioural reactions (C) to these events. Rational emotive behaviour therapists use concrete examples of A and C to help clients identify their irrational beliefs at B in the ABC model. In the assessment stage, therapists particularly look to assess whether clients are making themselves disturbed about their original disturbances as described earlier in this chapter.

Cognitive change techniques   Here both verbal and imagery methods are used to dispute clients' irrational beliefs. Verbal disputing involves three sub-categories. First, therapists can help clients to *discriminate* clearly between their rational and irrational beliefs. Then, while *debating,* therapists can ask clients a number of Socratic-type questions about their irrational beliefs: for example, 'Where is the evidence that you must . . .?' Finally, *defining* helps clients to make increasingly accurate definitions in their private and public language. These verbal disputing methods can also be used to help correct their faulty inferences (Beck et al., 1979).

To reinforce the rational philosophy clients can be given books to read (bibliotherapy); self-help books often used in conjunction with REBT include *A New Guide to Rational Living* by Ellis and Harper (1975) and *Think Your Way to Happiness* (Dryden and Gordon, 1990). They can also employ written rational self-statements which they can refer to at various times; and they can use REBT with others – a technique which gives clients practice at thinking through arguments in favour of rational beliefs.

Written homework, in forms such as those presented in Dryden (1995a), is another major cognitive technique used in REBT as is rational emotive imagery (REI). REI is the major imagery technique used in REBT. Here clients get practice at changing their unhealthy negative emotions to healthy ones (C) while keenly imagining the negative event at A; what they are in fact doing is getting practice at changing their underlying philosophy at B. Some cognitive techniques (like REI) are particularly designed to help clients move from 'intellectual' insight (i.e. a weak conviction that their irrational beliefs are irrational and their rational beliefs are rational) to 'emotional' insight (a strong conviction in those same points) (Ellis, 1963). Others included in this category are a range of rational–irrational dialogue techniques described in Dryden (1995a).

Emotive-evocative change techniques   Such techniques are quite vivid and evocative in nature, but are still designed to dispute clients' irrational beliefs. Rational emotive behaviour therapists unconditionally accept their clients as fallible human beings even when they act poorly or obnoxiously: they thus act as a good role model for clients. In this they judiciously employ self-disclosure, openly admitting that they make errors, act badly, etc., but that they can nevertheless accept themselves. Therapists employ humour at times in the therapeutic process, believing that clients can be helped by not taking themselves and their problems too seriously; such humour is directed at aspects of clients' behaviour, never at clients themselves.

Clients are often encouraged to do shame-attacking exercises in which they practise their new philosophies of discomfort tolerance and self-acceptance while doing something 'shameful' but not harmful to themselves or others: examples might include asking for chocolate in a hardware shop, and wearing odd shoes for a day. Repeating rational self-statements in a passionate manner is often employed in conjunction with shame-attacking exercises and also at other times.

Behaviour change techniques Rational emotive behaviour therapists can employ the whole range of currently used behavioural techniques (see Chapter 12); however, they prefer *in vivo* (in the situation) rather than imaginal desensitization. Ellis (1979d) favours the use of *in vivo* desensitization in its 'full exposure' rather than its gradual form, because it offers clients greater opportunities to change profoundly their ego and discomfort disturbance-creating philosophies. This high-lights the fact that behavioural methods are used primarily to effect cognitive changes. Careful negotiation concerning homework assignments, where clients aim to put into practice what they have learned in therapy, is advocated, and it should be realized that clients will not always opt for full-exposure, *in vivo* homework. Other behavioural methods often used in REBT include: (a) 'stay-in-there' activities (Grieger and Boyd, 1980) which help clients to remain in an uncomfortable situation for a period while tolerating feelings of chronic discomfort; (b) anti-procrastination exercises which are designed to help clients start tasks earlier rather than later, thus behaviourally disputing their dire need for comfort; (c) skill-training methods, which equip clients with certain key skills in which they are lacking (social skills and assertiveness training are often employed, but usually after important cognitive changes have been effected); (d) self-reward and self-penalization (but not, of course, self-damnation!) which can also be used to encourage clients to use behaviour change methods.

These are the major treatment techniques, but rational emotive behaviour therapists are flexible and creative in the methods they employ, tailoring therapy to meet the client's idiosyncratic position. A fuller description of these and other REBT treatment techniques is to be found in Dryden and Neenan (1995).

The change process in therapy

Rational emotive behaviour therapists are quite ambitious in setting as their major therapeutic goal helping clients to effect what Ellis often calls a 'profound philosophic change'. This primarily involves clients surrendering their 'demanding' philosophy and replacing it with a 'desiring' philosophy. In striving to achieve these changes in philosophy, such clients are helped in therapy to:

(a) adhere to the idea that they manufacture and continue to manufacture their own psychological disturbance;

(b) acknowledge fully that they have the ability to change such disturbance to a significant degree;

(c) understand that their psychological disturbance is determined mainly by irrational beliefs;

(d) identify such irrational beliefs when they disturb themselves and distinguish these from rational beliefs;

(e) dispute such beliefs using the logico-empirical methods of science and replace these with their rational alternatives (more specifically, such clients work towards unconditional self-acceptance and raising their frustration tolerance);

(f) reinforce such cognitive learning by persistently working hard in employing emotive and behavioural methods. Such clients choose to tolerate the discomfort that this may well involve because they recognize that without acting on newly acquired insights, change will probably not be maintained;

(g) acknowledge that as humans they will probably have difficulty in effecting a profound philosophic change and will tend to backslide. Taking such factors into account, such clients re-employ and continually practise REBT's multi-modal methods for the rest of their lives. In doing so, they learn to experiment and find the methods that work especially well for them. They specifically recognize that forceful and dramatic methods are powerful ways of facilitating philosophic change and readily implement these, particularly at times when they experience difficulty in changing. (Ellis, 1979e)

In helping clients achieve such profound change, effective REBT therapists are unswerving in their unconditional acceptance of their clients. They realize that the achievement of profound philosophic change is an extraordinarily difficult task, and one which frequently involves many setbacks. Consequently, while tolerating their own feelings of discomfort they dedicate themselves to becoming a persistent and effective change agent. They (a) identify and work to overcome their clients' resistances (Ellis, 1985); (b) interpret and challenge the many defences that their clients erect against such change; (c) continually encourage, persuade and cajole their clients to keep persisting at the hard work of changing themselves; and (d) generally experiment with a wide variety of methods and styles to determine which work best for individual clients.

Rational emotive behaviour therapists acknowledge that not all clients can achieve such far-reaching philosophic change. This knowledge is usually gained from clients' responses to the therapeutic process. When deciding to settle for less ambitious outcome goals, REBT practitioners limit themselves to help clients effect situationally based philosophic change; correct distorted inferences (Beck et al., 1979); and effect behavioural changes so that they can improve negatively perceived life events. Profound philosophic change would, of course, incorporate these three modes of change.

Limitations of the approach

I have been practising REBT now for almost 20 years in a variety of settings and I have seen a wide range of moderately to severely disturbed individuals who were deemed to be able to benefit from weekly counselling or psychotherapy. While I do not have any hard data to substantiate the point, I have found rational emotive behaviour therapy to be a highly effective method of individual psychotherapy with a wide range of client problems.

However, I have of course had my therapeutic failures, and I would like to outline some of the factors that in my opinion have accounted for these. I will use Bordin's (1979) useful concept of the therapeutic working alliance as a framework.

Goals I have generally been unsuccessful with clients who have devoutly clung to goals where changes in other people were desired. (I have also failed to involve these others in therapy.) I have not been able to show or to persuade these clients that they make themselves emotionally disturbed and that they are advised to work to change themselves before attempting to negotiate changes in their relationships with others. It is the devoutness of their beliefs which seems to me to be the problem here.

Bonds Unlike the majority of therapists of my acquaintance, I do not regard the relationship between therapist and client to be the *sine qua non* of effective therapy. I strive to accept my clients as fallible human beings and am prepared to work concertedly to help them overcome their problems, but do not endeavour to form very close, warm relationships with them. In the main, my clients do not appear to want such a relationship with me (preferring to become close and intimate with their significant others). However, occasionally I get clients who do wish to become (non-sexually) intimate with me. Some of these clients (who devoutly believe they need my love) leave therapy disappointed after I have failed either to get them to give up their dire need for love or to give them what they think they need.

Tasks As Bordin (1979) has noted, every therapeutic method requires clients to fulfil various tasks if therapy is to be successful. I outlined what these tasks are with respect to REBT earlier in this chapter. In my experience, clients who are diligent in performing these tasks generally have a positive therapeutic outcome with REBT, while those who steadfastly refuse to work towards helping themselves outside therapy generally do less well or are therapeutic failures.

It may of course be that I am practising REBT ineptly and that these failures are due to my poor skills rather than any other factor. Ellis (1983b), however, has published some interesting data which tend to corroborate my own therapeutic experiences. He chose 50 of his clients who were seen in individual and/or group REBT and were rated by him, and where appropriate by his associate group therapist, as 'failures'. In some ways, this group consisted of fairly ideal REBT clients in that they were individuals of

[1] above average or of superior intelligence (in my judgement and that of their other group therapist); (2) who seemed really to understand RET and who were often effective (especially in group therapy) in helping others to learn and use it; (3) who in some ways made therapeutic progress and felt that they benefited by having RET but who still retained one or more serious presenting symptoms, such as severe depression, acute

anxiety, overwhelming hostility, or extreme lack of self-discipline; and (4) who had at least one year of individual and/or group RET sessions, and sometimes considerably more. (Ellis, 1983b: 160)

This group was compared to clients who were selected on the same four criteria but who seemed to benefit greatly from REBT. While a complete account of this study – which, of course, has its methodological flaws – can be found in Ellis (1983b), the following results are most pertinent:

1. In its cognitive aspects, RET . . . emphasizes the persistent use of reason, logic, and the scientific method to uproot clients' irrational beliefs. Consequently, it ideally requires intelligence, concentration, and high-level, consistent cognitive self-disputation and self-persuasion. These therapeutic behaviours would tend to be disrupted or blocked by extreme disturbance, by lack of organization, by grandiosity, by organic disruption, and by refusal to do RET-type disputing or irrational ideas. All these characteristics proved to be present in significantly more failures than in those clients who responded favourably to RET.
2. RET also, to be quite successful, involves clients' forcefully and emotively changing their beliefs and actions, and their being stubbornly determined to accept responsibility for their own inappropriate feelings and to vigorously work at changing these feelings (Ellis and Abrahms, 1978). But the failure clients in this study were significantly more angry than those who responded well to RET; more of them were severely depressed and inactive, they were more often grandiose, and they were more frequently stubbornly resistant and rebellious. All these characteristics would presumably tend to interfere with the kind of emotive processes and changes that RET espouses.
3. RET strongly advocates that clients, in order to improve, do in vivo activity home-work assignments, deliberately force themselves to engage in many painful activities until they become familiar and unpainful, and notably work and practice its multimodal techniques. But the group of clients who signally failed in this study showed abysmally low frustration tolerance, had serious behavioral addictions, led disorganized lives, refrained from doing their activity homework assignments, were more frequently psychotic and generally refused to work at therapy. All these characteristics, which were found significantly more frequently than were found in the clients who responded quite well to RET, would tend to interfere with the behavioural methods of RET. (Ellis, 1983b: 165)

It appears from the above analysis that the old adage of psychotherapy applies to REBT: that clients who could most use therapy are precisely those individuals whose disturbance interferes with their benefiting from it. At present, it is not known whether clients who 'fail' with REBT are likely to benefit more from other therapies. Finally, as discussed by other contributors to this book, the practice of REBT is limited by the poor skills of the REBT practitioner.

As I have often said: 'REBT is easy to practise poorly.' There is no substitute, then, for proper training and supervision in the approach.

Case example

The client

Keith is a 26-year-old single man who works as an insurance salesman. He was referred to me by his GP whom he had consulted about angry outbursts at work. Apparently he had lost his temper with his supervisor at his appraisal when the supervisor had given him feedback which Keith viewed as 'demeaning and unfair'. He had sworn at his supervisor and stormed out of the appraisal meeting. Afterwards, Keith received an official written warning with regard to his future conduct and was told that he should 'get some anger management to sort yourself out'.

Keith comes from a small, close-knit family. His parents are both alive and live with his younger sister in south London. Keith lives in a flat, also in south London, with two friends. He sees his family at least twice a week and is very close to them. Keith says that he has always had a short fuse and in this respect resembles his father who, according to Keith, often lost his temper at work and while driving. Keith said, however, that his father never lost his temper with his family and Keith too says that he only gets angry at work and with strangers when they frustrate him or act selfishly towards others.

The therapy

In the referral letter, Keith's GP wrote that since the practice was fund-holding my fees would be met by them. I was asked in that letter to let the GP know how many sessions of therapy I thought Keith needed. At the first meeting I explained all this to Keith and suggested that he spend that initial meeting telling me about the concerns that he wanted help with. I also suggested that I would tell him a little about the therapy that I practised so that he could judge whether or not he thought it would be useful to him. Keith agreed with this plan.

Keith told me in detail about the trouble he was having at work and said that he was glad to have the opportunity to talk about his 'anger problem'. In addition to this problem, Keith reported that he was having trouble setting up appointments with prospective clients and that he thought he was becoming increasingly anxious about doing so. Other than these two problems, Keith said that his life was going well. He has a steady girlfriend to whom he was planning to get engaged. He has good relationships with his flat-mates and other male friends and he is actively involved in a local sports club where he plays football and squash. In addition, Keith said that he previously had had no reason to seek therapy. 'Although I've always had a problem with my temper this is the first time it has really gotten me into trouble,' he said.

After I elicited this information from Keith I explained the REBT model of emotion to him (Dryden, 1995b) and outlined in general terms what our respective tasks would be in REBT. Since this made sense to him and he met the criteria for brief individual REBT listed on pp. 314–15, I offered him a contract for another 10 sessions, which he accepted (see Dryden, 1995a for a thorough exposition of brief REBT with individuals).

Conceptualization of Keith's problems In REBT, we construct an understanding of a client's problems by assessing specific examples of them. In the beginning phase of REBT with Keith I did this, and the following irrational beliefs were revealed:

Anger
- 'My supervisor must not treat me unfairly and if he does, this proves that he is not good' (LFT anger towards others).
- 'My supervisor must not highlight my weaknesses and if he does, this proves that I am inadequate. He must not remind me that I am inadequate' (ego-defensive anger).
- 'People must not block me when I am pursuing important goals and if they do I can't stand it' (LFT anger towards others).
- 'People must not act selfishly towards me or others and if they do act selfishly they should be punished' (LFT anger towards others).

Anxiety
- 'I must be successful at attracting business from prospective new clients and if I don't then this will prove that I am a failure' (ego anxiety).
- 'Attracting new business should be easier than it is and until it is I won't do it' (discomfort anxiety).

Goals of therapy It has been my experience that when anger is a target problem, clients are often ambivalent about changing since quite frequently their anger 'works' for them, at least in the short term. I suggested that Keith complete a cost-benefit analysis form which helps clients to identify an alternative response to their anger and encourages them to specify the costs and benefits of both responses (a) to themselves and to others, and (b) from a short- and long-term perspective. First, though, I helped Keith to understand the difference between unhealthy anger (which stems from irrational beliefs) and healthy anger or annoyance (which stems from rational beliefs) (Dryden, 1996). When Keith had completed the cost-benefit analysis form, he saw clearly that in the long term his unhealthy anger was self-defeating and would get him into trouble with others, and that an assertive response based on healthy anger would be more functional.

With respect to Keith's anxiety, I helped him to see that it was healthy to feel concerned about the prospect of failing to attract new business and that such concern would motivate him to do well at work, while anxiety would lead him to avoid approaching new customers, which in fact was the case. I helped Keith to commit himself to work towards healthy anger in the first instance and concern in the second.

Therapeutic relationship and style As I discussed on pp. 316–17, REBT therapists strive to accept their clients as fallible human beings while focusing on the latter's problems in an acive-directive manner. This characterized my therapeutic style with Keith. Furthermore, my early interactions with Keith suggested that he would respond better to an informal therapeutic style than to a formal one. Our relationship could be described as relaxed and informal where humour was to the fore. We had no reason to focus on our relationship as a microcosm of Keith's problems and, indeed, our relationship was never a subject for direct therapeutic exploration.

Major therapeutic strategies and techniques During therapy I used most of REBT's major treatment techniques as described on pp. 318–19. For example, I made heavy use of standard disputing techniques where I helped Keith to see, through Socratic questioning, that his irrational beliefs were rigid, illogical, anti-empirical and self-defeating, while the rational alternatives to these beliefs were flexible, logical, empirically consistent with reality and self-enhancing. I instructed Keith in a variety of imaginal, emotive and behavioural techniques to help him to integrate these rational beliefs into his belief system so that they would effect constructive affective and behavioural change.

The change process My therapy with Keith got off to a shaky start when it turned out that he had not carried out three homework assignments that I had negotiated with him. On exploration, it transpired that Keith resented being told to come for counselling – he had denied this when I explored the issue with him in the first session. I handled this quite calmly and acceptingly and explained to Keith that he certainly did not have to come to see me, but that if he chose to do so that was his choice irrespective of what his employers had 'ordered' him to do.

Once he had truly accepted that his participation in therapy was *his* decision, therapy went quite smoothly and Keith worked hard at changing his irrational beliefs. In particular, he came to see that his self-worth was not defined on the basis of his achievement; rather to the extent that it could be said that he had self-worth, this could be more properly based on his aliveness and his humanity. This helped him to admit to himself and to his employers that his performance was not as good as he had previously (and defensively) claimed. On this point, Keith found devil's advocate disputing valuable. Here, I attacked his rational beliefs with irrational arguments to which he responded with more persuasive rational points.

Secondly, I helped Keith to acknowledge that while it was definitely preferable that others should not frustrate him or act selfishly, there was no earthly reason why they absolutely had to refrain from doing these things. Keith did have quite a lot of difficulty accepting this point (as most clients do), but he seemed to grasp it when I argued that while people would not frustrate him and would act thoughtfully on 'Planet Keith' on Planet Earth they didn't seem to behave that way.

Our brief therapy contract was spread out over six months, with the later sessions occurring at increasing intervals to enable Keith to use his REBT self-help skills independently. At the end of therapy, Keith had made quite a lot of gains. He was no longer avoiding approaching new clients and his supervisor was much happier with his performance. He was more self-accepting and more tolerant of life's frustrations.

Keith reported that he still made himself unhealthily angry about the selfishness of others and was having trouble fully accepting that others had the right to be wrong when they disregarded other people's feelings. However, he said that he was continuing to work on this issue even though it was difficult.

Notes

1   Where A stands for Activating event, B for Belief and C for the emotional/behavioural Consequences of holding that belief.

2   Where A stands for Activating event, B for Belief, C for the emotional/behavioural Consequences of holding that belief, D for Disputing irrational beliefs and E for the Effects of disputing.

References

Beck, A.T., Rush, A.J., Shaw, B.F. and Emery, G. (1979) *Cognitive Therapy of Depression*. New York: Guilford Press.

Beutler, L.E. (1979) 'Towards specific psychological therapies for specific conditions', *Journal of Consulting and Clinical Psychology*, 47: 882–97.

Bordin, E.S. (1979) 'The generalizability of the psychoanalytic concept of the working alliance', *Psychotherapy: Theory, Research and Practice*, 16: 252–60.

DiGiuseppe, R., Leaf, R. and Lipscott, J. (1993) 'The therapeutic relationship in rational-emotive therapy: some preliminary data', *Journal of Rational-Emotive and Cognitive-Behavior Therapy*, 11(4): 223–33.

Dryden, W. (ed.) (1984) *Individual Therapy in Britain*. London: Harper & Row.

Dryden, W. (1985) *Therapists' Dilemmas*. London: Harper & Row.

Dryden, W. (1995a) *Brief Rational Emotive Behaviour Therapy*. Chichester: John Wiley.

Dryden, W. (1995b) *Preparing for Client Change in Rational Emotive Behaviour Therapy*. London: Whurr.

Dryden, W. (1996) *Overcoming Anger: When Anger Helps and When it Hurts*. London: Sheldon Press.

Dryden, W. and Gordon, J. (1990) *Think Your Way to Happiness*. London: Sheldon Press.

Dryden, W. and Neenan, M. (1995) *Dictionary of Rational Emotive Behaviour Therapy*. London: Whurr.

Ellis, A. (1955a) 'New approaches to psychotherapy techniques', *Journal of Clinical Psychology* (Brandon, Vermont).

Ellis, A. (1955b) 'Psychotherapy techniques for use with psychotics', *American Journal of Psychotherapy*, 9: 425–76.

Ellis, A. (1958) 'Rational psychotherapy', *Journal of General Psychology*, 59: 35–49.

Ellis, A. (1962) *Reason and Emotion in Psychotherapy*. Seacaucus, NJ: Lyle Stuart.

Ellis, A. (1963) 'Toward a more precise definition of "emotional" and "intellectual" insight', *Psychological Reports*, 13: 125–6.

Ellis, A. (1973) 'Psychotherapy without tears', in A. Burton and associates, *Twelve Therapists: How They Live and Actualize Themselves*. San Francisco: Jossey-Bass.

Ellis, A. (1976) 'The biological basis of human irrationality', *Journal of Individual Psychology*, 32: 145–68.

Ellis, A. (1978) 'Personality characteristics of rational-emotive therapists and other kinds of therapists', *Psychotherapy: Theory, Research and Practice*, 15: 329–32.

Ellis, A. (1979a) 'Toward a new theory of personality', in A. Ellis and J.M. Whiteley (eds), *Theoretical and Empirical Foundations of Rational-Emotive Therapy*. Monterey, CA: Brooks/Cole.

Ellis, A. (1979b) 'The theory of rational-emotive therapy', in A. Ellis and J.M. Whiteley (eds), *Theoretical and Empirical Foundations of Rational-Emotive Therapy*. Monterey, CA: Brooks/Cole.

Ellis, A. (1979c) 'The rational-emotive approach to counseling', in H.M. Burks Jr and B. Stefflre (eds), *Theories of Counseling*. New York: McGraw-Hill.

Ellis, A. (1979d) 'The practice of rational-emotive therapy', in A. Ellis and J.M. Whiteley (eds), *Theoretical and Empirical Foundations of Rational-Emotive Therapy*. Monterey, CA: Brooks/Cole.

Ellis, A. (1979e) 'The issue of force and energy in behavioral change', *Journal of Contemporary Psychotherapy*, 10(4): 83–97.

Ellis, A. (1982) 'The treatment of alcohol and drug abuse: a rational-emotive approach', *Rational Living*, 17(2): 15–24.

Ellis, A. (1983a) *The Case against Religiosity*. New York: Institute for Rational-Emotive Therapy.

Ellis, A. (1983b) 'Failures in rational-emotive therapy', in E.B. Foa and P.M.G. Emmelkamp (eds), *Failures in Behavior Therapy*. New York: Wiley.

Ellis, A. (1985) *Overcoming Resistance*. New York: Springer.

Ellis, A. (1989) 'Ineffective consumerism in the cognitive-behavioural therapies and in general psychotherapy', in W. Dryden and P. Trower (eds), *Cognitive Psychotherapy: Stasis and Change*. London: Cassell.

Ellis, A. (1994) *Reason and Emotion in Psychotherapy*, revised and updated edition. New York: Birch Lane Press.

Ellis, A. and Abrahms, E. (1978) *Brief Psychotherapy in Medical and Health Practice*. New York: Springer.

Ellis, A. and Harper, R.A. (1975) *A New Guide to Rational Living*. North Hollywood, CA: Wilshire.

Eschenroeder, C. (1979) 'Different therapeutic styles in rational-emotive therapy', *Rational Living*, 14(1): 3–7.

Grieger, R. and Boyd, J. (1980) *Rational-Emotive Therapy: A Skills-Based Approach*. New York: Van Nostrand Reinhold.

Herzberg, A. (1945) *Active Psychotherapy*. New York: Grune & Stratton.

Jones, R.A. (1977) *Self-Fulfilling Prophecies: Social, Psychological and Physiological Effects of Expectancies*. Hillsdale, NJ: Lawrence Erlbaum.

Salter, A. (1949) *Conditioned Reflex Therapy*. New York: Creative Age.

Wachtel, P.L. (1977) *Psychoanalysis and Behavior Therapy: Toward an Integration*. New York: Basic Books.

Werner, E.E. and Smith, R.S. (1982) *Vulnerable but Invincible: A Study of Resilient Children*. New York: McGraw-Hill.

Wessler, R.A. (1978) 'The neurotic paradox: a rational-emotive view', *Rational Living*, 13(1): 9–12.

Wolpe, J. (1958) *Psychotherapy by Reciprocal Inhibition*. Stanford, CA: Stanford University Press.

Suggested further reading

Bernard, M.E. (ed.) (1991) *Using Rational-Emotive Therapy Effectively*. New York: Plenum.

Dryden, W. (1995) *Brief Rational Emotive Behaviour Therapy*. Chichester: John Wiley.

Dryden, W. and Neenan, M. (1995) *Dictionary of Rational Emotive Behaviour Therapy*. London: Whurr.

Ellis, A. (1994) *Reason and Emotion in Psychotherapy*, revised and updated edition. New York: Birch Lane Press.

Walen, S., DiGiuseppe, R. and Dryden, W. (1992) *A Practitioner's Guide to Rational-Emotive Therapy*, 2nd edition. New York: Oxford University Press.

14

Individual Therapy: Process and Outcome Findings Across Successive Research Generations

Michael Barkham

The preceding chapters have documented a wide range of theoretical approaches to the practice of individual psychotherapy. Whilst interest in psychotherapy as a profession has never been greater, there exists a considerable gap between practice and research which is long-standing and has been repeatedly documented in the psychotherapy literature (e.g. Barlow et al., 1984). Frustration at this gap arises because one of the central roles of psychotherapy research is to inform practice. However, it has tended to be the case that clinical insights have guided research. This situation is largely attributable to researchers and clinicians having different priorities and different paradigms within which they work. Research, as reported in the major international journals, tends to employ large-scale studies and focus on differences between group means representing the 'average' client. In contrast, practitioners work with individual clients and it is often difficult for practitioners to see the relevance of research findings to the clients seen in their practices.

The domains covered by research activity include making evaluative statements about the effectiveness, or not, of particular interventions: this has been the traditional domain of 'outcome' research. In addition, research can attempt to explain why improvement or deterioration occurs: this has been the traditional domain of 'process' research. The knowledge that a specific therapy is effective together with an understanding of what makes if effective can then inform practitioners' decisions ranging from planning and implementing an effective psychotherapy service delivery system to informing the moment-to-moment interventions by therapists with individual clients. However, attempts have been made to identify the practical implications of findings from psychotherapy research in the domains of outcome research (e.g. Whiston and Sexton, 1993) and process research (e.g. Dryden, 1996).

It is important at the outset to appreciate that, much like psychotherapeutic practice, the quality of research varies considerably. In the same way that practitioners aim to learn and integrate into their practice those ingredients which enhance the effectiveness of psychotherapy, so researchers seek to adopt those methods and procedures which lead to good research. These two activities are not mutually exclusive: the endeavour of psychotherapy will be progressed by some *rapprochement* between the two such that researchers are informed by the questions that practitioners want addressed while practitioners inform their practice by implementing ongoing evaluation. One central component of both these activities is 'method'. The skill of the psychotherapy researcher is reflected in issues of design; it is not the result of any study *per se* which is important. Texts which incorporate methodological issues include Bergin and Garfield's *Handbook of Psychotherapy and Behavior Change* (4th edition, 1994b) which, in addition to reviewing specific content domains, contains chapters on methodology (Kazdin, 1994) and process and outcome measurement (Lambert and Hill, 1994). Hill (1991) has summarized a range of methodological issues relating to process research. Recent texts emanating from Britain include Aveline and Shapiro's *Research Foundations for Psychotherapy Practice* (1995), and Parry and Watts's *Behavioural and Mental Health Research: A Handbook of Skills and Methods* (in press). There are also two excellent and complementary texts on research methods: Barker, Pistrang and Elliott's *Research Methods in Clinical and Counselling Psychology* (1994) and McLeod's *Doing Counselling Research* (1994). Finally, methodological issues pertaining to quantitative and qualitative research have been addressed by Barkham (1996) and McLeod (1996) respectively.

Against this background, the purpose of this chapter is twofold: to provide an overview of current international research on individual psychotherapy, and to provide an overview of individual psychotherapy research in Britain.

Psychotherapy findings across successive research generations

The first part of this chapter presents findings from the international scientific community as a series of three, or possibly four, successive but overlapping research generations beginning with Eysenck's (1952) critique of psychotherapy. These generations can be summarized as follows. Generation I spans the period 1950s to 1970s and addresses the outcome question 'Is psychotherapy effective?' and the process question 'Are there objective methods for evaluating process?' Generation II spans the period 1960s to 1980s and utilizes scientific rigour to address the outcome question 'Which psychotherapy is more effective?' and the process question 'What components are related to outcome?' Generation III spans the period 1970s to the present and addresses the outcome question 'How can we make treatments more cost-effective?' and the process question 'How does change occur?' A possible fourth generation can be seen as originating in the mid-1980s onwards and addresses the question of clinical significance in process and outcome research. Research addressing outcome and process domains is addressed under separate subheadings within each generation.

Generation I

Effectiveness in outcome research Although psychotherapy research was being carried out well before the 1950s (see Orlinsky and Russell, 1994), it was the publication of Eysenck's (1952) critique of the effectiveness of psychotherapy which marshalled activity leading to a generation of research focusing on the issue of effectiveness. As such, the overarching theme of this generation is one of 'justification' for psychotherapy and focuses on the question 'Is psychotherapy effective?' and subsequently 'If so, how effective is it?' Eysenck (1952) claimed that approximately two-thirds of all neurotics who received non-behavioural psychotherapy improved substantially within two years and that an equal proportion of neurotics who had not received treatment also improved within the same time period. Bergin and Lambert (1978) made a number of observations about the way Eysenck had analysed his data. For example, they noted that the most stringent improvement percentage was used for psychotherapy while the most generous was used for calculating spontaneous remission rates. Also, differing rates could be deduced depending on the criterion used. In general, their view was that conclusions drawn from the studies used by Eysenck were suspect due to their inherent limitations (not surprising, given their date). In looking at subsequent data, Bergin and Lambert (1978) found the rate for spontaneous remission to be 43 per cent rather than 67 per cent. Importantly, these authors also noted the finding from outcome studies that substantial change generally occurred within the initial 8–10 sessions, considerably quicker than the two-year time frame of spontaneous remission.

The response of researchers to Eysenck's critique was to incorporate a no-treatment control group into the research design, and one exemplar design of Generation I is the study of Sloane, Staples, Cristol, Yorkston and Whipple (1975). They contrasted psychodynamic versus behavioural treatments, each with an average 14-session duration of treatment, with a wait-list control group. The total sample size used for the analysis was 90 clients, with 30 clients randomly assigned to each of the three treatment conditions. The setting was a university psychiatric outpatient centre in which 54 per cent of the clients were students. The design used three experienced therapists in each of the two psychotherapy treatment conditions. The results, using interview-based measures, showed improvement in all three conditions but with the two active treatments being broadly similar and both superior to the wait-list condition. These gains were maintained at various follow-up intervals.

The findings from the Sloane et al. (1975) study were 'confirmed' later by the publication of the original meta-analytic study of psychotherapy carried out by Smith and Glass (1977) and elaborated upon in their book *The Benefits of Psychotherapy* (Smith et al., 1980). The book provides a considered way through the claims and counterclaims of various researchers. Smith and Glass (1977) collated 475 controlled studies (i.e. treatment versus no treatment) across 18 differing therapy types (including placebo treatment and undifferentiated counselling). The average effect size (ES) across all studies was 0.85, indicative of a large effect for psychotherapy over no psychotherapy, indicating that the average treated person was better off than 80 per cent of non-treated people. The effect sizes ranged from small (0.14 for reality therapy) to large (2.38 for cognitive therapies other than rational-emotive therapy). The authors found little evidence for negative effects, with only 9 per cent of the measures being negative (i.e. control groups were better than treated groups). In terms of overall effectiveness, the subsequent refinements of meta-analytic procedures and greater specificity, as well as the inclusion of more recent and more accomplished studies, have not delivered substantially different results, with the ESs remaining relatively stable.

In subsequent years, beyond the time frame of Generation I, many further studies have been included in meta-analytic reviews addressing the issue of effectiveness. Lambert and Bergin state: 'There is now little doubt that psychological treatments are, overall and in general, beneficial, although it remains equally true that not everyone benefits to a satisfactory degree' (1994: 144). The most concise summary of findings derive from meta-analytic studies. In the area of depression, the number of studies (N) included in the meta-analysis and the effect sizes (ES) for three major meta-analytic reports are as follows: Nietzel, Russell, Hemmings and Gretter (1987), N = 28, ES = 0.71; Robinson, Berman and Neimeyer (1990), N = 29, ES = 0.84; and Steinbrueck, Maxwell and Howard (1983), N = 56, ES = 1.22.

In terms of more diverse presenting problems, Lambert and Bergin (1994) provide a summary table of 30 meta-analytic reviews covering a range of presenting problems and psychological interventions. Five studies (including that of Smith and Glass) are defined as 'mixed' and result in a large average ES of 0.90. The range of other studies is so diverse as not to warrant categorization. However, they show the smallest and largest ESs (excluding control conditions) to range from 0.00 (schizophrenia; Quality Assurance Project, 1984) to 1.30 (stuttering; Andrews et al., 1980). Using only those studies (N = 25) which report ESs, the median ES was 0.76, which is approaching a large ES. In terms of comparisons, an ES of 0.67 is obtained from nine months of instruction in reading, while the ESs for antidepressants range from 0.40 to 0.81. Thus, as Lambert and Bergin (1994) argue, there appears to be evidence that psychological interventions are as effective as, if not more effective than, medication. Apparently contrary to these substantial effects, it has been claimed that psychotherapy accounts for only 10 per cent of the outcome variance. This might appear small. However, it needs to be realized that 10 per cent variance arises from a correlation of 0.32 between psychotherapy and outcome. This is appreciably greater than other established correlations in the field: for example, correlations of 0.03 for the effect of aspirin on heart attacks, and 0.07 for service in Vietnam and alcohol consumption.

In relation to specifically psychodynamic therapies, randomized controlled trials (RCTs) are rare. However, the theme of Generation I research is still germane to psychodynamic therapies. For example, Shefler, Dasberg and Ben-Shakhar (1995) report on an RCT of Mann's time-limited psychotherapy (TLP) in which 33 patients were randomly assigned to one of two conditions: three-months of TLP immediately (experimental group), of delay for three months and then TLP (control group). Whilst the study reflects the increased wisdom acquired over time of carrying out RCTs, this design essentially belongs to Generation I in that it is comparing an active treatment against a wait-list control. No alternative therapy was involved in order to advance arguments of specificity, although measures of specific effects which would be predicted from the model of therapy were administered. Results showed the group receiving TLP immediately to have improved significantly more at end of treatment than the control group after the same elapsed time. The effect size for the treatment vs. no-treatment comparison (i.e. prior to the control group receiving therapy) was 0.99, which would be defined as a large effect size, and is what would be expected when comparing an active treatment with a no-treatment condition.

An additional question that has been raised is whether psychotherapy is more effective than a placebo. In response, a critical point, well summarized by Lambert and Bergin, is worthy of reiteration: 'In interpreting this [placebo] research, it is important to keep in mind that failure to find incremental effects (effects beyond those attributable to common factors) for a specific therapy does not mean that psychotherapy is ineffective. Rather it means that no effect has been demonstrated beyond the effects of the common factors' (1994: 149). Lambert and Bergin (1994) provide a useful summary table of 15 meta-analytic studies whereby three two-way comparisons are made: psychotherapy vs. no-treatment; placebo vs. no-treatment; and psychotherapy vs. placebo. The first of these comparisons produces a mean/median ES of 0.82 (i.e., very similar to that stated previously). The placebo vs. no-treatment comparison produces a mean/median ES of 0.42, while the placebo vs. psychotherapy comparison produces a mean/median ES of 0.48. By way of comment on the use of placebo controls, Lambert and Bergin summarize:

> we have concluded that the typical placebo controls used in outcome studies are so conceptually and procedurally flawed that they have essentially failed in their purpose of helping to isolate the active therapeutic ingredients. It is time to discontinue placebo controls and design studies with more meaningful comparison groups. (1994: 152)

Measuring the process of therapy Within the domain of psychotherapy process, the major thrust of this generation focused on the question 'Can the therapy process (e.g. facilitative conditions) be measured?' The influence of Rogers was profound in Generation I's development of objective procedures for measuring events of recorded therapy sessions. His influence has been noted as deriving from his 'respect for the scientific method and dedication to the objective study of the efficacy of his methods' (Hill and Corbett, 1993: 5). Although there was a great surge of activity in an attempt to establish the effectiveness of psychotherapy, it was largely Rogers and his students who pursued research on the process of therapy. While the earlier process work had focused on verbal response modes as indicators of therapist techniques, attention turned to the evaluation of Rogers's facilitative conditions.

Examples of research in this early phase include the work of Rogers and Dymond (1954) who found evidence supporting the view that good outcome was associated with improvements in self-perceptions. Other research drew on the work of Whitehorn and Betz (e.g. 1954) who found, via a retrospective study of psychiatrists, that those who were successful in working with schizophrenic patients were warm and communicated with their patients in a personal manner. Similar findings arose from the various reports of the classic study of the therapeutic conditions with a group of schizophrenic patients carried out at the University of Wisconsin (e.g. Rogers et al., 1967). This study arose following publication of Rogers's (1957) paper on the necessary and sufficient conditions for change. The Wisconsin project was a major empirical investigation undertaken with schizophrenic clients (Rogers et al., 1967). However, Truax and Mitchell (1971), in a review of therapist variables, stated: 'it quickly became apparent to us that we were assuming that such variables are unitary when, in fact, they are not'. They went on: 'just as therapists are not unitary, neither are specific therapist variables', and concluded: 'Therefore, in our opinion, most if not all the research dealing with therapist characteristics needs to be re-done' (1971: 300). This was the call for specificity.

Generation II

Specificity in outcome research   Research characterizing Generation II began in large part as a search for greater specificity in response to what became known as the 'uniformity myth'. This myth reflected the held view that clients were thought to respond similarly to particular interventions. In other words, little attention had been paid to differences across clients, therapists, therapies, or across the course of therapy itself. In response to this situation, the archetypal question of Generation II research became encapsulated in Paul's litany: 'What treatment, by whom, is most effective for this individual with that specific problem, and under which set of circumstances?' (1967: 111). Clearly this was an important and logical step in research as it sought to address the issue of what was the most effective treatment. The question of whether psychotherapy is effective was seen as simplistic (Krumboltz, 1966) while process and outcome were increasingly viewed as differing across clients, therapists and therapies (Kiesler, 1966). Once the general theme of determining the overall effectiveness of psychotherapy was instigated, Paul's matrix of specifying the various components led researchers to focus most on the differing types of intervention (e.g. Luborsky et al., 1975). In addition, the 1960s saw the rapid development of behaviour therapy within the domain of clinical psychology and fed the logical question as to whether these newer therapies (or other brands of therapy) were more effective than, for example, the verbal (e.g. dynamically oriented) therapies.

Generation II studies can be summarized by referring to Bergin and Garfield who stated: 'We have to face the fact that in a majority of studies, different approaches to the same symptoms, (e.g. depression) show little difference in efficacy' (1994a: 822). This is the view reflected by Stiles, Shapiro and Elliott (1986) in their question 'Are all psychotherapies equivalent?' They posited three ways of understanding the supposed equivalence of outcomes. The first was methodological in that equivalence could be achieved by lack of stringency in research methodology. The second argument concerned the possibility that differing therapies may be broadly equivalent due to the overriding effects of common factors. The third argument revolved around the implementation of new research strategies to detect differences.

Generation II research is best characterized by the randomized control trial (RCT). The largest RCT to date has been the National Institute of Mental Health Treatment of Depression Collaborative Research Program (NIMH TDCRP; Elkin, 1994; Elkin et al., 1989). The design comprised three research sites in which 250 clients were randomly assigned to one of four treatment conditions. The four treatment conditions comprised the two psychotherapies which were of major interest: cognitive-behaviour therapy (CBT) and interpersonal psychotherapy (IPT). In order to provide a standard reference condition, the third condition comprised imipramine plus clinical management (IMI-CM). Finally, a placebo condition (PLA-CM) was used primarily as a control for the drug condition and also as an imperfect control for the two psychotherapies. Among the features of the design, expert therapists were used in the two differing psychotherapies; the particular treatments were documented in training manuals and the delivery of the treatments was investigated to check on therapists' adherence to the treatment protocols.

Findings showed that clients in the IMI-CM condition improved most, clients in the PLA-CM condition improved least, and clients in the two psychotherapy conditions fared in between but were generally closer to the IMI-CM condition. However, differences were not large. Indeed, there were no significant differences between the two psychotherapies or between either of them and the IMI-CM. Differences between the psychotherapies and the placebo condition showed only one instance of a trend towards lower scores for clients in the IPT condition as compared with PLA-CM and no significant or trend difference for CBT.

A recent meta-analysis of 28 RCTs (US DHHS, 1993) found improvement rates for individual and group treatments for depression to be comparable: 50 per cent for cognitive therapy, 52 per cent for interpersonal therapy, and 55 per cent for behavioural therapy but 35 per cent for brief dynamic psychotherapy. However, the latter group may have been adversely affected by the proportionally higher number of studies investigating group rather than individual psychotherapy. Overall, these findings have confirmed the view that technically different therapies result in broadly similar outcomes, a conclusion referred to as the 'equivalence paradox' (Stiles et al., 1986). It is not disputed that there is often a reported advantage to one particular method of therapy (invariably cognitive-behavioural), but what is important is that the size of this advantage is relatively small. How such a small advantage translates into clinical status or psychological health is unclear.

The theme of Generation II's research is being extended in terms of evaluating therapies for more challenging patients. For example, recent research on psychotherapy with borderline personality disorders has focused on the efficacy of dialectical behaviour therapy (DBT) and psychodynamic psychotherapy (Koenigsberg, 1995). The former is associated with the work of Linehan (1993), who found DBT to be superior to treatment in the community in a randomized trial over one year as defined by having fewer days in hospital and fewer and less lethal parasuicidal acts (Linehan et al., 1991). These results were largely maintained one year after treatment although there was no difference in patients' levels of general satisfaction, hence suggesting that the effects of DBT are quite specific and do not address non-behavioural symptoms or overall personality functioning (Linehan et al., 1993). Research on psychodynamic psychotherapy for borderlines has been carried out mainly on Kernberg's model (see Clarkin et al., 1992). In addition, Generation II research is also being applied to the study of child and adolescent psychotherapy; see for example, the special section in *Journal of Consulting and Clinical Psychology* (1995) on efficacy and effectiveness in studies of child and adolescent psychotherapy.

Specificity in process research Process research built its base on the 'recorded' session and in Generation II was dominated by the work carried out to investigate the 'facilitative' conditions (i.e. empathy, warmth and genuineness). This was a logical step deriving from a theoretical basis and employing observational and self-report measures. The core period for Generation II process research was the 1970s and there is a noticeable difference between Truax and Mitchell's (1971) review from the *Handbook of Psychotherapy and Behavior Change* reported above and the Mitchell, Bozarth and Krauft (1977) chapter published in *Effective Psychotherapy: A Handbook of Research*. The authors of the latter text acknowledged that the former had focused too much on gross outcome and not sufficiently on the potential correlates between, for example, empathy and outcome. Hence, they stated that 'demographic and process studies were ignored which might have answered the question: "Which therapists, under what conditions, with which clients in what kinds of specific predicaments, need to reach what levels of these interpersonal skills to effect what kinds of client changes?"' (1977: 482).

In contrast to the 1971 review which implied that the facilitative conditions were both necessary and sufficient, and that they were relatively invariant, Mitchell et al. stated that 'the mass of data neither supports nor rejects the overriding influence of such variables as empathy (1977: 483). They went on: 'their [the facilitative conditions] potency and generalizability are not as great as once thought' (p. 483). Hence, while the authors reported some studies which supported to varying degrees the positive role of the facilitative conditions, the majority of studies they reported showed little or no direct relationship between the facilitative conditions and outcome (e.g. Sloane et al., 1975).

While process research focused largely on the facilitative conditions, which in itself became the basis for subsequent research on the therapeutic alliance, it was, as Orlinsky and Russell (1994) observe, 'peculiarity flawed' to the extent that it virtually ceased by the late 1970s. The 'conceptual critique' of the facilitative conditions, combined with the increasing search for psychologically appropriate methods for investigating aspects of the therapeutic process, led to the demise of research in this area. In historical terms, the absence of a research centre linked to Rogers assisted the demise. More generally, there was probably a move away from investigating 'common' factors towards determining the more specific components of individual orientations. There was also an increasing move towards a reevaluation of the clinical utility of the single-case study (e.g. Strupp, 1980a, 1980b, 1980c, 1980d). Jones (1993) provides exemplars of current work using a single-case design.

Generation III

Cost-effectiveness and service delivery   The research included in Generation III spans the period from the 1970s through to the 1990s and incorporates what appear to be two quite diverse foci: cost-effectiveness, and change mechanisms. However, these two areas can be seen to be natural developments arising from the previous two generations of research. Cost-effectiveness has become a central concern, partly driven by research interest but also by the interest of a variety of stakeholders. As such, it is a natural extension of the outcome research carried out in Generation I. The focus on change mechanisms reflects an extension to the issue of 'specificity' which was a feature of Generation II process research, although it might equally be construed as a reaction to it. It is an extension in that it retains specificity as a hallmark, but a reaction in terms of refocusing research on to the process of change.

Information on service delivery systems has been derived from the 1987

National Medical Expenditures Survey (Olfson and Pincus, 1994a, 1994b) which has provided comprehensive data on the use of services by over 38,000 individuals in the United States. The results (usefully summarized by Docherty and Streeter, 1995) suggest that 79.5 million outpatient psychotherapy visits were made by 7.3 million people (representing 3.1 per cent of the US population). Women used the service at 1.44 times the rate of men. In terms of patient characteristics, 90 per cent of patients were white with the majority being either separated or divorced, aged between 35 and 49, and having more than 16 years of education. Two-thirds of psychotherapy visits were made for a mental health reason (mainly depression, anxiety disorders, and adjustment disorders). Outpatient psychotherapy accounted for 8 per cent of all expenditure on outpatient health care. The percentage of patients attending for specified numbers of sessions was as follows: 1–2 sessions, 33.9 per cent; 3–10 sessions, 37.0 per cent; 11–20 sessions, 13.4 per cent; and > 20 sessions, 15.7 per cent. This latter group accounted for 63 per cent of psycho-therapy outcome expenditure. The issue of the cost-effectiveness of psychotherapy has been addressed by Krupnick and Pincus (1992), who have provided a strategy for including this aspect in research studies.

The debate concerning length of treatment ('How much is enough?') has come to the fore in Generation II research. The major finding relating to the dose-effect literature derives from a study carried out by Howard, Kopta, Krause and Orlinsky (1986) which combined 15 outcome studies over a period of 30 years. These authors found that the percentage of clients showing measurable improve-ment following specified numbers of sessions was as follows: 24 per cent after a single session, 30 per cent after two sessions, 41 per cent after four sessions, 53 per cent after eight sessions, 62 per cent after 13 sessions, 74 per cent after 26 sessions, 83 per cent after 52 sessions, and 90 per cent after 104 sessions. This relationship between the number of sessions received by clients and the percentage of clients showing measurable improvement was best represented by a negatively acceler-ating curve. This means that while the curve 'accelerates' (i.e. the percentage of clients improving gets higher as a result of more sessions), it does so 'negatively' in that the greatest improvement occurs early in therapy and there are diminishing returns thereafter such that smaller and smaller gains are made later on in therapy in response to the provision of more sessions. However, it is worth noting that almost half of the studies reported by Howard et al. (i.e. seven) had a median of 15 or more sessions, considerably more than the often-quoted averages for attendance in service delivery systems (Taube et al., 1984). Further, the data set did not comprise cognitive-behavioural, behavioural, or cognitive therapy orien-tations. The findings from Howard et al.'s (1986) work are interesting in how they have been used by people espousing differing viewpoints. Howard et al. (1986) obtained two dose-effect curves: one based on therapist ratings and one on client ratings. Defence of longer-term therapy has utilized the former curve which suggests that diminishing returns only occur after about six months of therapy. In contrast, data from the client ratings suggests greatest improvements to be derived from the initial 8–10 sessions. More recently, the dose-effect findings have given rise to a three-phase model of psychotherapy (Howard et al., 1993). This model proposes that the first few sessions of therapy are characterized by *remoralization*, which then leads on to a phase of *remediation* of symptoms occurring upwards of about the fifth session, which then leads on in later sessions to *rehabilitation* (i.e. improvement in life functioning).

The growth of interest in brief therapies has been marked and research on brief therapies has been summarized by Koss and Shiang (1994). However, while findings indicate that for many clients the greater impact of counselling or therapy occurs during the initial time frame, with subsequent gains requiring more time, for many clients, especially those who have been severely damaged, effective therapeutic work may not be possible until considerable work has been carried out in establishing, for example, an effective therapeutic alliance. What this means is that there are clients for whom briefer therapies are appropriate and clients for whom longer therapies are appropriate. The issue is to determine what is best for each client. It is not necessarily true that more therapy is always the preferred option. Given limited resources, it is important to ensure that longer-term interventions are appropriately used and that they are evaluated in order to provide supporting evidence for their use.

Change pathways   The review of process and outcome in psychotherapy by Orlinsky, Grawe and Parks (1994) summarized a wealth of material relating to possible effective pathways. They identified stability of treatment arrangements and counsellor adherence to a treatment model as showing promise. They identified 'patient suitability' and 'therapist skill' as particularly robust, with over two-thirds of studies in each of these areas reporting significant findings. In terms of therapeutic operations, the authors summarized three areas: problem presentation; expert understanding; and therapist interventions. With regard to problem presentation, the cognitive and behavioural processes within the client's problem presentation are related to outcome. Findings on 'expert understanding' target client problems and client affective responses during sessions. In terms of therapist interventions, there appears to be substantial evidence supporting experimental confrontation as well as interpretations. In addition, paradoxical intention appears to show a consistent relationship with outcome. In terms of the therapeutic bond, this showed strong associations with outcome, especially when assessed from the client's perspective.

Specific techniques   The use of verbal response modes (VRMs) in various research studies has shown that therapists use responses which are consistent with their theoretical orientation (Elliott et al., 1987). Relating VRMs to immediate outcomes (i.e. in-session), a range of studies have identified 'interpretation' (or responses closely allied to it) as being 'effective'. For example, O'Farrell, Hill and Patton (1986) found interpretation to be related to a decrease in client problem description and an increase in experiencing and insight. However, the role of therapist 'intentions' is just as important. Horvath, Marx and Kamann (1990) found that clients' ability to identify the intention of the counsellor depended, in addition to other factors, upon the stage of therapy, with understanding increasing from initial to mid-therapy and then decreasing. A factor accounting for this may be that the intentions become more complex or tacit as therapy develops. The complex relationship between these factors (e.g. response modes and intentions) is summarized by Sexton and Whiston:

Based on a variety of complex factors (experience, training, client behavior), counselors develop intentions or goals that guide their choices of intentions or response modes. After each counselor response, the client reacts (decodes, interprets, and experiences) and responds. In response, the counselor develops an adjusted intention and subsequent response mode. Over time these patterns become stabilized in client and counselor expectations. (1994: 21)

However, it has been found that response modes account for very little of the outcome variance, even for immediate outcome. Hill reports that 'therapist intentions and client experiencing in the turn preceding the therapist intervention each contributed more to the variance than did response modes' (1990: 289). She cites her intensive analyses of eight single cases (Hill, 1989) in which she found that 'client personality, therapist orientation and personality, and adequate therapeutic relationship, and events external to therapy all influenced whether or not clients incorporated changes begun in therapy' (1990: 289).

Research into the effectiveness of interpretations has been summarized by Orlinsky et al. (1994). These authors cited a total of 38 findings from 16 studies, of which 24 findings were positively related to overall outcome, 11 showed no association, and 3 showed negative associations. Hence, while two-thirds of the findings showed a positive association between interpretations and outcome, inspection of their data (Orlinsky et al., 1994: 303) in which 11 studies yielded sufficient information for the reviewers to determine effect sizes, showed the average size of this effect to be small (ES = 0.21). Garfield (1990), albeit basing his views on a previous review (Orlinsky and Howard, 1986), when only half of the reported findings supported the link with a positive outcome, was also somewhat sceptical. Research into the accuracy of therapist interpretations has been carried out by Crits-Christoph, Cooper and Luborsky (1988), who found that accuracy of interpretation was the best predictor of outcome. However, rather surprisingly, it was not related to improvements in the therapeutic alliance. A useful summary of important domains related to change in psychotherapy are included in a special section of *Journal of Consulting and Clinical Psychology* (1993) which was devoted to curative factors in dynamic psychotherapy. Areas include interpersonal problems and attachment styles, the therapeutic alliance, psychodynamic formulations, transference interpretations, and patients' representations of psychotherapy. Generation III process research has combined much of the more 'technical' and quantitative research efforts, but difficulties undoubtedly occur when evaluating specific techniques and many researchers within this domain have contrasting views. For example, Garfield (1990) has stated that there is 'no truly strong support for the accuracy of interpretation as a process variable of importance . . . the interpretation of explanation that is accepted by the patient is the one that may have some positive therapeutic impact' (1990: 276). Others, for example Silberschatz and Curtis (1986), have argued that the interpretations which are important are those which are consistent with the client's unconscious plan for therapy rather than those relating, for example, to the transference.

The role of specific techniques in CBT has also been investigated. For example, patient change in the later stages of therapy has been linked specifically to the procedure of cognitive restructuring (DeRubeis et al., 1990). Further, evidence suggests that certain cognitive techniques (e.g. logical analysis and hypothesis testing) are linked with amelioration of symptoms in the mid-to-later phases of therapy (Jarrett and Nelson, 1987). In addition, the potential prophylactic effect of CBT has been suggested by results showing that patients who have received CBT are less likely to relapse than patients receiving medication (Evans et al., 1992). Hence, patients who have learned cognitive techniques appear to be offered a degree of protection against subsequent depressive experiences if they apply the learned techniques. These findings are congruent with the 'compensatory skills' model of change which suggests that CBT offers a set of effective coping strategies (i.e. compensatory skills) which are implemented by patients. This model appears to be more consistent with research evidence than that which suggests that CBT results in any permanent change in patients' schema. Recently, a review by Iliardi and Craighead (1994) suggested that non-specific factors may play a significant role in the early part of CBT. This suggestion arose from an analysis of a set of studies which showed that early response to CBT (i.e. symptomatic improvement) occurred prior to the formal introduction of cognitive restructuring techniques. The authors suggested that these findings are consistent with the three-phase model of therapy (see Howard et al., 1993) in which the early phase is characterized by remoralization (i.e. non-specific effects of expectancy and hope).

Common factors Process research has often been viewed as a dichotomy comprising common factors and specific techniques. As indicated above, research interest has moved from the facilitative conditions to investigating the therapeutic alliance. While the facilitative conditions have been viewed as a possible mechanism of change, the therapeutic alliance is best viewed as a mechanism which enables the client to remain in and comply with treatment (Bordin, 1979). Sexton and Whiston (1994) reviewed the research literature on the client–therapist relationship since 1985 using three domains: the 'real' relationship, the transference, and the working alliance. Findings summarized here focus on the last of these: the working alliance. A meta-analytic review of 24 studies (Horvath and Symonds, 1991) found that the working alliance was positively related to outcome and that client and observer ratings were better predictors of outcome than therapist ratings. However, the overall effect only approached medium size and it appears that findings from individual studies are affected by such factors as when the alliance was assessed and the particular outcome index used. Overall though, from the available evidence it appears that the therapeutic alliance might account for upwards of 45 per cent of outcome variance (Horvath and Greenberg, 1989).

The perspective taken by the rater influences the results and it is invariably the client's rating of the alliance that is most predictive of outcome. Further, if client change is the criterion for measuring outcome, then client ratings of process are the best. There is also evidence that clients have predispositions to the quality of the alliance they might develop. Horvath and Greenberg (1994) cite work suggesting that clients who have difficulty in maintaining their social relationships or have experienced relatively poor family relationships prior to therapy are less likely to develop strong alliances. Severity of presenting symptoms did not appear to impact on the quality of the alliance. In terms of the temporal nature of the therapeutic alliance, research findings are equivocal, with some researchers (e.g. Eaton et al., 1988) finding that it is constant while others (e.g. Klee et al., 1990) have suggested the opposite. This is an area requiring further research as it relates to the development and maintenance of the client–therapist relationship. While there has been considerable progress in the development of measures of the therapeutic alliance, there has been 'greater emphasis on interrater reliability and predictive validity and less emphasis on issues of dimensionality and convergent and discriminate validity' (Marmar, 1990). It is not clear that equivalent emphasis has been placed on furthering our understanding of what are the actual components of this 'umbrella' concept.

Nevertheless, it is clear that 'umbrella' or overarching models can be helpful in providing a framework for increasing our understanding of therapeutic processes. In an attempt to provide an overarching model for understanding the process of change through therapy, Stiles, Elliott, Llewelyn, Firth-Cozens, Margison, Shapiro and Hardy (1990) developed the assimilation model. This model presents change along a continuum comprising eight stages from 'warded off', through 'unwanted thoughts' and 'emerging awareness' and on to 'problem clarification' and 'insight/ understanding'. Thereafter come the stages of 'application/working through', 'problem solution', and 'mastery'. The model acknowledges that clients rarely experience difficulties in only one area of their lives. It supposes that the resolution of these problems will occur at different rates. Indeed, while some problems will be resolved at the end of therapy, others may only be partially resolved. Initial evidence for the model is encouraging (e.g. Stiles et al., 1994) and although the model requires considerably more rigorous testing, it does provide high face validity upon which to hang research questions.

Clinical significance in outcome and process research: a fourth generation?

When considering quantitative research alone, a three-generation framework suffices. However, when also considering qualitative research methods, it is open to debate whether or not another generation is required to incorporate new developments and foci. Some commentators have viewed the qualitatively based process research arising from the mid-1980s as Generation IV (Orlinsky and Russell, 1994). A key text in marking the divide is Rice and Greenberg's (1984) *Patterns of Change*. Interestingly, this appeared in the same year as Jacobson, Follette and Revenstorf's (1984) key paper on evaluating reliable and clinically significant change (subsequently 'corrected' in Jacobson et al., 1986). These two publications, representing process and outcome respectively, identify a move towards adopting more clinically relevant approaches to both clinical process and outcome research. Hence, while methods for analysing outcome research have increasingly incorporated more sophisticated multivariate statistics, there has also been a move to capture an index of change relevant to the clinician and service delivery manager. Jacobson and Truax (1991) have summarized the work on determining reliable and clinically significant change and have provided three methods for calculating this index. The principle they use is movement by the client from one population (i.e. dysfunctional) to another population (e.g. general population, or non-distressed population). Of course, it is only possible to determine membership of the 'normal' population when normative data is available. In the absence of such data, movement to two standard deviations below the intake mean would signify 'clinical' change (i.e. belonging to a different population, although not necessarily a non-distressed population). This approach enables clinicians to identify individual clients who have met a specified criterion of improvement.

In the same way that the above approach incorporates rigour and clinical utility there is a range of methods adopted in psychotherapy process research which are rigorous but remain sufficiently close to the clinical material to be seen as clinically relevant to practitioners. The traditional model of investigating process–outcome correlations has been challenged (Stiles and Shapiro, 1989) and there has been a movement towards the adoption of newer styles of research aimed at focusing on the 'change process' (Greenberg, 1986). In this paradigm, 'the process of therapy can . . . be seen as a chain of patient states or suboutcomes that are linked together on a pathway toward ultimate outcome' (Safran et al., 1988). A hallmark of qualitative research is that the data comprise 'vivid, dense, and full descriptions in natural language of the phenomenon under study' (Polkinghorne, 1994). For a good example of publications in this area, see the special section of the *Journal of Counseling Psychology* (1994) on qualitative research in counselling process and outcome.

The 'events' paradigm assumes that the intensive study of significant moments occurring during therapy is more informative than aggregating within and across sessions whereby considerable 'noise' is included in the data. It is a substantially better-informed strategy than sampling random segments of therapy sessions. The events paradigm emphasizes the experiences and perceptions of participating patients and therapists by focusing on a particular class of events (e.g. moments of perceived empathy, or insight). The events are usually derived from a variant of a procedure called interpersonal process recall (IPR; Elliott, 1984) which requires the patient, following a therapy session, to identify with an assessor a significant event that occurred during the session. This event then becomes the focus of subsequent intensive analysis. In order to make IPR less labour intensive, a brief format has been devised (see Elliott and Shapiro, 1988).

The events paradigm aims to investigate change episodes in therapy and to develop 'micro-theories' which explain how change takes place. The focus is on 'providing causal explanations of therapeutic change and on making explanation rather than prediction the primary goal of psychotherapy research' (Greenberg, 1994: 115). Task analysis is uniquely suited to the analysis of the psychotherapeutic change process. It attempts to explicate a model of the information-processing activities that the patient and therapist perform across time, which leads to the resolution of particular cognitive-affective tasks. The preliminary model, termed the rational model, can be developed by theoretical speculations and then its 'goodness of fit' verified against empirical examples of psychotherapy changes processes, termed the performance model. The rational model is then constantly revised in an iterative process between theoretical and performance models. The resulting model will potentially provide clinicians with information about the type of patient operations necessary for a therapeutic intervention to be effective or for a good outcome to be achieved. Further, the development of such models have clear implications for training and the manualization of therapies.

Therapy manuals comprise details of the components of particular therapies (e.g. CBT) as well as the procedures for administering them. The purpose of such manuals is to try and standardize the delivery of types of therapy across treatment settings (i.e. therapists) so that when researchers refer to, for example, CBT as carried out at different sites, they can be assured that the therapies are indeed similar. Of course, this can only really be checked by assessing the therapists' adherence to the written procedures.

Individual psychotherapy research in Britain

It is clear from the work reported above that a considerable proportion of research has derived from the United States. In addition, there has always been a strong research tradition in continental Europe, although it is only recently that this is becoming accessible through publications in the English language. Although it might be thought that research in Britain is very much a poor relation, there is indeed a wealth of high-quality research which has been, and currently is being, carried out. The aim of the second part of this chapter is to provide an overview of past and present work on individual psychotherapy research in Britain.

Generation I

Initial response to Eysenck Generation I research began in Britain, as elsewhere, with Eysenck's (1952) critique of the effectiveness of psychotherapy. The response in Britain came from work by Malan and his colleagues based at the Tavistock Clinic who investigated rates of spontaneous remission in 45 untreated neurotic clients (Malan et al., 1968, 1975). Malan and his colleagues found that while 49 per cent of clients had improved using symptomatic criteria, only 24 per cent had done so when using dynamic criteria. However, the generalizability of these findings is compromised by the highly selective nature of the sample. Malan also carried out two series of studies on analytic psychotherapy (Malan, 1963, 1976). In the first of these, Malan (1963) investigated a sample of patients for whom psychodynamic formulations were devised based on disturbances in their social relationships which required a resolution between the id and the superego. Malan assessed therapy according to whether patients improved in their social relations consequent on their symptom improvement. Of the 21 patients in the sample, five met the criterion for substantial improvement. In the second series of studies, Malan (1976) studied the outcome of a further 30 clients and found significant improvement in five. In particular, he found a significant association between outcome and interpretations linking transference with patient or sibling. In reality, the value of these two studies lies more in their attempt to study the material of psychotherapy by keeping closely to the clinical material than in their value as definitive studies of the effectiveness of psychoanalytic therapy. Ironically, therefore, they might almost be seen to have come full circle and sit within the suggested fourth research generation.

The advent of meta-analytic techniques provided the field with a much-needed procedure for summarizing findings in a quantitative and replicable fashion. Following Smith and Glass's (1977) meta-analytic publication, Shapiro and Shapiro (1982) replicated and refined the analysis. They analysed the effects of 143 outcome studies in which two or more treatments were compared with a control group. The mean effect size for treated versus untreated groups approached one standard deviation unit (slightly higher than the 0.85 effect size obtained by Smith and Glass). When they compared a smaller data set in which two active treatments were compared with each other, they found cognitive and certain multi-modal behavioural treatments to be superior. However, they were very clear in pointing out that much of this research was analogue and hence unrepresentative of clinical practice. This research acted very much as a bridge between Generations I and II, with its call for comparative research to be carried out with clinical populations.

Generation II

Outcome research Shapiro and Shapiro's meta-analysis (and limitations identified in it) led to a series of comparative studies evaluating different modes of therapies carried out by Shapiro and colleagues (see Shapiro et al., 1991). A programmatic series of studies has been devised to evaluate the outcome of cognitive-behavioural and psychodynamic-interpersonal therapies as well as what is effective (i.e. processes) within each therapy. The first Sheffield Psychotherapy Project (Shapiro and Firth, 1987) compared eight-session phases of prescriptive (cognitive-behavioural: CB) and exploratory (psychodynamic-interpersonal: PI) therapy in which 40 professional and managerial workers diagnosed as depressed or anxious received either eight sessions of prescriptive followed by eight sessions of exploratory, or the same two therapies in the reverse order. All clients saw the same therapist throughout therapy. Findings showed a slight advantage to prescriptive therapy as well as an advantage to the initial phase (i.e. first eight sessions) of a 16-session therapy. This slight advantage to CB over PI therapy was also obtained in the larger second Sheffield Psychotherapy Project, but only on one out of seven client self-report measures (SPP2; Shapiro et al., 1994). The design called for 120 white-collar workers, diagnosed as depressed, to be randomly assigned to one of the four treatment conditions: either PI or CB therapy delivered in either eight- or 16-session durations. The study also found that 16-session therapy was only superior to eight-session for those patients presenting with more severe levels of depression (as measured by the Beck Depression Inventory; BDI). Follow-up data at one year showed that patients in the 8PI condition were faring worse than those in the other three treatment conditions (Shapiro et al., 1995). It was also found that clients presenting with cluster C personality disorders had significantly poorer outcomes than clients without a cluster C personality disorder following PI therapy but not CB therapy (Hardy et al., in press). The SPP2 has been extended to NHS settings in a Medical Research Council/NHS collaborative study acting as a replication (Barkham et al., 1995). The effectiveness of treatments was found to be similar to that of SPP2 with the exception that patients had not maintained their gains at three-month follow-up. Scott (1995) has provided an update on psychological treatments for depression.

The effectiveness of psychotherapy has also been evaluated against other forms of clinical management. This applies particularly in clients diagnosed with anorexia nervosa or bulimia nervosa. In one study of severe anorexia nervosa, clients were randomly assigned to either 12 sessions of dietary advice or 12 sessions of combined individual and family psychotherapy (Hall and Crisp, 1987). At one-year follow-up, the dietary advice group showed significant weight gain. In contrast, while clients receiving the combined psychotherapy did not obtain a statistically significant improvement in weight gain, they did make significant improvements in their sexual and social adjustment. In another study of bulimia nervosa, 92 women diagnosed as bulimics were randomly assigned to one of three treatment conditions (cognitive-behavioural, behavioural, and group therapy) while a further 20 women were assigned to a waiting-list control group (Freeman et al., 1988). All three treatments were effective compared with the control group. The researchers predicted that cognitive-behavioural therapy would be superior to the other two active treatments. However, where differences did occur, they tended to favour behaviour therapy.

The efficacy of cognitive therapy has been extensively investigated. Teasdale has written on a model of understanding depression within a cognitive-behavioural framework (Teasdale et al., 1984). Through both theoretical (Teasdale, 1985) and empirical (Fennell and Teasdale, 1987) work, Teasdale has developed a model of depression in which 'depression about depression' is a central component. Teasdale (1985) argues that depression about depression is best attacked by helping clients to view it as a problem to be solved rather than evidence of personal inadequacy. To test out this hypothesis, Fennell and Teasdale (1987) investigated the process of change in outpatients with major depressive disorder. Cognitive therapy was compared to treatment as usual. Cognitive therapy produced marked improvement within the initial two-week period which was maintained through the course of treatment. The study showed that when fast responders were analysed between the two treatment groups (i.e. cognitive therapy vs. treatment as usual), only the good responders in the cognitive therapy group maintained their level of improvement. Establishing predictors of improvement is an important aim of psychotherapy research. Using detailed session-by-session analysis, Fennell and Teasdale (1987) found the major differentiating factor between high and low responders to be clients' responsiveness to a booklet about depression. Clients who responded positively to the booklet improved most quickly. The authors argued that this was because the booklet addressed the issue of being 'depressed about their depression'.

Evaluations of the comparative effectiveness of cognitive therapy with pharmacotherapy have been carried out by Blackburn (for review, see Blackburn, 1995). Findings for hospital patients presenting with depression, although not statistically significant, tended to support the view that combined drug and cognitive therapy was more effective than cognitive therapy alone which was, in turn, more effective than drug treatment alone (e.g. Blackburn et al., 1981). However, this pattern of findings did not hold for general practice clients. Rather, patients receiving pharmacotherapy alone did significantly worse than the other two client groups, and further, there was little difference between the combined therapy and cognitive therapy groups. These findings suggested that drug and cognitive therapies failed to have the additive effect in the general practice group which occurred in the hospital patient group. Blackburn, Eunson and Bishop (1986) reported on the recurrence rate at two years for cognitive therapy, medication, and combined. Results showed appreciably lower rates of recurrence for cognitive therapy alone (23 per cent) and cognitive therapy/drug combination (21 per cent) as compared with medication alone (78 per cent).

A series of studies of cognitive therapy for anxiety have been carried out by Butler and colleagues. Butler, Cullington, Hibbert, Klimes and Gelder (1987a) treated a total of 45 clients making diagnosis of generalized anxiety disorder (GAD), with 22 receiving anxiety management immediately while a further 23 received the same treatment after a three-month wait period. The results suggested that clients in the immediate treatment group improved significantly more than the matched group waiting for treatment. When the wait group received treatment, a similar improvement was obtained. A subsequent study treated 57 patients diagnosed as GAD and compared three treatment conditions: cognitive-behavioural therapy (CBT), behaviour therapy (BT), and a wait-list (Butler et al., 1991). Results showed CBT to be superior to BT alone (relaxation training plus graded exposure), with both treatments superior to the wait-list control. Whilst the study had relatively low statistical power to detect differences between the two active treatments and the wait-list group (19 patients initially in each of the three conditions), the fact that differences were found for CBT over BT attests to the robustness of the findings. Hence, addressing the cognitions of those patients presenting with GAD is clearly beneficial. The authors note that this is one of the few examples where one form of psychological treatment has been found to be more effective than another as a treatment for GAD. However, inspection of the pre-post change effect size on one of the criterion measures of anxiety, the Beck Anxiety Inventory, suggests that it may not be so much a story of CBT being superior (the pre–post change ES of 1.35 is standard) but more a story of BT being inadequate (as indicated by the pre–post change ES of 0.65) and hence not a treatment of choice with GAD in a clinical population.

Salkovskis (1995) provides a summary of how cognitive-behavioural therapy has advanced in the area of panic disorder together with a very useful 'hourglass' model of how psychotherapy research progresses through various stages. Following on from Butler et al.'s (1991) assertion for non-equivalence of psychotherapies, Salkovskis states:

> The myth of psychotherapy equivalence is not helpful in the process of refinement. Like the idea that all swans are white, the range of exceptions is now too striking to be ignored. As more knowledge is acquired about maintaining factors involved in different types of psychological problems, the rate of progress increases. Of course, where research is not guided by attempts to understand the idiosyncratic nature of the factors involved in the maintenance of such problems, outcome studies may show that there is no difference between therapies. (1995: 224)

In a comparative trial, Blowers, Cobb and Mathews (1987) studied a sample of 66 clients diagnosed as suffering from generalized anxiety. Clients were randomly assigned to one of three conditions: wait list, non-directive counselling, or anxiety management training (combined relaxation and brief cognitive therapy). Surprisingly, perhaps, there were few significant differences in outcome between non-directive counselling and anxiety management training. Blowers et al. summarized their findings as follows: 'A reasonable conclusion would therefore be that anxiety management training is indeed effective, but that its superiority to a less structured and less directive alternative remains to be proven' (1987: 500). However, as Morley (1988) suggests, it can be no surprise that such studies find little differences between anxiety management training and non-directive counselling. These studies are not really evaluating cognitive therapy but rather cognitive components divorced from their behavioural concomitants.

The comparative effectiveness of cognitive therapy (CT) with other interventions has been investigated (Clark et al. 1994). A total of 64 patients were allocated (the report does not state that this was carried out randomly) to either CT, applied relaxation therapy, imipramine, or a waiting list. Patients on the waiting list received no treatment for the initial three months and were then randomly allocated to one of the three treatment conditions. Patients in the CT or applied relaxation conditions received up to 12 sessions in the first three months and up to three booster sessions in the next three months. Results showed CT to be the most effective treatment. However, as with the Butler study, finding CT to be superior is less impressive when the 'competing' therapy may not be as powerful as it should. Blanes and Raven (1995), in a review of psychotherapy of panic disorder, questioned the findings from Clark et al. given that over 80 per cent of their sample had some degree of agoraphobia and that the treatment of choice for this problem is systematic self-exposure with homework diaries.

A multinational study investigating treatments for panic disorder with agoraphobia has been carried out (Marks et al., 1993). A total of 154 patients presenting with a diagnosis of panic disorder were randomly allocated to one of four treatment conditions: alprazolam and exposure, alprazolam and relaxation, placebo and exposure, placebo and relaxation. Patients in all four treatment conditions improved when evaluation of panic was used as the single outcome indicator. In brief, the findings indicated that while alprazolam and exposure were more effective than placebo, the effect size for exposure was approximately twice that for alprazolam, with the gains from exposure being maintained whilst those for alprazolam were not.

There is an increasing empirically based literature on treatments for people presenting with psychosis. Studies have developed cognitive-behavioural strategies for problem-solving and coping (Tarrier et al., 1993, 1990). Cognitive-behavioural principles have also been developed and applied to aspects of psychosis (Chadwick and Lowe, 1990; Kingdon and Turkington, 1991). A pilot control trial of CBT for drug-resistant psychosis has been reported by Garety, Kuipers, Fowler, Chamberlain and Dunn (1994). Patients meeting a diagnosis of schizophrenia or schizo-affective psychosis and who presented with unremitting (i.e. for a period of at least six months) drug-resistant positive psychotic symptoms were assigned (but not randomly) to either the treatment group or a wait-list control group. Patients in the treatment group received on average 16 weekly sessions of cognitive-behavioural therapy (Fowler et al., 1994) and were found to report significantly less intensive conviction in the delusional thoughts than the control group at end of treatment. Overall, the treatment group fared better than the no-treatment control group. Given this was obtained using very low statistical power (a maximum of 13 treated vs. 7 no-treatment patients), it is likely that this low power masks differences which may actually exist given adequate statistical power. This issue is addressed in an ongoing study by the authors.

Fairburn and colleagues have carried out a series of studies on the effects of psychotherapy on bulimia nervosa (e.g. Fairburn et al., 1991). Fairburn, Jones, Peveler, Hope and O'Connor (1993) compared cognitive-behavioural therapy (CBT) with interpersonal therapy (IPT) and also with behaviour therapy (BT; construed as a simplified version of CBT) with 25 patients allocated to each treatment condition and receiving 19 sessions over 18 weeks. The results indicated a high rate of attrition and withdrawal (48 per cent) among patients assigned to BT, with few patients in this condition meeting the criteria for a good outcome. By contrast, patients in the CBT and IPT treatments made substantial, lasting, and broadly equivalent changes across the various domains measured. Interestingly, while IPT showed the lowest percentage of patients meeting criterion at the end of treatment, the rate increased monotonically across the three post-treatment assessments such that it was the highest (44 per cent) at one year follow-up compared with 36 per cent and 20 per cent for CBT and BT respectively. A follow-up study of 89 patients, assessed on average just under six years following treatment, from two consecutive studies (Fairburn et al., 1986, 1993) found patients who had received either CBT or interpersonal therapy (IPT of focal) had a better prognosis than patients receiving behaviour therapy (Fairburn et al., 1995).

Roth and Fonagy (in press), in a report submitted to the DoH, aimed to identify psychotherapeutic interventions which are of demonstrated benefit and also to draw implications for their delivery within the NHS. In drawing attention to a number of limitations in the available research literature, they identify systemic and psychodynamic models as requiring research effort. They also identify a number of methodological limitations which should be noted, including generalizing results from randomized controlled trials, the ambiguity of findings from less well-controlled studies, the relative absence of long-term follow-up, statistical analyses, and most importantly in their view, the complexity of mental health problems and issues of classification raised by such complexity. They conclude that meta-analyses and qualitative reviews of psychological treatments for depression strongly support CBT even for severe depression, and its superiority to alternative psychotherapeutic treatments. However, most importantly, they add the observation that 'the range of contrast therapies is sometimes rather limited and rarely includes psychodynamic treatments'. This reiterates the point made previously that some of the advantages shown for CBT may arise as a function of the weaker alternative treatment selected rather than the superiority *per se* of CBT.

The research reported so far has been based in a 'pure' treatment method (either CBT or PI, or BT). However, there has also been an increase in integrative therapies. For example, a comparison between more traditional 'interpretative' therapy versus cognitive-analytic therapy (CAT: Ryle, 1990) has been carried out (Brockman et al., 1987). Although the overall findings reported no difference, one aim of this study was to evaluate effectiveness as carried out by trainees. Accordingly, it could be argued that the finding of no difference is a function of inexperienced therapists rather than of similarly effective treatments. It is still valid to conclude that the two treatments are equally effective with trainee therapists.

However, as the authors acknowledge, an unequal attribution (i.e. dropout) rate led to the two groups differing in severity level at intake. Because the two groups were not equivalent in severity at intake, rigorous comparisons as to the comparative effectiveness of one condition with another is problematic. Subsequent reports on CAT have comprised single case studies showing the impact of CAT on patients presenting with borderline personality disorders (e.g. Ryle, 1995; Ryle and Beard, 1993). Shapiro, Barkham, Reynolds, Hardy and Stiles (1992) combined prescriptive (i.e. cognitive-behavioural) and exploratory (i.e. psychodynamic-interpersonal) therapies by administering them as 'pure' therapies within a session but alternating within certain constraints across the course of therapy in response to a match between client requirements and a particular overarching integrative model (the assimilation model). The outcome for this single case was successful but requires replication. Overall, there is a dearth of direct evidence for the equivalence in efficacy, let alone superiority, of integrative therapies. Much of the argument in support of their use derives indirectly from the broad equivalence of outcomes. In addition, it is not clear that skills and expertise gained in one particular method of delivery transfer to a more integrated method without additional training. The current interest in (and articles written about) this area is considerable and reflects the fact that integrative therapies are probably more palatable to practitioners than pure treatment methods. Following a major workshop which focused on the research required to move this area forward, little empirical work has been carried out (Wolfe and Goldfried, 1988). Indeed, considerably more work needs to be done in order to provide hard data on the comparative effectiveness of integrative therapies.

Fonagy (1995) has provided a very useful summary of problems emanating from outcome research but states that without them we would not know what the optimal effects of treatments would be. Taking this forward, he argues for outcome studies (i.e. research from Generations I and II) to be enhanced by clinical audit, thereby bringing it into the realm of every practitioner: 'outcome studies and clinical audit should be performed in tandem. The first will identify potentially useful interventions which may be adopted by clinicians for specific disorders, and the second will show clinicians how effective they are in implementing these procedures' (1995: 176). He continues: 'Without outcome studies, the design of clinical services will lack strategic direction; without clinical audit, services may be massively distorted in unknown ways based on findings of little relevance to work at ground level' (ibid.: 176). The domain of clinical audit is very much to the fore at present and it makes eminent sense that this agenda be carried forward collaboratively in the context of rigorous research in the area of psychotherapy.

Process research and therapist skills Generation II process research differs appreciably in Britain from the United States as there has not been the same momentum in Britain for investigating facilitative conditions as that provided by Rogers. A series of studies carried out by Shapiro (1969, 1970, 1973, 1976) which investigated the role of the facilitative conditions in psychotherapy offered little support for their central role in accounting for change. However, later work investigating the role of various verbal response modes found 'exploration' (a response between interpretation and reflection) to be associated with client and helper experiences of perceived empathy (Barkham and Shapiro, 1986).

An alternative activity in the later part of this research generation has focused on attempts to increase the quality of therapists' practice. An ongoing programme of psychotherapy teaching and training has been implemented and evaluated in Manchester, largely through the work of Goldberg, Hobson, Margison and colleagues. This work has arisen from Manchester's position as a regional centre for psychotherapy. Consistent with its teaching priority, there has been considerable research into teaching specific psychotherapeutic methods to other caregivers, in particular the development of the Conversational Model of psychotherapy, together with a comprehensive teaching programme (Goldberg et al. 1984; Maguire et al., 1984). The Conversational Model of therapy has been developed over the past 30 years as a therapeutic method for dealing with people who have experienced difficulties in their interpersonal relationships. Hobson, in some ways reflecting the impact of Rogers, not only developed the model, but has also been central in advocating its investigation through video recording and research. This method has been packaged for teaching purposes and has been shown to be transferable to junior doctors (Goldberg et al., 1984). The development of teaching methods was paralleled by the development of manuals for specified therapies (a defining hallmark of Generation II research). For example, Startup and Shapiro (1993) carried out an adherence study on the second Sheffield Psychotherapy Project in which each of 220 sessions (110 sessions from each of CB and PI therapies) was rated by two raters according to a rating manual. These authors found that 97 per cent of sessions were correctly assigned.

The extension of psychotherapy skills to people in a primary care setting emphasizes not only an increasing adoption of a psychosocial model of presenting problems but also the notion that providing primary caregivers with psychotherapeutic skills results in an increase in the detection of psychological illness. For example, Gask (Gask and McGrath, 1989) has worked extensively on the application of psychotherapeutic skills to general practitioners dealing with issues such as AIDS.

Research has also focused on therapist difficulties (Davis et al., 1987). These authors devised a taxonomy of nine categories in which they were able to classify reliably therapists' difficulties. The three most commonly occurring difficulties were therapists feeling threatened (i.e. the therapist feels a need to protect self against the client), feeling puzzled (the therapist cannot see how best to proceed), and damaging (the therapist feels that he or she may be injuring the client). Most interestingly, therapists showed internal consistency in the patterns of difficulties experienced. This led the authors to argue that these profiles would be highly related to therapists' personalities and consequently might help identify potential counter-transference problems for different therapists. This work is ongoing.

Generation III

Cost-effectiveness and service delivery There is currently considerable interest, both economic and clinical, in evaluating the cost-effectiveness of the psychotherapies (e.g. Healey and Knapp, 1995). For example, McGrath and Lawson (1987) have argued for the legitimacy of assessing the benefits of psychotherapy from an economic standpoint and conclude that it is possible to justify the provision of psychotherapy within the NHS on economic grounds. At a broad level, Parry (1992) has identified a range of issues which are pertinent in devising cost-efficient psychotherapy services.

A major feature of the studies detailed in Generation II is their attempt to combine both internal validity (i.e. the attempt to minimize bias, usually through random assignment of clients to particular conditions) and extrinsic validity (i.e. sampling a clinical rather than a student population). Perhaps the best single indicator of such attempts is the use of random allocation of clients to treatment conditions (RCT). Often, however, it is not possible to do this either for ethical or practical reasons. When it is not possible to incorporate high components of both forms of validity, researchers face a choice. They must either employ analogue studies (e.g. studying students with test anxiety) in which internal validity is high but which are problematic in generalizing the findings to clinical populations, or use more naturalistic studies (i.e. describing and evaluating clients referred to outpatient settings) which do not permit the researcher to manipulate specific variables. Naturalistic designs have been used and are a logical means for evaluating service delivery systems. A study using a naturalistic design and studying inpatients has been carried out by Denford, Schachter, Temple, Kind and Rosser (1983). These workers completed a retrospective study of 28 successive admissions for inpatient psychotherapy at the Cassel Hospital, a community using a combination of both individual and community psychotherapeutic methods. Their findings suggested that

> to maximise the proportion of patients who improve, the hospital should be inclined to accept patients who have neurotic rather than borderline or psychotic psychopathology, those who appear considerably depressed, those with a history of minimal out-patient psychiatric treatment, and possibly those judged to be of superior intelligence. (Denford et al., 1983: 235–6)

An important difference between successful clients and clients rated as failures and dropouts was that motivation for insight and change was high in 50 per cent of successful cases and lower in both failed (38 per cent) and dropout clients (13 per cent). Blind ratings of motivation tended to distinguish success and failed groups at triage, a finding consistent with the results obtained by Malan (1963, 1976).

Another retrospective study was carried out by Keller (1984), who investigated the applicability of brief psychotherapeutic methods developed at the Tavistock Clinic in NHS outpatient psychotherapy clinics. Fifteen clients in all were treated but the study produced no statistically significant results. At non-significant levels, however, the results indicated that outcome was better for those clients who experienced high levels of distress subjectively but who functioned well externally. In addition, outcome was better for those clients who had a supportive relationship outside therapy and for whom a psychodynamic focus could be formulated. Keller argued that the findings generally substantiate Malan's (1976) work. Interestingly, this study exemplifies the difficulties of practitioners carrying out research. In their favour, these practitioners set up a workshop to provide a framework for the participating practitioners to adapt their methods to the clients they saw in their own practices as well as providing an environment for research to be implemented and carried out. However, from the researcher's viewpoint it is difficult to have much confidence in the findings: they are non-significant, based on a small sample, and contaminated by other influences (including rater bias). In addition, the finding that more distressed clients fare better (a finding also reported by Denford et al., 1983) may be a function of scores regressing to the mean. Accordingly, this phenomenon should always be borne in mind when considering improvement in high scorers.

Research has also been carried out on specialized populations who are of particular concern to practitioners in service delivery settings. For example, the treatment of survivors of childhood sexual abuse (CSA) has been reviewed by Cahill, Llewelyn and Pearson (1991), who concluded that virtually all publications in this area to date take the form of therapists' experience of treating patients. They conclude that what is needed is the application of empirical research methodology to establish the most effective treatments. In a study of six survivors of CSA, Clarke and Llewelyn (1994) report on the changes achieved by patients following cognitive-analytic therapy. Similarly, Birchwood (1992) has proposed practical intervention strategies to help reduce the occurrence of florid schizophrenic relapse where the emphasis is on providing an early intervention service.

The issue of cost-effectiveness has been addressed in several studies in which very brief interventions have been devised (i.e. therapy is construed as assessment). One model delivers therapy in the form of two sessions one week apart and a third session three months later for clients presenting with mild levels of depression. This generic model of therapy, termed two-plus-one therapy, has been implemented in pilot studies using cognitive-behavioural and relationship-orientated therapies in a research clinic (Barkham and Shapiro, 1990) as well as cognitive-behavioural therapies in a field setting (Barkham et al., 1992). Results from a large randomized controlled trial are awaited. Other clinicians have devised variants of the original model, for example a model of intervention comprising a three-plus-one design for patients presenting with greater severity of problems (Aveline, 1995). Preliminary results based on analyses midway through this latter study, which compared a brief intervention and follow-up with a standard assessment for psychotherapy procedure, suggest that there are more discharges in the brief intervention model than in the standard assessment, with its attendant benefit on the waiting list, together with greater change at the four-month follow-up. However, as Aveline (1995) correctly cautions, care should be taken in analysing results midway through a trial, particularly if those results themselves are less than clear-cut. Such models of brief therapy are informed by the dose–effect curve which, for example, would predict 30 per cent of clients to show improvement after two sessions. Interests in cost-effectiveness are therefore focused on identifying, like Fennell and Teasdale (1987), those clients who are able to respond beneficially to such treatment models. This is consistent with attempts to match treatment-specific delivery models with clearly defined presenting problems.

However, cost-effectiveness is not synonymous with brevity. For example, while Freeman et al. (1988) acknowledged that improvement rate for bulimics in their study (77 per cent) was marginally less than in other studies, they argued that the greater intensity of treatment offered in other treatments (e.g. being seen several times a week or for half a day at a time) for marginally greater improvement was not necessarily cost-effective. Similarly, Peveler and Fairburn (1989) argued that while their treatment for a case of anorexia nervosa with diabetes mellitus lasted one year, 'the treatment was of relatively low intensity, amounting to just under 40 hours of therapist time in total'. More salient, perhaps, was the fact that the diabetes required only routine specialist input and no hospital admission, making the treatment cost-effective when compared with the potential cost of a single hospital admission. The issue of cost-effectiveness has become an increasingly central issue in the design and delivery of psychotherapy services.

Change pathways In the study of 'psychotherapeutic process', work on psychoanalytic therapy has been, traditionally, the most difficult to carry out. However, there are studies worthy of note. For example, Moran and Fonagy (1987) carried out a non-experimental single-case study of a diabetic teenager who received psychoanalysis five times weekly for three and a half years. They investigated the relationship between psychoanalytic themes and glycosuria (the presence of sugar in the client's urine). They found that the working through of psychic conflict predicted an improvement in diabetic control, both in the short and in the long term. Of particular importance to the authors were the findings occurring in the short term where, they argued, other common factors could not be viewed as competing explanations. This view appears to counter research evidence attesting to the potency of common factors irrespective of time. Importantly, however, an aim of this study was to attempt to apply scientific rigour to psychoanalytic processes. As the authors state: 'the present study is viewed as an initial step towards the increased systematization of the treatment of psychoanalytic data and . . . other workers using similar methodologies may be able to explore psychoanalytic hypotheses which eluded the current authors' (Moran and Fonagy, 1987: 370).

In an attempt to ascertain how cognitive therapy works, Fennell (1983) drew together the purported mechanisms of change in cognitive therapy for depression. She asked three questions: how does cognitive therapy achieve its immediate effect?; how does cognitive therapy affect depression over the course of the treatment as a whole?; and how are treatment effects maintained over the longer term? In answer to the first question, Fennell concluded that active thought modification in itself can bring about significant change. In addition, where the intensity or frequency of depressive thinking is reduced, a reduction in severity of depression occurs. In answer to the second question, Fennell concluded that the most powerful strategy for achieving change is a 'close interweaving' of thought-change and behaviour-change. 'Thought-change allows behaviour-change to occur and behaviour-change in turn provides evidence to further counter distorted negative thinking' (1983: 102). The third question is answered by suggesting that long-term improvement will be most effectively achieved with the widest range of clients by training in generalized coping skills rather than by modifying assumptions. This is due to the modification of underlying assumptions being less easy to acquire and more difficult to implement when depressed. In a study of clients diagnosed as anxious, Butler, Gelder, Hibbert, Cullington and Klimes (1987b) attempted to determine the effective components of anxiety management. These researchers found evidence to suggest that treatment-specific components included the control of anxiety-related cognitions and the confronting of anxiety-provoking situations (as compared with the previous strategy of avoidance).

The attempt to discover the therapeutic ingredients responsible for the effectiveness of psychotherapy has been undertaken in a series of studies deriving from detailed analyses of the first Sheffield Psychotherapy Project (Shapiro and Firth, 1987). For example, Stiles, Shapiro and Firth-Cozens (1988) investigated the impacts of exploratory and prescriptive sessions. Impacts refer to the participants' evaluations of the immediate effects of the therapy session (their evaluation of the session, how they feel immediately afterwards, etc.). The authors found these differing therapies to have different impacts. Both therapists and clients rated prescriptive sessions as smoother (i.e. smooth, easy, pleasant, safe) than exploratory sessions. However, while both therapists and clients rated exploratory sessions as rougher (the opposite of smoothness), therapists but not clients rated exploratory sessions as deeper (e.g. deep, valuable, full and special). Taken together, these results show different therapies to have different impacts. When these results are combined with the findings that there is a general equivalence of outcome, the most parsimonious explanation is that equivalence 'occurs' after the differing therapies have had their impact. That is, there are different routes (i.e. processes) to achieving broadly similar outcomes, with the processes differing as a function of the different goals of therapy.

Common factors and integration   The above sections have addressed therapies which are based on assumptions that they comprise specific techniques which can, or will, account for effective change. By contrast, research into common factors has provided a vehicle for arguing that the effective ingredients of therapy tend to be shared factors (i.e. the therapeutic relationship). Murphy, Cramer and Lillie (1984) asked clients to describe curative factors following individual therapy. Findings showed 'advice' and 'talking to someone interested in my problems' to be elicited by more than half the clients. Further, the study found that 'receiving advice' and 'talking with someone who understands' were both moderately correlated with outcome. The relationship of each of these to outcome accounted for approaching 20 per cent of the outcome variance.

In a study of phobic clients, Bennun and Schindler (1988) investigated therapist and client factors operative within behavioural treatments. Ratings on these factors by clients and therapists were positively correlated with outcome, suggesting that interpersonal variables may contribute to treatment outcome. The results showed that the more positive the participants' ratings of each other after the second session, the greater the amount of change achieved at the end of therapy. Bennun and Schindler concluded: 'Researchers and clinicians should not be too preoccupied with technique; favourable interpersonal conditions are also essential for therapeutic change' (1988: 151). In a study of clients' and therapists' views of therapy, Llewelyn (1988) sampled 40 therapist–client dyads participating in psychological therapy in standard British clinical settings. During the course of therapy, the most frequently reported helpful events for clients were 'reassurance' and 'problem evaluation' while at termination 'problem solution' was most frequently rated as helpful. By contrast, therapists rated 'insight' as the most common helpful event both during therapy and at termination. These findings suggest that clients and therapists have quite different perceptions of what is helpful during the course of therapy. Clients appeared to value the common ingredients of reassurance and relief. In contrast, therapists valued both the cognitive and affective insight felt to be attained by their clients during therapy. Of course, if insight 'leads' to problem solution, at least in the sense of preceding it, it may be that clients are focusing on the consequences of their insight while therapists value the more personal and dynamic component of insight itself rather than the action arising from it. In the final analysis, it is to be expected that two differing perspectives on the therapeutic process will provide two differing perceptions.

Ryle has carried out research spanning some two decades into psychotherapy. Underlying Ryle's work is the aim of establishing an understanding of psycho-therapy based within a cognitive framework. This was apparent in his early work using repertory grids. Ryle has developed three important constructs relevant to understanding change (Ryle, 1979): 'dilemmas' (the narrow way in which a client will see the possible alternatives), 'traps' (patterns of behaviour which are based upon and also serve to reinforce negative assumptions about the self), and 'snags' (the avoidance of change due to its effects, real or imagined). Ryle (1980) studied 15 cases in which clients received focused integrated active psychotherapy. The aim was to define therapeutic goals which were specific and individual to clients and yet which referred to underlying cognitive processes as well as to overt symptoms. In general, clients reported improvements both in target complaints as well as in target dilemmas, traps and snags. Results showed that in clients where a change in target dilemmas in the predicted direction occurred, this change was invariably accompanied by a change in the client's cognitive structure as well as in problems targeted at the beginning of therapy. This provided support for Ryle's view that a cognitive framework for understanding psychotherapeutic change is both feasible and informative. Further, Ryle argued that his research counter-balances the more narrow approaches to psychotherapy, stating that attending to deeper cognitive structures enables questions to be answered which have long interested dynamic therapists but which have eluded researchers. It is certainly true that psychotherapy research 'should attend with adequate subtlety . . . the funda-mental but less easily demonstrated changes aimed for' (Ryle, 1980: 481). These findings have led to the formalization of Ryle's cognitive integration of theory and practice (Ryle, 1982), and more recently, to the development of a form of brief therapy termed cognitive-analytic therapy (CAT).

Clinically significant research: A fourth generation Evidence of Genera-tion IV research can be seen as arising from the work employing the 'events' paradigm which has yielded findings that bridge the use of quantitative and qualitative approaches. Central to this approach has been interpersonal process recall (IPR) and its variants, which can be used as the method for obtaining events to carry out comprehensive process analysis (CPA; Elliott, 1989), as can having patients complete the Helpful Aspects of Therapy form (HAT; Llewelyn, 1988).

Llewelyn, Elliott, Shapiro, Hardy and Firth-Cozens (1988) investigated client perceptions of helpful impacts occurring in prescriptive and exploratory therapy. The most common impacts reported by clients as helpful at the session and phase level (i.e. after eight sessions) were (a) 'awareness' (the client getting in touch with feelings which may have been previously warded off) and (b) 'problem solution' (possible ways of coping being worked out or rehearsed in the session). Not surprisingly, 'awareness' was largely attributable to exploratory therapy and 'problem solution' to prescriptive therapy. As Llewelyn et al. (1988) argue, these findings suggest that clients are achieving the major types of therapeutic realization intended by the two different therapies. The least helpful was reported to be 'unwanted thoughts'. This latter finding, while not surprising, raises the point that clients and therapists have differential perspectives, with the clients experiencing 'unwanted thoughts' as negative while therapists may well see these as a necessary stage for the client to progress through towards improved psychological health.

CPA was used to analyse six client-identified significant insight events in cognitive-behavioural (CB) and psychodynamic-interpersonal (PI) therapy (Elliott et al., 1994). Results suggested a general model of insight events which involved a 'meaning bridge' that linked the client's reaction to its context. Elliott et al. (1994) proposed the following five-stage sequential model: (1) contextual priming, (2) novel information, (3) initial distantiated processing, (4) insight, and (5) elaboration. However, the contents of the insight events from the contrasting therapies were very different. CB events were primarily reattributional while PI events involved connection to a conflict theme from a previous session. Two further single-case studies combining the outcome and process components of a possible fourth generation have been drawn from the second Sheffield Psychotherapy Project. The first study tested the assimilation model using a very stringent procedure and found support for successful assimilation of a problematic experience to be associated with a positive outcome (Field et al., 1994). The second study reported a task analysis of a single case in which a rupture and subsequent resolution of the therapeutic alliance was investigated (Agnew et al., 1994). While it may appear that this new generation of research is more grounded in clinical material, and hence more appropriate to the concerns of practitioners, it is probably too early, historically, in this research generation to be able to evaluate fully whether or not it is successful in achieving its aims.

Conclusions

The field of psychotherapy research, despite continued problems of funding, is increasingly grappling with issues which are seen to be more salient to clinicians. This is reflected in the dual thrusts of Generation III (cost-effectiveness and change pathways) as well as in more clinically relevant approaches that might be characteristic of Generation IV. However, it is interesting to note that by far the largest section of this chapter has been taken up by Generation II research, particularly in Britain, which may reflect the currency of 'specificity' at this time. While these generations can be plotted according to a time-scale, it is also clear that in some areas Generation I research (albeit quite sophisticated) is only now being carried out. These generations are more conceptual and thematic and do not appear to have a definitive sell-by date. Indeed, there may well be a cyclical phenomenon in which early issues are revisited by a new research generation or in which some political or social movement gives renewed salience to a paradigm from a prior research generation. In terms of research domains, future research will need to accept that psychotherapy cannot be adequately summarized by either technique or common factors alone. It seems highly probable that while common factors are extremely potent, they are shaped and refined by the moment-to-moment interventions of the therapist.

References

Agnew, R.M., Harper, H., Shapiro, D.A. and Barkham, M. (1994) 'Resolving a challenge to the therapeutic relationship: a single case study', *British Journal of Medical Psychology*, 67: 155–70.

Andrews, G., Guitar, B. and Howie, P. (1980) 'Meta-analysis of the effects of stuttering treatment', *Journal of Speech and Hearing Disorders*, 45: 287–307.

Aveline, M. (1995) 'Assessing the value of brief intervention at the time of assessment for dynamic psychotherapy', in M. Aveline and D.A. Shapiro (eds), *Research Foundations for Psychotherapy Practice*. Chichester: Wiley. pp. 129–49.

Aveline, M. and Shapiro, D.A. (eds) (1995) *Research Foundations for Psychotherapy Practice*. Chichester: Wiley.

Barker, C., Pistrang, N. and Elliott, R. (1994) *Research Methods in Clinical and Counselling Psychology*. Chichester: Wiley.

Barkham, M. (1996) 'Quantitative research on psychotherapeutic interventions: methodological issues and substantive findings across three research generations', in R. Woolfe and W. Dryden (eds), *Handbook of Counselling Psychology*. London: Sage Publications. pp. 23–64.

Barkham, M. and Shapiro, D.A. (1986) 'Counselor verbal response modes and experienced empathy', *Journal of Counseling Psychology*, 33: 3–10.

Barkham, M. and Shapiro, D.A. (1990) 'Brief prescriptive and exploratory therapy for job-related distress: a pilot study', *Counselling Psychology Quarterly*, 3: 133–47.

Barkham, M., Moorey, J. and Davis, G. (1992) 'Psychotherapy in two-plus-one sessions: a pilot field trial', *Behavioural Psychotherapy*, 20: 147–54.

Barkham, M., Rees, A., Shapiro, D.A., Stiles, W.B., Agnew, R.M., Halstead, J., Culverwell, A. and Harrington, V.M.G. (in press) 'Outcomes of time-limited psychotherapy in applied settings: replicating the second Sheffield Psychotherapy Project', *Journal of Consulting and Clinical Psychology*.

Barlow, D.H., Hayes, S.C. and Nelson, R.O. (1984) *The Scientist-practitioner: Research and Accountability in Clinical and Educational Settings*. Oxford: Pergamon Press.

Bennun, I. and Schindler, L. (1988) 'Therapist and patient factors in the behavioural treatment of phobic patients', *British Journal of Clinical Psychology*, 27: 145–51.

Bergin, A.E. and Garfield, S.L. (1994a) 'Overview, trends, and future issues', in A.E. Bergin and S.L. Garfield (eds), *Handbook of Psychotherapy and Behavior Change*, 4th edition. New York: Wiley. pp. 821–30.

Bergin, A.E. and Garfield, S.L. (eds) (1994b) *Handbook of Psychotherapy and Behavior Change*, 4th edition. New York: Wiley.

Bergin, A.E. and Lambert, M.J. (1978) 'The evaluation of therapeutic outcome', in S.L. Garfield and A.E. Bergin (eds), *Handbook of Psychotherapy and Behavior Change*, 2nd edition. New York: Wiley. 139–90.

Birchwood, M. (1992) 'Early intervention in schizophrenia: theoretical background and clinical strategies', *British Journal of Clinical Psychology*, 31: 257–78.

Blackburn, I-M. (1995) 'The relationship between drug and psychotherapy effects', in M. Aveline and D.A. Shapiro (eds), *Research Foundations for Psychotherapy Practice.* Chichester: Wiley. pp. 231–45.

Blackburn, I-M., Bishop, S., Glen, A.I.M., Whalley, L.J. and Christie, J.E. (1981) 'The efficacy of cognitive therapy in depression: a treatment trial using cognitive therapy and pharmacotherapy, each alone and in combination', *British Journal of Psychiatry*, 139: 181–9.

Blackburn, I-M., Eunson, K.M. and Bishop, S. (1986) 'A two-year naturalistic follow-up of depressed patients treated with cognitive therapy, pharmacotherapy and a combination of both', *Journal of Affective Disorders*, 10: 67–75.

Blanes, T. and Raven, P. (1995) 'Psychotherapy of panic disorder', *Current Opinion in Psychiatry*, 8: 167–71.

Blowers, C., Cobb, J. and Mathews, A. (1987) 'Generalized anxiety: a controlled treatment study', *Behaviour Research and Therapy*, 25: 493–502.

Bordin, E.S. (1979) 'The generalizability of the psychoanalytic concept of the working alliance', *Psychotherapy: Theory, Research and Practice*, 16: 252–60.

Brockman, B., Poynton, A., Ryle, A. and Watson, J.P. (1987) 'Effectiveness of time-limited therapy carried out by trainees: comparison of two methods', *British Journal of Psychiatry*, 151: 602–10.

Butler, G., Cullington, A., Hibbert, G., Klimes, I. and Gelder, M. (1987a) 'Anxiety management for persistent generalized anxiety', *British Journal of Psychiatry*, 151: 535–42.

Butler, G., Gelder, M., Hibbert, G., Cullington, A. and Klimes, I. (1987b) 'Anxiety management: developing effective strategies', *Behaviour Research and Therapy*, 25: 517–22.

Butler, G., Fennell, M.J.V., Robson, P. and Gelder, M. (1991) 'Comparison of behavior therapy and cognitive behavior therapy in the treatment of generalized anxiety disorder', *Journal of Consulting and Clinical Psychology*, 59: 167–75.

Cahill, C., Llewelyn, S. and Pearson, C. (1991) 'Treatment of sexual abuse which occurred in childhood: a review', *British Journal of Clinical Psychology*, 30: 1–12.

Chadwick, P. and Lowe, F. (1990) 'The measurement and modification of delusional beliefs', *Journal of Consulting and Clinical Psychology*, 58: 225–32.

Clark, D.M., Salkovskis, P.M., Hackman, A., Middleton, H., Anatasiades, P. and Gelder, M. (1994) 'A comparison of cognitive therapy, applied relaxation and imipramine in the treatment of panic disorder', *British Journal of Psychiatry*, 164: 759–69.

Clarke, S. and Llewelyn, S.P. (1994) 'Personal constructs of survivors of childhood sexual abuse receiving cognitive analytic therapy', *British Journal of Medical Psychology*, 67: 273–89.

Clarkin, J.K., Koenigsberg, H.W., Yeomans, F., Selzer, M., Kernberg, P. and Kernberg, O.F. (1992) 'Psychodynamic psychotherapy of the borderline patient', in J.F. Clarkin, E. Marziali and H. Munroe-Blum (eds), *Borderline Personality Disorder: Clinical and Empirical Perspectives.* New York: Guilford Press.

Crits-Christoph, P., Cooper, A. and Luborsky, L. (1988) 'The accuracy of therapists' interpretations and the outcome of dynamic psychotherapy', *Journal of Consulting and Clinical Psychology*, 56: 490–5.

Davis, J.D., Elliott, R., Davis, M.L., Binns, M., Francis, V.M., Kelman, J.E. and Schroder, T.A. (1987) 'Development of a taxonomy of therapist difficulties: initial report', *British Journal of Medical Psychology*, 60: 109–19.

Denford, J., Schachter, J., Temple, N., Kind, P. and Rosser, R. (1983) 'Selection and outcome in in-patient psychotherapy', *British Journal of Medical Psychology*, 56: 225–43.

DeRubeis, R.J., Evans, M.D., Hollon, S.D., Garvey, M.J., Grove, W.M. and Tuason, V.B. (1990) 'How does cognitive therapy work? Cognitive change and symptom change in cognitive therapy and pharmacotherapy for depression', *Journal of Consulting and Clinical Psychology*, 58: 862–9.

Docherty, J.P. and Streeter, M.J. (1995) 'Advances in psychotherapy research', *Current Opinion in Psychiatry*, 8: 145–9.

Dryden, W. (ed.) (1996) *Research in Counselling and Psychotherapy: Practical Applications*. London: Sage Publications.

Eaton, T.T., Abeles, N. and Gutfreund, M.J. (1988) 'Therapeutic alliance and outcome: impact of treatment length and pretreatment symptomotology', *Psychotherapy*, 25: 536–42.

Elkin, I. (1994) 'The NIMH Treatment of Depression Collaborative Research Study', in A.E. Bergin and S.L. Garfield, (eds), *Handbook of Psychotherapy and Behavior Change*, 4th edition. New York: Wiley. pp. 114–39.

Elkin, I., Shea, M.T., Watkins, J.T., Imber, S.D., Sotsky, S.M., Collins, J.F., Glass, D.R., Pilkonis, P.A., Leber, W.R., Docherty, J.P., Fiester, S.J. and Parloff, M.B. (1989) 'National Institute of Mental Health Treatment of Depression Collaborative Research Program: general effectiveness of treatment', *Archives of General Psychiatry*, 46: 971–82.

Elliott, R. (1984) 'A discovery-oriented approach to significant events in psychotherapy: interpersonal process recall and comprehensive process analysis', in L.N. Rice and L.S. Greenberg (eds), *Patterns of Change*. New York: Guilford Press. pp. 249–86.

Elliott, R. (1989) 'Comprehensive process analysis: understanding the change process in significant therapy events', in M. Packer and R.B. Addison (eds), *Entering the Circle: Hermeneutic Investigation in Psychology*. Albany: State University of New York Press. pp. 165–84.

Elliott, R. and Shapiro, D.A. (1988) 'Brief structured recall: a more efficient method for studying significant therapy events', *British Journal of Medical Psychology*, 61: 141–53.

Elliott, R., Hill, C.E., Stiles, W.B., Friedlander, M.L., Mahrer, A.R. and Margison, F.R. (1987) 'Primary therapist response modes: a comparison of six rating systems', *Journal of Consulting and Clinical Psychology*, 55: 218–23.

Elliott, R., Shapiro, D.A., Firth-Cozens, J., Stiles, W.B., Hardy, G.E., Llewelyn, S.P. and Margison, F.R. (1994) 'Comprehensive process analysis of insight events in cognitive-behavioural and psychodynamic-interpersonal psychotherapies', *Journal of Counseling Psychology*, 41: 449–63.

Evans, M.D., Hollon, S.D., DeRubeis, R.J., Piasecki, J.M., Grove, W.M., Garvey, M.J. and Tuason, V.B. (1992) 'Differential relapse following cognitive therapy and pharmacotherapy for depression', *Archives of General Psychiatry*, 49: 802–8.

Eysenck, H.J. (1952) 'The effects of psychotherapy: an evaluation', *Journal of Consulting Psychology*, 16: 319–24.

Fairburn, C.G., Kirk, J., O'Connor, M. and Cooper, P.J. (1986) 'A comparison of two psychological treatments for bulimia nervosa', *Behaviour Research and Therapy*, 24: 629–43.

Fairburn, C.G., Jones, R., Peveler, R.C., Carr, S.J., Solomon, R.A., O'Connor, M.E., Burton, J. and Hope, R.A. (1991) 'Three psychological treatments for bulimia nervosa: a comparative trial', *Archives of General Psychiatry*, 48: 463–9.

Fairburn, C.G., Jones, R., Peveler, R.C., Hope, R.A. and O'Connor, M. (1993) 'Psychotherapy and bulimia nervosa: the longer-term effects of interpersonal psychotherapy, behavior therapy, and cognitive behavior therapy', *Archives of General Psychiatry*, 50: 419–28.

Fairburn, C.G., Norman, P.A., Welch, S.L., O'Connor, M.E., Doll, H.A. and Peveler, R.C. (1995) 'A prospective study of outcome in bulimia nervosa and the longer-term effects of three psychological treatments', *Archives of General Psychiatry*, 52: 304–12.

Fennell, M.J.V. (1983) 'Cognitive therapy of depression: the mechanisms of change', *Behavioural Psychotherapy*, 11: 97–108.

Fennell, M.J.V. and Teasdale, J.D. (1987) 'Cognitive therapy for depression: individual differences and the process of change', *Cognitive Therapy and Research*, 11: 253–71.

Field, S., Barkham, M., Shapiro, D.A. and Stiles, W.B. (1994) 'Assessment of assimilation in psychotherapy: a quantitative case study of problematic experiences with a significant other', *Journal of Counseling Psychology*, 41: 397–406.

Fonagy, P. (1995) 'Is there an answer to the outcome question? ". . . waiting for Godot"', *Changes*, 13: 168–77.

Fowler, D., Garety, P. and Kuipers, L. (1994) *Cognitive Behavioural Therapy for People with Psychosis: A Clinical Handbook*. Chichester: Wiley.

Freeman, C.P.L., Barry, F., Dunkeld-Turnbull, J. and Henderson, A. (1988) 'Controlled trial of psychotherapy for bulimia nervosa', *British Medical Journal*, 296: 521–5.

Garety, P.A., Kuipers, L., Fowler, D., Chamberlain, F. and Dunn, G. (1994) 'Cognitive behavioural therapy for drug-resistant psychosis', *British Journal of Medical Psychology*, 67: 259–71.

Garfield, S.L. (1990) 'Issues and methods in psychotherapy process research', *Journal of Consulting and Clinical Psychology*, 58: 273–80.

Gask, L. and McGrath, G. (1989) 'Psychotherapy and general practice', *British Journal of Psychiatry*, 154: 445–53.

Goldberg, D.P., Hobson, R.F., Maguire, G.P., Margison, F.R., O'Dowd, T., Osborn, M.S. and Moss, S. (1984) 'The clarification and assessment of a method of psychotherapy', *British Journal of Psychiatry*, 14: 567–75.

Greenberg, L.S. (1986) 'Change process research', *Journal of Consulting and Clinical Psychology*, 54: 4–9.

Greenberg, L.S. (1994) 'The investigation of change: its measurement and explanation', in R.L. Russell (ed.), *Reassessing Psychotherapy Research*. New York: Guilford Press. pp. 114–43.

Hall, A. and Crisp, A.H. (1987) 'Brief psychotherapy in the treatment of anorexia nervosa: outcome at one year', *British Journal of Psychiatry*, 151: 185–91.

Hardy, G.E., Barkham, M., Shapiro, D.A., Stiles, W.B., Rees, A. and Reynolds, S. (1995) 'Impact of Cluster C personality disorders (Avoidant, Dependent, Obsessive-Compulsive) on outcomes of contrasting brief psychotherapies for depression', *Journal of Consulting and Clinical Psychology*, 63: 997–1004.

Healey, A. and Knapp, M. (1995) 'Economic appraisal of psychotherapy', *Mental Health Research Review*, 2: 13–16.

Hill, C.E. (1989) *Therapist Techniques and Client Outcomes: Eight Cases of Brief Psychotherapy*. Newbury Park, CA: Sage Publications.

Hill, C.E. (1990) 'Exploratory in session process research in individual psychotherapy: a review', *Journal of Consulting and Clinical Psychology*, 58: 288–94.

Hill, C.E. (1991) 'Almost everything you ever wanted to know about how to do process research on counseling and psychotherapy but didn't know who to ask', in C.E. Watkins, Jr. and L.J. Schneider (eds), *Research in Counseling*. Hillsdale, NJ: Lawrence Erlbaum Associates. pp. 85–118.

Hill, C.E. and Corbett, M. (1993) 'A perspective on the history of process and outcome research in counseling psychology', *Journal of Counseling Psychology*, 40: 3–24.

Horvath, A.O. and Greenberg, L.S. (1989) 'Development and validation of the Working Alliance Inventory', *Journal of Counseling Psychology*, 36: 223–33.

Horvath, A.O. and Greenberg, L.S. (eds) (1994) *The Working Alliance: Theory, Research, and Practice*. New York: Wiley.

Horvath, A.O. and Symonds, D.B. (1991) 'Relation between working alliance and outcome in psychotherapy', *Journal of Counseling Psychology*, 38: 139–49.

Horvath, A.O., Marx, R.W. and Kamann, A.M. (1990) 'Thinking about thinking in therapy: an examination of clients' understanding of their therapists' intentions', *Journal of Consulting and Clinical Psychology*, 58: 614–21.

Howard, K.I., Kopta, S.M., Krause, M.S. and Orlinsky, D.E. (1986) 'The dose–effect relationship in psychotherapy', *American Psychologist*, 41: 159–64.

Howard, K.I., Lueger, R., Maling, M. and Martinovitch, Z. (1993) 'A phase model of psychotherapy: causal mediation of outcome', *Journal of Consulting and Clinical Psychology*, 61: 678–85.

Iliardi, S.S. and Craighead, W.E. (1994) 'The role of nonspecific factors in cognitive-behavior therapy for depression', *Clinical Psychology: Science and Practice*, 1: 138–56.

Jacobson, N.S. and Truax, P. (1991) 'Clinical significance: a statistical approach to defining meaningful change in psychotherapy research', *Journal of Consulting and Clinical Psychology*, 59: 12–19.

Jacobson, N.S., Follette, W.C. and Revenstorf, D. (1984) 'Psychotherapy outcome research: methods for reporting variability and evaluating clinical significance', *Behavior Therapy*, 15: 336–52.

Jacobson, N.S., Follette, W.C. and Revenstorf, D. (1986) 'Toward a standard definition of clinically significant change', *Behavior Therapy*, 17: 308–11.

Jarrett, R.B. and Nelson, R.O. (1987) 'Mechanisms of change in cognitive therapy of depression', *Behavior Therapy*, 18: 227–41.

Jones, E.E. (1993) 'Special section: single-case research in psychotherapy', *Journal of Consulting and Clinical Psychology*, 61: 371–430.

Kazdin, A.E. (1994) 'Methodology, design, and evaluation in psychotherapy research', in A.E. Bergin and S.L. Garfield (eds), *Handbook of Psychotherapy and Behavior Change*, 4th edition. New York: Wiley. pp. 19–71.

Keller, A. (1984) 'Planned brief psychotherapy in clinical practice', *British Journal of Medical Psychology*, 57: 347–61.

Kiesler, D.J. (1966) 'Basic methodological issues implicit in psychotherapy research', *American Journal of Psychotherapy*, 20: 135–55.

Kingdon, D.G. and Turkington, D. (1991) 'Preliminary report: the use of cognitive behavior therapy with a normalizing rationale in schizophrenia', *Journal of Nervous and Mental Disease*, 179: 207–11.

Klee, M.R., Abeles, N. and Muller, R.T. (1990) 'Therapeutic alliance: early indicators, course, and outcome', *Psychotherapy*, 27: 166–74.

Koenigsberg, H.W. (1995) 'Psychotherapy of patients with borderline personality disorder', *Current Opinion in Psychiatry*, 8: 157–60.

Koss, M.P. and Shiang, J. (1994) 'Research on brief psychotherapy', in A.E. Bergin and S.L. Garfield (eds), *Handbook of Psychotherapy and Behavior Change*, 4th edition. New York: Wiley. pp. 664–700.

Krumboltz, J.D. (1966) *Revolution in Counseling: Implications of Behavioural Science*. Boston, MA: Houghton Mifflin.

Krupnick, J.L. and Pincus, H.A. (1992) 'The cost-effectiveness of psychotherapy: a plan for research', *American Journal of Psychotherapy*, 149: 1295–305.

Lambert, M.J. and Bergin, A.E. (1994) 'The effectiveness of psychotherapy', in A.E. Bergin and S.L. Garfield (eds), *Handbook of Psychotherapy and Behavior Change*, 4th edition. New York: Wiley. pp. 143–89.

Lambert, M.J. and Hill, C.E. (1994) 'Assessing psychotherapy outcomes and processes', in A.E. Bergin and S.L. Garfield (eds), *Handbook of Psychotherapy and Behavior Change*, 4th edition. New York: Wiley. pp. 72–113.

Linehan, M.M. (1993) *Cognitive-behavioral Treatment of Borderline Personality Disorder*. New York: Guilford Press.

Linehan, M.M., Armstrong, H.E., Suarez, A., Allmon, D. and Heard, H.L. (1991) 'Cognitive-behavioral treatment of chronically parasuicidal borderline patients', *Archives of General Psychiatry*, 48: 1060–4.

Linehan, M.M., Heard, H.L. and Armstrong, H.E. (1993) 'Naturalistic follow-up of a behavioral treatment for chronically suicidal borderline patients', *Archives of General Psychiatry*, 50: 971–4.

Llewelyn, S.P. (1988) 'Psychological therapy as viewed by clients and therapists', *British Journal of Clinical Psychology*, 27: 223–8.

Llewelyn, S.P., Elliott, R., Shapiro, D.A., Hardy, G.E. and Firth-Cozens, J. (1988) 'Client perceptions of significant events in prescriptive and exploratory periods of individual therapy', *British Journal of Clinical Psychology*, 27: 105–14.

Luborsky, L., Singer, B. and Luborsky, L. (1975) 'Comparative studies of psychotherapies: is it true that "everyone has won and all must have prizes"?', *Archives of General Psychiatry*, 32: 995–1008.

McGrath, G. and Lawson, K. (1987) 'Assessing the benefits of psychotherapy: the economic approach', *British Journal of Psychiatry*, 150: 65–71.

McLeod, J. (1994) *Doing Counselling Research*. London: Sage Publications.

McLeod, J. (1996) 'Qualitative Research Methods in Counselling Psychology', in R. Woolfe and W. Dryden (eds), *Handbook of Counselling Psychology*. London: Sage Publications. pp. 65–86.

Maguire, G.P., Goldberg, D.P., Hobson, R.F., Margison, F.R., Moss, S. and O'Dowd, T. (1984) 'Evaluating the teaching of a method of psychotherapy', *British Journal of Psychiatry*, 144: 576–80.

Malan, D.H. (1963) *A Study of Brief Psychotherapy*. New York: Plenum Press.

Malan, D.H. (1976) *Toward the Validation of Dynamic Psychotherapy: A Replication*. New York: Plenum Press.

Malan, D.H., Bacal, H.A., Heath, E.S. and Balfour, F.H.G. (1968) 'A study of psychodynamic changes in untreated neurotic patients: I. Improvements that are questionable on dynamic criteria', *British Journal of Psychiatry*, 114: 525–51.

Malan, D.H., Heath, E.S., Bacal, H.A. and Balfour, F.H.G. (1975) 'Psychodynamic changes in untreated neurotic patients: II. Apparently genuine improvements', *Archives of General Psychiatry*, 32: 110–26.

Marks, I.M., Swinson, R.P., Basoglu, M., Kuch, K., Noshirvani, H., O'Sullivan, G., Lelliott, P.T., Kirby, M., McNamee, G., Sengun, S. and Wickwire, K. (1993) 'Alprazolam and exposure alone and combined in panic disorder with agoraphobia', *British Journal of Psychiatry*, 162: 776–8.

Marmar, C.R. (1990) 'Psychotherapy process research: progress, dilemmas, and future directions', *Journal of Consulting and Clinical Psychology*, 58: 265–72.

Mitchell, K., Bozarth, J. and Krauft, J. (1977) 'A reappraisal of the therapeutic effectiveness of accurate empathy, nonpossessive warmth, and genuineness', in A.S. Gurman and A. Razin (eds), *Effective Psychotherapy: A Handbook of Research*. Oxford: Pergamon Press. pp. 482–502.

Moran, G.S. and Fonagy, P. (1987) 'Psychoanalysis and diabetic control: a single case study', *British Journal of Medical Psychology*, 60: 357–72.

Morley, S. (1988) 'Status of cognitive therapies', *Current Opinion in Psychiatry*, 1: 725–8.

Murphy, P.M., Cramer, D. and Lillie, F.J. (1984) 'The relationship between curative factors perceived by patients in their psychotherapy and treatment outcome: an exploratory study', *British Journal of Medical Psychology*, 57: 187–92.

Nietzel, M.T., Russell, R.L., Hemmings, K.A. and Gretter, M.L. (1987) 'Clinical significance of psychotherapy for unipolar depression: a meta-analytic approach to social comparison', *Journal of Consulting and Clinical Psychology*, 55: 156–61.

O'Farrell, M.K., Hill, C.E. and Patton, S. (1986) 'Comparison of two cases of counseling with the same counselor', *Journal of Counseling and Development*, 65: 141–5.

Olfson, M. and Pincus, H.A. (1994a) 'Outpatient psychotherapy in the United States, I: volume, costs, and user characteristics', *American Journal of Psychiatry*, 151: 1281–8.

Olfson, M. and Pincus, H.A. (1994b) 'Outpatient psychotherapy in the United States, II: patterns of utilization', *American Journal of Psychiatry*, 151: 1289–94.

Orlinsky, D.E. and Howard, K.I. (1986) 'Process and outcome in psychotherapy', in S.L. Garfield and A.E. Bergin (eds), *Handbook of Psychotherapy and Behavior Change*, 3rd edition. New York: Wiley. pp. 311–81.

Orlinsky, D.E. and Russell, R.L. (1994) 'Tradition and change in psychotherapy research: notes on the fourth generation', in R.L. Russell (ed.), *Reassessing Psychotherapy Research*. New York: Guilford Press. pp. 185–214.

Orlinsky, D.E., Grawe, K. and Parks, B.K. (1994) 'Process and outcome in psychotherapy – Noch einmal', in A.E. Bergin and S.L. Garfield (eds), *Handbook of Psychotherapy and Behavior Change*, 4th edition. New York: Wiley. pp. 270–376.

Parry, G. (1992) 'Improving psychotherapy services: application of research, audit and evaluation', *British Journal of Clinical Psychology*, 31: 3–19.

Parry, G. and Watts, F.N. (in press) *Behavioural and Mental Health Research: A Handbook of Skills and Methods*, 2nd edition. Hove: Lawrence Erlbaum Associates.

Paul, G. (1967) 'Strategy in outcome research in psychotherapy', *Journal of Consulting Psychology*, 31: 109–18.

Peveler, R.C. and Fairburn, C.G. (1989) 'Anorexia nervosa in association with diabetes mellitus: a cognitive-behavioural approach to treatment', *Behaviour Research and Therapy*, 27: 95–9.

Polkinghorne, D.E. (1994) 'Reaction to special section on qualitative research in counseling process and outcome', *Journal of Counseling Psychology*, 41: 510–12.

Quality Assurance Project (1984) 'Treatment outlines for the management of schizophrenia', *Australian and New Zealand Journal of Psychiatry*, 18: 19–38.

Rice, L.N. and Greenberg, L.S. (eds) (1984) *Patterns of Change*. New York: Guilford Press.

Robinson, L.A., Berman, J.S. and Neimeyer, R.A. (1990) 'Psychotherapy for the treatment of depression: a comprehensive review of controlled outcome research', *Psychological Bulletin*, 108: 30–49.

Rogers, C.R. (1957) 'The necessary and sufficient conditions of therapeutic personality change', *Journal of Consulting Psychology*, 21: 95–103.

Rogers, C.R. and Dymond, R.F. (eds) (1954) *Psychotherapy and Personality Change*. Chicago: University of Chicago Press.

Rogers, C.R., Gendlin, E.T., Kiesler, D.J. and Truax, C.B. (1967) *The Therapeutic Relationship and its Impact: A Study of Psychotherapy with Schizophrenics*. Madison: University of Wisconsin Press.

Roth, A. and Fonagy, P. (in press) *The Search for Effective Psychotherapy: Implications and Limitations of the Research Evidence*. New York: Guilford Press.

Ryle, A. (1979) 'Focus on brief interpretative psychotherapy: dilemmas, traps, and snags as target problems', *British Journal of Psychiatry*, 134: 46–54.

Ryle, A. (1980) 'Some measures of goal attainment in focused integrated active psychotherapy: a study of fifteen cases', *British Journal of Psychiatry*, 137: 475–86.

Ryle, A. (1982) *Psychotherapy: A Cognitive Integration of Theory and Practice*. London: Academic Press.

Ryle, A. (1990) *Cognitive-analytic Therapy: Active Participation in Change*. Chichester: Wiley.

Ryle, A. (1995) 'Transference and counter-transference variations in the course of the cognitive-analytic therapy of two borderline patients: the relation to the diagrammatic reformulation of self-states', *British Journal of Medical Psychology*, 68: 109–124.

Ryle, A. and Beard, H. (1993) 'The integrative effect of reformulation: cognitive analytic therapy with a patient with borderline personality disorder', *British Journal of Medical Psychology*, 66: 249–58.

Safran, J.D., Greenberg, L.S. and Rice, L.N. (1988) 'Integrating psychotherapy research and practice: modeling the change process', *Psychotherapy*, 25: 1–17.

Salkovskis, P.M. (1995) 'Demonstrating specific effects in cognitive and behavioural therapy', in M. Aveline and D.A. Shapiro (eds), *Research Foundations for Psychotherapy Research*. Chichester: Wiley. pp. 191–228.

Scott, J. (1995) 'Review of treatments for depression', *British Journal of Psychiatry*, 167: 289–92.

Sexton, T.L. and Whiston, S.C. (1994) 'The status of the counseling relationship: an empirical review, theoretical implications, and research directions', *The Counseling Psychologist*, 22: 6–78.

Shapiro, D.A. (1969) 'Empathy, warmth and genuineness in psychotherapy', *British Journal of Social and Clinical Psychology*, 8: 350–61.

Shapiro, D.A. (1970) 'The rating of psychotherapeutic empathy: a preliminary study', *British Journal of Social and Clinical Psychology*, 9: 148–51.

Shapiro, D.A. (1973) 'Naive British judgements of therapeutic conditions', *British Journal of Social and Clinical Psychology*, 12: 289–94.

Shapiro, D.A. (1976) 'The effects of therapeutic conditions: positive results revisited', *British Journal of Medical Psychology*, 49: 315–23.

Shapiro, D.A. and Firth, J.A. (1987) 'Prescriptive vs. exploratory psychotherapy: outcomes of the Sheffield Psychotherapy Project', *British Journal of Psychiatry*, 151: 790–9.

Shapiro, D.A. and Shapiro, D. (1982) 'Meta-analysis of comparative therapy outcome studies: a replication and refinement', *Psychological Bulletin*, 92: 581–604.

Shapiro, D.A., Barkham, M., Hardy, G.E., Morrison, L.A., Reynolds, S., Startup, M. and Harper, H. (1991) 'Sheffield Psychotherapy Research Program', in L.E. Beutler (ed.), *Psychotherapy Research Programs: An International Review of Programmatic Studies*. Washington, DC: Society for Psychotherapy Research/American Psychological Association.

Shapiro, D.A., Barkham, M., Reynolds, S., Hardy, G.E. and Stiles, W.B. (1992) 'Prescriptive and exploratory psychotherapies: toward an integration based on the assimilation model', *Journal of Psychotherapy Integration*, 2: 253–72.

Shapiro, D.A., Barkham, M., Rees, A., Hardy, G.E., Reynolds, S. and Startup, M. (1994) 'Effects of treatment duration and severity of depression on the effectiveness of cognitive-behavioral and psychodynamic-interpersonal psychotherapy', *Journal of Consulting and Clinical Psychology*, 62: 522–34.

Shapiro, D.A., Rees, A., Barkham, M., Hardy, G.E., Reynolds, S. and Startup, M. (1995) 'Effects of treatment duration and severity of depression on the maintenance of gains following cognitive-behavioral and psychodynamic-interpersonal psychotherapy', *Journal of Consulting and Clinical Psychology*, 63: 378–87.

Shefler, G., Dasberg, H. and Ben-Shakhar, G. (1995) 'A randomised controlled outcome and follow-up study of Mann's time-limited psychotherapy', *Journal of Consulting and Clinical Psychology*, 63: 585–93.

Silberschatz, G. and Curtis, J.T. (1986) 'Clinical implications of research on brief dynamic psychotherapy: 2. How the therapist helps or hinders therapeutic progress', *Psychoanalytic Psychology*, 3: 27–37.

Sloane, R.B., Staples, R.F., Cristol, A.H., Yorkston, N.J. and Whipple, K. (1975) *Psychotherapy versus Behavior Therapy*. Cambridge, MA: Harvard University Press.

Smith, M.L. and Glass, G.V. (1977) 'Meta-analysis of psychotherapy outcome studies', *American Psychologist*, 32: 752–60.

Smith, M.L., Glass, G.V. and Miller, T.I. (1980) *The Benefits of Psychotherapy*. Baltimore, MD: Johns Hopkins University Press.

Startup, M. and Shapiro, D.A. (1993) 'Therapist treatment fidelity in prescriptive vs. exploratory psychotherapy', *British Journal of Clinical Psychology*, 32: 443–56.

Steinbrueck, S.M., Maxwell, S.E. and Howard, G.S. (1983) 'A meta-analysis of psychotherapy and drug therapy in the treatment of unipolar depression with adults', *Journal of Consulting and Clinical Psychology*, 51: 856–63.

Stiles, W.B. and Shapiro, D.A. (1989) 'Abuse of the drug metaphor in psychotherapy process-outcome research', *Clinical Psychology Review*, 9: 521–43.

Stiles, W.B., Shapiro, D.A. and Elliott, R. (1986) '"Are all psychotherapies equivalent?"', *American Psychologist*, 41: 165–80.

Stiles, W.B., Shapiro, D.A. and Firth-Cozens, J.A. (1988) 'Do sessions of different treatments have different impacts?', *Journal of Counseling Psychology*, 35: 391–6.

Stiles, W.B., Elliott, R., Llewelyn, S.P., Firth-Cozens, J.A., Margison, F.R., Shapiro, D.A. and Hardy, G.E. (1990) 'Assimilation of problematic experiences by clients in psychotherapy', *Psychotherapy*, 27: 411–20.

Stiles, W.B., Shapiro, D.A. and Harper, H. (1994) 'Finding the way from process to outcome: blind alleys and unmarked trails', in R.L. Russell (ed.), *Reassessing Psychotherapy Research*. New York: Guilford Press. pp. 36–64.

Strupp, H.H. (1980a) 'Success and failure in time-limited psychotherapy. A systematic comparison of two cases: Comparison 1', *Archives of General Psychiatry*, 37: 595–604.

Strupp, H.H. (1980b) 'Success and failure in time-limited psychotherapy. A systematic comparison of two cases: Comparison 2', *Archives of General Psychiatry*, 37: 708–16.

Strupp, H.H. (1980c) 'Success and failure in time-limited psychotherapy. With special reference to the performance of a lay counselor', *Archives of General Psychiatry*, 37: 831–41.

Strupp, H.H. (1980d) 'Success and failure in time-limited psychotherapy. Further evidence (Comparison 4)', *Archives of General Psychiatry*, 37: 947–54.

Tarrier, N., Harwood, S., Yusopoff, L., Beckett, R. and Baker, A. (1990) 'Coping strategy enhancement (CSE): a method of treating residual schizophrenic symptoms', *Behavioural Psychotherapy*, 18: 283–93.

Tarrier, N., Beckett, R., Harwood, S., Baker, A., Yusopoff, L. and Ugarteburu, I. (1993) 'A trial of two cognitive behavioural methods of treating drug-resistant residual psychotic symptoms in schizophrenic patients: I Outcome', *British Journal of Psychiatry*, 162: 524–32.

Taube, C.A., Burns, B.J. and Kessler, L. (1984) 'Patients of psychiatrists and psychologists in office-based practice: 1980', *American Psychologist*, 39: 1435–7.

Teasdale, J.D. (1985) 'Psychological treatments for depression: how do they work?', *Behaviour Research and Therapy*, 23: 157–65.

Teasdale, J.D., Fennell, M.J.V., Hibbert, G.A. and Amies, P.L. (1984) 'Cognitive therapy for major depressive disorder in primary care', *British Journal of Psychiatry*, 144: 400–6.

Truax, C.B. and Mitchell, K.M. (1971) 'Research on certain therapist interpersonal skills in relation to process and outcome', in A.E. Bergin and S.L. Garfield (eds), *Handbook of Psychotherapy and Behavior Change*. New York: Wiley. pp. 299–344.

US DHHS (US Department of Health and Human Sciences) (1993) *Depression in Primary Care: Treatment of Major Depression*. Depression Guideline Panel. Rockville: AHCPR Publications. pp. 71–123.

Whiston, S.C. and Sexton, T.L. (1993) 'An overview of psychotherapy outcome research: implications for practice', *Professional Psychology: Research and Practice*, 24: 43–51.

Whitehorn, J.C. and Betz, B. (1954) 'A study of psychotherapeutic relationships between physicians and schizophrenic patients', *American Journal of Psychiatry*, 3: 321–31.

Wolfe, B. and Goldfried, M.R. (1988) 'Research on psychotherapy integration: recommendation and conclusions from an NIMH workshop', *Journal of Consulting and Clinical Psychology*, 56: 448–51.

15

The Training and Supervision of Individual Therapists

Mark Aveline

Overview

The purpose of training in psychotherapy is to facilitate the exercise of natural abilities and acquired skills to' best effect. This statement, which is based on my experience as a practitioner and trainer in psychotherapy in the National Health Service over 21 years, asserts two propositions, each of which is central to this chapter. First, that therapists bring to their work a greater or lesser degree of natural talent for psychotherapy.[1] Two subsidiary propositions are that the possession of talent is an essential foundation on which expertise can be built in training and that the talent is not a unitary predisposition; it may be for one of the individual therapies or for some other form such as group or family therapy. Second, psychotherapy is a purposeful activity in which trainees and trainers share a professional and ethical commitment to evaluate and refine their work. Thoughtful therapists will ask themselves three questions again and again: (1) *what in the therapy and this person's life actually helped the patient?* (2) *could the end have been achieved more expeditiously?* and (3) *was anything done that was to the patient's ultimate detriment?*

In this chapter, it is impossible to do justice to the fine detail of training in each of the many forms of individual therapy. Instead, attention is drawn to important issues in each area of training. After the introduction, I present a checklist of training objectives, then discuss motivating factors in therapists and selection for training before considering the sometimes neglected but universally important dimensions of counter-transference and the abuse of power. The three cardinal elements of theoretical learning, supervised clinical work, and personal therapy are discussed in turn. The move towards National Vocational Qualifications (NVQs), the registration of psychotherapists and the need for continued education is then considered. A section on supportive therapy concludes the review.

Introduction

'In what is called "individual psychotherapy", two people meet and talk to each other with the intention and hope that one will learn to live more fruitfully.' This deceptively simple statement by Lomas encompasses the central dimensions in psychotherapy practice – meeting, talking (I prefer the form 'talking with' rather than 'talking to') in a hopeful spirit and the purposeful intention of achieving more fruitful living in the patient's everyday life (Lomas, 1981: 5). The statement sets out in ordinary language the parameters of a kind of psychotherapy with which I can identify, a rather ordinary encounter between two people but one of exceptional promise. However, as is so often the case, the results of our intentions frequently do not measure up to our hopes. Training is intended to enhance the competence of the therapist but in itself is no guarantee of success. Please note that types of training which emphasize the apparent substantial difference in form between therapies may obscure underlying, powerful similarities.

Luborsky et al. (1975) in a survey of the effectiveness of different approaches to psychotherapy subtitled *Is it true that 'Everyone has won and all must have prizes'?* call attention to the fact that in research studies all the psychotherapies are similarly effective and none pre-eminent, a sobering conclusion for partisans of any school or faction. In other words, what effective therapies across schools have in common is more important than what divides them, a theme I return to later. This is not to say that certain therapies are not particularly suitable for a given person or problem, nor that a therapist will not function especially well in the approach that she finds most congenial. What are the best applications of the different therapies is a matter for research, while the natural affinity of a trainee with particular approaches is a key aspect to be identified in training.

The findings of Luborsky and other researchers certainly have not stilled debate about who is or is not a psychotherapist or which theoretical system if any approximates most closely to the truth of being human. Or can one variant, for example psychoanalysis and psychoanalytic psychotherapy which share so many features, consistently and with enhanced therapeutic effect be distinguished from the other? Sandler (1988), a distinguished psychoanalyst, thinks not. In such debates, questions of power, prestige and authenticity lurk in the shadows and threaten to upstage the essential question of *how appropriate and effective are the approaches with which patients and what problems.* When, as all too often, the tribes in the psychotherapy nation go to war with one another, they yield to the temptation of vested interest in promoting ascendancy over competitors and, within their own ranks, in stilling dissident voices; in such struggles, the pursuit of truth may be neglected. They neglect the communality of interest on the larger stage of developing a profession of psychotherapy where effective practice may be refined through the twin, opposite processes of differentiation and integration. In selecting a training programme, trainees need to bear these points in mind.

Given the wide range of approaches that may be gathered under the generic title of individual psychotherapy, and the partisanship that goes with differences that are often more apparent than real, I am mindful of the hazard of this chapter being dismissed by adherents of one approach on the grounds of irrelevance to their practice, ignorance of what they do or believe, and partiality to my own bias. In contrast, my intention is to address important issues for trainees and trainers which I hope will be heard across the spectrum. But first I must state what is central to my approach. I will be declaring my bias and setting out a synthesis, derived from my experience as a therapist, with which readers may compare their own conclusions (Aveline, 1979).

Psychotherapy attends both to the vital feelings of hope, despair, envy, hate, self-doubt, love and loss that exist between humans and to the repeated pattern of relationships that a person forms; in particular, to those aspects of the patterns for which that person has responsibility and over which they can come to exercise choice. As a therapist, I encourage my patient to take personally significant action in the form of new ways of relating, both in the consulting room and in his relationships outside, which, once succeeded in, will begin to rewrite the cramped fiction of his life. This therapeutic action challenges the determining myths that a person has learned or evolved to explain his actions; commonly, these myths are restrictive and self-limiting. I work with the psychological view that a person takes of himself, his situation and the possibilities open to him; essentially, this is the view that has been taken of him by important others and that he has taken of himself in the past, and it will go on being the determining view unless some corrective emotional experience occurs. The view that the person takes of himself is illuminated by the relationship patterns that form between the patient and the people in his life, including me; jointly, the patient and I examine the meaning of the patterns. Importantly, it is change in the external world of the patient, rather than inferred intrapsychic change, against which I judge the success of our mutual endeavour. Lest this sound too demanding, let me balance the statement by the recognition that many patients with deep problems of self-doubt and a negative world view need sustained care in order to gather the courage to change.

On one level, I make no distinction between enlightened analytic and cognitive-behavioural theory and practice that both recognizes and utilizes the therapeutic factors they have in common; both offer encouragement, the one covertly, the other overtly. In the former, intrapsychic terrors are faced and the treatment proceeds by analogy; if a new end to the old sad story can be written in the relationship with the therapist, the same new chapter can be written in the natural relationships outside the consulting room. In the latter, direct action is taken, perhaps after a period of rehearsal, often undertaken with the therapist. What characterizes good psychotherapy of any sort is a sustained, affirmative stance on the part of an imaginative, seasoned therapist who respects and does not exploit (Schafer, 1983). I hope that my relationship with the patient is both passionate and ethical, for both these elements are necessary if personal change is to occur. In the interplay of therapy, I influence and am influenced by what passes between us. It is the other person's journey in life, but it is a journey for us both and one in which I may expect to change as well as the patient. It is a journey and not an aimless ramble: though the ultimate destination may be unknown, the way-stations are known by the therapist and aimed for; the therapist has expertise in guiding the other through terrain which is new to them. It is, also, a journey in which I do not expect to be the guide for the whole way; someone may enter therapy for a while, gain what they require to get their life moving, go away to try their modified approach and return later if they need; in this, I am a minimalist. I do not aim, even if it were possible as early psychoanalysts hoped, to exhaust through the psychotherapy the patient's potential for neurosis or, necessarily, to locate the locus of change wholly in the relationship with me.

I have presented my conclusions in summary form. The constraint of space means that I cannot spell out the significance of each point, but I offer these conclusions as a personal point of reference for the following discussion of the elements in training. Let us begin by recognizing the formidable task that awaits the trainee therapist.

What the individual therapist has to learn

Despite the plethora of texts and manualized procedures whose clinical purpose is to lend assistance to both experienced and novice therapists, the practice of psychotherapy is challenging in its elusive complexity, ambiguity and frustratingly slow pace of change. Even in the more procedure-dominated cognitive and behavioural therapies, the ambiguous, uncertain reality of practice is disconcerting to those (and this includes many with medical, nursing and psychology backgrounds) who are used to the predictable clarity in the physical sciences of structure, intervention and consistent outcome. In physical science at a macro-level, lineality is the rule. In psychotherapy, chaos theory is a more apt model; change being the product of a complex and uncertain interaction between the form and severity of problems, the patient's personality, developmental stage and motivation, the appropriateness, intrinsic power and dose of the therapy, the skill, motivation and healing capacity of the psychotherapist, the malleability of the life situation and the operation of chance and good or ill-fortune.

Furthermore, what happens between therapist and patient is complicated by the often unrecognized involvement of the therapist during therapy in the patient's self-limiting fiction and by the arousal in the therapist of unresolved personal conflicts; this phenomenon of transference and counter-transference has the central place in the analytic therapies (and, of course, is fostered by their techniques) but to a greater or lesser extent is also part of any human interaction and, certainly, of any therapy where the participants have a close relationship. Yet, I trust, for readers of this volume, the struggle to become proficient therapists is worth while, not least because psychotherapy is a fundamentally important activity in our technological and materialistic age: it attends to individual and shared experience and meaning and it attests to the ability of people to support and help each other. But this practical discipline and creative art is not easily learned.

What a therapist has to learn depends on the level and intensity at which she has to practise, be it at the level of beginner gaining a limited appreciation of what psychotherapy is or of qualified professional who as a generalist needs psycho-therapeutic skills as part of her work, or of career psychotherapist and future trainer of therapists. The caveat is that, at all levels, the same lessons are repeated again and again. The individual therapies vary substantially in theory, focus and technique and there is much to be learned. However, the trainee who quite appropriately immerses herself in one approach risks being ignorant of others. The alternative, when faced with such variety, is to attempt to learn simultaneously two dissonant approaches which may cause trainee confusion and a degree of trainer alienation. Yet not to look widely at the therapy spectrum during the formative period of training is to risk premature closure in thinking and mental ossification, an eventuality to be guarded against.

From the point of view of the trainee therapist, the objectives in training can be stated as follows:

General
- to make progress towards the optimal use of natural ability and acquired skills;

- to identify the type(s) of therapy and range of patient problem and personality with which the therapist can work effectively.

Specific (in approximate order of priority)
- to learn to listen to what is said and not said by patients and to develop with them shared languages of personal meaning;
- to develop the capacity to keep in contact with patients in their pain and anger-filled explorations;
- in interaction with patients, to learn to move between participation and observation; to get a sense of when and when not to intervene;
- to gain a coherent conceptual frame within which to understand what happens and is intended to happen in therapy;
- to study human development, the process of learning, and the functioning of naturally occurring personal relationships between friends, couples and in families and the artificial, constructed relationships in psychotherapy where strangers are brought together;
- to understand and bring to bear both the therapeutic factors that types of therapy have in common (these, which are often referred to as non-specific factors, are detailed in the section on theoretical learning) and those that are approach specific;
- to gain confidence in the practice of the preferred type of therapy; to make full use of the therapist's emotional responses, theoretical constructs and techniques in resolving the patients' problems;
- to increase the therapist's level of self-awareness and to work towards the resolution of personal conflict which may interfere with the process of therapy;
- to come to know personal limitations and be able to obtain and use supervision;
- to know the features of major psychiatric illness and the indications and contra-indications for psychotropic medication;
- to make valid diagnostic assessments psychiatrically, psychologically and dynamically (Malan, 1995: Chs 18–23);
- to be sufficiently knowledgeable about other types of therapy so as to match therapy to patient need by referring on;
- to consider ethical dilemmas and internalize high ethical standards;
- to cultivate humility, compassion and modesty as well as a proper degree of self-confidence;
- to be familiar with the chosen theoretical system and aware of its areas of greatest utility and its limitations; to appreciate the significance of cultural and social factors and to adjust therapy accordingly;
- to evaluate critically what is enduring truth and what is mere habit or unsubstantiated dogma in the practice of psychotherapy through the experience of clinical practice, being supervised, and studying the research literature;
- to be able to evaluate outcome;
- to set standards of practice and systematically evaluate these by clinical audit;
- to understand the implications of the employment context in which practice is to occur (philosophical, political, institutional, economic, and contractual);

- to become committed to continuous professional development;
- at the level of career psychotherapist, to acquire that professional identity.

For the trainer, the objectives are:

- to assess accurately both the stage at which trainees are in their development as therapists and their strengths and weaknesses. At different stages, this may involve the normative functions of selection for training and evaluation for graduation. (In educational terms, 'normative' refers to entry/exit, pass/fail criteria, whereas 'formative' refers to non-examined elements that enrich the educational experience of training);
- to help trainees secure the formative learning experiences which will clarify and develop their natural affinity with particular types of therapy and problem;
- to hold the balance of interest between the learning needs of trainee therapists and the clinical needs of their patients until such time as the trainee therapists can do this for themselves.

This long list is not intended to be intimidating but it does serve to underline the seriousness of embarking on training to be a therapist. It provides a framework with which to assess training needs, progress and the suitability of the training programme for a particular trainee.

Training has no end-point or single path. An individual's training over time is the result of personal and occupational choices. The choices may mark a progression from the expertise needed by a generalist with an interest in the subject to that required by a career psychotherapist, and within psychotherapy from one type to another as the trainee's interest changes. Further training will be necessary to update the therapist with advances in practice and to maintain existing expertise at a good level. Just as therapy should meet the needs of the patient, so should training meet the requirements of the therapist's practice, those that stem both from the type of therapy and from the work setting. What a therapist working in brief therapy in a clinic with a long waiting list needs to know is very different from one specializing in long-term therapy in independent practice who only takes on new work when she has a vacancy.

The reader at this point may be eager to plunge into the detail of the three cardinal elements of training, namely theoretical learning, supervised clinical work, and personal therapy. To accede to this wish would be premature. It would collude with the view that proficiency in psychotherapy is a simple, acquired technical skill. Instead, I argue that the wish to train in psychotherapy arises from events in the trainee's personal history and their consequent effect on character structure. The reflective therapist will want to take stock of what she brings from her inheritance and experience of life to this work before she becomes deeply committed to it. Two things are certain. In the work of psychotherapy, whatever the type, the personal, unique reactions of the therapist will complicate and illuminate the relationship that she and the patient have, and being a therapist will expose her to the temptation of abusing that powerful position. What I mean by these strong statements is spelt out in the next four sections which deal with motivating factors in therapists, selection for training, counter-transference and the abuse of power.

Motivating factors in the therapist

The trainee therapist has been long in the making before he or she formally enters training. Family circumstance, life events, gender, race and culture combine with inherited predisposition to form a unique individual who may or may not be suited to the practice of some or all of the psychotherapies. Each potential therapist will be special in their values, expectations and sensitivities; each will have natural ability in different measure for the work and a natural affinity with particular types of therapy and patient problems.

Being a psychotherapist offers many satisfactions: the opportunity to develop a unique personal style of practice with a substantial degree of professional independence, to share at close hand an endless variety of human activities far beyond that generally encountered in the therapist's own life, to satisfy the desire to help others, to be intellectually stimulated, to gain in emotional growth . . . and to have prestige and be paid! (Bugental, 1964; Burton, 1975; Greben, 1975; Farber and Heifetz, 1981; Farber, 1983).

Guy (1987) distinguishes between functional and dysfunctional motivators. In fact, his items encompass both motivating factors and functional attributes of effective therapists. Functional motivators include a natural interest in people, the ability to listen and talk, the psychological-mindedness of being disposed to enter empathically into the world of meaning and motivation of others, and the capacities of facilitating and tolerating the expression of feelings, being emotionally insightful, introspective and capable of self-denial, as well as being tolerant of ambiguity and intimacy and capable of warmth, caring and laughter (see also Greben's six functional attributes in the next section).

Dysfunctional motivators draw people to the role of therapist and may prove to be functional, but when present to excess subvert the process for the therapist's own ends. There is a well-established tradition in dynamic psychotherapy, clearly articulated by Jung, that only the wounded healer can heal. Thus, Storr writes: 'Psychotherapists often have some personal knowledge of what it is like to feel insulated and injured, a kind of knowledge which they might rather be without, but which actually extends the range of their compassion' (1979: 173). Guy (1987) lists six dysfunctional motivators, the first of which is the most common:

1. emotional distress: therapists may seek – and gain – self-healing through their work; the crucial question is one of magnitude. Some acquaintance with emotional pain is essential; an over-preoccupation with unresolved personal needs hinders the therapist from giving full attention to the patient;
2. vicarious coping as a lifestyle which imparts a voyeuristic quality to the therapy relationship;
3. conducting psychotherapy as a means of compensating for an inner sense of loneliness and isolation; this is self-defeating as it is life lived at one remove;
4. fulfilling the desire for power and fostering a false sense of omnipotence and omniscience (Marmor, 1953; Guggenbuhl-Craig, 1979);
5. a messianic need to provide succour; one positive aspect of psychotherapy is that it is an acceptable way for a person to show their love and tenderness, but this becomes dysfunctional when it is carried to excess;

6 psychotherapy as a relatively safe way of expressing underlying rebellious feelings in the therapist through getting the patient to act them out.

These dysfunctional motivators give rise to counter-transference problems which are considered later (counter-transference means distortions derived from unresolved conflicts in the therapist's life which she unconsciously introduces into the therapy relationship).

The prevalence of dysfunctional motivators among psychotherapists is not known. In a major survey of 4,000 American psychotherapists (Henry, 1977), most reported good relationships with their families though 39 per cent said that their parents' marriage was not good. Childhood separations, deaths and incidence of mental illness were similar to that of other college-educated populations. These global statistics doubtless conceal much individual variation. Thus Storr's (1979) impression may be true that many therapists (and here he means dynamically oriented therapists) have had depressed mothers to whose feelings they may have developed a special sensitivity, together with an urge not to upset or distress; their childhood experiences may well have prompted them to seek out in adult life the role of therapist. In Kleinian terminology, the need to make reparation will be great in these therapists; they may be especially adept at making contact with timid and fearful patients. There is some evidence that within the occupation of psychotherapy a history of personal conflicts and a greater experience of mental illness in the family of origin inclines practitioners more towards dynamic rather than behavioural orientations (Rosin and Knudson, 1986). I know of no research that distinguishes between the personal backgrounds of therapists choosing to work in individual therapy and those choosing family and group therapy.

These factors and attributes constitute the natural ability for which selection has to be made and which is built on in training.

The selection of therapists for training

Trainers have a dual responsibility in selecting their trainees: the responsibility to help that person avoid taking on work for which she is not suitable; and the responsibility to the patients – from whom the trainee will learn – to ensure that they have optimal care.

Selection is a matter for both the trainee and the trainer: the trainee will want to test out what is on offer and the trainer will test the trainee's readiness for each level of training. Introductory trainings offer the trainee, through workshops and brief courses, the opportunity to try different types of therapy and to discover the ones for which she has a natural affinity. Little or no attempt is made to select at this level. Another formative route into formal psychotherapy training is to be supervised by therapists whose style and orientation vary and, either before or as a supplement to this, to be in personal therapy; both experiences form and clarify aptitude. With advancing level, selection procedures become correspondingly complex. Commonly, for analytic training, candidates will have to complete an autobiographical questionnaire and undergo two extended interviews with different assessors, one more factual and the other explorative in the analytic style; the results will be considered by a panel of assessors so as to reduce individual bias (a detailed explication of the process and criteria used in one institute can be found in Fleming, 1987: Chs 3 and 7). Later, the candidate's progress will have to be approved before entry to each further stage of training is allowed. In the case of psychoanalysis, this would commence with the candidate beginning their five times a week training therapy, being in therapy for at least a year, and having to secure satisfactory reports from their therapist before proceeding to the next stage of participating in theoretical seminars, and, then at a later date, embarking on their training cases, a meticulous and extended procedure.

Sadly, the correlation between training and effectiveness as a therapist is low (Auerbach and Johnson, 1977); this finding may reflect deficiencies in research methodology but is also a function of the overwhelming importance in promoting personal change of pre-existing personality factors such as decency, a respectful, empathic concern with others, neutrality, persistence and optimism. Reflecting on my own experience as a therapist and trainer, a therapist's effectiveness over the years of her career often seems to follow a U-curve and is a function of different attributes. Early on, patients benefit especially from the therapist's energy and enthusiasm and later from her acquired wisdom and skill as a therapist (Orlinsky and Howard, 1980). In the middle phase, as therapists become more self-conscious and aware of the complexity of the subject, performance may decline temporarily. Trainees should not feel dismayed by feeling de-skilled when they enter the next level of training, and may with justice on their side ask the training organizers what help they propose to provide in overcoming this common reaction.

The above should not be taken to imply that putting effort into selection is worthless. Personality is all-important. 'The greatest technical skill can offer no substitute for nor will obviate the pre-eminent need for integrity, honesty, and dedication on the part of the therapist' (Strupp, 1960). As a selector, I look for the functional motivators listed by Guy (1987), and also the six qualities identified by Greben (1984): empathic concern, respectfulness, realistic hopefulness, self-aware-ness, reliability and strength of character. These are the qualities that are necessary if the therapist is to win the patient's trust; they give him the sense of being tended to and valued. Women often seem to have these qualities in greater abundance than men. It must be stressed that no one is perfect: what is required for this work is a sufficiency of these qualities. In addition, I look for two markers of maturity in life: that the trainee has struggled with some personal emotional conflict and achieved a degree of resolution, and that she has enjoyed and sustained over years a loving, intimate relationship. The first may bring in its wake humility and compassion, the second an active commitment to and capacity for good relation-ships, so well summed up in Fairbairn's concept of mature dependence (Fairbairn, 1954). I am wary of aspiring therapists who have a scornful, rejecting or persecu-tory cast to their nature or who are not emotionally generous in their interaction.

My impression is that therapists who prefer to work in individual therapy rather than in, for example, group therapy have a number of identifying characteristics. They seem to have a greater interest in the vertical or historical axis of *there-and-then* exploration into the childhood origins of adult problems and their re-creation within the therapy relationship, as opposed to the horizontal axis of *here-and-now* interactions which is central to the focus of the group therapist (and increasingly of the modern psychodynamic therapist). They are more interested in fantasy, prefer to take a passive role and like the immediacy of the one-to-one relationship and the scope to work in depth. These impressions may help the trainee in the choice of which type of therapy to train in, though other factors will also be influential. The high patient demand for individual therapy and its greater economic viability in private practice, especially with the advent of powerful, focal therapy (Ryle, 1990), may powerfully reinforce natural affinity for the dynamic way of working.

A controversial issue concerns whether or not therapist should have as a pre-requisite for being a psychotherapist a qualification in one of the core health care professions; these are generally taken to be medicine, psychology and social work, all degree occupations, but should also include nursing (now more often a degree occupation) and occupational therapy and, perhaps, the new categories of art and drama therapy. Talent as a psychotherapist is not the exclusive preserve of any profession. The development in the NHS of the new *ad hoc* grade of Adult Psychotherapist, open to all with aptitude and training, testifies to the truth of this proposition. However, the possession of a core qualification indicates that the trainee has a certain level of intelligence and ensures familiarity with the symp-toms and signs of major psychiatric illness. It will also have offered the trainee the opportunity to internalize high ethical standards and, through membership of a professional group, ensures that she is subject to disciplinary procedures which help maintain good practice. Qualifications in literature, philosophy and religion are relevant but trainees with these backgrounds will need special training in the features of major psychiatric illness and in what may be gained from pharma-cological treatment, especially if they intend to practise independently. I return to this question in the sections on theoretical learning, supervised clinical practice, and registration.

I have written at some length about the personal qualities and qualifications that a trainee therapist brings to the work. In order to bring out two important consequences that stem from the intensity of the closed, asymmetrical personal relationship between patient and therapist that lies at the heart of individual therapy, the next two sections deal with the importance of counter-transference reactions and the temptation for the therapist to abuse her power in all types of psychotherapy.

Counter-transference

Unconsciously mediated transference and counter-transference reactions inevitably feature in any relationship, and especially in the intimate, prolonged relationship of individual therapy. Even in the symptom-oriented, individual cognitive and behaviour therapies, these powerful distortions are present. However, many cognitive-behavioural training programmes pay scant attention to these processes, a deficiency shared by some more psychodynamically based individual therapies. Trainees are advised to check that attention is given in the training to this aspect of the therapy relationship.

Individual therapists need to be as aware as possible of how these distorting processes are operating, their possible meaning and the implications for the work.

Let us illustrate this with the consequence of a positive transference reaction in two types of individual therapy, a supportive and a behavioural therapy, and the way that understanding the process could enrich practice. In a positive transference, the patient transfers on to the therapist idealized, dependent feelings which commonly derive from the relationship with his parents but which may also signify an unresolved, intrapsychic conflict and a dependent style in relationships. In a supportive psychotherapy, deep probing of mental defences and intrapsychic conflicts is by definition avoided. The consequence of understanding what was happening in the transference, and why, would be to bear in mind the hazard of fostering unnecessary dependence and to make use of the transference in mobilizing the patient's sense of hope and expectation of benefit from the therapy, rather than addressing and trying to resolve it. In other words, the aim is maintainance of best function, not development. In a behavioural therapy, the positive transference might manifest itself in a passive compliance which on a developmental level would signify that the patient has not mastered the maturational task of separation and individuation. The therapist, understanding the meaning of the transference, would probably not address it on the level of its historical significance but would circumvent it by encouraging the patient to take the initiative in devising behavioural tasks. Of course in the analytic therapies, directly examining these reactions and counter-reactions is the focus of the work.

The term counter-transference is used in two senses; it may refer (a) to feelings that are the counterpart of the patient's feelings and (b) to feelings that are counteractions to the patient's transference (Greenson, 1967). Counterpart feelings are part of empathy; they provide valuable information about the other, as when the therapist feels in herself the disowned, hidden sadness or anger of the other, technically a manifestation of projective identification, in Kleinian parlance. Thus the therapist's unconscious mind understands that of her patient (Heimann, 1950). Counteractions are situations where the patient's communications stir up unresolved problems of the therapist. An example would be a therapist who fears her own aggression and placates the patient whenever she detects hostile feelings towards her. In addition, the patient, through some combination of age, gender or other characteristics, may be a transference figure for the therapist; examples would be as parent or rival. Furthermore, the dependence and intimacy of the role relationship of therapist and patient will have a personal meaning for the therapist for good or for ill, based on past and childhood experiences of psychologically similar situations.

Consider the following list of counter-transference reactions and their consequences (Bernstein and Bernstein, 1980: 48) and see how each limits the therapeutic potential of the encounter.

1. Do I require sympathy, protection and warmth so much myself that I err by being too sympathetic, too protective toward the patient?
2. Do I fear closeness so much that I err by being indifferent, rejecting, cold?
3. Do I need to feel important and therefore keep patients dependent on me, precluding their independence and assuming responsibility for their own welfare?
4. Do I cover feelings of inferiority with a front of superiority, thereby rejecting patients' need for acceptance?
5. Is my need to be liked so great that I become angry when a patient is rude, unappreciative, or uncooperative?

6. Do I react to the patient as an individual human being or do I label him with the stereotype of a group? Are my prejudices justified?
7. Am I competing with other authority figures in the patient's life when I offer advice contrary to that of another health professional?
8. Does the patient remind me too much of my own problems when I find myself being overly ready with pseudo-optimism and facile reassurance?
9. Do I give uncalled-for advice as a means of appearing all-wise?
10. Do I talk more than listen to a patient in an effort to impress him with my knowledge?

Counter-transference problems are signalled by intensifications of departures from the therapist's usual practice. At the time, they seem plausible, even justifiable; yet, when considered in supervision or in the routine self-scrutiny ('internal supervision': Casement, 1985) that is the mark of responsible psychotherapy, their obstructive nature becomes apparent. Menninger (1958) lists among the items that he has 'probably experienced': repeatedly experiencing erotic feelings towards the patient, carelessness in regard to appointment arrangements, sadistic unnecessary sharpness in formulating interpretations, getting conscious satisfaction from the patient's praise or affection and sudden increase or decrease in interest in a certain case.

Items like the above can serve as a checklist to help identify counter-transference problems that arise from conflicts in the therapist's unconscious mind. This is different from the equally problematic feelings that are manifestations of the therapist's involvement in the patient's determining fiction or, in language of psychoanalysis, the *transference* and *transference neurosis*. One example of these processes is the way in which a patient who has been brought up in a persecutory environment expects others to persecute him, perceives the therapist as being persecutory (*transference*) and actually prompts the therapist to act in a persecutory way (*transference neurosis*); another example is when the therapist finds herself not respecting the boundaries of a patient whose boundaries as a child have been breached by a parent in incestuous acts. This is an *acting-out* of counter-transference feelings, an enactment of formative events from the patient's past, re-created by the interaction of patient and therapist. A golden route of promoting change lies in identifying these involvements, exploring their meaning and disentangling both therapist and patient from them. Both sets of involvements are encompassed within a taxonomy of therapist difficulty devised by Davis et al. (1987). This allows therapists to compile their own distinctive profile of difficulty on nine categories. Trainees might benefit from plotting their profile and using this to highlight their idiosyncrasies; these could then be focused on in training, including their work in personal (training) therapy.

A particularly common form of noxious therapy relationship results from the abuse of power.

The abuse of power

Therapists are all too easily seduced into abusing the therapy relationship. When this occurs, the relationship is no longer therapeutic. During training, trainees need to learn how to recognize when abuse is likely to happen and is happening and take corrective action. In this respect, the work that is done in supervision is crucial. How does the abuse of power come about? It results from the conjunction of the patient's transference wishes and dysfunctional motivators in the therapist; it is encouraged by the inequality of power between the two.

The arena in which individual therapy takes place is constructed essentially by the therapist. Though subject to negotiation, the therapist decides the duration, frequency and form of the therapy. Ultimately, beginning and ending is in her hands, ending being a powerful threat to the patient who is dependent or not coping. With rare exceptions, the meetings take place on the therapist's territory. The therapist, whether trainee or trained, is held to be expert in what goes on in the arena, certainly by the patient who is relatively a novice in this setting. Whatever procedures the therapist propounds, the patient is predisposed to accept. Because the sessions take place in private, the therapy is not subject to the natural regulation of the scepticism, and even incredulity, of outsiders. All this gives the therapist great power and, consequently, exposes her to great temptation.

Ideological conversion through a process analogous to brainwashing is one hazard. When Scientology was investigated (Foster, 1971), its practices of 'auditing' and 'processing' were seen to be so dangerous that statutory regulation of psychotherapy was called for (see section on registration, p. 389). More commonly, eccentric, unsubstantiated beliefs are peddled as truths and clung on to by vulnerable, uncertain people who deserve better.

Another hazard for the patient is the conjunction of his need for an ideal parent who will protect, guide and succour with the therapist's wish to be idealized. What Ernest Jones (1913) termed the 'God-complex' lies in wait for the unwary (Marmor, 1953). The therapist's ego is boosted by transference admiration; this seductive pitfall is compounded by the common tendency in psychotherapy and especially in individual therapy for therapists to mystify the process through the use of esoteric jargon and the adoption of an aloof, all-knowing stance. Therapists run the risk of coming to feel superior, free of the struggles, conflicts and defeats of their patients. From a detached position – which may be bolstered by viewing all the patient's communications as manifestations of transference and, as such, only needing to be put back to the patient for his sole consideration – the therapist is tempted to be a bystander in life, vicariously involved but spared the pain and puffed up by the patient's dependent approval. Progress towards separation and individuation is obstructed. In the artificial, time-limited world of the therapy session, the therapist may have the pretence of having all the answers.

Guggenbuhl-Craig (1979) asserts that within us all is the archetype of the patient and healer. In order to reduce ambivalence, the archetype may be split and either polarity projected on to others. But both are necessary for healing. The sick man needs an external healer, but also needs to find the healer in himself; otherwise he becomes passive through handing over his healing ability to the other. This is obviously antithetical to the spirit of good psychotherapy. For the healer, the danger is to locate the polarity of the 'patient in herself' in her patients and not recognize it in herself. Then, she will come to see herself more and more as the strong healer for whom weakness, illness and wounds do not exist. As a healer without wounds, she will be unable to engage the healing factor in her patients. Traditional medical education can reinforce the division (Bennet, 1987).

The therapist who locates weakness in others becomes powerful through their failure. In Jungian language, the *charlatan shadow* of the therapist has been constellated. Guggenbuhl-Craig doubts that personal therapy or case discussions are sufficient to reduce the split in the archetype. The *analytic shield* carefully acquired in training is too effective, the risk of loss of self-esteem or prestige too great, the need to maintain one's allegiance to a school of therapy against outside attack too pressing. In some therapists, the split in the archetype is minimal; their patients' problems illuminate their own and are consciously worked on; they remain a patient as well as a healer. The best way of reducing the split is through involvement in ordinary life in un-analytic, symmetrical relationships which have the power to touch deeply, and to throw off balance, relationships which are quite different from the asymmetrical ones of therapy. Friendships – loving, forceful encounters with equals – develop the therapist as a whole person. What the therapist advocates for others is good for herself.

Not surprisingly, given the intensity and privacy of individual therapy, some therapists become sexually involved with their patients. It is hard to conceive of circumstances when this is not abusive in its impact or when it is not a dereliction of the responsibilities of being a therapist. One can understand how it happens but it should not be condoned. Many more male therapists have sexual involvements with female patients than do female therapists with male patients but all combinations occur, including with the same sex. Eroticized transferences and counter-transferences are common in therapy and may be acted out (Holroyd and Brodsky, 1977). In the transference, the patient may be looking for a loving parent. This wish may connect with the therapist's need to be a helping figure but subsequent sexual action represents a confusing of childhood wishes, albeit expressed in adult language, with mature intent; sexual action disregards the boundaries that are necessary if the therapy arena is to be psychologically safe.

Lust is a relatively straightforward motivation in acting-out; its intensity depends on the urgency of the therapist's biological drive, age, state of health, recency of drive satisfaction, general satisfaction with personal life and, of course, the attractiveness of the patient. Darker motivations such as unconscious hostility towards women or reaction-formations against feared homosexuality or gender inadequacy may be present (Marmor, 1972). Sexual action may be rationalized as being for the patient's benefit but this self-deception should not survive the monitoring of self-scrutiny, supervision and personal therapy.

Occasionally, therapist and patient fall in love and form a long-term relationship. Though one may wonder about the basis of a personal relationship founded in the strange circumstances of the therapy room, when the two are in love the ethically correct action is to suspend the therapy and arrange for it to be continued by a colleague if necessary.

Cardinal elements in training

Theoretical learning, supervised clinical practice and personal therapy are the cardinal elements in training. It is difficult to discuss one without making an artificial distinction from the others, as the three are so interrelated. The section on each should be read with the others in mind. The reader is also invited to refer back to the section on what the individual therapist has to learn. The order of discussion reflects my priority. Many analytic therapists might wish to give primacy to personal therapy; many cognitive-behaviourists might dispute its relevance to their work. Academic courses awarding certificates, diplomas and Master's degrees are likely to emphasize theory and research, though this is a changing scene as universities realize that they have to incorporate supervised practice if their graduates are to be registered as practitioners by one of the national registering bodies. Many of the points made here are also relevant to training in other modalities of psychotherapy such as group therapy (Aveline, 1988).

Theoretical learning

Purpose and content The purpose of training is to facilitate the exercise of natural abilities and acquired skills. To do this the therapist needs to gain extensive experience in the type(s) of therapy required for her practice and for which affinity has been shown, in this case individual therapy. But to begin with the trainee needs to acquire a conceptual framework of what therapy is about, how people mature and learn, and the role of the therapist. Later in training, theory will be critically examined to discover its areas of greatest applicability and limitations. Studying theory means that therapists do not reinvent the wheel. Assimilating theory into practice provides the therapist with an internalized rationale for the comprehension of clinical phenomena, the derivation of technique and the formulation of testable, clinically relevant hypotheses.

Learning theory is part of a broad educational process in which, in enlightened training, the development of informed, critical thinking is being encouraged. Theory tends to be taught in an approach-specific way but general, overlapping and complementary perspectives also ought to be studied. Both specific and general learning need to be presented in the quality and level appropriate to the trainee's need and ability. Ideally, theoretical learning would encompass the following:

Theory and techniques specific to the therapy approach being learned. In most types of training this is the major component but, as has been indicated, the well-educated therapist needs to consider other aspects.

The common therapeutic factors. Frank (1973) has argued convincingly that in all effective therapies six influential factors are operative. The therapy provides (1) an exploratory rationale and (2) facilitates the exploration of traumas and conflictual issues in a state of emotional arousal. The effect is strengthened (3) when the therapist is sanctioned as a healer by the society. Responding to the patient's request for help (4) encourages that person to be hopeful about themselves and counters the demoralization which typifies most patients' state. Therapy provides or prompts (5) success experiences, which enhances a sense of mastery, thus countering demoralization. Finally psychotherapy provides (6) an intense confiding relationship with a helping person. These factors have a much greater influence on outcome than the contribution made by approach-specific theory and technique; in Lambert's review of empirical studies, common therapeutic factors accounted for 30 per cent of the therapeutic effect, technique 15 per cent, expectancy (placebo-effect) 15 per cent and spontaneous remission 40 per cent (Lambert, 1986).

The necessary conditions. Rogers (1957) promoted research studies to support his proposition that three therapist conditions were necessary and sufficient for personality change: *genuineness, unconditional positive regard* and *accurate empathy.* The contention that these conditions are sufficient in themselves, are always helpful and should be taken as absolutes has been much investigated and caveats placed on the original proposition. However, a sufficiency of each constitutes the basis of a helpful relationship. In passing, it should be noted that Freud took it as read that the analyst would be a decent, understanding, non-judgmental, respectful and neutral person. These qualities formed the basis of the therapeutic alliance and gave, in Sandor Ferenczi's word, 'stability' (*Tragfestigheit*) to the relationship (Strupp, 1977).

The evolution of psychotherapy ideas. How the concepts of psychoanalysis, analytical psychology, individual psychology, existentialism, humanism, Gestalt psychology, psychodrama, learning and systems theory have developed, their interrelationship and the implications for practice. In the analytic tradition, how an instinct-based theory has evolved to ego-psychology and then to self-psychology with the increasing emphasis on object relations (human relations) and, especially in North America, on cultural and interpersonal aspects.

Human development. How individuals develop over the lifespan with particular reference to maturational tasks, attachment theory, and the elements that contribute to being able, in Freud's definition of maturity, to love and to work.

Mental mechanisms, character structure and the concept of conflict. How to make a dynamic formulation of the origin and meaning of the patient's problems. The meaning and significance in clinical practice of the technical terms: process, content, therapeutic alliance, transference, counter-transference and resistance. When and how to make effective interpretations and other interventions. Good examples of the practical application of these concepts may be found in Malan (1995) and Casement (1985).

Learning and systems theory. The role of shaping, modelling, generalization and *in vivo* learning and faulty cognitions in determining human behaviour. The importance of problem definition and behavioural analysis in making a diagnostic assessment. How behavioural, system and dynamic processes operate in marriage and in families and result in disturbed functioning. The contribution of psychological theory on cognitive dissonance, attribution theory and crisis theory to the understanding of change and resistance to change.

Ways in which therapists need to take account of linguistics, philosophy, religion and ethics in formulating a comprehensive model of human aspirations and functioning.

Cultural relativity, with special reference to race, gender, sexual orientation, age and culture itself. The specific contribution made to 20th-century understanding of role relationships and psychology by feminist psychology.

Physical disease presenting as mental disorder. In addition, the trainee will need to know the signs and symptoms of major psychiatric illness, the likely benefits and side-effects of psychotropic medication and when and to whom to refer on. As a counterpart of this medical knowledge, the ways in which the sociological concepts of stigma and labelling further our understanding of alienation and isolation.

Indications and contra-indications for different kinds of psychotherapy.

The vital role of support in therapy.

Preparation for therapy and patient–therapist matching. How negative effects arise through therapy and may be minimized.

Research methodology and classic studies. How to evaluate the research literature and derive implications for clinical practice.

Clinical audit. How to set standards of practice and systematically monitor them through the audit cycle.

Format Theory orders the great mass of clinical information and helps orientate the therapist in finding a way forward. This useful function should not curtail curiosity and the spirit of enquiry that is necessary for the development of the professional and the profession. Theory should always be relevant and, dependent on the level at which the training is pitched, comprehensive in coverage.

How theory is presented varies greatly. Commonly the span of knowledge to be studied is set by the training organizers, which has the virtue of making it clear what is to be learned. Then, there may be set readings either by author or topic, an approach which specifies the route of study and makes it easy for trainer or trainee to spot omissions. Curriculums, while reassuringly solid for trainers and trainees, may have the negative effect of not engaging the student's active participation. An alternative which we employed for a time in the South-Trent Training in Dynamic Psychotherapy, a specialist NHS training, is to have a planning event each year where the trainees and seminar leaders jointly decide what is to be studied and how this is to be done. Instead of the conventional study of topics and authors, the question may be posed: 'What do I need to know in order to understand a specified psychotherapy process or problem?' This is the approach of researching a topic rather than simply reading someone else's selection of what is relevant.

At the advanced level, when many topics will have to be studied, teacher enthusiasm may be retained by offering a menu of courses in the teachers' areas of expertise; the trainee may select from these, with the training committee having the responsibility of ensuring that a balanced choice has been made. Here, an over-inclusive curriculum can be helpful. When every subject listed manifestly cannot be studied formally within the time available, a trainee in conjunction with a personal tutor can plan a more personal course of learning that takes account of prior learning and present interest.

Theory is not just to be found in textbooks. Novels, plays, films and poems portray the human condition more vividly, complexly and, often, more sensitively than do dry texts. Biographies and autobiographies trace individual lives (Holmes, 1986). All these should be studied.

Whatever the format, the trainee should return again and again to the fundamental, practical question: *what are the implications of this theory or portrayal of life for my practice in my working environment with the patients that I see?*

Supervised clinical practice

Clinical practice Appropriate supervised practice is the central learning experience in training. The trainee needs to learn what can be achieved in brief (up to 10 sessions), focal work (16–25 weekly sessions), medium (40–70 sessions) and long-term therapy (upwards of 2–3 years). Weekly therapy is the most common mode in NHS psychotherapy and in many other settings; this has its own rhythm and intensity and is quite different from more frequent therapy, where intensity may accelerate the process of change or be necessary in order to contain major personal disturbance. Weekly therapy tends to be more reality oriented; two, three or five times a week therapy affords greater scope for exploration and regression. The two ends of the spectrum present different learning experiences and need to be sampled.

The supervisor has a key role in ensuring that patients with a wide range of problems and character structure are seen during the training period. Both breadth and depth of experience are important for the development of trainees. Breadth develops flexibility and highlights to the trainee problematic counter-transferences and personal limitations that need either to be addressed in supervision, further experience and personal therapy or to be avoided. Depth fosters stamina, the ability to contain intense feelings and to have the patience to move at the pace of someone whose sense of basic trust and confident autonomy is poorly developed; often this will mean enduring feeling powerless and helpless as the reality of the patient's inner world is engaged (Adler, 1972).

In intermediate and advanced training, the trainee should gain supervised experience in making assessments. While the thrust of this chapter is towards individual therapy, I strongly favour a required element in training being the conduction of therapy groups, e.g. a small group over 18 months. A degree of competence in group therapy or, at the very least, a favourable familiarity with the approach should be part of the skills of an individual therapist. This can only be gained through direct experience.

What is judged to be an adequate training for a fully trained, autonomous practitioner in terms of duration, frequency and amount of clinical practice varies between the psychotherapies. At the level of career psychotherapy, it is hard to see that less than 900 hours of conducting therapy over three whole time equivalent years plus 300 hours of supervision divided between one main and two subsidiary supervisors could be sufficient, and this would need to be built on a foundation of less intensive, preliminary training in psychotherapy over two or more years; to learn well, one needs to immerse oneself in the subject. This is the standard set by the Royal College of Psychiatrists for the training of consultant medical psychotherapists. In addition, the College specifies that of the 900 hours, 700 should be in the main branch of psychotherapy being studied and 100 in each of the other two branches; currently, the branches recognized are psychodynamic/interpersonal, cognitive-behavioural and systemic (JCHPT, 1996). The British Association for Counselling specifies 450 hours of practice and 250 hours of supervision for accreditation as a counsellor. The United Kingdom Council for Psychotherapy requires a full programme of training over three years for registration but does not stipulate the number of hours of the elements in the training.

The same principle of breadth and depth in practice adduced above applies to supervision. To gain alternative perspectives against which the trainee's own view may develop, several supervisors need to be worked with for a year at a time. In order for the trainee to know one perspective in depth and to feel safe enough to explore certain doubts and conflicts, one main supervisor needs to be engaged with over two or three years. The choice of main supervisor is clearly a matter of great import.

In addition, trainees who are not qualified in one of the core mental health care professions need to gain through clinical placements sufficient acquaintance with major psychiatric illnesses to be able to recognize their presence; knowledge of the effects and likely benefits of pharmacological and physical treatments is also necessary. One example of why therapists need to be familiar with such matters is the high risk of suicide and depressive homicide in severe depressive illness; in such cases, antidepressants or ECT (electro-convulsive therapy) can be life-saving measures which restore normal functioning. Psychotherapists should not persist in interpreting psychopathology when a speedier and more effective biological remedy is at hand. When the patient is once more accessible to verbal interaction and the risk of harm to himself and his family has receded, then the precipitants and psychological vulnerabilities can be explored in psychotherapy with the benefit of greater self-understanding and reduced likelihood of recurrence.

The role of the supervisor The supervisor has a privileged, responsible position as mentor, guide and, often, assessor. From the advantageous position of hearing about therapy at second hand and generally after the event, the supervisor places his accumulated experience and knowledge at the service of the trainee. He helps the trainee work out with the patient the meaning and significance of the patient's communications, the nature of his conflicts and, certainly in the more dynamic therapies, brings into sharp focus the way in which patient and therapist engage and how this may be turned to good account. In the beginning, the trainee will feel an ambivalent mixture of excitement and dread in taking on a new role. During this time of insecurity and fearing being inadequate, she will need the support of the supervisor. As training progresses, the supervisor has to encourage the trainee to let go of the early, perhaps necessary, idealization of the supervisor so that identification can be replaced by an internalization of professional skills (Gosling, 1978). In successful training, the trainee moves through the stages of inception, skills development and consolidation to mutuality of expertise with the trainer (Hess, 1986).

When patient and therapist concur in their appreciation of the aims of therapy and when there is clarity in understanding accurately the structure of the conflicts and the process of the session, two major contributions have been made to the success of the endeavour. Many psychotherapy centres use a pre-assessment interview questionnaire to help clarify the purpose of the therapy; in Nottingham, this has questions on what the problems are, how the patient thinks they have come about and in what ways they have been shaped in their life, their self-concept, the characteristic form of their relationships and what has prompted them to seek help now. Of course, in cognitive-behaviour therapy, goal definition and objectification of problem severity as a baseline for therapy is an integral part of the approach. In every type of individual therapy, a formulation of the underlying dynamics is beneficial and, I would argue, necessary. Though different approaches will use their own vocabulary, schemas for the content are to be found in Aveline (1980), Cleghorn et al. (1983), Perry et al. (1987), Friedman and Lister (1987) and Mace (1995). I now favour an interpersonal formula which identifies a personally characteristic narrative of recurrent acts of self. This is an adaptation of Strupp and Binder's (1984) and Luborsky's (Luborsky and Crits-Christoph, 1990) approach: it records conscious and unconscious wishes, formative responses from others, and responses to self and to others as well as restorative actions and prediction of clinically significant patterns in therapy (Aveline, 1995); though derived from analytic and cognitive approaches, the formula is atheoretical and may be used by all.

Whichever conceptual schema is used, the supervisor helps the supervisee to make fuller use of the session and, crucially in my view, to see how she is getting caught up in the self-limiting relationship patterns of the patient. Getting caught up is inevitable; the skill in psychotherapy is in recognizing what is happening and using it constructively (Aveline, 1989). In the phenomenon called 'negative fit', therapists act in ways that fit the patient's negative preconceptions, which have been formed by how important people in his past have responded to him. Luborsky and Singer (1974) demonstrated two major patterns of negative fit when the tape recordings of experienced therapists were studied. One pattern was confirming the patient's fear of rejection by being critical, disapproving, cold, detached and indifferent, and the other was confirming the patient's fear of being made weak by being too directive, controlling and domineering. Clearly every effort should be made in supervision to identify these two patterns and to turn the potentially negative impact to therapeutic effect. Often the supervisor will be able to guide the trainee in selecting suitable patients for her stage in training. In this situation, the supervisor may consider selecting pairing that promise well, as when the therapist has resolved in her life a similar conflict to the patient's or avoiding pairings where the therapist seems likely only to reinforce the patient's pattern (Aveline, 1992a).

Ways of supervising Pedder (1986) sees supervision in three ways: as being analogous to gardening, that is as a process of promoting growth, as a place for play in the Winnicottian sense,[2] and as being like therapy in that it provides a regular time and place for taking a second look at what happened in the therapy session. Supervision aims to bring to the fore the creative potential of the therapist. It should be noted that supervision is not the same as therapy, though at times the distinction may become blurred.

Broadly speaking, the focus of supervisory interest can be on one of three areas: the process and content of the patient's concerns and communications, transference and counter-transference reactions between therapist and patient, and the supervisee–supervisor relationship. The focus on the last is justified by Doehrman's (1976) classic study which demonstrated the re-creation in the supervisee–supervisor relationship of the dynamics between patient and therapist. At least theoretically, this supports the view that, if the dynamics in supervision can be comprehended and resolved, blocks in the therapy relationship will be undone (for an example see Caligor, 1984). In practice, all these foci are useful though, in my practice, I incline towards the first as it is the patient's life that is my primary concern.

Much debate rages in psychotherapy circles about how the supervisory material should be presented. Classically in psychoanalytic training, a free-flowing account of the session is given with much attention being paid to what is said and not said and the elucidation of counter-transferences and associations as ways of illuminating unconscious processes. This is listening with the third ear (Reik, 1949). That the report may factually correspond poorly to the observable events of the session is held to be of little importance; indeed some supervisors argue that factually precise reporting both misses the point and may positively obscure it. I cannot accept this position. All ways of capturing the facts and essence of what went on are useful. Aids to supervision are just that: servants, not masters. They can be adapted to meet the needs of the moment.

After each session, trainees will write notes detailing content, process and feeling issues. It is advantageous to have audio or video recordings of the session which may be viewed from the beginning or at a point of difficulty or interest – or not at all. Such recordings document the actual sequence of events and bring the dimensions of non-verbal and paralinguistic communication and change in emotional tone into the arena of supervision (Aveline, 1992b). Other means may be utilized. Transcripts allow the leisurely study of process and form of verbal intervention; as a semi-research exercise, the method of brief structured recall (Elliott and Shapiro, 1988) may be used to go over with the patient the most significant events in a session; the significant events are identified by the patient immediately after the session, then therapist and patient listen to the tape just before, during and after the event, and amplify through discussion the associated feelings, meaning and impact of that segment of interaction. Live supervision from behind a screen with either telephone contact or a 'bug in the ear' may also be employed, though such measures reduce the scope for the therapist to grapple on her own as a person with the patient's issues. There is more to be said for the supervisor leading the way in openness by occasionally putting his own tapes forward for discussion.

Being supervised is supposed to be helpful, but it can be persecutory (Bruzzone et al., 1985) and intrusive (Betcher and Zinberg, 1988). The trainee's self-esteem is vulnerable and there needs to be room in the training for privacy and for mistakes to be made and discussed without dire penalty or excessive shame. Counter-transference reactions on the part of the supervisor must not be forgotten. The trainee may represent the coming generation why may equal or overtake the supervisor in skill and knowledge. Rivalry and the struggle for power may constitute a subtext for the supervisory meetings and, if not resolved, prove detrimental to professional development. Training for supervisors and a forum for them to discuss problems in supervision is beneficial (Hawkins and Shohet, 1989). In the training, it is also sensible and desirable in its own right to have group supervision as well as individual supervision, since the former provides multiple perspectives, peer support and the morale-enhancing opportunity of being of assistance to colleagues.

Skills development   While I favour weekly supervision over months and years as the best complement to the work of individual therapy, workshops and role-plays quickly lead to the acquisition of fundamental skills (structured examples of exercises are to be found in Tolan and Lendrum, 1995; Jacobs, 1985; Egan, 1982a, 1982b; Jacobs, 1991). Without risking any harm to the patient, difficult situations that therapists commonly face can be practised, the effects of different inter-ventions observed and the model presented by more experienced therapists evaluated. Micro-counselling training courses, first described at the end of the 1960s, have retained their promise for the relatively inexperienced trainee; they provide structured, focused learning over periods of one, two or three days with a strong emphasis on skills acquisition through role-play. At the more advanced, approach-specific level, the use of detailed treatment manuals for such diverse approaches as supportive-expressive psychoanalytic psychotherapy, cognitive and interpersonal therapy of depression and short-term therapy is an interesting, effective new method of skill development (Matarazzo and Patterson, 1986).

Personal therapy

'The therapist can only go as far with the patient as he can go himself', so the maxim runs. What the therapist can bear to hear in herself, she can hear in the patient. What the therapist can find in herself, she can recognize in the other. Thus in addition to the resistance by the patient to dismantling defensive, outmoded but originally adaptive patterns, the therapist contributes a resistance of her own to free exploration. The therapist's resistance may take the form of avoidance or over-interest; the former limits the opening up of areas of concern for the patient, the latter diverts the focus of the discourse to the therapist's own conflictual issues; these processes largely take place out of consciousness. Examples have been given in the sections on counter-transference and the abuse of power of some common personal conflicts which may limit or adversely distort the engagement of the therapist. All therapies at some stage confront the reflective therapist with the dilemmas in her own life and the partial solutions that she has adopted. An overlap of conflictual issue between therapist and patient often results in a blocked therapy, but may generate a particularly fruitful dyad when the therapist's conflict is not too great and the overlap enhances empathic contact (Aveline, 1992a).

Life experience and the practice of psychotherapy educate the therapist about herself. Self-scrutiny takes the learning about conflicts and their resolution one step further but the therapist's own internal security measures operate to maintain blind spots and protect self-esteem from sobering self-realizations; these defences limit what can be done alone. Personal therapy offers the therapist the same opportunity as the patient has to explore, understand and resolve inner conflicts. It brings together theoretical learning and psychotherapy practice in an experience that makes personal sense of the two. At a practical level, personal therapy provides a means through which sufficient self-understanding can be gained for the therapist to recognize how her personality and life experience affects her ability to be objective and to reduce her tendency to impose her own solutions on the life problems of the patient. The nature of the conflicts that interfere with the therapist's work predicate her requirement for therapy in terms of type, duration and frequency, and the achievement of sufficient resolution in order to work more effectively indicates the end-point of personal therapy on the practical level. At the next level, therapy aims to enhance the therapist's ability to relate, empathically and creatively, to her patients. One element in this is knowing at first hand what it is like to be a patient; another is the loosening through therapy of the self-limiting grip of personal conflicts. Beyond that, as was detailed in the section on motivating factors in the therapist, therapy offers an opportunity for the therapist to heal herself, an unmet need which may have been of prime importance in the selection by the trainee therapist of this kind of work. At a sociological level, personal therapy has the function of a rite of passage, forming and affirming her identity as a psychotherapist and as a member of her professional group.

Perhaps the most compelling argument in favour of personal therapy is that every therapist, like every patient, sees the world through the perspective of her guiding fictions and is impelled to impose that order, those patterns and her solutions on others. Thus, the more the therapist is aware of her personal, determining fictions, the more likely she will be able to engage with the reality of the other.

Personal therapy in varying intensity and duration is a required component of most formal, advanced trainings in psychotherapy. In psychoanalysis, full personal analysis is mandatory: the sequence of engagement in training is being in therapy, then theory seminars and finally conducting analyses. In Henry's (1977) survey of 4,000 North American psychotherapists 74 per cent had been in personal therapy and nearly 50 per cent had re-entered therapy for two to four periods; conversely, 26 per cent had chosen not to pursue that course. Despite the consensus in favour of personal therapy, especially at the psychodynamic end of the spectrum, there is little published evidence of its efficacy in enhancing therapeutic ability. Surveys of the literature by Greenberg and Staller (1981) and Macaskill (1988) conclude that (a) 15–33 per cent of therapies have unsatisfactory personal therapy experiences, e.g. damage to marriage, destructive acting-out and excessive withdrawal from the outside world; (b) therapy early in the therapist's career may have deleterious effects on work with patients; and (c) there is no positive correlation between either the fact of having been in therapy or its duration on outcome of the therapist's professional work. The level of reported dissatisfaction is in line with that generally expected for negative effects in psychotherapy, and, as such, emphasizes the importance of the trainee's making a sage choice of therapist.

When personal therapy is decided upon, its form, intensity and duration should parallel the form of psychotherapy that the therapist is going to practise. Generally for training in individual therapy, this will be one or more times a week for three or more years. It is important that the therapist enters therapy not just because the training requires it but to resolve personal conflicts or difficulties that are being encountered in her work and life. Advice on whom to consult should be sought from an experienced adviser who can steer the trainee away from pairings that are less than optimal and towards those of greater promise (Coltart, 1987). Exploratory sessions should be held with several potential therapists before the choice is made. This counsel of perfection could well apply to patients if ever they were in the position of being able to choose whom to see.

Evaluation

During training, there should be opportunities for evaluation, both formative and normative. It will be recalled that, in educational terms, 'formative' evaluation refers to non-examined elements that enrich the educational experience of training, whereas 'normative' refers to entry/exit, pass/fail criteria. The aims of the training should be clearly stated and be attainable within the learning experiences of the scheme. A system for monitoring progress both by self-assessment and by the trainers is necessary, as is the giving of feedback so as to help the trainee improve the quality of her psychotherapy. Individual and psychometric assessments of severity of patient problem can form a baseline for the evaluation of the success of therapy. Casebooks recording progress and any alteration in formulation of the patient's problems document the range of therapy experience and the lessons to be learned from actual practice as opposed to the fine rhetoric of texts. Detailed written case accounts of one or more psychotherapies carried out by the trainee demonstrate the degree of the trainee's development and bring into focus how difficulties have been encountered and struggled with. A personal tutor has a key role as adviser and appraiser to the trainee finding her way through the training. Ultimately, evaluation should address the question of therapist competence: *how effective is this therapist in aiding the quest of her patients towards more fruitful living?* The methodology to assess this does not yet exist, though the Mental Health Foundation in the UK is currently funding research into one way of evaluating competence. Only partial progress has been made towards the subsidiary but important question of what this training has added to the therapist's ability; one example is the quantification of the improvement in interviewing skills acquired through micro-counselling courses (Matarazzo and Patterson, 1986).

National Vocational Qualifications

Since 1987, the British government has been committed to introducing National Vocational Qualifications (NVQs) for as many occupations as possible. NVQs are based on a functional analysis of what a competent worker does. They describe competencies at five levels of increasing complexity of activity. Level one describes routine and predictable tasks where the worker follows rules set by superiors, and level five the application of fundamental principles or complex techniques across a wide range of unpredictable contexts by someone operating with substantial, personal autonomy. Level five would equate to the standards of the established professions like law or medicine, though these occupations have yet to be mapped by this process. The declared purpose of NVQs is to provide an alternative pathway to qualification other than traditional university courses and to help employers judge that their employees have the competencies to discharge the duties of a specific post.

After much deliberation, the British Association for Counselling (BAC) joined with the Department of Employment in 1992 to map and devise standards in the fields of work covered by BAC. The organ for this project is the Lead Body for Advice, Guidance, Counselling and Psychotherapy. After an enormous amount of work, competency statements have been agreed for advice, guidance, and counselling and contracts placed with awarding bodies to turn these into NVQ qualifications for advice and guidance. The agreed competencies for therapeutic counselling have been put on hold while psychotherapy is mapped. After an ambivalent period, the United Kingdom Council for Psychotherapy (see next section) voted to join the Lead Body in 1994. Once the mapping and standard devising is complete, probably by the end of 1996, areas of overlap with therapeutic counselling will be examined and there will be an amalgamation of standards and possibly a differentiation. NVQs in psychotherapy may be available from 1997.

The development of functional standards has aroused many anxieties. Critics argue that the approach is atomistic, and risks losing the sum of the parts by splitting the whole into so many elements, slavishly to be checked off during training. They fear that it will emphasize action over reflection, 'doing to' over 'being with', and is all too cognitive, rather than emotional. They say that the method misses out synthesis and intuition, and falsely suggests that the practice of psychotherapy is algorithmic when, truly, it is heuristic. The participating sceptics, myself among them, value the healthy emphasis on outputs and anticipate that it will bring out commonalties and differences between the psychotherapies. It should lead to a clearer definition of the competencies to be developed through training and promote equivalence of trainings.

Depending on the attitude of the professional bodies and training organizations to the finished standards, NVQs may become another route to qualification for psychotherapists.

Registration

At present, anyone in Britain may practise as a psychotherapist and advertise their services as such. Unlike the situation in North America and many European countries, psychotherapy is not a regulated profession. No formal training or subscription to a code of ethics is required by statute. Some titles such as psychoanalyst and child psychotherapist are protected. Within institutions such as the NHS, and university counselling services, the patient as consumer of psychotherapy has the protection of knowing that for the most part the therapist will have been appointed in open competition with other applicants, and has the sanction of being able to initiate an official complaint through the institution's code of practice and complaints procedure. Membership of professions that are regulated by statutory bodies (as for example is medicine by the General Medical Council) or have chartered status, such as psychology, or of training institutes with regulatory powers affords some assurance that the standards of the therapist are adequate and will be maintained. But in the private sector, members of the public have little protection against the misinformed or unethical therapist. This is bad for the consumer and bad for the profession.

The Foster Report (Foster, 1971), the result of a government appointed inquiry, recommended that the profession of psychotherapy be regulated by statute. Seven years later, the Sieghart Report (Sieghart, 1978) proposed the establishment of a council which would draw up and enforce a code of professional ethics and approve training courses. Registration of individuals as psychotherapists would be *indicative* rather than *functional*; that is, on the basis of titles associated with various forms of psychotherapy in which the therapist was qualified rather than the content of the work. The desirable goal of registration as some guarantee of integrity and competence, at present on a voluntary basis, has since made significant progress, especially in the last five years.

During the 1980s, psychotherapists and psychotherapy organizations from across the spectrum of practice met each year in Rugby (the Rugby Conference), initially under the auspices of the British Association for Counselling, and latterly in Canterbury. In 1989 the conference adopted a formal constitution as the United Kingdom Standing Conference for Psychotherapy (UKSCP), metamorphosing into the United Kingdom Council for Psychotherapy (UKCP) in 1993. UKCP is an organization of organizations, grouped into eight sections: Analytical Psychology; Behavioural and Cognitive Psychotherapy; Experiential Constructivist; Family, Marital and Sexual Therapy; Humanistic and Integrative Psychotherapy; Hypnotherapy; Psychoanalytic and Psychodynamic; and Psycho-Analytically based Therapy with Children. In 1993 UKCP established a register of its qualified members, now some 3,500, grouped for competence by the title of the section in which they are registered. Registrants have to meet a common standard of training and ethics and are subject to disciplinary procedures (Pokorny, 1995). UKCP is committed to seeking statutory registration. This is unlikely to happen for a few years and will be dependent on all the major psychotherapy organizations speaking with a common voice and showing evidence of being able to uphold high standards, investigate complaints and discipline malpractising registrants. Having successfully launched the register, the next step will be defining criteria for re-registration.

At the moment when UKSCP was preparing to vote UKCP into existence, a substantial proportion of the organizations from the psychoanalytic end of the spectrum withdrew from the conference. They were unhappy about the breadth of psychotherapy approach represented in UKSCP and, it would appear, about being one voice among many. They preferred to cluster round a psychoanalytic identity and formed the British Confederation of Psychotherapists in 1992. In 1994, they launched their register of 1,200 practitioners (Balfour and Richards, 1995). I regret that they turned away from the greater good of a representative profession of psychotherapy. Doubtless, a *rapprochement* will be necessary if statutory registration is to be achieved.

For many years, the British Association for Counselling has operated a system of individual accreditation of counsellors. In 1996, the counselling organizations will launch the United Kingdom Register of Counsellors; the register will be held by BAC. As well as individual registration, counsellors may be registered by sponsoring organizations who will guarantee the counselling that they do within that organization. Thus, a counsellor might be registered for independent practice and/or for work in, for example, Relate or Cruise.

All these moves help identify areas of competence among psychotherapists and therapeutic counselling and provide a useful measure of protection for the public and for employers of therapists.

Implicit in the above is the proposition that continued attention to maintaining and extending competence is part of the professional attitude of the psycho-therapist. The rubric for this further education is continuing professional develop-ment (CPD); it can help guard against burnout (Grosch and Colsen, 1994). This is particularly important for the individual therapist, who tends to work in relative or absolute isolation and, in the absence of challenging opportunities for further learning, may develop poor working practices. Feedback from colleagues in peer-group supervision of actual clinical work is especially helpful.

Supportive psychotherapy

The rhetoric of psychotherapy is towards fundamental change in people's feelings, attitudes and interactions; this has been the type of individual therapy for which training has been described in this chapter. The trainee therapist in her enthusiasm and inexperience of the struggle to survive that many patients face may be tempted to press for a pace and depth of change for which her patient is not ready. Fundamental change will not be possible or desirable for all or, if possible, no authorization may have been given by the patient for deep exploration that might profoundly challenge his view of himself. This situation has to be explicitly respected and the value of support recognized and taught in training. All therapy has to have in it a sufficiently supportive element in order to help the patient contend with the upheaval of change: most therapies will move between chal-lenging and supportive phases. Furthermore, supportive psychotherapy is a subject in its own right. It is indicated for the many individuals who need sustained support in order to return to their optimal level of adjustment and maintain themselves there. It has its own complex skills and needs to be learned by even the most therapeutically ambitious therapist.

Conclusion

The current practice of psychotherapy distils what is known about human healing. In its practice, it is both an art and a science; both elements need to be borne in mind in training. Training may occur in phases but is a lifelong commitment. Competence is achievable but there is always more for the therapist to learn. No end-point has been reached in the development of individual therapy as an agent of personal change. Further refinement in theory, scope and practice can be expected, especially if the practitioners of the different individual psychotherapies learn to speak with one another in pursuit of the common goal of assisting patients to lead more fruitful lives.

Notes

1   In this chapter, I use the word patient as a generic term for someone who suffers and is seeking help. Also, to avoid the cumbersome form of he/she, the male form is used unless a named authority is being referred to.

2   Winnicott derived many of his ideas from his work with children. He saw psycho-
    therapy taking place in the overlap of two playing areas, that of the patient and that of
    the therapist. The therapist's job is to help the patient move from a state of not being
    able to play into one of being able to play. Playing is a specially creative, intensely real
    activity which allows new syntheses to emerge.

References

Adler, G. (1972) 'Helplessness in the helpers', *British Journal of Medical Psychology*, 45:
315–25.

Auerbach, A.A. and Johnson, M. (1977) 'Research on the therapist's level of experience', in
A.S. Gurman and A.M. Razin (eds), *Effective Psychotherapy*. Oxford: Pergamon Press.

Aveline, M.O. (1979) 'Towards a conceptual framework of psychotherapy – a personal
view', *British Journal of Medical Psychology*, 52: 271–5.

Aveline, M.O. (1980) 'Making a psychodynamic formulation', *Bulletin of the Royal College
of Psychiatrists*, December: 192–3.

Aveline, M.O. (1988) 'Issues in the training of group therapists', in M.O. Aveline and W.
Dryden (eds), *Group Therapy in Britain*. Milton Keynes: Open University Press.

Aveline, M.O. (1989) 'The provision of illusion in psychotherapy', *Midland Journal of
Psychotherapy*, 1: 9–16.

Aveline, M.O. (1992a) 'Parameters of danger: interactive elements in the therapy dyad', in
M. Aveline (ed.), *From Medicine to Psychotherapy*. London: Whurr.

Aveline, M.O. (1992b) 'The use of audio and video tapes in supervision of dynamic
psychotherapy', *British Journal of Psychotherapy*, 8(4): 347–58.

Aveline, M.O. (1995) 'Assessment for focal therapy', in C.J. Mace (ed.), *The Art and
Science of Assessment*. London: Routledge.

Balfour, F. and Richards, J. (1995) 'History of the British Confederation of
Psychotherapists', *British Journal of Psychotherapy*, 11(3): 422–6.

Bennet, G. (1987) *The Wound and the Doctor*. London: Secker & Warburg.

Bernstein, L. and Bernstein, R.S. (1980) *Interviewing: a Guide for Health professionals*. New
York: Appleton-Century-Crofts.

Betcher, R.W. and Zinberg, N.E. (1988) 'Supervision and privacy in psychotherapy
training', *American Journal of Psychiatry*, 145: 796–803.

Bruzzone, M., Casaula, E. and Jimenz, J.P. (1985) 'Regression and persecution in analytic
training. Reflections on experience', *International Review of Psycho-Analysis*, 12: 411–15.

Bugental, J.F.T. (1964) 'The person who is the psychotherapist', *Journal of Counselling
Psychology*, 28: 272–7.

Burton, A. (1975) 'Therapist satisfaction', *American Journal of Psychoanalysis*, 35: 115–22.

Caligor, L. (1984) *Parallel and Reciprocal Processes in Psychoanalytic Supervision*. New
York: Plenum Press.

Casement, P. (1985) *On Learning from the Patient*. London: Tavistock.

Cleghorn, J.M., Bellissimo, A. and Will, D. (1983) 'Teaching some principles of individual
psychodynamics through an introductory guide to formulations', *Canadian Journal of
Psychiatry*, 28: 162–72.

Coltart, N. (1987) 'Diagnosis and assessment for suitability for psycho-analytical
psychotherapy', *British Journal of Psychotherapy*, 4: 127–34.

Davis, J.D., Elliott, R., Davis, M.L., Binns, M., Francis, V.M., Kelman, J.E. and Schroder,
T.A. (1987) 'Development of a taxonomy of therapist difficulties: initial report', *British
Journal of Medical Psychology*, 60: 109–19.

Doehrman, M.J.G. (1976) 'Parallel processes in supervision and psychotherapy', *Bulletin of
the Menninger Clinic*, 40: 1–104.

Egan, G. (1982a) *Exercises in Helping Skills*, 2nd edition. Belmont, CA: Wadsworth.

Egan, G. (1982b) *The Skilled Helper*, 2nd edition. Belmont, CA: Wadsworth.

Elliott, R. and Shapiro, D.A. (1988) 'Brief structured recall: a more efficient method for studying significant therapy moments', *British Journal of Medical Psychology*, 61: 141–53.

Fairbairn, W.R.D. (1954) *An Object-Relations Theory of the Personality*. New York: Basic Books.

Farber, B.A. (1983) 'The effects of psychotherapeutic practice upon psychotherapists', *Psychotherapy: Theory, Research and Practice*, 20: 174–82.

Farber, B.A. and Heifetz, L.J. (1981) 'The satisfactions and stresses of psychotherapy work: a factor analytic study', *Professional Psychology*, 12: 621–30.

Fleming, J. (1987) *The Teaching and Learning of Psychoanalysis*. New York: Guilford Press.

Foster, J.G. (1971) *Enquiry into the Practice and Effects of Scientology*. London: HMSO.

Frank, J.D. (1973) *Persuasion and Healing*, 2nd edition. Baltimore, MD: Johns Hopkins University Press.

Friedman, R.S. and Lister, P. (1987) 'The current status of the psychodynamic formulation', *Psychiatry*, 50: 126–41.

Gosling, R. (1978) 'Internalization of the trainer's behaviour in professional training', *British Journal of Medical Psychology*, 51: 35–40.

Greben, S.E. (1975) 'Some difficulties and satisfactions inherent in the practice of psychoanalysis', *International Journal of Psycho-Analysis*, 56: 427–33.

Greben, S.E. (1984) *Love's Labor*. New York: Schocken Books.

Greenberg, R.P. and Staller, J. (1981) 'Personal therapy for therapists', *American Journal of Psychiatry*, 138: 1467–71.

Greenson, R.R. (1967) *The Technique and Practice of Psychoanalysis*, Vol. I. New York: International Universities Press.

Grosch, W.N. and Colsen, D. (1994) *When Helping Starts to Hurt: a New Look at Burn Out among Psychotherapists*. New York: W.W. Norton.

Guggenbuhl-Craig, A. (1979) *Power in the Helping Professions*. Irving, TX: Spring Publications.

Guy, J.D. (1987) *The Personal Life of the Psychotherapist*. New York: Wiley.

Hawkins, P. and Shohet, R. (1989) *Supervision in the Helping Professions*. Oxford: Oxford University Press.

Heimann, P. (1950) 'On counter-transference', *International Journal of Psychoanalysis*, 31: 81–4.

Henry, W.A. (1977) 'Personal and social identities of psychotherapists', in A.S. Gurman and A.M. Razin (eds), *Effective Psychotherapy*. Oxford: Pergamon Press.

Hess, A.K. (1986) 'Growth in supervision: stages of supervisee and supervisor development', in F.W. Kaslow (ed.), *Supervision and Training: Models, Dilemmas, Challenges*. New York: Haworth Press.

Holmes, J. (1986) 'Teaching the psychotherapeutic method: some literary parallels', *British Journal of Medical Psychology*, 59: 113–21.

Holroyd, J.C. and Brodsky, A.M. (1977) 'Psychologists' attitudes and practices regarding erotic and non-erotic physical contact with patients', *American Psychologist*, 32: 843–9.

JCHPT (1996) *Implementation of the Calman Report: Royal College of Psychiatrists*.

Jacobs, M. (1985) *Swift to Hear. Facilitating Skills in Listening and Responding*. London: SPCK.

Jacobs, M. (1991) *Insight and Experience*. Milton Keynes: Open University Press.

Jones, E. (1913) 'The God-complex', in *Essays in Applied Psychoanalysis*, Vol. II. London: Hogarth Press.

Lambert, M.J. (1986) 'Implications of psychotherapy outcome research for eclectic psychotherapy', in J.C. Norcross (ed.), *Handbook of Eclectic Psychotherapy*. New York: Brunner Mazel.

Lomas, P. (1981) *The Case for a Personal Psychotherapy*. Oxford: Oxford University Press.

Luborsky, L. and Crits-Christoph, P. (1990) *Understanding Transference. The Core Conflictual Relationship Theme Method*. New York: Basic Books.

Luborsky, L. and Singer, B. (1974) 'The fit of therapists' behavior into patients' negative expectations: a study of transference–countertransference contagion'. Unpublished manuscript, University of Pennsylvania.

Luborsky, L., Singer, B. and Luborsky, L. (1975) 'Comparative studies of psychotherapies. Is it true that "Everyone has won and all must have prizes?"', *Archives of General Psychiatry*, 32: 995–1008.

Macaskill, N.D. (1988) 'Personal therapy in the training of a psychotherapist: is it effective?', *British Journal of Psychotherapy*, 4: 219–26.

Mace, C. (1995) *The Art and Science of Assessment in Psychotherapy*. London: Routledge.

Malan, D. (1995) *Individual Psychotherapy and the Science of Psychodynamics*, 2nd edition. Oxford: Butterworth Heinemann.

Marmor, J. (1953) 'The feeling of superiority: an occupational hazard in the practice of psychotherapy', *American Journal of Psychiatry*, 110: 370–3.

Marmor, J. (1972) 'Sexual acting-out in psychotherapy', *American Journal of Psycho-Analysis*, 22: 3–8.

Matarazzo, R.G. and Patterson, D.R. (1986) 'Methods of teaching therapeutic skill', in S.L. Garfield and A.L. Bergin (eds), *Handbook of Psychotherapy and Behavior Change*. New York: Wiley.

Menninger, K. (1958) *Theory of Psychoanalytic Technique*. New York: Basic Books.

Orlinsky, D. and Howard, K.I. (1980) 'Gender and psychotherapeutic outcome', in A. M. Brodsky and R.T. Hare-Mustin (eds), *Women and Psychotherapy*. New York: Guilford Press.

Pedder, J. (1986) 'Reflections on the theory and practice of supervision', *Psychoanalytic Psychotherapy*, 2: 1–12.

Perry, S., Cooper, A.M. and Michels, R. (1987) 'The psychodynamic formulation: its purpose, structure, and clinical application', *American Journal of Psychiatry*, 144: 543–50.

Pokorny, M.R. (1995) 'History of the United Kingdom Council for Psychotherapy', *British Journal of Psychotherapy*, 11(3): 415–21.

Reik, T. (1949) *Listening with the Third Ear*. New York: Farrer & Strauss.

Rogers, C.R. (1957) 'The necessary and sufficient conditions of therapeutic personality change', *Journal of Consulting Psychology*, 21: 95–103.

Rosin, S.A. and Knudson, R.M. (1986) 'Perceived influence of life experiences on clinical psychologists' selection and development of theoretical orientations', *Psychotherapy*, 23: 357–63.

Ryle, A. (1990) *Cognitive-analytic Therapy: Active Participation in Change*. Chichester: John Wiley.

Sandler, J. (1988) 'Psychoanalysis and psychoanalytic psychotherapy: problems of differentiation'. Paper presented at Psychoanalysis and Psychoanalytic Psychotherapy conference. (Association of Psychoanalytic Psychotherapy in the NHS), London, 22–23 April.

Schafer, R. (1983) *The Analytic Attitude*. London: Hogarth Press.

Sieghart, P. (1978) *Statutory Registration of Psychotherapists*. Tavistock Clinic.

Storr, A. (1979) *The Art of Psychotherapy*. London: Secker & Warburg.

Strupp, H.H. (1960) *Psychotherapists in Action*. New York: Grune & Stratton.

Strupp, H.H. (1977) 'A reformulation of the dynamics of the therapist's contribution', in A.S. Gurman and A.M. Razin (eds), *Effective Psychotherapy*. Oxford: Pergamon Press.

Strupp, H.H. and Binder, J.L. (1984) *Psychotherapy in a New Key*. New York: Basic Books.

Tolan, J. and Lendrum, S. (1995) *Case Material and Role Play in Counselling Training*. London: Routledge.

Appendix 1: Chapter Structure (for Authors of Chapters 2–13)

1 Historical context and development in Britain (1,000 words)

1.1 Historical context

Your aim here should be briefly to acquaint the reader unfamiliar with your approach with its *historical context*. Examine its historical origins, its intellectual roots and explain why it is called what it is.

1.2 Development in Britain

Your aim here should be to treat briefly the development of the approach in Britain (where this is different from 1.1 up to the time of writing).

2 Theoretical assumptions (2,500 words)

2.1 Image of the person

Outline the basic assumptions made by the approach about the person and human nature.

2.2 Conceptualization of psychological disturbance and health

Outline how the approach conceptualizes both psychological disturbance and psychological health. Explain in detail the *major concepts* utilized by the approach in accounting for psychological disturbance and health.

2.3 Acquisition of psychological disturbance

Explain the approach's view on how psychological disturbance is acquired.

2.4 Perpetuation of psychological disturbance

Explain the approach's position on how psychological disturbance is perpetuated. What *intrapersonal mechanisms* are utilized by individuals to perpetuate their own psychological disturbance; what *interpersonal mechanisms* are recognized as important in the perpetuation process; what is the role of the *environment* in the perpetuation process?

2.5   Change

You should use this section to outline briefly the approach's view on how humans change with respect to movement from psychological disturbance to psychological health. This section should orient the reader to what follows under 'Practice' but should not be limited to the change process in therapy (i.e. it should not duplicate section 3.6). Thus it should both complete the 'Acquisition–Perpetuation–Change' cycle and orient the reader to what follows.

3   Practice (5,500 words)

3.1   Goals of therapy

Your aim here is to set out the goals of the approach.

3.2   Selection criteria

What selection criteria are used to determine whether or not clients will benefit from the approach in its *individual therapy format*? There are two issues here: first, what clients (if any) are deemed unsuitable for the particular approach under consideration (refer back to 3.1 here where relevant), and second, what criteria are employed in deciding whether or not clients who are suitable for the approach would benefit from individual therapy (as opposed to couples, family and group therapy) at the outset. What criteria are employed when decisions concerning transfer from one modality (e.g. individual therapy) to another (e.g. group therapy) become salient? Indeed when do these issues become salient? What are the approach's views on the use of concurrent therapeutic modalities (e.g. where the client is seen in both individual and group therapy)?

3.3   Qualities of effective therapists

From the point of view of the approach under consideration, what qualities do effective therapists have? Focus on both personal qualities and skill variables. In writing this section what is the relative importance of personal characteristics vs. skill factors here?

3.4   Therapeutic relationship and style

Here you should outline the type of therapeutic relationship that therapists of your orientation seek to establish with their clients. You should also characterize the interactive style of the therapist in the conduct of the approach in action. (While you will no doubt use your own dimensions the following might be kept in mind: active–passive; formal–informal; self-disclosing–non-self-disclosing; humorous–serious.) How does the interactive style of the therapist change during the therapeutic process?

3.5 Major therapeutic strategies and techniques

List and describe the major strategies and techniques advocated as therapeutic by the approach. According to Marvin Goldfried, strategies lie at a level of abstraction between theory and techniques, so techniques are more *specific* than strategies. Please use this formulation in preparing this section and list the strategies first, showing how the techniques are specific ways of operationalizing the strategies. I am quite aware that some approaches cannot easily be described in these terms. Contact me if this is the case and we'll discuss how best to write this section.

3.6 The change process in therapy

Here outline the process of therapeutic change from beginning to end. What reliable patterns of change can be discerned in successful cases? Outline the major sources of lack of therapeutic progress and how these are addressed in the approach.

3.7 Limitations of the approach

Here describe the limitations of the approach. Where is there room for improvement? How should the approach develop in the future to rectify such deficiencies?

4 Case example (1,500 words)

Fully describe a case (a British client) which shows the approach in action, referring whenever possible to the above framework and dividing the section thus:

4.1 The client

Briefly describe the client and his/her presenting concerns.

4.2 The therapy

Here the emphasis should be on describing the process of change (i.e. how the therapy unfolded over time). Speculate on the sources of the therapeutic change. What, with hindsight, might you have done differently?

Please resist the temptation to select a 'brilliant success'. Choose a case that readers can relate to, i.e. one that had its difficulties and where the client had a realistic (not an idealistic) outcome.

NB: Those of you who contributed a chapter to *Individual Therapy: A Handbook* should present a *new* case.

Appendix 2: Useful Addresses

Contributors were asked to provide not more than two addresses for those wishing for information on therapy services and training opportunities in a particular approach. The organizations listed below will often give details of others not shown here.

Psychodynamic Therapy: The Freudian Approach

Therapy and training

The Chair
Psychoanalytic and Psychodynamic Psychotherapy Section
United Kingdom Council for Psychotherapy
167–169 Great Portland Street
London W1N 5FB

Psychodynamic Therapy: The Kleinian Approach

Therapy and training

Institute of Psycho-Analysis
63 New Cavendish Street
London W1M 7RD

The Tavistock Clinic
120 Belsize Lane
London NW3 5BA

Psychodynamic Therapy: The Jungian Approach

Therapy and training

Association of Jungian Analysts
Flat 3, 7 Eton Avenue
London NW3 3EL

Society of Analytical Psychology
1 Daleham Gardens
London NW3 5BY

Adlerian Therapy

Therapy and training

> Adlerian Society for Individual Psychology
> 77 Clissold Crescent
> London N16 9AR

> Institute for Adlerian Psychology
> 26 Biddulph Road
> London W9 1JB

Person-Centred Therapy

Therapy

> Norwich Centre for Personal and Professional Development
> 7 Earlham Road
> Norwich NR2 3RA

Training

> Person-Centred Therapy (Britain)
> Norwich Centre for Personal and Professional Development
> 7 Earlham Road
> Norwich NR2 3RA

Personal Construct Therapy

Therapy and training

> Ray Evans
> PCP Education
> 6 Fabyc House
> Cumberland Road
> Kew, Richmond
> Surrey TW9 3HH

Existential Therapy

Therapy

> Society for Existential Analysis
> c/o The School of Psychotherapy and Counselling
> Regent's College
> Inner Circle
> Regent's Park
> London NW1 4NS

Training

> School of Psychotherapy and Counselling
> Regent's College
> Inner Circle
> Regent's Park
> London NW1 4NS

Gestalt Therapy

Therapy and training

> The Gestalt Psychotherapy Training Institute in the UK
> 2 Bedford Street
> London Road
> Bath BA1 6AF

> The Gestalt Centre
> 64 Warwick Road
> St Albans
> Hertfordshire AL1 4DL

Transactional Analysis

Therapy and training

> The Administrator
> Institute of Transactional Analysis
> 32 Wilberforce Court
> Kings Drive
> Edgware HA8 8AZ

> Physis
> 12 North Common Road
> London W5 2QB

Cognitive Therapy

Therapy and training

> Institute of Psychiatry Cognitive Therapy Clinic
> Institute of Psychiatry
> De Crespigny Park
> London SE5 8AF

Behaviour Therapy

Therapy and training

> Psychological Treatment Unit
> Maudsley Hospital
> London SE5

400

Rational Emotive Behaviour Therapy

Therapy

> The Secretary
> Association of Rational Emotive Behaviour Therapists
> 1 Jenkinson Close
> Newcastle under Lyme
> Staffordshire ST5 2JP

Training

> Professor W. Dryden
> Department of Psychology
> Goldsmiths College
> New Cross
> London SE14 6NW

Further Information

> In addition, useful referral and training directories are available from:

> British Association for Counselling
> 1 Regent Place
> Rugby CV21 2PJ

> United Kingdom Council for Psychotherapy
> 167–169 Great Portland Street
> London W1N 5FB

> British Confederation of Psychotherapists
> 37 Mapesbury Road
> London NW2 4HJ

Feedback

> The editor welcomes feedback on the present volume.
> Correspondence should be addressed to:

> Professor Windy Dryden
> Department of Psychology
> Goldsmiths College
> New Cross
> London SE14 6NW

Index